RELIGIONS OF KOREA IN PRACTICE

RELIGIONS OF
KOREA
IN PRACTICE

Robert E. Buswell Jr., Editor

PRINCETON READINGS IN RELIGIONS

PRINCETON UNIVERSITY PRESS

PRINCETON AND OXFORD

Published by Princeton University Press, 41 William Street, Princeton, New Jersey 08540
In the United Kingdom: Princeton University Press, 3 Market Place, Woodstock,
Oxfordshire OX20 1SY

Library of Congress Cataloging-in-Publication Data

Religions of Korea in practice / Robert E. Buswell Jr., editor.
p.   cm.   —(Princeton readings in religions)
Includes bibliographical references and index.
ISBN-13: 978-0-691-11346-3 (hardcover: alk. paper)
ISBN-10: 0-691-11346-7 (hardcover: alk. paper)
ISBN-13: 978-0-691-11347-0 (pbk.: alk. paper)
ISBN-10: 0-691-11347-5 (pbk.: alk. paper)
1. Korea—Religion.   2. Buddhism—Korea.   3. Confucianism—Korea.
I. Buswell, Robert E.   II. Series. BL2233.5.R45 1997
200.9519—dc22   2006013072

British Library Cataloging-in-Publication Data is available

This book has been composed in Berkeley

Printed on acid-free paper. ∞

pup.princeton.edu

Printed in the United States of America

1   3   5   7   9   10   8   6   4   2

PRINCETON READINGS

IN RELIGIONS

———

Princeton Readings in Religions is a series of anthologies on the religions of the world, representing the significant advances that have been made in the study of religions in the last thirty years. The sourcebooks used by previous generations of students, whether for Judaism and Christianity or for the religions of Asia and the Middle East, placed a heavy emphasis on "canonical works." Princeton Readings in Religions provides a different configuration of texts in an attempt better to represent the range of religious practices, placing particular emphasis on the ways in which texts have been used in diverse contexts. The volumes in the series therefore include ritual manuals, hagiographical and autobiographical works, popular commentaries, and folktales, as well as some ethnographic material. Many works are drawn from vernacular sources. The readings in the series are new in two senses. First, very few of the works contained in the volumes have ever been made available in an anthology before; in the case of the volumes on Asia, few have even been translated into a Western language. Second, the readings are new in the sense that each volume provides new ways to read and understand the religions of the world, breaking down the sometimes misleading stereotypes inherited from the past in an effort to provide both more expansive and more focused perspectives on the richness and diversity of religious expressions. The series is designed for use by a wide range of readers, with key terms translated and technical notes omitted. Each volume also contains a substantial introduction by a distinguished scholar in which the histories of the traditions are outlined and the significance of each of the works is explored.

Religions of Korea in Practice is the thirteenth volume in the series. It has been designed, organized, and edited by the eminent scholar of Korean Buddhism Robert Buswell. The twenty-two contributors include many of the leading scholars of Korean studies from North America, Europe, and Korea. Each scholar has provided one or more translations of key works, many of which are translated here for the first time. These works include creation myths, miracle stories, ritual texts, and ethical instructions from the range of Korean religious traditions, including Buddhism, Confucianism, Shamanism, Christianity, and new religions, as well as the ideology of the Democratic Peoples Republic of North Korea. Each chapter begins with a substantial introduction in which the translator discusses the history and influence of the work, identifying points of particular difficulty or interest. Don Baker, who contributes several chapters to the volume, opens the book with a general introduction to the world of Korean religions.

The volumes *Zen in Practice* and *Islam in South Asia in Practice* are forthcoming in the series.

Donald S. Lopez Jr.
Series Editor

CONTENTS

Buddhism

Confucianism and Neo-Confucianism

Shamanism

Christianity

New Religions

North Korea

CONTENTS BY THEME

It is not always obvious with which religious tradition a specific chapter ought to be classified. Korean religions of both the premodern and modern eras interact with each other in areas as diverse as doctrine, practice, and ritual; hence, what makes a specific practice "Buddhist" rather than part of broader "folk religion" may not always be clear-cut. It is also common for religious traditions to draw freely from one another, such as the incorporation of Buddhist deities into shamanic rites, or the syncretistic tendencies seen in many of the Korean new religions. In order to suggest some of these manifold points of intersection between religious traditions, I provide here an alternative organization of the chapters by theme. This is only one of many possible arrangements, of course, and several chapters could easily be placed within other categories.

CONTENTS BY CHRONOLOGY

Dating the texts translated in this anthology is not as straightforward as it might seem. Tales from the Buddhist *Samguk yusa* (*Memorabilia of the Three Kingdoms*), for example, are dated to 1285, the official compilation date of that anthology, but these stories often derive from much older local histories and accounts of conduct that are no longer extant. Many of the shamanic songs translated in the anthology date from the twentieth century, when they were first recorded, but their antecedents clearly go back much earlier. Many of the chapters also include material from different eras; this chronology references only the earliest work translated in the chapter or will give an approximate range of dates for the materials (e.g., "early- to mid-20th century").

PREFACE

In addition to its attempt at offering a systematic overview of Korean religious practices, this book is also distinctive for being the first anthology on Korean religions ever to be attempted in any language, including Korean. While no such collection could ever hope to be comprehensive, the selections included herein make an important first step toward (1) providing a systemic overview of Korean religions as a whole, and (2) addressing the dearth of basic source materials on Korean religions in Western languages. Virtually all the material in this volume appears for the first time in English. Especially notable is the substantial coverage of contemporary Korean religious practice, especially in the various Christian churches and indigenous new religions that have been developing rapidly over the last century. Each chapter includes an extensive translation of original source material, accompanied by an introduction that frames the significance of the selections and suggestions for further reading.

Unlike in most of the other volumes in the Princeton Readings in Religions series, the material here is organized by religious tradition, in hopes of making the material more accessible to the reader, especially in classroom use. One decision may, however, warrant notice: because the extant sources included here on Shamanism, with one major exception, were not transcribed until the twentieth century, I have placed the section on Shamanism later in the anthology rather than at its presumptive place at the beginning. This arrangement also highlights the perhaps unexpected fact that the earliest body of religious literature in Korea is associated with Buddhism, not Shamanism. (My colleagues will naturally assume that this arrangement stems from the fact that I am a Buddhist scholar. I categorically deny all such allegations!) For readers interested in a thematic arrangement of the sources, which highlights the manifold points of intersection between the different Korean religious traditions, I also include among the front matter an alternative table of contents listed by theme.

With the Western study of Korean religions still very much in its infancy, an anthology such as this would not have been possible without the goodwill and cooperation of colleagues throughout the world. Unlike many of the other books in the series, which rely almost entirely on American scholars, this volume is truly an international effort. Even a quick perusal of our contributors will show that a substantial majority of the chapters are by scholars from outside the United States, from as far south as New Zealand and as far north as the Netherlands, and from disciplines as disparate as theology and geography. I thank all the translators for answering the call to contribute. I am especially grateful to Don Baker, who not only contributed much of the material on Korean new religions but also finally accepted my challenge to write the introduction to the volume. I would also like to thank the two reviewers for Princeton University Press, professors Don Clark of Trinity University and Vladimir Tikhonov of the University of Oslo, for their detailed comments, which were a great help to me and my colleagues as we refined our chapters for publication. I hope this volume will play its own small part in helping to build the field of Korean religious studies in the West and to broaden interest in Korean religions in all their diversity.

MAJOR PERIODS IN KOREAN HISTORY

Old Chosŏn (traditional dates 2333 B.C.E.–194 B.C.E.)

Three Kingdoms period (first century B.C.E.–668)
  Paekche kingdom (traditional dates 18 B.C.E.–661)
  Koguryŏ kingdom (traditional dates 37 B.C.E.–668)
  Silla kingdom (57 B.C.E.–668)

Unified Silla dynasty (668–935)

Koryŏ dynasty (918–1392)

Chosŏn dynasty (1392–1910)

Japanese colonial period (1910–1945)

Division between North and South (1945–present)

NOTE ON
TRANSLITERATIONS AND
CONVENTIONS

———

Transliterations of East Asian languages follow the systems commonly used in the Western scholarly community: McCune-Reischauer for Korean, pinyin for Chinese, revised Hepburn for Japanese. I have also adopted some of the modifications and enhancements of the McCune-Reischauer system proposed in Robert Austerlitz et al., "Report of the Workshop Conference on Korean Romanization," *Korean Studies* 4 (1980): 111–25. Most titles of Asian-language works appear together with an English translation. Although few works have standardized English renderings, I have tried to maintain some degree of consistency across the chapters in the translations used but have in some cases followed the preferences of the individual translators. Korean religious works (especially Buddhism, but also shamanic oral songs and new religions) use many transcriptions of originally Indian terms; these have been transcribed in their standard classical Sanskrit forms, for example, *samādhi*.

CONTRIBUTORS

Don Baker teaches in the Department of Asian Studies at the University of British Columbia.

Jonathan W. Best teaches in the Art and Art History Department at Wesleyan University.

Antonetta Lucia Bruno teaches in the Faculty of Oriental Studies at the University of Rome "La Sapienza."

Robert E. Buswell Jr., teaches in the Department of Asian Languages and Cultures at the University of California, Los Angeles.

Hyaeweol Choi teaches in the Department of Languages and Literatures at Arizona State University.

Chong Go Sŭnim is a Buddhist monk practicing at the Hanmaum Seon Center in Anyang, South Korea.

James Huntley Grayson teaches in the School of East Asian Studies at the University of Sheffield.

Hongkyung Kim teaches in the Department of Asian and Asian American Studies at the State University of New York, Stony Brook.

Youngmin Kim teaches in the Department of East Asian Studies at Bryn Mawr College.

Timothy S. Lee teaches at Brite Divinity School, Texas Christian University.

Younghee Lee teaches in the School of Asian Studies at the University of Auckland.

Richard D. McBride II, teaches in the Department of Asian Studies at Washington University in St. Louis.

Pankaj N. Mohan teaches in the Department of Japanese and Korean Studies at the University of Sydney.

Charles Muller teaches in the Faculty of Humanities at Toyo Gakuin University.

Jin Y. Park teaches in the Department of Philosophy and Religion at American University in Washington, D.C.

Franklin Rausch is a Ph.D. student in Korean religions at the University of British Columbia.

Eun Hee Shin teaches in the Department of Philosophy and Religion at Simpson College.

Patrick R. Uhlmann is a Ph.D. candidate in Buddhist studies at the University of California, Los Angeles.

Sem Vermeersch teaches in the Department of Korean Studies at Keimyung University.

Boudewijn Walraven teaches in the Asian Studies Program at Leiden University.

Hong-key Yoon teaches in the School of Geography and Environmental Science at the University of Auckland.

Inshil Choe Yoon teaches in the School of Asian Studies at the University of Auckland.

RELIGIONS OF KOREA IN PRACTICE

INTRODUCTION

Don Baker

For students of religion, especially those interested in religious pluralism and religious change, the Korean peninsula is a fascinating place to explore. The spectrum of religious beliefs and practices in Korea is wider than almost any other place on earth. The peninsula has been divided roughly in half since 1945, with the Communist People's Democratic Republic of Korea (DPRK) on the northern side of a demilitarized boundary and the democratic Republic of Korea (ROK) on the southern side, giving it an even more diverse religious culture today than it had during its thousand-plus years as a unified country. In the North, the Communist government has suppressed most religious activity and replaced it with the ideology of Juche (chuch'e), literally "self-reliance," an amalgam of Marxism and Neo-Confucianism with religious overtones. In the South, the opposite had occurred: since 1945, there has been an explosion of religious activity—particularly organized and self-conscious religious activity—leading to highly visible, vibrant, and growing Buddhist and Christian communities and expanding social roles for Korean new religions and traditional shamanism.

Comparatively little is said specifically about North Korea in this volume, for a couple of reasons. First of all, before 1945, there was little difference between religious beliefs and practices in the northern part of the peninsula and in the South, so what is said about Korea before 1945 applies to the entire peninsula. For the period after 1945, we have a lot more information about religion in the South than in the North, since North Korea is a closed society that does not allow many foreign observers in and does not let much information out.

What we do know about North Korea is that the government-promoted ideology of Juche claims at least the public allegiance of the vast majority of the population. We know that Juche teaches that human beings do not need to rely on any gods, since human beings are wise and strong enough to make decisions for themselves. We also know, however, that North Koreans are told to rely on the infallible guidance of Kim Ilsŏng (Kim Il Sung) and his son and successor, Kim Chŏngil (Kim Jung Il). We know that, although Kim Ilsŏng died in 1994, signs posted all over North Korea remind citizens that "he is with us forever," he is considered even in death to be the head of the North Korean state, and his birthday

is observed as the foundation day of the new "Juche era." In addition, North Koreans are told that they, too, can have eternal life, since, as Juche ideology explains, even after our individual physical body dies, we remain enmeshed in the
relational web of the sociopolitical community fostered by Juche; therefore, as
long as that community survives, so do we.

If Juche rhetoric sounds almost religious, that is intentional. The North Korean
government intends for Juche to completely replace religion in the not-too-distant
future. In the meantime, the state tolerates only limited practice of other religions.
That is why there is nothing in this volume on non-Juche religious activity in
North Korea after 1945. There are only about 35,000 people in North Korea officially recognized as having a religious affiliation (other than Juche). According to
government-controlled religious organizations, North Korea has around 10,000
Buddhists, 10,000 Protestants, a few hundred Catholics, and 15,000 followers of
Korea's oldest indigenous new religion, Ch'ŏndogyo (Religion of the Heavenly
Way). If shamanism still exists in North Korea, it has been driven deep under-
ground.

By contrast, in South Korea, the focus of most of the contemporary material in
this volume, there are reams of scholarly materials concerning religious activity.
The Republic of Korea enjoys one of the most complex and diverse religious cultures on the face of the globe. South Korea has the largest network of extant Confucian shrines of any nation and has a vibrant and active Buddhist community,
with hundreds of major monasteries scattered in scenic mountainous regions
around the peninsula. South Korea is additionally the most Protestant country in
Asia (in terms of the percentage of its population that identifies itself as Protestant), but it also ranks third in Asia, behind the Philippines and East Timor, in
the percentage of its population that attends Catholic worship services regularly.
On top of that, there are a number of indigenous new religions, many of them
large enough to operate their own universities and hospitals. And last but not
least, shamanism is still practiced in homes and offices in even the most fashion-
able sections of South Korea's most modern cities.

You can find ample evidence for this religious diversity just by walking the
streets of Korea's cities and towns and looking at the signs on the buildings
around you. The first thing you will probably notice, particularly in Seoul and in
its surrounding cities and towns, is the dominance of Christianity, obvious in the
many churches, both large and small, that can be found along Korea's streets and
alleys. However, an attentive observer would also notice the resurgence of urban
Buddhism, evident in the large number of temples being either built or rebuilt in
Korea's metropolitan areas. Close attention to the signs on homes, offices, and
apartment buildings will reveal that shamanism is also alive and well. Though the
offices of shamans usually lack the architectural distinctiveness of Christian
churches and Buddhist temples, they can be identified by reverse swastikas (a traditional Buddhist emblem for auspiciousness, which originated in India) on building walls or by placards on office buildings and apartment blocks proclaiming
that there is a "philosophy research center" (i.e., a fortune-teller) or a "bodhisattva"

(here meaning a shaman) inside. Not as obvious are the various worship halls and proselytizing centers for Korea's many indigenous new religions. Such religious diversity would not be surprising in a country inhabited by many different ethnic groups, since religious affiliation often serves as a marker of ethnic identity. Korea, however, is unusual in that it is one of the most ethnically homogeneous nations on earth, but also one of the most religiously diverse.

You do not need to travel the highways and byways of the peninsula to confirm this religious pluralism. Both government census data and Gallup survey results tell us that the South Korean population is divided into several religious groups. According to data gathered in the full census of 1995, 23.2 percent of South Koreans self-identify as Buddhists, 19.7 percent are Protestants, 6.6 percent are Roman Catholics, and 1.3 percent are followers of other religions. That leaves 50.1 percent with no religious affiliation, though we know that many of them patronize shamans, visit Buddhist temples, and may even attend a Christian church or Confucian shrine once in a while.

Snapshots of the religious population taken since 1995 tell us that more and more Koreans are proclaiming a specific religious orientation, but the respective divisions among them remain the same. In 2003 the South Korean government, based on a partial census, estimated that 54 percent of its citizens had a religious affiliation. Of those, 25.3 percent were Buddhist, 19.8 percent were Protestant, 7.4 percent were Catholic, 0.3 percent called themselves Confucians, 0.21 percent called themselves Wŏn Buddhists (a Korean new religion), and 0.75 percent had another religious affiliation. All three major religious communities had grown over the intervening eight years, a trend Gallup confirmed in 2004 with a survey of those living in Korea's largest cities. Gallup found 26.8 percent to be Buddhists, 21.6 percent to be Protestants, and 8.2 percent to be Catholics.

In that same period, the number of people who claimed to have no specific religious affiliation dropped to 46 percent, according to the government, or 43 percent, according to the Gallup survey. Such a decline does not necessarily mean that Koreans have grown more religious. Many of those who say they have no specific religious affiliation do not want to confine themselves to only one religious tradition. Instead, they want to be free to visit shamans and Buddhist temples and participate in the activities of new religious organizations without being told that by doing so they were no longer permitted to participate in the rituals and worship activities of other religious communities. It is also possible that some of the respondents to government or Gallup poll takers had a different understanding of "religion" than did the survey takers. Acts that observers considered religious, the respondents may not have viewed as religious at all. The term "religion" (Kor. chonggyo) is a relatively new term in Korean, having been imported from Japan as recently as the end of the nineteenth century. As a result, for some Koreans, the word "religion" does not necessarily embrace all the religious beliefs they hold or apply to all the religious activities in which they engage.

This may seem puzzling, at first. After all, defining what "religion" is appears to be a fairly easy task. Most of us know what religion is, or at least probably think we do. However, our definition of religion is often shaped by our particular religious orientation. In a religious culture as diverse as Korea, some of those concepts do not apply to the entire range of religious organizations and activities found on the peninsula. For example, many people assume that to be religious means to believe in God, or gods. But such a definition might leave out monastic Buddhism and Confucianism, since the existence or nonexistence of God is normatively irrelevant in the religious practice of these two traditions. Does that mean Confucianism and monastic Buddhism are not religions? Obviously not. Many people also assume that a religion must have its own moral code. But such a definition would exclude Korea's folk religion, which has no distinctive moral code of its own. It would also cause problems in discussing some schools of Buddhist practice, which teach that the truly enlightened have transcended the normal moral dichotomy separating good from evil actions.

Instead of trying to define religion in the abstract and then applying that universal concept to specific components of Korea's religious culture, we will be better served if, first, we identify the sorts of activities in which Koreans engage that might reasonably be called "religious"; and, second, ascertain the reasons Koreans engage in those sorts of activities. Only then will we come up with an understanding of religion that is generally applicable to the Korean situation.

The Religious Aims of Koreans

Koreans, like human beings in countries and cultures all over the world, have a wide range of reasons for engaging in religious activities. One common reason, which is easy to identify as religious, is the pursuit of salvation. However, salvation can mean different things to different people.

For some, such as Christians and Pure Land Buddhists, salvation means going to heaven or the Pure Land of Ultimate Bliss after you die. For them, the primary purpose of religious activity is to earn admission into paradise (though for the Pure Land Buddhists, paradise means a place where it will be easier to achieve nirvāṇa). However, for other Buddhists, being saved means not going anywhere after you die. Rather than rebirth in heaven, their ultimate religious goal is the achievement in this very life of nirvāṇa, the radical nonattachment to all the compounded things of this world, which brings a final end to the interminable cycle of birth, death, and rebirth and the concomitant inevitability of suffering.

An individual practitioner may seek his or her own salvation, but it is not unusual for religious activity to have as its intended aim the salvation of someone else. That someone else might be a recently deceased loved one, the whole of humanity, or even, in Buddhist circles, all sentient beings.

A common intended result of salvation, whether for oneself or for others, is an end to suffering. Those who believe in heaven look forward to eternal happiness in communion with God (or with Amitābha Buddha in Pure Land practice), in a realm in which there is no disease or pain, no hunger or thirst, no old age or death, and, therefore, no suffering. Those who believe in nirvāṇa anticipate an end to the illusions of permanence, happiness, individuality, and loveliness that bedevil us in this realm of the transitory, since such illusions give rise to attachments, which inevitably lead to suffering when their transitory nature becomes obvious. Freed from such unrealistic attachments, those who enter nirvāṇa will therefore be free of suffering.

Some Koreans prefer another route to salvation. Unlike those who look forward to going to paradise after they die or escaping from the illusions of this world, these religious prefer instead to work toward the creation of a paradise on this earth. Although they realize this world is not perfect, they believe it is perfectible: that is, they affirm the intrinsic value of this world rather than deny its ultimate value, as Christians and Buddhists appear to do. In some Korean religious traditions, such as Korea's new indigenous religions of Ch'ŏndogyo or Wŏn Buddhism, salvation will come through a Great Transformation (kaebyŏk in Korean) that will erase from this planet such imperfections as war, disease, poverty, and political and social injustice. After that Great Transformation, life on earth will be perfect and free of suffering, and there will be no need to seek escape into heaven or into nirvāṇa.

Salvation is not the only goal of religious activity in Korea. Koreans also seek self-perfection. Sometimes that self-perfection is a means to the end of salvation. In such cases, practitioners strive through their own efforts to eliminate as much human weakness as possible in order to gain the reward of a ticket to paradise. However, for other Koreans, self-perfection is a goal in itself. Neo-Confucians, for example, expressed disdain for anyone who tried to become a better person in order to receive some sort of reward for their accomplishment.

Self-perfection can aim at primarily physical perfection or primarily spiritual perfection. Usually, however, the two are interrelated. In fact, one standard way of saying "to pursue moral self-improvement" in Korean is momŭl takkta, which literally means to polish your body. Self-perfection as physical perfection can mean that you have control over your body, including control of your emotions, such that your body will not raise any barriers to fidelity with the laws of nature or obedience to the will of God (or the gods). At its most extreme, this would mean being willing even to sacrifice your physical life if that is the only way you can maintain fidelity to the dharma or God. Buddhist self-immolators and Catholic martyrs are examples of people who subordinated normal human desires to religious imperatives. Alternatively, physical self-perfection can mean that you have brought your body under such tight control that you can suppress individualistic emotions and align your actions with the movements of cosmic forces. This was the goal of Confucian self-perfection. A third meaning of physical self-perfection is to train your body until you have reached a point where you can reverse the normal process of aging and the physical decay that accompanies it. This is the goal of pursuit of physical self-perfection by members of the internal alchemy school of Daoism.

Spiritual self-perfection focuses on mind control, on attaining control over your thoughts so that no selfish or otherwise immoral idea is able to linger in your mind. This can be done either by emptying the mind of all ratiocination or by filling the mind with wholesome thoughts at all times. Such spiritual perfection may be cultivated by sitting in quiet meditation for long periods, as many Buddhists monks do, or by engaging in extensive periods of repetitive physical exercises such as chanting, as is done in some of the new religions in Korea.

Sometimes, however, spiritual cultivation is pursued through regular spiritual exercises that may not last an uncomfortably long time each they are performed, but that are done on a regular enough basis that they discipline both the body and the mind. One example would be rising regularly to pray before dawn, as many Korean Christians do. In such cases, both the body and the mind are disciplined at the same time, leading to both physical and mental discipline.

Sometimes Koreans engage in religious activity with less thought for such long-term goals as salvation or self-perfection than in more immediate goals, such as peace of mind. That peace of mind can come from listening to or reading religious explanations of how this world came to be the way it is. Creation stories, such as those in shamanic oral myths or the Christian Bible, tell us why we are in this world and what our roles are in it, giving us clarity about how we should behave. That clarity can provide peace of mind. Similarly, religious stories of supernatural intervention in human affairs can give us peace of mind, if those stories ease our fears of having no escape from the bad situations into which we may have fallen. The belief in the possibility of such intervention is one reason shamanism has remained such an important presence in Korean religious culture for so long. Another religious aid to peace of mind is the promise of a better life after this one. Many people find peace of mind when they are assured that they have nothing to fear from the inevitability of death. In addition, participation in communal religious activities can help us obtain peace of mind by raising our self-esteem, if participation in those activities raises our status in the eyes of others. Finally, some religious rituals themselves, by the very nature of the repetitive actions they require and the comfort people gain from familiarity with those actions, have a calming effect that can promote peace of mind.

Another goal of religious activities is the highlighting of important points of transition in life. Although such activities may not at first glance appear intrinsically religious, they nonetheless are often a goal of religious practice. Catholicism, for example, marks the joyful moment of the birth of a child with the ritual of baptism, welcoming a new arrival into the community. Another happy occasion whose importance is highlighted with ritual is marriage. Most Korean religious traditions (shamanism is one conspicuous exception) have ceremonies to both celebrate and sanctify the joining of two people to form a new family (though in Korea, neither shamans nor Buddhist monks traditionally officiated at weddings). Mournful occasions also are marked with religious ritual. When a loved one dies, religious ritual can provide a way to channel grief in a socially acceptable fashion and also can help us accept the fact that our beloved has left us before we were ready to say good-bye. Some religious traditions, such as Confucianism, go even farther to help the living deal with their grief by prescribing rituals of remembrance on the anniversaries of the deaths of parents and grandparents. In a society that puts as much emphasis as Korea does on filial piety, those rituals of remembrance also provide a way for descendants to lessen any guilt they might feel over not having done enough for their parents or grandparents while they were alive.

There are also more pedestrian reasons for engaging in religious activities. Though some religious leaders and thinkers express dismay at how often religion is used to pursue mundane, personal benefits, for as long as there have been human beings on this earth, men and women have turned to religion in the hope that it would make them healthier or wealthier (or, preferably, both). After all, religion promises to put us in touch with forces more powerful than we would otherwise have at our disposal. How many of us would resist the temptation to avail ourselves of a superior power that may be able to help us put enough money in our pockets to buy a better automobile or home? How many of us would not seek supernatural assistance if we thought that was the only way we could heal a chronic or life-threatening medical condition or even merely regain the energy of youth? It is therefore not surprising that Koreans of virtually all religious persuasions pray, perform rituals, tithe, or engage in other religious behavior in the hopes that, for example, their son or daughter will gain admission to one of the best universities in the nation, or at least marry a graduate of such a university.

Finally, since human beings are social beings and need friends and like-minded companions, some turn to religion for fellowship. Engaging in shared religious activities creates a sense of fellowship, of belonging to a community of shared ideals and values. Moreover, those who find themselves doubting their religious convictions may find that communal religious activities help to strengthen those beliefs. When we join with others in communal prayer, worship, or meditation, our trust in the efficacy of those activities is reinforced by seeing that other people share that belief.

These various goals of religious activities are not mutually exclusive. In fact, they usually overlap. For example, a Confucian may want to create a utopia on this earth, but he probably also believes that the best way to achieve that goal is to cultivate self-perfection. A Christian may want to go to heaven, but she may also want God to make life more comfortable for her and her family on this earth. And practices that help a Buddhist woman calm and focus her mind will also help ensure that her unborn baby is born healthy and wise.

Moreover, despite their different reasons for engaging in religious activities, most Koreans will have at least one reason in common: overcoming the frustrations produced by the inevitable limitations in human life. Religion usually involves either seeking the assistance of a supernatural force or being, or aligning oneself with some more powerful force. Either way, religion implies joining with something or someone more powerful than oneself in order to have a better chance of overcoming the obstacles life inevitably throws one's way. Koreans may seek that aid from a shamanic mountain deity, a Buddhist bodhisattva, or the Christian God. Or they may seek to overcome their own limitations by aligning themselves with the cosmic pattern Neo-Confucians believe governs the universe, by harmonizing their actions with the energy pattern in the geomancer's maps of the earth, or by breathing in such a way that their energy becomes one with the energy of the universe, as Daoist internal alchemy practitioners recommend.

Religion is obviously much more than just an attempt to benefit from cooperation with some force more powerful than oneself. After all, every time we get into an automobile and drive down the highway, we are using the power of the engine to get from one place to another faster than we could on our own. Yet we would not normally consider driving to be a religious act. It is not the desire to leverage our own power with some external power that defines religion. Rather, religion is identified by the techniques used to access that stronger power, as well as the type of power from which we seek to benefit.

The Religious Activities of Koreans

One technique used to gain the assistance of supernatural power is, of course, prayer. If you go to Buddhist shrines in the mountains on a day when the weather is nice enough for hiking, you will probably see quite a few people bowing over and over again before a statue of a buddha or a bodhisattva and asking for assistance in solving a health or financial problem. Such vocal petitionary prayer can also be seen in Christian churches. However, that is not the only form of prayer. In some of the new religions, such as Ch'ŏndogyo, prayer is a silent conversation with God within your own heart and is not audible to those around you. In folk religion, shamans not only converse aloud with their gods, they even negotiate and argue with them in their distinctive form of prayer.

There are other types of prayer as well, some of which are difficult to distinguish from worship. Producing religious objects by hand—making a lotus lantern for a Buddha's Birthday celebration, for example, or carving a statue of Jesus—could be seen as a form of prayer, if the aim is to gain merit for the lantern maker or the statue carver. However, if the purpose is primarily to express your devotion to the Buddha or to Jesus, then you are engaged in an act of worship. The same dual function applies to prayers that praise God or a god rather than asking him for a favor. When a Buddhist repeats over and over again, "Homage to the Buddha of Medicine," if she is simply expressing her belief in the existence, power, and benevolence of the Buddha of Medicine, she is worshiping that buddha; but if she is chanting his name over and over again, begging him to heal a family member dying of cancer, then she is praying. The same can be said of a Protestant who praises the Lord during Sunday services: if that is disinterested praise, it is primarily an act of worship; but if she is praising God in the hope that God will respond to her devotion by giving her husband a better-paying job, she is praying.

Pilgrimage is another form of worship popular among Koreans that can also be a form of prayer. Wŏn Buddhists and Catholics, for example, make the rounds of various sacred sites on Korean soil to show their devotion and reinvigorate their faith, and out of hope that they will thereby earn merit that will increase their chances of entering a supernal realm after they die. Some may have more immediate goals, such as hoping that their visits to sacred sites will be quickly rewarded with good luck in school, business, or their personal relationships. But for others, a pilgrimage is more than just a form of worship or prayer: it can also be a form of spiritual training, a way to cultivate both a better mental attitude and moral character.

Meditation is another form of spiritual training popular among Koreans. Meditation is of course a traditional part of Buddhist monastic practice, but businessmen, housewives, and university students also meditate, and not all of them are Buddhists. Meditation is different from prayer and worship in that it is focused inward. Rather than trying to communicate with God to ask a favor or show our devotion to him, when we meditate we try either to empty our minds of all deliberate conscious thoughts or to focus our minds on one thing to the exclusion of all else. Mainstream Buddhists in Korea tend to emphasize focusing the mind on the hwadu, or "keyword," of a kongan (a Zen conundrum) as a way of gaining direct access to the enlightenment inherent in the mind, though in recent years other forms of practice—such as silent meditation aimed at emptying the mind of all deliberate conscious thought, and Vipassanā (insight) practice derived from Southeast Asian traditions of Buddhism—have challenged the popularity of hwadu meditation. Neo-Confucians rejected both approaches, calling instead for a meditative focus on the unity of the cosmos. An efficient approach to meditation on which both agreed was to get out of our heads and focus attention instead on our breathing and on an invisible spot (known as the tanjŏn, or "cinnabar field") a little below our navel. Korean practitioners of internal alchemy would agree, though they are less interested in the mental states associated with meditation than they are with the physiological effects of slow and steady abdominal breathing.

The most popular form of meditation is quiet sitting. However, there are other ways to meditate. Some Koreans alternate periods of sitting with quiet walking meditation, or even standing upright but still. There are also some new Buddhist denominations in Korea, as well as some non-Buddhist new religions, such as Ch'ŏndogyo and the Chŭngsan family of religions, that meditate by chanting. Chanting aloud the same phrase over and over again can have a similar physiological and psychological effect as quiet sitting.

For those who find meditation boring or too demanding, there are livelier forms of religious activity. In addition to worship through verbal declarations of praise and devotion, through the production of sacred objects, and through visits to sacred sites, believers can also express their religious faith through song or dance. Congregational singing in religious services was introduced to Koreans by Christian hymnals, but music has long been a part of Korean religious practice. Shamanic rituals are filled with loud, sometimes even raucous, music, with the excuse that the spirits need to be entertained. Buddhist music is much more restrained, since it is intended to put its adherents in a contemplative mood. Confucian ritual music is even quieter, since Confucian music is designed to still emotions.

As may be expected, religious dance resembles its accompanying religious music. Confucian ritual dance hardly appears to be a dance at all, the performers move so slowly. Buddhist dance is well choreographed, like a Buddhist ritual at a somewhat faster speed. Shaman dances, on the other hand, do not appear at first glance to adhere to any set pattern, since the shaman is supposed to respond as the spirits move her, which sometimes means frenetically and wildly, rather than in the choreographed movements we typically associate with religious dance.

There are ways of worship more subdued than singing and dancing. A common way Koreans show respect to one another is through bowing. Koreans often bow where Westerners would shake hands, and the use of bowing has been extended into the religious sphere. Both Catholics and Buddhists bow from the waist before sacred statues, for example. Buddhists will also sometimes do a complete prostration, in which their head hits the floor when they want to show devotion to, and trust in, a particular buddha or bodhisattva. The same full prostration is used in the ancestor memorial services that originated in Confucianism.

Finally, there is one more form of worship that should not be overlooked: the presentation of gifts. Such gifts may be items offered as presents for a shaman's spirits, money tithed to a church, or offerings made to monks. They can even be donations of time, such as when believers demonstrate their faith and devotion by helping their church or temple prepare for formal worship services or by assisting with the daily tasks of keeping that church or temple open. For example, in many Buddhist monasteries, middle-aged women work in the kitchen, preparing food for the monks. (The monks commonly call these women "bodhisattvas," as if they are Buddhist saints incarnate.)

In addition to praying, worshiping, meditating, and going on pilgrimages, another common religious practice is ritual performance. There are nonreligious rituals, of course. Graduation ceremonies at secular institutions of higher education would not normally be considered religious, yet they are clearly rituals in that they adhere to a definite script that is followed every time a new class graduates. Nevertheless, rituals play a larger role in religious life than they do in other realms of human society. Moreover, its rituals are often what distinguish a religious community from other forms of human association.

Rituals can be stately or boisterous, as different as a Catholic high mass in Myŏngdong Cathedral or a *kut* in which a shaman stands in her bare feet on the sharp blades of two fodder knives. They can be as grand as the Sŏkchŏnje ritual performed twice a year on the grounds of the main Confucian shrine in Seoul to honor the spirits of Confucius and his most illustrious Chinese and Korean disciples, or as modest as the household rituals of some of Korea's new religions, in which a bowl of clean water is placed on a home altar and a brief prayer is said. Rituals can be a form of prayer, or a mode of worship. Rituals can also be used to show respect for a person or a spirit, as in the ancestor memorial services performed by most Korean families, or they can be used, as noted earlier, to mark significant occasions, such as weddings or the burial of a loved one. In Korean folk religion, rituals can be used to entertain spirits and keep them in a good mood so they will not cause any problems for the human beings in their purview.

In all these cases, religious rituals are like secular rituals in that they follow a standard format and in many cases adhere to a set script. However, they differ from secular rituals in the reasons they are performed (a secular ritual of prayer or worship is a contradiction in terms) or in the intended objects of the ritual (a secular ritual would not be directed at supernatural beings). Even when their purposes overlap with secular rituals, as in the case of marriages and funerals, religious rituals distinguish themselves by their aim of sanctifying the occasion for which they are performed or by their invocation of some supernatural power, such as God above.

Most, but not all, religions have ritual specialists. Whether they are called shamans, monks, or ministers, their function is basically the same: they are empowered to use their special knowledge of the rituals of their religious community to lead those rituals. Frequently, special ritual knowledge also empowers those leaders to offer the lay members of the community advice on how to behave. (In more tightly organized religious communities, that advice often becomes a command.)

Religious communities, like other human communities and organizations, have certain rules and regulations that help them function as a community and direct the actions of their members toward their common religious goals. In some religions, such as Christianity, those rules may take the form of commandments presented as laws of God that must be obeyed. To disobey those commandments is to sin, and sinners face divine punishment for eternity unless they repent and beg God's forgiveness.

In other religions, sin is not an important concept. Instead, their rules and regulations are primarily guidelines to tell you what you should do if you want to achieve certain goals. You can disregard those rules if you find that they are onerous, even though doing so will make it more difficult for you to achieve the ultimate goal of your religion. For example, if you are a lay Buddhist who happens to eat meat, most Korean Buddhists do not think you will be damned forever for giving into your carnivorous urges. However, your accumulated bad karma could drag you down into another cycle of rebirth instead of achieving liberation. Similarly, Confucians will not condemn you to eternal damnation if you do not honor your ancestors with the appropriate rituals. However, failing to honor your ancestors properly keeps you from being as good a human being as you should be, and that would bring shame to you and your family.

Korea's various religious traditions do not agree on what the rewards for good behavior are, or on what the punishments for bad behavior will be. Christians in Korea, like Christians elsewhere, believe the good will ascend to heaven after they die and the evil will fall into hell. Few other religions in Korea share that vision of the afterlife. However, even though they may not agree on what the penalties are for violating them, Korean religions generally share similar ethical standards.

They all agree that human beings should refrain from lying, stealing, cheating, sexual misconduct, murder, and any other selfish action that harms other human beings. They also agree that sons and daughters should respect their parents and grandparents, and that elders should guide their juniors. Korean religions also agree that we should treat our fellow human beings with compassion, helping those who are in need of assistance. They differ primarily in the behavioral expectations they add to that basic list. Shamans tell their clients to maintain good relations with their guardian spirits. Buddhists are urged to respect all forms of sentient life, including adopting a vegetarian diet if they are spiritually advanced enough. Believers in the new religion Ch'ŏndogyo are told to treat all human beings as though they were God. And many Protestant Christians are told not to smoke cigarettes or drink alcohol.

Religions in Korea, like religions elsewhere, do not just tell you how to behave. Most of them also tell you what you can do to cultivate the sort of moral character that will ensure that you will behave the way you should. Those prescriptions vary from religion to religion. Shamans tell their clients to sponsor rituals regularly. Buddhists tell believers to read and reflect on the sūtras or to meditate in order to develop the mind of compassion and nonattachment necessary to rise above their narrow self-interest. Christians tell their fellow believers to pray and read the Bible so that they can resist the temptations of the devil and be faithful to God's will. Confucians tell their students and disciples to read the writings of the sages and identify the moral lessons in them so that they can apply those lessons in their daily lives. Except for folk religions, it is normal for Korean religions to include the study of revered texts as an essential element in moral cultivation. Moreover, again except for folk religion, it is standard practice for religious specialists to give lectures to the laity to help them learn how to read those texts and apply them to religious practice.

In addition, Buddhists, Christians, and many of the new religions encourage lay believers to withdraw from everyday life for a few days at a time to pray, chant, or meditate, to discipline their bodies and minds through ascetic practices, and to strengthen their determination to lead a moral life. Buddhists go to mountain monasteries, Christians go to *kidowŏn* (retreat centers), and followers of new religions go to *suryŏnwŏn* (training ceners) or *sudowŏn* (centers for cultivating the Way). Despite differences in the specifics of what is taught during those periods of intense spiritual training, the essential idea is the same: there are times when it is helpful to withdraw from the world for a while to invigorate your ability to lead a moral life.

Objects of the Korean Religious Gaze

Despite the many similarities in their goals and activities, Korean religions are not all the same. Not only are the specifics of their goals and practices different from one religion to another, but so too are the objects of their religious gaze. Religions, by definition, look beyond the visible world for some underlying or overriding force or presence that unites the disparate phenomena of normal existence, gives meaning to human existence, and provides the foundation for the values that religions believe should govern our lives.

For some religions, the ultimate object of their religious gaze is God. For others, it is an impersonal governing pattern or energy pervading the cosmos. Scholars often classify religions into three categories: monotheistic, polytheistic, and nontheistic. Traditionally, Koreans were either polytheistic or nontheistic. Until the last couple of centuries, monotheism was not a significant presence in Korea.

Though Koreans today generally assume that their ancestors worshiped a supreme deity known as Hanŭnim, neither historical records nor artifacts provide any textual or archaeological evidence to support such an assumption. In premodern times, the Korean people were mostly polytheistic. They worshiped a number of different gods, mostly deified human heroes and deified personifications of nature. The educated elite, however, tended to be nontheistic. Neo-Confucians believed that there was one governing force in the cosmos, but that force, known as *li* (*i*; formative normative pattern) was immanent and impersonal and therefore does not correspond to the Western term "God." While the Buddhist laity tended to treat the various buddhas and bodhisattvas as inhabitants of a polytheistic spiritual universe, monks often viewed such theological descriptions of the buddhas as heuristic language that helps us to recognize the unitary nature of ultimate reality, which they called "buddha-nature."

Another way to distinguish popular religion and elite religion in traditional Korea is to note that gods in the popular imagination were anthropomorphic. In other words, they had personalities, and human beings could interact with them as though they were similar to human beings. On the other hand, the impersonal ground of reality in both the Neo-Confucian and the Buddhist monastic view was anthropocentric: rather than the object of a religious gaze outward, both *li* and buddha-nature could be sought within, since they filled the entire universe, both the stars externally and our minds internally.

If you pray to a god and expect a response, you have an anthropomorphic concept of that God, since only a supernatural personality can listen and respond to entreaties. In other words, anthropomorphic religion is religion that believes in divine persons with consciousness and intelligence, who interact with human beings. In anthropocentric religion, on the other hand, prayers would be a waste of time, since there is no supernatural personality to listen to those prayers. Instead, in anthropocentric religion, where religion is human-centered rather than god-centered, the focus is on self-cultivation, either on finding the real self within (such as the buddhahood that meditators seek to discover), or on linking with the impersonal forces in the cosmos without (such as in the Neo-Confucian drive to harmonize our minds with the principles of the cosmos).

The gods of shamanism and Korea's folk religion are definitely anthropomorphic (they have personalities, and human beings can interact with them). So too are the gods of popular Buddhism, though philosophical Buddhism is more often anthropocentric (in meditative monastic Buddhism, ultimate reality does not have a personality and, moreover, we can find it within as well as without). Neo-Confucianism was definitely not anthropomorphic, since ultimate reality was defined in terms of *li*, the cosmic network of appropriate relationships, and *ki* (*qi*, or *ch'i* in Chinese), the matter and energy that provide substance and motion to the cosmos. Though mainstream Neo-Confucians used a term, Sangje (the Lord on High), that can be translated as "God," they made it clear that that term was used metaphorically and did not refer to an actual supernatural personality.

When Christianity first appeared in Korea, at the end of the eighteenth century, it encountered a culture in which anthropomorphic polytheism coexisted alongside a nontheistic anthropocentrism, which was based on an assumption that behind the diversity of human experience lay a fundamental unity. At first, Christianity had a difficult time winning acceptance, since Christianity preaches an anthropomorphic monotheism, a combination Koreans had not encountered previously. However, this imported religion slowly began to win adherents and, in the process, began to change Korea's religious culture.

This first evidence of that change came with the birth of Korea's first indigenous organized religion in the middle of the nineteenth century. That religion was first known as Tonghak (Eastern Learning) to distinguish it from Western Learning, one of the early names given to Catholic Christianity. Early in the twentieth century, Tonghak changed its name to Ch'ŏndogyo, the Religion of the Heavenly Way. The God of Ch'ŏndogyo is not a supernatural personality like the God of Christianity. Nor is the God of Ch'ŏndogyo an impersonal metaphysical concept like the absolute of Neo-Confucianism. Rather, Hanullim, Ch'ŏndogyo's name for God, is something in between. He is often depicted in Ch'ŏndogyo scriptures as the animating force in the universe whom we can experience personally when we ask Ultimate Energy to fill our hearts with spiritual energy; but we should also recognize him as present not only in ourselves but also in all other human beings and animate objects.

This compromise between the nontheism of Neo-Confucianism and the theism of Christianity has not been very successful. Ch'ŏndogyo does not have many followers in Korea in the twenty-first century. Moreover, the premodern bifurcation remains strong. Meditative Buddhism is still nontheistic, and that more contemplative approach to Buddhism is spreading among the Buddhist laity. In contrast, popular Buddhism is still predominantly polytheistic, as is the folk religion. Even the new religions that followed Ch'ŏndogyo did not imitate its theological example. Wŏnbulgyo (Round, or Consummate, Buddhism), which as its name implies is a new Buddhist religion, takes a circle as its object of worship, giving concrete form to the Buddhist belief in the unity of all reality. Taejonggyo, on the other hand, though it claims to be a revival of Korea's ancient religion, is clearly monotheistic (though it, like Christianity, worships three persons in that one God). Another major new religion (which is actually a family of new religions, since it has many different denominations), the Chŭngsan group of religions, is polytheistic but with a monotheistic twist: the God of Chŭngsan'gyo is the Supreme Lord of

Heaven, but he presides over a large population of other spirits of various ranks. Moreover, he descended to earth at the beginning of the twentieth century to help humanity prepare for the coming Great Transformation from the current age, in which the gods dominate humanity, to the next era, in which human beings will run their own affairs and will no longer be subservient to the gods.

The Christian challenge to traditional Korean concepts of the absolute has not overcome those preexisting visions of multiple gods or an impersonal cosmic unity. Nor have those traditional concepts overcome Christian monotheism. Instead, since the introduction of Christianity to Korea, Korea's religious culture has grown even more complex, with polytheists and believers in impersonal, anthropocentric ultimate reality coexisting with monotheists. Korea's contemporary religious culture now includes shamanism and folk religion, various forms of Buddhism, Confucianism, and Christianity (both Catholic and Protestant), and new religions of various types.

Shamanism and Folk Religion

Folk religion, including shamanism, is typically considered Korea's original religion, representing the fundamental religious orientation of Koreans as long as there has been an identifiably Korean presence in northeast Asia. Moreover, it is sometimes asserted that shamanism has preserved unaltered the primal spirituality of the Korean people. However, though shamanism and the folk religion of which it is now the most visible manifestation have survived the challenges posed by both Christianity and modernization, their contemporary forms have been substantially transformed. For example, in the past most Korean families worshiped household gods. There were many such gods, including a god of the hearth, a god of the roof beam in the main room of the house, and even a god of the outhouse. However, that was when Koreans lived in traditional thatched-roof, clay-walled homes alongside dirt paths in villages or small towns. Now most Koreans have moved into high-rise condominiums or two-story concrete houses in towns and cities and have left their household gods behind.

Koreans have also left behind their village gods. Before the rapid urbanization that started in the 1960s, the vast majority of South Koreans lived in villages and hamlets. Each village had its own tutelary deity or deities. The guardian deities of an inland agricultural community would usually include the local mountain god as well as a pair of generals, the male general in charge of all above the earth and the female general in charge of all on and below the earth. (In fishing villages, the Dragon King who ruled the waters might replace the mountain god as the primary tutelary deity.) Once a year, usually at the beginning of the new year, villagers would come together in a community ritual to thank their guardian gods for keeping their village safe over the past year, and to pray that they continue to provide protection during the year ahead. Such rituals have disappeared as religious rituals in modern Korea, though some survive as cultural relics supported by local governments as a way of attracting urban tourists who want to see how their ancestors lived.

Mountains gods and dragon kings are examples of the importance of animism in Korea's traditional folk religion. Animism is the tendency to "anthropomorphize" natural objects that are normally inanimate. Animism animates mountains, bodies of water, stones, stars, and other normally inanimate natural objects so that human beings can interact with them. The world of animists is an enchanted world in which spirits inhabit many of the otherwise insentient natural objects people encounter in their local environment. Animism is prescientific, predating the view that the natural world is governed by impersonal forces operating according to laws of nature that operate independently of human will and behavior. Instead, animists view nature as filled with willful personalities, personalities that must be cajoled, entertained, flattered, and bribed to act in ways beneficial to human beings.

As the modern, scientific worldview has spread in Korea, penetrating even remote villages, inanimate natural objects have increasingly come to be seen as inert and more amenable to manipulation with tools than with flattery. Consequently, animism and the associated worship of, and ritual interaction with, the spirits of personified nature have almost disappeared. There remains one conspicuous exception, however. Because the Korean peninsula is so mountainous, mountain gods have always had a special importance in Korea. They retain much of their traditional authority even today. Though they no longer guard many villages, mountain gods can still be found in shrines behind most Buddhist monasteries built on the slopes of a hill or in the foothills of a mountain. Visitors to those monasteries will often visit the mountain god's shrine to ask him to continue to protect the temple as well as themselves and their family members.

Even though village rituals and household gods are becoming a thing of the past in modern Korea, and mountains are about the only inanimate natural objects that are still considered to be animated, another feature of Korea's folk religion has successfully resisted the challenge of modernity: shamanism has not only survived but is flourishing. Even the most modern sections of cities such as Seoul are dotted with shaman's offices.

In Korea, people we in English refer to as "shamans" actually belong to three different types of ritual specialists. The best-known type of shaman is the charismatic shaman, who in Korea is almost always a woman. A charismatic shaman enters a trance in order to be possessed by a spirit and then lets that spirit speak through her to members of her audience. (The spirits that possess shamans are not the animated natural objects of animism. Instead, they are usually the spirits of the recently departed or of long-dead figures from Korean and Chinese history.) Through the shaman's intercession, Koreans are able to plead with spirits to stop afflicting them with physical, financial, or personal problems, or are able to talk once again with recently deceased loved ones. Charismatic shamans are the most dramatic representatives of Koreans shamanism today and are thriving in

modern South Korea. In fact, they have been replacing the less dramatic hereditary shamans who, until the second half of the twentieth century, made up the
majority of shamans in the southern half of the peninsula.

During a ritual, or *kut*, a charismatic shaman will sing and dance in order to attract the attention of the spirits. She will also talk with the spirits who show up
and may even argue with them to determine which spirit is bothering her client,
and why it is doing so. In some cases, she will let herself be possessed by the
spirit that is causing trouble so that the offended parties can talk to that spirit and
convince it to change its behavior. (Money presented to the shaman channeling
the spirit is a particularly effective way to change a wayward spirit's behavior.)
Once she has determined the cause of her client's problems, the shaman may become possessed by a different spirit and, speaking through that spirit, order the
offending spirit to treat her client better. She may even threaten the offending
spirit and force it to flee. However, not all rituals involve threatening misbehaving
spirits. Sometimes shamans perform rituals to thank the spirits who have recently
helped them or their clients, or they perform rituals to seek the advice of spirits.

Hereditary shamans do not go into a trance and are not possessed by any spirits. They are ritual specialists who have inherited the knowledge necessary to perform certain *kut* that influence the behavior of spirits. In the past, they also inherited a clientele, regular customers from their home village or from neighboring
villages. However, when their clients began to move out of those villages into
towns and cities, the hereditary shamans did not follow them. City dwellers who
believe in shamanism tend to patronize charismatic shamans.

Those few hereditary shamans who still practice their craft in the countryside
are more often viewed as custodians of tradition than as effective masters of religious ritual. However, they may still be called on after a funeral to help the deceased accept the fact that they are no longer in the world of living. In Korean tradition, the line between the dead and the living could sometimes be crossed; but
when the dead tried to cross that line to contact the loved ones they left behind,
they could inadvertently bring misfortune on those loved ones. Therefore it was
important to make sure the dead realize they are truly dead. This would be done
through a ritual, the *Ssikkim kut*, in which the shaman entices the soul of the recently dead to follow along a white cloth that serves as a road to the realm of the
no-longer living. As the soul moves along that road in response to the induce-
ments of the shaman, the shaman cuts the cloth behind the deceased, assuring
that he or she cannot turn around and return to the realm of the living.

There is a third type of shaman that in the twenty-first century has become
more common than hereditary shamans. These are shamanic diviners. Unlike
nonshamanic fortune-tellers who use formulas based on Chinese techniques of
divination to calculate fate, shamanic fortune-tellers read the words of the spirits
in the throw of coins or rice grains. They do not necessarily go into a trance, nor
do they perform the elaborate rituals other shamans perform. Instead, they sit in
offices in Korea's cities and quietly offer advice to their customers based on their
inspired interpretation of signs from the spirits.

Is folk religion—with its mountain gods and toilet gods, its village rituals, and its shamans and diviners—really a religion? There is no clearly articulated theology for the gods of folk religion. Nor is there a folk-religion "bible" that all believers in the folk religion must read. There is not even a creed listing the various things shamans and their clients should believe. Because folk religion lacks theology, scriptures, and doctrine, it is usually not studied in religious studies departments in Korean universities. (Instead, it is studied in anthropology and literature departments.) Nor is "shamanism" or "folk religion" a category on the questionnaires about religious affiliation used by Gallup pollsters and government census takers.

Yet folk religion has many of the essential elements of a religion. It has prayer, it has worship, and it has rituals. Any study of Korean religious practices must include these folk practices to be comprehensive. However, sometimes it is difficult to distinguish folk religion from the other religious traditions of Korea. That job is made more difficult by the fact that many shamans, if asked what their religion is, will respond, "I am a Buddhist, of course." Moreover, many of the gods that appear in shaman rituals are borrowed from Buddhism.

Nevertheless, even if the boundary between them is not always clear, we can still talk in broad terms about Buddhism and folk religion as separate traditions. Buddhism, unlike folk religion, has clearly stated doctrines, has a standard collection of revered writings, and has standardized rituals. Moreover, Buddhism has a documented history on the Korean peninsula as a separate and distinct tradition.

Buddhism

When Buddhism entered Korea in the late fourth century, it initially took the guise of a more powerful form of folk religion. Korea's first Buddhist monks performed miracles that suggested that the Buddha could heal diseases that the less powerful gods of folk religion could not. Those displays of the Buddha's healing power occurred within the palaces of Korea's first kingdoms. Buddhism was brought to those palaces by Chinese, Central Asian, and Indian monks, who promised Korea's emerging royal families that its new spiritual technologies could help them stay healthy and long-lived, and also help them solidify and centralize their political authority.

Within just a couple of centuries, however, Buddhism became a religion for people beyond the palace walls as well. We can identify two main streams in Korean Buddhism as it developed in Korea. There are many Korean Buddhists, both in monasteries and in the secular world, who have been attracted to Buddhism primarily for its soteriological message: its promise of effective techniques for escaping suffering by developing insight that will dissolve the illusions that cause that suffering. However, there are also Buddhists who see Buddhism as a font of supernatural power for coping with the problems of everyday life in this world.

Such Buddhists visit Korea's monasteries not to meditate alongside monks but to pray to various buddhas (awakened ones), bodhisattvas (beings intent on enlightenment, who defer their own advance into full nirvāṇa in order to help other sentient beings achieve awakening), and other supernatural beings for assistance in overcoming intractable health, financial, or family problems.

Korean Buddhism is Mahāyāna (Great Vehicle) Buddhism. That means a couple of things. First of all, it means that the form of Buddhism that has become dominant in Korea derives from the same East Asian tradition out of which Japanese Zen was later born. Called Sŏn in Korea, this is meditative Buddhism. In the Korean context, it means first studying sūtras and commentaries on those sūtras that explain how human beings are caught in a web of illusion that misleads them into attributing permanence to phenomena that are only transitory. After this grounding in doctrine, Sŏn Buddhists will then seek to transcend a purely intellectual understanding of the nature of reality through meditation, so that the discriminating mind recognizes its limitations and lets go, allowing the meditator to experience the buddha-nature that is inherent in all things.

A second feature of Mahāyāna Buddhism as we find it in Korea is a result of the Mahāyāna focus on compassion. In Mahāyāna Buddhism, there are a large number of buddhas and bodhisattvas who, out of compassion, offer assistance to suffering humanity and, indeed, to all sentient beings. The more popular buddhas in Korea have included Śākyamuni (the Sage of the Śākyas, the historical Buddha Gautama), Amitābha (the Buddha of Limitless Light, or Limitless Life, who presides over the Western Paradise), Maitreya (the Buddha of the future), and Bhaiṣagyaguru (the Healing Buddha). A particularly popular bodhisattva throughout all periods of Korean history has been Avalokiteśvara, the Bodhisattva of Compassion.

Each of these beings in his own way offers hope to those who are looking for concrete solutions to specific problems. The Buddha Amitābha (Amit'a in Korean) recognizes how difficult it is for beings to achieve true insight when they are surrounded by the distractions of this world. Feeling compassion for the many who might otherwise find it all but impossible to achieve awakening, Amitābha promises that he will allow anyone who places his or her trust in him to be reborn in his Pure Land, the Western Paradise of Ultimate Bliss, where all the conditions will be perfect for attaining enlightenment. The promises of the Healing Buddha, Bhaiṣajyaguru (Yaksa yŏrae in Korean) are more concrete. He promises to heal all those who trust in him, and who also exhibit that trust through certain specified ritual displays of devotion. The Bodhisattva Maitreya (Kor. Mirŭk) offered hope that a Buddhist paradise will eventually be established on this earth, though in the meantime believers could ask Maitreya to help them add a healthy son to their family or to bestow health, wealth, and longevity on petitioners and their family members. The Bodhisattva Avalokiteśvara, known in Korea as Kwanŭm (the Chinese Guanyin and Japanese Kannon), "S/he Who Listens to the Cries of Humanity," was constantly on call to solve any problem a human being might face. She was sometimes depicted with multiple arms, the better to help simultaneously a multitude of beings in a multitude of ways. Two sūtras associated with Avalokiteśvara, the Heart Sūtra (P'anya simgyŏng) and the Thousand Hands Sūtra (Ch'ŏnsugyŏng), are particularly beloved by Koreans and are often chanted in Buddhist rituals.

"Buddhism" in Korea today is an umbrella term that covers a great variety of beliefs, practices, and schools. The largest contemporary denominations, the Chogyejong and the T'aegojong, identify themselves as Sŏn Buddhism, though their temples often have halls for chanting and halls for sūtra study alongside halls for meditation. However, South Korea also has many smaller, but thriving, denominations that focus on particular sūtras or on specific bodhisattvas or buddhas. One denomination run by nuns pays special attention to the Bodhisattva Kwanŭm. There are also denominations devoted to the Healing Buddha, Maitreya Buddha, or Amitābha Buddha, as well as denominations focusing on the Flower Garland Sūtra or the Lotus Sūtra. Moreover, Korea has at least two strong esoteric Buddhist denominations, which emphasize the chanting of mantras and the use of esoteric hand gestures, or mudrās, in their rituals. In addition, one of the largest of Korea's indigenous religions, Wŏn Buddhism, shares many beliefs and practices with traditional Buddhism, though it uses no Buddhist images in its worship halls and has its own sacred texts.

The large number of Koreans today who tell survey takers that they are Buddhist shows that Buddhism is successfully adapting to the urban environment of modern Korea. During Korea's lengthy Chosŏn dynasty, Buddhism was kept isolated in the mountains by the ruling Neo-Confucian elite, and any presence in the towns and cities of Korea was severely limited. Those mountain monasteries still flourish today and are frequently visited by pilgrims and others in search of a traditional Buddhist religious experience. However, Buddhist monks have also moved into the cities and have built urban temples. These temples often have Sunday morning services, in addition to regular monthly rituals dedicated to the Healing Buddha, the bodhisattva who assists the dead (Kṣitigarbha; Kor. Chijang), and the Bodhisattva of Compassion on the eighth, the eighteenth, and the twenty-fourth days, respectively, of the lunar month. Monks still chant sūtras, especially the Heart Sūtra and the Thousand Hands Sūtra, in the traditional style, using the Korean pronunciation of the Chinese characters that make up the text and following a tempo established by a monk striking a wooden clacker (mokt'ak). However, many urban temples now also have a piano along the wall in the main worship hall for leading lay congregations in the Buddhist hymns that are commonly sung in modern-day Korean. Temples hold meditation retreats for lay practitioners, but they also welcome laity who turn to Buddhism for supernatural assistance, such as a worried mother who might visit a temple a hundred days in a row, bowing 108 times on each visit, to pray that her eldest son will be accepted into one of Korea's top universities.

Buddhism's success in meeting the challenge of modernity is in sharp contrast to Confucianism. Once hegemonic on the peninsula, Confucianism today has shrunk to not much more that a source of ethical vocabulary and a guide to ancestor memorial services.

Confucianism and Neo-Confucianism

Confucian ideas first entered Korea in the fourth century along with institutional Buddhism, when Korea began importing written texts and administrative techniques from China, the bastion of advanced civilization in East Asia. However, Confucianism was imported primarily as a tool for government administration and a guide to writing poetry and histories, rather than as a religious tradition. It also provided a framework for discussing social obligations and the structure of society. A core assumption of Confucianism is that, if people learn to be loyal to their rulers, filial to their parents, deferential to their older siblings, correct in their relations with their spouses, and honest with their friends, then conflicts will be minimized and harmonious cooperation will prevail. Moreover, if everyone plays their assigned role within the social hierarchy, accepting the responsibilities of a superior toward an inferior and the duties of a subordinate toward a superior, then society could effectively work toward the collective good. This was an ethics of this world, which put aside questions of why we were on this earth in the first place, and what happened to us when we died. Answers to such questions were left for Buddhism to answer. Buddhism accepted responsibility for religious matters, since it provided answers to questions about the meaning of life and the nature of reality, and it provided rituals for interaction with supernatural beings.

That division of labor held for around a thousand years. Then, at the end of the fourteenth century, a new form of Confucianism was brought to Korea. Neo-Confucianism represented a metaphysical Confucianism that challenged Buddhist claims about the meaning of life and the nature of reality with counterclaims of its own. Neo-Confucianism turned on its head the Buddhist belief that things that change are inherently illusory and unreal. For Neo-Confucianism, it is precisely change that is real. To be more precise, patterns of change constitute reality. We should make sure our actions conform to that reality instead of striving to escape this realm of change into what Neo-Confucians considered the illusion of a static unity underlying change, à la the Buddhist concept of buddha-nature or nirvāṇa. In Neo-Confucian eyes, the pursuit of buddha-nature not only was a waste of time but also was selfish, since it put personal salvation ahead of the needs of society.

Neo-Confucians charged that Buddhist monks were immoral because they renounced their responsibilities to their families and fled into mountain monasteries to pursue enlightenment for themselves alone. When they entered a monastery, monks also left behind the land they were supposed to farm, and from which the government expected to collect taxes, and were exempted from corvée labor.

Their behavior, in Neo-Confucian eyes, was selfish. Monks placed their own spiritual advancement above the needs of the larger community. Someone who was
truly moral would obey his parents when he was young and take care of them
when they were old. He would not abandon them for the selfish pursuit of the
monastic life. Those who left for the monastery placed an unfair share of the responsibility for taking care of their parents on their brothers and sisters. Nor
would a moral subject abandon his fields. That made others pay for his pursuit of
enlightenment by forcing those who remained behind in his village to pay more
taxes to make up for what he was not paying.

The basis for the Neo-Confucian criticism of Buddhism was a new vision of the
world. Neo-Confucianism asserted, first of all, that the world of human experience was real. It was not created by our ignorant minds, as Buddhist philosophers claimed, but by the interaction of *li* (alt. *i*) and *ki*. *Ki* is the basic stuff, both
matter and energy, from which the universe is formed. *Li*, on the other hand, is
the Neo-Confucian name for the unifying pattern of appropriate interactions that
defines the world of human experience. Often misleadingly translated as "principle," *li* is much more active than that insipid translation implies. It is *li* that integrates the various bits of *ki* in the universe into a dynamic cosmic pattern of cooperation. It is also *li* that human beings should conform to so that their actions
will be consistent with those cosmic patterns of harmonious cooperation rather
than selfishly working against what is best for society and the universe as a
whole.

The Neo-Confucian prescription for self-cultivation, for becoming a virtuous
human being whose thoughts and actions are free of selfishness, was to cultivate
our innate goodness. We did this by activating the *li* within our hearts that told
us the correct way to behave. Neo-Confucians believed that we were born good.
Even if we had departed from the moral path over time and had let selfish desires
determine many of our actions, we could revive and strengthen our innate moral
sense. How could we do that?

One way was to study the Confucian classics and the explications of them by
later sages. Neo-Confucians respected wise men from the past and believed that
those sages not only knew what *li* was but also tried to pass that knowledge on to
later generations. By studying what the sages wrote, we too could learn to recognize *li*. Another way was to practice proper ritual and etiquette. Ritual and etiquette force us to put personal preferences aside and instead play whatever role is
assigned us by society at large, bringing us into conformity with *li*.

Neo-Confucians came to power in 1392 with the formation of the Chosŏn
dynasty (1392–1910) and established a Neo-Confucian government. That government lasted for more than five centuries and strengthened the grip of Confucian social values on the Korean heart. The impact of those five centuries of
Neo-Confucian dominance is still felt today. For example, Neo-Confucianism insisted that male dominance over women in the public sphere is *li*, a fundamental
pattern of the universe that human beings cannot change. The strength of the
patriarchy in modern Korea is at least partially the result of that Neo-Confucian

doctrine. Confucian ethics continues to provide the parameters for Korean concepts of the proper roles men and women should play in their families and their communities. The persistence of a collective orientation in Korea, favoring the family and the community over individual self-interest, is testimony to the continued relevance of Confucian values. Confucian ethics also provides the vocabulary Koreans use today when they discuss ethical issues. Koreans continue to use Confucian terms such as filial piety, loyalty, and sincerity when they evaluate human behavior. Moreover, for more than half the South Korean population, modernized Confucian rituals serve as the primary way to show respect for deceased parents and grandparents.

One other legacy of Confucianism, broadly defined, can still be seen in modern South Korea. Geomancy, the siting of graves and buildings according to the perceived patterns of the flow of ki through the earth, is not strictly speaking a product of Confucianism or Neo-Confucianism. Geomancy arose in China at least two thousand years ago and developed alongside rather than within Confucianism. Moreover, some of the most influential geomancers in Korean history have been Buddhist monks rather than Confucian scholars. Nevertheless, because both Neo-Confucianism and geomancy advocate aligning with cosmic patterns, and because both geomancy and Neo-Confucianism are textual traditions that require study before they are implemented, in the popular imagination, geomancy and Confucianism are connected.

At first glance, Confucianism does not look like many other religions. Though it accepts the existence of spirits, particularly ancestral spirits, it does not believe in an actual God above. Nor does it offer a vision of what awaits us after we die. However, especially when it was supported by the metaphysics of Neo-Confucianism, it served as a functional equivalent of religion. Confucianism told Koreans how to behave and how to cultivate a proper moral character. Moreover, as is the case with the vast majority of religions, rituals assumed a central role in Confucian practice. Even in the twenty-first century, when Neo-Confucianism metaphysics has vanished from almost everywhere in Korea except university philosophy departments, it is impossible to discuss the religious practices of Koreans without taking into account the influence of Confucianism. Koreans continued to be guided by the Confucian prescription to respect their parents and grandparents, and to show that respect by obeying them when they are alive as well as honoring them with appropriate rituals after they have died. Confucian values remain significant in Korea today, despite declines in the power of Confucian metaphysics and the number of Confucian organizations and institutions.

Daoism

Buddhism and Confucianism were not the only religions imported into Korea from China. Daoism was imported as well, but it never established a significant institutional presence and did not have the impact in Korea that Buddhism and

Confucianism had. There were no halls in Korea for the study of Daoism, though plenty of Confucian and Neo-Confucian academies were established on the peninsula over the centuries. Nor were there Daoist temples in Korea's mountains, though Buddhist monasteries were scattered all over the peninsula. The only Daoist temples in Korea were official ones located in the capital for the use of the court and government; the last such official Daoist temple was closed in the early seventeenth century, never to reopen.

One feature of Daoism, however, has influenced Korea's religious practices: internal alchemy. Internal alchemy refers to a constellation of breathing exercises and slow gymnastic movements, combined with meditation, that are intended to lengthen the practitioner's life span. Internal alchemy has its roots in the Daoist search for ways to enhance the quality of the *ki* (in this context, life-giving energy) in the body through physiological transformation (hence the term "alchemy"). Under the Chosŏn dynasty, quite a few prominent Confucian scholars practiced internal alchemy. They probably did not think of it as Daoist, however. To them, it was just another technique for enhancing health and longevity. Some internal alchemy techniques were discussed in the early seventeenth-century Korean medical classic the *Tongŭi pogam* (Treasury of Eastern Medicine), and thus they became an integral part of Korean spiritual practice.

Internal alchemy fell out of favor in Confucian circles in the last century or so of the Chosŏn dynasty. It was revived in South Korea in the last quarter of the twentieth century, but this time it is seen as an ancient indigenous Korean art. Internal alchemy is now associated with the new religions that worship Tan'gun, the mythical first Korean king and ancestor of the Korean people, its Chinese origins long forgotten.

Christianity

It is not Daoism, however, that is presenting the greatest challenge to the lingering influence of Confucianism today. This challenge also does not come from its old rival Buddhism, though Buddhism is thriving in contemporary Korea, or even from the indigenous folk religion, despite the pride Koreans have in their native culture and tradition. The biggest threat to traditional Confucian values is Korea's latest major religious import: Christianity.

Since the beginning of the twentieth century, it has been impossible to discuss the religious practices of Koreans without taking into account the presence and influence of Christianity. As noted earlier, Protestant Christians make up a larger percentage of the population in South Korea than in any other Asian country. More than 20 percent of South Koreans attend Protestant church services. In addition, at least another 8 percent of South Koreans call themselves Catholic, a higher percentage than in any other nation in Asia except the Philippines and East Timor. However, it is not just the number of Korean Christians that makes them so significant in Korea's modern religious culture. Christianity is also changing the way non-Christian Koreans think about religion and, in the process, is changing their own conceptions of appropriate religious behavior. The greatest force for change has been the Protestant community.

Protestants have become hugely influential in modern Korean society, although there have been Catholics in Korea for a century longer than Korea has had Protestant churches. One reason the Protestant model of religion and religious behavior is so powerful is that there are almost three Korean Protestants today to every one Korean Catholic. Ironically, Protestant Christianity has been so successful in Korea in part because Catholicism paved the way for Protestant missionary endeavors.

The Korean Catholic Church was born in 1784. In that year a young Korean Confucian scholar traveled to the Chinese capital of Beijing, where he met a French missionary priest, was converted and baptized, and returned to Korea to convert and baptize his friends. Within a decade there were four thousand Koreans calling themselves Catholic, even though a priest did not arrive until 1794. Under Father Zhou Wenmo's guidance, between 1794 and 1801, the Korean Catholic community more than doubled in size. However, in 1801, after the death of relatively tolerant king, the Chosŏn dynasty's staunchly Neo-Confucian government launched a full-scale persecution of Catholics, which would rage off and on for another seventy years. Thousands of Catholics were executed for putting their faith ahead of their duty to obey their king, who had decreed that Koreans should renounce that religion (which was denounced in official documents as "perverse teachings"). This was the first full-blown religious persecution in Korean history. What had the Catholics done to provoke such animosity?

Catholics were monotheists. They believed in one God and one God only. That belief, new to Korea, made confrontation with their government unavoidable. First of all, since they believed there was only one God, they refused to participate in rituals honoring other gods. That was a dangerous position to adopt in Chosŏn Korea. The pope had declared that ancestors were treated like gods in Confucian memorial services. (The standard English name then for such practices was "ancestor worship.") However, the government of Korea required all educated Korean men to honor their ancestors with precisely such Confucian rituals. The first Catholics to die for their faith, in 1791, were executed for failing to perform the mourning rites in the prescribed Confucian manner.

Monotheists, since they believe in one and only one God, also believe that God is the Supreme Being. That means God ranks ahead of any mere earthly king, and his orders take precedence over any orders handed down by a king or government. As a result, Catholics rejected the king's claim that he had the power to tell Catholics which rituals they could and could not perform. Catholics not only refused to perform "ancestor worship," but also held their own rituals, the Catholic mass, without official permission. This was a challenge to the traditional control over ritual by the state, which could not be tolerated by a Confucian government.

Moreover, as a consequence of their monotheism and the related rejection of state authority over their religious practices, Catholics formed religious communities with much clearer boundaries than those to which Koreans had been accustomed. In premodern Korea, it was not at all unusual for the same person to patronize shamans, pray at Buddhist monasteries, and perform Confucian rituals. The average Korean was not expected to identify exclusively with one religious tradition. Catholics changed that. They defined themselves as Catholics and even had an initiation ceremony (baptism) that indicated they had joined a new religious community and had severed ties with all other religious traditions.

Though the first generations of Korean Catholics were unsuccessful in getting the government to recognize their right to follow their own conscience, they introduced three new ideas to the Korean people that slowly gained respectability. The first idea was monotheism. The second was religious freedom, the notion that the state should not interfere in the religious beliefs and activities of its subjects. The third was the concept of an exclusive religious orientation (exclusive in the sense that it excluded involvement with other religious traditions, and that people with the same religious orientation formed a separate and distinct religious community).

By 1884, when the first Protestant missionaries arrived on Korean soil, Koreans had heard about monotheism for a century, not only from Catholics but also from the first organized indigenous religion in Korea, Tonghak (later called Ch'ŏndogyo), which formed in a sense as a response to Catholicism. They had also grown accustomed to hearing demands for religious freedom, first from Catholics but later from Tonghak adherents as well. And, thanks to Catholicism and Tonghak, the idea of a religious organization composed of both clergy and like-minded laity was not unfamiliar.

Protestant missionaries had an additional advantage in that, by the time they reached Korean soil, religious persecution was drawing to an end. Just a few years after their arrival, they were able to preach publicly, open churches for Korean converts, and build schools and hospitals for the general public. By 1910 they were drawing more Koreans into their churches than were Catholics, and they have had larger memberships than the Catholic Church ever since.

The Protestant version of Christianity was different from Roman Catholicism in several respects, differences that helped it to grow so quickly. First of all, Protestants introduced a new form of participatory worship to Koreans. In Korea's traditional religions, as well as in Catholicism, the ritual specialist dominated the service. Lay participants acted primarily as observers and passive participants. There were no hymns in traditional religious ceremonies. Moreover, except in the folk tradition, the language of rituals was a foreign one. In Buddhism, it was Sanskrit, an ancient Indian language used in East Asia for mantras and spells, and classical Chinese. In Confucianism, it was classical Chinese alone. And in Catholicism, it was Latin. Protestant services, however, were conducted in vernacular Korean. One of the first projects the early missionaries took on was the translation of the Bible into Korean. They translated hymnbooks into Korean as well.

Protestant churches offered the only worship services, outside of the folk religion, in which the average Korean not only could understand what was going on but also could join in. (The Korean Catholic Church did not start saying mass in Korean until after the Vatican II reforms of the 1960s.) Worship in Korean Protestant churches is congregational worship, in which everyone present is an active contributor to the service. This participatory model of religion was new to Korea and became extremely popular. Further enhancing the participation of the laity, many Protestant pastors handed over some of the responsibility for running their churches to laypeople, who were given titles corresponding to their responsibilities. Buddhism monasteries in Korea did not have any formal lay positions corresponding to the elders and Bible women of Korean Protestant churches. Even the Catholic Church did not have as clearly articulated a lay hierarchy as did Protestant churches.

Another feature of Protestant Christianity that set it apart from other religions in Korea a hundred years ago was its proselytizing zeal. The Korean Protestant community was determined to save as many souls as it could in the shortest amount of time possible, and, since it believed Protestant Christianity offered the only sure route to salvation, that meant bringing non-Christians into Christian churches. The result has been a rate of growth that has astonished Christians in the rest of the world. There were fewer than twenty-one thousand Protestant Christians in all of Korea in 1900. A little more than a century later, the Korean Protestant community is well over ten million strong.

Along with growth has come division. The imported idea that people with similar religious convictions should form their own independent and distinct religious organizations has led to a proliferation of Protestant denominations in South Korea. The major denominations, in terms of membership figures, are the Presbyterian Church, the Methodist Church, and the Holiness Church. However, almost every Christian denomination found in Europe or North America is also represented in Korea. Moreover, the larger denominations have splintered into subdenominations; there are, for example, more than fifty Presbyterian subdenominations on the peninsula.

Despite this organizational diversity, some common elements tie Korean Christians together across denominational lines and also help distinguish Korean Christianity from Christianity in other countries. Korean Christianity is overwhelmingly fundamentalist and evangelical. It is also very demanding. Just attending church on Sunday for an hour or two is not enough. Korean churches expect their members to come to worship services during the week as well, even if they have to attend a daybreak prayer devotional service at dawn on a weekday before leaving for their secular job. Moreover, the practice of tithing—contributing 10 percent or more of one's income to the church—is even more common in Korea than in many other countries, such as the United States, that are typically considered to be "Christian nations."

The primary division in Korean Christianity—one that is even broader than those that divide denominations—is the split between the few churches that promote the social gospel and the many that preach the gospel of wealth. Though the social-gospel churches remain a minority within the overall Protestant community, they contributed significantly to the democratization of South Korea in recent decades; they preached that God demanded that all human beings be treated with respect, and then acted on that conviction by leading public demonstrations for free elections and for better treatment for workers. The gospel-of-wealth churches, on the other hand, preach that political issues should be left in the hands of politicians. They also preach that God will reward the godly in this life with wealth and health. Their sermons that faith will be rewarded with wealth have brought large crowds into their pews. Some outside observers argue that the gospel of wealth has also inspired the rapid economic development of South Korea, as Christian Koreans have worked hard to increase their own and their country's wealth as a way of proving that they are the chosen people of God.

New Religions

Korea's traditional religions have responded to Christian proselytizing zeal by adapting aspects of Christianity that have made Christianity such a powerful force in modern Korea. Some of those responses have been more successful than others.

Modern Korean Buddhists, for example, have written Buddhist hymns that the laity can sing together and have encouraged greater lay participation in Buddhist activities. These responses have stimulated a boom in urban Buddhism, which has kept the number of Buddhists in Korea ahead of the number of Protestant Christians. Confucians, on the other hand, have not adapted well to their fall from power with the demise of the Chosŏn dynasty. The main Confucian organization in Korea officially declared itself a religious organization only in the 1990s and also published a one-volume guide to Confucian teachings and practice that at first glance looks a lot like a Christian Bible. However, although Confucian values remain strong in Korean society and most families still honor their ancestors with Confucian memorial rituals, Confucianism as an organization is very weak, and less than 1 percent of Koreans identify themselves as Confucians to survey takers. Internal alchemy is growing in popularity, though most of its practitioners are unaware of its ancient roots in Chinese Daoism and its modern connections to the worship of Tan'gun, and many of these adepts might not even consider themselves religious. Finally, Korean folk religion has not come up with a coherent response to Christian inroads, since it has no central organizations to formulate policies. Shamans, however, do not appear to have lost much of their appeal despite urbanization and the popularity of Christianity. According to the membership figures of national shaman organizations, there are as many practicing shamans in Korea today as there are Protestant pastors.

Rather than internal transformation, another response to the Christian challenge has been the creation of new religions, based on the Christian model of people with similar religious beliefs forming religious organizations to promote those beliefs. It is estimated that there are more than two hundred new religions in South Korea today, but only a few of them merit our attention. These include Ch'ŏndogyo, Wŏnbulgyo (Wŏn Buddhism), Taejonggyo, Tan (Dahn) World, Chŭngsando (Jeungsando), Taesŏn Chillihoe (Daesun Jinrihoe), and the Unification Church.

Ch'ŏndogyo, Wŏn Buddhism, Taejonggyo, and the Unification Church (which considers itself a Christian organization) appear to have been created with the Christian model of modern religion in mind. They all hold Sunday worship services in buildings that look like churches, buildings and they sing hymns at those services. However, the prayers they pray, the hymns they sing, and the doctrines they teach are unique to each of these religions.

Wŏnbulgyo (Round, or Consummate) Buddhism, as its name implies, is a new religion with Buddhist orientations. The language it uses sometimes is more modern-sounding than traditional Buddhist language, but its basic doctrines have many parallels with what is taught in mainstream monasteries. Wŏn Buddhists sing hymns and pray, but they also practice Sŏn meditation, seek enlightenment, and practice compassion. Ch'ŏndogyo, on the other hand, cannot be assigned to any of the traditional religious categories. The oldest of Korea's new religions, it began in 1860 as a response to Catholicism. That is clear not only in its monotheism but also in one of its early names for god, Ch'ŏnju (the Lord of Heaven), the name Catholics had coined for their God. However, Ch'ŏndogyo theology is not Catholic. Instead, Ch'ŏndogyo combines a belief in one God and in the equality of all human beings before God with a Confucian vision of the universe in which everything is related to everything else and the goal of religious endeavors is to live in harmony with the universe. Taejonggyo is equally difficult to classify. It considers itself to be the revival of the ancient religion of the Korean people, which would suggest that it has its roots in folk religion. However, many of its rituals resemble Christian, rather than shamanic, rites. Moreover, its theology shows clear Christian influence. Taejonggyo is the only indigenous Korean religion to worship a trinitarian God, even though its leaders insist that ancient Koreans shared their belief that Hwanin, Hwanŭng, and Tan'gun were three persons in one God. There are also elements in Taejonggyo that resemble elements of the Shintō religion that Japanese colonial powers introduced to Korea in the early twentieth century, including Taejonggyo's focus on Tan'gun as a divine founder of both the Korean state and the Korean race. Nevertheless, Taejonggyo adherents strongly resist any suggestion that their religious beliefs have in any way been influenced by Christianity or by the Japanese.

One thing all these new religions have in common is Korean nationalism. They represent assertions of pride in native Korean tradition in the face of the challenge wrought by Christianity and the West. That is particularly clear in the case of the Unification Church (T'ongilgyo). The Unification Church clearly derives from Christianity; its original name, in fact, was the Holy Spirit Association for the Unification of World Christianity. However, it differs from mainstream Christianity in several key doctrinal points. Of particular importance is the Unificationist belief that Jesus failed to complete the mission God assigned him. He was supposed to marry and bring sinless children into the world but was crucified before he could do so. That is why God decided to assign the Reverend Mun Sŏnmyŏng (Sun Myong Moon) the mission of completing that task and bringing salvation to humanity.

Wŏn Buddhism and Ch'ŏndogyo share the Unification Church's belief that the most recent spiritual leader of the human race was born in Korea. They disagree over who that spiritual leader is (each nominates its own founder), but they agree that Korea has become the spiritual center of the world, the place to which everyone today should turn for spiritual advice and guidance. That Korea-centric worldview is shared by Dahn World, an internal-alchemy organization that has opened branches all over the world but insists that its leader, Yi Sŭnghŭn (Seung Heun Lee), is a renowned spiritual leader who is leading humanity toward an "enlightenment revolution."

Taejonggyo goes even farther in its assertion of a leading role for Korea in modern religion. Because Taejonggyo worships Tan'gun, the mythical ancestor of the Korean people, it is able to claim that God is a Korean. That belief is shared by both Chŭngsando (Jeungsando) and Taesŏn Chillihoe (Daesun Jinrihoe), though they do not worship Tan'gun as the Supreme Deity. Instead, they worship Kang Chŭngsan, whom they believe is the incarnation in human form on earth of the Supreme Lord Above. Chŭngsando and Taesŏn Chillihoe, though they worship the same God, disagree on many of the details of what their God taught in the first decade of the twentieth century, when he walked on Korean soil. However, they are alike in at least one important aspect. Neither Chŭngsando nor Taesŏn Chillihoe shows much Christian influence in their doctrines, their architecture, or their practices. Neither their services nor their worship halls look anything like Christian services or churches. They do not sing hymns or sit in pews. Instead, they chant sacred mantras taught by their God. Both religious organizations have grown rapidly in the last two decades of the twentieth century, a possible sign of greater self-confidence among the indigenous Korean religious traditions.

Korean Religious Practice Today

A few decades ago, many scholars around the world predicted that the growing importance of science and technology in the modern world would lead to a lessening of interest in religion and shrinking memberships in religious organizations. Most have now changed their tune and admit that secularization is not the wave of the future. It instead seems clear that religion will continue to play an important role in human society, religious values will continue to influence how people behave, and people will continue to find satisfaction, hope, and peace of mind in religious practice. Korea is certainly an example of this continuing importance of religious even in modern, technological societies: as Korea has modernized, it has also become more religious (if in this case we define "religious" as membership in a religious organization and regular participation in organized religious activities).

Koreans are more likely now to attend religious services on a weekly basis than they ever were before. They are more likely now to identify with a specific religious orientation than they have ever been. And they are also more likely to try to convince others to share their religious orientation, as other religions begin to imitate Christian proselytizing techniques. In short, with recent polls showing that, for the first time in history, more than half of the population of South Korea says it believes in a specific religion, Korea has become a consciously religious nation.

This does not mean, however, that all Koreans share the same religious beliefs and engage in the same religious practices. As this survey of contemporary South Korean religion argues, and as the chapters that follow in this book will demonstrate, South Korea has an extremely diverse religious culture. It is the very model of religious pluralism. Koreans define salvation in a number of ways and pursue it using an even greater number of techniques. Many Koreans also seek to become better human beings, a goal they also define in different ways and pursue in different manners. They celebrate and mourn with religious rituals, but those rituals vary across the religious spectrum. They also seek supernatural assistance in solving a wide variety of pressing issues, but they differ over how best to seek that assistance and where best they should look. And Koreans join religious associations in search of fellowship, but those associations may satisfy one Korean's desire for a sense of community, but not another's.

Koreans worship, pray, and mediate, but they do not worship, pray, and meditate the same way. Some sit quietly, some speak to supernatural beings, some entertain spirits and gods, and still others participate in solemn ritual to show their devotion to their God or gods or to convince those deities to help them. (The same person may do all four, depending on the situation.) Many Koreans go on pilgrimages to holy sites, but they do not all agree on which sites are holy. Many Koreans study sacred texts, but they do not all agree on which texts are sacred. And many Koreans follow religious rules defining proper behavior, but they do not all agree on what those rules are.

All these activities, and all these goals, despite their diversity, have one thing in common: they all are examples of Korean religious practice. They suggest that religion in Korea is whatever Koreans do when they use religious means to seek religious goals. From shaman purification rituals to Buddhist exorcisms, from Confucian rites for the spirits to Christian rituals for expressing grief, from chanting incantations to celebrating the birthdays of holy persons, Koreans engage in such a wide variety of religious practices that only a few can be included in this one volume. This book can, however, provide a brief, tantalizing glimpse into the religious practices of Koreans so that we may come to a better appreciation of the complexity and rich diversity of Korea's religious culture.

Buddhism

1

King Mu and the Making and
Meanings of Mirŭksa

Jonathan W. Best

King Mu—or, literally, the "Martial Monarch" (r. 600–641)—is the honorific title (Kor. *shi*) posthumously bestowed by the court of Paekche (early fourth century–663) upon the ruler who during his lifetime reigned under his personal name of Chang. The posthumous title presumably was chosen in recognition of the dramatic reversal effected in the kingdom's military fortunes in its bitter conflict with the neighboring state of Silla (early fourth century–675) during the four decades of his rule. Mu's notable achievements were not, however, restricted to his armies' repeated victories in battle; it is evident from both written and archaeological records that generous patronage of Buddhism was another hallmark of his reign. Building on the pious precedent of his father, King Pŏp—the "Dharma King" (r. 599–600)—Mu not only completed construction on the great metropolitan Wanghŭngsa, or the Monastery of Royal Propagation, begun by his father, but also initiated construction on several other important temples, including most notably Mirŭksa, or the Monastery of Maitreya. Mu's many political and military accomplishments apparently won him a special place in the minds of his contemporaries at home and abroad. He is, for instance, the only Paekche king whose passing is known to have been formally mourned by a Chinese ruler. The *Xin Tang shu* reports that, upon learning of Mu's death in 641, Tai Zong (r. 627–50), emperor of the mighty Tang dynasty (618–907), made a ritual demonstration of grief at the Xuan Wu Gate in the northern wall of the imperial capital of Chang'an.

Mu is also the only ruler of Paekche known to have been celebrated in peninsular folk legend. His fabulous biography, preserved in the thirteenth-century *Samguk yusa* (Memorabilia of the Three Kingdoms; *Taishō* no. 2039), claims that he was sired by a dragon and relates a multiplicity of marvels associated with his building of Mirŭksa. The *Samguk yusa* was compiled by the Korean monk Iryŏn (1206–89), and its text consists largely of Buddhist miracle tales set in both the Three Kingdoms period (first century B.C.E.–668) and the succeeding Unified Silla period (668–935). Although this text's beguiling account of King Mu's youthful years and their relevance to the construction of Mirŭksa clearly belongs to the realm of folklore, it also provides the earliest surviving written evidence relating to the temple's construction, plan, and symbolic significance. To appreciate the historically important political and Buddhological implications of this mildly risqué biography of Mu, however, requires extensive contextualization of its narrative.

In pursuing policies of aggressive military action and generous patronage of Buddhism, Mu was likely motivated in significant part by contemporary Chinese example, especially that of the Sui dynasty (581–618), the regime whose brief but historically critical reign overlapped with the formative years of his own rule. Having initially risen to power as suzerains of northern China in 581 and then vanquished the southern Chinese state of the Chen (557–89) less than a decade later, the Sui emperors became the first masters of a unified China in almost three hundred years. This momentous accomplishment was to have profound repercussions upon the course of Korean history. As rulers of all of China, the Sui emperors proudly assumed the imperial mantle of the Han dynasty (206 B.C.E.–220 C.E.), a regime whose control had extended from western Central Asia into northern Korea. The Sui attainment of imperial hegemony meant that for the first time in centuries there existed a powerful government in China that, being unhindered by any rival Chinese regime, was both predisposed and able to take an aggressive interest in the Korean peninsula. The strength of this interest was forcefully demonstrated in 598 when the Sui court unleashed a massive military assault upon Koguryŏ (late first century B.C.E.–668 C.E.), the third and northernmost of the Three Kingdoms. This campaign proved costly and unsuccessful, yet the Sui leadership was undeterred and subsequently launched three more equally monumental—but also equally abortive—campaigns against this same northeast Asian state between 612 and 614.

The mounting of these attacks on Koguryŏ—like the similar, though more successful, Sui campaigns in Central Asia, Mongolia, and Vietnam—was made possible by the dynasty's centralized control of the vast resources of China. Although the unification of the Central Kingdom had been accomplished through Sui force of arms, the dynasty's founder, the emperor posthumously known as Wen Di (r. 581–605), made effective use of both political and cultural means to weld the long-divided country into a single mighty state. Although Wen Di also utilized Daoism and Confucianism to sanction his dynasty's authority and to foster ideological harmony within the empire, without question his patronage of Buddhism was the most important and prominent factor in these efforts. Not only was the persecution of the religion by the previous regime in northern China an outrage for which he, as a Buddhist, wished to make amends, but there also was a long history of lavish governmental support of Buddhism in southern China that, for sound political reasons, he sought to emulate. Wen Di strove through proclamation and patronage to translate into actuality his vision of the potently beneficial reciprocity between the authority of Buddhism and the authority of the state, especially as the latter was manifest in the person of the ruler.

During the first year of his reign (581), Wen Di ordered the erection of Buddhist monasteries at battle sites that had been critical in his family's ascent to imperial majesty. He further commissioned the regular observance at these battlefield temples of rituals for the benefit of those who had died there. Two years later, Wen Di also ordered the construction of state monasteries in the capital and throughout the empire, where services would be performed at government expense three times a year for a span of eight days. In addition, he forbade the population from killing living things during the periods when these services were being enacted and thereby, theoretically at least, made everyone in China participants in the particular sacredness of those days. Comparable acts designed to advance Buddhism as a means to promote the unity of the state and the sacrosanct authority of the emperor continued to characterize Wen Di's endeavors throughout his lengthy reign. Between 601 and 604, for instance, he ordered the construction of a network of pagodas throughout China and dispatched delegations of eminent monks to supervise the enshrinement of Buddhist relics therein. The relics and the costly reliquaries that contained them were provided by the government and, in some cases, Wen Di himself presided over the ritual placement of the sacred remains within the reliquaries.

Through his grand acts combining imperial largesse and personal devotion, Wen Di was overtly casting himself simultaneously in two of Buddhism's most revered roles for the pious potentate: the *cakravartin*, the devout, all-conquering "wheel-turning emperor," and the *mahādānapati*, the munificent patron of the faith. By assuming these roles, he consciously linked himself both to the legendary Indian paragon of Buddhist kingly virtue, King Aśoka (r. 274–237 B.C.E.?), and to the recent Chinese imperial champion of the dharma, Wu Di (r. 502–50), the ostentatiously pious emperor of the southern Chinese Liang dynasty (502–557). In the following passage from his edict ordering the building of the battlefield memorial temples in 581 as reported in the *Lidai sanbao ji* (Record of the Three Jewels through Successive Generations), Wen Di declares himself a *cakravartin* and credits his military successes to his devotion to the Dharma. He then asserts that the world will be transformed through his conjoining of temporal power with Buddhism's divine power.

> With the armed might of a *cakravartin* king, We spread the ideas of the Ultimately Benevolent One [the Buddha]. With a hundred victories in a hundred battles, We promote the practice of the ten Buddhist virtues. Therefore We regard the weapons of war as having become like incense and flowers [presented as offerings to Buddha] and the fields of this visible world as becoming forever identical with the Buddhaland. [*Taishō* no. 2034, vol. 49, p. 107c, A. F. Wright, tr.].

Paekche's rulers prudently maintained cordial, if rather circumspect, relations with the powerful and aggressive Sui court. Mu's great-uncle, best known by his posthumous appellation of King Widŏk (r. 554–599), sent the first of the kingdom's repeated embassies to the dynasty during its initial year of power (581). The alacrity of Widŏk's dispatch of this embassy is distinctive: among the ten

Chinese regimes with which the kingdom had relations over the course of its history, only the ascendancy of the Sui was so promptly acknowledged. Wen Di evidently appreciated Widŏk's ready recognition of his authority because he forthwith reciprocated by conferring upon the Paekche monarch the impressive double title of "Senior Palatine with Dignities Equal to Those of the Three Ministers, and Duke of Daifang Commandery." Widŏk, in apparent appreciation of the honor done him, sent a second mission to the Sui court in the following year. The mission of 582, however, constituted Paekche's last official contact with this Chinese government until 589, the year of the Sui unification of China through its triumph over the southern Chen dynasty. Toward the end of 589, the appearance of a storm-buffeted Sui warship in Paekche waters inspired the dispatch of Widŏk's third embassy to Wen Di's court, a mission whose dual purpose was to escort the ship home and to felicitate the Sui emperor on his army's historic achievement. It is also reported that at this time an ensemble of the kingdom's musicians accompanied the embassy and performed at the imperial court in Chang'an. Wen Di was evidently gratified by Widŏk's actions on this occasion because he issued an edict absolving him henceforth of the obligation of providing yearly tribute—an obligation to which the king had, in any case, paid scant heed in the past. Consistent with the privilege granted him and his own previous behavior, the Paekche monarch thereafter refrained from further diplomatic intercourse with the dynasty for nine years.

In 598, however, Widŏk did send a fourth embassy to the Sui court. His envoy carried a memorial to Wen Di urging the strengthening of the Sui armies in Liaodong and offering to provide guides to participate in the Chinese punitive expedition against Koguryŏ that had been launched earlier that year. Widŏk's offer of military assistance was appreciatively declined because, by either chance or design, it reached the Sui emperor after the campaign had been terminated. Yet Widŏk's actions in this instance—actions that not many years later would be closely emulated by his grandnephew, King Mu—reveal a clear cognizance on the Paekche monarchy's part that the realpolitik of East Asia had fundamentally altered. China for the first time in centuries had demonstrated a willingness to take a forceful role vis-à-vis Korea. Widŏk not only sought to ingratiate his government with the emperor through the offer of military guides but also directly encouraged armed Chinese intervention as a means of weakening one of his northeast Asian enemies.

The enormous resources—including, for instance, an army said to number three hundred thousand men—that the Sui government was able to marshal for the 598 attack upon Koguryŏ constituted a formidable lesson whose implications were evidently not lost on the rulers of Paekche. It demonstrated convincingly that the wide-scale unification of adjoining territories coupled with effective centralization of political authority could result in an exponential increase in the power of the state. An equally obvious corollary to this lesson was that the best chance for Paekche, or any Korean kingdom for that matter, to resist aggression from a unified China would be to control a unified peninsula. Although it could be reasonably argued that Korean monarchs had long harbored hegemonic ambitions toward their peninsular neighbors, the combined inspiration and threat of Sui power nonetheless served dramatically to intensify the already active struggle among the three kingdoms.

In Paekche the martial King Mu, who ascended the throne just two years after Widŏk's 598 mission to the Sui, clearly took these lessons to heart. He strove both to maintain his great-uncle's amicable relations with the Sui emperors and to move strategically against his Korean neighbors, especially Silla, which at this time confronted Paekche across all its land frontiers. The overall cordiality of Mu's relations with the Chinese government notwithstanding, the *Sui shu* indicates that he delayed sending his first diplomatic mission for almost a decade after his accession to the throne. An authoritative Buddhist record dating to the Sui period and preserved in the early Tang *Guang hongming ji* (Expanded Record of the Transmission of the Lamp; *Taishō* no. 2103, vol. 52, p. 217a), however, reports that official representatives from Paekche came to the Sui court in 601, the second year of Mu's reign, to request relics of the Buddha. It will be recalled that also in this year Wen Di initiated his program of distributing relics and establishing pagodas throughout China to enshrine them, an undertaking no doubt modeled upon the revered Aśoka's mythical building of eighty-four thousand stūpas throughout his South Asian empire.

The *Sui shu's* first report of the arrival of a formal diplomatic mission from Paekche during Mu's reign is dated to 607. In fact, as if to make amends for the belated opening of his relationship with the Sui, Mu in this year sent two embassies to the Sui capital. This was the first time in the kingdom's recorded history that more than one embassy was dispatched to the same Chinese court in the course of a single year. The second Paekche mission of 607 presented a memorial from Mu encouraging the Chinese government to undertake another campaign against Koguryŏ. The new Sui emperor, Yang Di (r. 605–17), who had ascended the throne just two years earlier and was personally inclined to undertake such an offensive, promptly ordered Mu to gather military intelligence concerning his northern neighbor. The *Sui shu* asserts that at the time, however, Paekche was secretly in league with Koguryŏ, and that Mu's request for Chinese intervention was simply a ruse to gain Sui confidence in order to learn their military plans. Whatever the truth of this assertion, it is clear that this time Paekche's leadership had greater cause to be concerned with the immediate threat posed by the adjacent kingdom of Silla than with the more distant challenge of Koguryŏ.

Mu sent yet a third embassy to Yang Di's court in the following year (608), and during the same year Paekche was also visited by a Sui envoy traveling to Japan. The eighth-century *Nihon shoki* reports, moreover, that a year later (609) a storm-driven Paekche ship found safe anchorage in a western Japanese port. On board were a number of Buddhist monks who informed the Japanese authorities that they had been dispatched at royal command to advance their understanding of the religion through studies at monastic centers in southern China. This record, like that concerning the representatives that Mu sent to obtain relics from the Sui court eight years earlier, both suggests his willingness to use Buddhism to foster international relationships and provides evidence of the breadth of his program to promote the religion within his domain.

In 610, just a year after the monk-bearing Paekche ship found safe harbor in Japan, the Sui emperor ordered that preparations be made for a second assault on Koguryŏ. Mu, apparently aware of the Chinese emperor's intentions, is said to have sent an envoy in the following year (611) to request that he be kept apprised of developments regarding the forthcoming attack. Yang Di, evidently gratified by this demonstration of apparent loyalty, dispatched a special envoy to Paekche to inform the king directly of the campaign's objectives and, presumably, to supervise the kingdom's expected participation in the endeavor. Both Chinese and Korean sources indicate, however, that when the Chinese army attacked Koguryŏ early in 612, Mu deployed his troops in a manner designed to simulate support for the Sui cause while in fact putting pressure on Silla's border positions. Whether or not this attribution of duplicity on Mu's part is accurate, it is clear that the Paekche king desired to maintain congenial relations with the powerful Sui government, but that he was also ever mindful of the challenge posed by Silla. In 614 Mu dispatched what proved to be the kingdom's final embassy to the Sui court; subsequent civil unrest within China made further diplomatic contact with the dynasty impossible.

The mounting disturbances in China were triggered in large part by the stresses caused by the staggering costs of the repeated—and in all cases unsuccessful—Sui attacks on Koguryŏ between 612 and 614. The unrest ultimately resulted in the Sui government's downfall and its replacement in 618 as suzerain of an unified China by the long-ruling Tang dynasty. Mu's diplomatic contacts with the Tang court were largely amicable and much more frequent than his official interactions with the preceding regime. He dispatched his first embassy to the Tang in 621 and, according to the Chinese historical record, was responsible for sending twelve more missions to their court prior to his death in 641. Although some tensions arose with the Tang government due to Paekche's increasingly successful offensive warfare against Silla during the latter half of Mu's reign, when the emperor Tai Zong was informed of the king's death, he not only formally mourned his passing, as noted previously, but also posthumously conferred upon him an honorific title and contributed generously to the expenses of his funeral.

At the start of Mu's reign, however, Paekche's military situation had been vulnerable. The loss of the Han River valley to Silla fifty years earlier, followed shortly by the battlefield death of King Sŏng (r. 523–54) and Silla's forceful annexation of the intervening territory of Kaya in 562, had left the kingdom much weakened and exposed to aggression from Silla across all its land frontiers. The twelfth-century *Samguk sagi* (Histories of the Three Kingdoms) reports that although Paekche twice attacked Silla during Widŏk's reign, both offensives had ended in failure with heavy losses. Over the course of Mu's forty-year reign, however, Paekche's military position vis-à-vis Silla improved dramatically. After mounting an unsuccessful siege in 602 upon Silla's Amaksan Fortress in the

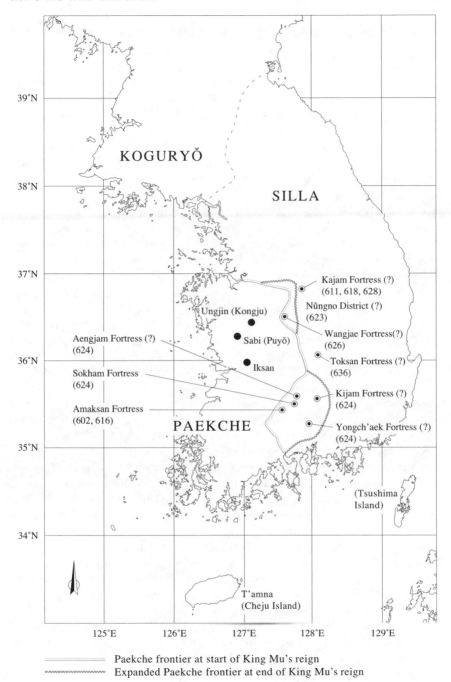

Figure 1.1. Paekche-Silla battle sites and changes in Paekche's borders during
the reign of King Mu (600–641).

southeast (see figure 1.1), Mu's army in 611 scored its first recorded victory, the capture of the neighboring kingdom's strategic Kajam Fortress. Five years later (616) Paekche troops launched a second—and this time triumphal—attack on the Amaksan Fortress. The strategic importance of the Kajam Fortress, which evidently was located near Paekche's northeastern border, is apparent from its history as an object of repeated contention. Having been seized by Paekche in 611, it was retaken by Silla in 618, and then ten years later (628) Paekche's troops strove unsuccessfully to regain possession of it.

The failure to retake the Kajam Fortress is one of just two setbacks that appear in the record of Paekche's otherwise wholly successful military record during the latter half of Mu's reign. In 624 his armed forces captured six of Silla's southwestern fortifications, including the Sokham, Kijam, and Yongch'aek Fortresses. These victories enabled Paekche to annex a substantial portion of former Kaya territory in south-central Korea. Nor did the kingdom's armies relent in applying pressure along its northeastern border with Silla. In 623 a daring raid was made on the neighboring kingdom's Nŭngno district, and three years later Silla's Wangjae Fortress (also known as the Chujae Fortress) was overrun, a victory that resulted in the expansion of Paekche's territory in the northeast as well. In 627 two additional, though unnamed, Silla frontier fortifications fell to Paekche. These losses, coupled with the series of earlier conquests made by Paekche's armies and Mu's evident intentions of further aggression, led the reigning Silla king, Chinp'yŏng (r. 579–632), to send a special envoy to the Tang court in 627 to decry his kingdom's perilous condition. The Tang emperor, Tai Zong, responded immediately with a letter to Mu ordering him to desist from further attacks on his neighbor. The *Samguk sagi* indicates that the imperial Chinese reprimand did prompt a pause in the warfare between the two Korean kingdoms, but in 633 Mu's army renewed its campaigning in the northeast by capturing Silla's Sŏgok Fortress, and three years later it mounted an unsuccessful assault on the strategic Toksan Fortress. With regard to Silla's successful diplomatic maneuvering in 627 and indicative of the folkloric character of the *Samguk yusa*'s biography of Mu, it is notable that in the latter text Chinp'yŏng, the Silla king who complained to the Tang court concerning Paekche's aggression, appears improbably as Mu's father-in-law and temple-building helpmate.

All in all, Paekche's troops were markedly successful over the course of Mu's long reign. The *Samguk sagi* relates that the kingdom launched one raid and eight substantial campaigns against Silla during this period. In five of the eight campaigns Paekche's forces prevailed, and their victories on the battlefield resulted in the acquisition of ten Silla fortifications and sizable concomitant gains in territory. Silla, in contrast, is reported to have only launched one raid and one offensive during the forty-year span of Mu's rule. The offensive succeeded, but the object gained was only the retaking of its own Kajam Fortress that Paekche had previously captured.

Like Wen Di of the Sui dynasty, Mu balanced his aggressive military policy with an assertive program of official patronage of Buddhism. Active governmental promotion of the religion had a lengthy history in Paekche. Mu's father—posthumously entitled during Mu's reign as King Pŏp or literally, as mentioned previously, the "Dharma King"—during his first year on the throne (599) had made the pious gesture of prohibiting the killing of living things within the kingdom. The same gesture had earlier been made by the devout Wu Di of the Liang dynasty and, as also mentioned earlier, by Sui Wen Di. In 600 Pŏp had initiated the building of the Wanghŭngsa, the Monastery of Royal Propagation, a great temple located in the Paekche capital of Sabi (the present city of Puyŏ) that in time came to serve as a virtual national cathedral. Mu continued construction of Wanghŭngsa after his accession to the throne later in 600 and saw the project through to completion in 634. Texts also credit Mu with the building of two other major Buddhist temples, Mirŭksa and the Chesŏk-chŏngsa (or the Monastery of Indra), both located on the outskirts of the present city of Iksan or about thirty-five kilometers to the southeast of Mu's capital of Sabi. Although no surviving record provides a date for the construction of either of these monasteries, it is reasonable to assume that such major building projects would not have been initiated in the Iksan area until after Paekche's extensive southeastern conquests of 624. An early Tang account in the *Guanshiyin yingyan ji* (Record of the Miraculous Responses of Avalokiteśvara) concerning miracles associated with a disastrous lightning strike at the Chesŏk-chŏngsa in 639 states that Mu had intended to relocate the Paekche capital to the Iksan area. Accordingly, the construction of such a concentration of large temples in this region can be understood as preparation for the relocation of the capital that Mu contemplated, but seemingly never realized.

Although none of these monasteries has survived, material evidence recovered from their sites supports the written evidence of their shared royal heritage. The double-lobed petals of the lotus-flower designs on the circular eave-end roof tiles unearthed at the Wanghŭngsa site in Puyŏ conform closely to the decoration on tiles excavated from the sites of Mirŭksa and Chesŏk-chŏngsa. Likewise, the petals of the lotus decoration on an eave-end tile excavated from the site of the royal citadel on Mount Puso in Puyŏ closely resemble this type, especially as represented by the roof-tile for Chesŏk-chŏngsa (see figure 1.2). Given Mu's strong advocacy of Buddhism, the apparent appearance of the lotus motif on the roofs of palace buildings further suggests that more than mere happenstance or the convenience of preexisting molds for Buddhist tiles was involved here. Use of this core Buddhist symbol on the roofs of royal and religious structures alike gave silent expression to the correspondence between the ordering of political power in the kingdom and the universal power of the Buddha. Mu and his late father, Pŏp, like their imperial Chinese contemporary, Sui Wen Di, sought through their open support of Buddhism to project an image of their devout striving toward the establishment of the ideal symmetry between the temporal and the divine.

Mu's intention to identify royal authority in Paekche with the sacred authority of the cosmos is proclaimed on a more spectacular scale through the imposing and unique ground plan of Mirŭksa's primary ritual compound (figure 1.3). The

Figure 1.2. (a) Eave-end circular roof tile with lotus design from Mirŭksa site; North
Chŏlla province, Iksan-gun, Kumma-myŏn. D. 14 cm. Mirŭksa Excavation Storage.
(b) Eave-end circular roof tile from Wanghŭngsa site; Shingu-ri, Puyŏ. D. 14.2 cm.
Puyŏ National Museum. (c) Eave-end circular roof tile from Chesŏk-chŏnga site; North
Chŏlla province, Iksan-gun, Wanggung-ni. D. 13.3 cm. Puyŏ National Museum.
(d) Eave-end circular roof tile from Mount Puso citadel site; Puyŏ. D. 15.5 cm.
Seoul National Museum.

Samguk yusa's biography of Mu relates that construction of this monastery resulted
from a miracle witnessed by the monarch and his consort (improbably presented as
a Silla princess, the third daughter of King Chinp'yŏng) while they were on their
way to visit Chimyŏng (fl. early seventh century?), a monk possessed of great magical powers. It is reported that as the royal couple was passing a large lake near the
foot of Yonghwasan (Dragon Flower Mountain, a peak located near Iksan and the
site of Chimyŏng's monastery), three images of the Buddha Maitreya suddenly appeared above its waters. Swayed by this divine vision and the importunings of his
spouse, Mu determined to build a temple at the very spot where the images had ap-

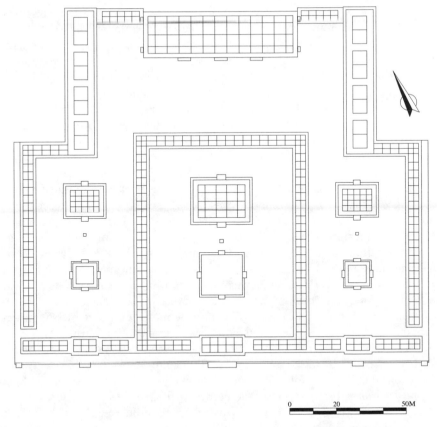

Figure 1.3. Plan of primary ritual compound of Mirŭksa: North Chŏlla province,
Iksan-gun, Kumma-myŏn. Approximately 155×175 m.

peared. The *Samguk yusa* account relates that his vow was expeditiously realized
through the aid rendered by Chimyŏng's supernatural powers and by the assistance
provided by Mu's putative royal Silla father-in-law. The former is said to have used
his powers to upend a nearby mountain into the lake to provide sound footings for
the temple's foundation, and the latter to have sent a hundred artisans to speed its
completion. The *Samguk yusa*'s account further states that the great monastery contained the Halls of Maitreya's Three Assemblies (Kor. Mirŭk Samhoe Chŏn), each
with its own pagoda and courtyard, and that Mirŭksa was still standing and functioning at the time of the text's composition in the mid–thirteenth century. Other
textual and archaeological evidence indicates the temple continued to function as
late as the early centuries of the Chosŏn era (1392–1910), but that it had fallen into
disuse by the start of the eighteenth century.

One of the most important results of the archaeological investigation of
Mirŭksa's site in the 1980s was the verification of the accuracy of the *Samguk yusa*'s

description of the temple's ground plan. Excavation confirmed that Mirŭksa was indeed possessed of three image halls (i.e., the Halls of Maitreya's Three Assemblies) and that each was provided with a separate pagoda and walled courtyard. Excavation also revealed that these three adjacent, parallel, and functionally separate precincts were enclosed within a single large walled temple compound measuring approximately 155 by 175 meters that, in turn, constituted the monastery's primary ritual center. Each of the three precincts contained, from north to south, an axially aligned entry gate, pagoda and image hall, and each gave access to the commodious lecture hall centrally positioned in the northern section of the compound's encircling wall.

The iconographic rationale underlying this seemingly unprecedented parallel tripling of the pagodas and image halls at Mirŭksa is clearly indicated in the *Samguk yusa*'s succinct description. It was intended to provide three discrete ritual precincts to correspond symbolically to the three grand assemblies, or public dharma lectures, to be held by Maitreya after he emerges, fully enlightened, as the next earthly Buddha from his meditation beneath a dragon-flower tree (Skt. *nāgapuṣpa*; Kor. *yonghwasu*). In this context, the significance of the siting of Mirŭksa at the base of Dragon Flower Mountain becomes apparent. As foretold in a number of sūtras, beginning at least as early as the Āgama and Nikāya literature, Maitreya is expected to initiate his ultimate mortal existence by being born into the family of a high official in the service of a mighty king, a true *cakravartin*. According to later and more elaborate prophecies of Maitreya's final incarnation, such as that found in Kumārajīva's early fifth-century rendering of the "Grand Sūtra on Maitreya Becoming a Buddha" (Ch. *Mile dazhengfo jing*; Kor. *Mirŭk taesŏngbul kyŏng*: Taishō no. 456), the particular dragon-flower tree of Maitreya's enlightenment will stand within a grove of these beautiful trees located near the *cakravartin*'s capital city. Sūtras also presage that the three grand assemblies of Maitreya will take place within this same sacred grove and that the Future Buddha's enlightenment-evoking discourses will be delivered from a multistoried hall. It is these beliefs relating to Maitreya's last mortal existence that provide the iconological justifications for Mirŭksa's unique architectural layout and for its siting beneath Dragon Flower Mountain.

It is also these beliefs that provide the key to understanding both why Mu assumed the extraordinary expense of constructing the unusually large and complex Mirŭksa in Iksan, and why he contemplated the even more expensive project of moving the royal capital to the vicinity of the new monastery. In building Mirŭksa, Mu was proclaiming Paekche to be the *cakravartin* state where Maitreya was destined to incarnate. At the time of Mu's undertaking the building of Mirŭksa, the past military and governmental successes of Sui Wen Di, a self-proclaimed *cakravartin* who had made most effective political use of his ardent patronage of Buddhism, formed an inspirational model familiar to all East Asian rulers. Yet it was clear that Maitreya had not chosen to incarnate in Wen Di's Chinese empire, since the Sui government had fallen in 618, just thirteen years after the emperor's death. Paekche's national prospects, in contrast, had improved steadily over the course of Mu's reign, especially in the kingdom's struggle against Silla for the domination of southern Korea. There were also good strategic reasons for Mu to undertake the relocation of the Paekche capital from Puyŏ to the Iksan area. On the one hand, the area was closer to the restive former Kaya territory, a region traditionally more friendly toward Paekche than Silla, and which, moreover, had been forcefully annexed by the latter kingdom just half a century earlier. Significantly, it was in the former territory of Kaya that the Paekche army made the greatest territorial gains during Mu's reign. On the other hand, the Iksan area was farther from the Yellow Sea than the existing capital of Sabi, and thus the proposed new capital would have been less susceptible to a waterborne attack from an increasingly assertive China—and indeed just such an attack was instrumental in Paekche's abrupt destruction less than twenty years after Mu's death.

According to the *Samguk yusa*'s narrative at least, Mu also had good theological reasons for relocating the capital to the vicinity of Iksan. The visionary manifestation of the three images of the Buddha Maitreya could readily be interpreted as a sign that this place would be the chosen locale for that Buddha's promised three grand assemblies. Hence the unprecedented tripartite design of the temple created at Mu's command can be understood as being intended not only to honor Maitreya but also to provide the sanctified setting for the Buddha's liberating oratory. The sūtras declared that the dragon-flower grove where Maitreya would both gain enlightenment and give his three dharma lectures would be located near the capital of a *cakravartin* king. In an attempt to actualize this prophecy of the sūtras and thereby to cause Paekche to be the land where the Future Buddha would preach and an all-conquering *cakravartin* ruler would appear, Mu undertook both to build the exceptional Mirŭksa and to relocate the kingdom's capital to the area adjacent to that monastery's supernaturally designated site. Mu himself might not be the promised *cakravartin*, but the propitious victories of his armies lent reason to believe that one of his near successors on Paekche's throne might well be the unifying conqueror whose advent the sūtras had foretold.

The following translation of the biography of King Mu is based on Iryŏn's *Samguk yusa*, edited by Ch'oe Namsŏn (Seoul: Minjung Sŏgwan, 1947). Iryŏn's brief intralineal textual commentaries concerning alternative versions of the names of Mu and his queen have been omitted. The earlier quotation from Sui Wen Di's edict of 581 that is preserved in Fei Zhangfang's *Lidai sanbao ji* of 597 (T 2034) is taken from Arthur F. Wright, "The Formation of Sui Ideology, 581–604," in *Chinese Thought and Institutions*, edited by J. K. Fairbank (Chicago: University of Chicago Press, 1957). The illustration of the eave-end circular roof tile from Mirŭksa (see figure 1.2a) and the plan of the temple's primary ritual compound (see figure 1.3) have been adapted from Munhwajae Kwalliguk, ed., *Mirŭksa yujŏk palgul chosa pogosŏ*, 2 vols. (Seoul: Koryŏ Sŏjok Chusikhoesa, 1989). The illustrations of the eave-end roof tiles from Wanghŭngsa and the Chesŏk-chŏngsa as well as that from the site of the royal Paekche citadel on Mount Puso in Puyŏ (figure 1.2b–1.2d) have been adapted from Paekche Munhwa Kaebal Yŏn'guwŏn, ed., *Paekche wajŏn torok* (Seoul: Samhwa Inswae Chusikhoesa, 1983). I am grateful to the Los Angeles County Museum of Art for its kind assistance in facilitating the publication of this text.

Further Reading

Jonathan W. Best, "Diplomatic and Cultural Contacts between Paekche and China," *Harvard Journal of Asiatic Studies* 42 (1982): 443–501, esp. 470–80; Jonathan W. Best, "Early Korean Buddhist Bronzes and Sui Regional Substyles: A Contextual Study of Stylistic Influence in the Early Seventh Century," in Sambul Kim Wŏllyong Kyosu Chŏngnyŏn T'oeim Kinyŏm Nonch'ong Kanhaeng Wiwŏnhoe, ed., *Sambul Kim Wŏllyong Kyosu chŏngnyŏn t'oeim kinyŏn nonch'ong* (Festschrift in Honor of Kim Won-yong), 2 vols. (Seoul: Ilchisa, 1987), 2:476–512; Joseph M. Kitagawa, "The Many Faces of Maitreya—A Historian of Religions' Reflections," and Lewis Lancaster, "Maitreya in Korea," both in *Maitreya, the Future Buddha*, edited by A. Sponberg and H. Hardacre (Cambridge: Cambridge University Press, 1988), pp. 7–22, 135–153; Alexander C. Soper, "Maitreya," in his *Literary Evidence for Early Buddhist Art in China* (Ascona, Switzerland: Artibus Asiae Publishers, 1959), pp. 210–219; Arthur F. Wright, "The Formation of Sui Ideology, 581–604," in *Chinese Thought and Institutions*, edited by J. K. Fairbank (Chicago: University of Chicago Press, 1957), pp. 71–104.

King Mu

King Mu, whose personal name was Chang, was the thirtieth monarch [in the Paekche royal line]. His mother was a widow who made her home beside a lake to the south of the capital. The dragon that inhabited the lake had a liaison with her and, as a consequence, she gave birth to the future king who, as a youth, was called Sŏdong [Sweet-Potato Boy]. Even though his natural talents far exceeded the norm, the people of the day gave him that nickname because he made his living by every day digging wild sweet potatoes and selling them.

Having heard that Sŏnhwa . . . , the third daughter of Silla's King Chinp'yŏng, was beautiful beyond compare, Sŏdong shaved his head [to disguise himself as a monk] and made his way to the Silla capital. Once there he made use of gifts of sweet potatoes to befriend the band of street urchins who frequented the city's palace district, and consequently they came to regard him as their leader. This end attained, he composed a verse and got the urchins to sing it aloud in the thoroughfares of the district. The ditty went as follows,

> The noble Princess Sŏnhwa has secretly ceased to be chaste;
> in the dark of night she enfolds Sŏdong in her loving embrace,
> and then, only then, does she return to her palatial estate.

The urchins' song spread throughout the city and came to be known within the palace itself, and because the court officials remonstrated vociferously against the princess' reputed behavior, she was discreetly ordered into banishment at a site far removed from the capital. At the time appointed for her departure, the queen gave her a peck of gold nuggets as a parting present. Subsequently, when the princess was approaching her place of banishment, Sŏdong came forward and, having greeted her with due formality, proposed that he be permitted to serve as her protector on her travels. Even though the princess did not know him or from whence he came, she trusted him and welcomed his company. Thus it happened that they began to travel together and, after a time, covertly became lovers. It also happened that the princess only learned Sŏdong's name after their intimate bond had been fashioned, and so it was that she accepted their union as the fulfillment of the fate foretold in the street urchins' song.

Together the two lovers journeyed to Paekche, and when the princess, intending that they should give some thought to the practicalities of life, brought out the gold that her mother, the queen, had given her, Sŏdong laughed uproariously and queried, "What good is this stuff?" She replied, "This *stuff* is pure gold. Just this bit that you see before you is a fortune sufficient to last a hundred years!" Sŏdong then exclaimed, "Why, when I was a child and went out digging wild sweet potatoes, I used to cast aside piles of this stuff as if it was dirt!" When the princess heard this, she declared in absolute amazement, "That much gold would be a treasure worth the price of the world itself! If you still know where those nuggets are, and if we could somehow convey them as a gift to my parents' palace, then surely that would mend the breach between them and me!" Sŏdong replied that all that she wished to be done, could be done.

Accordingly, he gathered together the nuggets that he had once thrown away, making a mound as big as a hill. He then went to Saja Monastery on Dragon Flower Mountain where Master of the Law Chimyŏng resided, and asked the priest how the gold might be transported to Silla. The priest responded, "By my sacred power, I could surely convey it thither. Bring the gold here!" The princess at this time also prepared a letter to her parents and it was placed before the priest together with the gold. [Chimyŏng] then employed his supernatural power and in the course of a single night both the letter and the mound of golden nuggets were delivered to the royal palace of Silla. King Chinp'yŏng marveled at the miracle wrought by the priest's power and his veneration for the cleric became all the more profound; thereafter he sent repeated missives to Chimyŏng expressing his esteem and solicitude for the priest's well-being. As for Sŏdong, because of the events narrated above, he gained the regard of the people and eventually succeeded to the royal throne.

Sometime afterward, King Mu and his wife made a journey to Saja Monastery [in order to pay their respects to Chimyŏng]. They had proceeded as far as the edge of the large lake that lay at the foot of Dragon Flower Mountain when suddenly three images of Maitreya appeared in the midst of the lake. They

forthwith halted their carriage and made obeisance to the sacred manifestations. The queen then addressed the king, saying, "We must raise a great
monastery at the very place where these images have appeared. To do so is my
ardent desire!" The king agreed, and they continued on to Chimyŏng's temple
abode, where they asked the priest that he contrive to fill in the lake [so that
the monastery could be built just where they had vowed]. Once again the
priest completed the task in the course of a single night; by using his sacred
power he caused a mountain to collapse into the lake and transform it into
level ground. Then, by order of the royal couple, three images of Maitreya
were sculpted in strict conformity to the prescriptions of the Dharma. In addition, in order to enshrine the images, they had raised three paired sets of
buildings consisting of a Hall of Maitreya's Three Grand Assemblies and an accompanying pagoda. Each set of these structures was, moreover, contained
within its own separate courtyard bounded by a roofed colonnade. The entire
complex was named Mirŭksa [Monastery of Maitreya]. . . . King Chinpyŏng
sent one hundred artisans to assist in its construction, and at the present time
the monastery is still standing. <Iryŏn: Although the *Samguk sagi* states that
Mu was the son of King Pŏp, the tradition recounted here holds that he was
the son of a solitary widow. The truth of the matter cannot be determined.>

2

Wŏn'gwang and Chajang in the Formation
of Early Silla Buddhism

Pankaj N. Mohan

Wŏn'gwang (555–638) and Chajang (ca. mid–seventh century) are seminal figures in the history of early Silla Buddhism. They nurtured and shaped Silla Buddhism during its incipiency by forging close links between the secular and ecclesiastical establishments, a hallmark of Korean Buddhism through history, and equipping it with a firm institutional foundation. And apparently because of their influence at home and abroad, they are the only two Silla monks from the late sixth and early seventh centuries whose detailed biographies are available both in Korean works, the *Samguk yusa* (Memorabilia of the Three Kingdoms) and the *Haedong kosŭng chŏn* (Lives of Eminent Korean Monks), and in the Chinese *Xu gaoseng zhuan* (Continued Biographies of Eminent Monks), dating to the seventh century.

Wŏn'gwang went to China in the late sixth century and earned such renown for his virtue, theurgy, and Buddhist scholarship that the Silla monarch sent several petitions to the Chinese emperor of the Sui dynasty to send him back. The emperor bestowed munificent rewards on Wŏn'gwang and allowed him to return to his native land. Though Wŏn'gwang continued his monastic career in Silla, he was entrusted with the responsibility for drafting all the court's important reports, memorials, and correspondence, and the exchange of state orders. The sources note that "though his duties were not those of a state official in silk robes, he was requested to care for the country like an official."

Since the late sixth and early seventh centuries represented a period of domestic political tumult and uncertainty, as well as the threat of an increasingly aggressive Koguryŏ kingdom to the north, King Chinp'yŏng asked Wŏn'gwang to write a letter to Emperor Wen of the Sui, seeking military help to pacify Koguryŏ. The monk replied: "To seek one's own profit and destroy others is not the way of a monk. But since I, a poor monk, live on your majesty's land, eat your majesty's grain, and drink your water, how dare I disobey [your command]?"

This statement of Wŏn'gwang's is commonly cited as evidence of the nation-protecting tradition of Silla Buddhism in its early phase. However, it may be more

appropriate to view the statement as an attempt by the state to domesticate Buddhism and to appropriate the human and material resources of the Buddhist establishment in order to advance the political interests of the state. Wŏn'gwang
did not redefine the norms of Buddhism; indeed, he realized that the royal command amounted to an infringement of the monastic precepts. Nonetheless, like
monks during the strong Chinese dynasties of Northern Wei, Sui, and Tang, he
submitted to secular authority and allowed monarchical power to prevail.

The Five Secular Precepts that the monk Wŏn'gwang bestowed on Kwisan and
Ch'uhang, two members of the Hwarang, an order of youth in Silla, also testify to
the subordination of Buddhism to the dominant political impulse of the age.
According to the *Samguk sagi* (Histories of the Three Kingdoms), these two Hwarang
youths pledged together to cultivate virtuous minds and train strong bodies. At the
time Wŏn'gwang had returned from China and was residing in Kasil monastery,
where he was universally admired and respected by his countrymen. The two
youths visited him and requested him to give them precepts that could serve as a
moral guide for them until their last breath. Wŏn'gwang remarked, "The Buddhist
vinaya prescribes ten Bodhisattva precepts, but since you are subjects [of the king]
and sons, you will not be able to adhere to them." Instead, he gave the two young
men the Five Secular Precepts. These were

1. Serve the king with loyalty.
2. Serve one's parents with filial piety.
3. Be faithful to one's friends.
4. Do not retreat in battle.
5. Do not kill indiscriminately.

Although Wŏn'gwang seems to have modeled his precepts on the Confucian
principles of the five human relationships, they need not be pigeonholed as either essentially Buddhist or Confucian in character. Filial piety, trust between
friends, and loyalty to the state constitute universal values. Besides, as fundamental underpinnings of the Chinese civilization from which Silla was energetically
borrowing, they were crucial to the stability of the new political structure of a
centralized monarchy. The last two precepts, concerning discriminate killing and
display of valor in the battlefields, seem to be derived from Wŏn'gwang's understanding of the significance of the martial spirit to the Hwarang tradition and its
relevance to the contemporary needs of the state. In other words, his modifica-
tion of the traditional Buddhist precept against injuring living creatures and his
emphasis on displaying valor on the battlefield were directly relevant to the interests of Silla, which was engaged in a bitter war of peninsular conquest. It is also
important to note that "trust between friends," the last precept in the Five Cardinal Confucian Principles of Human Relations, was in the third place in Wŏn'g-
wang's prioritization. Kim Ch'ŏlchun, professor emeritus of history at Seoul National University, has correctly explained that this was because Wŏn'gwang
realized the significance of youthful camaraderie and fellowship to the contemporary political and social needs of Silla.

Chajang, another great Silla monk and originally a scion of Silla nobility, spent seven years in Chinese monasteries. In 643, upon his return home at the behest of the contemporary ruler of Silla, Queen Sŏndŏk, he became active in both ecclesiastical and secular affairs of state. He is believed to have advised Queen Sŏndŏk to build a nine-story pagoda at Hwangnyong monastery. Quoting from the *Tongdo sŏngnip ki* (Record of the Establishment of the Eastern Capital), which is now lost, Iryŏn, the author of this account of Chajang's life, interprets the nine stories of the stūpa as representing conquest over the nine contiguous states, including China and Japan. This could well be Iryŏn's own interpretation, a projection of the concerns of this thirteenth-century monk who suffered through the invasion of Korea by the Mongols (then in power in China) and lived under constant fear of their depredations. The near-contemporary *Hwangnyongsa kuch'ŭng mokt'ap ch'alchu ki* (The Record [Inscribed on a Pillar] of the Nine-Storied Wooden Stūpa of the Hwangnyong Monastery) paints a considerably more modest picture of the territorial ambition of Silla:

> Dhyāna Master Yuanxiang of Nansan said [to Chajang], "If a nine-storied stūpa is constructed at Hwangnyong Monastery in your country, the whole of Haedong [East of the Sea, a term referring to the Korean peninsula] will surrender to your kingdom." Hearing these words, Chajang returned home and, on [royal] command, the stūpa was built by Chief Mason Abi (Abiji) of Paekche and 200 assistant masons under the supervision of Ikan (Ich'an) Yongshu.

Chajang is also claimed to have contributed to a change in Silla's dress code. The *Xu gaoseng zhuan* states that there were differences between the Chinese and the barbarians (viz., Koreans) in customs and clothing, but since Chajang revered only the true tradition (of China), he successfully petitioned the court to abandon native clothing and take Tang styles as standard. It needs to be noted, however, that the *Xu gaoseng zhuan*'s statement is not corroborated in Korean sources. It is possible that Kim Pusik, the author of *Samguk sagi* (1145), omitted Chajang's role in developing Silla's new political orientation because of Kim's Confucian worldview. It is also likely that Daoxuan (596–667), the author of *Xu gaoseng zhuan*, exaggerated the influence of Chajang on the contemporary Silla ruler, since the Buddhist hagiographies often tended to overemphasize the power, privilege, and political patronage enjoyed by the eminent monks.

Chajang is also credited with having proclaimed that the contemporary ruler of Silla belonged to the Kṣatriya caste, the warrior caste of India to which the Buddha himself belonged. In an age of great internal turmoil and external threat, there is an obvious political dimension in employing Buddhist elements to enhance the sanctity and sacredness of Queen Sŏndŏk's lineage by tracing it to the Buddha's own clan. Because she was the first female ruler in Korean history, her gender might also have prompted misgivings about her strength and influence. Attributing Kṣatriya status to Queen Sŏndŏk would have established a direct linkage between her and Buddhism, the shared religious belief of the Silla elite in the early seventh century, and would evidently have been an effective strategy to shore up her authority. Seen from the perspective of Buddhist political theory, proclaiming her status as a Kṣatriya also meant that she had a legitimate claim to the throne. In Buddhist thinking the first ruler, *mahāsammata*, is also called Kṣatriya, and unlike Brahmanical sources, Buddhist works gives preeminence to Kṣatriya in the caste hierarchy. In addition, perhaps because Kṣatriya is described in the Brahmanical scriptures as the only caste with a legitimate claim to political power, many rulers in early and medieval Indian history fabricated their geneology to arrogate Kṣatriya (also known as Rajput) status to themselves and their ancestors.

Chajang is also said to have proclaimed that Silla was a Buddha land (*pulgukt'o*), an abode of past buddhas. According to the *Samguk yusa*, when Chajang arrived at Mount Wutai in China, he experienced a manifestation of the Bodhisattva Mañjuśrī, who transformed himself and appeared before him to tell him that Hwangnyong monastery of Silla was built on the site where Śākyamuni and Kāśyapa buddhas had preached in the past. As evidence, he pointed to a rock on which Śākyamuni and Kāśyapa had sat and which still existed at the site. Chajang's idealized construct of Silla as a Buddhist realm or Buddha land falls neatly into a recognizable pattern in the history of Buddhism. Buddhist societies invoked precedents of the "mytho-historical" past in order to arrogate to their lands the attribute of karmically predestined connections with the buddhas, bodhisattvas, and Buddhist divinities and, thereby, sacralized and legitimized their contemporary concerns. The legend of Silla's own Buddhas of Antiquity was presumably aimed at transforming the status of Hwangnyong monastery, a cathedral of the state, into "archaeological sacra," as has been pointed out by Herbert Durt, and enhancing Silla's prestige vis-à-vis Paekche and Koguryŏ. This enhancement could well have provided spiritual comfort to the war-weary people of Silla.

Chajang's other major contribution was the systematization of ecclesiastical organization under the guidance of the state. He took resolute steps to institute a uniform code of monastic rules, based presumably on the *Dharmaguptakavinaya*, which the East Asians called the *Four-Part Vinaya* (*Sabunyul*), throughout the kingdom. To quote from the *Samguk yusa*, "The Silla court deliberated that, although it had been long since Buddhism was transmitted to the East, the state did not yet have the law and regulations to discipline the monastic order. Without guiding principles, the order and purity of the saṃgha could not be maintained, and therefore the queen issued an edict appointing Chajang to the post of *taegukt'ong* (Chief of Clerics)."

The *Xu gaoseng zhuan* (Continued Biographies of Eminent Monks) also states that "when Chajang, the chief of clerics, was entrusted by the state with creating regulations for the saṃgha, he ordered each of the five divisions of the saṃgha to strengthen their [adherence] to the old interpretation [of the *Dharmaguptaka-vinaya*] and established an administrative mechanism to supervise and maintain the saṃgha's adherence to monastic rules."

Indeed, an episcopacy or central monastic officialdom was first instituted during the reign of King Chinhŭng, as epigraphic evidence corroborates. The Ojak stele in Taegu (578) refers to Buddhist monks that hold the rank of Doyuna

(*Karmadāna*, or rector, of the capital). This reference implies that Buddhist monk-officials were dispatched by the state to the provinces, apparently to help expand monarchical control over Buddhism in the outlying areas and to spread Buddhist dogma centered on the institution of kingship. Expansion of monasteries and the monastic community and the enhanced power of the central government in the middle of the seventh century made it imperative to reorganize the system as to bring it under tighter state control.

A divided and disorganized saṃgha would be a source of instability for the state, because different religious factions may affiliate themselves with contending political factions at the court and forge a mutually empowering relationship. The highly centralized imperial government of Tang, a model of state-saṃgha relations in East Asia, created elaborate institutions to regulate its religious establishments. The Tang emperors, as Arthur Wright wrote, carefully "guarded against the resurgence of a Buddhist church as an imperium in imperio." The monastic community, particularly its activities that involved the lay community, was brought under tighter govermental supervision and control. It was also made mandatory that monks and nuns renewed their registration every three years. A copy of their registration papers was kept by the local municipal administration, the prefectural government, and the central government's Bureau of Rites.

In his capacity as chief of clerics, Chajang established a new administrative mechanism to supervise the saṃgha's strict adherence to monastic rules. He enforced the Poṣadha rite—the fortnightly assembly of the monastic community on full- and new-moon days to recite the *prātimokṣa* (the Buddhist monastic rules) and confess their violations of the *vinaya*. Chajang also introduced a comprehensive examination system, which twice a year in spring and winter sought to determine who had kept and who had violated the *prātimokṣa* rules. Overseers were appointed and entrusted with the task of undertaking tours of all the monasteries in the kingdom to admonish errant monks and enforce the teachings of the dharma, as well as to ensure proper maintenance of Buddha statues and correct management of saṃgha affairs. The *Xu gaoseng zhuan* notes that "thanks to Chajang discipline became an established norm" and praises him as a "dharma-protecting bodhisattva."

Apparently, Wŏn'gwang and Chajang were able to blend seamlessly Confucian and Buddhist values. It has been pointed out by several scholars that early Korea and Japan regarded Buddhism as but one part of an integrated "Chinese cultural package" that included other systems of thought and institutions. When early Korean monks went to China and lived in the Chinese cultural environment, their vision of Chinese culture as an integrated blend of Buddhism and Confucianism became reinforced because of Confucian influences on Buddhist monastic education. It appears that because of their early training in the Confucian classics and their immersion in Chinese culture, Wŏn'gwang and Chajang came to appreciate the significant roles Confucian-Buddhist values could offer to the social and political needs of their states, and upon their return home, they actively pursued and promoted a "civilizing" agenda, in which Buddhism and Confucianism were integral parts. Their spiritual leadership sustained and promoted a simultaneous respect for Confucian and Buddhist ideas among the Silla elite and enhanced the ideological cohesion of Silla society.

The translations of the biographies of Wŏn'gwang and Chajang are from the *Xu Gaoseng Zhuan* (Continued Biographies of Eminent Monks) by Dao-xuan (596–667), included in *Taishō Shinshū daizōkyō* (Tokyo, 1924–34), no. 2060, vol. 50. The biography of Wŏn'gwang appears at *Taishō* no. 2060, vol. 50, pp. 523c1–524b4; the biography of Chajang at *Taishō* no. 2060, vol. 50, pp. 639a8–640a8.

Further Reading

For an overview of the history of Buddhism in Korea, see the introduction to the pioneering work by Robert E. Buswell Jr., *The Korean Approach to Zen: The Collected Works of Chinul* (Honolulu: University of Hawaii Press, 1983); reprinted in paperback abridgment as *Tracing Back the Radiance: Chinul's Korean Way of Zen*, Kuroda Institute Classics in East Asian Buddhism, no. 2 (Honolulu: University of Hawaii Press, 1991). Wŏn'gwang's biography from the *Haedong kosŭng chŏn*, compiled by the monk Kakhun in 1215, and Chajang's biography from the *Samguk yusa*, dating from the thirteenth century, have been translated into English by Peter H. Lee and Robert E. Buswell Jr., respectively; they appear in Peter H. Lee and Wm. Theodore de Bary, eds., *Sources of Korean Tradition*, vol. 1 (New York: Columbia University Press, 1997). For discussions of the Hwarang order of Silla, see Richard Rutt, "The Flower Boys of Silla," *Transactions of the Korea Branch of the Royal Asiatic Society* 38 (1961): 1–66; and Pankaj Mohan, "Maitreya Cult in Early Shilla: Focusing on Hwarang as Maitreya-Incarnate," *Seoul Journal of Korean Studies* 14 (2001): 149–74; For an understanding of the character of Wŏn'wang's thought, see Lee, Ki-baik, "Wŏn'gwang and His Thought," in *Korean Thought*, edited by Korean National Commission for UNESCO (Seoul: Si-sa-yong-o-sa, 1983). For a critical perspective of the role of Chajang in the formation of Silla Buddhist institutions, see Kim Jong Myung, "Chajang and 'Buddhism as National Protector' in Korea: A Reconsideration," in *Religion in Traditional Korea*, edited by Henrik H. Sorensen (Copenhagen: Seminar for Buddhist Studies, 1994). Herbert Durt has also discussed related issues in his article "The Meaning of Archaeology in Ancient Buddhism: Notes on Stupas of Asoka and the Worship of the 'Buddhas of the Past,'" in *Pulgyo wa che-kwahak: kaegyo yuksimnyŏn kinyŏm nonch'ong* (Seoul: Tongguk Taehakkyo, 1987).

The Biography of Wŏn'gwang

The monk Wŏn'gwang was a native of Chinhan, one of the three Han leagues (Samhan) of Pyŏnhan, Mahan, and Chinhan. His secular family name was Pak. His family lived for generations in Haedong [the Korean peninsula], carrying forward without interruption the scholastic traditions of its ancestors. His supernal vessel was brilliant and wide-ranging and he was fond of learning. As he was well versed in Daoist and Confucianist works and had delved deep into philosophical as well as historical texts, his fame radiated all over the domain of Han. Although he was widely read and erudite, he felt humbled by the Chinese world of scholarship. Consequently, he set his mind on bidding farewell to his relatives and friends and crossing the sea. At the age of twenty-five he boarded a ship and reached Jinling [present-day Nanjing]. It was the era of the Chen dynasty, which was renowned as a realm of culture. He was now able to probe deeper and resolve the doubts he previously held. Initially he attended lectures of the disciples of Master Min of Zhuangyan monastery [who was also known as Sengmin or Lord Min, 474–534, a renowned monk active in the Liang dynasty]. In the past he had read secular books and reckoned their principles as extraordinary, but after he learned Buddhist doctrines, he felt on the contrary that the former were no more than rotten mustard seeds. In his empty pursuit of Confucianism he was really only [motivated] by fears about his livelihood. He petitioned to the ruler of Chen, seeking his permission to take refuge in the dharma, which was granted through an imperial edict. Thereupon he took the tonsure and accepted the monastic precepts. He toured all the lecture places and learned all the noble doctrines. He understood all the subtleties of the texts and was assiduous in his pursuit of knowledge. He stored in his heart the *Tattvasiddhi* and the *Nirvāṇa Sūtra*. He was particularly devoted to the various doctrines of the Tripiṭaka.

Later he went to Huchiu mountain in Wu where he adhered ceaselessly to right mindfulness and was always circumspect about perception and view. Believers assembled around his hermitage like clouds. When he explored all the four Āgamas [Dīrghāgama, Madhyāgama, Saṃyuktāgama, and Ekottarāgama—Āgama literally means what has come down/handed down from tradition] he bent his efforts toward the eight samādhis. He made goodness clear and thinking easier. He was as straight and flawless as a bamboo tube [this expression may allude to the straightness of bamboo, or alternatively to precepts, instructions, or edicts, which were stored in bamboo tubes]. Since the place profoundly met his original intention, he decided to remain in the faith till his death. Therefore, he severed his ties with worldly affairs and followed the footprints of the sages; with his thoughts as clear as the cloudless sky, he reflected from afar on all ages.

At that time a lay believer lived at the foot of the mountain. He invited Wŏn'gwang to deliver lectures. Wŏn'gwang firmly declined, but when he made insistent and ardent entreaties, Wŏn'gwang finally yielded. First he discoursed on *Tattvasiddhi* and then on the *Prajñāpāramitā-sūtra*. All his interpretations were excellent and insightful, and his fame spread afar. Moreover, he used such fine rhetoric that his audience felt highly delighted and understood the core point of his talks. From then on following the ancient texts, he took upon himself the duty of proselytising. Every time he turned the wheel of dharma [i.e. gave religious discourses], his message spread far and wide. Although it was not his native land, his fame spread all over the country.

People with sacks on their shoulders crossed bushes and brambles and came one after another as densely as the scales [on a fish]. At that time the Sui had assumed power [in 581] and its authority spread to the southern kingdom as well [589]. When the Chen calendar came to an end, Sui soldiers marched into the Yang capital [the capital of Chen]. In the chaos and confusion of the times, Wŏn'gwang was about to be executed by unruly soldiers. At the time the chief of the army generals saw a temple stūpa in flames. But when he went to the rescue, there was no trace of fire. He only saw Wŏn'gwang in front of the stūpa, tied up and about to be killed. Wonder-struck at the miracle, he untied his bonds and set him free. When confronted with danger, Wŏn'gwang manifested such miracles.

Wŏn'gwang's learning permeated the Wu and Yue regions and now he wanted to travel and spread his teachings in the Zhou and Qin regions [in north China]. In the ninth year of the Kaihuang era he visited the imperial capital. This happened to be the time when Buddhism was reviving and interest in the *Mahāyānasaṃgraha* [Compendium of the Great Vehicle] was beginning. Won'gwang cherished its style and treasured its excellent thought. He went about and explained it with great insight. His fame spread in the capital. Now that he had established his meritorious karma, it was necessary to transmit the Law eastward [to Silla]. His homeland heard about him from afar and sent repeated petitions [to the Sui] for his return. The emperor bestowed munificent rewards on him and allowed him to return to his native land. When Wŏn'gwang returned after a lapse of many years, old and young alike were jubilant. Even the king of Silla, from the Kim clan, paid him deep reverence and treated him like a sage.

Wŏn'gwang's temperament was humble and calm; he was affectionate and overflowing with love. He always spoke with a smile and there was no trace of anger on his face. The reports, memorials, and official documents, as well as diplomatic correspondence were all written by him. The reigns of government in this corner [of the world] were placed squarely in his hands, but he used the opportunity to propagate dharma. Though he was not a state official in brocade silk robes, he was requested to look after the country like an official. He took advantage of this opportunity and offered advice. He set an example that is relevant even today.

When he was advanced in age, he went to the palace by carriage. The king personally took care of Wŏn'gwang's clothes, medicine, and food and did not seek the assistance of his servants, thereby hoping to monopolize the blessings for himself. Such was his devotion and respect for Wŏn'gwang.

When Wŏn'gwang was about to die, the king held his hands and consoled him. He asked Wŏn'gwang to bequeath his teachings, which might bring benefit to the people. His fine and auspicious teachings spread even to the corners of the sea.

In the 58th year of the Kŏnbok era [640, but this seems to be an error because the Kŏnbok era ended in the fiftieth year with the death of King Chinp'yŏng—it should be the ninth year of Queen Sŏndŏk], he felt slightly uncomfortable and during the course of the subsequent seven days he gave his dharma talks in a lucid voice. Then sitting upright at his residence in Hwangnyong monastery, he breathed his last. He was ninety-nine years old. This was the fourth year of the Zhen'guan era of Tang China. At the time of his death, music filled the sky northeast of the temple and a strange fragrance pervaded the monastery. Monks and laymen were struck with grief and wonder and respectfully realized that this was a numinous response to the event. He was buried in the outskirts of the capital with funeral rites befitting a king.

Later a commoner's child was born dead. There was a local saying that if such a stillborn child were buried in the grave of a blessed one, [the family's] line would not come to an end. So the parents secretly buried the child beside the tomb of Wŏn'gwang. However, on that day an earthquake hurled [the child's] corpse from the tomb. Because of this incident, his tomb remained undefiled. Those who honored him were all full of respect and admiration.

He had a disciple named Wŏn'an. He was wise and intelligent and by temperament loved traveling and enjoyed delving into the mysteries of religion. He went north to Hwando [formerly the territory of East Ye and the Koguryŏ capital—the shift of capital from Hwando to P'yŏngyang occurred in 427] and east to Pulnae [modern Anpyon in Hamgyŏng province]. He also traveled to the lands of Western Yan and Wei. Later when he reached the imperial capital, he familiarized himself with the local customs and studied various sūtras and śāstras. He was well versed in their fundamentals and was perceptive about even their subtlest meanings. Though he took refuge in Buddhism late in his life, he was highly distinguished for his efforts to save humankind. When he was first living in a monastery in Chang'an, he became renowned for his attainment of the Way. Tejin ["Lord Specially Advanced"] Xiao Yu petitioned [to the emperor] and had him reside at Jinliang monastery in Lantian. He was provided with the four daily necessities [clothing, food, bedding, and medicine] without fail.

He once wrote about Wŏn'gwang as follows: Once the king of Silla was seriously sick and no medicine could cure him. He requested Wŏn'gwang to come to the palace and stay in special quarters. Every day he had Wŏn'gwang teach the mysteries of the dharma. The king accepted the precepts [of the faith] and repented. The king became a devout believer in Buddhism. One day in the early hours of evening the king saw Wŏn'gwang head's resplendent with a golden halo, as if the disc of the sun were following him. The queen and the court ladies also witnessed it. Because of this, the king developed even greater devotion, and asked him to stay with him in his sickroom. Soon the king recovered. Wŏn'gwang propagated the faith in the land of Chinhan and Mahan. The dharma flourished. He gave two courses of sermons every year and mentored younger scholars. Whatever offerings he received he donated to the maintenance of temples and the only things he kept were a robe and a bowl.

The Biography of Chajang

The monk Chajang, surnamed Kim, was from the Silla kingdom. His ancestors were descendants of the Three Hans and during the mid-ancient period, Chinhan, Mahan, and Pyonhan were all their vassals. Each had its chieftain. According to *Lianggong zhi tu*, this kingdom of Silla was called *Silu* during the Wei, and during the Song (420–477) it was called Xinluo [Silla, in Korean]. It was originally one of the countries of the Chinhan league, the Eastern Yi.

The name of Chajang's father was Murim. His official career reached that of *sop'an* [variously, first or third rank in the Silla civil service hierarchy]. Having attained high office, he considered retiring to a quiet place. He was without progeny. His worries increased with each passing day. He always believed in Buddhism and extended it special protection. He invited large numbers [of monks] and made generous donations to them. He was devoted to the Buddhadharma. He commissioned images of the Thousand-Armed Bodhisattva Avalokiteśvara in the hopes that he would be blessed with a son. He hoped if he had a son he would take the vows of a monastic career upon attaining adulthood and strive to liberate all sentient beings. Numinous omens manifested in response and the mother [of Chajang] had a dream that a star fell and entered her bosom. Consequently, she became pregnant and on the morning of the eighth day of the fourth month [the full-moon day in the month of Vaiśākha, which corresponds to the Buddha's birthday] gave birth to a son. Monks and laity all rejoiced and celebrated a rare blessing. He spent years in basic studies. He possessed a wonderful [spiritual vocation] and perceptive mind and read almost all the secular historical works. Though his sentiments were vast, he was not soiled by worldly interests. When he lost both his parents, he came to detest the vanity of mundane life. He became profoundly aware of the impermanence of life and finally became a hermit. He left his wife and children and gave away his houses, fields and orchards. Whenever it was necessary, he made gifts. He practiced mercy and respected [the principle of] karma. He went to live all alone by a forest ravine, determined to exhaust his remaining karmic retribution by wearing coarse clothes and straw shoes. Chajang climbed further up to a dangerous and remote site to practice meditation in silence, not avoiding dangerous wild animals and always thinking of acts of arduous charity.

Sometimes, when his heart and actions had almost reached completion, he would fall asleep from fatigue. He moved to a small cell that had thorns and brambles on all the four sides. He sat upright, naked, so that when he moved, the thorns immediately tore his flesh. He tied his head to the roof-beam to help eliminate sluggishness. He practiced *paekkolgwan* (lit. "white-bone contemplation"), focusing his meditation on a skeleton's bones [the *Samguk yusa* calls this practice *kogolgwan*, a form of meditation dating back to the early history of Buddhism in India, which was intended to help realize the impermanence of life and overcome worldly attachments]. He turned his mind away from fame and worldly success. Meanwhile his hidden acts of virtue were revealed and people looked up to him and expected him to return to secular life. Chajang's status meant that it was assumed he would be appointed to a top ministerial position. But he insistently refused to accept repeated summons. The ruler of Silla [Queen Sŏndŏk] was furious. She ordered her men to go to his hermitage and use violence on him. When Chajang heard, he replied, "I would rather keep the Vinaya for one day and die than live for a lifetime while breaking it." When the messengers heard, they did not dare use their swords on him. When this was reported to the queen, she felt ashamed and yielded to Chajang's wish, permitting him to become a monk and engage in cultivating the dharma. Thereupon he lived in remote obscurity, cutting off all communications with the outside world. His grain was exhausted and he was destined to die. Thereupon strange birds felt moved to bring various fruits in their beaks and place them in his hands. The birds joined Chajang in eating from his hands. They always came on time, though Chajang had nourished no such unusual expectations beforehand. His actions had caused a mysterious response and there were rarely any connected phenomena. Always full of compassion and pity for sentient beings, he pondered what expedients he should employ so as to enable them to escape from the cycle of life and death.

He happened to see in his dream two [celestial] beings who asked him, "Venerable Sir, what profit do you seek by living deep in the mountains?" Chajang replied, "I merely seek to benefit all sentient beings." They then conferred on Chajang the five precepts and said, "With these five commandments you can help the masses." They also said to Chajang that they had descended from the Heaven of the Thirty-three especially to give him the precepts. Then the divine beings soared up and vanished into the sky. Chajang then left the mountain. Over a one-month period, gentlemen and ladies of the country all flocked to receive the five precepts from him. Nonetheless, Chajang deeply reflected on the fact that he was born in a peripheral region where Buddhism had yet to flourish. He had not read Buddhist teachings with his own eyes nor were there famous mountains [monasteries] in Silla where he could receive and honor Buddhist teachings. He petitioned to the Silla ruler to permit him to travel west to witness the great transformation [of Buddhism in China]. In the twelfth year of the Zhenguan era of the Tang Emperor Taizong (638), together with over ten of his disciples, including the monk Sil, he set out to the West and reached Chang'an. The emperor issued an official edict for his comfort and well-being. Chajang was accorded warm treatment in the special cloister of Shengguang monastery and treated with exceptional generosity. People flocked to him and offerings piled up with each passing day. At that time, a thief came from outside. When he was about to take [Chajang's] things, he trembled with shock and came back to confess his sin and receive the precepts from Chajang. A man born blind visited Chajang and confessed his sins. Later he recovered his eyesight. As a result of such happy miracles, there were more than a thousand people a day who received precepts from him.

By nature Chajang was fond of solitude. His petition to the throne to retire to the mountains was granted. To the east of Yunji monastery in the Zhongnan mountains he built himself a hut on the top of the cliff. The whole day humans and spirits thronged to him to receive ordination. Once, when he was afflicted with measles, one of the spirits to whom he had given precepts massaged him where he was suffering and he was immediately healed. While three summers came and went, he remained on this mountain.

Chajang now wished to serve the cause of Buddhism in his own eastern frontier land and left Yunji monastery. At that time, a huge demon appeared with an enormous retinue of minions, all wearing armor and wielding cudgels. The specter said, "I have to fetch Chajang in this golden chariot." Then another big deity appeared and fought him. He blocked the demon from approaching Chajang. Chajang smelled an overwhelmingly foul stench choking the valley. He climbed up to his rope-bed and took his leave. The specters had struck one of the disciples of Chajang, crippling him and killing him, but he came back to his life. Chajang then donated all his clothes and belongings, exemplifying the monastic virtue of charity. A sweet fragrance pervaded his entire body and mind. The deity said, "As you did not die today, you will live to be over eighty." Thereupon he returned to Chang'an. The emperor once again issued an imperial decree for his well-being and gave him 200 rolls of silk to be used for his clothing.

In the seventh year of the Zhenguan era (643) his country Silla sent a petition to the Tang emperor asking for his return. The emperor sanctioned this. He invited Chajang to the palace and bestowed on him a robe and 500 *duan* [one *duan* is equivalent to eighteen feet] of various-colored silk. The crown prince also gave him 200 *duan* of silk. A vegetarian feast was organized under the auspices of the state at Hongfu monastery. In this assembly of eminent monks eight people were ordained. It was also decreed that the Chancellor of the Board of Rites make donations. As the Buddhist scriptures and images that Silla possessed were patchy and incomplete, Chajang obtained a full set of the Buddhist canon, holy images, Buddhist banners, and embroidered canopies. He returned to his country wth all these objects, which would bring happiness and benefit. When he reached his native land, the whole country rejoiced. This was the flowering of Buddhism during that age.

Because of Chajang's prestige in the great land [of China] and his adherence to the true teaching, the monarch felt that, without his guiding principles, the order and purity of the saṃgha could not be obtained, and therefore, appointed him to the post of chief of clerics. He resided in Wangbun monastery [the *Samguk yusa* records that Wangbun is an error for Punhwang monastery]. The monastery was built by the monarch. A special cloister was constructed for him, and ten people were ordained especially to attend permanently to Chajang. One summer he was invited to the palace to lecture on the *Mahāyānasaṃgraha*. In the evenings he lectured at Hwangnyong monastery on the Bodhisattva Precepts for seven days and nights. Heaven dropped sweet dew, and clouds and mist enveloped the lecture hall. The fourfold congregation [of monks, nuns, and male and female laypeople] rose up to congratulate him. His fame spread far. On the day the dharma assembly dispersed, a large number of people flocked to him like clouds to receive precepts. Owing to this epochal event, nine out of ten households received the dharma. This auspicious turn of events was due to Chajang, who had always been brave and perspicacious. He donated all his clothes and possessions and dedicated himself solely to *dhūta* [the ascetic exercises].

Although it had been exactly a century since Buddhism was transmitted to the East [Silla], abbots were deficient in their adherence to discipline. Chajang held detailed discussions with ministers and elders on the issue of the rectification of discipline. At the time the ruler and ministers, both high and low, all examined and discussed how it should be ordered. The entire [system of] the Buddhadharma needed regulations and Chajang, the chief of clerics, was entrusted with [creating] them. Chajang ordered each of the five divisions of the saṃgha [monks, nuns, male novices or *śrāmaṇera*, female novices or *śrāmaṇerikā*, and female postulants or *śikṣamāṇā*] to strengthen its adherence to the Old Interpretation [of the *vinaya*]. He established an administrative mechanism to supervise and maintain the saṃgha's adherence to monastic rules. Twice a month the monastic community was required to recite the precepts and to expatiate their sins according to the *vinaya*. A comprehensive examination was held each spring and winter to ensure that it would be known who had obeyed and who had violated [the rules of the *pratimokṣa*].

Chajang also appointed commissioners who toured all the monasteries to admonish [errant monks] and to teach the dharma, to ensure proper decoration [i.e., worship and maintenance] of Buddha statues and management of saṃgha affairs. Now discipline became permanent, and on this account it was said that Chajang was indeed a dharma-protecting Bodhisattva.

Also, he constructed over ten new monasteries and stūpas, and every time a new monastery was built the entire country unitedly worshiped at it. Chajang then made the following vow, "If what has been constructed possesses numinous power, let some miraculous signs appear. And, influenced by his vow, there were invariably *śarīra* [relics] in all the sheets and begging bowls. The crowd were so moved and enraptured that their donations piled up like mountains and they sought the precepts. The practice of virtue spread widely.

In addition, there were differences between the Chinese and the barbarians in customs and clothing. Chajang revered only the true tradition. How could he have two minds about it? After this matter was discussed [at court], Silla changed its frontier clothing and took Tang norms as standard. Every year when tributary envoys assembled [at the court of Tang], Silla was placed in the rank of highest tributaries. Appointments to office and transfers of officials also tallied with that of China. If one makes comparisons on the basis of what was done, this had no precedent in history.

Chajang compiled more than ten fascicles of commentaries on sūtras and precepts. His one-fascicle *Guanxingfa* [Kor. *Kwanhaengbŏp*, Methods of Contemplation Practice] was popular in his own land.

3

A Miraculous Tale of Buddhist Practice
during the Unified Silla

Richard D. McBride II

There are few primary sources for the study of Buddhist practice in Korea during the Unified Silla period (668–935). While a number of scholarly works by Silla monks on Buddhist scriptures have been preserved, none of the edificatory and faith-promoting literature composed for the Buddhist monks, nuns, and laity of Silla has been preserved in original form. A number of inscriptions on Buddhist images and stone monuments have been discovered by archaeologists, but these by themselves do not provide a distinct picture of Buddhist belief and practice on the Korean peninsula at this time. Despite this dearth of material, *Samguk yusa* (*Memorabilia of the Three Kingdoms*), a collection of myths, anecdotes, and short stories from ancient Korea, mostly from the kingdom of Silla, has been preserved from the succeeding Koryŏ period. The text was compiled around 1285, after the Mongol subjugation of Korea in about 1260, by the Buddhist monk Iryŏn (Kim Kyŏnmyŏng, 1206–89) and contains at least two later insertions by his disciple Mugŭk (Hon'gu, 1250–1322). Little is known about the text prior to 1512. The word *yusa* (*yishi* in Chinese) in the title suggests the text was conceptualized as belonging to a loose genre of works that preserve local anecdotes and traditional narratives in a freer style different than that of "official records" commissioned by the royal family and central government. Hence, *Memorabilia of the Three Kingdoms* may be seen as preserving local discourse in contradistinction to the official discourse of the *Samguk sagi* (*Histories of the Three Kingdoms*) compiled by Kim Pusik (1075–1151) between 1136 and 1146 by order of the Koryŏ court.

Like most collections of hagiography and narratives in East Asia, *Memorabilia of the Three Kingdoms* is not a work of fiction that was conceived in the imagination of one writer. Instead, it is a selective, edited compilation based on earlier collections of miracle tales in circulation, stele inscriptions, and local narratives passed down in both oral and written form. In this respect, the composition of the text is roughly modeled after the earlier Chinese texts in the *yishi* genre, although in form and content it borrows from the panoply of literary, historical, and Buddhist hagiographical materials of the time. For the most part Iryŏn clearly and conscientiously states the documentary sources of his information. Furthermore, there are few inconsistencies when the information in these stories about Buddhist practice in Korea is placed in context with Chinese and Japanese writings dealing with the same time period. Both of these points suggest the general reliability of this late work. However, since the writing style Iryŏn employs in the *Memorabilia of the Three Kingdoms* is more like the nonparallel, simple, direct "ancient writing style" (*guwen* in Chinese, *komun* in Korean) that gained ascendancy in the Sinitic cultural sphere in the Northern Song period (960–1127)—rather than the refined and well-crafted parallel prose of texts in "dual-harnessed style" (*pianwen* in Chinese, *pyŏnmun* in Korean), which was prevalent earlier in the Chinese medieval period (317–907) and which was probably the style of some of the original Korean documents—we can be sure that Iryŏn and perhaps others exerted a strong editorial and stylistic hand.

The received version of the *Memorabilia of the Three Kingdoms* is composed of five chapters. The first chapter begins with a dynastic chronology and follows with the foundation myths of the native Korean kingdoms and other traditional narratives dating from before Silla's conquest of the other kingdoms. The second chapter contains tales from the peninsular wars for unification, as well as post-unification dynastic and other tales. The third chapter consists of two sections, subtitled "The Flourishing of the Dharma" and "Stūpas and Images," which present the Buddhist perspective on the transmission of the religion to the peninsula and tales about the miraculous founding and history of particular sacred or cultic sites. The fourth chapter, "Exegetes," contains hagiographies of eminent Silla scholastic monks. The fifth chapter is divided into four subsections entitled (1) "Divine Spells," hagiographies of Buddhist monks who specialize in working miracles through chanting dhāraṇī and sūtras; (2) "Thaumaturges," stories of individuals, particularly Buddhist monks, who possess magical powers; (3) "Escape and Seclusion," stories of people who escaped this mortal realm; and (4) "Filial Piety and Virtue," traditional narratives of filial sons and virtuous daughters.

The tale translated here, "The Two Saints of White Moon Mountain," is contained in the third chapter of *Memorabilia of the Three Kingdoms*. White Moon Mountain (Paegwŏlsan) is located in the vicinity of the present-day city of Ch'angwŏn in South Kyŏngsang province in the southeastern part of the Korean peninsula near the southern coast. The remains of a monastery, called "Nambaeksa" (South White [Moon Mountain] Monastery) for short, have been unearthed at the base of White Moon Mountain. Ancient roof tiles and ceramic shards have been found at the site, as well as an image of the Buddha incised on a rock face and a three-story stone pagoda. These data suggest that White Moon Mountain was an active cultic site during the Unified Silla period.

Buddhist practice in Silla Korea during the seventh and eighth centuries C.E. may be described as a rich combination of many kinds of devotional practices, rituals for repentance and the eradication of unwholesome karma, and contemplative techniques to focus the mind on the qualities and characteristics of buddhas and bodhisattvas and on the sacred realms associated with them. It was particularly associated with the cults of Maitreya, Amitābha, and Avalokiteśvara. Images of these cultic figures in wooden, gilt-bronze, or stone form, as well as in paintings, played an important role in enabling the monks and laity to visualize the physical characteristics of these figures and served as a focal point for meditative and devotional activities.

Maitreya is an important figure because he is both an advanced bodhisattva and the future Buddha. He dwells in meditative absorption in Tuṣita heaven in our world system, which was believed by Koreans and other East Asians to be located in the northwest region of the heavens. The *Scripture on Maitreya's Advent* (*Mile xiasheng jing*) explains that in the distant future, after a long period of warfare, Maitreya will be born into the world, preach the Buddhist Law to congregations of beings prepared to hear the Buddhist truth, and establish a long period of lasting peace. In Silla times, believers vowed to be reborn in Tuṣita heaven, where they could hear the Buddhist Law in its purity; they also vowed to be reborn in the world in the future when Maitreya would reestablish the Buddhist teaching in its purity. Their worship included thinking about Maitreya's appearance and characteristics, performing pious deeds, and chanting his name. Some people, mainly monks who had the leisure time, cultivated special meditative trances in which they visualized themselves in Tuṣita heaven in Maitreya's presence, as explained in the *Scripture on Maitreya's Advent*. In these various ways the people of Silla sought to form karmic connections to Maitreya.

Amitābha (also called Amitāyus) is the Buddha who presides over a Buddha-land in a distant world system located in the western direction called Sukhāvatī or "Extreme Bliss" (*Kŭngnak*). The *Scripture on the Buddha Amitāyus* (Ch. *Emituo jing*; *Taishō* no. 363) recounts how when he was a bodhisattva he made forty-eight vows that caused this Pure Land to come into being, and the *Scripture on the Visualization of the Buddha Amitāyus* (Ch. *Guan Wuliangshoufo jing*; *Taishō* no. 365) explains various practices by which one may be reborn in this Western Paradise. As with the Maitreya cult, aspirants in the Silla period vowed to be reborn in Sukhāvatī after they died by relying on the power of Amitābha. Though many practices—including mental recollection of that Buddha's qualities, offering worship through bows and prostrations, chanting scriptures, and cultivating visualizations of one's rebirth in the Pure Land—were originally employed to ensure rebirth, verbal recitation of the name of the Buddha Amitābha began to emerge as the dominant form of Buddhist practice in China in the seventh century, and this practice soon spread to Korea. The efficacy of verbally chanting Amitābha's name is found in the scriptures, but it was intended originally for aspirants with the most deficient spiritual capacities and ensured rebirth in the lowest possible level in the Pure Land.

Avalokiteśvara (Kuanŭm; Guanyin in Chinese) is the popular and powerful Bodhisattva of Compassion who looks down upon the world and responds to the cries of people in distress. The chapter of the *Lotus Sūtra* dealing with this bodhisattva, which circulated separately in East Asia as the *Scripture on Avalokiteśvara*

(*Guanyin pusa jing*), describes many ways in which he aids the Buddhist faithful and also provides a list of the apparitional forms that Avalokiteśvara may assume to provide appropriate assistance according to the needs of each individual. These may include the shapes of gods or goddesses, lay men or lay women, monks or nuns, boys or girls, dragons or demons, and so forth. Along with Mahāsthāmaprāpta, Avalokiteśvara is one of the main assistants of Amitābha, who appears before people who will attain rebirth in Sukhāvatī and escorts them as they pass from this realm of existence into the Pure Land. Avalokiteśvara is also the transmitter of numerous scriptures on Buddhist spells (dhāraṇī) and the ritual procedures for their efficacious use, such as for the eradication of unwholesome karma, wish fulfillment, protection from snakebites, and cures for skin diseases.

The narratives preserved in *Memorabilia of the Three Kingdoms* mainly concern the capital-based aristocrats and local elites. We can distinguish people in these elite groups from people in the lower social ranks because they possessed Chinese-style family names consisting of one character, such as Kim, Pak, or Sŏl. Commoners for the most part did not have family names, and the names they did have were simple and unadorned, and often contained repeated sounds. The names of the two saints of White Moon Mountain, Nohil Pudŭk and Taltal Pakpak, suggest humble social origins, but they became famous for their spiritual attainments.

Although Nohil Pudŭk and Taltal Pakpak were probably both commoners, the narrative makes special mention of their parents' names. The names of their parents appear to have been altered to suggest a relationship with the names given to the parents of Maitreya and Amitābha in Buddhist scriptures. Nohil Pudŭk's father's name was purportedly Wŏlchang and his mother's name, Misŭng. Taltal Pakpak's father's name was reportedly Subŏm and his mother's name, Pŏmma. In the *Scripture on Maitreya's Advent*, Maitreya's parents are Xiufanma (Subŏmma in Korean) and Fanmayue (Pŏmmawŏl in Korean), and in the *Dhāraṇī on the Drum Sound King Amitābha* (*Emituo guyinsheng wang tuoluoni jing* in Chinese; *Taishō* no. 370), Amitābha's parents are Yueshang Zhuanlun Shengwang (Wŏlshang Chŏllyun Sŏngwang in Korean) and Shusheng Miaoyan (Sulsŭng Myoan in Korean). Although these correspondences have been indicated previously by scholars, they have not emphasized that names of the parents of Pudŭk, who worships Maitreya, correspond more closely to the names of Amitābha's parents, and that the names of the parents of Pakpak, who worships Amitābha, correspond to the names of Maitreya's parents. Nor is this the first case in which symbolic Buddhist names have been attributed to Koreans. For example, according to the *Histories of the Three Kingdoms*, the given names of King Chinp'yŏng (r. 579–632), his wife, and his younger brothers were made to correspond to the Chinese translations of the names of the family of the Buddha Śākyamuni (Siddhārtha Gautama), namely, the Buddha's father, Śuddhodhana, the Buddha's mother, Lady Māyā, and the Buddha's uncles Śuklodana and Drotodana. Considering that the finale of the tale is that Pudŭk and Pakpak become both Maitreya and Amitābha in their present bodies, it may have been an editorial mistake that Amitābha's parents should give birth to Maitreya and Maitreya's parents give birth to Amitābha. Or perhaps we may understand this as evidence for the interrelationship between these two cults and the relative interchangeability of Maitreya and Amitābha in the minds of some Korean Buddhists. Both figures are lords over sacred lands where the Buddhist Law may be heard and understood with greater ease than in our world. More important, however, the narrative concerning Nohil Pudŭk and Taltal Pakpak's practice suggests a close and friendly relationship between the practitioners of the cults of Maitreya, Amitābha, and Avalokiteśvara in eighth-century Silla.

Nohil Pudŭk and Taltal Pakpak are great examples of a type of Buddhist practitioner that was common in East Asia from the fifth through the tenth centuries: the śramaṇa (samun in Korean, shamen in Chinese), a person who left his family and renounced the world but who probably did not receive full ordination to the Buddhist monastic precepts, did not reside in a state-sponsored monastery, and was not recognized by the government as a "monk." In Indian literature, a śramaṇa, or "striver," was described originally in contrast to a brāhmaṇa, the high-caste Vedic priest in ancient India. In the Buddha's time there were primarily two classes of religious practitioners: brahmaṇas and śramaṇas. The term brahmaṇa is found in the Upaniṣads, an ancient Indian religious commentarial collection, which describes the traditional path of a religious practitioner in the priestly caste. Ideally, a brahmaṇa's life was divided into four stages: student, householder, forest dweller, and wanderer. The śramaṇa also abandoned the householder life to become a wandering mendicant but did so against the prevailing social order, often because he did not belong to the priestly caste. Many śramaṇas left their families while they were young, and there was no requirement that they pass through the other stages mentioned for the brahmaṇa. The śramaṇa was celibate and usually concerned with purity, devoted himself to controlling and limiting his desires and passions, practiced meditation, and often endured severe austerities in order to obtain liberation from the cycle of rebirth and death.

The Buddha Śākyamuni became a śramaṇa when he renounced his life in his father's palace, his family, and his warrior-caste status, and went forth to find the answers to the questions of old age, sickness, and death. His followers, the monks in the Buddhist order he founded, were also śramaṇas, since they too renounced their homes, families, and inheritances to pursue the path leading to wisdom, awakening, and nirvāṇa. However, the term was not exclusively Buddhist. Many other non-Buddhist religious leaders of the Buddha's day, including Mahāvīra, the founder of Jainism, were also śramaṇas.

The most common and generic term for a Buddhist "monk" in East Asian Buddhist literature is sŭng (seng in Chinese), the Korean pronunciation of the Chinese character that probably transliterates the Prākṛit saṃgha. This is a complex term usually understood as the congregation of monks but which can also refer to the larger congregation of all Buddhist faithful, including monks, nuns, and laypeople. Other common terms are samun, a transliteration of śramaṇa, which was treated previously, and pigu, a transliteration of bhikṣu, a fully ordained monk. The problem is that while all fully ordained monks are technically śramaṇa, the term śramaṇa more correctly refers to a broad range of Buddhist renunciants that includes all strata of ordained and unordained monks and mendicants.

Iryŏn uses the term "monk" (sŭng) to refer Nohil Pudŭk and Taltal Pakpak, which means that they were probably śramaṇas rather than fully ordained bhikṣus. The beginning of the narrative contains some conflicting information that I will attempt to clarify. Once Nohil Pudŭk and Taltal Pakpak turn twenty years old, the narrative says that they move to another settlement, cut their hair, and "become monks" in the Office of Dharma Accumulation (Pŏpchŏkpang). This office is mentioned nowhere else in Korean Buddhist literature. However, as the narrative continues there are hints at a different situation: they were engaged in farming on land owned by a Buddhist monastery. Being humble commoners who had no inherited lands to farm, it appears that they registered as dependents with the office overseeing the management of arable monastery land. They (and their families) would have been viewed as "monastery households," clients of the monastery who paid rent to the Buddhist church. The rent they paid to the monastery managing this estate would have been conceptualized in spiritual terms: as offerings to the Buddhist church that accumulated merit. As members of the broad community under the jurisdiction of the monastery, they would, in this respect, be listed as members of the saṃgha, the Buddhist community. We cannot be certain whether they really shaved their heads. If they did, it could have been a symbolic practice to signify or solidify the covenant relationship between the client and the monastery; or it could merely be an editorial addition to bring the two men clearly into the fold of orthodox Buddhist practitioners: "to cut one's hair and become a monk" is a common phrase.

They could not have been celibate monks as Nohil Pudŭk and Taltal Pakpak are then described in the narrative as devout Buddhist laymen who were married and had families. They had made commitments to assist each other in completing the path to Buddhahood, becoming "saints." The word "saint" (sŏng in Korean) here refers to the bodhisattva, a powerful yet sylphlike being on the path to Buddhahood who has escaped from the cycle of rebirth and death and who vows to save all other beings and uses various skills and strategies to aid and assist beings. The Bodhisattva Avalokiteśvara is referred to in this story as the "Great Saint." Becoming a bodhisattva was the common goal of Mahāyāna Buddhists—monks, nuns, and laypeople—in East Asia at this time. Nohil Pudŭk and Taltal Pakpak probably approached their goal of becoming bodhisattvas by vowing to be reborn in Tuṣita heaven and Sukhāvatī, respectively, since Pudŭk later "diligently sought after Maitreya" (kŭn'gu Mirŭk) and Pakpak "religiously recollected Amitābha" (yenyŏm Mit'a). They led simple lives as faithful householders for a time but eventually decided to reject the world of men for a reclusive life in a deep mountain valley. There is no indication that they ever became fully ordained monks, and no special term is used to describe them. They just settled their family affairs and became śramaṇas in the original sense of the term described earlier in this chapter.

As śramaṇas they were concerned with abiding by the precepts and rules of the fully ordained monks (numbering 250 for monks), though they had never officially "received" them from the Buddhist church at an ordination platform in a ritual procedure with government approval. Regardless, the idea of spiritual or ritual purity through observing the precepts is an important motif in the story. However, although it is important to keep the monastic precepts, those who are really enlightened like the buddhas and bodhisattvas must transcend or overcome dualistic conceptualizations of pure and impure, wholesome and unwholesome, male and female, and so forth, and become awakened to the emptiness of all such dualistic constructions. This is a standard Mahāyāna understanding of the nature of enlightenment acquired through cultivating bodhisattva practices. In the story that follows, the śramaṇas Nohil Puḍŭk and Taltal Pakpak are tested and guided to enlightenment through the unusual ministration of one who has fundamentally completed the path to Buddhahood. They are hence able to complete the path themselves, becoming transformed manifestations of Maitreya and Amitābha in their present bodies.

The translation is from *Samguk yusa kyogam yŏn'gu* (Critical Edition of the *Samguk yusa*), by Ha Yŏllyong and Yi Kŭnjik (Seoul: Sinsŏwŏn, 1997), 327–34 (internal page numbering 3:270–77); cf. *Samguk yusa* 3:155–58, Ch'oe Namsŏn edition (Seoul: Minjung Sŏgwang, 1954; rpt., Seoul: Sŏwŏn Munhwasa, 1990), *Taishō* no. 2039, vol. 49, pp. 995b–996b, and *Han'guk Pulgyo chŏnso*, vol. 6, pp. 328c–330b.

Further Reading

For an often periphrastic translation of *Memorabilia of the Three Kingdoms*, see Ha Tae-Hung and Grafton K. Mintz, trans., *Samguk Yusa: Legends and History of the Three Kingdoms of Ancient Korea* (Seoul: Yonsei University Press, 1972). For a detailed discussion of the practices and development of the cults of Maitreya, Amitābha, and Avalokiteśvara in Silla, see Richard D. McBride II, "Buddhist Cults in Silla Korea in Their Northeast Asian Context" (Ph.D. diss., University of California, Los Angeles, 2001).

The Two Saints of White Moon Mountain:
Nohil Puḍŭk and Taltal Pakpak

The *Record of the Two Saints of White Moon Mountain Who Completed the Path* (*Paegwŏlsan yangsŏng sŏngdo ki*) says: White Moon Mountain lies north of Silla's Kusa Commandery (the ancient Kulcha Commandery; the present Ŭian Commandery). With peaks of surpassing uniqueness stretching several hundred *li*, it is aptly called enormous Chin [Mountain]. . . . In the settlement there were two men: one named Nohil Puḍŭk (or Puḍŭng), whose father's name was Wŏlchang and whose mother's name was Misŭng; and the other was named Taltal Pakpak, whose father's name was Subŏm and whose mother's name was

Pŏmma. They were of uncommon bearing and physique and, since they both had lofty aspirations beyond the remote region [of their hometown], they were good friends for each other. In the year when they both went through the capping ceremony [at the age of twenty], they traveled over the ridge to the northeast of their settlement, cut their hair, and became monks in the Office of Dharma Accumulation (Pŏpchŏkpang). Not long afterward they heard that there were old monasteries to the southwest [in the vicinity] of Ch'isan Settlement, Pŏpchong Valley, and Sŭngdo Settlement. Being able to turn themselves to the truth, they traveled together to the two vicinities of the Great Buddha Field and the Small Buddha Field and dwelt therein.

Pudŭk stayed in Embracing Truth Hermitage (Hoejinam), also called Mud Monastery (Yangsa). (This is, in fact, the foundation of an old monastery presently called Hoejin Cave.) Pakpak dwelt in Crystalline Glow Monastery (Yurigwangsa). (This is the present-day monastery ruins on Pear Mountain [I san].) They both brought their wives and children to dwell [in this remote area]. They passed their time in farming, coming and going to visit each other, disciplining their minds, and training themselves. Their wills that [sought that which is] beyond this world [realized that] nothing was permanent and everything would eventually decay. They viewed their mortal frames has impermanent. For this reason, they said to each other, "Fertile fields and prosperous harvests are good benefits, but they are not as good as having clothing and food to suit one's whims and being satiated and warm spontaneously. Wives and woman and houses and dwellings are good for the senses, but they are not as good as wandering with the thousand saints in lotus ponds and flower storehouses to amuse oneself as parrots and peacocks. Moreover, learning the [path of the] Buddha one rightly becomes a Buddha; cultivating the truth one must necessarily obtain the truth. Presently we have already cast aside worldly pursuits to become monks, we have just stripped ourselves of trifling entanglements, and we have completed the unsurpassed path [to Buddhahood]. How would we flow or sink in the wind and dust [of the mundane world] and be no different than the vulgar beings of this world?"

Eventually they rejected the world of men and were about to conceal themselves in a deep valley. At night they dreamed of a thin ray of white light that came from the west. In the midst of the light hung a golden arm that touched the foreheads of the two men. When they awoke and related their dreams, they both matched the other's exactly. They were both struck with wonder at this for a long time. Eventually they entered Mudŭng Valley (presently South Cave) on White Moon Mountain. Master Pakpak divined that he should reside on the northern ridge at Lion Rock (Sajaam), so he dwelt there in a chamber eight Chinese-feet wide (p'alch'ŏk) made of wooden boards. Hence, it was called "the Wooden Board Room" (P'anbang). Master Pudŭk divined that there was a spot with water beneath a pile of rock on the eastern ridge, so he also built a residence ten feet (chang) square and dwelt therein. For this reason it was called "the Rock Pile Room" (Noebang).

Each dwelt in his own hermitage. Pudŭk diligently sought Maitreya and Pakpak religiously recollected Amitābha. Before a full three years had passed it was the eighth day of the fourth month of *kiyu*, the third year in the Jinglong reign period [of the Tang dynasty emperor Zhongzong], eight years since King Sŏngdŏk ascended the throne of Silla (21 May 709). When it was about to become night, there came a young woman about twenty years of age, whose form and figure were of surpassing exquisiteness. The scent of orchid musk wafted around her body. When she by chance arrived at the northern hermitage and coyly requested to spend the night, she offered the following poem:

> While traveling, the sun set and the thousand mountains grew dark;
> The road was blocked and the city far away, cutting me off from my four
>   neighbors.
> Now I ask that you let me spend the night in your hermitage—
> A compassionate *upadhyāya* [*hwasang*, a monk] would not be perturbed.

Pakpak replied, "An *āraṇuya* (hermitage) endeavors to protect its purity. Do not remain in this vicinity. Go! Do not stop in this place." Shutting the gate he went inside. (In the *Record* [*of the Two Saints of White Moon Mountain*] he says, "I have let the ashes of my hundred passions grow cold. Do not tempt me with your bag of blood!")

The young woman then went to the southern hermitage and made the same request as before. Pudŭk said, "Where did you come from in breech of nighttime safety?"

"I am transparent and of the same essence as vacuous space, so how could I come and go!" the young woman replied, "I merely heard that a worthy gentleman's will and wishes were profound and circumspect and that his virtuous observances were noble and resolute. I want to help him perfect the *bodhicitta*." For this purpose, she composed a gāthā that said:

> The sun sets over the road through a thousand mountains,
> Out traveling, I am separated from my four neighbors.
> The shadows of bamboo and pine turn into something profound,
> The sounds of the stream and cave are as if refreshed.
> I beg for lodging, not losing myself in the maze,
> You, revered master, desire to be pointed to the ferry.
> My desire is that you merely fulfill my request,
> And that you do not ask who I am.

When Master [Pudŭk] heard this, he was astonished and replied, "This land is not corrupted by womankind but, being in accord with all sentient beings, it is also a place for [cultivating] bodhisattva practices. Nevertheless, how did you suddenly appear in this remote valley in the dark of the night?" He then courteously welcomed her into his hermitage and seated her. As night approached he purified his mind and sharpened his integrity. He hung a small lamp halfway up the wall and chanted assiduously.

When the night grew late the young woman said, "Unfortunately I must give birth here. I beg of you, noble monk, to spread out some straw mats for me."

Pudŭk felt compassion for her and did not refuse her request. When he had brightened the candlelight politely the young woman had already given birth and requested a bath. Nohil was both embarrassed and afraid at heart, nevertheless, his feelings of compassion and pity were more selfless. So, he prepared a bath for her, placed the young woman in it, and stoked up the bath water to bathe her.

As soon as she got into the bath, an elegant and beautiful fragrance wafted from the water and the water turned into liquid gold. Nohil was flabbergasted. The woman said, "You, my master, must also bathe herein." Nohil made a strong effort to follow her instructions when suddenly he realized that his vital essences were cool and refreshed and his skin had become the color of gold. Gazing to his side there suddenly appeared a lotus throne on which the young woman encouraged him to sit. For this reason she spoke, saying, "I am the Bodhisattva Avalokiteśvara. I have come to assist you, oh great master, to achieve *mahābodhi* (great enlightenment)!" When she finished these words she disappeared.

Pakpak thought that Nohil had certainly sullied the precepts this past night and was about to go make fun of him. But as soon as he arrived he saw Nohil seated on a lotus throne, composed as a revered image of Maitreya, emitting bright light, and his body was the color of sandalwood and gold. Without thinking he kowtowed and respectfully inquired, "How were you able to attain this state?"

When Nohil had completely detailed the causes, Pakpak lamented, saying, "My hindrances are now serious indeed. I had the good fortune to encounter the Great Saint (Avalokiteśvara) but, to the contrary, did not actually meet him. Oh sir of great virtue and ultimate benevolence: although I deserve first to be whipped, I hope you will not forget the pact we made so long ago that we would do all things together."

Nohil replied, "In the bath there is some remaining liquid. You only need to bathe in it."

Pakpak then bathed in it and just as expected he became Amitābha. These images of these two revered ones faced each other in a dignified manner. When the people of the settlement down the mountain heard about this, they raced to gaze upon them, marveled, and said, "How uncommon! How rare!" While the two saints were preaching to them the essentials of the Dharma, their bodies rose up on clouds and departed.

In *ŭlmi*, the fourteenth year of the Tianbao reign period [of Xuanzong] (755), the Silla King Kyŏngdŏk assumed the throne and heard about this event. In the *chŏngyu* year (757), he dispatched commissioners to build a great monastery, which he called the Southern Monastery of White Moon Mountain. On the fifteenth day of the seventh month of *kapchin*, the second year of the Guangde reign period (16 August 764), the monastery was completed. Then, a clay image of Maitreya was enshrined in the Golden Hall, the face board of which read: "Hall of Maitreya Who Completed the Path in This Present Body." Furthermore, a clay image of Amitābha was enshrined in the Lecture Hall. Since the remaining liquid was insufficient to completely cover the image in this paint, the Amitābha image also has flaws, giving it a mottled, spotted look. The face board of this hall read: "Hall of Amitābha Who Completed the Path in This Present Body."

4

Buddhism as a Cure for the Land

Sem Vermeersch

We tend to think of religions as organic, self-sufficient systems that offer a comprehensive interpretation of the world. Yet not all religions have developed a theology, cosmology, or other systems of interpretation to set them apart from other systems of thought and belief. In premodern Korea, it is also the case that many religions existed side by side, each claiming specific areas of efficacy while sharing many common elements in their conception of the universe. A case in point is geomancy, or what Koreans call *p'ungsu* (lit. "wind and water"; *fengshui* in Chinese): on the one hand, it may not seem to qualify as a religion, since it lacks, for example, a church and a priesthood; but on the other hand, it offers solutions to people's physical and spiritual needs by mediating with the hidden forces contained in the earth. In Korean history, geomantic techniques initially developed in close conjunction with Buddhism, since Buddhism was thought to have the power to correct negative flows of terrestrial energy or to enhance positive ones.

Originating in China, the East Asian practice of geomancy has become popular in the West, too, where it is usually known by its Chinese name, *fengshui*, but there are still many misunderstandings about what it entails. In contemporary Korea (and elsewhere, in fact), geomancy is often represented as a protoscience, a body of knowledge and wisdom to divine the ideal site for a dwelling or grave. While geomancy is indeed concerned with divining such locations, and has developed principles to deduce auspicious sites, objective geographic conditions are only part of the equation. Besides the physical environment, in the form of mountains and watercourses, the site should also be correlated with cosmological factors and the astrological or numerological constitution of the person(s) for whom the site is intended. And despite the existence of objective criteria to determine a site, these are often conflicting or open to interpretation, so ultimately the geomancer's own impression based on his experience and insight may be conclusive. Finally (as illustrated in the accompanying chapter by Hong-key Yoon), it is important to understand that the auspiciousness sought was not always an abstract feeling of well-being, but often the expectation of very concrete benefits.

The translations presented in this chapter do not concern specific cases or techniques of Korean geomancy, but rather provide a discourse on geomancy that links it to the fate of the nation. Especially during the Koryŏ period (918–1392), the fate of the dynasty was intimately tied to the manipulation of this discourse, and it is presumably during this time that the perception of the peninsula as a unified geomantic system took hold. In other words, whereas the practice of geomancy is typically considered to involve only the immediate surroundings of a specific site, a distinctive feature recurring throughout the history of geomancy in Korea is the relationship of a site to the whole array of mountain ranges fanning out from Mount Paektu over the peninsula. This view had important political implications: since every single spot was connected to the whole geomantic array, the state had to guard against any attempts at manipulating this discourse by the construction of harmful or conducive sites that would challenge the center. In this respect, Buddhism played an important role, as it was regarded as the main force to regulate the flow of energy throughout the country. This explains why the construction of monasteries was an integral part of the political system, for these Buddhist edifices literally helped to construct the "nation."

Korean tradition credits the monk Tosŏn (827–98) with being the first to apply Buddhism as a corrective to geomantic forces. Tosŏn supposedly said that if pagodas or other Buddhist edifices were built in places where the flow of energy was adverse, they could function in the same way that needles do in acupuncture: applied in the right places, they could cure diseases of the land. This is called pibo, literally "assisting and supplementing," or remedying. Although Tosŏn was a historical figure living at the end of the Silla era, many myths have accrued to this figure. Many works are attributed to him, but since none are extant, it is perhaps more realistic to say that the preceding interpretation developed over time.

Looking at the traditions preserved regarding Tosŏn and the idea of Buddhism as a remedial force, a certain evolution can be discerned. Though pibo is nowadays interpreted as a specific geomantic term and the expression of a unique Korean form of geomancy, originally it probably did not have such a specific meaning. Moreover, although pibo is not attested as a geomantic term in Chinese sources, to some extent a similar concept is operative in Chinese expressions of geomancy. Also, there are many different legends involving Tosŏn, and many different representations of exactly how he interpreted the Korean landscape.

What is certain is that there is a core of historicity in the legends and accounts of Tosŏn. He was a prominent Sŏn monk, living during the golden age of Korean Sŏn Buddhism. During the ninth century, many Korean monks gained prominence in the lineages of the major Chinese Chan (Jpn. Zen) schools, and after returning to their native Silla enjoyed the patronage of court and local aristocrats alike, which allowed them to found their own monasteries and train lineages of disciples. During their long sojourns in China, it is likely that these monks also learned about geomancy, and since most of them studied in the Jiangxi region of the Chinese mainland, one can assume that they were exposed to the Jiangxi tradition of geomancy, which relies heavily on interpreting the shape of the land-scape to determine the location of auspicious dwelling sites.

While probably a fairly obscure figure during his lifetime—Tosŏn never traveled to China and did not found an important new mountain school of Sŏn—he posthumously rose to prominence soon after the founding of the Koryŏ dynasty (918–1392). Tosŏn was revered by the Koryŏ court for prophesying the rise of the dynastic founder, Wang Kŏn (r. 918–43), later known as King T'aejo. According to Tosŏn's official biography and the dynasty's founding legend, the extant forms of which were both composed in the twelfth century, he not only foretold the crowning of Wang Kŏn but also advised Wang Kŏn's father on where and how to build his palace to make maximum use of the terrestrial forces. The founding legend thus attempts to legitimize the Wang family dynasty by representing them as both masters and products of the country's numinous energy: because of the illustrious deeds of the founder's ancestors, the geomancer Tosŏn chose them as worthy recipients of the geomantic forces, which they harnessed in the most auspicious place, the capital Kaesŏng.

Neither the founding legend of Koryŏ nor Tosŏn's biography makes any mention of Buddhism and its remedial role in manipulating the land, suggesting that this was not yet considered an important part of Tosŏn's legacy. Yet the Koryŏsa, the official history of Koryŏ compiled in 1453, makes it clear that Tosŏn was an important figure as far as the construction and founding of Buddhist monasteries was concerned: an injunction issued by Wang Kŏn, reputedly on his deathbed, states explicitly that Buddhist structures could be built only at spots Tosŏn designated, for otherwise the earth's energy could be damaged. Most comments in the Koryŏsa focus on the potentially harmful effects of building pagodas or temples, although their potentially positive influence is also acknowledged. Also, it is clear that the term pibo, though it appears frequently in the sources, was not only used in a geomantic sense but also could refer to temples that had distinguished themselves in the founding of the dynasty. Thus the term was employed mainly to designate an official category of monastery; records kept on these temples were known as Pibo ki (Records of Geomantic Remediation) or Sanch'ŏn pibo ki (Records of Remedying the Geography), while Tosŏn's list of temples was known as the Milgi (Secret Record). Seventy monasteries are said to have been listed on this Secret Record, but unfortunately the list has not come down to us. Only the names of a few monasteries, such as Pojesa or Manŭisa, can be confirmed as pibo temples.

Tosŏn's influence was acknowledged even in the Chosŏn dynasty, as is evident in the translations from the Chosŏn annals included here. Although the new authorities, under pressure from Neo-Confucian elites, confiscated temple assets and eliminated many monasteries, those on the Secret Record were all allowed to exist. This probably explains why there are a number of temple records dating to the early Chosŏn period that identify a monastery as an ancient pibo temple; officials such as Kwŏn Kŭn were probably entreated by monks to write these records to further their claims to such status and thereby ensure a temple's survival. That the anti-Buddhist Chosŏn authorities accepted the special status of *piho* temples was apparently in deference to the previous dynasty, though it is also possible that geomancy was not regarded in such a negative light as Buddhism. Although critical comments were voiced on the practice of geomancy and the ideas underpinning it, especially in the later half of the dynasty, geomancy was probably thought to be much less inimical to Neo-Confucian orthodoxy, perhaps even compatible with it in many ways. Thus the late Chosŏn period saw a resurgence of interest in geomancy, and also the first works in which an exposition of Tosŏn's geomantic principles is given. In one of these examples, it is alleged that Tosŏn was schooled by the Chinese monk Yixing (683–727), who instructed him in the way to read the earth veins and where to insert temples as if they were acupuncture needles in a body. According to another text, Tosŏn saw the Korean peninsula as a ship, which needed ballast—in the form of Buddhist structures—to keep it on an even keel. It is not certain how far back these concepts go (they may well recycle older material eschewed by official historiographers), but at the very least they reflect the attitudes of late Chosŏn Koreans toward the landscape, revealing that they looked at the environment with a lively imagination in terms of an organic whole.

The translated material is drawn from the following sources, listed in the same order as the translations: Chŏng Inji et al., *Koryŏsa* (rpt., Seoul: Asea Munhwasa, 1990), 2:15a, 7:36a–b, 95:6b–7a, 18:36b, 129:6a–b, 77:26b, 78:27a; Sŏ Kŏjŏng, *Tongmun sŏn* (Keijō [Seoul]: Chōsen Kosho Kankōkai, 1914; rpt., Masan: Minjok Munhwa Kanhaenghoe, 1994), 4:42 (*kwŏn* 68), 227–29 (*kwŏn* 78); *T'aejong sillok* 3:23a–b, 10:25b–28a; *Sejong Sillok* 28:22b, both from *Chosŏn wangjo sillok*, 48 vols. (rpt., Seoul: Kuksa P'yŏnch'an Wiwŏnhoe, 1955–58); *Chōsen jisatsu shiryō* (Keijō: Chōsen Sōtokufu, 1911; rpt., Seoul: Chungang Munhwa Ch'ulp'ansa, 1968), 2:377, 1:205.

Further Reading

Choi Byŏng-hŏn (Ch'oe Pyŏnghŏn), "Tosŏn's Geomantic Theories and the Foundation of the Koryŏ Dynasty," *Seoul Journal of Korean Studies* 27, no. 2 (1989): 67; Marion Eggert, "P'ungsu: Korean Geomancy in Traditional Intellectual Perspective," *Bochumer Jahrbuch zur Ostasienforschung* 26 (2002): 243–57; Michael C. Rogers, "P'yŏnnyŏn t'ongnok: The Foundation Legend of the Koryŏ State," *Journal of Korean Studies* 4 (1982–83): 3–72; Sem Vermeersch, "The Relation between Geomancy and Buddhism in Koryŏ: Pibo Sasang Reconsidered," in *History, Language and Culture in Korea. Proceedings of the Association of Korean Studies in Europe (AKSE)*, compiled by Pak Youngsook and Jaehoon Yeon (London: Saffron Books, 2001), pp. 186–98; Yi Pyŏngdo, *Koryŏ sidae ŭi yŏn'gu—t'ŭk'i toch'am sasang ŭi palchŏn ŭl chungsim ŭro* (Seoul: Asea Munhwasa, 1980); Yoon Hong-key, *Geoman-*

tic Relationships between Culture and Nature in Korea (Taipei: Chinese Association for Folklore, 1976).

SELECTED SOURCE MATERIALS ON GEOMANCY AND BUDDHISM

FROM *KORYŎSA* (HISTORY OF KORYŎ)

King T'aejo's Second Injunction (943)

All the temples have been established following Tosŏn's fathoming of the properties of the landscape. Tosŏn has said: "Except for the places I have designated, no construction ought to be added, or else the virtue of the land will be damaged and the dynasty will not reign eternally." We consider that if, in later generations, kings, princes, consorts, concubines, and court ministers designate their personal prayer temples or build temples, there will be reason to worry! At the basis of Silla's collapse lies the building of stūpas toward the end of the dynasty, making the land's virtue diminish. We should guard against this!

Chancellery's Protest against the Construction of Hŭngwangsa (1055)

Moreover, our Holy Ancestor [the Koryŏ founder King T'aejo] built temples first to reward [Buddhists] for their earnest wish for unification, second to suppress the wayward elements of the landscape. Now if you want to build more temples, you will make the people toil at unnecessary projects, resentment and slander will compete for first place, and you will damage beyond repair the vital arteries of the landscape so that calamities will arise and the spirits will all be angered. This is not the way to establish peace.

Ch'oe Yusŏn's Memorial against the Construction of Hŭngwangsa (1055)

The Injunction of our divine royal ancestor T'aejo says, "State Preceptor Tosŏn surveyed the [wayward or conducive] patterns of the country's geography (*sanch'ŏn*), and wherever temples can be erected, something has been built. Later kings, dukes, lords and aristocrats, queens, consorts, ministers, and officials should not fight to build shrines, because it will damage the earth's virtue."

King Ŭijong's New Statutes (1168)

[Second Statute] Reverently attend to Buddhist affairs. As these are the Latter Days when the Buddhist Law declines, if there are derelict establishments among the *pibo* temples built by our ancestors, the old dharma seats, and special prayer temples, the officials should repair them.

Reform Measures by Ch'oe Ch'unghŏn (1196)

At the time of our hallowed ancestors, Buddhist temples had to be built according to the conduciveness of mountains and rivers to suit the earth['s virtue] After pacification, ministers and unreliable monks built temples they called votive shrines, disregarding the auspiciousness of the landscape and thus damaging the earth veins again and again. Please let your majesty appoint *ŭmyang* officials to investigate this. All nonremedial (*pibo*) temples should immediately be destroyed.

[Entry on the establishment of the *Sanch'ŏn pibo togam*, the Directorate for Geographic Remediation] In 1196 the Privy Council and the Military Governor Ch'oe Ch'unghŏn convened diviners (*sulsa*) and consulted them on extending the remedial basis of the nation's mountains and rivers, and then set up this agency.

Cho Chun's Memorial (1386)

Concerning temple lands, since the time of [T'aejo, it is customary to] grant grain stipends to the five great temples and the ten great temples to assist and supplement the nation (*kukka pibo so*), if they are in the capital, and cultivation land and forest land, if they are in the provinces. The temples built in Silla, Paekche, and Ko[gu]ryŏ and those recently built are not in Tosŏn's *Secret Record* (*Milgi*) and therefore do not receive grants.

FROM *TONGMUN SŎN* (ANTHOLOGY OF KOREAN LITERATURE)

Record of the Reconstruction of Yongamsa (written by Pak Chŏnji between 1318 and 1325)

Long ago our nation-building patriarch (*kaeguk chosa*) Tosŏn received from the owner of Mt. Chiri, the holy mother celestial monarch, a secret instruction: if you build three cliff (*am*) temples, the three countries will become one, and the war will automatically cease. Thereupon the three *am* temples were built: Sŏnam, Unam and Yongam temples. Therefore these temples made a great contribution (*pibo*) to the nation, as everyone knows.

Record on a Dharma Assembly in Manŭisa (1392, by Kwŏn Kŭn)

Several tens of *ri* [one *ri* is approximately 400 meters] east of Suwŏn there is a temple called Manŭisa. It is an ancient *pibo* temple. Derelict for a long time, it had become completely overgrown when in the Huangqing reign (1312–1313) the abbot of the Ch'ŏnt'ae temple Chingusa, Great Sŏn master Hongi, came upon the ruins and rebuilt everything as new.

Record of the Reconstruction of Yŏnboksa stūpa (CA. 1392, by Kwŏn Kŭn)

According to the way of the Buddha, compassion and liberal giving are the highest virtues. The recompense to everyone without discrimination serves as evidence for this. How extremely vast are these words! After the Buddha's words were translated and transmitted to China, they spread continuously in the course of a thousand years across the four seas. And as time passed, more and more came to believe in these words. From the king, princes, and ministers of state above to foolish housewives below, all hope for blessings; there is no one who does not truly believe this. Therefore, temple pagodas and shrines were erected, so imposing and grand to behold that they seemed to fill the universe. In our Eastern Country, people since the time of Silla have been particularly diligent in upholding Buddhism. The monastic buildings in the cities were indeed more numerous than people's houses, and their halls were vast and majestic. To this day they still exist, so that one can see and imagine how great the worship of Buddhism was at that time! When the Koryŏ Wang dynasty had just united the country, all this was adopted and continued. To facilitate the secret assistance [of Buddhism], many temples were established, both in the center and in the provinces. What is meant by the term *pibo* is nothing but this. Yŏnboksa was actually built adjacent to a city gate [of Kaesŏng] and was originally named Tangsa. But since in the vernacular the pronunciation of "Tang" (Tang China) and "Tae" (big) are similar, it is also known as Taesa (big temple). [Note: this temple was actually known as Pojesa in early Koryŏ, so both Tangsa and Taesa were likely popular names.]

FROM THE CHOSŎN DYNASTY'S *T'AEJONG SILLOK* (ANNALS OF KING T'AEJONG'S REIGN)

Memorial by the Office of Divination and Astronomy (1402)

When T'aejo of the previous dynasty united the three [kingdoms], someone advised him "If one establishes temples and holds Buddhist rituals in places where the mountains are treacherous and the water adverse, it would help to pacify the nation." Thereupon [T'aejo] ordered an official to establish temples according to the terrain and grant fields and slaves. Those with pure [conduct] and few desires were appointed as abbots so as to offer to the Buddha and the saṃgha, but only to pacify the gods of the earth (*sajik*). It was not like the case of Liang Wudi [Emperor Wu of Liang, r. 502–49], who was in awe of sins and blessings and sought to ingratiate himself with the Buddha. Later rulers and ministers increased their faith and built big temples, calling them votive shrines (*wŏndang*) and endowing them with fields and cultivators. The [shrines] increased with every generation and, because of this, in the course of 500 years more temples were built than can be recorded. For this reason, the Sŏn and Kyo orders are fighting over temples with fields and slaves and strive to get them included in the *pibo* register. Monks' disciples collect the rent of fields and covet the tribute of slaves; they do not offer these to the Buddha or the saṃgha but [sport] fat horses and light clothes. The worst cases are infatuated with drink and passion; their desire is double that of laypeople. Although there are perhaps thousands of temples, and tens of thousands of monks, their behavior is still like this. Although the Buddhist faction propounds the doc trine of pacifying the nation, how could they contribute even a little to this? . . . We humbly presume that it would be difficult for the ruler to eliminate Buddhism. Instead, we should unite the Sŏn sects into the Chogye order and the Five Kyo sects into the Hwaŏm order. The seventy temples included in the *Secret Record* (*Milgi*) should be divided among the two orders. . . . As for the other *pibo* temples that are not among the seventy listed in the *Secret Record*, their land rents should be allocated to the military to prepare for a "three-year stock" and their slaves should be distributed among the different government agencies and provinces and prefectures.

Memorial by the State Council (1405)

[This memorial urges the court to confiscate temple land, the pretext being the alleged sexual misdemeanors of some abbots. The State Council argues that Buddhists had deviated from their ideal of purity and from their task of seeking blessings for the country.] The rulers and ministers of the Three Kingdoms competed with each other in the building of temples, and the previous dynasty [Koryŏ] made additional constructions in the name of *pibo*. Now our country, with all its land and people, is supporting the shrines of rulers and ministers of four defunct countries and, besides these, there are the so-called *pibo* [temples] that cannot be abolished. . . . T'aejo of the previous dynasty pointed out in his injunctions for posterity that Silla built so many temples that it perished. T'aejo's building projects were confined to what the *Secret Record* stipulates. [But] later rulers and ministers all built personal shrines. King Ŭijong visited up to ten temples every month and annually gave food to over 30,000 monks in the palace, yet he could not avoid calamity. . . . The arguments about *pibo* and blessings are definitively untrustworthy, but since they have been prevalent for years and since many believe in them, the [*pibo* temples] cannot be hastily abolished. Drawing from the *pibo* temples of the previous dynasty that feature in the *Secret Record* and all the outlying temples featuring in the official *Record of Surveying Mountains* (*Tapsangi*), the Five Sects and Two Orders will each get one temple in the new and old capitals; in the outlying circuits and districts, the Sŏn and Kyo orders will each get one temple.

FROM SEJONG SILLOK (ANNALS OF KING SEJONG'S REIGN)

Request by Office for Annals Compilation (1425)

Originally the official registers for *pibo* temples from all over the country were kept in the Ch'ungju archive. In 1402 they were moved to Kwanjipsa for the printing of Buddhist books. The aforementioned documents contain descriptions of the landscape of all the counties and prefectures. Now we need to consult these documents for the compilation of the treatise on geography. Please have Ch'ungju track down the documents and forward them to us.

FROM *CHŌSEN JISATSU SHIRYŌ* (HISTORICAL SOURCES ON KOREAN TEMPLES)

Biography of Koryŏ State Preceptor Tosŏn (attributed to the Koryŏ monk Hongin, but probably dating to the late Chosŏn period)

Previously Tosŏn traveled to Tang China to study with Chan master Yixing. Yixing was well versed in the Three Teachings [of Buddhism, Confucianism, and Daoism], and also excelled at reading the ways of heaven, yin-yang, and other forms of prognostication; he penetrated the principles of waterways and mountains, and above sealed the seven stars in a jar. Tosŏn was intent on learning all this before returning to his country. Yixing told Tosŏn, "I have a karmic connection with Koryŏ. I have heard that the Koryŏ rivers and mountains are treacherous toward the present rulers, leading to [the division into the] Nine Han states. Both inside and outside its borders, rebellious bandits swarm around; this is a disease caused by the arteries of heaven and earth being unharmonious. Because of this, many people in Koryŏ die due to diseases, hunger and warfare. What a shame, what a shame! Now I make a sincere wish to cure the disease of the landscape and make Koryŏ a land of peace. Now, why don't you draw a map of your country?" Tosŏn immediately handed him a map of the Koryŏ landscape. Yixing inspected it and exclaimed, "If the landscape is like this, Koryŏ will always be a battleground. When the sages of old controlled the floods, it took them nine years; how could it be achieved overnight!" Then he marked 3,800 places on the map and said, "If one has a disease, then one looks for the arteries and [applies] acupuncture or moxibustion to cure it. For a disease of the landscape, it is also like this. Now, on the spots I have marked, you should either build a temple, or establish a buddha [image], pagoda, or stūpa, which serve the same purpose that needles and moxa do for people. This is called *pibo*."

True Record of State Preceptor Tosŏn (published by Pak Chiso in 1743)

When [Tosŏn] returned from studying with Yixing, he wanted to apply what he had learned to cure the land's diseases and correct the leaking of *ki* to the wind, so as to consolidate the state and pacify the life of all the people and animals. He thought the topography resembled a moving ship, with T'aebaek and Kŭmgang as its bow, Wŏlch'ul and Yŏngju as its stern, Pyŏnsan near Puan as its rudder, Chirisan in the Yŏngnam area as its oar, and Unju near Nŭngju as the hull. In order to float on the water, a ship needs ballast to keep its bow and stern down. On its board and hull it needs rudder and oars to keep its course. Only then can it avoid capsizing and float in safety. Thereupon he built tem-

ples and stūpas to keep the ship down, and established buddha images to sta
bilize it. Especially below Unju, on places where the terrain was irregular, coil-
ing, and jutting out, he established a thousand buddhas and a thousand stūpas
to strengthen the sides and hull, and in Wŏlch'ul and Kŭmgang he built temples as ballast for the bow and stern.

5

The *P'algwanhoe*: From Buddhist Penance
to Religious Festival

Sem Vermeersch

One of the hallmarks of Buddhist religious practice during the Silla and Koryŏ periods was the proliferation of rituals. More than a hundred different rituals are attested in the literature, covering a wide variety of Buddhist practices, from initiation rites to memorial rites, to scripture readings and apotropaic rituals. Most of these were held at court or court-sponsored temples, and though similar rites may have been held among the ordinary people, there is very little evidence for this. Sources do describe an event called Myriad Buddha gatherings, where people calling themselves "fragrant followers" chanted the Buddha's name and read sūtras, but give no further information beyond this of rituals performed outside of the court elite. A few fragmentary remains of Buddhist spells and communal pledges to gather funds in support of a Buddhist project show that there was considerable fervor among ordinary people, but these sources are silent about any specific activities that accompanied these votive acts.

If there is one ritual event that could have been observed by both the court and ordinary people, however, it must have been the winter festival known as *p'algwanhoe*, together with its spring counterpart, the *yŏndŭnghoe*. At first sight, both seem to designate Buddhist lay practices that are common in most countries where the religion spread. *P'algwanhoe* can be translated literally as the "Assembly of the Eight Commandments," referring to the special observance of Buddhist precepts on the *poṣadha* holy days, days when people's actions were thought to be scrutinized by gods. The *yŏndŭnghoe* corresponds to the Lantern Festival, the lighting of lanterns in celebration of the Buddha's Birthday. However, these two Koryŏ rites clearly deviated from what was practiced in other Buddhist countries. The assemblies of the eight commandments were originally not meant to be celebrated only once a year and were certainly never meant to be an event where officials toasted the king and foreign merchants presented tribute, as was the case with the Koryŏ *p'algwanhoe*. While the Lantern Festival has always been celebrated only once a year, in East Asia it has mostly been held on the eighth day of the fourth month, which was believed to be the Buddha's Birthday, not on the first full moon of the second month, as in medieval Korea. Both festivals—for they were certainly that, involving performances, processions, and banqueting—are thus unique to Koryŏ and tell us a lot about Koryŏ society. Unfortunately, there are very few substantial sources on the yŏndŭnghoe, so the translations presented here deal mainly with the p'algwanhoe, which is somewhat better documented. But since it is difficult if not impossible to talk about one but not the other, this introduction will also cover the Lantern Festival.

The idea of laypeople gathering under the supervision of religious seekers on certain days of the month for ritual purification has long antecedents in Indian culture and was adopted by Buddhism. These poṣadha days were the 8th, 14th, 15th, 23rd, 29th, and 30th (or 1st) of the lunar month (two days each for the full moon and the new moon, and one day each for the quarter-phase moons), the days when evil ghosts were thought to prey on people's weaknesses. Several Buddhist sūtras devoted to the precepts for the laity stipulate that, on such days, the believers should gather near a monastery and, under the guidance of a monk, observe three special precepts (in addition to the normal five precepts for the laity) for one day and one night so as to be able to enjoy the same karmic benefits as monks. The five precepts are (1) do not kill, (2) do not steal, (3) do not engage in sexual misconduct, (4) do not lie, and (5) do not use intoxicants. The three additional precepts that make up the eight commandments are (6) do not sit on elevated and spacious, lavish beds or seats, (7) do not wear adornments or jewelry or take part in singing and dancing, and (8) do not eat after noontime.

Several short sūtras such as the Foshuo zhaijing (Sūtra on Fasting Spoken by the Buddha, T. 87), translated into Chinese in the third century A.D., explain how these ritual assemblies were to be conducted and what their meaning was. And from the mid–fourth century onward, Chinese lay believers are known to have practiced assiduously these fasts—for in China they were usually designated as zhai, the Chinese rendering of poṣadha, fast. In Japanese history, they make their first appearance toward the end of the sixth century, when the famous Buddhist prince Shōtoku Taishi decreed that it was forbidden to kill any living beings on the six fasting days of the month. In Korea, the eight commandments as a form of religious practice make their appearance in 551. In that year, Silla invaded Koguryŏ, and among the people taken captive was the monk Hyeryang: in the same year, Hyeryang for the first time established the "Hundred Seats Assembly" (based on the Renwang jing, the Benevolent Kings Sūtra) and the "Way of the Eight Prohibitions" in Silla.

It is not clear how this first ritual of the eight commandments was conducted, but obviously it soon developed into a court-sponsored ritual. In 572, on the twentieth day of the tenth lunar month, a seven-day-long "Banquet Congregation of the Eight Commandments" was held in a temple to pacify the spirits of those who had fallen in battle. So from the very beginning the Silla p'algwanhoe seems to have been a state ritual that had little to do with personal religious merit. Actually, a similar development can be observed in China, where eminent monks frequently administered the eight commandments to the first Sui emperor (Wen Di, r. 581–605) in large ceremonies designed, among other things, to pray for rain. It is possible that in these ceremonies the original intent of the ritual, that is, to create merit and purify the mind, was still present but was turned from a very personal devotional ritual into one with a national dimension. In the case of the 572 *p'algwanhoe*, the commandments were most likely bestowed on the spirits of the deceased soldiers; in the case of the Chinese emperor, the commandments were probably administered to absolve the emperor of his sins, which had caused a negative response of heaven (in the form of a drought).

A *p'algwanhoe* was also mentioned in connection with the construction of the nine-story pagoda at Hwangnyongsa around 645, which was intended to obtain the subjugation of Silla's enemies, but it is not recorded at all throughout Unified Silla (668–935). Yet the founders of new states that emerged as Silla disintegrated were keen to hold this ritual. Kungye did so right after founding the T'aebong state in 898, and his successor, T'aejo, did the same when he founded Koryŏ in 918. To T'aejo, the *p'algwanhoe* was a venerable tradition and thereby something that was needed to substantiate his authority. If it was indeed a continuation of a *p'algwanhoe* ritual held regularly by Silla kings, then it evidently had developed enormously in the course of Unified Silla. It had now become a large festival, in which nothing remained of the original purpose of bestowing the eight commandments.

Descriptions of the festival in the *Koryŏsa*, the official history of the Koryŏ dynasty, are brief and elliptic, but they nevertheless allow us to piece together some details of what was undoubtedly one of the highlights of the medieval Korean calendar. The source should be used with caution, as its Chosŏn dynasty compilers did not hide their disdain for an event like the *p'algwanhoe*, which they considered a wasteful extravagance; even though they were only allowed to select material verbatim from the Koryŏ veritable records while compiling the official history of the previous dynasty, a careful selection process could nevertheless severely distort the actual meaning of this ritual.

The *p'algwanhoe* was part of the ritual agenda of Koryŏ kings; together with the *yŏndŭnghoe*, it was classified among the "various congratulatory ceremonies," and thus one of the less important ritual functions to which the king had to attend. The chapter on rites in the *Koryŏsa* contains an elaborate description of the ceremonial actions in which the king and his officials engaged, but it seems to be more of a script for the participants than a description: as shown by the translation of the opening part of the chapter on the *yŏndŭnghoe*, which outlines the procedures leading up to the king's departure for Pongŭnsa temple, it contains detailed instructions for the movements of people, where they should stand, when they should bow, and so on, but nothing pertaining to the ritual itself. In other words, it is like a script telling actors where to move but not what to say. We do learn from this, however, that the festival was spread over two days and consisted of both a minor festival and a major festival. In the case of the *p'algwanhoe*, the major festival always took place on the full moon of the eleventh month (i e , the fifteenth day), and the minor festival on the day before, except if it clashed with the memorial day of a deceased king or the winter solstice, in which case it could be moved to an earlier or later date. Also, a separate *p'algwanhoe* took place in the Western Capital, P'yŏngyang, on the fourteenth and fifteenth of the tenth month. Occasionally the king attended this ceremony as well, but mostly he just sent high-ranking ministers.

The practice of the *yŏndŭnghoe*, on the other hand, was slightly more complicated. Originally, it took place on the fifteenth of the first month, but after 1010 it was moved to the fifteenth of the second month. Also, there were irregular celebrations of the Lantern Festival, held for special events such as the completion of a temple, but these also took place mostly in the second month. The Lantern Festival as we know it today, celebrating the Buddha's Birthday, only occurs from the late-Koryŏ period onward.

In fact, we know from other entries in the *Koryŏsa* that much more happened at these festivals than just the exchange of congratulations between the king and his ministers. Most important, there were performances, mainly of plays connected with the legacy of the Silla kingdom. For example, when the very first *p'algwanhoe* festival was held in 918, the plays performed were based on Silla legends. Also, more important, there were performances by "the four immortals": although this could refer to Daoist Perfected, it is more likely to refer to the four main *hwarang*, who went by the same title. The *hwarang* (lit. flower boys), originally an elite youth corps and a key institution in helping Silla unify the peninsula in approximately 668—most of the key players in the peninsular unification wars had belonged to the *hwarang* corps in their youth—originally embodied both martial and spiritual values. In the course of time, however, only the spiritual, educational, and cultural dimension remained, and this tradition was maintained in the *p'algwanhoe*. In fact, the *p'algwanhoe* seems to have helped to preserve a moribund tradition: these cultural reenactments were constantly under threat, being at one time abolished by King Sŏngjong (r. 981–97), while later kings, such as King Ŭijong (r. 1146–70), had difficulty finding people of noble descent to represent the tradition of the "immortal lad" (*sŏllang*), a title for a member of the *hwarang*.

Even though the chapter on ritual in the *Koryŏsa* makes no mention of it, this Silla tradition was a core component of the *p'algwanhoe*, which defined it as a native Korean tradition. Thus when King Sŏngjong abolished the performances, one of his ministers urged their reinstatement, impressing on the king the need to maintain such traditions as emblems of Koryŏ identity in the face of claims on their territory by the Khitan Liao dynasty, which controlled much of northern China. But the reenactment of the *hwarang* tradition was not the only thing celebrated here. It was also intended to serve heavenly spirits and the deities of mountains and rivers, although there are unfortunately no records of how these were worshiped. Furthermore, effigies were made of merit subjects who contributed to the founding of the dynasty, which were then presented to the king. Apparently, these "idols" upset some envoys of other countries, providing another pretext for King Sŏngjong to abolish the performances. The commemoration of the spirits of these merit subjects appears to be a continuation of the earliest *p'algwanhoe* of Silla, held to pacify the spirits of those fallen in battle. Finally, another important clue is provided by the account of a twelfth-century Chinese envoy, Xu Jing, who saw the *p'algwanhoe* as simply a re-creation of the ancient Koguryŏ Tongmaeng festival, thought to have been a harvest thanksgiving festival, which was held in the tenth month. Rather than seeing these as conflicting and mutually exclusive accounts, it is more likely that these are all elements of a highly syncretic festival, which celebrated the various traditions on which the Koryŏ state was built.

Held under the purview of the Koryŏ king, who was toasted by all his officials and who in turn bestowed wine and food on them, these rites probably served as symbolic expressions that the ruler presided over a variety of cultural traditions and served as their unifier. It is important to note in this context that the king also took over some of the trappings of imperial rule in this ceremony: the presence of foreigners, albeit traders rather than envoys, presenting tribute, clearly reminds one of the Chinese emperor's role as the center of the universe. This implication is further underscored by the imperial yellow worn by the king on this occasion. Perhaps Buddhism, from which the ritual was ultimately derived, also served as a unifying force amid this cultural diversity: even though there are no explicit Buddhist elements to be noted, after the festival—which took place on the polo court, the biggest space in the royal palace compound—the king invariably went to a Buddhist temple. Indeed, even when King Sŏngjong abolished all the festivities, he still maintained the tradition of going to a temple, in this case Pŏbwangsa, the Monastery of the Dharma King, on the days of the *p'algwanhoe*. Something of the original spirit of the eight commandments was thus probably maintained, even in the margins of the festival, but all the same the Buddhist origins of the *p'algwanhoe* were always evident to the participants and, as the biggest institution besides the state, Buddhism was able to subsume many of the other, less organized cults and traditions.

The Buddhist associations of the Lantern Festival remained more evident, as the practice of lighting lanterns was always perceived as a Buddhist merit-making act. While performances took place at this festival, too, it is not certain what these entailed. Except for the lighting of lanterns, the format of the *yŏndŭnghoe* seems to have been in fact very similar to the *p'algwanhoe*. The accounts in the *Koryŏsa* chapter on rites differ only in the level of detail, in that the *p'algwanhoe* appears to have been more elaborate. Also, however, the account of the *yŏndŭnghoe* reveals some facts left out in the account of the *p'algwanhoe*: mention is made of a music troupe, of the king paying his respects to the portrait of an ancestor, and of his visit to Pongŭnsa. Such elements have been carefully excised from the *p'algwanhoe* account but for some reason were included here; this fact, together with the slightly more succinct description of events that are otherwise very similar, makes the Lantern Festival account a bit more interesting than that of its counterpart.

While it is not certain for what purpose the king went to Pŏbwangsa—according to one source, there was a "spirit cloister" there, which would fit in with the *p'al-gwanhoe's* stated purpose of revering spirits and deities—he visited Pongŭnsa to worship the statue of the dynastic founder, Wang Kŏn (r. 918–43). Thus royal ancestor worship played an important part in the Lantern Festival, perhaps in an attempt to associate the dynastic founder with the Buddha himself. Although the traditional date for the Buddha's Birthday is considered to be the eighth day of the fourth lunar month, there were other traditions placing it on the eighth of the second month. Combined with a traditional date for his nirvāṇa on the fifteenth of the second month, the Lantern Festival could thus have served to reenact the Buddha's life.

Perhaps it is for this reason that King Hyŏnjong (r. 1009–31) sought to move the festival from the full moon of the first month to the full moon of the second month. It had probably been held previously during the first month in accordance with Chinese practice, where the Lantern Festival was amalgamated with the Daoist tradition of the "three primordials," the first of which fell in the middle of the first month. It has also been suggested that this move was motivated by the agricultural calendar: whereas the first signs of spring would burst forth in the first lunar month in central China, it would have been about a month later in central Korea, the sites of the respective capitals at that time.

This difference points to an important fact about these two festivals, namely, their close connection with the calendar. The *p'algwanhoe*—a word that has often been interpreted by Korean scholars as a transcription for a native Korean term related to the modern word for "brightness"—always fell close to the winter solstice, and it is likely to have played a role in praying for the return of light. Thus a poem by Yi Illo (1152–1220) on the *p'algwanhoe* suggests that the "full regalia of the officials' robes . . . is appropriate for a full summer day" and closes with the line "But the spring colors [of the festival] spread across a thousand homes." The literal words for "summer day" are "yang-heaven," that is, weather full of yang, the positive life force characteristic of summer. Whereas in the tradition of Chinese antiquity this period would have been spent in the quietude of one's own home, where one would devote oneself to self-cultivation and fasting, the Koryŏ people saw things differently. According to Kim Pusik (1075–1151), the festivities of the *p'algwanhoe* were "not for one's own pleasure, but because of a desire to have Heaven and humanity rejoice together." In other words, heaven was to be induced not through quiescence but through merriment. In the same vein, the Lantern Festival probably celebrated the successful renewal of life. Korean scholars such as Hŏ Hŭngsik have therefore likened the *p'algwanhoe* to Christmas and the *yŏndŭnghoe* to Easter, and indeed in many years they fall on almost the same dates as these two Western, Christianized festivals.

Although it is fairly certain that these two festivals had a seasonal nature and a unique connection to Koryŏ society, many questions remain. It is not certain, for example, if these were also popular festivities. At the very least, even if they were not observed in the rest of the country, people were certainly aware of it;

for example, for the *p'algwanhoe*, officials from all the provinces sent letters of congratulation to the king, so that those regions were in some way represented as well. For the Lantern Festival, several accounts stress that all the houses of the capital hung out lanterns; and at one occasion, during a special edition of the Lantern Festival held to celebrate the completion of Hŭngwangsa, the memorial temple for King Munjong's (r. 1046–83) parents, the whole road from the temple to the capital was hung with lanterns. Since memorial temples dedicated to kings were spread across the country, it is likely that people all over the country celebrated the festival in these and other temples, and also at home.

The translated material is drawn from the following sources, listed in the same order as the translations: Kim Chongsŏ, *Koryŏsa chŏryo* (rpt., Seoul: Asea Munhwasa, 1973), 1:15a; Chŏng Inji et al., *Koryŏsa* (rpt., Seoul: Asea Munhwasa, 1990), 2:15a, 3:1b, 93:16a, 69:33a, 94:2b–3b, 4:6a, 6:1a–b, 18:36b–37a, 100:26a–27a, 69:1a; Sŏ Kŏjŏng, *Tongmun sŏn* (Keijō: Chōsen Kosho Kankōkai, 1914; rpt., Masan: Minjok Munhwa Kanhaenghoe, 1994), 6:147; Xu Jing, *Xuanhe fengshi Gaoli tujing* (Illustrated Account of Koryŏ) (rpt., Seoul: Hongikchae, 1997), 173–74.

Further Reading

An Chi-wŏn, "Koryŏ Yŏndŭnghoe ŭi kiwŏn kwa sŏngnip" (Origin and Establishment of the Lantern Festival in Koryŏ) *Chindan hakpo* 88 (1999): 87–114; An Chi-wŏn, "Koryŏ sidae kukka Pulgyo ŭirye yŏn'gu: Yŏndŭng–P'algwanhoe wa Chesŏk toryang ŭl chungsim ŭro" (A Study on Buddhist State Rituals of the Koryŏ Period—Focusing on the Lantern Festival, *P'algwanhoe* and *Chesŏk toryang*) (Ph.D. diss., Seoul National University, 1999); Jongmyung Kim, "Buddhist Rituals in Medieval Korea (918–1392)" (Ph.D. diss., University of California, Los Angeles, 1994).

The *Koryŏsa Chŏryo* (Essentials of Koryŏ History) on the *P'algwanhoe*

ELEVENTH MONTH, 918

The *p'algwanhoe* was instituted. An official said, "Every year in the second month of winter, the former king(s) organized a grand fast of the eight commandments to pray for blessings. I beg you to honor this institution." The king said: "We lack in virtue, and therefore must protect the great enterprise. By relying on Buddhism, the realm can be pacified." Then in the polo court a circle of lamps was made, flanked by rows of incense burners, so that the whole place was brightly lit at night. Also two colored tents were made, each more than fifty feet high; and, furthermore, a platform was constructed in the shape of a lotus, which was dazzling to behold. In front of it, a hundred plays, songs and dances were held; the music troupe of the four immortals, cart-ships of dragons, phoenixes, elephants and horses, all old stories of Silla. All the officials paraded in full dress, carrying their insignia. The whole capital came to watch, and feasted day and night. The king watched from the Wibongno. It was nominally a gathering to make offerings to the Buddha and to entertain the spirits. After this it became an annual event.

From the *Koryŏsa* (History of Koryŏ)

T'AEJO'S SIXTH INJUNCTION, 943

My greatest vow concerns the *yŏndŭng* and *p'algwan* [festivals]. The purpose of *yŏndŭng* is to serve the Buddha, the purpose of *p'algwan* is to serve the heavenly spirits, the dragon gods of the Five Peaks, the famous mountains and great rivers. If in later generations there are treacherous ministers who propose to alter anything at all [regarding the festivals], they ought to be stopped. Also, from the beginning, I made an oath that the days of the festival should not coincide with days of mourning. When the ruler and his ministers celebrate together, one should still proceed with respect.

ELEVENTH MONTH, 981

In this month, because the various arts performed at the *p'algwanhoe* were uncanonical, and moreover noisy and bothersome, they were all suspended. The king [Sŏngjong] went to Pŏbwangsa to offer incense and then returned to the polo court to receive the congratulations of all the assembled ministers.

MEMORIAL BY CH'OE SŬNGNO, 982

In our country, for the Lantern Festival in spring and the *p'algwanhoe* in winter, people are mobilized far and wide to labor in corvée duty, causing everyone lots of trouble. I submit that their [performances] should be limited, so as to lessen the people's exertions. Also, various images are constructed for these festivals; their manufacture not only requires huge expenses, but once they have been presented, they are destroyed. Isn't this an unspeakable waste! Moreover, the images should only be used for inauspicious [e.g., mourning] rites. Once, when the envoys from the Western Dynasty [the Liao] saw them, they regarded them as inauspicious and passed by, covering their faces. Henceforth, I submit that they should no longer be used.

TENTH MONTH, 987

In this month, the king [Sŏngjong] instructed the officials to suspend the *p'algwanhoe* in the two capitals.

BIOGRAPHY OF SŎ HŬI, EVENTS OF 993

[In court deliberations on how to resist the 993 Khitan encroachment from northern China, Sŏ Hŭi takes a firm stance and advises King Sŏngjong not to yield to demands to hand over fortresses on the northern border: "They may claim to want Koguryŏ's former territories, yet I fear that they want to grab all of our land. Handing over all the territory north of P'yŏngyang just because of their military strength is not a good strategy. Also, everything north of Sam-gaksan is former Koguryŏ territory; and since they are extremely avaricious, they will keep demanding for more, and be unsatisfied however much we give." Yi Chibaek then chimes in:] "Since T'aejo founded the country, through the generations there was not a single loyal minister who rashly considered handing over territory so easily. . . . Rather than handing over territory, it would be better to restore the acts of previous kings, such as the *yŏndŭng* and *p'algwan* festivals and the divine lad (*sŏllang*) tradition, instead of different customs from other countries, to protect the state and establish a reign of peace. If you agree with this, then we should first of all report this to the spir-its and then either fight [the Khitan] or negotiate peace; that is for your high-ness to decide." King Sŏngjong agreed with this. At the time, the king was in-fatuated with Chinese customs, displeasing the people. That is why Yi Chibaek brought this up.

ELEVENTH MONTH, 1010

[In the first year, eleventh month, of King Hyŏnjong's reign (1010), the *p'al-gwanhoe* was resumed, at the suggestion of Ch'oe Hang.] Before, because the performances at the *p'algwanhoe* were considered inappropriate and bother-some, King Sŏngjong suspended them, but merely went to Pŏbwangsa to offer incense and then to the ball court to receive the congratulations of the assem-bled ministers. Then Ch'oe Hang requested its reinstatement.

TENTH MONTH, 1034 [YEAR OF KING
CHŎNGJONG'S ENTHRONEMENT]

In the tenth month, high ministers were sent to the Western Capital to hold the *p'algwanhoe* for two days and to conduct the libations.

On the *kyŏngin* (4th) day of the eleventh month, the king climbed the Sin-bongnu, declared a pardon, and received congratulations from ministers from the center and the regions.

Traders from Song [China], East and West Jurched, and T'amna [Cheju Is-land], offered local products.

On the *kyŏngja* (14th) day the *p'algwanhoe* was held. The king went to the Sinbongnu and gave a feast for the officials. In the evening he went to

Pŏbwangsa. On the second day of the festival, during the Great Assembly, he gave another grand feast and enjoyed the music. Then the military commanders (pyŏngmasa) of the western and eastern capitals, and the two northeastern provinces (Kangwŏn and P'yŏngan), and the four regional military commands (tohobu) and eight provinces (p'almok) sent petitions with congratulations. The Song traders, the East and West Jurchens, and people from T'amna offered local products and they were given a seat to assist in the festival. This subsequently became a regular custom.

THIRD MONTH, 1168 [22ND YEAR OF ŬIJONG]

[Sixth of seven reform measures proclaimed during the king's visit to the Western Capital:] We have to honor the old tradition of the immortals. Of old, the Silla tradition of immortals flourished greatly. Because of this, the protective dragons and heaven were pleased and the people were at ease. Since the time of our dynastic forefathers, this custom has been worshiped for a long time. Recently, the p'algwanhoe in the two cities has failed to live up to its former standard, and the transmitted customs have become gradually depleted. From now on, for the p'algwanhoe, I will choose landed families from both sections of officialdom and designate them "immortal families" (sŏn'ga), and through them the old customs will be enacted, so that humankind and heaven will be pleased.

BIOGRAPHY OF CH'OE CHŬNGNYŎL (D. 1181)

Together with Yi Kwangjŏng and Mun Kŭkkyŏm, Ch'oe proposed: "Formerly the yŏndŭng festival was held on the full moon of the second month, but because the king's father died in that month it was moved to the first month. But this is a distortion of the intentions of former kings. Now we witness irregularities in the sun, moon, and stars, and the imbalance of yin and yang, and it is probably because of this. Even if we cannot perform the full ceremony with all the ritual music, I still hope that officials and private people will appropriately hang lanterns on this day." The king agreed with this proposal. Then they also proposed "During the p'algwanhoe, the tables spread with delicacies for the officials and the clothes worn by the royal guards are too luxurious; please forbid this." The king followed this advice. Not long after this, an irregularity in the stars occurred and Ch'oe requested to be removed from office, but the king instead promoted him.

According to the customs transmitted from old, during the yŏndŭng and p'algwan festivals, high officials of the secretariat-chancellery were to be dispatched to the Western Capital to perform the ceremonies on behalf of the king. But since the Kabo incident [the 1170 military coup] there were troubles in the Western Capital and this was stopped. Only third-rank officials were henceforth sent. Since Ch'oe Ch'ungnyŏl would get a windfall if he was sent as special envoy, he became greedy, so he suggested: "The reason why former kings sent high officials of the secretariat-chancellery to the second capital was to show respect for it, so I hope you will follow this custom." The king guessed his intention and sent him to P'yŏngyang to hold a lavish festival. When he returned, he carried thirty wagons of bribes.

LANTERN FESTIVAL OF THE FIRST PRIMORDIAL
(*SANGWŎN YŎNDŬNGHOE*) (CHAPTER 11
OF THE SECTION ON RITUALS)

On the day of the small assembly, before the king takes his seat in his [temporary] throne hall, the Caretakers' Office (Togyosŏ) places a movable platform in front of the steps of the Kangan hall, while the subordinates of the Keepers of the Premises (Sangsaguk) install a royal tent above the hall, install convenient seats in the east of the tent, and place two wild-animal braziers outside the front posts. The Keepers of the Robes (Sangŭiguk) place decorated tables on both sides of the throne in front of the posts. The Department of Palace Affairs (Chŏnjungsŏng) places rows of lanterns above and below, and to the left and right, of the movable platform, and a colored mountain is placed in the courtyard. Storehouse employees (*kosa*) place rows of wine cups on either side of the courtyard.

On the day itself, the king wears reddish-yellow robes, and first goes to the convenient seats. The horse pages and other royal guards, and all the guards of the palace gates let out a great huzzah and everyone bows. Then the edict transmitters (*sŭngjewŏn*) and palace attendants take up their robes in both hands for convenience's sake and in order of rank go up toward the king; when they reach their appropriate places, the person at the head of the file then shouts and they all bow. Then they withdraw to stand on the western side of the platform, facing east and going up toward the north. Next, the officials of the Ceremonial Affairs Academy (Kangmunwŏn) enter the courtyard moving sideways, facing north and going up toward the east; the person at the head of the file then shouts and they all bow. Then everyone goes to take places at the east of the courtyard, facing west and going up toward the north. Next, guardsmen below the rank of general enter the court moving sideways, facing north and going up toward the north; the person at the head of the file then shouts and they all bow. They then divide up to take places to the west and east. Next, the officials of the Department of Palace Affairs, the Agencies of the Six Ministries, and all the rear palaces enter the court and take their places to bow. They then go to stand at the west of the courtyard, facing east and going up toward the north. Next, the various artists of the 100 plays enter the courtyard in sequence, and perform successively, retiring [after their performance]. Next, the ward commanders (*kyobang*) call for music, and the dance troupe comes and goes. Everything proceeds as at normal ceremonies.

The king goes to [perform] the ancestral portrait ceremony, and then the [palace] hall rituals are over.

An official of the [Board of] Rites then announces the "first warning." Everyone holds their tablet and office insignia and lines up along the polo court, where parasols and fans have been placed. Guards line the whole way on both sides from the Kangan hall to the Taejŏng gate. The Keepers of the Premises then install the palanquin-mounting place in the middle of the court, close to the northern part and facing east. They also install the seats where the crown prince, queens, nobles, and top ministers will bow south of the palanquin mount, close to the southern part and all facing east and going up toward the north. The palanquin bearers pull up the small cart bearing the palanquin and place it on its mount.

Then the official of the [Board of] Rites announces the "second warning." Courtiers and ministers below the ranks of Royal Secretariat then enter the courtyard and line up to the left and right. The edict transmitters of the left and right, and the generals of the Thousand Bull Division go to the east and west stairs of the [palace] hall to protect it with their bodies. Royal guards from several different corps all climb up the movable platform and stand all around it. Later the king, wearing ochre-yellow robes, leaves the throne hall. With shouts and the striking [of drums], the palace guards produce a great roar and everyone bows. The Board of Astronomy announces the time [with a] board, and the edict transmitters of the left and right, and the generals of the Thousand Bull Division, descend from the east and west stairs and take their places near the axe-screen. Official secretaries (sain) of the left and right shout, and all courtiers and ministers below the rank of Secretary bow. Next, the [members of] the Ceremonial Affairs Academy lead the crown prince, queens, nobles and top ministers to their places; the attendants shout and everyone below the crown prince bows. Then the [members of] the Ceremonial Affairs Academy lead the crown prince, queens, nobles, and high-ranking officials of the secretariat-chancellery around the assembled officials, and left through the west. Next, the prime minister is led to the middle of the courtyard where he kneels in prostration and requests the "outside affairs." Rising, he retreats to his original place. The king then descends from the hall and proceeds to the cart bearing the palanquin. The keeper of the robes helps the king enter and arranges his robes, and then brings a table into the palanquin. . . .

Kim Pusik, "On the Scripture Reading of the Eight Commandments at Pŏbwangsa," from the Tongmun Sŏn (Anthology of Korean Literature)

Though the moon may be reflected in three different places, it is but one. Although all dharmas return to a single [source], among the five nectars in the one thousand bottles [of Avalokiteśvara?], only the pure commandments of the eight prohibitions have [inspired] deep faith since the time of our dynastic founder. These important instructions have not been cut off and, after memorizing them, their format is followed sincerely, according to the model. During the full moon of the midwinter month, lavish rituals are held in the broad courtyard [of the palace]. Attending to the correct performance of drumming and beating is not for one's own pleasure, but because of a desire to have heaven and man rejoice together. Thus an era of great peace is ushered in. This is when [the king] goes to the "fragrant city" [the palace of the gandharvas; here referring to Pŏbwangsa]: truly magnificent Buddhist rites bring forth the "opening of people," as in the lecture delivered on Vulture Peak. Setting forth the transcendent words from the Dragon Palace, we humbly wish for the protection of Buddha's power. Seeking people's hearts and minds and making them healthy and happy, establishing the grand enjoyment of the multitudes—nobody will be excluded no matter how far, and the joyful foundation will be preserved for ten thousand generations. The benefits received will be immeasurable.

Xu Jing, *Gaoli Tujing* (Illustrated Account of Koryŏ)

CHAPTER 17, SHRINES

I have heard that Koryŏ people commonly believe in spirits and fear them, and that they are also restrained by superstitious beliefs in yin and yang. When they fall ill, they do not use medicine; even if it is their father, son, or close relative, they do not look at each other but merely [chant] magic spells and incantations in order to overcome [the illness].

Previous histories regarded their customs as vulgar, [because] in the evening and at night men and women gathered without regard for ceremony to sing and enjoy themselves, and [then] make offerings to ghosts, earth and grain deities, and numinous stars. In the tenth month, there was a great offering to heaven called *Tongmaeng*. In the east of the capital there was a hole called "*susin*" (lit. "god of the grave-clothes"), where also in the tenth month [the spirits] were welcomed and given offerings.

From the time the Wang dynasty [Koryŏ] ruled the country, they built a fortress along the mountains south of the capital, and during the first month officials were taken [there] with presents to offer to heaven. Later, Koryŏ kings were invested by the Khitan in this place, while the crown prince also performed rituals here. The *Tongmaeng* assembly of the tenth month is now called the "fast of the eight prohibitions," a vegetarian banquet which takes place on the full moon (15th day) of the same month. The rituals are sumptuous. The [royal] ancestral shrine is located outside the capital's east gate. Only upon the king's accession, and then once every three years hence, there is a great sacrifice, for which the king dons his full regalia to conduct the offerings himself. For the rest, officials are dispatched [to perform the sacrifices]. [Note: Xu Jing seems to have mistaken the *p'algwanhoe* of the tenth month, which took place in P'yŏngyang, with the one in the eleventh month, which took place in the capital.]

On the first day of the year, the first days of every month, and the vernal and autumnal equinoxes, sacrifices are presented to the portraits of deceased royal ancestors. Their likenesses are kept in the palace. Monks' disciples are taken there to chant day and night without interruption.

Also, their preference for the Buddha is a deeply engrained custom, so on the full moon of the second month all the Buddhist temples light candles; it is extremely resplendent and extravagant. The king together with the queen and his consorts all go out to watch the spectacle, while the local people throng the streets, making lots of noise.

For the spirit shrines within a 100-*ri* radius [of the capital], officials are dispatched with sacrificial animals for all the meal offerings. Also, once a year there is a great sacrifice within their precincts, but at this time, on the pretext of sacrificing to the spirits, the [officials take] and hoard the people's treasures: white gold in the amount of a thousand taels is amassed, while other products are also raised. This is given to the ministers, who distribute it among themselves. This is laughable indeed!

Except for the palace halls where the king lives, only the shrines are luxurious. But among the temples, Anhwasa crowns them all, because it honors the imperial signature. [Note: the temple held a plaque that was personally inscribed by Emperor Huizong of the Song dynasty.]

Now I have drawn what I saw and heard while passing through the streets they use, and while visiting the shrines. For the rest, those institutions I did not see have been omitted.

—6—

Hell and Other Karmic Consequences:
A Buddhist Vernacular Song

Younghee Lee

Kasa are discursive vernacular songs/poems that reached the apex of their expression during the Chosŏn period (1392–1910). Having no restrictions on length and closely conforming to natural Korean speech patterns and rhythms, the *kasa* form readily lends itself to a wide variety of uses and subject matter. The most widely recognized examples of *kasa* poetry are written compositions by the scholar-official elite of Chosŏn, but the earliest and necessarily oral examples of the genre are attributed to priests and other members of the Buddhist clergy of the Koryŏ period. These "Buddhist *kasa*" (*Pulgyo kasa*) were composed and made available to the general populace with the apparent purpose of propagating the word of Buddhism to a broader audience.

The invention of the phonetic writing system *han'gŭl* in early Chosŏn times meant that Korea's rich literature in the vernacular, sustained by its oral tradition, could now be freely represented in written form as well. It is interesting to note, however, that *kasa*'s rhythmic structure does not appear to have originated solely from within Korea's own linguistic and oral heritage. Scholars of the genre now believe that Korean Buddhist monks, in composing these vernacular songs, employed the four-line rhythms of Buddhist verses (*gāthā*) in Chinese. This borrowing would suggest that one of Korea's most important, popular, and versatile poetic forms is indebted for part of its structural and rhythmic formation to a larger Buddhist tradition extending well beyond Korea's immediate cultural sphere. This presumption would thence apply to all religious *kasa*, including those with Confucian, Daoist, Eastern Learning (Tonghak; viz., Ch'ŏndogyo), Catholic, or other devotional content. Here too it bears repeating that Buddhist *kasa*, by virtue of their being the very first known examples in the genre, are therefore the first examples of devotional *kasa* as well.

Scholars differ in the way they include, organize, and count extant Buddhist *kasa*, making it difficult to pinpoint their precise number. However, it is not unreasonable to say that there are more than 70 and fewer than 120 of them, composed over a period spanning roughly seven hundred years, beginning with the first in the fourteenth century and the latest in the twentieth century. These can be found in general *kasa* compendiums, formal Buddhist *kasa* collections, and other Buddhist writings. It is thought that eminent priests composed the majority of such *kasa*, but it is important to note that more than one-third are without attribution. One explanation for such prolific anonymity may lie in the Sŏn (Zen) tradition of favoring practice over doctrine, with a priest risking censure and/or ridicule for devoting too much of his time to the written word. On the other hand, it is almost certain that some *kasa* were falsely attributed to famous masters to lend them greater authority.

Buddhist *kasa* can be grouped in various thematic categories. Some are concerned with the promise of rebirth in the Pure Land through the repeated recitation of Buddha's name (*yŏmbul wangsaeng ryu*). Others describe the fleeting, ephemeral nature of all earthly life (*musang ryu*) and the principle of karmic cause and effect (*in'gwa ryu*). The translation included in this chapter falls under the "conversion" category (*hoesim ryu*). This type of Buddhist *kasa* exhorts the listener to "convert" from a life of undiscerning immorality to a life of insightful virtue. The consequences of pursuing the latter are highly propitious, whereas the consequences of pursuing the former are dire indeed.

Although they were written down or even published in woodblock-print editions at different times, Buddhist *kasa* of the premodern period usually were listened to rather than read. They could be part of Buddhist rituals performed in temples, such as those held for the well-being of souls of the departed, or they might be sung while the faithful circumambulated a temple's pagoda to show their devotion. Monks who traveled around to collect alms might sing these songs as well. There were also groups of monks, the so-called *kŏllipp'ae*, who performed music, sang, and danced while they toured the countryside to collect money for the restoration of their monasteries. Buddhist *kasa* would be part of their repertoire. In this way some of the songs became very well known. A number of them came to be performed outside a purely Buddhist context as well, as, for instance, by singers who would accompany pallbearers at funerals, and by shamans.

Conversion Song: A Variation (*Pyŏrhoesim kok*) is a vivid example of the kind of didactic, cautionary, censorious religious literature to which the common Buddhist faithful were exposed. This song is far removed from the contemplative and metaphysical writings we more commonly associate with the Sŏn Buddhist tradition. It relates in explicit terms the consequences for acceptable and unacceptable behavior during one's privileged yet fleeting incarnation as a human being in this world. A life spent in appropriate action and moral behavior carries with it the promise of reaching the Pure Land in the next life, whereas a life spent in inappropriate action and immoral behavior consigns one to a virtual cornucopia of Buddhist hells.

This *kasa* also provides strong evidence of the all-pervasive Neo-Confucian ideology underpinning Chosŏn political and social institutions. Proper behavior for men and women is expressed in Confucian terms. Women's subservient position to men in Chosŏn's patriarchal Confucian society is readily apparent here as

well. Men can prove their good behavior by being filial and performing any number of meritorious deeds on behalf of society and country. Women, by contrast,
must prove their virtue by acting appropriately within the much more restrictive
environment of the household. Women's sins, and the variety of hells to which
they could be consigned, are described in greater number and detail than are
those of men.

The apparent devotion of much of the text to women's concerns and behavior
also reflects the importance of the female gender to the survival of Buddhism in
Chosŏn times. Stripped of official sanction and support, the Buddhist institution
was publicly eschewed by the great majority of the ruling elite. Women of all
classes and men in their private lives, however, still found comfort and hope in
Buddhism's promise of enlightenment and universal entry into the Pure Land for
those who adhered to the True Path. Buddhist *kasa* like this *Conversion Song* support the assumption that members of the Buddhist elite felt compelled by strait-
ened circumstances to make special overtures to women, with whom their teachings continued to resonate.

A robust informality and dramatic sensibility further inform such vernacular
songs. Ostensibly composed by members of a marginalized Buddhist elite, they
are a welcome contrast to the vast corpus of Chosŏn literature so very much mo-
nopolized by the scholar-official class and their more restrained aesthetic.

The *kasa* translated here, *Conversion Song: A Variation (Pyŏrhoesim kok)*, exists
in numerous manuscript versions. As with many other *kasa* of this kind, it is often difficult to pinpoint its exact date of origin. It is one of numerous "conversion" Buddhist *kasa* publicly circulated in manuscript form during the nineteenth
century, and it bears a distinctly popular character. It was first printed only in the
1930s. In the first lines the listeners are addressed as "almsgivers." Thus it is reasonable to assume that, as an oral song, it was chanted by monks going door to
door collecting alms while beating a wooden handbell or small gong.

The first part of the song contains a description of how a child comes to be
born, to which the deities Ch'ilsŏng and Chesŏk both contribute. Ch'ilsŏng
(Seven Stars) refers to the asterism of the Big Dipper, which was originally worshiped in China in Daoist circles. From there, however, the worship of Ch'ilsŏng
spread to Buddhism, and it was in this form that it came to Korea, where eventually Ch'ilsŏng also became one of the most important gods of the shamans.
Ch'ilsŏng's special domain was the birth and protection of children, and therefore
he was a deity to whom women would often pray. The same holds for Chesŏk,
who had very similar duties, and who also became an indispensable member of
the shamanic pantheon. Originally Chesŏk (Śakro devānām Indraḥ) was a god of
the Indian Vedas who, with thunder and lightning, would fight the forces of evil;
but for Buddhists this heavenly ruler became a protector of their faith, and as
such he is often depicted in Buddhist paintings, together with Brahmā, who was
assigned the same role. It is probably because of his position as ruler of one of the
Buddhist heavens that Indra was ascribed the capacity to grant certain blessings,
such as life and good fortune. Other protectors of the faith were the Sinjang,

"Divine Warriors," who also often appear in Buddhist paintings of the Chosŏn period. They too were adopted into the pantheon of the shamans.

Conversion Song: A Variation also refers to a numinous being of non-Buddhist origin, the Chinese "Queen Mother of the West" (Xiwangmu), who resides in the Kunlun mountains and possesses the "peaches of immortality." Also mentioned is the mythical pond of Yaojiyan (Yojiyŏn), the Lake of Gems, where she is said to enjoy herself. Xiwangmu is associated with Daoism, as is the Jade Emperor, the highest deity, who is also referred to in the song. Figures with a more Confucian resonance are not lacking either. Longfeng (Yongbang) was a vassal of the legendary Chinese Xia dynasty who was executed for dutifully remonstrating against the cruel rule of his king, while Bigan (Pigan), a loyal retainer of the Chinese Yin dynasty, was executed for dutifully criticizing his king's lewd and immoral behavior.

The central part of *Conversion Song: A Variation*, however, is the description of the Underworld, where ten judges (the Ten Kings of Hell) examine the records of the recently deceased. The representation of the Ten Kings, the courts over which they preside, and the hells in which sinners undergo gruesome punishments was developed in China (where it had established itself as part of popular religion by Song times), although it incorporated Indian elements as recorded in sūtras as well. In their capacity as judges these kings have at their disposal an assortment of choices. Some of the judged they send to a new reincarnation in the world after first requiring that they spend a relatively short time in a kind of purgatory to be spent in expiation of their misdeeds. Others have been so sinful that they are sent to one of the hells for their next reincarnation. Finally, those who have led truly pious lives are sent to be reborn in the Pure Land of Amitābha.

Each of the Ten Kings of the Underworld has his own court and his own duties. The dead move from one court to another, remaining seven days in each court. Those with less grievous sins and thus undeserving of rebirth in hell are mostly dispatched to a new existence from the seventh court after forty-nine days. During this period, surviving relatives may enhance the chances of obtaining a favorable rebirth for the deceased by offering Buddhist masses. Of particular importance in this respect is the mass on the forty-ninth day. In charge of light and darkness, good fortune and bad, is King Chin'gwang (the Far-Reaching King of Chin), who supervises the dead's first seven days in the Underworld. From him the dead pass to King Ch'ogang (King of the First River), who presides over the great hell beneath the sea. Preliminary judgments of the sinner are first determined here. Third is King Songje (the Imperial King of Sung), who presides over Frozen Hell (Hanbing Chiok). Sinners are punished there by being encased in blocks of ice. King Ogwan (King of the Five Offices) is entrusted with punishments, their severity being determined through intense investigation of the sinner's life on earth. The fifth judge, King Yŏmna (King Yama), metes out rewards and punishments for good or bad behavior during one's lifetime, and the next judge, King Pyŏnsŏng (King of Transformations), investigates any sins King Yŏmna may have overlooked. Then King T'aesan (King of Mount Tai) determines the manner and place where the sinner, having died, will be born again. The next three judges deal with the worst offenders. King P'yŏngdŭng (Impartial King), for whom a mass is said a hundred days after death, is known for his fairness in judging the dead. The special domains of King Tosi (King of the Capital) are the three worst forms of reincarnation: as a hungry ghost, as an animal, or as a denizen of hell. A mass is addressed to him exactly one year after someone has died. Finally there is King Chŏllyun, who, as King of the Five Paths, is general arbiter over the five possible choices for rebirth (heavenly being, human being, hungry ghost, animal, or the hell denizens). King Chŏllyun, also acts as a general administrator for the spirits of the dead in all the courts, counting them, recording their monthly totals, and sending those sinners among them to Fengdao (P'ungdo) hell prison. This hell, incidentally, was originally not a Buddhist hell described in the sutras. Fengdao was a place in China with Daoist associations, which gradually came to be regarded as a spot that gave access to the Underworld. Another term for the Other World used in this song is Beimangshan (Pungmangsan), originally the name of a place in Henan province in China, where many famous people were buried. In Korean folk literature it is used much more generally to refer to the grave or to the world of the dead.

The following translation is taken from Im Ki-chung, *Pulgyo kasa wŏnjŏn yŏn'gu* (Seoul: Tongguk Taehakkyo Ch'ulp'anbu, 2000), pp. 392–404. Im offers the original pure *han'gŭl* text, a mixed Sino-Korean text, and a modern Korean rendering of the original. Im's commentary in this comprehensive volume on the subject is an important source for some of the introductory material on Buddhist *kasa* presented in this chapter as well. The translated *kasa* texts themselves are presented as paired hemistiches, with the second of each pair always indented. In this regard the translation differs from Im's presentation of the original *han'gŭl*, text where paired hemistiches constitute a single line.

Further Reading

At present no writings devoted to Buddhist *kasa* are available in English. For an introduction to and translated selections from the *kasa* genre in general, see Peter H. Lee, ed., *A History of Korean Literature* (New York: Cambridge University Press, 2003). For a discussion of Confucian influence in Korean Buddhism, see Robert E. Buswell Jr., "Buddhism under Confucian Domination: The Synthetic Vision of Sŏsan Hyujŏng," in *Culture and the State in Late Chosŏn Korea*, edited by Jahyun Kim Haboush and Martina Deuchler (Cambridge, Mass.: Harvard University Asia Center, 1999), pp. 134–59. For the worship of Ch'ilsŏng, see Henrik H. Sørensen, "The Worship of the Great Dipper in Korean Buddhism," in *Religions in Traditional Korea*, edited by Henrik H. Sørenson (Copenhagen: Seminar for Buddhist Studies, 1995), pp. 71–105. Chinese representations of the Ten Kings are discussed in Stephen F. Teiser, *"The Scripture of the Ten Kings" and the Making of Purgatory in Medieval Chinese Buddhism*, Kuroda Institute Classics in East Asian Buddhism (Honolulu: University of Hawai'i Press, 1994).

Conversion Song. A Variation

Of all the myriad living things in the universe,
    what can compare to man?
Hey, you almsgivers!
    Listen to these words of mine!
By whose grace
    did we enter this world as human beings?
By the grace of Śākyamuni
    I prayed for my bones before my father,
For my flesh before my mother,
    For my life before Ch'ilsŏng in the heavens,
And for blessings and good fortune before Chesŏk,
    whereupon I was born.
Innocent at age one or two,
    could I know of my parents' kindness and care?
Even after age twenty or thirty,
    how can I repay them for all their acts of love?
How ineffably sad!
    Heartless time passes by like rushing water.
Enemy white hairs come around,
    along with previously absent senility.
People regard senility with disfavor;
    their derisive laughs heard in every corner.
How utterly sad!
    How vexatious and acutely painful!
But what can be done about it?
    White hairs replace youth's blossom, and we grow old.
Who among us
    can obstruct this order of nature?
"Spring grasses renew themselves year after year,
    but the royal grandson does not return."
As we advance in years
    we cannot reclaim our youth.
One hundred years yield a mere forty of life
    when conceding days spent ill or asleep, worried or stressed.
The sound body of today and days past
    becomes frail and ill in the twilight of life,
Illnesses that enter this failing body
    become like great mountains,
And it is for our mothers that we cry
    and a drink of cold water that we seek.
We take ginseng and deer-horn medicine
    but are they efficacious?

We call the blind fortune-teller to recite incantations,
    but does any good come of it?
We call for the shaman to perform an exorcism,
    but is it of any help?
We polish and re-polish the offertory rice
    and take it with us to noted mountains and famous rivers.
In the upper hot pool we prepare the rice offering,
    in the middle hot pool we bathe,
And in the lower hot pool we wash our hands and feet
    and set out two lighted candles.
Taking incense burner and incense case, we light the offertory paper.
    As smoke from the consumed offering blows away,
We pray before God,
    saying, "I beg of you, I beg of you."
Before Ch'ilsŏng we offer a prayer,
    and to the Sinjang we present a rice offering.
But what kind of wisdom or knowledge do we acquire,
    what kind of response from on high can we expect?
In the first palace is King Chin'gwang,
    in the second palace is King Ch'ogang,
In the third palace is King Songje,
    in the fourth palace is King Ogwan,
In the fifth palace is King Yŏmna,
    in the sixth palace is King Pyŏnsŏng,
In the seventh palace is King T'aesan,
    in the eighth palace is King P'yŏngdŭng,
In the ninth palace is King Tosi,
    and in the tenth palace is King Chŏllyun.
In service to the ten kings
    are the day messengers and the night messengers.
At the command of the ten kings, the messengers,
    each with an iron cudgel in one hand,
Wielding a sword in the other,
    and girded about with lengths of iron chain,
Move quickly along the tortuous twisting path
    like straight-flying arrows.
The locked gates are kicked open
    to a thunderous, clamorous sound.
They call us in by our full names,
    saying, "Let's go. Quickly now!"
Who would dare disobey these commands?
    Who would be so bold as to delay?
Around our slender threadlike necks
    they hang an iron chain a forearm thick

Pinning our arms behind us we are led forth,
    as some cry in terror "all is lost!"
Others shout, "You messengers!
    Have you any expenses on this journey that I can help defray?"
We plead, remonstrate, and wrangle in so many ways,
    but what messenger will heed any of this?
Overwhelmed, we wail this and lament that,
    for what else, after all, can we do?
How immeasurably pitiful is this body
    taking its leave of humankind.
Your roses along the shore of Myŏngsasimni
    will wither and fade, but don't despair.
Next year in the third month, when spring arrives,
    you will blossom once again,
But for us humans, having once departed
    it is difficult to return.
Upon our deaths we go to Beimangshan,
    but how can we travel the steep and dangerous road?
The road to the afterlife is without end,
    so when will we return?
Taking leave of this world
    is indeed sorrowful and pitiable.
No longer can you take the hands of wife and child in yours,
    and regale them with tales.
Coming to your senses and looking around,
    you will surely see that the herbal tea,
Brewed in the open medicine pot with such care
    Will not save your body from death.
The old men of times past
    say the road of the afterlife is distant,
But today I have come to see that just through those gates
    lies the road to the afterlife.
Many friends have I,
    but which of them would accompany me on this journey?
I depart the old ancestral shrine
    and bow before the new one.
When I pass through the gate, [a relative] takes out my jacket,
    lifts it up in his hand,
And performs the rite of calling back the spirit,
    and from everywhere moaning breaks the silence.
The day messenger takes my hand,
    the night messenger presses me in the back,
Their demands on me are like wind-driven rain,
    and as we are swept onward helter-skelter,

The high places are become low,
  and the low places are become high.
Can I first consume my hard-earned assets,
  and then take my leave of this world?
"Esteemed messenger! Esteemed messenger!
  Please take a moment to hear what I say."
"I am hungry, let's stop for lunch."
  "I have to adjust my shoes."
"Let's rest before going on,"
  are all pleas that go unheard.
They just beat our backs with iron chains, saying,
  "Let's move along, move quickly now!"
Traveling in one direction, then another,
  after several days we arrive at the gates of Hell.
The horseheaded and cowheaded *rākṣasa* demons
  come running in, shouting.
They are begging for a bribe!
  But we've nary a halfpenny with which to bribe them.
Can savings earned by smoking less
  be used to make a bribe?
Can I transfer my assets to the afterworld?
  Can I convert it to coin and take it with me?
I remove my clothing, offering it as a bribe,
  and pass through the twelve gates.
Limitless is my fear.
  Unfathomable the depths of my terror.
The prison keeper awaits the royal command,
  Then hears the order sounded.
The waiting men and women sinners come to their senses
  and look about themselves.
The ten kings sit in a row,
  the court clerk holds some writing in his hand,
Men and women sinners are dragged before him,
  made to take an oath, and the inquisition begins.
Fish-headed *rākṣasa* demons stand fore and aft,
  to the left and to the right.
Armed to the hilt with swords and other weapons,
  they prepare their instruments of torture.
Awaiting the judge's command,
  the solemnity of the moment is beyond words.
Then they grab the men and women sinners in turn,
  applying torture as they ask,
Hear this, you contemptible men!
  Having vowed to be of a good heart,

What good deeds did you perform
   upon going out into the world?
Speak truthfully. Following the example
   of Longfeng and Bigan,
Did you do your utmost in loyal service
   to king and country?
Were you filial to your parents,
   and did you uphold family customs?
Did you give food to the famished
   and avert starvation?
Did you deliver from harm the one in rags
   by offering him some clothing to wear?
Did you build your house on a solid foundation,
   and were you charitable to passersby?
Did you perform the meritorious deed of building a bridge
   for those who cannot cross the deepest water?
Did you perform the meritorious deed of providing water
   to the person suffering from thirst?
Did you perform the meritorious deed of saving a life
   by giving medicine to the sick?
Did you perform the meritorious deed of public service
   by constructing a temple on a high mountain?
Did you plant melons in a prime field
   on behalf of thirsty travelers?
Did you hold a mass before the Buddha
   And strive to be pure and generous of heart?
Did you invoke the Buddha's name and perform acts of piety?
   You have schemed with malice against the kindhearted.
You have committed numerous unjust deeds,
   and have lusted after riches.
What should be done about these charges?
   for your sins are grievous indeed.
Lock them in Fengdao hell prison,
   and bring in the good-hearted ones!
Console and wait on them,
   while you men of contempt, observe this!
This person, being of good heart
   is going to the Land of Utmost Bliss.
Is it not wonderful
   that when you make known your wishes,
They will be fulfilled
   and you will go to Paradise?
Do you wish to go to the Lotus Pavilion?
   Do you wish to go to the world of the immortals?

Do you want a long and deathless life?
    Do you want to be Xiwangmu's messenger,
And deliver to her the peaches of immortality?
    Make known your wishes!
Do you want to stand before the Jade Emperor
    and ask that you become handsome without peer?
Do you want to go to Yaojiyen?
    Do you want to command one million soldiers?
Do you want to become a generalissimo?
    Then quickly say so!
Report this to the Jade Emperor.
    Have Śākyamuni and Amitābha save him.
Prepare a Letter of Transfer to the next life
    and discuss the matter with the Birth Goddess!
Then quickly see that it is carried out,
    For a man such as this, having a good heart,
Is become noble.
    Invite him to the Hall of Great Heroes.
Serve him with tea and cakes.
    But remove these worthless men of contempt!
You men of good heart, observe what follows!
    The sins of you contemptible men are severe.
Send them away to Fengdao hell prison!
    After thus ruling on the men sinners,
The women sinners are hauled in
    and the tortuous inquisition begins.
Listen to the sins you have committed!
    To your parents-in-law and to your parents,
Have you carried out your filial duties with a sincere heart?
    Have you been kind and loving to your siblings?
Have you lived in perfect harmony with your relatives?
    Crafty and villainous women sinners,
You went against your parents' advice,
    set your siblings one against the other,
Hindered harmonious relations between siblings,
    and committed all kinds of treachery.
Endlessly fickle and disobedient,
    you speak ill of people behind their backs.
The contemptible woman who gets angry after sitting with others,
    laughing and making uncalled-for remarks,
The contemptible woman who enjoys gossip, who is green with jealousy,
    I will lock you all in Fengdao hell!
After interrogating them on their sins, punishments are meted out
    in proportion to the severity of their transgressions.

Then they are consigned by turns
    to Knife Mountain Hell, Fire Mountain Hell,
Frozen Ice Hell, Tongue Extraction Hell,
    Needle Hell, and Dried Bones Hell,
After determining their offenses
    and consigning the sinners to their respective hells,
They prepare a great banquet,
    and invite the good and proper women.
While thus honoring them
    they ask them their fondest wishes.
Would you wish to be a fairy?
    Would you wish to go to Yaojiyan?
Would you wish to be a man?
    Would you wish to be the wife of a State Minister?
Would you like to be an empress in the Imperial household?
    Would you like to be a royal consort?
Would you like to have wealth, rank, and fame?
    We will do as you wish.
Just tell us your heart's desire.
    We will call a fairy and order that it be carried out.
Is it not wonderful
    that you are going to the Pure Land?
[Listeners,] be of a good mind, purify your heart,
    and refrain from committing sinful acts.
If you do not heed the words of this conversion song,
    to act in a virtuous and upright manner,
You will be unable to avoid the cow-headed and horse-headed forms,
    nor will you be able to avoid the serpent.
Be cautious and cultivate your morals.
    Attend to your own morals first, then morally lead your household.
Succeeding in this you must then do your utmost
    to help govern the country and secure the people's welfare.
If you do not accrue a record of such virtue,
    your days after death will be wretched indeed.
I hope, my brethren,
    that you will perform many charitable deeds,
Cultivate the proper path in the next life
    and go forth into the Pure Land.

Namu Amit'a Pul namu Kwanseŭm Posal [Homage to Amitābha Buddha, homage to Avalokiteśvara Bodhisattva].

———— 7 ————

A Buddhist Rite of Exorcism

Patrick R. Uhlmann

In contemporary Korea, healing rituals, especially treatments for spirit possession, tend to be associated primarily with the practices of shamans. However, this perception is far from accurate, since healing and exorcism are widely practiced within Protestant Christian denominations and so-called new religions as well. In fact, healing remains a major function of Korean religions, and exorcism is one of its most distinctive manifestations. This has also been the case with Buddhism since its introduction to the Korean peninsula. Such historical records as the *Samguk yusa* (Memorabilia of the Three Kingdoms), the *Koryŏsa* (History of Koryŏ), and, to a lesser extent, the *Chosŏn Wangjo sillok* (Veritable Annals of the Chosŏn Dynasty) attest to the primary role that healing played in propagating and securing the preeminence of Buddhism in Korea at all social levels. Buddhist monks engaged in the performance of a wide variety of healing rituals, ranging from state-sponsored exorcisms at the royal court to apotropaic rituals for the common people.

During the Chosŏn dynasty, the rejection of Buddhism as official ideology and the deprivation of state support for the religion brought the performance of these rituals to an end and resulted in many of the liturgical manuals being lost. During the first half of the twentieth century, criticism of these rituals as being merely "superstitious goblin-theater" and a deviation from the "essence" of Buddhism was voiced even by monks, who advocated their eradication. While a more positive reevaluation of Buddhist rituals in general has occurred during the last few decades, exorcisms and fortune-telling still do not exactly correspond to the self-image that the contemporary Korean Buddhist establishment wants to promote for itself. Therefore, although they continue to be widely practiced and tolerated, these activities remain controversial. Monks with experience and expertise in these activities thus avoid extensive publicity, which could buttress criticism of Buddhism as a backward and superstitious religion.

As a consequence, the ritual known as *Kubyŏng sisik* has emerged as the main Buddhist practice for treating cases of spirit possession and spirit-induced illness. This does not, of course, preclude the use of talismans (*pujŏk*), spells, or prayers, such as those invoking Bhaiṣajyaguru (Yaksa Yŏrae), the Medicine Buddha, to which monks often resort as preliminary or concomitant healing measures.

Literally meaning "rescuing from illness by offering food," the *Kubyŏng sisik* is a food-offering ritual performed to heal a patient diagnosed as suffering from an illness caused by spirits, whether one or many. In most cases, illness here refers to the most serious cases of spirit possession. Thus the ritual is also known as *kumyŏng sisik*, literally meaning "saving a life by offering food." Despite the homophony and interpretative affinity between *kumyŏng* with *kubyŏng*, the term *kumyŏng sisik* itself does not occur in liturgical manuals.

While slightly different versions of the liturgical text for the *Kubyŏng sisik* appear in most ritual manuals compiled by the major Korean Buddhist orders as well as those printed by individual monasteries, there is no one version of the text that is more authoritative than others. On the one hand, philological investigations concerning the genesis of the liturgy have not been made, by either scholars or monks. At the same time, the liturgical text only partially reflects the performance as it is actually enacted.

Perhaps the oldest extant version of the liturgical text, the *Kubyŏng sisik ŭimun* (Ritual Text for the Kubyŏng Sisik), is included in a larger manual that is only partially extant: the *Chŭngsu sŏn'gyo sisik ŭimun* (*Zengxiu chanjiao shishi yiwen* in Chinese), the *Revised and Augmented Ritual Manual for the Performance of Food Offerings in Sŏn and Kyo*. The undated manuscript dates from the late Chŏson period and claims to be authored by the Chinese Chan master Mengshan Deyi (1231–1308), who exerted a notable influence on Korean Buddhism. However, in addition to its being heavily edited by an unknown Korean monk, the attribution of its authorship to Mengshan Deyi is most probably wrong and results from confusing Mengshan Deyi with Ganlu *Dashi*, a master of esoteric Buddhism known as the compiler of the "Great Food Offering of Mengshan" (Mengshan here referring to a mountain in the Chinese province of Sichuan, not the monk Mengshan). For many reasons, which cannot be discussed here, it is safe to presume that the earliest versions of the text for the *Kubyŏng sisik* were compiled and circulated in Korea during the late Koryŏ period (ca. fourteenth century) and that this ritual has been performed from that period onward. However, the extant form of the liturgical text does not provide enough information to allow us to determine how the actual performance of the ritual evolved over the centuries. Indeed, while contemporary editions provide a more or less identical structure for the ritual, an ethnographic study of its performance reveals significant regional differences, as well as pronounced divergences among individual officiants. Specialists in performing this ritual tend to add, delete, insert, correct, or modify passages, procedures, prayers, and spells in their own copy of the liturgical text. Indeed, none of the printed editions of the ritual text currently available have been properly proofread or edited, so the officiants inevitably must correct spelling mistakes and textual inconsistencies. For example, most manuals mention a "Great Bodhisattva Manifesting the Traces," which is in fact a misreading for "Great Bodhisattva of

Unclean Traces," a reference to Ucchuṣma, who controls the spirits that abide in unclean places.

Further, the liturgical text does not reflect the great amount of improvisation that occurs during the performance of the ritual. Since the patient has been possessed by spirits, his or her behavior remains unpredictable (the liturgical text simply refers to the patient "striking the floor and moaning"). More often than not, the ritual sequence is interrupted by the patient's sudden outburst or violent behavior, which necessitates the intervention of assistants to keep him under control—and, depending on the "dharma-power" of the officiant, to engage in sometimes lengthy verbal confrontations with the possessing spirit(s).

The discrepancy between the prescriptive dimension of the text and the ritual's actual performance also results from the fact that the *Kubyŏng sisik* is not performed exclusively by properly ordained monks or nuns belonging to a specific Buddhist order but also by individual religious entrepreneurs of dubious background. This includes men and women who don monastic robes and call themselves "monks" or "nuns," even though they may have never been ordained; or laymen and laywomen pretending to be "dharma masters," even though their knowledge of Buddhist teachings, by any stretch of the imagination, is rudimentary at best. These entrepreneurs limit their remunerative practice almost exclusively to the performance of the *Kubyŏng sisik*, claiming that, because of their magical powers, their performance of the ritual is more effective than that of Buddhist monks and nuns. These individuals—who, for a lack of a better term, might be labeled "Buddhist shamans"—have attracted considerable popular interest through the publication of their experiences performing exorcisms using the *Kubyŏng sisik*.

The performance of the *Kubyŏng sisik* is thus located at the intersection, or the point of convergence, between Buddhism and shamanism. This also tells us that the liturgical text and the performance of the *Kubyŏng sisik* have been appropriated by different groups to serve different purposes, demonstrating the dynamism of the religious market in Korea.

As evident from its name, the *Kubyŏng sisik* belongs to the category of food-offering rituals, all of which are performed in the context of funerary practices. Therefore, a *Kubyŏng sisik* is usually preceded by a full-scale mass for the dead, known as *ch'ŏndojae* (sending on the spirits), performed either on the same or on previous days. However, unlike other *sisik*, which are regularly performed during funerary rites, the *Kubyŏng sisik* is performed only in special cases of spirit possession or spirit-induced illness. Nevertheless, the *Kubyŏng sisik* is similar to other food offerings that also use mantras for feeding spirits and place paper dolls on the altar. It is also related to the funerary mass in the sense that it includes an adaptation of the procedures for bathing the spirits, which otherwise is performed during the forty-nine-day death cerermony (*sasipkujae*).

The performance of the *ch'ŏndojae* before the *Kubyŏng sisik* is done in the belief that cases of possession or illness result from a dead relative whose funerary mass has not been properly performed. In most cases, the troublesome ghosts are identified as the patient's near or distant relatives rather than, say, the foxes or demons of popular lore. But the *chŏndojae* may also be omitted in the conviction that the "bathing" procedures, which otherwise form part of the *chŏndojae*, are enough. It is also common to perform *Kubyŏng sisik* in a short form, in which its "bathing" procedures are entirely omitted.

The "bathing," as well as the whole *Kubyŏng sisik*, ideally involves at least three officiants: a main officiant, labeled a dharma master (*pŏpchu* or *pŏbsa*), a first auxiliary aide (*paraji*), and a certifying dharma master (*chŭngmyŏng pŏbsa*). In most cases, however, only the dharma master and a close aide are present, and they are assisted occasionally by the relatives of the patient.

The officiant ideally has to maintain the unity of the three esoteric empowerments, that is, while forming hand gestures (*mudrā*) and reciting mantras, he or she also should be able to see or visualize the actions and behavior of the spirits. The mantras recited during the bathing and the entire *Kubyŏng sisik* are supposed to have a coercive force, allowing the officiant to maintain control over the situation and keeping the spirits at bay.

Stories of officiants who lost control and were attacked and/or possessed by spirits during such performances circulate among monks and individual entrepreneurs. Therefore, it is not uncommon that patients include monks and nuns who became possessed while they were performing a *Kubyŏng sisik*. The *Kubyŏng sisik* is also used to treat the "meditation-illness" (*sŏnbyŏng*) of monks and nuns.

Kwanyok, or "bathing," is an ablution ritual that aims to cleanse bad karma and defilements from the spirits—in this context troublesome ghosts and spirits, specifically those possessing the patient but also all other lonely spirits. A "bathing room," or *kwanyokpang*, usually created using a four-panel folding screen, is set up on one side of the dharma hall, and the following items are placed inside it: a large bowl of clean water infused with diluted perfume, a toothbrush, toothpaste, soap, a towel, sometimes a razor and shaving cream, properly folded paper clothes (including underwear, outer garments, socks, and shoes), one tile (on which to burn the paper clothes), and a pair of metal chopsticks (to hold up the burning clothes). Two sheet of paper with the inscriptions "gentlemen" and "ladies" (no ladies first in Korea!) are fixed on the outside, so as to faithfully replicate a Korean public bath with its separate entrances for male and female users.

The bathing process is carried out in four main steps. First, the spirit tablet either with the name of the possessing spirit, if known, or with the characters "troublesome ghost" written on it, is brought into the bathing room. Second, the officiant recites a set of four mantras by which the troublesome ghost and all the spirits are bathed. Third, the officiant recites another set of four mantras by which the spirits are clothed, while his aide burns the paper clothes, thereby transforming them into netherworld clothes for the spirits. Fourth, the aide comes out from the bathing room carrying the spirit tablet and hands it over to the relative of the patient, who then advances to the front of the dharma hall and performs prostrations to the Buddha on behalf of the spirit tablet.

While the bathing process may be carried out at any time of the day, the *Kubyŏng sisik* itself is traditionally performed in the darkness of night, preferably after ten o'clock. Also, whereas the "bathing" and most food offerings are performed in the main shrine or dharma hall of a monastery or the main room of a building, the *Kubyŏng sisik* is mostly performed in another room adjacent to the dharma hall. The *Kubyŏng sisik* is also one of the very few rituals in Korean Buddhism that is performed in secret, that is, its performance is not publicly announced and is carried out in private: only the patient and perhaps one or two of his close relatives is allowed to attend.

The preparations consist in setting up a "spirit altar" (*yŏnggadan*) on the left side of the room and a less elaborate "horse-stable altar" (*magudan*) at the entrance. The spirit altar consists of an unfolded screen set up behind an offering table. On the screen, the following paper items are fixed: in the middle, a strip of paper with the characters "Homage to Ghost King Great Saint Burning Face, Bodhisattva-Mahāsattva of Superior Compassion" written on it; left and right of it, two paper strips with the characters "male ghost" and "female ghost," respectively; seven paper-cut spirit dolls are pasted on the right and left; paper-cut horse dolls, or just blank papers with the character "horse" written on it, are fixed below the spirit dolls; and approximately ten sheets of paper money are fixed below each of the horse dolls. A spirit tablet, again either with the name of the possessing spirit or with the characters "troublesome ghost" written on it, is placed on the offering table with forty-nine small vessels in seven rows placed in front of it. Each row of vessels is filled with one particular kind of food: cooked rice, soup, fried vegetables, cooked potherbs, fruits, oil-and-honey pastry, or rice cakes. A large brass bowl filled with *toenjang* (fermented soybean paste) dissolved in water, is placed under the table. A much smaller table, with candles and a tea set on it, is placed in front of, or on the side of, the offering table.

The "horse-stable altar," a table with a bowl of water and fodder on it, is placed either outside or inside the entrance to the room.

The liturgical text(s) of the *Kubyŏng sisik* do not give directions on setting up the altars, and the officiants provide their own disparate interpretations. For example, the horses are explained either as carrying away the troublesome spirit(s) on their back to the Pure Land or to the netherworld, or as representing Hayagrīva, the horse-headed manifestation of Avalokiteśvara who subdues demons.

Avalokiteśvara assumes a primary role in the *Kubyŏng sisik*. He is invoked at the very outset of the ritual together with the Three Jewels of Buddhism. His function is to mediate and resolve the strained relations between the realm of human beings and the realm of the spirits. Following the request of the officiant, he manifests himself as the Ghost King Great Saint Burning Face and leads the troublesome ghosts and spirits to their destined rebirth.

The *Kubyŏng sisik* draws upon the motif of the Buddha's attendant, Ānanda, saving the Burning-Mouth Hungry Ghosts and is a variant on the esoteric food-offering rituals introduced by Amoghavajra in Tang China. This connection is another factor that strongly suggests that the extant recensions are based on a manual authored by Ganlu Dashi rather than Mengshan Deyi, for esoteric elements and similarities with the "Great Food Offering of Mengshan" appear throughout the text. The *Revised and Augmented Ritual Manual for the Performance of Food Offerings in Sŏn and Kyo* is a revised version of this "Great Food Offering" adapted to Korean circumstances: that is, it is an abridged version of a larger manual, with many parts omitted. This results in the linkage of Avalokiteśvara as Ghost King with Ucchuṣma, originally two separate figures.

Similar to the "bathing" process, the procedures of the *Kubyŏng sisik* can be roughly divided into four major sets of four mantras, and the recitation of a lengthy dhāraṇī.

The first set of mantras serves to destroy, or more literally to "open up," the hells and evil destinies so that all hungry or unsatisfied spirits (and not just those troubling the patient) are able to accept the invitation to the ritual space. Next follows the "bathing" process described earlier. The second major set of mantras serves to prepare food in a way to make it edible to the spirits. The third set of mantras involves the actual feeding process, whereby all spirits are fed indiscriminately. The fourth set serves to send off the spirits by burning their paper effigies and wishing them rebirth in the Pure Land or an auspicious realm of rebirth. This is done respectfully, and the merit of this food offering is transferred to all sentient beings. So far, the ritual has been conducted in a solemn but compassionate way, aiming at persuading the troublesome spirit(s) possessing and bringing illness to the patient to leave. The last step of the *Kubyŏng sisik*, in contrast, serves forcefully and violently to chase away the troublesome spirit(s) who refused to depart previously—a last measure, so to speak. The officiant hurls red beans at the spirit altar or at the patient himself, causing, according to the traditional interpretation, great pain to the spirits and forcing them out from the patient's body.

The apotropaic quality of red beans not only pervades a whole set of popular religious practices but also can be perceived in the preparation of a large variety of foods. Hurling red beans also occurs during shamanic rituals, and the fact that this practice occurs at the climax of the *Kubyŏng sisik* further nurtured the perception and criticism of this ritual as being a shamanistic practice. Officiants of the ritual tend to consider Buddhist exorcism to be different from its shamanic counterparts. From a doctrinal perspective, Buddhism views even troublesome spirits are nothing but deluded sentient beings who must be taught the dharma and shown compassion. Thus, exorcism is not merely about chasing away spirits; instead, it seeks to help spirits recognize their situation so that they may let go of their worldly attachments and take rebirth in either the Pure Land or another auspicious destiny. From a performative point of view, the Buddhists claim, the *Kubyŏng sisik* is also staged in an austere fashion that does not involve the "disorderly jumping around and dancing" of a shamanistic *kut*. Buddhists, therefore, are able to justify to themselves, at least, that the *Kubyŏng sisik* is an orthodox religious practice, not shamanic superstition.

The version of the *Kubyŏng sisik* translated here is from the *Chae ŭisik* (Mortuary Rituals), pp. 64–79, compiled by Venerable Ch'ŏnun and published by Hyangnim Monastery in 1994. The parentheses follow the original text, while square brackets are my additional comments. The mantras are given following the Korean pronunciation, as nobody in Korea recites them in Sanskrit. What is probably the oldest extant manuscript, the *Kubyŏng sisik üimun*, is partially preserved in the *Chŭngsu sŏn'gyo sisik üimun*; a photolithographic reprint is compiled in the third volume of Venerable Pak Semin's (secular name: Pak Kyŏngnyŏl) *Han'guk Pulgyo üirye charyo ch'ongsŏ* (Collection of Materials on Korean Buddhist Rituals) (Seoul: Pogyŏng Munhwasa, 1993), pp. 363–77.

Further Reading

Buddhist exorcism in Korea remains an unexplored field in both Korean and Western academe. On the importance of healing in the context of Korean Buddhism, see Don Baker, "Monks, Medicine, and Miracles: Health and Healing in the History of Korean Buddhism," *Korean Studies* 18 (1994): 50–75. For an overview of esoteric Buddhist food offering rituals in China, which clearly influenced the *Kubyŏng sisik*, see Charles D. Orzech, "Esoteric Buddhism and the *Shishi* in China," in *The Esoteric Buddhist Tradition*, edited by Henrik Hjort Sørensen (Copenhagen and Åarhus: Seminar for Buddhist Studies, 1994), pp. 51–72; and Sørensen's rather more accessible "Saving the Burning-Mouth Hungry Ghost," in *Religions of China in Practice*, edited by Donald S. Lopez Jr. (Princeton, N.J.: Princeton University Press, 1996), pp. 278–83.

Ritual for Healing through Offering Food

Initial Invocation (*repeat three times to the beat of a wooden block*) [and while ringing the handbell]:

> Homage to the Buddhas that constantly abide in the ten directions.
> Homage to the Dharmas that constantly abide in the ten directions.
> Homage to the Saṃghas that constantly abide in the ten directions.
> Homage to the Bodhisattva Avalokiteśvara, who, with great loving-kindness and compassion, saves [sentient beings] from suffering and afflictions.

(*Proclamation to Be Read Aloud*):
> Tonight, [this ritual is] directed especially to the troublesome ghost(s) and spirits possessing [insert name of patient], who lives in [insert name of town or village], Republic of Korea, the Land East of the Sea, on the Southern Continent Jambudvīpa, in the Sahā universe. May you, [oh troublesome ghosts and spirits], by relying on the divine power of the Buddha and the empowerment of the Dharma, come forward to this jeweled throne of purity, and be satiated with delicious food and the meditative joy of this Dharma-offering.

Verse for Ringing the Handbell:
  May the ringing of this handbell extend this invocation to the netherworld. May it be heard by all beings in the realm of the ghosts. May you tonight, sustained by the power of the Three Jewels, come forward to this
  gathering.

Brief Instruction [preceding the recitation of *The Great Dhāraṇī of Spiritually
Sublime Phrases*]
  Where the light of loving-kindness shines, lotus flowers blossom forth.
  When examined with the eye of wisdom, the hells are [realized to be] empty.
  Also, by the power of this Divine Spell of Great Compassion, all sentient be-
  ings will achieve buddhahood in an instant.

  As the *Thousand Hands [Spell]* is recited on your behalf, oh lonely spirits,
  singlemindedly listen to it carefully and singlemindedly accept it carefully.

The Great Dhāraṇī of Spiritually Sublime Phrases (Text omitted here) [but included in other recensions].

Brief Instruction [preceding the recitation of four mantras]:
  If someone wants to thoroughly know all the buddhas of the three time periods, he should examine the nature of the Dharmadhātu: everything is only
  a creation of the mind.

[The following four mantras are performed with the corresponding hand gestures and mental visualizations]:
  Mantra That Shatters the Hells: Namo atta sijinam samyak sammotta kuch'i-
  nam om ajana pabasi chirijiri hum (*repeat three times*).
  Mantra That Destroys the Evil Destinies of Rebirth: Om amok'a mirojana
  maha monara mani panama abarabara maldaya hum (*repeat three times*).
  Mantra That Invokes the Hungry Ghosts: Om chignajigna yehyehye sabaha
  (*repeat three times*).
  Mantra of Universal Invocation: Namu pobojeri karidari tat'a adaya (*repeat
  three times*).

[Now the procedure for bathing the spirits begins, which is often omitted during abridged performances of the ritual:]
[*Threefold Invocation of Lonely Spirits*:]
Invocation of Lonely Spirits (part one):
  Singlemindedly, I respectfully invoke you. The [principle according to
  which] causes and conditions gather and scatter is the same in both past and
  present. It is empty and penetrating, vast and great, numinous and pervasive,
  coming and going, autonomous and free of constraints.
    It is with the utmost sincere mind that, today, [insert name of donor(s)]
  bestow(s) a feast for sending off the troublesome ghost(s) and spirits possessing [insert name of patient] [to the Pure Land]. Relying on the divine
  power of the buddhas and the empowerment of the Dharma, may you come

forward to this incense-offering altar, receive the Dharma offering and realize the principle of non-origination.

Invocation of Lonely Spirits (part two):
Singlemindedly, I respectfully invoke you. The conditions [sustaining] your life were exhausted and your life force suddenly moved on. Being dead, a "traveler to the yellow spring," you have turned into a spirit for whom [your relatives] performed memorial services. Your appearance has become faint and your features are barely recognizable [anymore].

It is with the utmost sincere mind that today, [insert name of donor(s)] bestow(s) a feast for sending off the troublesome ghost(s) and spirits possessing [name of patient] [to the Pure Land]. Relying on the divine power of the buddhas and the empowerment of the Dharma, may you come to this incense-offering altar, receive the Dharma offering and realize the principle of non-origination.

Invocation of Lonely Spirits (part three) [identical to part one]:
Singlemindedly I respectfully invoke you. The [principle according to which] causes and conditions gather and scatter is the same for the time past and present. It is empty and penetrating, vast and great, numinous and pervasive, coming and going, possessing self-mastery, and free of constraints.

It is with the utmost sincere mind that today, [name of donor(s)] bestow(s) a feast for sending off the troublesome ghost(s) and spirits possessing [name of patient] [to the Pure Land]. Relying on the divine power of the buddhas and the empowerment of the Dharma, may you come to this incense-offering altar, receive the Dharma offering, and realize the principle of non-origination.

Invocation by Burning Incense (*repeat three times*):
Spirits! You have reached the limit [of your life span] and discarded your dead body. Time flies like a stone-generated spark, as in a dream.

To where did the "three spirits (*samhon*)" silently return? The "seven souls (*ch'ilpaek*)" departed for a faraway and distant land.

Troublesome ghost(s) and spirits possessing [name of patient]! You came down to this incense-offering altar after receiving this earnest invocation. [Now,] abandon all conditions and condescend to taste from this food offered to you.

Troublesome ghost(s) and spirits possessing [name of patient]! This pure incense-stick is in fact you departed spirits' original face. These several bright lamps are in fact the moment that is right before your eyes.

[*Offering of Chan Master Zhaozhou's Tea:*]
First, you will be offered Zhaozhou's tea. Later, you will be offered heaps of fragrant food. Do you see all these different offerings [piled up] here [on this altar]?

(*After a while, ring the handbell three times.*)
    Whether you bow your head or raise your face, there is no place for you to
hide. Clouds are in the blue sky and water is in a bottle.
    Troublesome ghost(s) and spirits possessing [name of patient]! Having
received the offering of incense and listened to the sound of the Dharma
[preached to you], [prepare yourself to] go and worship the Golden Immortal [i.e., the Buddha] with palms together and mind focused.

Guiding [the Ghosts] to Take a Perfumed Bath:
    Relying on the power of the buddhas, the power of the Dharma, and the ma-
jestic and divine power of the Three Jewels, all human beings, all lonely
spirits without a master, and all other sentient beings have been invoked in
this human realm. [Spirits!], having arrived at the site of enlightenment, the
congregation [of monks] invites you, by the sound of cymbals, to advance
toward the bathing room.

Recitation of the Great Dhāraṇī of Spiritually Sublime Phrases (omitted here)

    Mantra for Purifying the Way [to the bathing room]: "Om sosidji najaridara
najaridara moradaye charajara mandamanda hanahana hum pat'ak" (*repeat
three times*). [The officiant or his aide carries the spirit tablet into the bathroom.]

*Stanza for Entering the Bathing Room (recited after striking the metal plate an-
nouncing that the bath has been prepared)*
    Having once turned your back on the Original Mind King, how many times
have you lapsed into the three [evil] destinies and undergone the four modes
of rebirth?
    Today, the stain of your defilements will be washed away and eradicated.
In accordance with your [karmic] conditions, you will return to your ancestral home [i.e., your original mind].

Section on Bathing [the Spirits] through Empowerment:
    To state it plainly: for purifying the three kinds of karmic acts, nothing is
better than a purified mind; for purifying all the myriad things, nothing is
better than pure water. Therefore, it is with respect and solemnity that fragrant hot water has been specially prepared in this bathing room, hoping
that your defilements (lit. "dust and troubles") will be washed away in a single cleansing and you will obtain purity that will last a myriad aeons.

What follows below is the *Ablution Verse (to be repeated by the congregation, following the intonation of the officiant)*:
    By means of this fragrant hot water, I now bathe the lonely spirits and [other]
sentient beings.
    Your body and mind being thus cleansed and purified, may you enter into
the realization of true voidness and [return to] the land of Everlasting Bliss
[i.e., the Pure Land].

[The officiant recites the following four mantras while simultaneously making the appropriate hand gestures and visualizations:]

Mantra for Bathing: "Om padamo sanisa amokka are hum" (*repeat three times*).

Mantra for Brushing the Teeth (lit. "masticating the willow branch"): "Om pa-araha sabaha" (*repeat three times*).

Mantra for rinsing the mouth: "Om todori kuruguru sabaha" (*repeat three times*).

Mantra for washing hands and face: "Om samanda pari sutje hum" (*repeat three times*).

Section on Clothing [the Ghosts] through Empowerment:

[Addressing the spirits:] Disciples of the Buddha! By means of this bath, both your body and mind have been thoroughly cleansed.

Now, through the empowerment of the Tathāgata's supreme and secret words, the clothes for [your journey to] the netherworld [will be provided to you].

May this single suit of clothes be transformed into many suits of clothes, and may these many suits be transformed into infinitely many suits of clothes.

May these clothes fit the stature of the [spirits'] bodies, be neither too long nor too short, neither too tight nor too loose. May their quality be superior to anything they have ever worn before.

To transform [these clothes] into the clothes of liberation, I therefore respectfully will publicly recite the Buddhas' and tathāgatas' dhāraṇī for the transformation of clothes.

[While the aide enters the bathroom and burns the paper clothes, the officiant recites the following four mantras, simultaneously making the appropriate hand gestures and visualizations:]

Mantra for the Transformation of Clothes: "Namu samanda mottanam om pajana pirogije sabaha" (*repeat three times*).

Mantra for Giving the Clothes [to the spirits]: "Om parimara paba-arini hum" (*repeat three times*). [The officiant makes a fist with his right hand and sprinkles water on the bathroom.]

Mantra for Dressing [the spirits]: "Om pa-ara pasase sabaha" (*repeat three times*).

Mantra for Fitting the Clothes [of the spirits]: "Om sammanda padarana padame hum pak" (*repeat three times*).

Section on Visiting the Saint [i.e. the Buddha] after Bathing:

[The aide carries the spirit tablet out of the bathing room and hands it over to a relative of the patient, "the main mourner."]

[The officiant addresses the spirits:] Disciples of the Buddha! Now that you are completely dressed, it befits you to advance to the altar site, worship the Compassionate Worthies of the Three Jewels [alt. worship the Three

Jewels and go to the Compassionate Worthy One (the Buddha)] and listen to the sublime Dharma of the One Vehicle. We invite you to leave the bathing room and advance to the pure altar. Advance at a slow pace, with your palms together and your mind focused.

[The officiant recites the following mantra pointing with the second finger of his right hand to the Buddha altar:]

Mantra for Pointing to the Altar: "Om yeihye pirojanaya sabaha" (*repeat three times*).

Verse on the Dharmakāya:

The Dharmakāya pervades tens of billions of worlds, everywhere radiating a golden light that illuminates the realm of humans and gods.

It manifests in accordance with the capacity of things (i.e., sentient beings), like the moon reflecting on the bottom of a pond. [But] its essence is perfect and sits in correct posture on the Jeweled-Lotus Platform.

Mantra for Bestowing a Universal Offering: "Om a-ana sambaba pa-ara hum" (*repeat three times*).

[This concludes the procedures for bathing the spirits.]

Statement Explaining the Motive for Invoking [the Spirits]:

Be it announced that: on the [insert] day of the [insert] month, in the [insert] year, the individual named [insert patient's name], living in [name of town or village], having been afflicted with an [hitherto] incurable illness, is striking the floor and moaning.

Incense, candles, boiled rice, rice cakes, [paper-]money, and [paper-]horses have been respectfully prepared to invoke the troublesome ghost(s) and spirits, including all ghosts and spirits in the five directions. An offering to these ghost(s) and spirits shall [now] be made.

Prostrating myself, I wish that you spirits, the troublesome ghost(s) and spirits possessing [name of patient], come to this offering site and receive the dharma offering, and dissolve your smoldering grudges. May you extinguish and remove the illness [affecting the patient] and restore his/her health [lit. "have the patient's body reinvigorated"]. May each of these wishes be fulfilled.

I earnestly hope:

The way to the netherworld being vast and boundless, the lonely spirits are confused. Some of them enter into the gloomy prison of the netherworld, where they suffer for an eternity. Some of them abide in the intermediate state between death and rebirth [Skt. *antarābhava*], starving for long aeons, experiencing calamities and suffering that are difficult to bear and difficult to sustain. After a thousand years, they still have not found a way out. During all four seasons, there are never any memorial services performed on their behalf.

Even if they wander in all the four directions trying to live from hand to mouth, there is no way for them to be satiated even once. They randomly cling to possessions and sex, bringing harm to people, and also cling to alcohol and food, thus possessing people. Some of them cannot forget their [former] affection and love and stalk their [once-beloved]. Some of them have not yet resolved their grudges and hatred, and keep persecuting [their enemies]. Some of them [stick] to tripod cauldrons or wine jars, causing accidents after these have been sold. Some of them are connected to tiles, stones, soil, or trees, so that, if these are moved, they produce an outflow of calamities.

Ordinary men do not know the roots of such illnesses and thus experience great suffering. Unaware of the signs of their wrongdoing, ghosts and spirits attack and trouble [human beings]. Not knowing the suffering and affliction [they cause] of human beings, ghosts recklessly unleash their anger [at them]. But human beings are unaware of the hunger of these ghosts and merely detest them.

[Hence,] if not for the divine power of Avalokiteśvara, how could the knot of hatred between human beings and ghosts [ever] be untied?

In the end, it is with an impartial mind that [this] food offering is made, without discrimination [toward any spirit]. May all lonely spirits who have no master [i.e., no relatives who perform rituals for them] rely on the sublime power of Avalokiteśvara and escape from the painful destinies [of rebirth]. Please come to this dharma feast.

Respectfully and singlemindedly, this request is presented [to you] three times [by the officiating monk].

[*Invocation of Avalokiteśvara as the Ghost King Great Saint Burning Face*:]

Homage [to Avalokiteśvara]. Singlemindedly, I respectfully request that you uphold the provisional and promote the [Buddhist] teachings; that you universally relieve [the ghosts and spirits] from starvation, and save all sentient beings in the evil realms of rebirth. May you therefore manifest yourself as the weak and emaciated appearance of the Ghost King Great Saint Burning Face. Oh Bodhisattva-Mahāsattva of Superior Compassion, may you not abandon your original vow and descend to this enlightenment site, and certify the merit [of this ritual].

Invocation [of the Ghost King] by Offering Incense and Flowers (*repeat three times*):

Great Bodhisattva of Unclean Traces [i.e., referring to Ucchuṣma, who controls the unclean demons] and Superior Compassion, as an expedient, may you manifest yourself in the form of the King of Ghosts.

Do not linger in your venerable position, [for your compassion] is vast like a bright moon shining on reed flowers.

Consequently I singlemindedly take refuge and prostrate [before you].

[*Remarks before the*] *Mantra for Offering a Seat* [to Avalokiteśvara as the King of Ghosts, which follows below]:

The seat of sublime awakening (*bodhi*) has been splendidly adorned; all the buddhas who have sat there have attained right enlightenment.

The seat I now offer you is also like this. May oneself and others complete the path to buddhahood at the same time.

[*Mantra for Offering a Seat to the King of Ghosts*]: Om pa-ara minaya sabaha (*repeat three times*).

Mantra for Cleansing the Dharmadhātu: Om nam (*repeat twenty-one times*).

Verse for Offering Tea [to the King of Ghosts]:

I now transmute pure water into sweet-dew tea.

I respectfully offer it to [you, King of Ghosts, as] the certifying [master]. May you honor my sincere wish. May you honor my sincere wish. May you honor my sincere wish. May you honor my sincere wish with loving-kindness and compassion.

Invocation [of the following long list of ghosts and spirits]:

Singlemindedly, I respectfully invoke: the troublesome ghost(s) and spirits possessing [name of patient], followed by the spirits of his [the patient's] deceased parents, his teachers and elders over many lifetimes, the spirits of his five families [i.e., the paternal and maternal sides of one's family, the paternal and maternal sides of one's spouse's family, and the maternal side of the family of one's mother] and six relatives [i.e., father and mother, brothers and sisters, spouse and children], the great deity King of the Kitchen who protects the interior [of the household], the great deity King of the Mountain who protects the exterior; the earth deities of the five directions, the dragon kings of the five directions, the saints [i.e., spirit-generals] of the five directions [and Ten Celestial Stems, namely:] the blue-colored god of the first and second Celestial Stem in the eastern direction, the red-colored god of the third and fourth Celestial Stem in the southern direction, the white-colored god of the fifth and sixth Celestial Stem in the western direction, the black-colored god of the seventh and eight Celestial Stem in the northern direction, the yellow-colored god of the ninth and tenth Celestial Stem in the center.

[Furthermore, I invoke:] the ghost of a bachelor followed by seven other ghosts: the blue killer-god in the east, the red killer-god in the south, the white killer-god in the west, the black killer-god in the north, the yellow killer-god in the center, the ghosts wandering around with a body made of the five aggregates [*skandha*], and the ghosts of those who died far away from home.

[Furthermore:] The ghosts living in neighboring realms [such as]: ghosts living in the soil, ghosts living on pounding stones, ghosts dwelling in toilets, ghosts living on roads, ghosts living in courtyards, ghosts living on fences.

[Furthermore:] the hosts of ghosts attached to specific places: ghosts in the sky, ghosts on the earth, ghosts inside human beings, ghosts in the aggregates, ghosts wandering around, ghosts in places [of those who died] away from home, ghosts on roads, ghosts in mountains, ghosts in the water, as well as the entourage belonging to each of them.

May [all of you], relying on the power of the Three Jewels, come forward to this place of offerings. May you obtain the offering of the dharma and realize the understanding of the principle of non-origination.

Invocation by Incense Smoke (repeat three times):
Troublesome ghost(s) and spirits harboring grudges against human beings: when will your hate and love come to rest?

Now, having been provided with food and this Dharma exposition, may all of you troublesome ghost(s) and spirits instantly awaken to the principle of non-origination and dissolve your enmity.

Mantra for Assigning a Seat and Be Seated in Order: Om mani kundari hum hum sabaha (*repeat three times*).

Verse for Offering Tea:
To how many people did Zhaozhou offer tea, a new taste among the hundreds of herbs and plants?

Having boiled water from the middle of a river in a stone-tripod cauldron, may you, spirits of the dead, put an end to the painful wheel of rebirth [by drinking this tea].

May you, lonely souls, put an end to the painful wheel of rebirth. May all of you spirits put an end to the painful wheel of rebirth.

[Here the officiant covers the body of the sitting patient with a monk's robe for a short moment, while reciting the following remarks preceding the set of four mantras for preparing food:]

By bestowing this secret empowerment, may your body and mind become invigorated, the karmic fire cool down, so that each of you will seek liberation.

Mantra for Transforming Food [to become edible for spirits]: Namak salba tat'a-ada parogite om sambara sambara hum (*repeat three times*).

Mantra for Bestowing Sweet-Dew Water: Namu sorobaya tat'a adaya tanyat'a om sorosoro parasoro parasoro sabaha (*repeat three times*).

Mantra for Visualizing the One-Syllable Water-Wheel: Om pam pam pam pam (*repeat three times*).

Mantra for Making an Ocean of Milk: namu samanda mottanam om pak (*repeat three times*).

Praise of the Holy Epithets [of the five Tathāgatas]:
Homage to the Tathāgata Prabhūtaratna. May you prompt all lonely spirits to annihilate stinginess and greed, and become endowed with the wealth of the dharma.

Homage to the Tathāgata Surūpa. May you prompt all lonely spirits to leave behind their filthy appearance, and to become completely endowed with the major and minor marks [of an enlightened one].

Homage to the Tathāgata Vipulakāya. May you prompt all lonely spirits to discard the six kinds of bodies of ordinary men, and awaken to the body of empty space.

Homage to the Tathāgata Abhayaṃkara. May you prompt all lonely spirits to leave behind all fears, and to obtain the bliss of nirvāṇa.

Homage to the Tathāgata Amṛtarāja. May you prompt the throat of all lonely spirits to be opened so that they can get the taste of sweet dew.

May this empowered food pervade all the ten directions. May whoever eats from it eliminate his hunger and thirst, and be reborn in the [Pure] Land of Peace and Sustenance.

Mantra for Feeding [Hungry] Ghosts: "Om migi migi yaya migi sabaha" (*repeat three times*).

Mantra for Bestowing the Food of Dharma Indiscriminately [to all beings]: "Om mogyŏngnŭng sabaha" (*repeat three times*).

Mantra for Universal Offering: "Om a-ana sambaba ba-ara hum" (*repeat three times*).

Mantra for Universally Transferring Merit: "Om sammara sammara mimana sara maha chagaraba hum" (*repeat three times*).

Having receiving this dharma food from me, how could it be any different from the food that had been prepared by Ānanda [for saving the hungry ghosts]?

All those with starving intestines will be completely satiated and the karmic fire will be immediately cooled.

Do immediately reject [the poisonous afflictions of] greed, hatred, and delusion, and forever take refuge in the Buddha, Dharma, and Saṃgha.

Maintain the bodhicitta in every single thought-moment, and wherever you may be will be the Land of Peace and Bliss.

Whatever has characteristics is all empty and false.

If you see all characteristics as being devoid of characteristics, you will immediately see the Tathāgata.

The Ten Epithets of the Tathāgata:
"Thus-come" [Sanskrit, *tathāgata*], "one worth of alms-giving" [*arhat*], "the fully enlightened one" [*samyaksambuddha*], "one endowed with both wisdom and practice" [*vidyācaraṇasampanna*], "well-gone" [*sugata*], "knower of the world" [*lokavid*], "the unsurpassed" [*anuttara*], "tamer of men" [*puruṣadamyasārathi*], "teacher of gods and men" [*śāstā devamanuṣyāṇam*], "the awakened and world-honored one" [*buddhalokanātha*].

[*Dharma Sermon Delivered to the Spirits:*]
From the beginning, all dharmas have always been marked by the characteristic of extinction.

Having practiced the path [accordingly], a disciple of the Buddha will become a buddha in a future existence.

All formations are impermanent: this is the dharma of production and cessation.

With the cessation of production and cessation: this calm extinction is bliss.

[Here follows a lengthy section praising the Buddha Amitābha, the ten adornments of the Pure Land, the eight major events in the Buddha's life, and so on. I do not translate this section, since it tends to be omitted by most officiants, unless they have a special devotion to Amitābha.]

Section on Respectfully Sending Off [the Spirits]:
Memorial text for Respectfully Sending Off [the Spirits]:
Verse for Sending Off the Spirits:
Lonely spirits, sentient beings, hell denizens, hungry ghosts, and beasts: I respectfully send you off.

I will set up this site of enlightenment [i.e., perform this ritual again] on another day, so do not abandon your original vow and come again!

Verse on Walking [to the Pure Land]:
[Addressing the spirits:] Move across a thousand *li* so as to fill up the empty space; being on your way home, forget your passions, and you will reach the Pure Land.

Abandon the three kinds of karmic acts and sincerely worship the Three Jewels; [then] saints and ordinary people alike will gather together in the palace of the Dharma King.

Flowers Are Strewn [on the road of the spirits] (*repeat three times*). [Note that this verse is rarely performed anymore.]

Homage to the Bodhisattva-mahāsattva Great Saint and King Guiding [the Spirits on] the Road [to Rebirth] (*repeat three times*).

Having Reached the Incineration Platform [for burning the spirit tablets, say]:
By the merit of having respectfully invoked you, offered you food, recollected the Buddha's name, and recited sūtras, may all of you quickly realize the sublime fruition of the joy of the Dharma, especially you troublesome ghost(s) and spirits possessing [name of patient], accompanied by your entire family of spirits and the spirits who are disciples of the Buddha; and you who harbor grudges and are afflicted. May those of you who, because of your hunger, attack and possess [human beings], be forever satiated by the exquisite food of meditative joy.

May you receive the powerful light of the great compassion of Avalokiteśvara, and may you all enter the ocean of awakening of Amitābha's great vow.
Recollect all the buddhas and venerable bodhisattva-mahāsattvas in the ten directions and the three time periods, and the *Mahāprajñāpāramitā* [the Great Perfection of Wisdom].

May you all take rebirth in [the Pure Land of] Ultimate Bliss, see [the Buddha] Amitābha, and have the top of your head rubbed by him as a prediction [of your future buddhahood].

May you all take rebirth in [the Pure Land]. May you sit among Amitābha's assembly, and may you always carry with you incense and flowers for making offerings.

May you all take rebirth in the Lotus-Womb World, where oneself and others complete the path to buddhahood at the same time.

Mantra for Burning (Paper-)Money/Dolls: Om pirogite sabaha (*repeat three times*).

[The aide rapidly detaches all paper items fixed on the screen of the spirit altar, including the spirit tablet of the Ghost King and the paper dolls, and burns them above the brass bowl.]

Mantra for Respectfully Sending Off: Om pa-ara sat'a mogch'a mok (*repeat three times*).

Mantra for Being Reborn among the Highest Class [of aspirants for the Pure Land]: Om mani tani hum hum pat'ak sabaha (*repeat three times*).

Mantra for the Universal Transfer of Merit: "Om sammara sammara mimana sara maha chagaraba hum" (*repeat three times*).

Verse for Merit Transfer:

Even if heaven and earth are destroyed by blazing fire and blustery winds, desolate quiescence long remains among the white clouds.

The walls of the Iron City are destroyed in a single shout. Just face toward the Seven-Jeweled Mountain in front of the Buddha.

Homage to the Buddha Heaping Treasures of the Jewel Storehouse of Joy (*make one prostration*).

Homage to the Bodhisattva-Mahāsattva Storehouse of Perfection (*make one prostration*).

Homage to the Bodhisattva-Mahāsattva Storehouse of Merit-Transfer (*make one prostration*).

Dhāraṇī for Dispelling the Grudges of a Hundred Lifetimes (*put out the light and throw red beans*): Om a-a amak (*repeat 108 times*).

[The aide again rapidly empties all the forty-nine vessels one after another, turning them upside down and throwing their contents into the brass bowl filled with dissolved soybean paste. He then rushes outside and throws away the content of the brass bowl into a river or onto a trash dump.]

——— 8 ———

"A Crazy Drunken Monk": Kyŏnghŏ and
Modern Buddhist Meditation Practice

Jin Y. Park

"An Account of Sŏn Master Kyŏnghŏ's Activities" ("Sŏnsa Kyŏnghŏ Hwasang haengjang") is a hagiography of Kyŏnghŏ Sŏngu (1857/alt. 1849–1912), written by his disciple Pang Hanam (1876–1951) in 1930. Widely acknowledged as one of the founders of modern Korean Sŏn (Zen in Japanese) Buddhism, Kyŏnghŏ is well known for his practice of *hwadu* (critical phrase, or keyword) meditation and his liberal lifestyle. Hanam's biography of Kyŏnghŏ offers a panoramic view of the life of a man who began his Buddhist practice with scriptural studies and went on to become a leading lecturer on Buddhist sūtras. Later he turned to *hwadu* meditation and attained enlightenment. Eventually, he ended his life as a wandering layperson.

The progression of Kyŏnghŏ's life and practice contains inherent contradictions. On the one hand, Kyŏnghŏ's condemnation of a doctrinal approach to Buddhist practice and his emphasis on *hwadu* meditation set the course for modern Korean Buddhism. Kyŏnghŏ's endorsement of *hwadu* meditation and his subsequent enlightenment are especially important in Korean Buddhism because they occurred when Korean Buddhism was in deep decline after a long period of governmental suppression and social disdain. Kyŏnghŏ provided a positive role model that was much needed at the time. In this way, he has been regarded as a revivalist of meditation practice for modern Korean Buddhism. On the other hand, Kyŏnghŏ's extremely liberal lifestyle has raised much doubt about his integrity in the minds of both Buddhist practitioners and scholars up to the present.

Usually translated as a "critical phrase," or "keyword," *hwadu* (*huatou* in Chinese) is a branch of what is known as the practice of "encounter dialogue" between Sŏn masters and students (Korean, *kongan*; Chinese, *gong'an*; Japanese, *kōan*). In practicing *hwadu* meditation, the practitioner employs one word or passage (the "critical phrase") given by ancient masters as a focus on which the practitioner can concentrate and eventually realize the nature of his existence. The Korean Buddhist tradition considers Sŏn meditation, especially on the *hwadu*, to be its main type of contemplative practice. *Hwadu* meditation was introduced to Korea in the thirteenth century and was advocated by National Master Pojo Chinul (1158–1210) as the fastest way to attain enlightenment. By the late nineteenth century, when Kyŏnghŏ joined the monastery, *hwadu* practice was moribund, since Buddhist practitioners were more involved with discussing the nature of Sŏn Buddhism than in actually practicing *hwadu* meditation. Kyŏnghŏ himself was a renowned lecturer on Buddhist sūtras before he completely gave up the doctrinal approach to Buddhism to focus on *hwadu* meditation at the gravest stage of life and death.

In Kyŏnghŏ's case, his *hwadu* was a phrase mentioned by the Chinese Chan Master Lingyun Zhiqin (d.u.): "The work of a donkey has not yet gone; the work of a horse has already arrived." This phrase illustrates that a *hwadu* is generally characterized by the mysterious or inexplicable nature of the statement. The idea is that the impenetrability of a statement will defeat the familiar logic of our thinking and will prevent practitioners from indulging in the habitual and dualistic views that pervade ordinary modes of thought. By creating a dead-end situation for our mental functioning, *hwadu* forces practitioners to directly face their existential condition. Since logical speculation is no longer relevant, practitioners have no other choice but to look inside themselves and face their own reality.

Kyŏnghŏ's life fits into what some have called the "hippy monk" tradition in East Asian Buddhism. In many ways, Kyŏnghŏ's life resembles that of the seventh-century Korean monk Wŏnhyo (617–86), one of the most liberal monks in the history of Korean Buddhism. The fact that Wŏnhyo and Kyŏnghŏ continue to inspire fiction writers and television dramas attests to the controversial nature of their lives. At the center of this controversy lies their relationship with the secular world. Both Wŏnhyo and Kyŏnghŏ not only openly violated the vow of celibacy incumbent on monks but also maintained liberal sexual relationships with women; both Wŏnhyo and Kyŏnghŏ frequently mingled with people from various social groups and in diverse situations that may not always have seemed appropriate for monks. In one of his poems, Kyŏnghŏ even described himself as "a crazy drunken monk." It is not difficult, then, to see why Kyŏnghŏ's personal conduct has been an object of controversy, despite the important role he played in revitalizing modern Korean Sŏn Buddhism.

In his "Account," Pang Hanam also addresses this controversy surrounding Kyŏnghŏ's life. Hanam's interpretation of Kyŏnghŏ's conduct is thoughtful and persuasive, addressing the issue on several levels. On a superficial level, Hanam strongly warns practitioners not to follow Kyŏnghŏ's lifestyle but only to learn from his dharma teaching. Hanam, however, qualifies his warning as a concern that practitioners might try to imitate Kyŏnghŏ's liberal lifestyle without first embodying his teaching. On a deeper level, Hanam tries to explicate Kyŏnghŏ's life within the context of the Mahāyāna Buddhist teaching of freeing oneself from all kinds of artificially constructed rules, theories, and constraints. These include monastic settings, Buddhist precepts, and even such fundamental teachings as the four noble truths. These are provisional and thus only have temporary value as they are dressed up in common parlance, logical structures, and social customs. Moreover, they provide only short-term frames of reference to guide practitioners to the ultimate teaching, which Hanam identifies as the teaching that mind is the Buddha and that, ultimately, all teachings are themselves empty. Hanam claims that in defying all forms of constructed precepts as well as social conventions, Kyŏnghŏ demonstrates that he himself was free from the artificiality of life. Thus Kyŏnghŏ's liberal lifestyle was one way of teaching the nonobstruction between all things. Hanam concludes that by freeing himself from the monastic setting and rules imposed by tradition, Kyŏnghŏ was able to practice the bod-hisattva path and realize the Mahāyāna teaching of the nonduality between bud-dhas and sentient beings.

Hanam further elaborates on the issue by considering the social and historical impact on Kyŏnghŏ's behavior. Hanam wonders whether Kyŏnghŏ's lifestyle was his reaction to the extremely impoverished state of Buddhism at the time. In the "Account," Kyŏnghŏ is quoted as having said that he wished not ever to set foot in the capital city. Given that Buddhist monks were not allowed to enter the cap-ital city for centuries until 1895, when the anti-Buddhist decree was lifted, Hanam had a good reason to interpret Kyŏnghŏ's wish as a reflection of the latter's awareness of the humiliation that Buddhism suffered during his time. For Hanam, it thus followed that practicing Buddhism in such dire conditions was tantamount to Kyŏnghŏ's placing himself in the humblest position in the society.

Whether one agrees with Hanam's interpretation of Kyŏnghŏ's life as a practice of nonduality between buddhas and sentient beings, and between a monastic set-ting and the secular world, Kyŏnghŏ's life itself poses important questions as to the relationship between wisdom and compassion in Mahāyāna Buddhism. How does a Sŏn practitioner transform his wisdom obtained through practice and awak-ening into compassion for others? The former (gaining wisdom) is a solitary en-deavor, whereas the latter (compassion for others) is a communal act. Both Wŏn-hyo and Kyŏnghŏ chose to transform their wisdom into compassion by putting themselves in the lowest possible position, going far beyond social convention. Is this the ultimate way of practicing nonduality between "myself" and others, or is this an "anything-goes" way of life?

As Hanam states, it may not be possible for those who are bound by provi-sional truths to fathom the state of the mind of masters who have liberated them-selves from all the world's constraints. In this sense, the account of Kyŏnghŏ's life provides us with rich resources regarding Sŏn practice, its influence on an indi-vidual, and its social implications in modern times.

This translation is based on Pang Hanam's "Sŏnsa Kyŏnghŏ Hwasang haengjang" and included in Pang, *Kyŏnghŏ chip (Collected Works of Kyŏnghŏ)* (Korea: Kŭngnak Sŏnwŏn, 1991), pp. 399–405.

Further Reading

Accounts of Kyŏnghŏ's life and practice appear in Henrik H. Sørensen, "The Life and Thought of the Korean Sŏn Mater Kyŏnghŏ," *Korea Journal* 30, no. 1 (1990):

17–27; Henrik H. Sørensen, "Buddhist Spirituality in Premodern and Modern Korea," in *Buddhist Spirituality: Later China, Korea, Japan and the Modern World*, edited by Takeuchi Yoshinori (New York: Crossroad, 1999), pp. 109–33; and Mu Seong Sunim, *Thousand Peaks: Korean Zen—Tradition and Teachers* (Cumberland, R.I.: Primary Point Press, 1991), pp. 162–78.

An Account of Sŏn Master Kyŏnghŏ's Activities

It is said in the *Diamond Sūtra*: "If, five hundred years later in this world, a sentient being keeps his faith pure upon hearing this sūtra, and thus sees reality, this being will achieve the most rare kind of meritorious virtue." Master Dahui states: "If a few individuals did not awaken their minds and achieve success in spite of difficult situations, how would it be possible for the Buddhadharma to remain alive today?" The Buddha and the patriarch made these statements because, even in the final dharma age, there were individuals strong-willed and courageous enough to penetrate to the foundation of dharma. These statements also suggest that such individuals are so rare that continuing the wisdom of the dharma is difficult. Which individual had the will of a great man to realize thoroughly the self-nature, to achieve the unsurpassed merit, and to transmit the light of great wisdom through the next five hundred years? My teacher Sŏn master Kyŏnghŏ was this person.

His posthumous designation was Sŏngu, his secular name, Tonguk, and his soubriquet, Kyŏnghŏ. His family name was Song and he was from Yŏnsan. His father's name was Tuok, and his mother's family name was Pak, from the Miryang region. He was born in Chadong village in the city of Chŏnju, on the twenty-fourth day of April in the Year of the Snake [1857], the eighth year of King Ch'ŏlchong's reign. He astonished people, it is said, because he did not cry for three days after he was born, and only when given a bath did he begin to make sounds. He lost his father when he was young. At the age of nine, his mother took him to Ch'ŏnggye monastery in Kwangju. With Master Kyehŏ as his teacher, he shaved his head and received precepts. His brother also received precepts at Magok monastery in Kongju. Their mother took refuge in the Three Jewels and chanted incantations with devotion. This resulted in the brothers joining the monasteries.

Even in his youth, Master Kyŏnghŏ's will was as strong as an adult's. The monastery was destitute, but he did not express any fatigue or aversion but instead collected firewood, drew water, and prepared food for his master.

He did not have a chance to learn Chinese characters until he turned fourteen, when a Confucian scholar came to stay at the monastery for the summer. The scholar, as a way of passing time, began teaching the boy the text of the *Thousand Character Classic*. The boy learned by heart what was taught. The scholar then taught him history and other texts, and the boy amazed the scholar by memorizing five to six pages per day. The scholar said to himself: "This boy

JIN Y. PARK

has remarkable talent. There is an old saying that a horse capable of running hundreds of miles pulls a salt-cart with fatigue, but only because its owner fails to recognize its capacity. This boy will grow up to be a figure who will deliver all the people in the world."

Soon after that, the boy's dharma master Kyehŏ disrobed. Having recognized Kyŏnghŏ's talent and not wanting the boy's education to stop with his own disrobing, Kyehŏ sent Kyŏnghŏ to Master Manhwa at Tonghak monastery on Kyeryong Mountain with a recommendation letter. Master Manhwa was a well-known lecturer at the time. Manhwa recognized Kyŏnghŏ's capacity and accepted him with delight. Within a few months of studying with Manhwa, Kyŏnghŏ demonstrated his talent in composition and was able to discuss the teachings of the Buddha. Kyŏnghŏ memorized in one glance the sūtras and śāstras assigned for the day's study and then slept the rest of the day. The following day, when he was asked about the material, his interpretation was as sharp as the splitting of wood and as clear as the light of a candle.

Disapproving of his excessive sleep and intending to test his talent, the lecturer assigned Kyŏnghŏ anywhere from four to ten pages to study, including commentaries, from the *Sūtra of Perfect Enlightenment* (Kor. *Wŏn'gak kyŏng*; Ch. *Yuanjue jing*). Kyŏnghŏ continued to sleep most of the day and still memorized all the assignments, thereby amazing people at the monastery who had never witnessed such aptitude. Since that period, Kyŏnghŏ's name and talent became widely known. Having frequently attended lectures held in the southern part of the Korean peninsula, his scholarship matured every day, and his knowledge expanded to such an extent that he became an expert even in the subjects of Confucianism and Lao-Zhuang Daoism.

Master Kyŏnghŏ was a man with a free and easy disposition inwardly, while being active and unadorned outwardly. When reading sūtras on hot summer days, other members at the monastery would be dressed up and sitting up straight, sweating all over. Kyŏnghŏ alone took off his clothes without being bothered by his appearance or informality. Noticing this, a lecturer named Iru acknowledged to other practitioners: "He is truly a person of the Mahāyāna dharma. Others cannot compete with him."

At the age of twenty-three, Kyŏnghŏ began to lecture at Tonghak monastery at the request of its members. His discussion of Buddhist doctrine was like waves in the ocean, attracting people from all over.

One day, Kyŏnghŏ thought about his former teacher Kyehŏ, who took care of him as if he were his own child. Kyŏnghŏ wanted to visit him. After informing the monastery members of this plan, he went on his way. In the middle of the journey, Kyŏnghŏ was caught in a rainstorm. Hurriedly he tried to take shelter from the rain under the eaves of a nearby house. But the owner of the house hurriedly drove him out, and he tried another without success. Dozens of houses in the village treated him in the same manner. As they sent him away, they shouted in rage: "The village is contaminated by a contagious disease that spares no living soul. Why would you want to come to such a deadly place?" Upon hearing these words, Kyŏngho found himself shivering all over. Both his body and mind became feeble as if death had attacked him at that very moment. Life, it seemed, was equivalent to the breath he was breathing, and all the things in the world looked like mountains in a dream.

Kyŏngho thought about the situation and told himself: "I pledge that even though I have to remain a fool in this life, I will not be constrained by letters. I will seek the path of the [Sŏn] patriarchs and deliverance from the three realms of existence." Having made this vow, Kyŏngho thought about the exchanges [kongan] between Sŏn masters and their students. Soon he realized that, because of his habit for analyzing and interpreting these exchanges, he was approaching the exchanges with rational thinking and usual knowledge. He could not find one case on which he could meditate. Eventually he came across a "critical phrase" [hwadu] given by Sŏn Master Lingyun: "The work of a donkey is not yet gone; the work of horse has already arrived." This phrase was difficult to interpret, and Kyŏngho felt as if he were facing a silver mountain and iron wall, which forced him to ask "what is this?" His journey with the hwadu meditation had finally begun.

Kyŏngho returned to his monastery and dismissed those assembled there with a statement: "I bid you farewell; please find your path according to your karma. My intentions and wishes do not lie in this [studying Buddhist scriptures]." Locking himself inside, he sat up straight, concentrating wholeheartedly on hwadu meditation. When sleep overwhelmed him, he would prick his thigh with a gimlet, or he would keep a sharpened knife below his chin. For three months, he meditated on the hwadu with no other thoughts.

One acolyte who attended Kyŏngho had a father, whose family name was Yi, who was known to have attained a degree of realization after having practiced meditation for several years. People called the father Layman Yi. An occasion came when the acolyte's dharma master went to visit Layman Yi at home. During their conversation, the Layman Yi stated: "A monk will eventually become a cow." The acolyte's teacher responded, paraphrasing the remark: "If a monk fails to enlighten his mind and does nothing but receives almsgivings from believers, he will definitely become a cow and thereby repay the gratitude of almsgivings in that manner." Layman Yi rebuked the monk: "How can a monk's response be so inappropriate?" The monk responded: "I am not well versed in the teachings of Sŏn. How else should I have interpreted what you said?" Layman Yi said: "You should have said that a monk might become a cow, but he would have no nostrils."

Without responding further, the monk left Layman Yi. When he returned, he told the acolyte: "Your father told me such and such but I cannot understand what he means." The acolyte said: "The Abbot [Kyŏngho] has lost sleep and skipped meals in practicing meditation. The Master must understand what my father meant. Dear teacher, why don't you go ask the Abbot about what my father said?" The monk cheerfully went to see Kyŏngho, paid his respects and sat down. He told Kyŏngho about the conversation with Layman Yi.

When the monk mentioned the cow without nostrils, Master Kyŏnghŏ's expression changed. It was as if a message from the time before the Buddha's birth was suddenly revealed to him. The earth flattened, as subject and object were both forgotten. Kyŏnghŏ had arrived at the state which the ancient masters called the land of great rest. A hundred or a thousand dharma talks, and inconceivable and mysterious truths, opened themselves as if a layer of ice had been broken or a tile cracked. This happened on the fifteenth day of November in the Year of the Rabbit [1879], the sixteenth year of King Kojong's reign.

There is no dharma outside the mind; his eyes were filled with snow and the moon; water was flowing under pine trees on a high mountain; what should one do under the clear sky on this long night? This is truly a different state; unless one obtains it oneself, one cannot comprehend it.

Kyŏnghŏ lay down in the Abbot's room and was not concerned whether people came in or went out. Lecturer Manhwa entered the room, and Kyŏnghŏ would not sit up. Manhwa asked Kyŏnghŏ: "Why do you stay in bed?" Kyŏnghŏ responded: "Those who have nothing to do stay like this." Manhwa left the room without inquiring further. The next spring, Kyŏnghŏ moved to Ch'ŏnjang hermitage on Yŏnam Mountain where his brother, Sŏn master T'aehŏ, was staying with their mother.

Kyŏnghŏ described the experience of his enlightenment in a poem and a *gāthā*. Both pieces were as elevated as a canyon a thousand times deeper than two arms extended, and so wide that no names or words could reach across. These compositions did not fall short of the tradition kept by the patriarchs of old. His poem states:

> Upon hearing that there are no nostrils,
> I realized that the entire world is my home;
> On the path under Yŏnam Mountain in June,
> People in the field enjoy their time, singing a song of good harvest.

And the *gāthā* reads:

> Looking around, I find no one nearby,
> To whom shall I give this robe and bowl?
> To whom shall I transmit them?
> Looking around, I find no one nearby.

The four lines of the *gāthā* were added after the poem because the Master deeply deplored the situation in which no one could recognize his enlightenment, since the lineage of dharma teachers had been interrupted.

Earlier he had explained to his students, "In the school of the patriarchs [viz., Sŏn], there exists a principle and standard for transmitting the mind-dharma, which no one can disrupt. Historically, Huangbo received the dharma-transmission from Baizhang and attained enlightenment upon hearing Baizhang emulate Mazu's shouting. Xinghua attained enlightenment upon receiving Dajue's hit, which reminded him of Linji's being hit; this amounts to Xinghua receiving the dharma-transmission from Linji, even though Linji had been dead by that time. In our country, Pyŏkkye traveled to China and received transmission from Zongtong. Chinmuk was a sage representing the Buddha's transformation body and received dharma transmission after Sŏsan died. The recognition of the transmission of dharma from teacher to disciple has been strict because dharma has been transmitted from mind to mind, and mutual recognition takes place through mind.

"Alas! It has been a long time since the Sage [the Buddha] came to this world and the dharma has already deteriorated. However, from time to time a serious monk would revive the dharma by shooting the arrow of birth and death, which will result in the appearance of a perfect or half-perfect sage, who would maintain the right path with this teaching, like a lamp in the darkness, or like life in death.

"Even though I am not perfect in my dharma and have yet to examine its nature, all I have aimed to do in my life is to clarify dharma. But now that I am old, I am telling you my students that, in the future, with regard to the origin of my dharma lineage, you should record as its source the dharma of Master Yongam, whose dharma-transmission I have received, and Lecturer Manhwa should be recorded as my training teacher."

If we trace the dharma lineage in the way the dharma has been transmitted, Master Kyŏnghŏ received the dharma from Yongam Hyeŏn, who received the dharma from Kŭmhŏ Pyŏlch'ŏm. Pyŏlch'om in turn received the transmission from Yulbong Ch'ŏnggo, and Ch'onggo from Ch'ŏngbon Kŏae, and Kŏae from Hoam Ch'ejŏng. Ch'ŏnghŏ transmitted the dharma to P'yŏnyang, P'yŏnyang to P'ungdam, P'ungdam to Wŏltam, and Wŏltam to Hwansŏng. This makes Master Kyŏnghŏ the twelfth descendant from Ch'ŏnghŏ and the seventh descendant from Hwansŏng.

Master Kyŏnghŏ presided over monasteries in the western region of the Korean peninsula, including Kaesim and Pusŏk monasteries on Sŏ Mountain, and Ch'ŏnjang monastery in Hongju, all of which were well managed by him, and thus became good places for practicing the dharma. In the fall of the Year of the Boar [1899], the third year of Kwangmu's reign, Master Kyŏnghŏ moved to Haein monastery on Kaya Mountain in the southeastern part of the Korean peninsula. According to a royal order, Master Kyŏnghŏ had the Buddhist canon reprinted and established a Center for Sŏn Practice in order to provide a space for meditation practitioners. Both ordained and lay practitioners then respected him as head of the meditation school. When he gave a dharma talk on his dharma seat, he directly revealed the original nature. Using various methods he emphasized the importance of the issue of birth and death. He was truly like a diamond jewel sword and was as majestic as a lion. Those who heard his talks were able to remove all the biases and attachments as cleanly as if their bones were replaced or intestines washed.

At the beginning of a retreat for the monastic community, Master Kyŏnghŏ sat high on the dharma-seat and hit the floor of the dharma hall once with his dharma staff and said: "All the buddhas of the three time periods, all the generations of patriarchs, dharma teachers and masters in the world—they all will come and follow." Master Kyŏnghŏ struck down his dharma staff once again and said, "All the buddhas in the three time periods, all the generations of patriarchs, dharma teachers and masters in the world—they all have followed. Do you understand me?" There was no response from the assembly. The master threw away his dharma staff and came down from his dharma-seat.

A monk asked, "An ancient said, 'One can run along the old road all the while changing one's facial expressions, and one still does not fall into a feeble frame.' What does this old road refer to?" The master responded: "There are two meanings to the phrase 'old road': one is a plain path, the other, rough. What is a rough road? Below Kaya Mountain there are a thousand paths along which carts and horses pass from time to time. What is a plain path? In a canyon a thousand times wider than the distance of two arms extended, which humans cannot reach, only monkeys were hanging on the trees."

Ending a summer retreat, the master sat on the dharma seat and told the assembly, quoting a dharma talk by Dongshan: "Master Dongshan said, 'In the late summer and early fall when dharma brothers are traveling to the east and to the west, one should directly go to a place that is thousands of miles away, and where there is not even one blade of grass.' I do not say that. I say, 'In the late summer and early fall when dharma brothers are moving to the east and to the west, one should step on each and every blade of grass along the way.' Is what I say the same as or different from what Dongshan said?" There was no response from the assembly. Kyŏnghŏ waited for a while in silence and said, "Since there is no response from the assembly, I will answer the question myself." He suddenly stepped down from his dharma-seat and returned to his room. This is the way that the master directly revealed his truth.

The monasteries where the master stayed include T'ongdo monastery on Yŏngch'uk Mountain, Pŏmŏ monastery on Kŭmjŏng Mountain, Hwaŏm monastery and Songgwang monastery in the western region of the Korean peninsula. At this time, meditation halls began to spring up all over the country as if there were a competition. The number of practitioners who began to explore their faith rose up like clouds. It was very impressive. No time has been more active than this period in which the light of the Buddha shone once again and opened up people's eyes and ears.

In the fall of the Year of the Tiger [1902], the master was staying at Kŭmgang hermitage at Pŏmŏ monastery. During that time at Maha monastery, which was located east of Pŏmŏ monastery, an event was held to venerate the repainting of an arhat statue, and the Master was invited to witness the event. As Master Kyŏnghŏ arrived at the entrance to the monastery, darkness prevented him from continuing on. At that time the abbot of the monastery was dozing off. In his dream an old monk appeared and said, "Big Master is on his way. Hurry out and receive him." The abbot woke from the dream and went to the entrance of the village with a torchlight in his hand. As expected, Master Kyŏnghŏ was on his way. The abbot then realized that the old monk in his dream was the arhat. The abbot told the story to the assembly, which took all by surprise. Hearing this story, those who had earlier defamed and refused to trust Master Kyŏnghŏ came to see him and repent.

In the fall of the Year of the Rabbit [1903], on his way from Pŏmŏ monastery to Haein monastery, Master Kyŏnghŏ composed a poem:

> My knowledge remains shallow, as my name becomes high,
> The world is rough and I do not know where to hide this body.
> Fishing villages and taverns can be found wherever I go,
> But I am afraid that my name will become better known, the more I try
> to hide it.

A poem usually expresses one's will. The will of the master in this poem is to hide himself, and people whose goal lies in seeking fame would not understand this. The following year, which was the Year of the Dragon [1904], Master Kyŏnghŏ moved to Odae Mountain and then to Sŏgwang monastery in Anbyŏn village via Kŭmgang Mountain. At the time, an event to venerate the repainting of the five hundred arhats was about to be held at Sŏhwang monastery. Renowned monks from various places attended the dharma meeting in order to witness the event. When Master Kyŏnghŏ went up to the podium and gave a dharma talk, he was so eloquent that people assembled there put their palms together and expressed their admiration of the uniqueness of his talk. After the event, Master Kyŏnghŏ disappeared and nobody knew his whereabouts.

Ten years later, Chŏnghae Sŏn Center received a letter from Master Suwŏl, which stated that Master Kyŏnghŏ was seen around places like Kapsan and Kanggye with his hair grown out, wearing the attire of a Confucian scholar. Sometimes he was seen teaching people in a village, other times having a drink in a marketplace.

In the spring of the Year of the Rat [1912], the news arrived that our master had entered nirvāṇa at a village teaching room in Toha village, Ungibang in Kapsan. Two of his disciples, Hyewŏl and Man'gong, immediately left for Kapsan. They moved the master's body to Nandŏk Mountain, where it was cremated. They also retrieved a poem Master Kyŏnghŏ had composed on his deathbed. This happened in the twenty-fifth day of July in the Year of the Ox [1913], which was the year after Master Kyŏnghŏ's death.

Village elders reported that one day, Master Kyŏnghŏ was sitting under the bamboo fence, watching schoolchildren weeding. He then suddenly lay down and was not able to sit up. The Master said: "I am really tired." People carried him to his room. He refused to either eat, speak, or murmur a sound. He was lying with his legs stretched. The next morning, at about the time of sunrise, Master Kyŏnghŏ suddenly sat up, and began to write a poem with a brush.

> The moon of the mind is round all alone,
> Its light has engulfed ten thousand things in the world.

Light and things are both forgotten,
And what is this thing?

Having written this, Master Kyŏnghŏ drew an image of a circle after the poem. He then threw away the brush, lay on his right side, and passed away. That was the twenty-fifth day of April in the Year of the Rat (1912). The villagers paid their respects and held a funeral.

How sad it is! The appearance of a great dharma teacher into this world is an event that rarely takes place in ten thousand kalpas. Though brief, we had a chance to meet the dharma teacher, but failed to fully serve him and fully learn his teaching. Even on the day when he entered nirvāṇa, we were not able to take care of what was left behind by him. As in the case of the death of ancient sages, we again created reasons for regret.

Master Kyŏnghŏ was born in the Year of the Snake and died in the Year of the Tiger. He joined the monastery at the age of nine. He was fifty-six years old in secular age and his dharma age was forty-eight. Four people received his dharma transmission. Ch'imun taught his dharma at P'yoch'ung monastery located in the southeastern part of the Korean peninsula. During his later years, he gave dharma talks at Pŏmŏ monastery and left behind a poem written on his deathbed. Speaking of Hyewŏl Hyemyŏng and Man'gong Wŏlmyŏn, these two Sŏn masters served and practiced under Master Kyŏnghŏ from early on, and thus were able to fully receive the master's teaching. Each became a teacher in his own region and played an important role in edifying the people.

As for me, although I am not smart, I had a chance to meet the master and learn his teachings. Now all I can do is to show my respect to the master, since I am not capable of teaching his dharma. Nevertheless I would not dare be ungrateful to the benefit of the dharma I learned from the master. This makes four of us.

"An Account of Activities" is a record of facts, and no fictional elements are to be included. What has been stated so far regarding Master Kyŏnghŏ's enlightenment and his effort to deliver others is all truthful. If we talk about his life, we can say that he was a tall and big man. His will and spirit were strong, his voice was as loud as the sound of a bell, and he was an eloquent speaker. If he had met wind coming from all eight directions, he would have remained firm like a mountain. If he thought he would take action, he would indeed take action, and if he thought he would stop, he would indeed stop. He would not be swayed by others' influence. He showed no constraint in eating or with regard to sex. He enjoyed himself thoroughly, which caused doubts and criticisms from people. Did our master attest to the nonduality with his unbound mind as did Li Tongxuan (635–730)? Or did the feeling of suppression, as well as his awareness of adverse conditions, and his lamentation at the situation, make him hide himself in a lowly place, thus accustoming himself to humble situations? Was he making such training his own pleasure? If one is not a big bird, how can one know the elevated state of that bird? If he had not attained great awakening, how would it be possible for him not to be distracted by trivial things? In one of his poems, Master Kyŏnghŏ wrote:

Drinks emanate light, and so do women;
Will there really be a time when I say good-bye to greed, anger, or afflictions?
I do not care about the Buddha or sentient beings.
I am spending my whole life as a crazy drunken monk.

In this poem is reflected an aspect of the life of Master Kyŏnghŏ.

However, in ordinary times, Master Kyŏnghŏ ate only just enough to maintain his energy. He was quiet, said little, and did not enjoy meeting people. People sometimes recommended him to teach in cities, and Master Kyŏnghŏ usually responded: "My wish is that I won't have to set foot in the capital." This demonstrates how distinguished and notable Master Kyŏnghŏ was.

When he stayed at Ch'ŏnjang hermitage, he wore the same rugged clothes through summer and winter. Mosquitoes surrounded his body as his clothes were full of lice. Bitten by mosquitoes and infested with lice day and night, his skin was abscessed and inflamed, but he remained calm without moving, sitting like a mountain. One day a snake coiled its upper body around the master's back and shoulder. A person nearby gave him a warning, but Master Kyŏnghŏ did not care. Shortly afterward, the snake retreated by itself. Unless one was deep in concentration, and one's degree of awakening highly refined, how could anyone behave that way?

In one sitting, he would spend years, which would pass by like a moment for him. One morning, Master Kyŏnghŏ wrote the following poem:

Which one is right, the secular world or the green mountains?
Around the castle in the springtime flowers bloom all over.
If someone asks me about my concerns,
It is a song beyond the *kalpa* in the voice of a barren woman.

Master Kyŏnghŏ broke his dharma staff and threw it out. Abruptly he left his residence in the mountain. Wandering from village to village, he delivered sentient beings without resorting to habitual methods of teaching or to formalities. Sometimes he would loiter with people at the marketplace; other times he would take time alone, lying in a pine tree arbor, enjoying the wind and the moon. His capacity to transcend cannot be measured by the standard of common people.

When he gave instructions, his method was extremely tender and elaborate. When he expounded the subtle meaning of the Inconceivable, he reached the foundation of goodness and, at the same time, the abyss of evil. He had transcended the stage of overcoming good and evil by avoiding them through practice. He distinguished himself in both composition and calligraphy. He was truly the owner of a master-mind rarely seen in this world.

Alas! If all the people who left the secular world firmly proceeded along their paths with the courage of Master Kyŏnghŏ, if they clearly attended to great affairs, and thus continued the dharma transmission, the flourishing of the dharma teaching, as happened in the Nine Mountains Sŏn schools, and the continuation of the dharma transmission through the sixteen national masters will not be things of the past! Not only have the transmission of the dharma and the prosperity of dharma teaching been forsaken, but helping all the sentient beings cut off the five defilements of the world by using their bright seed of original wisdom has also been suppressed. How can we not say that to serve the secular world from deep in one's heart is the way to recompense one's debt to the Buddha? Hence I burn incense and pray from the bottom of my heart.

However, practitioners in later generations should follow only Master Kyŏnghŏ's deliverance of dharma, not his way of life, for people might believe in him but would not understand [his behavior]. Also, "to rely on dharma" means to rely on the true, correct, and unfathomable dharma. "Not to rely on the person" means not to rely on rules and ceremonies or those who go against rules and ceremonies. "To rely on" means that one takes someone as a teacher and learns from him. "Not to rely on" means that one does not take account of gain or loss, or right or wrong. Practitioners of dharma will eventually have to abscond with the dharma itself. What more can we say about gain or loss, right or wrong of an individual's behavior?

Therefore, the *Sūtra of Perfect Enlightenment* states: "Sentient beings who have aroused their minds and who have practiced dharma in the degenerate age should seek a person who owns a perfect right view. The mind of such a person will not rest on forms; though staying in the secular world, his mind will always be pure. Though appearing to have errors, he would praise holy conduct, and will not lead sentient beings to fall into improper rules and ceremonies. If one meets such a person, one will immediately attain the unsurpassed wisdom."

Such a teacher will always reveal purity whether he is walking, standing, sitting, or lying down. If sentient beings make various faults or create anxiety, such a person would not raise a despising mind or evil thought. The *Diamond Sūtra* states: "If someone tries to see me in form, or find me by sound, the person is following an evil path, and will not be able to see the Tathāgata." Also the National Master Pojo Chinul states: "When awakening their minds, practitioners should first plant right causes. Teachings such as the five precepts, the ten good acts, the four noble truths, the twelvefold chain of dependent co-arising, and the six destinies are not right causes. Believe that one's mind is the Buddha. Do not raise one thought of delusion. Know that endless kalpas of time are all empty. If one believes these, they are the right causes." If teachings such as precepts, the four noble truths, and dependent co-arising are not to be considered as right causes, what more can we say about improper precepts and ceremonies? Therefore, only search for the person who owns the correct knowledge and view, and by doing so you will find your own pure dharma eyes. Do not be deluded and search for evil faith and spoil this grave matter.

Hence, an ancient sage said: "Value only correct view, not one's behavior." And he added: "In my dharma teaching, I discuss neither meditation, nor liberation, nor observing or violating precepts, nor practice or enlightenment. I discuss only how to acquire the Buddha's insight." Doesn't this mean that one should first realize insight and only then discuss behavior? In other words, practitioners should learn Master Kyŏnghŏ's embodiment of dharma, but not his behavior. I say so in order to warn those who try to learn the unobstructed behavior of Master Kyŏnghŏ without first being equipped with the insightful dharma eye. I also caution people who are bound by views based on temporary forms and thus fail to penetrate the source of one's mind. If one is able to earn the right dharma eye, the source of one's mind will be penetrated, and then one's behavior will naturally be authentic. If this happens, whether one is walking, staying, sitting, or lying down, one will always reveal purity. In that situation, how would it be possible to be deluded by outwardly appearances, to harbor affection or hatred, and claim that "I" am right?

In the winter of the Year of the Horse [1930], dharma brother Man'gong was serving as abbot at the Sŏn center of Yujŏm monastery on Kŭmgang Mountain and sent a letter to me to Odae Mountain, asking me to write an account of Master Kyŏnghŏ's activities. I have no talent in writing, but since it is an account about Master Kyŏnghŏ, I did not dare say such a thing and appropriately wrote the facts about the master, so that future generations can read them. First, I praised the master's merit for coming into this degenerate age and accomplishing the difficult job of spreading the dharma widely. Secondly, I reproached our own fault in damaging the Buddha's teaching by being attached to deluded thoughts, keeping us outside the dharma and wasting our time. I included our teacher's poems and writings in my record of his activities. The draft was thus created, printed, and is now made available to the public.

9

Educating Unborn Children: A Sŏn Master's Teachings on *T'aegyo*

Chong Go Sŭnim

The idea that parents' behavior, thought, and virtue can influence the development of their unborn child is an old one in Korea. Called *t'aegyo*, or prenatal education, this notion is as old as Korea's recorded history. Through t'aegyo, one could help ensure that one's child would be healthy and wise, and perhaps even become a great being who would bring honor and fortune to the family. Well understood by the common people, t'aegyo was also practiced by the royal family, with its need to produce wise and intelligent rulers. Even in Buddhist circles, monks and nuns occasionally emphasized the importance of t'aegyo when giving dharma talks to laypeople.

T'aegyo: A Traditional View

For centuries it has been understood in Korea that a mother's and father's thoughts and actions affect the development of their unborn child. This influence could be either positive or negative; thus, the focus of t'aegyo was upon creating a good and nurturing environment for the unborn child.

Instructions about t'aegyo tended to vary widely. They could be straightforward, such as simply urging a daughter-in-law to maintain a gentle attitude during pregnancy, to much more complex lists of do's and don'ts. For example, expectant mothers were encouraged to surround themselves with beautiful sights and smells, while refraining from harsh or frivolous speech. Impure behavior was to be avoided at all costs. Similarly, it was said that pregnant women should eat only fruit that was free from blemish or disfigurement. Nor should a woman kill any animals while she was pregnant because that violent intention would have a negative impact on her unborn child. Likewise, it was universally understood in Korea that a pregnant woman would never attend any sort of funeral.

For fathers, the instructions tended to be simpler. Because half of the child's makeup comes from the father, the father was told to maintain a pure and upright attitude prior to pregnancy, and even afterward. He was also reminded of his responsibilities to help ensure that the mother was surrounded with a caring and nurturing environment.

These are typical examples of instructions for t'aegyo and were usually the result of both direct observations and deeply held belief structures. With families living in the same villages for generation after generation, there was plenty of opportunity for people to observe a mother's behavior and environment while pregnant, and how that child turned out. In this way, people derived cause-and-effect information on how t'aegyo worked.

For example, in one modern story, a woman was raped on her way to school, and it was several months before she realized she was pregnant. She tried all kinds of methods to cause a miscarriage but was unsuccessful. Although she greatly resented the child, after he was born she grew to love him. They had a close and loving relationship for many years, but when her son was in his early twenties he suddenly became verbally abusive toward his mother. Screaming and cursing her, he was so unlike himself that he seemed to have gone insane. This continued for a long time, and finally the mother told a Buddhist monk about this. He told her that her son's behavior was the result of the violent thoughts she had directed toward her son while she was pregnant. The monk's answer reflects the Buddhist view of cause and effect: the woman had planted a certain seed, and eventually it sprouted. The ending of this story is as interesting as the beginning: on the monk's advice, when her son would yell at her, the mother would bow very sincerely to him and apologize for her past thoughts and behavior. Gradually his abuse lessened, and eventually he returned to normal.

Confucian writers, on the other hand, often chose to place special emphasis on the role played by the mother's demeanor and virtue, reflecting the belief that virtue is the source of all success and happiness. Another Confucian perspective viewed the child as being essentially pure and uncorrupted at the moment of conception, and the direction it thenceforth takes depends on the influences it receives from the mother and father. Other themes, such as the mother needing great virtue in order to become pregnant with a child of similarly great virtue, also touched upon Buddhist ideas of karmic affinity. A common aspect of teachings about t'aegyo is the view that the unborn child is a distinct being, who, like any other being, is influenced by the behavior of the people around it.

Information about t'aegyo was generally transmitted through two routes: word of mouth and texts. Most expectant mothers learned about t'aegyo in large part from the women in their family and their mother-in-law, with family traditions of t'aegyo being handed down from one generation to the next. These often included family stories illustrating the effects of a pregnant woman's actions on the development of her unborn child. The second way information about t'aegyo was transmitted was through texts.

From ancient times in Korea, texts that focused on medical care, farming methods, and animal husbandry have played a major role in the prosperity of the Korean people. Often, these types of books were developed and published by order of the king, as part of an effort to improve the lives of the people. For example, in 1393, the first king of the Chosŏn dynasty sent instructors to every province to train medical practitioners. At about the same time, he ordered the compilation and publication of *Hyangyak chesaeng chipsŏng pang* (Collection of Native Prescriptions to Save Life), which was finished in 1397. Other texts were the work of individuals, such as the extremely influential *Tongŭi pogam* (Exemplars of Korean Medicine), which was written by the famous medical practitioner Hŏ Chun (1546–1615), and published in 1610. These types of books all contained basic information about t'aegyo, but their readers were generally highly educated medical practitioners.

Another category of texts were those written for ordinary people. These were written in *han'gŭl*, the indigenous Korean writing system, which made them accessible to virtually everyone. These also included books about farming methods, basic medical treatment, and even novels. A major type of such *han'gŭl* texts was known as *kyubang chip* (texts for the women's quarters). They were written for women and addressed topics of importance to them, such as how a good wife should behave, how to raise children, how to run a household, how a woman should cultivate virtue, and so forth. Some *kyubang chip* were published and distributed through book manufacturers; others were written by family members. These family *kyubang chip* were handwritten and conveyed the family's traditions, experiences, and philosophy from one generation to the next. These books generally remained within the family and contained, in some sense, family secrets.

One of the most famous of the *kyubang chip*–type books was *T'aegyo sin'gi* (New Theory of Prenatal Education), by Yi Sajudang (1546–1615). Written by a woman for women, it sets forth many of the principles of t'aegyo that are observed even today by pregnant women in Korea. For example, it is the earliest recorded example of the Korean saying, "Ten months in the womb have more influence upon a child than ten years with a good teacher." Published in *han'gŭl*, this book appears to have been very influential when it first appeared. Even today in Korean bookstores, modern translations of *T'aegyo sin'gi* are still among the best-selling books about t'aegyo.

An interesting footnote to t'aegyo is the role played by birth dreams. Traditionally in Asia, a woman's dream about her future child was considered to be a good indicator of that child's character. As such, auspicious dreams were highly prized, though they were said to lose their power if told too many times or told to the child.

These kinds of dreams can also be seen as a form of t'aegyo: if parents have a certain image of their unborn child, their child will be more likely to develop according to that expectation. Research in the social sciences has shown similar effects, where students will tend to perform up to a teacher's expectations, regardless of whether those expectations are based on fact. The traditional view of t'ae-gyo assumes that this effect would be just as true for unborn children.

Modern Trends in Korea

Beginning in the 1980s, t'aegyo became much more visible outside the family. This was the result of several influences, in particular Korea's rapid economic growth and the development of the commercial print and media industry. Although there had always been books about t'aegyo, the numbers and types began to increase dramatically. Further, many of the ideas that were popular began to be featured on various morning television programs, and with the growth of the Internet, there are now even web sites and chat rooms dedicated to t'aegyo.

In the late 1980s, some of the most popular books about t'aegyo were translations of European and U.S. books, many of which belonged to the popular "how to make your baby a genius" variety. However, these gradually became less popular. As one mother complained, "They didn't tell me anything about how to help my child be well adjusted and happy." Perhaps in response to feelings like this, t'aegyo books written from an oriental medicine perspective, and those translated from Japanese, became more popular. One aspect of both these types of books is that they are more likely to include concepts and approaches that reflect Buddhist or Confucian perspectives.

Books written about t'aegyo in Korea generally fall into three categories: books written by medical doctors, books written by social scientists, and those based on traditional perspectives, including oriental medicine. When medical doctors in Korea write about t'aegyo, they tend to present a biological, mechanistic view of it, emphasizing things such as the role the mother's mood plays on hormones and their effects on the child's development. One interesting thing about modern Korea is that, although only about a quarter of the population is Christian, the vast majority of doctors and pharmacists are Christians. (Reliable survey numbers are hard to find, but interviews with people holding medical degrees usually cite figures of between 70 and 80 percent.) So even when Korean doctors write books about the more spiritual aspects of t'aegyo, they tend to avoid touching upon ideas that might seem Buddhist or Confucian, such as karmic affinities or the importance of virtue.

The second category of t'aegyo book common in Korea includes those written by social scientists. Most of the ideas contained in these books have been derived from studies on the effects of early childhood experiences. For example, research found that listening to classical music as a child positively affects one's intellectual development. This has been extrapolated to presume that, if classical music can aid a child's development between the ages of one and five, it must be even better to be exposed to classical music as a fetus. This highlights a key difference between this type of prenatal instruction and conventional t'aegyo: the traditional view is that the unborn child is affected by what the *mother* experiences. People who are playing music for their unborn child are instead trying to convey the music directly to the child.

The third category of books about t'aegyo includes those based on traditional texts, which often include principles of oriental medicine. These works put the focus back on the mother's influence on the child. These are often modern versions of traditional ideas. They tend to emphasize the role that the mother's experiences and thought play in the development of the child's temperament, health, intelligence, and spirituality. Often, books of this type include explanations and worldviews that reflect themes that might be categorized as Buddhist or Confucian.

These are some of the general trends in Korean books about t'aegyo, but in reality there are many different kinds of books, which can include anything from strictly traditional methods to methods derived from an author's personal experiences. There are medical descriptions of t'aegyo, books and Web sites that emphasize Christian or Buddhist perspectives on the practice, and any combination of these. The appearance in recent decades of so much information about t'aegyo, through books, television, and the Internet, has created the sense of a t'aegyo "boom" in Korea. However, only the media have changed; the importance of t'aegyo to Korean parents has continued unabated since ancient times.

Daehaeng Sunim

As an innovative, female Sŏn Master, Daehaeng Sunim (Taehaeng *sŭnim*; b. 1927) occupies a unique place in contemporary Korean Buddhism. (*Sŭnim* is the polite form of address for a Buddhist nun or monk in Korea.) Born in 1927, she awakened at an early age and lived in the mountains for years, experimenting with what she realized. It was there that she determined to teach spiritual practice in such a way that anyone, regardless of his or her gender or occupation, could practice and awaken. The Sŏn (Jpn. Zen) center she founded, Hanmaum Seonwon (Hanmaum Sŏnwŏn; "One-Mind Zen Center"), has twenty-five Korean and international branches, with more than thirty thousand families registered as members.

T'aegyo, as Daehaeng Sunim teaches it, is really education for both parents and children. Although parents may start out practicing t'aegyo with the welfare of their unborn child in mind, it helps them to evolve spiritually as well. Further, because the unborn child reacts so quickly to the parents' practice of t'aegyo, the parents can learn a lot about spiritual practice in a relatively short time. As for the child, Daehaeng Sunim emphasizes that t'aegyo is important because the child's development in the womb will have a major influence on its life. She teaches that through t'aegyo it is possible to help one's child develop spiritually and also to dissolve the seeds of bad karma and harmful affinities.

The fundamentals of Daehaeng Sunim's teachings about t'aegyo mirror those of her teachings about spiritual practice. She begins by teaching people to have faith in their inherent nature, which she describes as Buddha-nature or Juingong (*chuin'-gong*; which, in Daehaeng Sunim's interpretation, means the true host, or doer, which is empty). Next she teaches people to entrust whatever confronts them, both good and bad, to that fundamental nature. As she says, "It has been guiding you over billions of years of evolution, so trust it now!" Thus, parents should let go of all their hopes and fears, and trust that their inherent nature is taking care of things. Further, Daehaeng Sunim teaches that when parents want to tell their unborn child something, if they entrust that to their inherent nature, all of those things will be instantly communicated to their child. This is possible because of both the nondual nature of all existence and, in the case of t'aegyo, the direct physical connection between mother and child. The next thing people need to do is continue to observe, while experimenting with what they know, and applying what they have experienced. In this way, people can develop a self-sustaining practice that will take them beyond the initial stages of awakening.

According to Daehaeng Sunim, t'aegyo is possible because every thing and life in the world reacts to the thoughts we input into our foundation, which can be called Buddha, Buddha-nature, Juingong, *hanmaum* (one mind), inherent nature, or God. This foundation has been guiding our development over countless billions of years. It is the fundamental nondual connection of all life. All beings, both living and dead, are connected through the inherent foundation they all share; what happens at one point can thus be instantly communicated to all others. When we entrust the things that confront us to our foundation, it responds to them in a comprehensive way that includes both the material realm and the unseen realms.

T'aegyo is also possible because the universe and every single thing in it are always in a constant state of flux. Nothing is fixed and immobile, so everything is free to grow and develop, including the unborn child. Regardless of what karma and genetics a child may have, those need not dictate its destiny.

In Daehaeng Sunim's teachings about t'aegyo, the effects of the mother's spiritual practice on her unborn child parallel those of traditional teachings about t'aegyo. The main difference is in the spiritual quality of Daehaeng Sunim's instructions and the underlying framework of such ideas as interconnectedness and impermanence. Many traditional teachings about t'aegyo rely greatly on observations without necessarily understanding the reasons for the observed results. This tends to limit the ability to extrapolate those teachings of t'aegyo more widely.

Daehaeng Sunim's teachings on t'aegyo are notable for their practicality. There is no need for expensive equipment or special foods, as required in forms of t'aegyo oriented toward oriental medicine or social science. Another important aspect is that in order to be able to help one's child, one must first help oneself. Although parents may have started t'aegyo out of concern for their child, in the end, they benefit as much from its practice as does their child. Further, both children and parents take with them what they have learned and experienced, and in so doing they become a force for positive change in society.

T'aegyo: Spiritual Practice and Prenatal Education is a compilation of Daehaeng Sunim's oral teachings about t'aegyo, and is drawn from both Daehaeng Sunim's public Dharma talks and interviews with laywomen who received personal instruction on t'aegyo directly from Daehaeng Sunim.

Further Reading

English translations of Daehaeng Sunim's teachings have been published in several books, two of which are *No River to Cross, No Raft to Find* (Anyang, South Korea: Hanmaum Seonwon, 2005), and *Wake Up and Laugh* (Anyang, South Korea: Hanmaum Seonwon, 2005). *No River to Cross, No Raft to Find*, is a collection of her Dharma talks that have been translated in their entirety. T'aegyo and raising children are addressed occasionally within the context of spiritual practice and daily life. *Wake Up and Laugh*, which is organized by topic and contains Daehaeng Sunim's teachings across a wide variety of issues, has a short section on t'aegyo.

    Fred Jeremy Seligson's *Queen Jin's Handbook of Pregnancy* (Berkeley, Calif.: North Atlantic Books, 2002) is the best presentation of the traditional Korean view of t'aegyo available in English. Seligson's *Oriental Birth Dreams* (Seoul: Hollym, 1989) is also an outstanding collection of mostly Korean birth dreams, and indicates their importance in Asian cultures. In Korea today, one of the most popular works on t'aegyo continues to be a modern *han'gŭl* edition of Yi Sajudang's *T'aegyo sin'gi* (New Theory of Prenatal Education) by Ch'oe Samsŏp and Pak Ch'an'guk (Seoul: Sŏnbosa, 2002). The editors, both doctors of oriental medicine, provide a modern commentary to the main text.

T'aegyo: Spiritual Practice and Prenatal Education

If you have thought about your role as a parent or future parent, you will realize that one of the most important things you can ever do is to raise a wise and good child. Unfortunately, most people don't try to do this until after their child is born. *T'aegyo*, or prenatal education, is possible before, during, and even after pregnancy, and should be done by both the mother and the father. This time is a unique opportunity to help raise the consciousness of your child, while dissolving the karmic, genetic, and spiritual hindrances that it has accumulated over countless lives. The time before birth, and even the months after, is when what you teach your child and what you expose it to will have deep and lifelong effects.

T'aegyo is possible because everything and every being are directly connected to each other, and t'aegyo's effects are possible because nothing in the
universe is fixed and unchanging. Every single thing is constantly changing and
manifesting anew. Further, the essentials of spiritual practice are basically the
same for prenatal education. Ideally, every parent would have a well-developed
spiritual practice before trying to get pregnant, so perhaps it would be best to
begin by talking about the essentials of spiritual practice.

THE ESSENTIALS OF SPIRITUAL PRACTICE

All beings, living and dead, and everything in the universe share an inherent
foundation that has guided us over aeons of evolution. Through it, everything
is connected. Through it everything, including the spiritual and material realms,
works together as one. This inherent foundation gives rise to all things and all
things return to it, and it has the ability to take care of everything we encounter in our daily life. Sometimes this foundation is called Buddha-nature,
sometimes it's called Juingong ("the true doer, which is empty"), inherent nature, or true self. Many names have been used to describe it, but these words
are just attempts at pointing people in the right direction; you have to understand for yourself what these names are trying to express. Sometimes people
ask, "If I could just see my foundation for myself, it would be so much easier
to have faith," but our foundation is not a fixed, material thing that can be
grasped with the senses.

The very first step of spiritual practice is to trust the ability of your inherent
foundation. It has guided you through all your lives, it is endowed with abilities beyond your imagination, and is the source and destination of everything,
so have faith in it and trust that it can take care of whatever it is that confronts
you. You must believe in the ability of your inherent foundation. It surrounds
us and is present throughout our lives; it is so close and ever-present that
many people overlook it.

The second step is letting go: let go of all of the things that confront you and
entrust them to your foundation. Let go of everything that arises from outside
or inside, and trust that your foundation will take care of all of that. Even if
things seem to be going well or going badly, let go of that and entrust it to your
foundation. Try to learn to rely upon your inherent nature rather than your
fixed ideas about what constitutes something going well, or not.

The third step is to observe. Observe what happens when you let go. Let go
and bravely go forward in your life while observing. See what happens after
you let go, and pay attention to how things develop and turn out. And be sure
to let go again of the results of what you experience. If things go well, let go
with gratitude, and when they don't, let go and think of that as your home-
work. Let go of all thoughts such as "I did," "I experienced," "so and so did
this or that to me," and so forth. Letting go doesn't mean pushing away thoughts
or feelings; it means that once you become aware of them you turn them over

to your foundation. By experimenting and applying yourself like this, you will awaken to your foundation. Faith in your inherent foundation, letting go and entrusting, observing, and applying what you understand form the essentials of spiritual practice.

EVERYTHING IS ALWAYS CHANGING

Inherently everyone and everything is changing and manifesting every instant. There is nothing that is stationary and unchanging. This is also the true meaning of the words "nothingness" and "emptiness." It is not that there is a void or vacuum; rather there is no unchanging essence or substance that remains the same from moment to moment. There is nothing that carries over from one instant to the next. But instead of some great vacuum, everything everywhere is filled with change and potential and ability. Everything is always changing from one thing to the next; even time is not absolute. There is no fixed future or present; not even the past is fixed and unchanging. This is why it is said that everything is empty.

The fact that everything is empty also means that even our karma is not fixed and unchanging. What has already manifested is already gone, what is here is passing away every instant, and what has yet to manifest is not inevitable. Even if a cave has been dark for a thousand years, the darkness still vanishes the instant you shine a light in it. No matter how bent and twisted a piece of metal may be, once you throw it into a blast furnace, it is melted down so that pure metal is reborn from it. In the same way, when we entrust the things that confront us to our foundation, they melt down and are transformed into bodhisattvas. The light and ability of your inherent nature is beyond anything you can imagine—please don't ignore it. Too many people treat this fact casually, without thinking about what this truly means and implies.

EVERYTHING IS CONNECTED

Through the inherent foundation, Buddha-nature, all consciousnesses and matter are connected to each other. Inherently all beings are sharing the same life, the same mind, the same body, working together as one, and sharing all things together. Everything and everybody, both living and dead, are connected; nothing is separate. Your inherent foundation encompasses all of the lives in your body; it encompasses both the realm of the living and the dead; it encompasses the past, present, and future; and it encompasses this universe and every other universe.

In addition to the spiritual connection they share with all other beings, a mother and her unborn child also share a direct physical and emotional connection. If a mother drinks alcohol, the alcohol circulates in the baby's body. If the mother is under a lot of stress while pregnant, there is a greater chance that her baby will have a low birthweight. What a mother does and thinks while pregnant influences her child. The traditional belief that expectant mothers should avoid being exposed to things like violence, harsh speech, or even the killing of fish or chicken, isn't some old superstition.

HOW T'AEGYO WORKS: RELYING UPON THE FOUNDATION AND DISSOLVING OBSTACLES

T'aegyo, educating your unborn child, is possible because of this inherent connection between all beings. When you let go of the things that confront you and trust your foundation, your Buddha-nature, you and all beings become one through the foundation. When this happens, your thoughts and feelings are communicated to all beings, both living and dead. Thus the thoughts and outlook that you give rise to are perceived by the child's consciousness and the lives that make up its body.

Further, when you rely upon the foundation and entrust it with what confronts you, energy and light circulate and your level of consciousness is raised, together with that of your child. When you connect with the foundation like this, your spiritual level raises, and you become like a bright light that raises the level of the people around you. Because your unborn child is still a part of your body and is also developing so rapidly, it is very susceptible to the influences it is exposed to within the womb. Thus, it is much easier to help your child at this stage than after its growth and development have slowed.

Even if you receive a child with a lot of bad affinities, you can dissolve that karma through prenatal education. Everything is constantly changing; nothing is fixed. This is the meaning of "everything is empty." Through letting go and entrusting while having faith in our foundation, we can dissolve the seeds of accumulated karma. We change our future when we stop re-inputting that karma. Suppose I am short-tempered and always fighting: if I learn about my foundation and practice entrusting it with whatever arises from both inside and out, then gradually I'll become a more patient and flexible person. These actions and thoughts also greatly affect your child. A fetus gets its oxygen and food from the mother; how could her spiritual state not affect the fetus? If the mother is habitually short-tempered and irritable, that is what the child is going to learn. You can even see this same thing with young children. Look at how they learn from their parents: if dad swears a lot, the child will start using those words. Children absorb their parent's fears, values, and even their political views. It's easy to imagine how much stronger this effect is with the mother and unborn child sharing so many spiritual and physical connections.

Relying on and returning to our foundation actually causes our karma to dissolve. Why? The source of all bad karma is ignorance of the foundation and ignorance of the nondual nature of everything. When one becomes aware of this foundation, the roots of all evil karma and bad affinities naturally dissolve. Everything arises from our foundation, so that is the place we have to return things to. It's like throwing various types and pieces of metal into a furnace that melts them all down and turns them into pure gold. The ability of your foundation is infinite and profound beyond anything you can imagine. Because the mother and fetus don't exist separately, if the mother has faith in her inherent nature and practices entrusting and observing, the karma of the fetus will also melt away, and its level of consciousness will be uplifted. This is a wonderful chance for the child, a chance to move in a new direction, free from the impulses of karma. It's like being in a classroom for nine months. If mom understands and practices prenatal education, then her fetus is spending nine months listening to a good teacher. Imagine spending nine months bathed in the light of your inherent nature, being reminded that nothing is separate from you, that there is nothing to fear, and that you are complete as you are, lacking nothing. In this way, your child's karmic hindrances are naturally dissolved and your child becomes more aware of its fundamental nature. Thus, your child naturally lives a wise and good life.

In many ways, pregnancy is a good time for mothers to take up spiritual practice. Because of their connection with their child, they can see the effects of their thoughts almost immediately. And if the mother has had more than one child, she can see how prenatal education has affected each of her children as her ability and understanding of t'aegyo have increased.

EVERYTHING DEPENDS UPON MIND

If the mother thinks something is sublime and beautiful, then that is the environment the child is bathed in. But if she just listens to music, feeling impatient or thinking about how tired she is, then those thoughts and feelings, not the music, are what is communicated to the child. It is the same for what she sees, tastes, and feels. This is the key to t'aegyo, for it is the mother's thought and intention that are communicated to the child. For example, there was a woman who really couldn't stand cockroaches, and when her first child was born, that child also was afraid of them. However, when she was pregnant with her second child she understood t'aegyo better, so every time she saw a cockroach she remembered to say to herself, "Oh, you are sharing this world with all of us, as part of one big family." This child was born completely unafraid of bugs like cockroaches, spiders, ants, and so forth. Imagine a child that, through mind, has heard "Oh, you are sharing this world with all of us, as part of one big family," ever since it was conceived. Imagine how welcome and connected to all other life that child would feel.

Because the unborn child responds to the mother's mind, anyone, regardless of her circumstances, can practice t'aegyo. Even if a woman is too poor to afford good food or the medical care that is often associated with pregnancy, this doesn't have to be a problem, because through t'aegyo, she can help compensate for those things. Wise and kind thoughts from the mother will have a tremendous, positive effect upon her unborn child. Although the mother may live in a run-down, ugly area, if her thoughts are beautiful, that's what the baby feels.

More beautiful than pictures or music is the wisdom that sees everything as not separate from yourself. Beauty is knowing that "I also used to be like that" or "this is something sent from my foundation in order to teach me" when something hateful or frustrating confronts you. Everything depends upon the thoughts you raise.

By the way, too much aspiration for your child is not good. Too much ambition regarding your child's future can be like giving too much fertilizer to a plant: it can damage and deform both your child and yourself. Often these kinds of ambitions represent an attitude that places excessive value on social status or material things. It's okay to have great hopes for your child, that he or she will be happy, wise, virtuous, successful, and so forth. However, as your child grows up, be aware of its own level and don't force it too much. If you could choose only one thing for your child, let it be wisdom. A child in touch with its fundamental nature will naturally avoid bad things or harmful acts, and will instead develop affinities with good things and grow up into a good person.

EXPERIMENTING

Merely knowing something is not enough—you have to be able to put it into practice and use it whenever you need to. It is only by applying what you know and experimenting with it that you can truly make it your own. Try to let go and rely upon your foundation, and observe how a single thought can affect your child. For example, if your baby is in a bad position in your womb, then by raising the thought, "my baby needs to move so that it can be born head-first," and entrusting that thought to your inherent nature, the baby will move into the proper position before being born. Really! This very example has happened to so many members here! Everything depends upon mind. All matter follows mind. Few people believe this anymore. Material things have become so important. People these days think that material things came first, but before that there was mind, what's sometimes called One Mind, or inherent mind. Sometimes it's called our foundation, or sometimes Juingong, but everything, both material and immaterial, follows this One Mind. It is taking care of everything, both spiritual and material, and when we entrust it with what confronts us, it takes care of things so that they turn out for the best. Even if the doctor tells you there is something wrong with your baby, by wholeheartedly entrusting that situation to your inherent foundation, the situation will improve much easier. If you keep thinking "my baby is sick," and so forth, this will make it harder for your baby to change.

If you plan to have children, you should learn ahead of time how to practice prenatal education. Everything takes practice. Start with what belief you possess and try to entrust what arises in life to your foundation. Pay attention and observe what happens. As you try to apply this, you will see the results of your practice and your faith will increase. Never cling to the results: whether they're good or bad, just keep letting go and trusting your inherent nature. If you try to cling to what you experience, it will become a problem and will prevent you from growing. Everything is flowing, everything is changing. There is nothing you can stick thoughts of "I" or "mine" to. "I did . . . ," "it's mine," "She did this or that to me," these types of thoughts are the source of so much suffering. They are attempts to cling to and immobilize what is always changing. So just let them go with a laugh and trust your foundation. These teachings are useless unless you try to apply them to the things in your life. As you experiment and understand the nature and ability of your fundamental mind, your own practice will become your guide for practicing t'aegyo, and by practicing t'aegyo you will deepen your own practice. Start with small steps, with the things right in front of you.

Several years ago there was a couple that came here. They were both quite good looking, but it was because they had cosmetic surgery. When their first child was born, it was kind of ugly, to be frank, because it resembled its parents' original appearance. This led to several awkward situations. By the way, once something manifests in the material realm, it's harder to change. It's easier to solve these things before they are made manifest. Anyway, when the wife became pregnant again, this time she and her husband tried to visualize the image of the husband's grandfather, who had been very handsome, and entrusted that image to their foundation. This child turned out to be quite good-looking and resembled the grandfather. By entrusting and letting go of everything to Juingong, their foundation, they were able to influence the appearance of their child. The ability of our fundamental mind is truly infinite and profound. Raise an image of a healthy child, a wise child, a kind child, and if you have not become pregnant yet, this is the kind of child who will be attracted to you. If you are already pregnant, this is the direction your child will develop. Let go of greed and fear and thoughts of "I" or "mine," and try to experiment with this in your daily life.

THE ROLE OF THE FATHER

Prenatal education isn't for just the mother. The father also plays an important role. Although the mother, obviously, is more connected to the unborn child, the father provides 50 percent of the child's genetic material, and also has a special karmic affinity with the child. Thus, it's better if the father is spiritually and physically prepared before the mother becomes pregnant. This can have a deep impact upon the baby's development. If both parents are working together to practice prenatal education, in addition to greatly helping their child, the energy of both of their practice will increase. Further, the quality of their relationship will naturally affect the mother, and thereby the child. So it's important to be kind and generous with each other.

You should know that one of the principles of this universe is that like tends to attract like. So you will attract, and be attracted to, beings with a similar level of spiritual development. It is important to be aware of this before you become pregnant. Thus, the health and level of development of both the father and the mother affect what kind of child is attracted to them. The parents' level of spiritual development even influences which particular egg and sperm are attracted to each other. In this way, the spiritual practice of both the mother and the father affects even the baby's genetic structure.

WHEN TO START PRACTICING T'AEGYO

Ideally, t'aegyo should start before you become pregnant. Parents and children are drawn together according to their karmic affinity, so the time before you become pregnant is vitally important. Just as we clean and level the ground before erecting a building, it's important to prepare for the embryo before getting pregnant. Similar things gather together, so your level of consciousness, of spirituality, along with the karma you have, will play a big role in what kind of child you receive. This is why it's important for the parents not to drink or smoke too much before becoming pregnant. If your mind is cloudy or influenced by foreign substances, a child with a similar level will be attracted to you. Let go of dualistic thoughts such as "you" and "I," don't blame others, and try to practice relying upon your inherent foundation. Try to be harmonious, kind, and generous. Take care of your body and try not to worry too much. It's much better if you can have a relaxed and generous mind. Also, if you are very sincere, you can even receive a child whose level of development is higher than your own.

You should continue practicing t'aegyo even after your child is born. For the first few months or so after birth, the connection between the child and mother is almost the same as it was in the womb. Because your baby is developing so rapidly, t'aegyo while pregnant and even after birth is very effective. So don't stop just because your baby has been born. Even after this period, the same principles that you applied during pregnancy—relying upon your foundation, entrusting everything to it, and observing—can help you to raise a good and healthy child while being a wonderful mother. When you interact with someone, in addition to what you say or your body language, that person also feels your mind. People can feel the difference if you just say "I love you," versus entrusting that "I love you" to your foundation. We are all connected through our inherent foundation, our Buddha-nature, so if you input that thought into your foundation, it will be communicated to your child or spouse at the deepest level. They will truly feel it. It's the same for family arguments. Things often reach a point where nothing you say can help the situation. Instead of trying to solve the situation through words, try entrusting it to your foundation with the thought, "It's my foundation that can let us live together harmoniously," or "All beings should live together harmoniously." If you entrust things to your foundation like this, then your foundation will naturally work toward finding the solution or path that's best for everyone. Your sincere and humble mind will help melt others' stubbornness.

So many mothers have come here crying, saying that their children are behaving badly, skipping school, sleeping away from home, hanging out with bad friends, and so forth. Those problems have arisen from mind, and so must be cured through mind. Don't yell or treat your child harshly; if you do, they'll behave exactly as you treat them. If you look upon them as someone who behaves badly, that is how they will behave. Your mind and your child's mind are connected to each other—your mind and your child's mind are not two—so you should raise the thought that "Juingong, only you can brighten my child's mind," and release that thought to your foundation. If you keep doing this, the light will be turned on instantly. Like two electrical wires connecting, peace, harmony, hope, and energy are transmitted back and forth.

CHOOSING PARENTS AND CHILDREN

Everything and everyone gathers together according to their similar karma and level of development. We can see this everywhere in our daily lives. Go into any store and the apples are kept with apples, pears are displayed with other pears, and tin cans are shelved with other tin cans. Likewise, politicians assemble together with other politicians, artists naturally mingle with one another, and fishermen enjoy each other's company. In the very same way, parents gather together with their children. Even though parents and children may seem very different in this life, in past lives they created similar karma. Parents and children choose each other. You chose your parents and your parents chose you, so there's no one else to blame.

Be very careful about blaming others. One of the most spiritually damaging things you can do to yourself is to blame other people for the things that occur to you. By blaming others you are denying the law of cause and effect, and the principle of nonduality. In effect, you are saying that you had no role in causing what happened, that you had no connection with it whatsoever. When you blame someone else, you are reinforcing the false sense that someone completely separate from "you" caused you to suffer. Further, by carrying around that fixed image of someone, you are in conflict with the law of impermanence, that all things change. When you treat someone according to your fixed image of them, you also make it harder for them to grow and change. This also applies to the statements and thoughts you have about yourself.

People receive things exactly as they have made them, and how they lived in the past gives rise to the things they encounter now. There's no need to beat yourself up, but you also have to be honest with yourself about your role in causing what happened. Moreover, now is the time to correct the mistakes we made when we lacked wisdom. Entrust all of those things to your foundation and bravely go forward while observing and letting go. Inherently nothing is fixed, nothing is unchanging: this is also one of the secrets of t'aegyo. All of these things that confront us are like recordings: if we just react to them, clinging to the things we like and trying to avoid the unpleasant things, then we just perpetuate the recording. We reinput the exact same thing. However, when we entrust the things that confront us to our foundation, it's like erasing the recording. By letting go of these things and trusting our inherent nature, we dissolve those causes and stop re-creating them. And by observing and experimenting with this process we learn how our fundamental mind works.

People often ask why their children suffer, "What did she do to deserve this?" But even a child is a being with a past. It has already lived countless lives and has accumulated its own unique karma. However, each one of us is endowed with the inherent nature, the foundation, which has the ability to dissolve that karma. Everything arises from this inherent nature, and everything returns to it. It is the source of all ability and wisdom; but what will become of us if we live our lives ignoring this, always searching for something outside of us? If we just live according to the karma we've created in the past, just reacting to it as it confronts us, we will be enslaved and bound by it. If you just react to it, clinging to the things you like, and trying to push away things you don't like, when can you be free? You just keep re-creating the same karma over and over. You should let go of both the things you like and what you dislike, and instead learn to rely upon your foundation. By doing so, you will free yourself as well as your unborn child, allowing him or her to live a wise and better life.

CONCLUSION

When children are born into this world, they are bound to experience various difficulties, but through practicing t'aegyo you can give them the wisdom and awareness of their foundation that will help them to overcome those things wisely.

Not only is t'aegyo, prenatal education, possible, but its effects are greater than most people imagine. Through t'aegyo you can help dissolve your child's bad karma, raise its level of spiritual development, and help it to have affinity with good things. T'aegyo can be done before you become pregnant, while you are pregnant, and even in the months after your child is born. Ultimately, the essence of t'aegyo is not different from the essence of spiritual practice.

All parents want what is best for their children. All parents hope that their children will grow up to be healthy, happy, and successful. And yet, how many parents have shed bitter tears over their children? If offered a chance, they would instantly take their child's hardships upon themselves. But that is not possible. So, instead, teach your child to rely upon and return to the foundation. Teach your child that everything arises from there and returns there. Teach your child to return all of the things that confront him or her to that place, the foundation.

Let your children know, including those who have been born and those who are not yet born, that everything in the universe is connected through the same inherent foundation. Everything works together as one. So never view things dualistically. Other's minds are not separate from your mind. Teach them to completely entrust whatever confronts them to their foundation and go forward bravely, regardless of whether things seem to be going well or not. If, by practicing t'aegyo, you can help your child become aware of this, then he or she will naturally sense whether something is good or not, and will make positive and constructive choices.

Thus, even though your children experience some hardships, they will not make it worse through bad choices. Even if they suffer, by entrusting everything to their foundation they will dissolve the seeds of harmful karma and will strengthen good affinities. Then, not only will the level of consciousness of your children improve, the overall spiritual level of society will also improve; the world that your children will live in will become better and wiser. If you can convey this wisdom to your children, how could they not but live good and happy lives?!

Confucianism and Neo-Confucianism

—10—

A Party for the Spirits:
Ritual Practice in Confucianism

Hongkyung Kim

Confucianism in Korea today is practiced as a "religion" on three levels. These levels progress from formal institutionalized practices, to practice within the household, and to practice as it informs personal ideology, which then influences individual actions.

Formal, institutionalized Confucianism is performed by socially recognized religious organizations that focus on disseminating Confucian ideology widely in order to revive Confucianism as a "glorious" tradition. Compared with other religious groups in Korea, these institutions are loosely organized and less closely linked to the general public. However, it is these very organizations that formally represent contemporary Confucianism in Korea. Building on the identification of Confucianism with Korean tradition, these organizations have strived to escape from the predicament caused by modernization and have periodically performed diverse activities, including the rituals that symbolize contemporary Korean Confucianism.

The best-known Confucian organization today is the Sŏnggyun'gwan, named after the National Confucian Academy of the Chosŏn dynasty. This institution represents a legitimate succession within the tradition and has been mostly recognized as such by the Korean public, recognition additionally merited by the fact that it is located in the same place where the academy used to be. The Sŏnggyun'gwan is also loosely connected with several local Confucian organizations affiliated with traditional Confucian academies (Hyanggyo) and private academies (Sŏwon). Beyond this network of institutional affiliations, there are quite a few private organizations that have been founded to disseminate Confucian ideology, some of which even challenge the authority of Sŏnggyun'gwan by asserting their superior orthodoxy.

Among the most popular Confucian rituals performed by the Sŏnggyun'gwan is a state-level worship ritual for Confucius called Sŏkchŏn, which refers to the setting and presenting of offerings. The translated version of some of the praises used in the Sŏkchŏn ritual will be introduced later in this chapter.

Another core component of contemporary Confucian practice involves individual households. The goal of this practice is to maintain Confucian social traditions, especially its notion of the family. Thus, giving priority to the family over
the individual, they seek to preserve values that will sustain the traditional family
order. Confucian rituals performed in the household are broadly of four types:
the initiation ceremony, wedding ceremony, funeral rites, and ancestor worship.
However, if Confucian family units can be distinguished from other households
of Korea, the primary criterion here would be their commitment to ancestor worship ritual, as it surpasses the other three in its significance within Confucianism.
Even though today's practice of ancestor worship is somewhat simplified so as to
be more relevant to modern life, it still carries Confucian influence and represents the true vitality of Korean Confucianism. Confucian household procedures
will be introduced in the second part of this chapter.

The last form of Confucian practice is more or less disputable depending on
one's perspective, as this relates more to general Confucian culture, its value system and mentality, rather than to activities typically conceptualized as religious.
At this stage, followers may be identified as Confucian merely because they constitute a collective force that orients Korean society and culture toward Confucianism. Thus, many such followers may hesitate to identify themselves as Confucian. Nevertheless, considering that Confucianism is both social and cultural in
nature, we may view them as important examples of the continued influence of
Confucian values on contemporary Korean society. The third section of this chapter concerns the norms imposed on Confucian scholars in the Chosŏn dynasty,
norms that are still influential to those who would loosely be identified as Confucian. The way of life it describes may be considered "Confucian" in the context of
Korean history, whereas the same aspects might be attributed to other religions in
a different historical context.

Institutionalized Practice: "Praises in
the Ritual for Confucius"

"Praises in the Ritual for Confucius" (Akchang), which is the first set of translations in this chapter, are musical texts used in the National Confucian Shrine
(Munmyo), a Korean sanctum, during sacrificial rites commemorating Confucius
(551–479 B.C.E.). Ever since its foundation in 1397, the National Confucian
Shrine in the capital of Seoul has been a symbol of Korean Confucianism and has
sponsored a ritual worshiping Confucius two times a year, in spring and autumn.
The shrine is located in the central precincts of the Sŏnggyun'gwan. This ritual reflects the belief that worshiping the ancient sages and maturing scholars into re-
spectable Confucians are two inseparable processes.

The most important figure worshiped in the ritual is unquestionably Confucius, but all other Confucian sages are also consecrated in the ceremony. The ritual

is performed in the main sanctuary, the most sacred place among the dozens of buildings of the National Confucian Shrine. In the sanctuary, many sacred tablets representing various Confucian sages are enshrined, with the one for Confucius holding the top seat. In accordance with the Confucian guide on installing such tablets in a shrine, the tablets of Confucius's four important successors, Yanzi, Zengzi, Zisi, and Mencius, are displayed next, the order of whose names represents the hierarchy in Confucian circles according to their putative proximity to the Way of Confucius. Next to them are Confucius's ten major disciples, as listed in the Confucian *Analects* (11:2). However, since Yanzi is also included in the more important four disciples' group, his slot among the ten disciples was allocated to Zizhang instead. These ten disciples are followed by the six Neo-Confucian scholars who contributed to the development of Neo-Confucianism. Besides them, ninety-four tablets of less important Chinese Confucian scholars and eighteen tablets of Korean Confucian scholars are installed in a separate building in the shrine. Thus the worship service in the shrine is, in a broader sense, dedicated to all the sages of Confucianism.

The rituals are performed on a *ding* day of the ten heavenly trunks (*Tian'gan*) in early February and August according to the lunar calendar. On this day, not only the National Confucian Shrine in Seoul but also 330 county Confucian shrines all over the country perform the same ritual simultaneously, regardless of their size. This ritual originated in China and was known to have been held there throughout the imperial period until the early twentieth century, when many of its traditional practices were discontinued. For this reason, Korea is now the only country that has preserved this Confucian tradition. Recognizing the rarity and antiquity of the ritual, the Korean government has designated the dances, the music, and the detailed procedures of the ritual to be the country's official cultural properties. Thus, the ancestral rites have become a culturally significant event for Korean people generally.

The more fundamental purpose of the ritual is to encourage people to align themselves with Confucian teaching through recollecting the virtues and sacred lives of the great Confucian sages. In previous times it served to invest peoples' lives with a great deal of authority and significance, as Confucian edification and promotion had been closely intertwined with the traditional Korean social system for more than five hundred years, until a new era of modernization was instituted in the twentieth century. Today, however, it invokes no sense of religious obligation. Even Koreans who strictly subscribe to Confucian teachings in their daily lives do not feel any obligation to attend this national Confucian ritual. On the one hand, this impression reflects the serious failure of contemporary Korean Confucianism to institutionalize its practices. On the other hand, it represents Confucianism's own propensity to serve as a teaching or guide to live life rather than to strive to establish itself as a religious institution. Therefore, even though Confucius is from time to time addressed with the kind of splendid rhetoric used in referring to gods in other religions, he is more often commemorated as a teacher-sage. In addition, the praises are dedicated to the ritual in honor of the virtues of this great teacher, as experienced by humankind, rather than seeking to imbue him with glory of a god.

The ritual can be viewed as a genteel type of party for the spirits of the various great teachers in Confucianism. In the ritual, the virtues of the sages are glorified over and over again by praises such as the ones translated here and augmented by repeated bowings from attendants toward the shrine. Good food and wine, along with music and dance, are offered as tokens of gratitude. However, just as Confucius stated in the *Analects*, "Sacrifice to the spirits as if the spirits were present" (3:12), people only pretend that the spirits of the sages have descended on the ritual rather than believing that they are really present among them. Despite this projected existence of the spirits, anyone who has ever participated in this ritual would hardly doubt the religiosity that surrounds it.

Family Practice: *Multifarious Rites* *for Worshiping the Ancestors*

The second text translated here, *The Multifarious Rites for Worshiping the Ancestors*, was written by Yi Ŏnjŏk (1491–1553), a Confucian scholar of the early Chosŏn period. This little booklet was written as a guideline for his own family on how properly to conduct ancestor worship rituals. These rituals are one of the most important religious activities in Confucianism, and this booklet paved the way for later Confucian scholars to publish private manuals designed for the same purpose.

Confucianism in Korea eventually would prosper after the newly established Chosŏn dynasty adopted it as its state ideology in 1392. In order to promote Confucian culture, the Chosŏn government strongly propagandized its subjects to establish family shrines in individual households and to observe strict ancestor worship rituals before these shrines. However, it is doubtful that many households willingly responded to this policy during the fifteenth century. Prior to the foundation of the Chosŏn dynasty, Korean culture had been under the strong influence of Buddhism for a millennium, and the old religious lifestyle of the people would not have changed so drastically, despite the government's active promotion of Confucianism. Chosŏn society in the fifteenth century was in the midst of a transition from Buddhist traditions to Confucian ones. However, Korea witnessed a new phase in the development of a Confucian state during the sixteenth century when scholar-officials, called *sadaebu*, became infatuated with Neo-Confucianism. Yi Ŏnjŏk was one of the scholar-officials who were immensely devoted, both culturally and philosophically, to the successful transformation of Chosŏn society into a strictly Confucian one. He is among the eighteen sages of Korean Confucianism whose ancestral tablets are worshiped at the National Confucian Shrine.

Today, despite some seven hundred years of development, it is still not easy to determine how many people in Korea have accepted Confucianism as their

religion. This is primarily because Confucianism, unlike Christianity and Buddhism, is not a typical religious organization supported by the two pillars of believers and clergymen. The Sŏnggyun'gwan uses as its religious barometer the issue
of whether a household performs rituals for ancestors. Based on this barometer, it
has boldly declared that more than half of the entire population in Korea could be
considered Confucian. This conclusion may of course be an exaggeration, since
many people who observe ancestor worship rituals identify themselves with other
religions, such as Catholicism or Buddhism. (Unlike Catholicism, Protestantism in
Korea doesn't allow its believers to participate in ancestor worship in general.)
However, their declaration reflects the fact that a significant number of Korean people participate in ancestor worship rituals, which are the core religious activity of
Confucianism. Since the family is the basic unit of the Confucian community, Confucianism confers hallowed status on the elders in a family, who become ancestors
after their deaths, and promotes the holiness of families through periodic rituals to
the ancestors.

   Confucian families observe many different rituals for ancestors. In his primer,
Yi Ŏnjŏk introduces four kinds: seasonal rituals (*sije*); the memorial ritual exclusively dedicated to the deceased father (*nyeje*); memorial rituals dedicated to
close ancestors on the anniversary of their deaths (*kije*); and the grave ritual performed at the grave sites of deceased ancestors (*myoje*). Of course, these do not
represent all the rituals observed by a Confucian family throughout the year.
However, just these four kinds alone would yield four seasonal rituals, one paternal ritual performed in September of the lunar calendar, one grave ritual observed in March of the lunar calendar, and possible memorial services for parents, grandparents, great-grandparents, and sometimes great-great-grandparents
(Yi Ŏnjŏk extends the lineal range of offering rituals only to great-grandparents),
totaling at least ten rituals a year per household. Therefore, a strict Confucian
household would perform a ritual for its ancestors almost every month. Though
only a few people may observe all the stipulated obligations to their ancestors in
the hustle and bustle of contemporary life, this practice still remains as a desirable one for most Confucians.

   The translation here is preceded by a foreword encouraging the establishment
of a family shrine and the practice of ancestor worship rituals in the shrine. It is
followed by a detailed introduction to the procedures for conducting one of the
four main seasonal rituals. Other rituals were intentionally omitted in the translation, as all the Confucian rituals follow similar procedures. Like the state-level rituals performed at the National Confucian Shrine, those performed in private
households also follow several general steps, such as inviting the spirit or spirits
to whom the ritual is dedicated, greeting them with good food and fragrant wine,
making deep bows repeatedly to show respect and politeness, and saying farewell
to the spirits at the end of the ritual.

   As a matter of course, there exist minor differences among the various rituals.
For example, unlike other rituals, memorial services do not include stages in
which the spirits of the ancestors give blessings to their siblings or in which

people share the food served in the ritual. This is based on the natural reluctance to combine the partylike atmosphere of sharing food and being blessed with the sadness of commemorating one's ancestors' memorial days. As an alternative, an offering to the land spirits around the grave is a special performance that may be practiced during a grave ritual performed outdoors. However, these differences are relatively insignificant, and it may be said that most procedures are common to all household rituals. For readers who might not have experienced such rituals, the translation tends to be somewhat expository rather than literal.

Individual Practice: "Behavioral Rules of the National Confucian Academy"

Is Confucianism a religion? One of the issues frequently asserted by those who take a negative view is that Confucianism does not have a full-time clergy. If a desideratum of a religion is a full-time clergy that, from time to time, removes themselves from the secular world, then Confucianism is not a religion. But if a clergy refers to religious specialists who aspire to the holy and who strive to build a bridge between people in the secular world and the divine, thus guiding people to something beyond themselves, then Confucianism is clearly a religion. The only difference would be that it is difficult to recognize in a successful Confucian community the stray sheep that need to be guided by shepherds, since Confucianism requires that everyone involved in the religion must become a shepherd to lead this world to an eternal realm of morality. Most Confucians proudly esteem themselves as the "light and salt" of the world. If a stray sheep exists at all, it would be in our minds, which are susceptible to recurring seduction. Outside the Confucian community, however, there will be many people who need to be guided and edified. Their relationship with good Confucians is not much different from that of sheep with their shepherd.

In their rituals, the Confucians perform a role resembling that of an experienced priest in those rituals commemorating the great sages of the religion and the ancestors of the family. Like priests in other religions, they invite the gods or spirits to appear, and then appease them and communicate with them through the rituals. One must not assume, though, that an ordinary secular man adopts the airs of a dignified cleric for the sake of a successful ceremony. If we look closely at their daily lives, we may see that Confucians seek continuously to imbue themselves with a sincere religiosity that carries over into the ritual. Even though their lives are focused on cultivating such humanistic values as morality, knowledge, and social righteousness, they nevertheless abound in religious divinity. Their commitment to a moral life is as religious to a Confucian as are the worship and praise of gods to people of other religions.

"Behavioral Rules of the National Confucian Academy" (Hakkyo mobŏm) is a short primer written in 1582 by Yi Yi (1536–84), one of the most renowned

Confucian scholars in Korea, in order to advise students in the National Confucian Academy on how to lead their daily lives as aspiring Confucians. To enter the academy, students were required to pass licentiate examinations on Confucian precepts and writings and to agree to live strictly according to the rules as listed in this primer during their study at the academy. This document introduces sixteen codes of conduct with recommended practices, five of which are translated here. The sixteen codes are: (1) becoming resolute, (2) regulating conduct, (3) reading, (4) prudence in speech, (5) preserving the mind, (6) being devoted to parents, (7) being devoted to teachers, (8) discretion in friendship, (9) behavior at home, (10) behavior in serving people, (11) behavior for the civil service examination, (12) conserving righteousness, (13) respecting loyalty, (14) cultivating reverence, (15) behavior at the academy, and (16) recitation of these behavioral rules.

The praises used in each important stage of the Confucian ritual were compiled in a government document called *The Record of the National Confucian Academy* (*T'aehakchi*), which was published on the order of King Chŏngjo (1752–1800) to document the affairs of the Sŏnggyun'gwan. This book, consisting of fourteen chapters, covers all matters regarding the academy, including the history of its construction, the structure of its buildings, the procedures for Confucian rituals, and its educational programs. Among several photolithographic editions of this book that are available, this chapter uses *Kugyŏk T'aehakchi* (Seoul: Sŏnggyun'gwan, 1994), pp. 225–28. These praises are translated in the order in which they are recited in the ceremony. The first, the second, and the last ones have been used since 1397, when this ritual began; the others were added later, in 1609, according to the suggestions of Confucian scholars who felt that the existing praises were not sufficient for such a magnificent ceremony.

The Multifarious Rites for Worshiping the Ancestors (*Pongsŏn chabŭi*) was included in the *Collected Works of Hoejae*, published in 1565 by his grandson Yi Jun, after Yi Ŏnjŏk's death. Hoejae is Yi Ŏnjŏk's pen name. The translation in this chapter is based on *Hoejae chŏnsŏ* (Seoul: Taedong Munhwa Yŏn'guwŏn, 1973), pp. 579–83. According to his own testimony, Yi Ŏnjŏk's sources range from articles on ancestor worship by Sima Guang and Cheng Yi, Confucian scholars in Northern Song China, to a book entitled *Family Rites of Master Zhu Xi* by Zhu Xi in Southern Song China, to many vernacular customs common in Chosŏn at the time. This twenty-five-page primer is divided into two parts; the following excerpt is from the first part. The second part consists mainly of quotations from the Confucian scholars mentioned earlier and Yi's annotation regarding the philosophical basis for the ancestor ritual.

"Behavioral Rules of the National Confucian Academy" (*Hakkyo mobŏm*) is a short primer prescribing a normative daily life for Confucian followers. It was written in 1582 by Yi Yi (1536–84) and included in the *Complete Works of Yulgok*, which was first published in 1611. Yulgok is the pen name of Yi Yi. The edition consulted for the translation in this chapter is *Yulgok Chŏnsŏ*, Han'guk munjip ch'onggan vol. 44 (Seoul: Minjok Munhwa Ch'ujinhoe, 1990), pp. 331–34.

Further Reading

For general background on Korea's Confucian tradition and the development of the Neo-Confucian tradition of the Chosŏn dynasty, see William Theodore de Bary and JaHyun Kim Haboush, eds., *The Rise of Neo-Confucianism in Korea* (New York: Columbia University Press, 1985); Martina Deuchler, *The Confucian Transformation of Korea: A Study of Society and Ideology* (Cambridge, Mass.: Harvard University Press, 1993); and James Palais, *Confucian Statecraft and Korean Institutions* (Seattle: University of Washington Press, 1996). For the continuing impact of Confucianism in modern Korean society, see John Duncan, "Confucian Social Values in Contemporary South Korea," in *Religion and Society in Contemporary Korea*, edited by Lewis R. Lancaster and Richard K. Payne (Berkeley: Institute of East Asian Studies, 1997); and Chai-shik Chung, "Confucian Tradition and Values: Implications for Conflict in Modern Korea," in *Religions in Korea: Beliefs and Cultural Values*, edited by Earl H. Phillips and Eui-young Yu (Los Angeles: Center for Korean-American and Korean Studies, California State University, Los Angeles, 1982). For a general survey of the rituals of Korean Confucianism, see Spencer Palmer, *Confucian Rituals in Korea* (Berkeley: Asian Humanities Press, 1984).

Among the materials translated in this chapter, two are by the important Confucian scholars Yi Ŏnjŏk and Yi Yi. Although Yi Ŏnjŏk greatly influenced the formation of Yi Hwang's philosophy, he is much less well represented in Western writings on Korean Confucianism than is Yi Hwang or Yi Yi. Some valuable references concerning the philosophy of Yi Hwang and Yi Yi are Michael C. Kalton, ed., *The Four-Seven Debate: An Annotated Translation of the Most Famous Controversy in Korean Neo-Confucian Thought* (Albany: State University of New York Press, 1994); Edward Y. J. Chung, *The Korean Neo-Confucianism of Yi T'oegye and Yi Yulgok: A Reappraisal of the "Four-Seven Thesis" and Its Practical Implications for Self-Cultivation* (Albany: State University of New York Press, 1995); and Sasoon Yun, *Critical Issues in Neo-Confucian Thought: The Philosophy of Yi T'oegye* (Honolulu: University of Hawaii Press, 1991). For a collection of translated original texts on Korean Confucianism, see Peter H. Lee and Wm. Theodore de Bary, eds., *Sources of Korean Tradition, vol. 1 From Earliest Times through the Sixteenth Century* (New York: Columbia University Press, 1996).

"Praises in the Ritual for Confucius"

DEDICATION

Since the beginning of humankind, who else could have achieved such glory? The divinity of the King (Confucius) alone surpasses that of all the sages of the past. The grain for sacrificial offerings is being presented and supplemented with the highest decorum. Though the broomcorn millet and the millet are still not fragrant enough, please, King, be merciful and accept our dedication.

WELCOMING THE SPIRITS

How great the former sages were! They exalted the Way and its virtues and assisted in the kings' edification. Therefore, the people also respect and admire them so that these institutionalized rituals may be performed with adequate courtesy. Refinement and genuineness being widespread, please come and brighten us with your holy appearance, oh spirits!

THE FIRST LIBATION

Greatest of the sage kings, truly did heaven confer virtues on you! None of us would ever refuse to praise you by dedicating these songs and performing these timely worship rituals for you. The pure wine smells fragrant and the beautiful sacrificial animals are piled high like a mountain. Please come down to this sacred place as we offer the votive. (*Praise to Confucius*)

Your rice bin being so frequently empty, how deeply rooted you were! As the sage only second to Confucius unravels the way, it is dutiful for us to make sacrificial offerings to him. At this time of good fortune and purity, we have prepared all the vessels for food and wine. With glasses full of tasty wine, please come and stay with us, oh spirit! (*Praise to Yanzi*)

Binding loyalty and empathy transmitted by the mind-and-heart with one single thread, you composed *The Great Learning* and taught the world how to be righteous. You brought us a bright light, respected what you heard, and practiced what you knew. As you succeeded the former sages and enlightened those who follow after you, you naturally deserve our worship. (*Praise to Zengzi*)

What you transmitted was derived from Zengzi, while what Mencius transmitted was derived from you. There is a successive thread of chief descendants in the tradition, the backbone of which was truly secured for you. Grasping the core, you revealed the accumulated teaching and thereupon wrote *The Doctrine of the Mean*. Your harmony with Confucius will be compensated by people's veneration for billions of years. (*Praise to Zisi*)

As the Way flourished thanks to your efforts, you have glorified the King, Confucius. Based on your transmission of the Way, people began to proceed in the right direction. You are enshrined with the other sages; your accomplishment and position are really correspondent indeed. How beautiful the mandate of heaven is! The beauty has continued to be conveyed for thousands of years. (*Praise to Mencius*)

THE SECOND AND THE LAST LIBATION

You are the teacher of all kings and the paragon of all the people and of all creation. When we look up, you are overflowing everywhere; your spirit stays comfortably with us. We dedicate to you in a golden cup this wine that is so pure and tasty. We also dedicate praises to you three times and, oh, we extend proper courtesy to you out of our joy.

FAREWELL TO THE SPIRITS

Here we see the grandiose Academy, to which people offer their reverence. In this dedication to a sincere and polite ritual, prestige and procedures are harmonious and peaceful. Having been served with a fragrant sacrifice, the spirits are about to return back to their places, driving their carriages. Upon closing this beautiful ritual, we are all blessed with great fortune.

CLEARING AWAY THE RITUAL UTENSILS

In front of the offering table are a grail in the shape of an ox and another in the shape of an elephant, and in the rear row are vessels for fruit and nectars. Serving wine and food in them is fragrant and uncluttered. The proper courtesy is observed and the music is played in the background so that people are cooperative and the spirits are delighted. The ritual produces blessings; thus let us perform it without breaking courtesy.

Multifarious Rites for Worshiping the Ancestors

Build a family shrine on the east side of the main building of a house and enshrine the ancestors' tablets there. Relatives who have died without descendants are also invited to the family shrine depending upon the person's rank in the family lineage.

Secure land to pay off expenses for the rituals and prepare proper utensils to be used in the rituals.

The head of the family begins each day by taking bows to the ancestors in the shrine while burning incense.

Each outing and homecoming should be reported to the ancestors.

Each first and fifteenth day of the month are observed as the occasion for a formal visitation to the shrine.

When festive days arrive, seasonal foods should be dedicated to the ancestors first.

Major family business should also be reported to the ancestors.

In case of natural disasters such as flood or fire, or unfortunate events like robbery, save the family shrine first. Relocate all the tablets and bequeathed books first, and keep the utensils for ancestor worship ritual in a safe place; then, only after assuring their security, other household goods may be saved. In the event of the death of the head of the household, thus precipitating a change of generation, the tablets in the shrine should be reorganized, sending off the oldest ones to their respective tombs and ushering in new ones.

SEASONAL RITUALS

Seasonal rituals are performed in the middle month of each three-month season. Specific dates for the rituals are chosen by divination, usually during the last ten days of the previous month.

Before the ritual, an observation of three days of purification is required.

An altar should be set up one day before the ritual, and other memorial items, such as an incense burner, should be put in place.

Men sacrifice animals for offerings while women occupy themselves with preparing food and utensils.

At dawn, a selected assortment of food, such as fruits, sweets, and dry meat, is first served on the altar.

At daybreak, the tablets should be brought in from the shrine and placed on the altar by the host.

All participants should make two big bows to the spirits of the ancestors.

The spirits are greeted by a rite of pouring wine into the ritual vessels on bent knees following the burning of incense.

The host and hostess proceed to the altar and with help from a butler set the table with prepared foods, such as fish, grilled meat, rice cakes, noodles, rice, soup, and so forth.

The host then takes the wine from the butler and serves the first round of libation to the ancestors, beginning with the great-grandparents. After the host serves the wine, the invocator, who kneels next to him, recites a prayer.

The wife of the host proceeds to the altar and takes the wine from the butler to serve the second round of libation to the ancestors, beginning with the great-grandparents. No prayer will be recited at this time.

One of the other participants, such as the eldest sibling, the first son of the host, or one of guests, takes the wine to serve the last round of libation to the ancestors, with no prayers read.

The host goes forward again and fills the cups with wine while his wife opens the lid of the rice bowl, places a spoon in it, and changes the position of the chopsticks. All of the participants should leave the room, close the door, and remain outside for a while so that the spirits of the ancestors may take their meals.

After a period of time, the host clears his throat three times, alerting the spirits to their reentrance, and opens the door.

The host proceeds to the altar, takes the wine and food served on the altar from the invocator acting on behalf of the ancestors, and announces that those participating in the ceremony have all been blessed by the ancestors.

As a farewell to the ancestors, the host and all the other participants make two large bows and say good-bye.

The host and hostess proceed, put the tablets in a wooden coffer, and take it to the shrine.

All ritual utensils should be properly cleaned and stored under the direction of the hostess.

The host and hostess share all the offered food with people they know; this symbolizes the sharing of the good fortune they have received from the ancestors with others.

Master Zhu Xi said, "As host of the ancestor worship ritual, you must do your best to manifest the sincerity of your love and respect for your ancestors. If you are poor, make the ceremony harmonious within circumstances. If you are sick, do as much as your legs and arms allow you to. If you have sufficient wealth and strength, then you should follow all due procedures."

"Behavioral Rules of the National Confucian Academy"

The first code refers to becoming resolute. A student should first become resolute in following the Way as his responsibility. The Way is not far away, yet people do not practice it. As thousands of virtues reside within, there is no need to search for them elsewhere. Do not hesitate or doubt, waiting for something to happen, and do not be frightened or flurried. One should make it his immediate aim to raise his mind for heaven and earth, to erect moral standards for people, to resume the discontinued studies of the sages in the past, and to help create peace for the entire world. One should not entertain, in one's mind, a bit of thoughts or habits of withdrawal, of setting limits beforehand, of putting things aside, or being overindulgent with oneself. As for other occasions, such as defamations and compliments, honors and dishonors, benefits and disadvantages, or harm and fortune, one should maintain one's state of mind, not being agitated by them. Just strive to solve problems and latch on to yourself only with the resolution to become a saint until this process comes to an end.

The second code is about regulating conduct. Once a student creates the desire to become a sage, he must erase all his bad habits, fully dedicate himself only to study, and regulate his body and behavior accordingly. On normal days, he should wake up early in the morning and stay up late at night; his clothes and hat should be kept clean and tidy. His features and face should look solemn, his attitude when watching and listening should be decent, his deportment indoors should be polite, and his posture while walking and standing should be straight. One should be moderate when eating and drinking and pious when writing. Make sure that the desk and the armrest are well arranged and the room is cleaned. Abide always by nine features: the feature of the feet should be heavy; the feature of the hands should be gentle; the feature of the eyes should be calm; the feature of the mouth should be firm; the feature of the voice should be quiet; the feature of the head should be straightforward; the feature of the breathing should be silent; the feature of the standing should be virtuous; and

the feature of the complexion should be earnest. Do not look unless it is in accordance with the rites, do not listen unless it is in accordance with the rites, do
not speak unless it is in accordance with the rites, and do not take action unless
it is in accordance with the rites. The so-called things that go against the rites are
whatever violate the heavenly principle, however slightly. Should some of the
details emerge in the uncouth realm of life, behaviors or occurrences such as the
indecent faces of clowns or entertainers, the lewd voices of popular music,
games with vulgar and impudent manners, or parties with reckless drinking and
bawdy interactions should all be seriously prohibited. . . .

The fifth code is to preserve the mind. If a student desires to cultivate himself, he must rectify the mind so that he protects himself from external seduc-
tions. Only then can his mind remain calm and all aggression fade away, enabling him to attain real virtue thereafter. Thus a student should first strive to
preserve his mind in serene meditation and prevent the core of this tranquil
mind from being distracted or obscured in order to erect this great basis. If a
thought is about to arise in the mind, one must essentially contemplate the in-
cipient activating force of good and evil. If it is good, one should investigate
the moral principles in it, and if it turns out to be evil, one must completely
eradicate its root. If one continues in this way to preserve and cultivate the
mind, contemplating its movement unbrokenly, all of one's behavior will become compliant with the principle of naturalness.

The sixth code is to be devoted to one's parents. Of the hundreds of codes
for a scholar to live by, filial piety for one's parents and respect for one's elders
are the most fundamental. Of the three thousand sins, disobedience to one's
parents is the worst. Being devoted to one's parents is as follows: in the matter
of living, accomplish the rites of obeying and following the parent's order by
maintaining reverence for them; in the matter of serving, support their bodies'
physical needs by pleasing them; in the event of sickness, perform methods of
treatment and medication with apprehension about them; in the event of a funeral, fulfill the Way of meticulously observing the last moment with sorrow-
fulness; and in the event of an ancestor worship ritual, achieve the sincerity of
memorizing rites for the deceased ancestors with solemnity. Keep in mind the
sage's admonitions such as keeping the parents warm in cold weather and cool
in hot weather, arranging their beds at night, bowing to them in the morning,
notifying them when leaving and returning home, so that not a single detail is
overlooked. When everything is deemed by the student as being provided and
also no stain is added to his inherited life as a result of completing the virtues
consistently, he may be considered proficient in the matter of being devoted to
his parents. . . .

The twelfth code is to conserve righteousness. The most important thing for
a student is to distinguish righteousness from profit. Righteousness does not
aim for anything but itself. If one aims for anything else, however small, he
must be considered identical to those who pursue profit or steal. How can one
be sufficiently cautious about this? To practice goodness while seeking fame

originates in minds that pursue profit; for that reason, a virtuous man sees this as worse than making a hole in another's fence in order to break into his property: even this is not justified, much less so is the action of one who performs evil and pursues only profit. Therefore, a student should not possess even the tiniest mind of pursuing profits. In ancient times, people striving to feed their parents did not hesitate to peddle and borrow rice from others. Nevertheless, their minds were so unperturbed and pure that profits could not taint them. However, these days scholars cannot avoid the mind that pursues profit, even though they may read the books of the great sages all day long. How can this not be regretful? Although one's family exists in such poverty that he must engage in some business to feed it, he should not allow the mind of pursuing profit to sprout. In matters of refusing, accepting, taking, and giving things, it is imperative that one investigate whether it is proper. Always question if it is correct in the sight of gain and do not be indulgent, so that even a small incident will not be transgressed inappropriately.

——11——

The Great Confucian-Buddhist Debate

Charles Muller

A prominent characteristic of Korean religious and philosophical thought is its proclivity for sustained and open intellectual debate regarding fundamental principles—especially phenomenological issues that deal with the origins and manifestations of evil and goodness, soteriology, ethics, and so forth. Although Korean religious debates were never institutionalized in a formal manner comparable to a tradition like that of the Tibetan Gelukpa school of Buddhism, to which the Dalai Lama belongs, it can still be said that such debates assume a distinctive measure of importance in Korean history. For example, when one begins to study Buddhism and Confucianism in the context of Korean intellectual history, one will notice quickly that religious practice was framed in terms of such seminal debates as the Buddhist "sudden-gradual" and "doctrine-meditation" debates, the Confucian "four-seven" debate, and so forth. It can further be observed that this Korean proclivity for religious debate tends to be delimited by a well-defined and distinctly repeated pattern of discourse: that of essence-and-function (*ch'e-yong*).

Essence-and-function is a traditional East Asian approach toward interpreting the spiritual and material aspects of human existence, which understands all phenomena to have two contrasting, yet contiguous, aspects: (1) an underlying, deeper, more fundamental, hidden aspect, called "essence" (Kor. *ch'e*), and (2) a visibly manifest, surface aspect, called "function" (Kor. *yong*). This pair has many analogues in East Asian thought, one of the earliest and most readily apprehensible being the "roots and branches" paradigm taught in the *Great Learning*. The essence-function paradigm is applied as an interpretive tool to articulate a wide range of situations in human behavior and society at large, but its most common application is seen when classical East Asian philosophers are attempting to describe the complex relationship of the substance of the human mind as juxtaposed with people's manifest (moral) behavior and physical appearance.

While there are a few notable exceptions, the pervasive view regarding the human being that developed within the classical East Asian tradition is that despite all the obvious evil and suffering in the world, the human mind is, at its most fundamental level, something good and pure. This notion is expressed in the "humaneness" (Kor. *in*; Ch. *ren*) of Confucius, the "four beginnings" of Mencius, as well as such images as the "uncarved block," "newborn babe," and so on, of the *Daodejing* (*The Way and Its Power*), as well as the "buddha-nature" in East Asian Buddhism. As a rule, people's minds (interpreted as the "essence" of human beings) are presumed to be basically good. But whether or not this goodness actually ends up being reflected in their day-to-day activities, and if so, to what extent, depends on a wide variety of factors, including the degree of one's own effort/attention, along with contingent factors—especially the quality (or "orthodoxy") of the religious instruction with which one has been inculcated. This basic essence-function approach is followed and elaborated upon by generation upon generation of scholars and commentators in the Confucian, Daoist, and Buddhist systems in China, Korea, and Japan.

The articulation of this paradigm and its analogues first appears in classical Chinese philosophical works. But the close geographic proximity of Korea, along with the concomitant extensive and continuous exchange of commodities and ideas, enabled Koreans to participate in the Chinese philosophical world at a relatively early period—and even to make serious contributions to the greater East Asian religious discourse, as many Korean thinkers traveled to the Tang and Song Chinese centers of learning and made their own mark. Thus, Koreans learned Chinese religion and philosophy well and, bringing it back to their homeland, made their own enhancements and even took off in some novel directions of their own. One of these enhancements or divergences is an even stronger degree of attention paid to the essence-function paradigm, and this is coupled, as mentioned earlier, with a pronounced affinity for open philosophical confrontation.

Philosophical confrontation becomes a notable dimension within Korean Buddhist practice, especially in the context of the development of the Sŏn (Ch. Chan; Jpn. Zen, or "Meditation") school. The advent of this school in Korea led to an ideological conflict between the older, established, doctrinal schools of Buddhism and the newly imported Meditation school, whose adherents regularly opined that textual studies were an impediment to the attainment of the Buddhist goal of enlightenment.

In Korea, the relation between the doctrinal teachings of Buddhism and meditation practice was an issue that has been debated in almost every generation, including the current one. The arguments for the pro-meditation group were initiated by early Sŏn teachers, and such positions are still expressed in Korean Sŏn Buddhism today. What eventually became more common in Korean Sŏn, however, was a discourse from within the tradition that sought a middle ground, advocating an approach to cultivation that included both meditation and textual study in a balanced format. This sort of position was advocated through the centuries by numerous leading Buddhist figures, including Kyunyŏ (923–73), Ŭich'ŏn (1055–1101), Chinul (1158–1210), Kihwa (1376–1433), and Hyujŏng (1520–1604).

A roughly parallel Korean intra-Buddhist debate—which involved many of the same participants as in the doctrine-versus-meditation debate—can be seen in the controversy regarding whether enlightenment was something that is attained suddenly or gradually. Again, this argument also has its roots in China, but after fading away on the continent, it was taken up with fervor in Korea, where it has continued to spur debate within the Korean Chogye school of Sŏn down to the present day.

The greatest of the Korean debates regarding the nature of the mind, strikingly analogous to the previously-introduced Buddhist doctrinal-meditative and sudden-gradual oppositions, is the Neo-Confucian question of the precise character of the relation of the "four beginnings" (four good qualities of the mind that Mencius understood as being latent in all people) and seven feelings (seven kinds of mixed-quality emotions that arise secondarily to the four beginnings), which was first taken up between the Neo-Confucian scholars Yi Hwang (T'oegye; 1501–70) and Yi Yi (Yulgok; 1536–84), and later rejoined by their disciples.

All three of the preceding debates are framed by a clear thematic pattern: (1) the degree to which the goodness, purity, or enlightenment that exists within the human mind can said to be innate, or even originally complete; (2) based on this innate purity, what specific factors (if any) are necessary to bring about its completion; and (3) what the relationship is between the innate (good, enlightened, pure) nature of the mind, and the discordance, affliction, and evil that we see appearing in everyday human activity. No matter what the degree of divergence in the interpretation of the various aspects of the previously-expressed pattern, the soteriological discourses of the mainstream early and classical period Korean philosophical/religious systems operate within this framework. They all basically agree on the point that the fundamental nature of the mind is good, and that there is a problem somewhere that leads that fundamental nature not to manifest itself properly—that is, to function discordantly. Thus, it is a problem that can be identified as lying within the conceptual framework of essence-function.

The Buddhist-Confucian Debate

In this chapter, we will read representative selections from another significant debate that occurred in the Korean philosophical arena—that which occurred between the Neo-Confucians and the Buddhists in the late Koryŏ and early Chosŏn periods. This also happens to be a debate that is wholly grounded in the core points of the issues introduced earlier. We will look at the two most important, roughly contemporary, representative works that emerged from each side. These are the Pulssi chappyŏn (Array of Critiques of Buddhism) by the Neo-Confucian scholar Chŏng Tojŏn (Sambong; 1342–98), and the Hyŏnjŏng non (Articulation of Orthodoxy) by the Buddhist monk Kihwa (Hamhŏ Tŭkt'ong; 1376–1433).

These two treatises do not actually constitute a direct, ongoing dialogue between contemporaries as does the four-seven debate, since Kihwa probably wrote his piece sometime after Chŏng's death. But since the *Hyŏnjŏng non* is clearly written as a direct response to the *Chappyŏn*, as well as a response to the entire gamut of critiques lodged by Confucians against Buddhists since the dawn of their conflicts, the juxtaposition of the two texts can certainly be seen as one of the major philosophical debates of the Korean tradition. This case is especially interesting, since, even though the argument was ostensibly conducted between two distinct, competing philosophical/religious traditions, the degree to which both sides automatically ground their basic arguments in the structure of essence-function makes an even clearer point about the role of that structure as an a priori framework of classical Korean philosophical debate.

As a philosopher, Chŏng Tojŏn was the product of a long-developing Neo-Confucian tradition, which started in China and worked its way into Korea, and which had as a major part of its raison d'être the project of exposing the harmful nature of the Buddhist teachings to both the moral well-being of the individual and the stability of society in general. Although Confucian criticisms of Buddhism start as far back as the Tang dynasty with the Chinese literatus Han Yu (768–824), it is in the works of the Song Neo-Confucian masters, most importantly the Cheng brothers (Cheng Hao [1032–85] and Cheng Yi [1033–1107]) and Zhu Xi (1130–1200), that the critique takes on its mature philosophical form. The target of the Song Neo-Confucian critique was particularly Chan (Sŏn) Buddhism, the school that had distinguished itself for its ostensive rejection of book learning and societal norms.

During the two centuries after Zhu Xi, a roughly analogous confrontation between the Neo-Confucians and Buddhists developed in Koryŏ dynasty Korea, but with some important distinctions. One of the most critical differences between the two scenarios was the markedly greater degree to which the Korean Buddhist establishment was embedded into the state power structure as compared with the situation in Song China. Leaders of the Buddhist establishment owned large tracts of tax-free territory, traded in slaves and other commodities, and were influential at all levels of government. There were too many monks who were ordained for the wrong reasons, and corruption was rampant. Thus, the ideological fervor with which Neo-Confucianism arose in Korea had a special dimension, since the ire of the critics of Buddhism not only was fueled by the earlier philosophical arguments of the Cheng brothers and Zhu Xi but was exacerbated by the extent of the present corruption. There was a decadent, teetering government in place, inextricably wrapped up, in the view of these critics, with a dissolute religious organization.

With this less-than-exemplary Buddhist establishment as its target, the Korean Neo-Confucian anti-Buddhist polemic grew during the twelfth and thirteenth centuries, reaching its zenith at the end of the fourteenth century when, with the 1392 coup d'état directed by the Confucian-backed general Yi Sŏnggye (1335–1408), which led to the founding of the Chosŏn dynasty (1392–1910), the Buddhists were pressed out of the seat of political power. The Buddhists over time lost much of their influence with the government, becoming far less visible in the metropolitan areas. The final polemical push for the Buddhist purge came in the form of the essays of Chŏng Tojŏn, Yi Sŏnggye's main political adviser, who would play a major role in the development of the political structure of the new Chosŏn dynasty. Chŏng wrote a few philosophical essays that were critical of Buddhism, but his final and most directly anti-Buddhist polemical work (completed shortly before his assassination in 1398) was the *Pulssi chappyŏn*.

The Confucian Attack: The *Pulssi Chappyŏn*

In his *Array of Critiques of Buddhism,* Chŏng focused on comparisons of Buddhist and Confucian positions on issues of doctrine and practice, with the main intention of demonstrating that Buddhist doctrine was internally contradictory and even deceptive. In Chŏng's view, it was not only necessary to restrain the Buddhist establishment at the present moment: it was desirable to seriously curtail and, if possible, permanently put a stop to the activities of this dangerous belief system. His critique is extensive, covering every aspect of the Buddhist tradition as it was generally understood at the time. Given the composition of Korean Buddhism at this time, the primary object of his criticism was the Sŏn school, which the Neo-Confucians perceived as being nihilistic, denying the importance of human relationships, denying respect for the state, and even denying Buddhism's own principle of cause and effect.

The Arguments of the Pulssi chappyŏn

Chŏng starts off, in the first two chapters of the treatise, with a critique of the Indian notions of karma and transmigration, arguing against these "foreign" Indian paradigms, favoring instead Chinese cosmological schema that were developed in connection with the *Yijing* (*Book of Changes*) and its commentaries: yin/yang, the five phases (*wuxing*), the material (*hun*) and spiritual (*po*) souls, and so forth. He points out that, when it comes to such practical matters as healing disease, virtually all people, Buddhists included, rely on Chinese yin/yang cosmology in the form of traditional medicinal practices—a tendency that is still evident in East Asia today.

In the third through fifth chapters, Chŏng moves into the core of his philosophical argument, attacking Buddhism at one of its traditional weak points: that of the contradictory character of its discourse on the nature and the mind. He cites passages from the *Śūraṃgama-sūtra* and from the writings of the Koryŏ scholar-monk Chinul that show a wide range of inconsistency between the various accounts of the relation between the mind (*xin*) and the nature (*xing*). As Chŏng leads us through these citations, in one Buddhist text, the nature is said to be equivalent to the mind; in another, it is an aspect of the mind; then it is a principle contained in the mind; and then, in another text, a function of the mind. This line of criticism is carried into chapter 6, where the focus comes to be placed directly on the relationship between the mind and its external, functional manifestations. To clarify the Confucian position (which Chŏng claims is consistent, both rationally and metaphysically), he cites the Mencian "four beginnings" that are innate to humans, along with their four associated functions of humaneness, propriety, justice, and wisdom.

Chŏng's argument continues on through several more chapters, addressing issues such as the Buddhists' abandonment of societal obligations, their perverted application of the notion of "compassion," criticism of the Buddhist idea of two levels of reality, the practice of begging, and, most of all, the escapist/nihilistic views of Sŏn. All can be summarized in his view that the components of Buddhist doctrine are disconnected from each other and incongruous. They are conveniently used for excusing responsibility, the converse of providing a viable system of values. Confucianism, by contrast, is completely aligned between essence and function, is unitary and without contradictions, teaches a concrete system of values, and articulates a clear relationship between inner and outer.

The Buddhist Response: The *Hyŏnjŏng Non*

Kihwa, born in 1376, was thirty-four years Chŏng's junior. The son of a diplomat, he was considered to be one of the brightest young scholars of his generation, excelling at the recently established national academy of Confucian studies, the Sŏnggyun'gwan—where Chŏng also was on the faculty for a time—quite likely even during the period that Kihwa was enrolled as a student. During the course of his studies there, however, Kihwa was continually attracted by the Buddhist teachings, passing through a phase during which he was confused about which course he should follow. (Kihwa describes this period of his life and how he came to his final decision in a passage from the *Hyŏnjŏng non* that is translated later in this chapter.)

When Kihwa was twenty-one, the trauma he experienced at the death of a close friend finally tilted the scales irreversibly in the direction of Buddhism, and he joined the order. He eventually became the disciple of the leading Sŏn master of his generation, Chach'o (Muhak; 1327–1405), under whose tutelage he learned the approach to *kongan* (Sŏn cases) training derived from the Imje (Ch. Linji; Jpn. Rinzai) school of Sŏn. Yet at the same time, despite this affiliation with the ostensibly "antitextual" Imje tradition—due, no doubt, to the influences of his literary training—Kihwa went on to become one of the most prolific Buddhist writers of his period, exerting significant influence on the subsequent character of Korean Sŏn, most notably through his commentaries to the *Perfect Enlightenment Sūtra* and the *Diamond Sūtra*.

Kihwa's life span was almost exactly divided between the years prior to and after the dynastic transition from the Koryŏ to the Chosŏn, during the course of which the Buddhists were ejected from their long and intimate relationship with the rulership. During his career as a Sŏn teacher, Kihwa rose to the position of being the leading Buddhist figure of his generation. While the Confucians had succeeding in bringing enough pressure to bear to eliminate the title of National Teacher, which had for centuries been granted to the leading Buddhist figures, he was still posthumously awarded the title of Royal Preceptor, which reflects the degree of respect that Kihwa commanded, despite the changing atmosphere. This also means that Kihwa, as the leader of the Korean *saṃgha* during this period, was the one who ended up being faced with the primary responsibility of responding (or not) to the Neo-Confucian polemic.

He did respond, composing the *Hyŏnjŏng non*. A date of composition is not attached to the version of the *Hyŏnjŏng non* in our possession, nor is there any clear dating provided in Kihwa's biographical sketch. We do know that he had to have composed it after the time of his conversion to Buddhism in 1396–97, and we might also assume, given the strong mastery of Buddhist doctrine demonstrated in the treatise, that it would have been composed at least a few years after this conversion, and thus probably subsequent to Chŏng's demise in 1398. Therefore, strictly speaking, this text probably cannot be seen as constituting a "live debate" with Chŏng.

On the other hand, however, the *Hyŏnjŏng non* directly responds to every one of the objections raised in the *Chappyŏn*, which represented the culmination of all the Confucian arguments that had been made against Buddhism from the time of Han Yu onward. And since the Neo-Confucian tradition in both China and Korea lacks any other overview comparable to the *Chappyŏn*, it can be said that it is primarily the *Chappyŏn* to which Kihwa is making his response.

Kihwa starts off by grounding his argument in an essence-function view of the mind and its activities. Elaborating on a general Buddhist approach, Kihwa tells us that the mind is originally pure, but as it engages in situations, it tends to become entangled in affliction. For the purpose of recovering the original mind, Buddhism has a wide spectrum of practices, which range from the most expedient and superficial, to the most profound. In outlining the teachings, starting from the most profound and extending to the most superficial, he ends up with the fundamental Buddhist doctrine of the law of cause and effect. Yet no matter how superficial the Buddhist teaching of cause and effect may seem within the East Asian Mahāyāna tradition, Kihwa judges it to be one level above the typical application of the Confucian teaching, which he characterizes as the mere conditioning of people through reward and punishment on the part of the state.

The centerpiece of Kihwa's argument lies in the presentation of what he takes to be the common denominator of all three traditions of Confucianism, Daoism, and Buddhism: a shared doctrine of "humaneness" (Kor. *in*, or "altruism"), which is in turn linked to the shared view that the myriad living beings of the universe are fully interlinked with one another. While the expressed doctrine of the mutual containment of all things is technically Buddhist in origin, it ended up being one of the central tenets articulated by the most influential of the Song Neo-Confucian founders, especially Cheng Hao, who declared, "The myriad things and I form a single body." Kihwa points out that Buddhism and (Neo-)Confucianism share in the view that it is fundamentally wrong to harm others. Buddhists have the doctrine of *ahiṃsā* (non-injury) at the core of their practice of moral discipline, and this is observed fully in all Buddhist practices. Confucians, on the other hand, take humaneness to be the most fundamental component of their path of cultivation. Confucius himself continually cited humaneness as the source of all forms of goodness. Mencius said that humaneness was innate to all people, explaining its function through a variety of metaphors, the most oft-cited being that of the stranger who automatically rushes to prevent a toddler from falling into a well.

However, Kihwa argues, the Confucian literary corpus is rife with inconsistencies on this matter. For example, in one of the more famous quotations from Song Neo-Confucianism, Cheng Hao asserts that humaneness means that we form a single body with the myriad things. Nonetheless, according to Kihwa, Confucius himself went only halfway in his practice of sharing in a oneness with other living beings, as he still enjoyed the sports of hunting and fishing. For Mencius, taking the life of an animal was not problematic for the humane man, as long as he did not hear the animal's screams in its death throes. And, in general, the Confucian tradition endorsed the practices of ritual sacrifice.

The charge, then, that Kihwa lays on the Confucians is strikingly similar to the one that Chŏng uses to assail the Buddhists, in that both want to show the other side to be guilty of inconsistency. There is a slight difference, however, in that, while Chŏng for the most part wants to point out inconsistencies in the Buddhist doctrine itself, Kihwa centers his argument on showing inconsistencies between Confucian doctrine and the actual behavior exhibited by the tradition's adherents. Simply put, Confucians say one thing but do another.

In the closing portion of his treatise, however, Kihwa concludes that the three teachings, when properly understood, should be seen as three different expressions of the same reality. In the passage that provides the strongest justification for presuming that Kihwa was responding directly to the *Chappyŏn*, he discusses two concepts of voidness and quiescence raised by Chŏng in his own summation, arguing instead that the connotations of these terms are basically the same throughout all three traditions and that, at their most fundamental level, the three are equally valid approaches to the same reality.

Chŏng Tojŏng's *Pulssi chappyŏn* is translated from the edition included in the *Sambong chip*, vol. 1 (Seoul: Minjok Munhwa Ch'ujinhoe, 1977), pp. 76–85. Kihwa's *Hyŏnjŏng non* appears in the *Han'guk Pulgyo chŏnsŏ* [abbreviated as *HPC*], vol. 7

(Seoul: Tongguk Taehakkyo Ch'ulp'ansa, 1985), pp. 217–25. Chinese source texts of both treatises, along with a complete English translation, can be found on the Internet at http://www.hm.tyg.jp/~acmuller/jeong-gihwa/index.html.

Further Reading

For the relationship between these two texts, see Charles Muller, "The Centerpiece of the Goryeo-Joseon Buddhist-Confucian Confrontation: A Comparison of the Positions of the *Bulssi japbyeon* and the *Hyeonjeong non*," *Journal of Korean Buddhist Seminar: Memorial Edition for the Late Professor Kim Chigyŏn*, September 2003, 23–47; and Muller, "The Buddhist-Confucian Conflict in the Early Chosŏn and Kihwa's Syncretic Response: *The Hyŏn chŏng non*," *Review of Korean Studies* 2 (September 1999): 183–200. The most comprehensive work that investigates the development of the Korean Neo-Confucian polemical movement against Buddhism remains John Goulde, "Anti-Buddhist Polemic in Fourteenth- and Fifteenth-Century Korea: The Emergence of Confucian Exclusivism" (Ph.D. diss., Harvard University, 1985). For further background on Chŏng and his role in the birth of the Chosŏn regime, see Chai-sik Chung, "Chŏng Tojŏn: 'Architect' of Yi Dynasty Government and Ideology," in *The Rise of Neo-Confucianism in Korea*, edited by JaHyun Kim Haboush and Theodore de Bary (New York: Columbia University Press, 1985), pp. 59–88. For a full-length monograph that provides a total picture of the gamut of forces involved in the transition from the Koryŏ to the Chosŏn, see John Duncan, *The Origins of the Chosŏn Dynasty*, especially chap. 6, "The Ideology of Reform," which offers extensive discussion of Chŏng Tojŏn. Michael Kalton's book *The Four-Seven Debate: An Annotated Translation of the Most Famous Controversy in Korean Neo-Confucian Thought* provides a detailed account of an intra-Confucian debate that shows many similarities to this one. From the Buddhist angle, for an understanding of the Sŏn tradition that produced Kihwa, standard reading is the introduction to Robert E. Buswell Jr., *The Korean Approach to Zen: The Collected Works of Chinul* (Honolulu: University of Hawaii Press, 1983), reprinted in paperback as *Tracing Back the Radiance: Chinul's Korean Way of Zen*, Classics in East Asian Buddhism, no. 2 (Honolulu: University of Hawaii Press, A Kuroda Institute Book, 1991). Kihwa's approach to the three teachings in the context of the *Hyŏnjŏng non* is also discussed in Robert E. Buswell Jr., "Buddhism under Confucian Domination: The Synthetic Vision of Sosan Hyujong (1520–1604)," in *Confucianism and Heterodox Religion in Late Choson Korea*, edited by JaHyun Kim Haboush and Martina Deuschler (New York: Columbia University Press, 1999), pp. 134–59. Additionally, extensive discussion of Kihwa's syncretic religious views appear in Charles Muller, *The Sūtra of Perfect Enlightenment: Korean Buddhism's Guide to Meditation*. Many of these and other materials from my own articles, conference presentations, and books on topics related to Kihwa, Chŏng, and Confucian-Buddhist related issues

can be found on my Web site at http://www.hm.tyg.jp/~acmuller/publications-etc
.html.

Array of Critiques of Buddhism (*Pulssi Chappyŏn*)

CRITIQUE OF THE BUDDHIST VIEW OF TRANSMIGRATION

We can test this concept [of transmigration] in the case of our own bodies, in
the space of a single inhalation and exhalation. When air goes out, we call it
"one breath." But that which goes out in one exhalation not what is taken in
with the next inhalation. In this way, then, the respiration of people is continually produced without end. The principle of the departing of that which goes
forth, and the continuation of that which comes in, can be seen in this fashion.
We can also test this on other living things in the world. In all kinds of vegeta-
tion, a single vital force penetrates from the roots through the trunk, the
branches, the leaves, flowers, and fruits. During the spring and summer, this vital force peaks in its activity, and flowers and leaves are abundant. Reaching
fall and winter, the vital force contracts, and the flowers and leaves fall away.
When the spring and summer of the next year arrive, they again grow apace.
But it is not the case that the fallen leaves return to their roots—back to their
origin to be reborn!

When we draw water from a well each morning to boil for cooking and drinking, it is eventually boiled away. When we wash our clothes and put them out to
dry in the sun, the water disappears completely without a trace. The water in the
well is drawn out continuously, but it never runs out. Yet it is not the case that
the water returns to its original place and is reborn. There is also the case of the
grains that we farm. In the spring we plant ten bushels, and in the fall we gather
one hundred bushels. We can keep going like this, multiplying the yield until we
reach one hundred thousand bushels. So these grains are also produced again and
again.

Now if we look at it from the point of view of the Buddhist theory of transmigration, all animate creatures come and go in fixed numbers—there is
never any increase or decrease [in the total]. But if this is the case, then the
creation of living beings by heaven and earth is not like the profitable work of
the farmer. Also, these animate creatures do not become human beings. This
being the case, then the total number of all of the birds, fish, and insects is
also fixed. That means that if one increases in number, the other must decrease. Or if one decreases in number, the other must increase. It should
not be the case that all simultaneously increase, or that all simultaneously
decrease.

From the present point of view, however, during times of prosperity, the
population of human beings increases, and at the same time, the population
of the birds, beast, sea creatures, and insects also increases. During a period of
decline, the population of human beings decreases, as does the popula-

tion of birds, beasts, sea creatures, and insects. This is because human beings and the myriad things are all born from the vital force of heaven and earth. Therefore, when the vital force is waxing, all things increase simultaneously. When the vital force is on the wane, all things decrease simultaneously. I have had it with the Buddhist's teaching of transmigration, which is nothing but a hideous deception to the people of the world! If we deeply fathom all the transformations of heaven and earth, and clearly examine the production of human beings, then we cannot but understand it as I have explained here. It would be best for those who share my views to reflect on this together.

CRITIQUE OF THE BUDDHIST NOTION OF KARMA

Some say, "Your criticism of the Buddhist notion of transmigration is extreme. You claim that human beings and the [myriad] creatures are born through the reception of the vital forces of yin/yang and the five phases." Well, in people there are the inequalities of wise and foolish, capable and incapable, poor and rich, noble and low-class, long and short-lived. In the case of the animals, there are those that are captured, raised as livestock, and made to suffer in labor, without respite until their death. There are some that cannot escape the angler's and bird catcher's nets, the fisherman's hook or the hunter's arrow. The large and small, strong and weak eat, or are eaten by, each other. In heaven's creation of the creatures, each receives its own lot. How can there be such a situation of inequality as this? With this in mind, are not the Buddha's teachings of the attainment of birth as a result of the good and evil actions of prior lifetimes on the mark? Those good and evil activities that one carries out in this life are called "causes." The rewards that appear at a later date are called the "fruits." Doesn't this explanation seem reasonable?

I answer this objection by saying that I have explained the matter in full in my earlier discussion on the continuous production of humans and things. Once you grasp this, one cannot but have doubts regarding the theory of transmigration. And even though the critique of the theory of transmigration is properly grasped, and the shortcomings of the theory of karma are self-evident without any special effort at making a critique, you still ask this question? I take the prerogative of not repeating my explanation from the beginning again. Now, in the activity of yin/yang and the five phases, the twists of fate and the alternations in patterns are uneven and unequal. Therefore in their related vital force, there are differences of free flow and congestion, imbalance and balance, purity and pollution, substantiality and insipidity, high and low, long and short.

And in the production of humans and animals, if the timing is right, they obtain free flow and balance, becoming humans. If they end up with congestion and imbalance, they become animals. The respective nobility and wretchedness of humans and animals is differentiated here. Furthermore, as humans, those who attain purity are the wise and the capable. Those who end up being polluted are the foolish and the incapable. The substantial attain wealth and the insipid end up in poverty. The high are ennobled and the low are miserable. The long are long-lived and the short die young. This explanation is greatly abbreviated, yet the case is the same with the things of the natural world. The *qilin*, dragons, and phoenix are spiritual, while the tigers, wolves, and snakes are poisonous. The camellia, cassia, iris, and epidendrum are auspicious, while the crow, long-beaked birds, poisonous herbs, and cogongrass bring suffering. Although these are all in the category of the congested and imbalanced, there are still distinctions among them in terms of relative good and evil.

ON CHINESE MEDICINE

People do not become congested and out of balance of their own accord. The *Book of Changes* says: "Heaven: The Way transforms, determining the constitution of each thing." (From the main text of the first hexagram.) An earlier scholar said: "Heaven's Way is distributed to the myriad things without discrimination." The same principle can be seen expressed in the minor arts of the physicians and fortune-tellers. When the fortune-tellers determine people's ill and good destinies, they must inevitably trace back to the basis in the rise and fall of the five phases. For example, some people's destinies are determined by the phase of wood. In the spring they will flourish, and in the autumn they will decline. Their appearance tends to be green and tall, and their hearts tend to be warm and compassionate. Other people's destinies are determined by the phase of metal. They do well in the autumn and falter in the summer. Their appearance tends to be whitish and square, their minds are strong and bright. The same sort of examples can be made from the phases of water and fire—there is no place where they do not have application. Also, ugliness in appearance, and coarseness and dullness of mind, are rooted as well in imbalances in the endowments gotten from the five phases.

When physicians diagnose people's sickness, they also must investigate to the root causes of the mutual influences of the five agents. This can be seen in the fact that sicknesses related to cold will be associated with the water-based kidneys, and the sicknesses of heat will be associated with the fire-based heart. The prescriptions given for treatment are adapted to the various natures of warm and cool, cold and hot, assigning tastes of salty and sour, sweet and bitter, which are in turn categories related to the five agents. In this, there are no remedies that are not perfectly matched to the disease and personal constitution. This is what our Confucian teachers mean when they say that the production of people and things occurs based on the attainment of the vital forces through yin/yang and the five agents. This is supported by direct testimony that is beyond doubt.

If you follow the explanations of the Buddhists, then fortune and misfortune, and sickness are not related to yin/yang and the five agents, but all are made manifest as the products of karma. If this is so, why is it that not a single person has abandoned our Confucian yin/yang—five agents paradigm and adopted the Buddhist theory of karmic results when it comes to the divination of fortune/misfortune, and the diagnosis of disease? Their theories are wild, empty, and error-laden, and not worth being adopted. How can you allow yourself to be bewildered by such teachings?!

CRITIQUE OF THE BUDDHIST NOTIONS OF MIND AND NATURE

The mind is the pneuma that the human being takes from heaven at birth. It is spiritually subtle and undarkened, and takes its position as lord of a single body. The nature is the principle that the human being takes from heaven at birth. It is pure and perfectly good—the endowment of a single mind. The mind possesses both awareness and activity, while the nature possesses neither awareness nor activity. Therefore it is said that the mind is able to fathom the nature, but the nature is not able to take stock of the mind. It is also said that the mind encompasses the emotions and the nature. The mind is also said to be the abode of the spiritual luminosity, while the nature is the principle with which it is endowed. Observing this, the distinctions between the mind and the nature should be understood!

The Buddhists take the mind to be the nature. But if you examine their theory thoroughly, it does not add up. They furthermore say that delusion is none other than the mind, and that awakening is none other than the nature. They also say that "mind" and "nature" are synonymous, just like the words *yan* and *mu* (in Chinese "eye" and "eye").

Pojo [Chinul] said: "Outside of the mind there is no Buddha" (*HPC* 4.742b 10–11) and "outside of the nature there is no dharma" (*HPC* 4.746c113–14). This also suggests a distinction in terms of Buddha and dharma, seemingly indicating that there is [a distinction] to be seen. Yet this is all done based on nebulous supposition, rather than on explicit facts. The teachings of the Buddhists have lots of wordplay but lack a definitive doctrine, and so their actual intentions can be understood. Our Confucian teachers say, "Exhaust your mind to understand the nature" (*Zhu Xi yulei*, 9). Here the original mind is used to fathom a profound principle.

The Buddha's teaching says, "Observe the mind and see the nature" (*Taishō* no. 2016, vol. 48, p. 656b7) and "mind is none other than the nature." This means that you use a separate one mind to observe this one mind. But how can a person have two minds? From this we can also readily know the impoverishment of their theories. We can sum it up by saying that using one's mind to observe the mind is like using the mouth to eat the mouth. What kind of nonsense is this to say that we will use the unobserving to observe?!

THE CONSISTENCY OF THE CONFUCIAN TEACHINGS

Moreover, our Confucian teachers say, "Within the space of a square inch, [all matters and all creatures have their definite principle]" (*Zhu Xi yulei*, 14) and "the rarefied spirit is undarkened, [including within it a multitude of principles and responding to a myriad circumstances]." The rarefied spirit which is undarkened is the mind. That which contains a multitude of principles is the nature. Those things which respond to a myriad circumstances are the sentiments. Now, since this mind is endowed with a multitude of principles, upon the arrival of all affairs and things, there are none that are not responded to appropriately. Therefore affairs and things are treated according to their correctness and incorrectness, and affairs and things follow the lead of the self. This is the learning of our Confucian masters. From inside the body and mind, extending out to all affairs and things—from the source, flowing out to the branch streams. All are penetrated by one, like the water that comes down from the fountainhead to flow out to a myriad streams: there is no place where it is not water. It is like holding the handle of the Big Dipper, which assesses the worth of all things under heaven. The relative worth of those things is just like the weighing of grams and ounces on a scale. This is what I mean when I say that there has never been an iota of inconsistency in the Confucian teachings.

Therefore I say: Buddhism is void, while Confucianism is substantial; Buddhism has two realities, while Confucianism has one; Buddhism has gaps, while Confucianism is consistent. This is something that learned people should clarify and discern.

THE BUDDHIST CONFUSION OF ESSENCE AND FUNCTION

It is like the saying "Essence and function spring from the same source; the manifest and the subtle have no gap between them." The Buddhist method of study addresses the mind, but does not address its manifestations. This can be seen in the Buddhists' saying things like, "The bodhisattva Mañjuśrī wanders through the taverns, but these activities are not his mind." Excuses like this for sloppy behavior abound in the Buddhist teachings. Is this not a separation of the mind from its activities? Chengzi said: "The study of the Buddhists includes reverence to correct the internal, but does not include justice to straighten the external." Therefore those who are stuck in these incorrect views will waste away.

THE BUDDHISTS' TREATMENT OF THE WORLD AS UNREAL

When [the Buddhists] see their Way as not distinct from concrete entities, they end up taking concrete entities to be the Way. Thus they say, "Good and evil [phenomena] are all mind. The myriad phenomena are nothing but consciousness." By according with all things, they go along with their activity without contrivance; acting wildly and arbitrarily, there is nothing that they do not do. This is what is Cheng Hao meant when he said "those who are rigid become like dry wood, and those who are unrestrained end up being arbitrary and reckless" (Cheng Hao, "Selected Sayings," no. 32). Yet when [the Buddhists] talk about their Way, they are referring to the mind. But they end up falling back down into the physical realm of concrete things, without even being aware of it themselves. How regrettable!

CRITIQUE OF THE BUDDHISTS' LACK OF THE APPLICATION OF "COMPASSION" TO STANDARD FAMILIAL NORMS

Heaven and earth take living beings as their mind; human beings take this mind of the living beings of heaven and earth to be born. Therefore people are uniformly endowed with the mind that cannot bear to watch the suffering of others. Even though the Buddha was a foreigner, he was still a human being. So how could he alone lack this mind? What we Confucians call the feeling of sympathy for the suffering of others, the Buddhists call "compassion." Both are functions of humaneness. Even though these two concepts are basically the same, significant differences can be seen in the way that they are actually carried out in practice.

My family members and I share the same vital force. Other people and I are of the same species. Other beings and I share in being alive. Therefore, in the actualization of the mind of humaneness, one starts with one's family, then extends to other people, and then to other beings. It is like water overflowing from one hole, and then to a second and third hole. The source of humaneness is deep, and its extent is far-reaching. Including all the creatures in heaven and earth, there is not one that does not exist within our heartfelt love. Therefore [Mencius] said: "[The Superior Man] loves his parents intimately and loves people as people. He loves people as people and cares about creatures" (*Mencius* 7A:45). This is the Confucian Way. Therefore it is unitary, it is substantial, and it is consistent.

The Buddhists are different. In their treatment of other living beings, even if they are fierce animals like tigers and leopards, or insignificant bugs like mosquitoes and flies, they shamelessly desire to feed them with their own bodies. In their treatment of people, if a man from Yue (i.e., a total stranger) is hungry, they are concerned about giving their food to him. If a man from Qin is cold, they want to donate their clothing to him. And this offering of clothing is the so-called charity [*dāna*]. But in the case of someone extremely close, like one's father or son, or someone to whom great respect is due, such as the prince or minister, they unfailingly seek to sever the relationship and run away. What is the meaning of this!?

Moreover, the reason that people learn to act with care and discretion is because they have fathers and mothers, wives and children. This causes them to learn proper values. The Buddhists regard human relationships as provisional combinations. The son does not treat his father as a father, and the minister does not treat his prince as a prince. Human warmth and justice go down the drain. People regard their most intimate family members like passersby on the street, and they treat the most venerable person like a capped boy. The original basis has already been lost. Therefore, if they try reach out to other people and beings, it is like a tree without roots, or a river without a spring, which easily dries up. In the end they succeeded neither in bringing benefit to people nor in giving aid to living beings . . . they haven't the slightest bit of feeling for them.

CRITIQUE OF THE SŎN PROCLIVITY TOWARD ANTINOMIANISM

The early Buddhist teachings did not go beyond the discourse of causes, conditions, and retribution, so that they could ensnare foolish people. Even though they took nothingness as their cardinal teaching, and abandoned the obligations of society, they still taught that the good obtain fortune while the evil reap misfortune. This engendered the custom of people choosing goodness over evil, of observing the rules of morality, and not falling into dissipation. Therefore, even though the importance of human relationships was disparaged, justice and reason were not completely stifled.

But when Bodhidharma arrived to China, he was aware of the shallowness of his own teachings and knew that they would not suffice to move the intellectual elites. Thus he proffered slogans such as "no establishment of words and letters," "cutting off the path of language," "directly pointing to the human mind," and "seeing the nature, one achieves buddhahood." Once these teachings had been released, they proliferated rapidly, and his followers continued to transmit and elaborate on them. Some said, "Goodness is none other than this mind, and you cannot use mind to cultivate mind. Evil is none other than this mind, and you can't use mind to eliminate mind." Alas, the practices of disciplining oneself against doing evil, and endeavoring to cultivate goodness, were extinguished.

Others said, "Even lust, anger, and ignorance are divine practices"; "regulating one's behavior through observing the precepts, one loses the Way." Regarding themselves as having avoided falling into the pit of entanglements, having released themselves from bondage and cast off the fetters, they arrogantly abandon themselves beyond the norms of propriety. Wholly absorbed in self-indulgence, they are as blind as madmen, never to return to humane principles. The so-called study of justice and principle, is, at this point, terminated.

Zhu Xi lamented this situation, saying: "The Western teachings of dependent origination and karma have agitated the foolish crowd, and have now been long disseminated into the world. Climbing the latter beyond the heavens, they look back and point to the mind's nature; their sayings transcend being and non-being." This led directly to the spread of confusion and disputation throughout the world. This is called emptiness, without producing concrete fruits. Treading through this brambled path, who will take up the mantle of the three sages? Would it be extreme for us to burn their books? Our grief over this situation is extreme, and I myself am depressed to the point of making the three lamentations.

BUDDHISM IS A RELIGION BASED ON NOTHINGNESS

Prior Confucian scholars have [already] shown that the Confucian and Buddhist paths differ with every single phrase and every single situation. Here I will elaborate based on these. We say voidness, and they also say voidness. We say quiescence, and they also say quiescence. However, our voidness is void yet existent. Their voidness is void and nonexistent. Our quiescence is quiescent yet aware; their quiescence is quiescent and negative. We speak of knowledge and action; they speak of awakening and cultivation. Yet our knowledge is to know that the principle of the myriad things is replete in our own minds. Their awakening awakens to the fact that the mind is originally empty, lacking anything. Our action is to return to the principle of the myriad things and act according to it, without error. Their cultivation is to sever connection with the myriad things and regard them as unconnected to one's mind.

If we follow the "in accordance with all things," as taught by Śākyamuni, then in the case of children, if they are filial, we just accept them as filial; if they are criminals, we just accept them as criminals. In the case of vassals, if they are loyal, we just accept them as being loyal; if they are rebellious, then we just accept them as being rebellious. As for the usage of cattle and horses, if they work in plowing and transport, then we use them for plowing and transport, and if they gore, butt, kick, and bite, then we let them gore, butt, kick, and bite. The Buddhist way is to follow the way things are, and nothing more.

Although we Confucians cannot accept this sort of thing, the Buddhist teaching is like this. It is natural that we should subject the beasts to our usage, and not be subject to their behaviors. Should the mere weight of a single gram sink us? Are not our and their manifest behaviors different? Thus, the reason that heaven gave birth to human beings is for them to serve as the guide for the myriad creatures. Placed in the role of assistant manager, how can we be at ease?

This kind of explanation can be repeated again and again, and although there are numerous points that can be made, we can sum them up by saying that the Confucian's manifest mind is at one with the principle, while the Buddhist's manifest mind is something other than the principle. Their manifest mind is empty, lacking principle, but our manifest mind, though empty, is re-

plete with the myriad things. Therefore it is said that our Confucianism follows a unified principle, while Buddhism is dualistic. Confucianism is consistent, while Buddhism is incoherent. Yet if the mind is one, how can there be
such differences between our and their ways of seeing things?

We cannot but regard Buddhism as a theoretical system that is shallow and
fragmentary, and which desires to conceal shape and hide form. It can be regarded a unique doctrine that is obscure, spellbinding, difficult, and obscur-
ing. It makes scholars carelessly place the mind outside the realm of text and
words. Yet they say that the Way must be like this, and that one can attain it afterward. Hence, modern scholars of Buddhism suffer from the faults of de-
pravity, lewdness, evil, and evasiveness, desiring to shift the meanings around.
They skew the true learning of the ancients who are of illuminating virtue and
renovating the people. This is certainly wrong! We should deliberate repeatedly on Zhu Xi's words, which are genuine and clear. If scholars would im-
merse their minds in these teachings, they will naturally attain them.

The Articulation of Orthodoxy (Hyŏnjŏng non)

THE BASIC BUDDHIST VIEW OF THE MIND

Though the mind's essence is neither existent nor nonexistent, it permeates
existence and nonexistence; though it originally lacks past and present, it permeates past and present: this is the Way. Existence and nonexistence are based
in nature and discriminations. Past and present are based in birth-and-death.
The nature originally lacks discrimination, but when you are confused about
the nature you give rise to discriminations; with the production of discriminations, wisdom is blocked—thoughts are transformed and the essence is differentiated. It is through this process that the myriad forms take shape and birth-
and-death begins.

Practitioners of the three vehicles and practitioners of the five vehicles each
have their own means of quelling discriminations. Humans and gods (etc.)
have their own means of quelling their impure defilements and those of the
three vehicles have their own means of quelling their pure defilements. Once
pure and impure defilements are both extinguished, one intimately creates the
state of great enlightenment. The five precepts lead to rebirth as a human being. The ten virtues lead to rebirth as a god. The practice of the four noble
truths and the contemplation on dependent origination result in the realization of the two vehicles. The practices of the six perfections lead to the production of bodhisattvahood. We can, then, summarize the gist of the entire
content of the Buddhist canon as none other than inducing people to abandon
discrimination and manifest their original natures.

The discriminations that are born out of original nature are just like clouds
appearing in the sky. The removal of discriminations and the manifestation of

the original nature is just like the dispersion of clouds and the clarity that appears. Among discriminations there are both light and heavy, in the same way that among clouds there are both thick and thin. But even though clouds show the distinction of thick and thin, they are all the same in that they obscure heavenly illumination. And although among discriminations there are differences between light and heavy, they are the same in their character of impeding the luminosity of the true nature. When the clouds appear, the illumination of the sun and moon is obstructed and the earth is darkened. When the clouds disperse, the illumination extends across the great chiliocosm and the universe appears limitless.

COMPARISON OF THE CONFUCIAN AND BUDDHIST APPROACHES TO MORALITY

The five precepts and the ten virtuous forms of behavior are the most shallow among the Buddhist teachings, originally designed for those of the weakest of spiritual abilities. Nonetheless, if one succeeds in practicing them, it is sufficient to bring about sincerity in oneself, and benefit to those around oneself. How much more so in the case of contemplation on the four noble truths and dependent origination? And how much more so again in the practice of the six perfections? The Confucians regard the five eternal principles to be the pivot of the Way. The moral precepts of Buddhism are none other than these five eternal principles of Confucianism: the Buddhist precept of "not-killing" is the same as humaneness (in); "not stealing" is the same as "justice" (ŭi); "not engaging in sexual excesses" is the same as "propriety" (ye); "not drinking alcohol" is the same as wisdom (chi); and "not speaking falsely" is the same as trust (sin).

However, the Confucians' way of teaching people is not through the example of virtuous action, but through laws and punishments. Therefore it is said, "If you lead them by laws and regulate them by punishments, the people will avoid these, but will be without shame. If you lead them by virtuous action and regulate them with propriety, the people will have a sense of shame and reflect on themselves" (Analects 2:3). Now "leadership by virtuous action and regulation by propriety" is something of which only sages are capable. Therefore the saying: "accomplishing silently; not speaking yet being trusted constitutes virtuous action" (Zhouyi, Xici zhuan, part 1). In the case of "leading by laws and regulating by punishments" one cannot avoid the clarification by reward and punishment. Therefore the saying: "reward and punishment are the great basis of the state."

"Accomplishing silently; not speaking yet being trusted" (Zhouyi, Xici zhuan, part 1) is strongly characteristic of the Buddhist method of teaching, where it is used in conjunction with the teaching of cause and effect. If you teach people by the method of reward and punishment, then there will invariably be some who will follow you only superficially. If you teach them with the concept of cause and effect, then they will be changed—and changed in their inner minds. Such a situation can be readily observed in this present world. How so? If you encourage them with rewards and discourage them with punishment, then the stopping of evil actions will merely be due to the people's fear of authority. Virtuous behavior will only occur as the result of seeking the benefit of rewards. Therefore the change that occurs will only be superficial. There will not be a change in their inner minds.

If people want to understand the reasons for the successes and failures in the present life, then teach them regarding the seeds sown in prior lifetimes. If they want to know about the fortune and misfortune to come in the future, then teach them regarding present causes. Then those who have enjoyed success will rejoice in the knowledge of the goodness of their seeds and redouble their efforts. Those who have failed will regret their lack of cultivation in prior lives and discipline themselves—and if they seek to invite good fortune in subsequent lives, they will apply themselves unstintingly toward goodness. Wanting to avoid misfortune in subsequent lives, they will grasp the necessity of being careful not to act in an evil way. If people are taught in this way, but are not influenced, then that will be the end of it. But if they are influenced, they will be influenced in their inner minds, and there will never be a case where someone merely goes along superficially.

Even so, how could you possibly cause every single person to change his inner mind? Therefore, those who are not able to change their hearts can be guided for the time being through reward and punishment. This will cause their hearts to become increasingly joyful and they will sincerely change. Therefore, in addition to the teaching of cause and effect, we may also retain the devices of reward and punishment. This concept is reflected in the [Buddhist] saying "gently lead those who can be gently led; force those who must be forced" (Taishō no. 353, vol. 12, p. 217c11–12)—which is close to the Confucian way. Seen this way, neither Confucianism nor Buddhism should be rejected.

The Buddha's way of transforming people is to take his dharma and confer it on the princes and ministers. If you want to use this Way to lead all the people and play a major role in governing the realm, causing all to tread together on the same path of cultivation of truth, then our Buddha's teaching does not advocate either remaining a householder or becoming a monk. All that is required is to have people not act contrary to the Way—and nothing more. It is not necessary to shave one's head or wear special clothes in order to practice. Therefore the sayings "loosening the bonds according to the situation is metaphorically called samādhi," and "there is no set entity named perfect enlightenment" (Diamond Sūtra; Taishō no. 235, vol. 8, p. 749b15). With the Buddha's mind being like this, why should there be such a limitation in approach? (HPC 7.218a).

DEFENSE OF THE BUDDHA'S "LEAVING HOME"

However, if one lacks self-control, then it is extremely difficult to live in the secular world without becoming polluted, and extremely difficult to accomplish the Way as a householder. Therefore people are taught to leave the secular world and are encouraged to cultivate the practices of detachment. The Confucian saying, "The man has his house and the woman has her family" (*Zuozhuan, Huangong*, Year 18) is taught in order to perpetuate the family business and not cut off the ancestral sacrifice—this can be called "filial piety." Well, the Buddha ended his marriage and abandoned the basic societal relationships, wandering long through the mountains and forests, severing his posterity. How could this be called filial? The classics say: "At night prepare the bed, in the morning inquire"; "be sensitive regarding their faces and accord with their expressions" and "when going out, let them know; when returning, announce yourself." Now the Buddha, without informing his parents, left the household by his own authority. Once he left home, he never returned for the rest of his life. While his parents were alive, he did not offer them sweet meats, and after they died, he did not provide a rich funeral. Is this not quite unfilial?

This can be tested, though, by observing: the constant and the expedient are the great factors of the Way. Without the constant there is no way to preserve eternal principles. Without expediency, there is no way to adjust to circumstances. When you are able to use the constant to maintain the principles and use the expedient to adapt to circumstances, you can attain to the great completion of this Way and there will be nothing that you cannot accomplish. But if you do not know how to maintain principles, there will be no way to correct the human mind. And if you do not understand adaptation to circumstances, there will be no way for you to accomplish great tasks.

People receive their lives from their parents. They are able to continue in life by the graces of the ruler and the state. "When inside the home, be filial; when out in society, be loyal." This is certainly the behavior appropriate to citizens and children. Furthermore, the ceremonies of wedding and ancestor worship are certainly the great bonds of human relationships. Without marriage, the connection of the continuity of life would be severed. Without the sacrifice, the method of honoring one's ancestors would be lost.

Nonetheless, it is not easy for ministers and children to be perfect in their loyalty and filial piety. It is also quite difficult to go through a lifelong marriage and maintain perfect constancy, or always to be able to offer the sacrifice in a state of perfect mental purity! One who is able to maintain perfect loyalty and perfect filial piety and at the same time conduct one's livelihood—to be constant in marriage and pure at the sacrifice and not waver in the slightest to the end of one's days will undoubtedly be spoken of highly after his death, and subsequent to his death, will be reborn as a human being. These are the merits of holding to the eternal principles.

Yet while one may not fail to attain a good reputation, those who go on to eliminate attached love and desire are exceedingly few. And although one may succeed in attaining a human rebirth, escaping cyclical existence is a far more difficult matter. Attached love is the root of transmigration and desire is the precondition for receiving life. So if someone has not yet escaped the fetters of spouse and children, how can that person eliminate attached love and desire? And if attached love and desire have not been eliminated, how can one escape from cyclical existence? If you want to escape cyclical existence you must first sever attached love and desire. If you want to sever attached love and desire, you must first forsake spouse and children. If you want to forsake spouse and children, you must first leave the secular world. If you do not leave the secular world, you cannot forsake spouse and children, sever attached love and desire, nor escape cyclical existence. Aside from the great expedient example of the Great Sage who offers his compassion, can ordinary, unenlightened people be capable of living in the world and attaining liberation?

This kind of person is difficult to meet, even in a trillion generations, and is hard to lay hold of, even among a hundred million people. The attraction of attached love is like that between steel and a magnet. If one is deficient in forbearance, it is quite difficult to avoid attached love while living in the secular world. To be able to do like our founding teacher Śākyamuni who abode in Tuṣita Heaven with the name "Protector of Luminosity Bodhisattva" and then descended into this world in the palace of the king, with the name Siddhārtha: how could he have been lacking in forbearance?! It would be like the sun being ashamed of its far-reaching illumination, or the formless realm's being embarrassed about its erasure of conditioning.

Even while passing through the clutches of attached love, Śākyamuni was never defiled by his entanglement in attached love. He aspired to become the example for future generations—the rightful heir to the golden wheel. Without announcement to his father and mother he slipped away, entering the Himalayas. Showing little regard for his own life, he practiced strict discipline, steadily, without wavering, waiting out the full exhausting of all his emotional afflictions. Only after the true luminosity had shown in its full brilliance did he return home for an audience with his father and ascend to heaven to pay respects to his mother. Through his teachings on the essentials of the dharma, he brought both of them to liberation. This is an example of the sages' merging with the Way by utilizing expedient methods to adapt to conditions even though they act contrary to eternal societal principles.

DEFENSE OF BUDDHIST "ANTISOCIAL" PRACTICES

The Confucians complain, saying: "The Buddhists roam idly, avoiding the responsibilities of society. Neither harvesting nor plowing, they depend on others for their food and clothing, and therefore the people bear this suffering, often being forced into destitution because of it. Is their decadence not great?"

In response to this, I say: The responsibility of the monks lies in spreading the dharma and elevating the consciousness of sentient beings. By their spreading of the dharma they cause wisdom and life not to be severed. By elevating the consciousness of the people, they cause each one of them to proceed toward goodness. This is the job of the monks. Who else is capable of performing this task? Therefore, there is no need for them to be embarrassed about receiving alms from the people. If a monk proves to be incapable of his responsibilities, it is an individual fault. How could it be the fault of the Buddha? Mencius said: "Here is a man who is filial at home and respectful to those he meets in the world. He preserves the Way of the ancient kings so that it may be picked up by later scholars. Yet he does not receive his sustenance from you. Why do you respect the carpenter and the wheelwright, and show disdain for the man of humaneness and justice?"

Why does it now suddenly become incorrect for those who preserve the Way and elevate the consciousnesses of people to receive food and clothing from those people? Whether one will be wealthy or poor in this life is based on his karmic predisposition. If one has an abundance of good seeds from prior lifetimes, then even if he spends money every day, he will always have extra. But if one lacks good seeds from the prior lifetime, then even if he saves every day, he will never have enough. There are people in this world, who, upon seeing a Buddha, do not show respect, and seeing monks, vilify them. They do not once in their whole lives offer a single cent for alms. They do not have enough clothes to cover their bodies, nor enough food to satisfy their stomachs. Have they also come to this condition because of the *saṃgha*?

DEFENSE AGAINST THE CHARGE OF DECADENCE IN THE *SAṂGHA*

The Confucians complain, saying: Purification and the reduction of desires; abandoning oneself in pursuit of the dharma; studying the scriptures widely and memorizing deeply; kindly instructing those who come after: these are definitely the proper activities of Buddhists. But the present-day monks do not engage in religious cultivation; they oppose and defile their teacher's dharma. When people question them as to their Way, it is like standing and facing to the wall. They peddle the Tathāgata to garner their necessary sustenance. They dwell in regular houses and act like secular people. They enrich themselves through the means of regular society and even become ministers in the government. How can the prince and the state stand for this?

In answer to this, I say: The Qilin and the Phoenix do not form flocks. The rarest of gems are not to be found in the local marketplaces. Among the three thousand disciples of Confucius, those who can be called men of truly outstanding acumen numbered no more than ten. Among the vast body of the Tathāgata's disciples, those who were categorized as first-rate also numbered no more than ten. Now, as the time of those sages passes further and further away, and the religious faculties of people grow ever weaker, how can you expect every single person to be able to possess the morality of Kāśyapa, or the breadth of learning of Ānanda? In the thousand or so years since the time of Confucius and Yan Hui, the likes of Yan Hui and Min Ziqian have not been heard of.

For a monk to live up to his name, once he has embodied the Five Virtues and cultivated the Six Kinds of Harmony—then he deserves to be called a monk. However, when it comes to the matter of matching the name with the reality, the problems lie with the individual. In the forest there is wood that is not fit for use as lumber; in the fields there are grains that do not bear fruit. Granted, there are monks who are not capable of acting as repositories and exemplars of the dharma, but one should not be alarmed to the extreme by these types. Even these persons, if they formally submit to the dharma, their seeds will gradually mature to infuse their nature, and they will not fail in following the Way. How can you castigate their dharma based on individual failings?

THE DOCTRINE OF CAUSE AND EFFECT IS FOUND IN THE CHINESE CLASSICS

As for the theory of karmic reward: how can it be suggested that this is only the teaching of Buddhism? The *Yijing* says: "When you accumulate virtue you will have abundant good fortune; when you accumulate evil you will have abundant calamity" (*Yijing, kun* [hexagram no. 2]). Another example is the teaching given in the *Great Plan* to the effect that when the people accord with ultimate principles, heaven rewards them with the five blessings. When they are at discord, then heaven responds by bringing about the six extremes (see James Legge, *Shoo King*, pp. 340–41). What is this, if not karmic reward? It is already obvious that there is karmic reward while the bodily form is still present. But also in death—even though the body disappears, the spirit remains to reap the good and evil fruits. How could it not be so? The Buddha once said: "Even after the passage of a hundred thousand aeons, the karma that one has created does not disappear. When the right causes and conditions are encountered, the fruits of each action return to oneself" (*Ratnakūṭa-sūtra, Taishō* no. 310, vol. 11, p. 335b14). How can you deceive people?

THE TRUE MEANING OF "HUMANENESS"

The Confucians argue, saying: People eat living creatures and living creatures sustain people—this is certainly the natural course of things. And if those in their seventies are not fed meat, their stomachs will not be filled. Therefore those who take care of the elderly cannot fail to serve them with meat. Also, the methods of hunting for spring, summer, fall, and winter are the means by which the ancient kings helped the people to avoid difficulty. These systems, which are established according to the change in seasons, cannot be altered. Furthermore, sacrificial animals have been used as the ceremonial objects for making offerings from ancient times to the present. This practice also clearly cannot be abandoned. The parents of the Buddhists become aged, but they do not feed them sweet foods, nor do they serve them with meats. They also teach people to abandon the systems established by the ancient kings and the ritual of sacrifice. Is this not excessive?

To this, I say: Violence toward heaven's creatures is something in which the sage will have no part. How much less so could one who manifests the heavenly Way and perfectly accomplished humanity encourage people to kill life in order to nourish life! The *Book of History* says: "Heaven and earth are the parents of all creatures, and of all creatures man is the most highly endowed with intelligence. Only the most intelligent among men becomes the great sovereign, and the great sovereign becomes the parent of the people." Since heaven and earth are already the mother and father of all things, then those things which are born within heaven and earth are all the children of heaven and earth. So the relationship of heaven and earth to its creatures is just like that between parents and children. Children naturally differ in terms of stupidity and intelligence, just like the difference in mental endowment between human beings and the myriad creatures. But even if a child is stupid, the parents will not turn away from it—in fact, they will love it and treat it with special care. They will even have special concern as to whether or not it is able to attain its proper sustenance. How could they possibly go as far as to inflict harm upon it?

Killing life in order to nourish life is like one's own children killing each other in order to nourish themselves. If children are killing each other in order to nourish themselves, how are the parents going to feel about this? To have their children killing each other is certainly not the wish of their parents. So how could the mutual inflicting of harm between human beings and the other creatures be the will of heaven and earth? Human beings and the myriad things already share in their possession of the vital energy of heaven and earth. They also share in their possession of the principle of heaven and earth, and dwell together in the space of heaven and earth. Sharing, as they do, in the same vital force and the same principle, how could there be a principle that condones the killing of life in order to nourish life? It is like the saying: "Heaven and earth and I share the same root; the myriad things and I share the same body" (*Taishō* no. 2016, vol. 48, p. 915a8). These are the words of the Buddha. "The man of humanity forms one body with heaven and earth and the myriad things" (*Henan ercheng ishu*, p. 15). These are the words of a Confucian. Only when one's actions fully accord with these words can we say that someone has fully achieved the Way of humaneness (*HPC* 7.219b).

The term in the medical texts for numbness in the hands and feet is "non-humaneness" (Kor. *purin*). The hands and feet are the extremities of the body. Even with a slight sickness the vital energy will not penetrate them. Therefore *humaneness* implies the interpenetration of heaven and earth and the myriad things into a single body, wherein there is no gap whatsoever. If you deeply embody this principle, then there cannot be a justification for inflicting harm on even the most insignificant of creatures. This can be called the actualization of the Way of the humane person.

The *Book of Odes* says: "One arrow for five boars" (see Legge, *She King*, p. 36). The *Analects* say: "When the master fished he would not use a net;

when hunting he would not shoot a perched bird" (*Analects* 7:26). Mencius said: "The superior man stays far away from the kitchen. If he hears the screams of the animals he cannot bear to eat their flesh" (*Mencius* 1A:7). These are all examples of incompletely actualized humaneness. Why don't they try to come up to the level of "forming a single body"? The *Doctrine of the Mean* says: "His words reflecting his actions, his actions reflecting his words—how can this Superior Man not be sincere through and through?" (*Doctrine of the Mean*, commentarial section 13). Who among those I have cited here comes up to this level? This is an example of the Confucians preaching about the goodness of the path of *humaneness* but not following through. If it is necessary to place limits on the killing of birds, why even shoot the arrow at all? If it bothers you to shoot a perched bird, why shoot it when it is flying? If the superior man is going to avoid the kitchen, why does he eat meat at all? [Here Kihwa digresses to tell an interesting story that explains how he came to develop the position he is presently articulating.]

One time, during the period when I still had not yet entered the Buddhist order, a monk named Haewŏl was reading the *Analects* to me. He reached the passage that says: "Zigong asked: 'Suppose there were a ruler who benefited the people far and wide and was capable of bringing salvation to the multitude, what would you think of him? Might he be called humane?' The Master said, 'Why only humane? He would undoubtedly be a sage. Even Yao and Shun would have had to strive to achieve this'" (*Analects* 6:28). Haewŏl commented, using the phrase "The man of humaneness forms a single body with heaven and earth and the myriad things." With this, he put the scroll aside and asked me: "Was Mencius a man of humaneness?" "Yes," I replied. "Are 'fowl, pigs, dogs and swine' to be counted among the 'myriad things'?" "Yes," I replied. Haewŏl continued, citing Cheng Hao: "The humane man forms a single body with heaven and earth and the myriad things." If this statement is to be taken as a true expression of the principle, how are we supposed to see Mencius as humane? If 'fowl, pigs, dogs and swine' are to be counted among the 'myriad things,' how could Mencius say: 'If, in the raising of fowl, pigs, dogs and swine, their breeding times are not missed, then people seventy years old can eat meat'" (*Mencius* 1A:3). I was completely stymied by this question, and could not answer. I pondered over all of the classical transmissions, and could not come up with a single text that could support a principle that condoned the taking of life. I inquired widely among the brightest thinkers of the day, but not one of them could offer an explanation that could resolve my perplexity.

This doubt remained buried within my mind for a long time without being resolved. Then, while traveling around Mount Samgak in 1396, I arrived at Sŭnggasa, where I had the chance to chat with an old Sŏn monk throughout the night. The monk said: "The Buddha has ten grave precepts, the first of which is not killing." Upon hearing this explanation, my mind was suddenly overturned, and I recognized for myself that this was indeed the behavior of the truly humane man. I was thereupon able to embody deeply the teachings of the Way of humanity. From this time forth, I was never again to be confused regarding the differences between Confucianism and Buddhism. I subsequently composed a verse, which went:

> Up till now, knowing only the teachings of the classics and histories, and the criticisms of Cheng and Zhu,
> I was unable to recognize whether the Buddha was wrong or right,
> But after reflecting deep in my mind for long years,
> Knowing the truth for the first time, I reject [Confucianism] and rely upon [the Buddhadharma].

The creatures that make nests understand the wind; those that dig holes understand the rain; spiders possess the skill of weaving, and dung beetles are adept at rolling things. All creatures are like this, sharing in the same inherent spiritual awareness. Furthermore in their sharing in the emotion of loving life and hating death, how do they differ from human beings? Hearing the sound of ripping flesh and the cutting of the knife, livestock are in utter fright as they approach their death. Their eyes are wild and they cry out in agony. How could they not harbor bitterness and resentment? And yet people are able to turn a deaf ear. In this way human beings and the creatures of the world affect each other without awareness and compensate each other without pause. If there were a man possessing humaneness present, how could he observe such suffering and continue to act as if nothing were wrong?

KIHWA'S CONCLUSION: THE UNITY OF THE THREE TEACHINGS

You ask: What are the points of sameness and difference and the relative strengths and weaknesses of Daoism, Confucianism, and Buddhism?

The answer is this: Laozi said: "No doing and no not-doing; eternally doing, yet not-doing." The Buddha said: "Quiescent, yet eternally luminous; luminous, yet eternally quiescent." Confucius said: "The Changes have neither thought nor activity; still and unmoving they extend throughout and penetrate the world." Now this "stillness" that has never failed to "extend" is the same thing as the "quiescence" that is "eternally luminous." The "extend throughout and penetrate" that has never not been "still" is exactly the same as the "luminous, yet eternally quiescent." "No doing and no not-doing" is none other than "still, yet eternally extending." "Eternally doing, yet not-doing" is none other than "extending, yet eternally still."

If you can grasp this, then the words of the three teachers fit together like the broken pieces of the same board—as if they had all come out of the same mouth! If you would like to actually demonstrate the high and low among these teachings, exposing their points of similarity and difference clearly in their actual function, then you must first completely wash the pollution from your mind and completely clarify your eye of wisdom. Then you can study all of the texts contained in the Buddhist, Confucian, and Daoist canons. Compare them in your daily activities, at the times of birth and death, fortune and misfortune. Without needing words, you will spontaneously nod in assent. Oh, King, how strongly do I need to make my argument to get you to listen?

— 12 —

Confucianism and the Practice

of Geomancy

Hong-key Yoon

Geomacy, or *p'ungsu* (lit. wind and water, best known in the West through the Chinese pronunciation *fengshui*), is an essential element in the practice of every major Korean religion in regulating relationships with the environment. The use of land, including building houses, planning cities, siting graves, and locating temples and shrines, has especially been affected by the art of geomancy.

Geomancy originated in China, especially in the region of the Loess Plateau. It is thought to have been developed by the early Chinese as a technique for selecting auspicious cave-dwelling sites. The technique must have been introduced from China to Korea during ancient times, but at least since the later part of the Silla period (ca. eighth century), geomancy has significantly affected Korean society, including politics and religion. For instance, the impact of geomancy on the three major traditional religions of Korea, Buddhism, Confucianism, and Shamanism, is plainly visible in the sites they have selected for their temples and shrines and in their religious writings. Folk narratives describing their religious values also demonstrate that geomancy has been incorporated in the practice of their beliefs. Thus, geomancy and traditional Korean religion have been in symbiotic relationship with one another for more than a millennium. In this chapter, I will briefly examine the relationships between geomancy and Confucianism, mainly through folklore and the writings of Confucian scholars, before assembling and translating relevant source material.

Many Confucian scholars of the Chosŏn dynasty were experts on geomancy and accepted the practice of geomancy to varying degrees, sometimes claiming that the great Confucian scholars of China such as Confucius and Zhu Xi (1130–1200) accepted geomantic ideas. Zhu Xi, one of the principal architects of Neo-Confucianism, seemed to have embraced geomancy, as he was interested in searching for auspicious grave sites for his family and wrote a (Geomantic) Discourse on Royal Tombs (*Shanling yizhuang*), which was presented to the Chinese emperor in 1194. A Korean Confucian scholar-court officer, Ha Ryun (1347–1416), was an expert on geomancy and played an important role in searching for the new capital site during the reign of the first king of the Chosŏn dynasty (1392–1910). Another Confucian scholar–court official of the early Chosŏn dynasty, Chŏng Inji (1396–1478), also had good knowledge of geomancy and was involved in determining King Sejong's original tomb site. The *Annals of King Sejong* in the *Chosŏn wangjo sillok* (Veritable Records of the Royal Family of Chosŏn) includes Chŏng Inji's letter reporting his geomantic fieldwork to examine an auspicious tomb site for the king. His letter was based on a field survey he had conducted at the proposed royal tomb site together with a group of court officials. In his letter, Chŏng Inji listed eleven geomantic reasons why the royal tomb should be located at a site near the present-day eastern outskirts of Seoul. His letter is a good example of the degree of geomantic knowledge common among highly esteemed Korean Confucian scholar–officials, as it evaluated the geomantic quality of the proposed site using technical geomantic terms while citing specialized geomantic manuals. (The first part of his letter is translated later in this chapter.)

Korean geomancy came from China, and the principles that were applied in the search for an auspicious site were more or less identical to those used by the Chinese. The geomantic classics and manuals used in Korea generally either were imported directly from China or were edited and translated versions of the Chinese texts. However, Koreans sometimes interpreted and applied the Chinese geomantic principles in a distinctly Korean style. One of the most important geomantic discourses in Korea is by the Sirhak scholar Yi Chunghwan (1690–1756). His book, *Taengniji* (Book on Choosing Settlements) is a widely read classic on siting auspicious settlements and is sometimes treated by geomancers as esoteric geomantic literature. Yi Chunghwan lists four important factors to be considered in the selection of an auspicious settlement site. These factors are geomantic, economic, social, and scenic. In his discussion of the geomantic conditions of a settlement, Yi Chunghwan presents the following six aspects of the geomantic landforms of an auspicious settlement:

1. an outlet for the water's flow, or an outgoing direction for that flow;
2. the shape of the plain;
3. the shape of the mountain or hill;
4. the color of the soil;
5. beneficial shapes of water flow;
6. *chosan chosu,* or the homage-paying mountains and waters (i.e., locations of distant mountains and waters in front of a proposed settlement site).

These six geomantic conditions for a desirable settlement are in fact a Korean interpretation and application of Chinese geomantic principles. What Yi Chunghwan suggested as ideal is a site with both a suitable amount of flat land and water, which is surrounded by horseshoe-shaped hills in the background. (The full text of Yi Chunghwan's discussion of the geomantic conditions of a desirable settlement is translated later in this chapter.)

The close relationships between geomancy and Korean Confucianism are also well reflected in the locations of Confucian shrines, academies, or schools throughout Korea. For instance, Sŏnggyun'gwan, the Korean National Shrine and Academy of Confucianism in Seoul, is located in an obviously auspicious site. It is located between Korean palaces with appropriate background hills and an open front. These landform conditions fulfill the geomantic requirements. Various regional Confucian schools and academies (hyanggyo) throughout Korea are generally located in geomantically ideal sites. An example is the site of Tosan Sŏwon (the Tosan Academy), the Confucian school and academy in Andong County commemorating Yi Hwang (1501–70), a renowned Confucian scholar of the Chosŏn dynasty, which is known to be an auspicious site in terms of geomancy.

The Practice of Geomancy and Confucian Ethics

During the later period of the Chosŏn dynasty, the practice of geomancy, especially that of grave geomancy, became very common at all strata of Korean society.

Korean geomantic tales, including various folk narratives, reveal important aspects of how Koreans practiced geomancy. The idea that "an auspicious place can be found only by an ethical person" is deeply rooted in Korean geomancy. Because these tales are authored anonymously, they may be considered communally authored and owned. In folklore, people's wishes, feelings, and thoughts are more freely expressed than in scholarly writings, which typically would identify their authors. For this reason, the ethical values reflected in geomantic tales can be considered genuine expressions of the ethical values of the Korean people as a whole. Geomancers often cite folk narratives in the process of practicing geomancy, and these geomantic tales have been some of the most popular tale motifs in Korean folk narratives. These facts also add more value to the geomantic tales as credible sources for examining the ethical values inherent in geomancy as it was practiced in Korea.

It is generally recognized that Confucian family relationships were dominated by patriarchal, patrilineal, and patrilocal relationships. This means that family members submit themselves to their father's authority and should heed his leadership; family inheritance passes from father to son rather than to daughters; daughters become an integral part of their husbands' family after marriage and are excluded from their own natal family. These Confucian values and Koreans' fanatical practice of geomancy are well reflected in the Korean geomantic tales. Through some of these representative geomantic tales, I will now seek to explain the important aspects of Confucian ethos in the practice of geomancy in Korea.

A Married Woman's Attitudes toward Her Husband's Family

Confucian ethics insists that married daughters should live in the village or town where their husbands' families live. A married woman becomes an integral part of her husband's family by resuming the full privilege and responsibilities. These Confucian values teach the Korean woman to be faithful to and devote herself to the well-being of her husband's family rather than her own natal family, values that are well reflected in Korean geomantic tales. In the story "The Grave of the Yu Family of Andong" (translated below), a married woman secures an auspicious grave site for her husband's family at the expense of her own birth family by tricking her own mother and brothers. The married woman literally deceives her own birth mother and steals the auspicious grave site that was prepared for her own birth father. Slightly modified versions of this tale are found throughout Korea. The wide distribution of this type of tale signifies that a married woman in Chosŏn dynasty Korea was expected to identify herself fully with her husband's family, not her birth family. Koreans generally thought that this Confucian attitude toward one's husband's family was not only acceptable but commendable. For this reason, Koreans often joke that married daughters are thieves of their father's home.

Patrilineal Delivery of the Energy from the Deceased Father to the Living Son

In Chinese geomancy, parents are considered the main body of their children, just as if they were a tree trunk that may have many branches. This principle has been illustrated and transmitted to Korean folk society as a geomantic tale. When the bodies of deceased parents or ancestors are suffused with vital energy, the remaining branches of the living family tree may also receive benefits from that energy. By extending this geomantic logic, one can also say that if a dead ancestor's body suffers in its grave, the living descendants will suffer as well. This aspect of geomantic belief is effectively described in the legend "The Skull of the Prime Minister's Father," which is translated in full below. In the story, poking the deceased father's skull with a stick caused pain in the eye of the living descendant who was the prime minister, and pulling the stick out of the skull immediately relieved the pain. This story effectively represents the folklorized version of the geomantic principle that there is a mystic connection between the bones of deceased parents and their living descendants, and that descendants are directly affected by the conditions of a deceased father's bones.

According to this logic, however, the following paradox is possible: people never really die, but live on in the world after their death through their descendants. Prosperity for the ancestors therefore means prosperity for the descendants, and expecting prosperous descendants is also a hope these ancestors may have. In this sense, as Freedman points out, even a filial son who moves his parents' graves in the sincere hope of giving them peaceful rest at an auspicious site could also hope for blessings for himself from the grave. This hope, of course, would not go against the principle of filial piety but would support the importance of patrilineal continuity in the Confucian family structure.

Filial Piety

Filial piety (*hyodo*) may have been the most important ethical principle among traditional Koreans. In practice it is the most important obligation any child has toward his or her parents. However, the act of filial piety is an unconditional obligation to respect and look after one's parents. In traditional Korean society the concept of parents can be extended to include grandparents, great-grandparents, and other direct ancestors. In spite of its importance, however, geomantic tales with this ethical theme have not been very popular in Korea. Most geomantic tales are about how to acquire an auspicious site, as well as what kinds of blessings an auspicious site has made manifest. I have been able to find only a few geomantic tales that emphasize filial piety. One of them, "Tiger Mountain," is translated here from Ch'oe Sangsu's *Han'guk Min'gan chŏnsŏl chip* (Anthology of Korean Folk Legends).

> About five hundred years ago, a Mr. An lived in Hosan Village in Hwanghae Province. He was so filial to his parents that after his father's death, he went to his grave with a bowl of rice and bowed to the grave every day.
>
> One day a tiger was in front of his father's grave. The tiger had been helped once by Mr. An, who had taken a stake out of its mouth. Mr. An was surprised at seeing the tiger again. He pushed the tiger to make it go back to its cave, but it would not move. When the tiger started walking, it kept looking back at him and Mr. An realized that this was a sign for him to follow. At a certain place, the tiger stopped and dug in the soil with its paw. Mr. An understood that the tiger was offering a good place for Mr. An to bury his father. Thus, he moved his father's grave to that place.
>
> Afterward, Mr. An's family became prosperous, and eventually was the richest family of the region. This is why the people call the mountain "Pŏmmoe" or "Hosan," both of which literally mean "Tiger Mountain."

This story suggests that a filial son will somehow be helped to find an auspicious burial site for his father, which will guarantee prosperity for himself and his descendants. In fact, many unfilial Korean sons who did not care for their parents while they were alive suddenly became filial after the death of their parents when it comes to searching for an auspicious grave site. This action was clearly for one's personal selfish gain, and was not necessarily an expression of filial piety toward the deceased parents. Even in such cases, however, it is assumed that the well-being of the deceased ancestor is actually being taken into consideration, since the offspring will take better care of their graves and offer worship ceremonies when they become prosperous. Based on this discussion, one could go so far as to say that Koreans' practice of grave geomancy is mainly for the benefit of the living descendants and their future generations to come, rather than the deceased ancestors. This view is well reflected in Korean geomantic tales.

Criticisms against the Practice of Grave Geomancy

Koreans during the Chosŏn dynasty were so preoccupied with burying their ancestors in geomantically auspicious sites that geomancy-related crimes were rampant. Eventually a number of Confucian scholars came to criticize the practice of grave geomancy. These concerned scholars were often associated with the Sirhak, or Practical Learning School, including such well-known figures such as Yi Ik (1681–1763), Chŏng Yagyong (1762–1836), Pak Chega (1750–1805), and Chŏng Sŏn (1676–1759). For example, Chŏng Yagyong severely criticised the practice of grave geomancy and lamented its tragic social consequences:

> Presently, litigation in the courts regarding grave sites has become a troubling problem. About half of the [recent] fighting and assaults resulting in death are due to this [conflict over grave sites]. Since it is said that the unfortunate act of excavating graves [to move them to better places] is considered an act of filial piety, one [local magistrate] must investigate the practice of geomancy and appropriately deal with this.

Chŏng Sŏn even more vividly described the crimes and litigations that resulted from people's fanatical pursuit of geomancy in their desperate search for auspicious grave sites for their own selfish benefits (see translation in the anthology section). During the Chosŏn dynasty, the practice of grave geomancy became popular among the people, causing a negative impact on Korean society. A Sirhak scholar during the later Chosŏn dynasty, Pak Chega, lamented that Koreans of his time indulged in the selfish pursuit of good fortune by placing an ancestor's grave in an auspicious site rather than caring for the well-being of their ancestors. Moving one's ancestral grave to a geomantically superior place is mainly motivated by the hope of blessings for one's descendants, he says, rather than the well-being of one's ancestors. As the British anthropologist Maurice Freedman once commented concerning the Chinese practice of grave geomancy:

> Indeed, we may say that, in the traditional Chinese setting, there is more involved than a mere desire to procure good fortune; there is a moral obligation to seek a future of happiness for those for whom one is responsible. If I select my grave site in anticipation of my death, it is for the benefit of my sons and remoter agnatic issue. If my sons choose my grave, they are intent not only on their own prosperity but also on that of their descendants, each his own.

Freedman accurately understood the purpose of practicing grave geomancy in China and noticed a critically important aspect of the theory of geomancy: that the graves of ancestors can channel blessings to descendants. Freedman's comment on Chinese geomancy is also applicable to the practice of geomancy in Korea. The fact that the main purpose of practicing grave geomancy was to extract blessings from the grave site was discussed at the Korean royal court during the fifteenth century. *Chǔngbo Munhǒn Pigo* (The Revised and Enlarged Edition of the Comparative Review of Records and Documents) recorded that during the first year of King Yejong (1469), Yŏngnŭng (King Sejong's tomb) was relocated to its present location in Yŏju. However, moving the tomb had already been discussed during King Sejo's reign (r. 1455–68). During that discussion, Sŏ Kŏjŏng (1420–88), a well-known Confucian official, objected to the plan by saying that moving the ancestor's grave to a more auspicious site was an attempt to seek blessings for the living descendants and a king cannot expect any more blessings, since he has already received every possible good fortune. Accepting the official's reasoning, the king decided not to proceed with relocating his father's tomb. (A full translation of the text appears later in this chapter).

By moving graves, people expected to receive such blessings as enhanced social status, greater wealth, or more sons. Most geomantic tales reflect these wishes and very rarely convey any information regarding the descendants' concern for the well-being of their deceased ancestors' life after death. In fact, geomancy textbooks declare that the benefits manifested via auspicious grave sites were concerned only with the well-being of the living and their future descendants to come.

The Contemporary Practice of Geomancy

Despite concerned scholars' criticisms of the practice of geomancy, people's enthusiasm for the practice did not wane. Geomantic ideas firmly occupied Koreans' minds, and the practice of geomancy continued to be popular during the Japanese colonial period (1910–45), even though the Japanese attempted to enforce a public cemetery system that circumvented all geomantic manipulation. Following the liberation from Japanese colonial rule in 1945, geomancy was not officially recognized by the government, but many Koreans still continued to practice it. Following the Korean War and throughout the 1960s and 1970s, when Korea was relatively poor, Koreans had little time to be concerned with aspects of their cultural heritage that were not essential to the urgent task of improving the standard of living. However, since the 1980s, as rapid industrialization and modernization led to unprecedented wealth in the society, Koreans have had the leisure time to develop nostalgic feelings toward their traditional cultural values. In my view, economic prosperity reawakened interest in such traditional practices as grave geomancy and filial piety and left many Koreans with the discretionary funds they needed to hire geomancers and search for auspicious grave sites, or to improve grave decorations with stone works. For these reasons there seems to have been a popularization of geomancy in Korea since the 1980s.

South Korea

The practice of geomancy in South Korea is as popular as ever, especially among the rich. A large number of professional geomancers are available for hire in any city of Korea. This popularity can be measured in several ways. First, one can list the number of geomantic manuals and guidebooks published in recent years. In the 1970s I was able to find fewer than ten titles published on the principles and practice of geomancy written by professional geomancers. In the latter 1980s, however, I was able to find about two dozen such books on geomancy, filling several bookshelves at Kyobo Books, the largest bookstore in Seoul. In 2004, in the same bookstore, I was astonished to find that the book section on geomancy had expanded tremendously: I counted 183 different books on geomancy filling six shelves of a bookcase, and twenty-nine additional titles of "overflow" geomancy books were shelved in the "divination" section. A total of 212 different geomancy books were available for sale in the bookstore that day. When I typed in the keyword *p'ungsu* (wind and water) into the bookstore computer, 184 book titles were retrieved; the keyword *myŏngdang* (auspicious land), another commonly used Korean term to connote geomancy, yielded another 47 book titles.

Second, the current practice of geomancy by leading politicians in South Korea is also evidence of the continuing popularity of the practice in Korea. It is well known to Koreans that before his 1995 election campaign, the former president of Korea, Kim Dae-Jung, shifted his family graves from his home island in South Chŏlla province to an auspicious site in Yong-in, near Seoul. His new family cemetery site was chosen by hiring probably the best-known geomancer in Korea, Son Sŏg-u, who predicted that the site was auspicious enough to make Kim the president of Korea. It is not clear, however, how relocating his family graves became public, or how word spread that the site would be so auspicious for Kim's political fortunes. It would not be surprising if this operation and prediction were deliberately revealed by Kim's campaign staff to present him as destined for the presidency.

There were widespread rumors that several presidential hopefuls in 2002 had shifted their ancestral graves to more auspicious sites before the campaign. Kim Tugyu, a contemporary scholar of geomancy, perceptively commented that, during major electoral campaigns, people often talk about candidates who have moved their ancestors' graves to auspicious sites. Some of these geomantic rumors seem to have been deliberately fabricated and spread by prospective candidates as a means of influencing public opinion. In this sense, Korean politics and society today continue to be influenced by geomancy.

The practice of geomancy continues to thrive in South Korea. People's belief in geomancy affects the contemporary South Korean government's national environmental planning. As one example, the government's attempts to encourage cremation and limit the expansion of graves and cemeteries have attracted intractable opposition from many quarters because of the geomantic consequences. Geomantic ideas are more important to older generations in rural areas than to younger generations in urban areas. As I mentioned earlier, since the 1980s, the practice of geomancy in Korea, aided by the improving economy and living standards, has been popularized and a number of geomantic manuals and related literature have been published. Currently, geomancers in Korea are still important as grave and house site consultants, although their role has significantly weakened in society. Many Korean intellectuals regard geomancers as superstitious sorcerers, although some view geomancy as a traditional system of ecology that offers vital lessons for modern environmental planning. Geomancers are, however, still persuasive authorities in selecting the sites for graves and houses in South Korea.

North Korea

North Korea, which was thought to have suppressed or even eradicated the practice of geomancy, has recently published a heavily edited legend about the geomancy of Kŭmsusan Mausoleum, the burial site in P'yŏngyang of the deceased leader of North Korea, Kim Ilsŏng (Kim Il Sung; 1912–94). The story tells us that an overseas Korean geographer who taught at a North American university attempted to examine Korean geomancy in light of world geography in order to develop geomancy as a science. The geographer was said to have been disappointed with the geomantic qualities of South Korean cities, but when he visited P'yŏngyang after the death of Kim Ilsŏng, he immediately recognized that the North Korean capital, and especially the Kim Ilsŏng Mausoleum, was the most auspicious site in the entire world.

In the legend of Kŭmsusan, the place was said to be so auspicious because of its geomantic landscapes known as "Washing Silk under the Bright Moonlight" and "A Golden Turtle Immersed in the Muddy Field." The legend argues that this site, which is naturally endowed with extraordinary auspiciousness, was enhanced even more by Kim Ilsŏng and his son Kim Chŏngil (Kim Jong Il; 1942–) thanks to their construction of a dam at the mouth of the Taedong River, which flows through the city of P'yŏngyang. This legend thus implies that Kim Ilsŏng was a sage who could mysteriously change the geomantic conditions of a place to turn it into the most auspicious site in the world. By saying that the Great Leader Kim could mysteriously influence the auspiciousness of nature, the traditional geomantic theory that "an auspicious site is able to help people give birth to great personalities" is also extended. The legend suggests, at very least, that North Korean society today employs geomantic ideas in its deification and mystification of Kim Ilsŏng. But it may even be interpreted as implicitly deifying Kim Ilsŏng, by attributing to him the divine power to remake the geomantic quality of the land around his mausoleum. From this story, we can suspect that the North Korean attitudes toward geomancy must have changed significantly in recent years, to the point that geomancy would even have been used as a means of deifying Kim Ilsŏng.

"Chŏng Inji's Letter Regarding the Examination of King Sejong's First Tomb Site" is translated from the *Annals of King Sejong* (*Sejong sillok*), chŏngmi day, fourth moon, twenty-seventh reign year [1445]; quoted in Kim Tugyu, *Chosŏn p'ungsu hagin ŭi saengae wa nonjaeng* (The Lives and Discourses of Geomancer-Scholars during the Chosŏn Dynasty) (Seoul: Kungni, 2000), pp. 140–57. "The Legend of the Skull of the Prime Minister's Father" is translated from Sin Wŏlgyun, *P'ungsu sŏrhwa* (Folk Narratives on Geomancy) (Seoul: Miral, 1994), pp. 42–43; different versions of this tale are found in Han'guk chŏngsin munhwa yŏn'guwŏn, *Han'guk kubi munhak taegye* (Grand Anthology of Korean Oral Literature) (Seoul: Han'guk Chŏngsin Munhwa Yŏn'guwŏn, 1979–81), vol. 3–2, p. 449; vol. 7–7, p. 793; vol. 8–1, p. 105; vol. 8–3, p. 36. "Yi Chunghwan's Discourse on the Locational Factors for Settlements" is translated from Yi Chunghwan, *T'aengniji* (Book of Choosing Settlements), Geomancy Section, Part II: Discourse on Locational Factors for Settlements (Seoul: Chosŏn Kwan'gunhoe, 1912), pp. 42–44. "The Story of the Grave of the Yu Family of Andong" is translated from Ch'oe Sangsu, *Han'guk Min'gan chŏnsŏl chip* (Anthology of Korean Folk Legends) (Seoul: Tongmun'gwan, 1958), pp. 256–57. "Graves of the President's Ancestors" is translated from Kim Tugyu, *Han'guk p'ungsu ŭi hŏ wa sil* (Falsities and Truths in Korean Geomancy) (Seoul: Tonghaksa, 1997), pp. 268–69. "Chŏng Sŏn's Criticisms of the Practice of Grave Geomancy" is translated from Chŏng Yagyong, *Kugyŏk Mongmin simsŏ* (Criticisms and Advice on Governing the People: A Modern Korean Translation) (Seoul: Minjok Munhwa Ch'ujinhoe, 1969), vol. 2, p. 393. "Sirhak Scholar Pak Chega's Criticism of Geomancy" is translated from Pak Chega, *Pukhak ŭi* (Discourse on Northern Learning), translated into modern Korean by Yi Sŏkho (Seoul: Taeyang Sŏjŏk, 1972), p. 402. "The Debate on Moving King Sejong's Tomb" is translated from Hongmun'gwan, comp., *Chŭngbo Munhŏn Pigo* (The Revised and Enlarged Edition of the Comparative Review of Records and Documents) (Seoul: Hongmun'gwan, 1908), vol. 71, Yego section, p. 5. "The Earth Vein of Kŭmsusan, a Contemporary North Korean Legend" is translated from Kim Ugyŏng, Tong Kich'un, and Kim Chongsŏk, *Kŭmsusan kinyŏm Kungjŏn chŏnsŏl chip* (Collection of Legends Regarding Kŭmsusan Mausoleum) (P'yŏngyang: Munhak Yesul Ch'onghap Ch'ulpansa, 1999), vol. 1, pp. 12–14.

Further Reading

The most important classical literature on geomancy in China is the *Zangshu* (Book of Graves), which is attributed to Guo Pu (276–324) during the Jin dynasty (265–420). This book is written in classical Chinese and included in *Dili zhengzhong* (The Cardinal Principles of Geomancy), commentary by Jiang Guo (Shinchu: Chulin Shuchu, 1967). In the English language, the principles and practice of Chinese geomancy were first discussed in E. J. Eitel, *Fengshui: or the Rudiments of Natural Science in China* (Hong Kong: Lane, Crawford, 1873). A more recent work on Chinese geomancy is Stephan D. R. Feuchtwang, *An Anthropological Analysis of Chinese Geomancy* (Bangkok: White Lotus, 2002). Perhaps one of the most perceptive essays describing the nature of Chinese geomancy and its practice in China is a short paper by Maurice Freedman, "Geomancy: Presidential Address 1968," *Proceedings of the Royal Anthropological Institute of Great Britain and Ireland* (1968), pp. 5–15. In this paper, Freedman points out that grave geomancy was mainly intended to procure good fortune for the living rather than for the well-being of the deceased. For a brief discussion of the nature and theory of Chinese geomancy as a method of choosing auspicious cave-dwelling sites in the Loess Plateau, see Hong-key Yoon, "The Nature and Origin of Chinese Geomancy," *Eratosthene-Sphragide* 1 (1986): 88–102, and Hong-key Yoon, "Lun Zhongguo Gudai Fengshui de Qiyan he Fazhang (A Theory on the Origin and Development of Ancient Chinese Geomancy)" [in Chinese with English abstract], *Ziran Kexueshi Yanjiu (Studies in the History of Natural Sciences)* (Beijing, China), 8, no. 1 (1989): 84–89.

For geomancy as practiced in Korea, the best-known recent academic work is Ch'oe Changjo, *Han'guk ui p'ungsu sasang* (Korean Geomantic thought) (Seoul: Minŭmsa, 1984). One of the earliest and most comprehensive works reflecting modern scholarship on geomancy in Korea is by Murayama Chijun, a Japanese scholar working for the Japanese colonial government of Korea, who carried out a field study of Korean folk customs. His book was originally published in Japanese, Murayama Chijun, *Chōsen no fusui (Korean Geomancy)* (Seoul: Chōsen Shōtofu, 1931); his work has been translated into Korean by Ch'oe Kilsong, *Chosŏn ŭi p'ungsu* (Seoul: Minŭmsa, 1990). One of the few English-language studies of the nature and principles of geomancy in Korea is by Hong-key Yoon, *Geomantic Relationships between Culture and Nature in Korea* (Taipei: Orient Culture Service, 1976).

The contemporary practice of geomancy in South Korea has been reported in Korea through the news media, including newspapers, TV, and radio. Some of the more interesting stories of how prominent politicians have practiced geomancy are included in Kim Tugyu and An Yŏngbae, "Myŏngdang ch'aja nammollae Yijanghago taegwŏn tojŏn" (Running for the Presidency after Secretly Moving Their Ancestral Graves to Auspicious Sites), *Sin Tonga* (New East Asia) 45, no. 2 (February 2002): 181–93, and Kim Tugyu, *Han'guk p'ungsu ŭi hŏ wa sil* (Falsities and Truths in Korean Geomancy) (Seoul: Tonghaksa, 1997).

Legends and folktales involving geomancy are popular, and any collection of Korean folklore will include some stories relating to the practice of geomancy in Korea. One of the first books exclusively on geomantic tales is Sin Wŏlgyun, *P'ungsu sŏrhwa* (Folk Narratives on Geomancy) (Seoul: Miral Ch'ulp'ansa, 1994). Geomantic tales are found in every volume of the one-hundred-volume *Han'guk kubi munhak taegye* (Grand Anthology of Korean Oral Literature) (Seoul: Han'guk Chŏngsin Munhwa Yŏn'guwŏn, 1979–81). This is the largest unabridged collection of Korean folk narratives covering most parts of South Korea. Therefore, it provides original versions of Korean tales that have been transmitted orally among the common people throughout Korea. Geomantic legends and folktales are also an important part of an earlier collection of Korean folk narratives: see Ch'oe Sangsu, *Han'guk min'gan chŏnsŏl chip* (Anthology of Korean Folk Legends) (Seoul: Tongmun'gwan, 1958). An appreciation of Koreans' wishes and ethical values as reflected in Korean geomantic tales is in Hong-key Yoon, "An Analysis of Korean Geomancy Tales," *Asian Folklore Studies* 34, no. 1 (1975): 21–34.

A number of scholars of the Chosŏn dynasty belonging to the Sirhak, or Practical Learning, school criticized the practice of geomancy in their writings. Some of the best examples are Chŏng Yagyong, *Kugyŏk Mongmin simsŏ* (Criticisms and Advice on Governing the People: A Modern Korean Translation) (Seoul: Minjok

Munhwa Ch'ujinhoe, 1969); Pak Chega, *Pukhak ŭi* (Discourse on Northern Learning), translated into modern Korean by Yi Sŏkho (Seoul: Taeyang Sŏjŏk, 1972); Yi Ik, *Sŏngho sasŏl* (Sŏngho's Encyclopedic Discourse), vol. 9, "Insamun, Kamyŏjo (Section on Geomancy)."

Yi Chunghwan, who is considered a Sirhak scholar, wrote *T'aengniji* (Book of Choosing Settlements) (Seoul: Chosŏn Kwangmunhoe, 1912). Some scholars consider this book to be not geomantic literature per se, but human geography in the traditional Korean style. However, geomancy was a key factor in Yi's evaluation of Korean settlements, and the book should be considered as a part of geomantic literature. The book was studied by Hong-key Yoon, "*Taengniji*: A Classical Cultural Geography of the Korean Settlement," *Korea Journal* 16, no. 8 (1976): 4–12; Inshil Choe Yoon, Yi *Chunghwan's T'aengniji: The Korean Classic for Choosing Settlements* (Sydney: Wild Peony, 1998).

Chŏng Inji's Letter Regarding the Examination of King Sejong's First Tomb Site

This official (Chŏng Inji) went with others to the auspicious site at the west of the Hŏnnŭng Royal Tomb and surveyed the orientation and shapes of the place's main mountain and other surrounding hills and waters. With the reference to a report prepared by a person, I will discuss (the geomantic quality of the site) one by one as below:

First, the *Shiyi* (*Sŭbyu*) ([The Geomantic Manual] Repairing Omissions) states, "In a place that has a gentle and flat shape embracing a geomantic vein, the auspicious spot is located in the center. In such a case, blessings will gather at the central site, while the fringe sites will cause the family [occupying it] to perish." The *Zhixuan lun* (*Chihyŏn non*) (Treatise on the Utmost Arcane) also states, "Auspiciousness is in the center, not the fringe." In *Repairing Omissions*, the subsequent paragraph states, "A flat site on high ground is a concave site surrounded by projected mountains that are extensions of low lying landforms, while a projected spot in a hollow land is the convex site on the low ground." A commentary on this statement declares, "The center of a place is the most auspicious spot, but it does not need to be the [physical] center of the place. The center means the concave of the high ground and the convex of the low ground. The *qi* (*ki*, vital energy) expresses itself depending on the feature [of the landscape]." The distance from the main auspicious site of the Royal Tomb of Hunnŭng to the White Tiger [Paekho, viz., the mountain on the right], the slope of Kuryong (Nine Dragon) Mountain, is 3,264 *chŏk* (about 989 *m*: 1 *chŏk* = 0.303 meters); to the slope of Azure Dragon [Chŏngryong, viz., the mountain on the left] is 1,873 *chŏk*. The distance from the west auspicious site to the outer White Tiger is 2,328 *chŏk*; to the slope of Azure Dragon (the mountain on the right side) is 2,817 *chŏk*; to the Inner Peace mountain,

2,751 *chŏk*. The distance between the eastern and western auspicious sites is 944 *chŏk*. Therefore both eastern and western auspicious sites are located at the center of the geomantic landscape, not the fringes.

The Legend of the Skull of the Prime Minister's Father

On his way down from a remote mountain after completing his decade-long study of geomancy, a geomancer found an extremely auspicious grave site worthy of producing a prime minister. An exposed skull was lying there on the site, so he poked a stick through an eye of the skull to see what would happen.

At that very moment, the prime minister of the nation suddenly suffered severe pain in his eye. No medicine was effective for his pain and he went searching for a doctor who could cure it. The same geomancer went to the prime minister and promised to cure his sickness within three days, and told him that he needed to see his ancestor's graves. When the geomancer examined the graves of the prime minister's family, he realized that all had been well maintained but were not located in geomantically good places. Therefore, the geomancer went to the mountain where the auspicious site with the exposed skull was lying. He pulled out the stick from the skull, and the pain in the prime minister's eye suddenly went away.

The geomancer then told the prime minister everything he had done and advised him that the grave that he originally thought was his father's was not his real father's grave; rather, the exposed skull at the auspicious site was his real father's. Astonished, the prime minister asked his mother for an explanation. Then his mother told him her secret and shameful story: the prime minister had been born out of wedlock to her and a male slave in the family. After this incident the slave ran away from the family and she did not know what had happened to him. The prime minister then made a decent grave for the skull and maintained it well.

Yi Chunghwan's Discourse on the Locational Factors for Settlements

How should the geomantic conditions of a site be examined? First, observe *sugu*, the mouth of a watercourse; then *yase*, the features of a field; *sanhyŏng*, the forms of mountains; *t'osaek*, the color of the soil; *suri*, the availability of water; and finally *chosan chosu*, homage-paying mountains and waters.

[WATERCOURSES]

If the mouth of a watercourse is warped, organized loosely, empty, or broad, prosperity cannot extend to the next generation even if the place has a lot of farmland and big houses on it. Those who live there will naturally disperse and disappear. Therefore, when people search for a house site, they should look for a stream whose water discharge cannot be observed and a field enclosed by mountains. Although it is easy to find such a watercourse in a mountainous area, it is not easy to find it in a plain. . . . Whether it is a high mountain or a low land (yin hill), if water flows nearby in a direction away from the place, it is auspicious. . . .

[THE FEATURES OF A FIELD]

Generally, humans are born by receiving the yang force. Since the sky is the yang light, a place surrounded by high mountains with only a small part of visible sky is not a good place to live. For this reason, a broad field is a lovely place to live. Here, the light of the sun, moon, and stars will always shine brightly with various mild and moderate weather conditions of wind, rain, heat, and cold. In such a place there will be many great people born and few diseases. [The place that] should be avoided most is an area which has a late sunrise and early sunset due to being obstructed by high mountains in the four directions.

If the spiritual light of the Big Dipper is not seen at night, it will always have a small yin force. The ascendancy of the yin force results in many ghosts, inauspicious power [atmosphere] in the mornings and evenings, and people easily becoming ill. For these reasons, living in a narrow valley is worse than living in an open field. Low mountains surrounding a big field are not called mountains; rather, they are also called fields, because such areas are not cut off from the light of the sky, and the power of water flows distantly. If there is an open field amid high mountains, it is also a good place to live.

[THE FORMS OF MOUNTAINS]

Generally, the best features of mountains are, as geomancers say, a high projection for an Ancestral Mountain and a beautiful, neat, clean, and soft appearance for a Main Mountain. . . . The feature that one should avoid the most is an Oncoming Dragon [mountain range], which lacks vital energy due to the dragon's weak shape. . . .

[THE COLOR OF THE SOIL]

Generally, in rural settlements, the soil should be firm in structure and fine in texture not only at the bottom but also on the edge of the water. This will result in cool and clean wells, and makes the most ideal living conditions for one's livelihood. If the soil is red clay, black sand, gravelly soil or fine yellow soil, it is considered "dead," and water from such soil will be unpleasant without exception. Such a place is not suitable for human life.

[THE AVAILABILITY OF WATER]

Generally, humans cannot live in a place with no available water. A mountain should have streams, then it can engender the sublimity of auspicious transforming power. The outlets and inlets of the water flow should be in accordance with the principles [of geomancy]. Such a place is auspicious. . . .

[HOMAGE-PAYING MOUNTAINS AND WATERS]

If a Homage-Paying Mountain is a rugged and ugly stone mountain, a tilted lonely hill [a shape caused by landslides], or a spying or thief mountain [suggested by the summit of a mountain partly visible behind a mountain range] . . . it is not a good place to live. If the mountain profile does not have a rugged and hateful appearance, it is an auspicious mountain. Homage-Paying Waters are also called Outer [distant] Waters. . . . The oncoming waters should flow in the direction to meet the dragons [mountain ranges], to combine yin and yang forces, and should flow slowly with many turns; they should never flow in a straight line.

For these reasons, if one desires to build a house and pass it on to his descendants, he should select the location by observing its geomancy. The above six factors are the essence [of geomantic principles].

THE STORY OF THE GRAVE OF THE YU FAMILY OF ANDONG

During the Chosŏn dynasty (1392–1910), a girl of the Kim family of Andong District married into the Yu family, which also hailed from the same region. On the very same day, the woman's father and father-in-law both died. Therefore, both families were looking for a grave site. Her father's family was rich and was able to search for and choose an auspicious grave site by hiring famous geomancers from all over Korea. However, her husband's family could not do this, for they were poor and powerless.

In the meantime, the woman who had married into the Yu family overheard a geomancer reporting to her brother that he had found an auspicious location and prepared a grave site on it. The geomancer said that if water did not spring from the site by noon the next day, the place would produce prime ministers of the nation for three generations. After overhearing this news, the woman secretly went to the grave site and poured water into it during the night.

Next day at noon, when the Kim family went to see the grave site, there was water in it. So they abandoned the place and chose another. At this point, the woman begged her mother to give her the abandoned grave site for her own father-in-law's burial. The mother allowed her daughter to do so. After the grave was prepared, the Kim family gradually lost their fortune and the Yu family became prosperous. Indeed the prime minister Yu Sŏngnyong (1542–1607) was born from the Yu family.

Graves of the President's Ancestors

When Ch'ŏn Tu-hwan was the president of the Fifth Republic, many thought-less geomancers visited and examined the graves of his ancestors, for it was thought that he had become the president due to auspiciousness manifested from such grave sites. It may be natural for Koreans who are filled with geo-mantic ideas to talk about the [auspicious] grave sites associated with success-ful electoral candidates or powerful people. However, this phenomenon may not be a simple matter, as such rumors may have been intentionally spread by people in power or candidates to manipulate the public in their favor. They at-tempted to sway public opinion by hiring influential fortune-tellers and geo-mancers. They spread rumors that a certain someone would become king or was destined to be elected as the president, in order to influence the people to accept a particular candidate as the one with the Mandate of Heaven to be-come the ruler of the country. . . .

Chŏng Sŏn's Criticisms of the Practice of Grave Geomancy

Chŏng Sŏn said, "People in the world are brainwashed and seduced by Guo Pu's art of geomancy and do not bury their deceased parents for several years while they covetously look for auspicious grave sites. Some people, even after burying their deceased, doubt the quality of the grave site and shift the corpse to different places up to three or even four times. Some families quarrel over grave sites and cannot decide where to bury their ancestor's corpse, turning family relationships sour. In some cases, brothers, taking different geomantic advice, have disputes and become enemies." He also said, "People who bury their parents while indulging in the art of geomancy end up illegally invading grave sites in mountains belonging to other people. In some cases they ille-gally dig up other people's graves and throw their bones away [in order to bury their own ancestors there]. This kind of behavior leads people to extreme ani-mosity and ends up causing serious litigation, which people are determined to win at all costs. Therefore some people waste their wealth and ruin their busi-nesses this way while not being able to secure an auspicious site. Such behavior brings misfortune instead of the blessings they seek. How has the people's fool-ishness reached this degree?"

Sirhak Scholar Pak Chega's Criticism of Geomancy

The idea of geomancy has had a more adverse influence [on Korean society] than even Buddhism or Daoism. Even the scholar-gentry class followed this idea and made it a custom. It is said that moving an ancestor's grave to a better location is an act of filial piety. Since the scholar-gentry class considered the location of its ancestor's graves to be important, the common people imitated their behavior. . . . Generally, it is a bad intention to depend on one's deceased parents for one's fortune. Moreover, occupying other's mountains illegally and destroying other's burial tumuli are not the right things to do. To hold more splendid worship ceremonies at grave sites than at home during special occasions is abhorrent [lit. against proper principles]. It is not possible to list all the stories about people who have performed such abhorrent deeds [lit. deeds against proper principles] as wasting all of their wealth [in looking for auspicious places] without taking care of their ancestor's bones, and yet expect good fortune to come to them.

The Debate on Moving King Sejong's Tomb

In the first year of King Yejong (1469), Yŏngnŭng [King Sejong's tomb] was moved to Yŏju. Originally the tomb was near to Hŏnnŭng [King Taejong's tomb]. During King Sejo's reign, there was discussion that Yŏngnŭng should be moved, since it was not located at an auspicious place. Therefore, King Sejo summoned Sŏ Kŏjŏng and asked him about the matter. Sŏ said, "The art of 'mountains, waters, and directions' [viz., geomancy] is used to receive blessings and avoid misfortune among descendants. I do not know much about the art, but people's relocating their ancestors' graves is an attempt to seek and acquire fortune [for the descendants]. What more fortune do you, as a king, expect?" The king then said, "I no longer wish to move the tomb."

The Earth Vein of Kŭmsusan, a Contemporary North Korean Legend

. . . As the evening approached, the view of Kŭmsusan District became even clearer and the geographer's eyes turned brighter. He exclaimed, "How mysterious this land is. This really is the geomantic landscape of 'Washing Silk under Bright Moonlight' and 'A Golden Turtle Immersed in a Muddy Field.' The Great Taedong River that embraces this land flows in a southwesterly direction and powerful cliffs exist there that form the world's most auspicious mountains. How can this place not be an auspicious geomantic site." . . .

In the geomantic landscape of a Golden Turtle Immersed in a Muddy Field, the most important element is water. Tortoises and turtles are associated with water, and there should not be too much or too little water. Now I realize that our nation suffered the misfortune of wars and natural disasters whenever we had floods such as the one in the Ŭlmyo year or a great drought. Such misfortunate times occurred when the golden turtle was twisting in discomfort [caused by flood and drought]. The river as [the geographer] knew it when he was little was a river of death that took people's lives due to flooding and mudflows. Kim Ilsŏng and his son Kim Chŏngil have provided eternal comfort to this golden turtle. They built the West Sea Dam at the mouth of the Taedong River and stopped its flow. Therefore the Taedong River became a great artificial lake that enjoys everlasting stability without any change.

However, this old scholar's view changed the moment he saw the great leader (Kim Ilsŏng's) mummified appearance. As he passed the hall that enshrined Kim's standing figure and paid homage, he suddenly came to realize that the place was a genuine geomancy cave [auspicious site] of the first degree.

It has been long since the formation of this place, but the reason why this site became a genuine auspicious site of "the geomantic landscape of a golden turtle" was because the body of the savior of Korea, Kim Ilsŏng, lies here. [The geographer] had been familiar with this place since his boyhood, but he had not seen it as an auspicious site; the site only became genuinely auspicious after Kim Ilsŏng was laid to rest there. He thought that only auspicious land could influence people and produce a great person. However, he now realized that the Great Leader Kim Ilsŏng was able to transform this place into an auspicious site, because he was a great sage.

—13—

Voices of Female Confucians
in Late Chosŏn Korea

Youngmin Kim

The Chosŏn dynasty (1392–1910) marks the ascendancy in premodern Korean history and religion of the tradition of Neo-Confucianism ("Neo-Confucianism" here being used in the narrow sense of *Daoxue*, the "Learning of the Way"). Indeed, Korean society underwent significant changes as Neo-Confucian mores became deeply rooted in Chosŏn society and culture. These changes especially affected women. Despite the consensus of scholarly opinion concerning the general rubric of "Confucianization," however, the multidimensional quality of late-Chosŏn culture in general, and women's history in particular, demands further investigation.

The existence of female Confucian philosophers in the late Chosŏn period suggests that the relationship between Confucianism and women in this period is actually much more nuanced than often assumed. Indeed, given that Confucianism is often reputed to have a demeaning attitude toward women, "female Confucian philosopher" may sound like a contradiction in terms. If Confucianism is a gyno-oppressive ideology, it seems self-defeating for a woman to aspire to become a Confucian philosopher.

The translation in this chapter aims to restore the multidimensional significance of Confucianism in the intellectual lives of late Chosŏn women through the writings of two female Confucian philosophers, Im Yunjidang (1721–93) and Kang Chŏngiltang (1772–1832). These writings are instrumental in exploring the following questions regarding Confucianism and Korean women's history: (1) What elements of Confucianism were taken up by female intellectuals? (2) How did these intellectuals deploy these elements to forge their self-understanding? (3) How did they reinterpret Neo-Confucian philosophy in pursuing their interests in social relationships? And (4) how did female Confucians of this period differ from those of earlier eras?

The translation includes five short poems, one letter to Kang's husband, brief notes for Kang's husband, the preface to Kang Chŏngiltang's literary collection, and one philosophical essay written by Im Yunjidang.

Kang Chŏngiltang was born in Chech'ŏn, Ch'ungch'ŏng province, in 1772 and married Yun Kwangyŏn when she was twenty years old. Yun did not pass the civil service examination, and his family was quite poor. According to various biographies in Kang's literary collection, despite the extreme poverty in which she lived, Kang not only completely fulfilled her domestic duties but also applied herself to a thorough study of the Confucian classics like the *Four Books*. The fruition of her study of the classics produced scholarly essays, letters, and poems. Soon after Kang's death at the age of sixty-one, her husband collected her writings and published her works in a literary collection.

Im Yunjidang was born in Yangsŏng in Kyŏnggi province. She was a sister of Im Sŏngju (1711–88) a famous Neo-Confucian philosopher of the late Chosŏn period. In the funeral oration for her brother, Im Yunjidang wrote that her brother served as her lifetime intellectual companion in studying the Confucian classics. She married Sin Kwangyu at the age of nineteen but was widowed at age twenty-seven. Even after her husband's death, it is said that she fulfilled all the traditional duties of a daughter-in-law in the Sin family until she died at the age of seventy-two. During her lifetime, she studied the Confucian classics and wrote several philosophical essays and commentaries on the *Doctrine of Mean* and the *Great Learning*. Her literary collection was posthumously published by her other brother Im Chŏngju and her brother-in-law Sin Kwangu.

On a social level, both of these women were admired by their family members and friends for being exceptionally virtuous human beings. In addition, it was quite rare during the Chosŏn dynasty for women to have their literary collections published—that theirs in fact were published, even if posthumously, speaks to their influence. In this regard, it is most likely that both these women enjoyed happy lives. However, their personal lives did not live up to their reputations as exemplary virtuous women. For example, neither Im Yunjidang nor Kang Chŏngiltang had children. In fact, Kang Chŏngiltang gave birth to nine children, but all of them died before they could speak. Given the tremendous significance of bearing children in Confucian social norms, this would seem to reveal at least a flaw in their social persona, if not also in their personal lives. Thus while some scholars have praised their scholarly achievements as the result of overcoming personal misfortune, it seems more likely that such misfortune freed them to invest more time and energy in scholarly pursuits rather than performing such household tasks as caring for children.

Extant Chosŏn governmental tablets celebrating virtuous women attest that Im Yunjidang and Kang Chŏngiltang were not the only women believed to have attained Confucian moral ideals through virtuous conduct. However, what makes them extraordinary is that they apparently wanted to be Neo-Confucian philosophers. In other words, they were Confucian not only as women were defined in Confucian family ritual, but enacted male protocols of scholarly Confucianism, studying theories of Neo-Confucianism and writing philosophical essays and commentaries on the Confucian classics. It is because they pursued scholarly work and contributed to the body of Confucian philosophy that we can call them Neo-Confucian philosophers. In particular, Im's philosophical essays are proof of her firm grasp of Neo-Confucian principles. Her mastery of the theories of human nature shows that Im was able to comprehend and ponder Confucianism as deeply as were male intellectuals.

As is well known, however, it is not easy to discover many female intellectuals of the Chosŏn period, since opportunities for specialized education were not widely available to women. Although there are a handful of female intellectuals with extant literary collections, it appears that very few women were interested in philosophy. The vast majority of female intellectuals were most likely encouraged toward literary pursuits, especially poetry. For these two exemplary women, however, philosophy was their preferred means of religious practice.

The source references for the translations are the literary collections of Kang Chŏngiltang and Im Yunjidang, which were reproduced in Yi Young-ch'un's Korean translation, *Kang Chŏngiltang* (Seoul: Karam Kihoek, 2002). Poems by Kang Chŏngiltang appear at Yi Young-ch'un, pp. 201–6. Kang Chŏngiltang's letter to her husband appears at pp. 211–22. For Kang's brief notes to her husband, see Yi Young-ch'un, pp. 224–25. The preface to Kang Chŏngiltang's literary collection appears at Yi Young-ch'un, pp. 198–99. For Im Yunjidang's philosophical essay "On the Mind of Man, the Mind of Dao, the Four Beginnings, and the Seven Emotions," see Yi Young-ch'un, trans., *Im Yunjidang* (Seoul: Hyean, 1998), pp. 309–10.

Further Reading

The significance of Im Yunjidang (1721–93) and Kang Chŏngiltang (1772–1832) has yet to be satisfactorily explored. Their literary collections are translated into modern Korean by Yi Young-ch'un, *Im Yunjidang* (Seoul: Hyean, 1998) and *Kang Chŏngiltang* (Seoul: Karam Kihoek, 2002). The first scholarly paper in English on these writers will appear in *Confucianism and Women in Late-Chosŏn Korea*, a volume to appear in the Series on Korean Studies from the International Center for Korean Studies, Korea University.

POEMS BY KANG CHŎNGILTANG

Human Nature Is Good

Human nature is primordially good without exception.
Actualizing it fully makes for a sage,

No sooner do I desire humanness than it is before me.
Make the self sincere by illuminating the pattern of the universe.

Reading *The Practice of the Mean*

Zisi [ca. 483–ca. 402 B.C.E.] passed down this treatise.
It weaves a thousand years together and opens the minds of multitudes.
When the heart's essence is established, there is no imbalance.
When the heart function is at work, there is no error.

For the Wife of Kŭn Chin, a Great-Grandson

Female virtue is of prime importance.
Submissiveness is a duty.
This is the way of a woman.
You should follow it diligently.

A Poem Offered to My Husband

A long time ago, you studied with the master Kan Chae,
There has been no other path to seeking the way since then.
Thirty years have now passed.
What is the level of your achievement?

Concentrating on Reverence

Myriad patterns originate from Heaven-and-Earth.
One mind unites nature and emotions.
Without concentrating on reverence,
How can you manage the long trip to sagehood?

Kang Chŏngiltang's Letter to Her Husband

. . . I heard that on this visit with your teacher you received his calligraphy—
"Look at nothing contrary to ritual, listen to nothing contrary to ritual, say
nothing contrary to ritual, do nothing contrary to ritual"—and planned to
carve it on a board to hang in your study. I am extremely happy about this.
These four sentences were Confucius's response to Yan Hui. Yan Hui, a disciple of Confucius, put this teaching into practice during his lifetime and thus

entered the realm of sagehood. Great-grandfather-in-law copied the statements for his self-discipline and passed them down to younger generations. Please respect the exchange between Confucius and Yan Hui. Keep in mind your ancestor's serious self-discipline. Appreciate your teacher's encouragement. Day and night, never slacken your moral discipline and always concentrate on this. "Selfish ego"—the heart likes it, but it does not correspond to the Heavenly pattern. Ritual propriety—deportment of the Heavenly pattern. First clarify what corresponds to ritual propriety and what does not, cut out selfishness courageously, and follow the heavenly pattern all along. Then you can reach the Dao.

Kang Chŏngiltang's Brief Notes for Her Husband

A. The Confucian gentleman is attentive to the Dao because he wants to govern society by cultivating himself. The Confucian gentleman should do his best day and night in fulfilling this task, constantly worrying that he is not self-cultivated enough. How could you indulge in idle fancies, careless speech, meetings with guests, and loitering? How could you forget that the Confucian gentleman's responsibility is heavy and the road to the Dao is long? Reproach yourself and work harder in order to cultivate yourself. Life span and success in career depend on fate. Influenced by vulgar sayings in the world, parents do not educate their daughters. As a consequence, women often do not know moral principles. How ridiculous this is!

B. Im Yunjidang said, "Even if I am a woman, there is no difference between a man and woman's human nature." "If a woman does not wish to be like Tairen [the mother of King Wen, the founder of the Zhou dynasty in China, whose virtuous conduct, the *Odes* say, contributed to her son's success] and Taisi [King Wen's wife, who is said to have helped her husband establish the Zhou dynasty], she abandons herself. If a woman tries, she can reach the level of sagehood. What do you think about this?"

C. I am a mere housewife stuck in the inner quarters. I do not hear and learn many things. But while sewing and cleaning, I study ancient classics, probe their principles, and learn the conduct of ancient peoples, hoping to achieve the ancients' level of sagehood. You are a grown man. If you commit your will to sagehood, seek the Dao, follow your teachers, make good friends, and proceed diligently in this way, what learning are you not capable of, what lecture is there that you do not understand, what actions can you not accomplish? If you pursue humanness and rightness, and establish equilibrium and rectitude, who can prevent your pursuit of sagehood? Sages and worthies were once ordinary men. You are also an ordinary man. What fear can stop you? Please renew your virtue daily and take the state of the sages and worthies as your goal.

Preface to Kang Chŏngiltang's Literary Collection

Generally speaking, human beings can enjoy fraternal harmony through brotherhood, and social harmony through friendship. These are consummate delights obtained through relationships with others. However, from the ancients to now, only a few have been able to achieve these delights.

How much more delight can be had if husband and wife admonish one another for self-cultivation and continue to do so even when they are at leisure and sharing food. They become each other's mutual resources for moral development!

When my relative T'anwŏn Myŏngjik was young, he was too high-spirited, so his conduct was not without problems. But since the age of twenty, he has gradually turned to the Dao. Studying with Master Kangjae Song Ch'igyu, he was seriously engaged in scholarly erudition, putting what he learned into earnest practice with genuine resolve. So, I paid attention to him.

Recently, his poverty has worsened. His wife passed away. His life is so wretched, so much so that people almost cannot bear it. Nonetheless, he exerts himself all the more and does not waver from his original goal of improving his morality. I, thus, find him all the more extraordinary. One day, all of sudden, he showed me a small manuscript, the "Posthumous Manuscript of Chŏngiltang." He sobbed:

> This is my late wife's manuscript, which she kept in her silk box. She thought that writing was not women's business so she did not publish it. I do not want to go against her wishes in death, but I cannot bear to see her writing disappear from this world. The poems are few, but they are admonishments to those who seek learning. Her style is not flamboyant and is without embellishment. And yet her writing is relevant to self-cultivation. When discussing learning, she focused on sincerity and reverence. When discussing self-cultivation, she emphasized "the extension of knowledge through investigating things" and earnest practice. Her words mesh well with the Confucian classics to the smallest detail. While weaving and making cloth, she studied the ancient classics. She must have had profound insights. I do not fully know the level of refinement and depth she achieved, but I credit my wife for making me transform my disposition, follow my teacher, enjoy the companionship of my friends, and obeying the law.

I listened to my relative with respect. At first, I smacked my lap with great joy; and at the end I was on my knees with reverence. I said, "I paid my attentions to you and found you extraordinary. Now I know what made it possible. Your wife's admonishment and advice in daily life made you virtuous. This is indeed an extraordinary case!"

In the past, there were bright and wise women whose reputations were known throughout the generations. They attracted public attention through their excellence in things like filial piety, chastity, virtuous actions, or effectiveness in speaking. How remarkable to find among women a sophisticated understanding of moral principles and high attainments in learning as seen in this manuscript. Given that desirable relationships among brothers and friends are difficult, this case is extraordinary! Myŏngjik wanted to publish this manuscript in order to immortalize it for subsequent generations. It cannot be prevented! Myŏngjik asked me to write a preface because of our intimate relationship. I cannot dare to ignore this request. I am happy to write this preface but I do not deserve to do so.

Im Yunjidang's "On the Mind of Man, the Mind of Dao, the Four Beginnings, and the Seven Emotions"

QUESTION: The Emperor Shun said to the Emperor Yu, "The mind of man is unstable, the mind of the Dao is unapparent; be of true insight and maintain unity, hold fast to the mean." Why does Emperor Shun speak of two things—the mind of Dao and the mind of man—when the mind is one?

ANSWER: It is not that there is a duality of mind but that there are two modes in which the mind issues forth. Human nature is the most noble because it earns the most refined material force of the five phases when it comes into being. However, human nature does not exist without the mind. Without the mind, [human nature as] pattern cannot exist as pattern. Therefore, it is said, "It is man who is capable of broadening the Way. It is not the Way that is capable of broadening man." The Dao here means human nature; Man means the mind.

What is the mind? On the one hand, it is the mind of heaven-and-earth when it produces material things. It is spiritual intelligence, which is clear and unitary. This spiritual intelligence, which is clear and unitary, is embodied in human beings and makes up an unobstructed intelligent consciousness. It carries human nature and becomes the master of the self and the foundation of myriad affairs. This is the so-called mind of Dao. On the other hand, human beings cannot help possessing individual forms, and thus cannot avoid having the mind of man. The mind of man comes from the selfish and private elements, which are formed by physical endowments. By contrast, the mind of Dao originates from the impeccable aspects of innate endowments.

Even sages cannot escape the mind of man because they also have physical endowments. Even villains possess the mind of Dao because they share the principle of the supreme ultimate. But for villains, the mind of Dao is nothing more than the four beginnings of morality [see below] issuing forth sporadically. As for the sages, although their minds of man are founded on physical endowments, they do not transgress what is proper even when they follow their heart/mind's desire. Thus for the sages the mind of man is identical with the mind of Dao.

As for ordinary people, what comes from physical endowments surpasses what comes from the impeccable aspects of innate endowments. The mind of Dao tends to be clouded and has difficulties manifesting itself. The mind of man tends to be arbitrary and is difficult to control. Thus, it is said, "The mind of man is unstable, the mind of Dao is unapparent."

When the mind issues forth, there is an emotion. Human beings are able to examine what the mind issues forth, and watch the subtle activating forces of good and bad. They should choose goodness and stick to it, recognize badness and eliminate it without fail. In this way, they make the mind of Dao their master and the mind of man obeys. Only then will what is unstable become stable and what is unapparent become apparent. As a result, there will be no problem of excess or deficiency in speech and deeds. Thus, it is said, "Be of true insight and maintain unity, hold fast to the mean."

QUESTION: The four beginnings are also what the mind issues forth. They are also emotions. This being so, why are they distinguished from other feelings?

ANSWER: The four beginnings refer to humanity, rightness, decorum, and wisdom. They are what human nature directly issues forth when it is stirred. The seven emotions refer inclusively to what human nature and the physical endowments issue forth. The four beginnings are not independent of the seven emotions. One should not misunderstand their meanings because of the [seeming confusion in the terms].

QUESTION: Do you mean that human nature and the mind/heart both issue forth?

ANSWER: No. Human nature is a pattern with which the mind is equipped. The mind is the vessel in which human nature resides. They are two different things in certain contexts and one whole in other contexts. The mind is what is unobstructed, intelligent, spiritual, and transformative, without being predictable. The pattern makes such features possible. The pattern is not involved in actions, while the mind is. The pattern does not leave traces, while the mind does. If there is no pattern, there is nothing to be issued forth. If there is no mind, there is no mechanism to make issuing forth possible. How can human nature issue forth without the mind, and the mind issue forth without the pattern, given that the pattern and material force are intertwined? Although there are many existing theories on this issue by former worthies, I cannot accept them. So, I wrote this and will wait for the one who has a better understanding.

Shamanism

—14—

Yi Kyubo's "Lay of the Old Shaman"

Richard D. McBride II

Yi Kyubo (1168–1241) was a prominent civil official and literary figure during the Koryŏ period (918–1392). He passed the civil service examination in his twenty-first year and served diligently at a minor post in southwestern Korea before he caught the eye of the military dictator Ch'oe Chunghŏn (1149–1219) in 1207. After being transferred to the Koryŏ capital, present-day Kaesŏng in North Korea, he distinguished himself during the ensuing years between 1210 and 1230 as a literatus of the Hallim Academy, the government-sponsored Confucian university; as a drafter of proclamations; and as a member of the Ministry of Rites, the body of officials that directed state rituals, interpreted decorum for the dynasty and the state, and oversaw all interstate relations. He then served during the 1230s as the administrator of the Chancellery, minister of revenue, and grand academician of the Academy of Worthies, and supervisor of the Ministry of Rites before retiring with the highest honors given by king and country in 1237.

Since Yi Kyubo was schooled from his youth in the curricula of the Confucian classics, similar to the civil bureaucracy and literati in China, the views and opinions expressed in his writings are representative of the educated elite in medieval Korea. As one of the prominent literati elite, Yi Kyubo's life was dominated by the writing of *hansi*, poems written with Chinese logographs that follow established Chinese poetic patterns. Like most of the intelligentsia in his day, he was first greatly influenced by the writing style of the great Song dynasty poet Su Shi (Su Dongpo, 1036–1101), who reintroduced and further developed the simple yet elegant style of Tao Qian (Tao Yuanming, 365–427) to the cultured elite of China and East Asia. Building from this foundation while living in the Koryŏ capital of Kaesŏng, Yi Kyubo developed his own vigorous and direct poetic style.

The poem translated here, the "Lay of the Old Shaman," demonstrates what we may define roughly as the Confucian rejection and denunciation of shamans, shamanism, and native religious practices. Although Yi Kyubo's poem is written with a negative view of shamans, it is still a crucial piece of evidence in any scholarly attempt to reconstruct the role and activities of shamans in Koryŏ society, and the relationship between shamanism and Buddhism in medieval Korea, because it is the single longest treatment of shamans prior to the Chosŏn period (1392–1910).

Scholars typically characterize pre-Buddhist Korean religion as "shamanism," but the nature of ancient shamanism in Korea is notoriously difficult to define. The historical sources from which the brief accounts of shamans and shamanic activities are gleaned and used to cobble together a sketch of early Korean shamanism were written by Korean literati who, following Chinese historical tradition and convention, did not treat them as important and generally considered them barely worthy of mention. These writers were at best ambivalent and at worst hostile toward shamans and practitioners of local or native religious traditions. Such figures were excluded from conceptualizations of appropriate official state ritual in Chinese elite culture from at least the third century C.E. onward, after the Chinese generalissimo Cao Cao (155–220) enacted a general proscription against shamans and autochthonous religious practices. This official act was met with approbation by the educated elite in the Sinitic cultural sphere and was adopted over time by the Korean aristocracy. Since Cao Cao's proscription of shamans was promulgated from his power base in the city of Ye (in southern Hebei along the Yellow River), during the Guanghe period of the Latter Han period (178–84) and reinforced by his son Emperor Wen (r. 220–26) of the succeeding Wei dynasty in 225, it became known in the literature as the "Edict of Ye District." However, this edict was more than just an attack on shamans: it was a law forbidding the performance of local religious rituals, pejoratively labeled "licentious sacrifices" (ŭmsa in Korean, yinsi in Chinese), which for the most part were composed of blood sacrifices to local gods and spirits. In Yi Kyubo's poem, however, the edict of Ye is placed in conjunction to an allusion to a famous anecdote in Sima Qian's (d. ca. 85 B.C.E.) Historical Record (Shiji), which tells about the discontinuation of rites to the River Earl (He Bo), the spirit ruler of the Yellow River. The River Earl purportedly demanded yearly tribute of virgin brides, and Confucian bureaucrats, like Yi Kyubo in his poem here, celebrate Ximen Bao, an official of the ancient state of Wei at Ye during the Chinese Warring States period (fourth and third centuries B.C.E.), for throwing into the river the female shamans who officiated in this ancient ritual of human sacrifice.

If we define "shamanism" as a religion in which the guiding belief is that the unseen world of gods, spirits, demons, and ancestral spirits is responsive only to the shaman, there is also little literary evidence to support the proposition that shamanism was the ancient religion of the Korean people. The earliest accounts of the tribes and small city-states that eventually coalesced into the Korean people derive from accounts by Chinese generals, travelers, merchants, and diplomats included in short didactic essays in Chinese dynastic histories describing the barbarians on the frontier of successive Chinese states. Although the word scholars translate as "shaman" (wu in Chinese, mu in Korean) was used to describe certain religious leaders and diviners of various Turkic and Mongolian tribes, as well as the Wa state in ancient Japan, the term was never used in reference to those who officiated over religious observances such as worship of objects worthy of veneration (mountains, waters, trees, and special animals), worship of founding kings and ancestors, and seasonal and yearly rituals among any of the Korean tribal peoples and ancient states recorded in Chinese sources.

In the two primary sources of Korean history and lore of the Three Kingdoms period (traditional dates, 57 B.C.E.–668 C.E.)—the *History of the Three Kingdoms* (*Samguk sagi*), compiled by the scholar-official Kim Pusik (1075–1151) between 1136 and 1146, and the *Memorabilia of the Three Kingdoms* (*Samguk yusa*), compiled by the Buddhist monk Iryŏn (1206–89) around 1285 and later revised— there are a combined total of eleven references to "shamans" (*mu*), a few of which duplicate the information. These texts include five references to the activities of shamans in the northern kingdom of Koguryŏ (traditional dates, 37 B.C.E.–668 C.E.). Shamans are here depicted in roles very similar to those in which they comport themselves today: spirit-mediumship, exorcism and the pacification of the vengeful spirits of people who had been executed by the king, divination regarding royal pregnancies and auspicious and inauspicious actions of the king, and the performance of ancestor commemoration rituals at the shrine of the founder king. The citations concerning the southwestern kingdom of Paekche (traditional dates, 18 B.C.E.–661 C.E.) also portray the shaman in a divinatory role: recounting how a shaman solves a riddle written on the back of a turtle shell, foretelling the downfall of Paekche in 660.

The four accounts dealing with the southeastern kingdom of Silla (traditional dates, 57 B.C.E.–935 C.E.) provide the best literary evidence regarding the presumed exalted station of shamans in ancient Korea, yet they also demonstrate one aspect of the extant sources' ambivalent attitude toward shamans. Both of the literary works just mentioned contain similar accounts of the native title given to the legendary second ruler of Silla, King Namhae (r. 4–24 C.E.): *ch'ach'aung*. They repeat a gloss on the word putatively given by the Silla aristocrat Kim Taemun (active late seventh and early eighth centuries C.E.), who says that *ch'ach'aung* means "shaman" (*mu*) in the language of Silla. Kim also says that people serve the spirits and make offerings to ancestors through shamans; therefore, they are revered by the people. The association between shamans and kings in Silla, though anachronistic, may have some archaeological support as well. Elaborate golden crowns (*kŭmgwan*) dating to the fifth and sixth centuries have been excavated from some of the royal tombs of Silla in Kyŏngju (as well as from other sites in southeastern Korea associated with the ancient Silla and Kaya kingdoms [traditional dates 42–562 C.E.]). The golden crowns of Silla are characterized by deer-antler shapes and tree shapes adorned with small golden bangles and curved pieces of jade. Scholars suggest that this is a symbolic representation of the king's virility and his responsibility to ensure the fertility of the state's lands. Since these crowns resemble the headdresses worn by some shamans and shamanic tribal leaders excavated from tombs in Siberia and Manchuria and currently in use there, some scholars speculate that the Silla kings may have functioned as shamans, mediating between the gods and ancestral spirits on behalf of the people. Nevertheless, whatever shamanic characteristics scholars may wish to impute to Silla's kings, these appear to have diminished as Silla's royalty and aristocracy embraced Buddhism as an official state cult and personal faith in the sixth century and absorbed Sinitic social and cultural practices in the process of forging a centralized, bureaucratic state like those of China. One account in Buddhist-inspired materials suggests that the shamans of Silla were ineffective in controlling harmful spirits when compared with an adept Buddhist monk. Buddhist literature suggests that during the seventh century, monk-thaumaturges specializing in sūtra chanting and dhāraṇī rituals superseded shamans in their abilities to control native spirits and in the deployment of gods to protect the Korean state of Silla.

A broader picture of the role of shamans can be ascertained for the Koryŏ period (918–1392). The number of references to shamans in the *History of the Koryŏ* (*Koryŏsa*), which was compiled under the direction of Chŏng Inji (1396–1478) and completed in 1451, is more than three times that of the allusions to shamans found in the earlier documents. Since this text is the official history of the Koryŏ period, it deals predominantly with court-centered activities, though it also contains some stories dealing with aristocratic families. As with the materials treating the Three Kingdoms period, shamans are also treated ambiguously in this work. They are shown favor and relied upon by the royal family in times of difficulty, but they are also seen as an embarrassing aspect of low culture to be controlled and eradicated.

The *History of the Koryŏ* records more than twenty occasions in which Koryŏ kings gathered shamans and had them pray for rain in officially sponsored ceremonies. On at least one occasion, the older sister of a high-ranking official became a shaman, receiving the title "sylph official" (*sŏn'gwan*). We are told that she was permitted to officiate over some sacrifices during the P'algwanhoe (Festival of the Eight Prohibitions), an important state-sponsored religious ceremony that contained Buddhist and native religious elements. Shamans were often favorites of palace women (queens, secondary royal wives, and princesses) and sometimes taught their songs in the palace compound. However, there are also a few occasions in which members of the royal family were charged with the crime of employing shamans to influence dynastic succession through the use of curses and black magic to induce virulent infection (*mugo*) in opponents.

A few accounts are preserved in which shamans explain the underlying supernatural causes of illness and give advice that certain man-made objects, such as levees, are causing disturbances among the native spirits and must be dismantled. Some shamans claimed that important native Korean gods, the mountain god (*sansin*) and the god of walls and moats (*sŏnghwangsin*), sometimes referred to as "the city god," descended into and possessed them during their shamanizing. One female shaman was said to have bedazzled the common folk by making pronouncements in strange whistling sounds she claimed to be the voice of the spirit possessing her. The shaman portrayed in Yi Kyubo's poem seems to have possessed similar attributes. Skilled shamans often enjoyed financial success and could receive prize possessions as payment for their services. One account relates that a horse (an expensive possession in traditional Korea and usually reserved for top-ranking officials, aristocrats, and military leaders) was given as a distinctive payment for a successful shamanic ceremony. Nevertheless, unlike the official patronage enjoyed by the Buddhist church in Koryŏ, shamans were not tax exempt and, along with other skilled, wealthy, lowborn people—such as artisans—are said to have had their taxes extracted in bolts of hemp cloth.

As I mentioned previously, the literati-officials of Koryŏ generally despised shamans and periodically attempted to eliminate their role in defining popular beliefs by submitting memorials to the Koryŏ king outlining the abuses perpetrated by shamans and suggesting policies to diminish their influence. One government official submitted a memorial suggesting that all shamans be removed from the capital and large cities in the state and ten reservations be made in the countryside to quarantine them so that they could continue to do their shamanizing without infecting the population—presumably in hopes that they would eventually die out. On a few occasions, memorials submitted by the literati influenced royal domestic policy sufficiently that shamans were driven out of the Koryŏ capital and shamanic exorcisms were prohibited. The Minister Ham Yuil (1106–85) was one of the most outspoken and active officials who worked hard to prohibit rituals and blood sacrifices for the propitiation of native gods and spirits, destroyed their altars, and promoted the expulsion of shamans, diviners, and other religious specialists deemed charlatans by the state from the capital. Minister Ham was most active in this role during the reign of King Ŭijong (1146–70), right around the time of Yi Kyubo's birth in 1168. Yi alludes to Minister Ham's anti-shaman campaign in his poem as being a more or less contemporary event, but this policy would probably have been impossible to enforce during the political and social chaos that emerged during the first twenty-five years of military rule in Korea. Although I have no firm evidence, my suspicion is that the "Lay of the Old Shaman" was composed between 1210 and 1230, when Yi was a literatus in the Hallim Academy in the capital.

Yi Kyubo anchors his didactic poem with many allusions to the *Classic of Mountains and Seas (Shanhai jing)*, an important work of ancient Chinese literature, the oldest parts of which were composed during the Warring States period and the latest parts as late as the Han (202 B.C.E.–220 C.E.) and Wei-Jin (220–317) periods. For instance, Yi establishes what he considers to be a proper shaman by referring to Wu Xian, a famous shaman of ancient China who stationed himself on Wu shan (Shaman Mountain), and to several shamans who assisted him by gathering medicinal drugs and herbs on Wu shan, which, according to many commentators, also went by the name Ling shan (Spirit Mountain). Ling shan, in the east of present-day Sichuan province, was full of male and female shamans during the time of the ancient Chinese state of Chu. Chu shamans were also active in the area of the Yuan and Xiang rivers. The Yuan jiang is a long river originating in the east at Guizhou and flowing westward in Hunan into Lake Tongting. The Xiang jiang, also known as the Xiang shui, is a large tributary of the Yangzi River in Hunan province, originating in the vicinity of Jilin in Guangdong prefecture and flowing northward; ultimately arriving at Lake Tongting. The Yuan and Xiang rivers appear in poems with shamanic themes preserved in the *Elegies of Chu* (*Chu ci*, fourth to third century B.C.E.), specifically in poems dedicated to the "Princess of the Xiang" (Xiang jun) and the "Lady of the Xiang" (Xiang furen). Traditional commentary, though debated by modern scholars who suspect the two poems may merely be alternate versions of the same song, suggest that the "Princess" and "Lady" of the Xiang allude to deified daughters of the mythical sage emperor Yao.

Since Yi conceptualizes the ancient shamans of China as sagacious recluses who dwell in mountains and as producers of elegant poetry in honor of gods, he speaks disparagingly of the pronouncements of the shamans of his day who attribute life's troubles and mishaps to such bothersome animals as rats, raccoons, and mythical nine-tailed foxes (*kumiho*). Koreans have a special affinity for the nine-tailed fox because it is said to hail from Ch'ŏnggu (Green Hillock; Qingqiu in Chinese), presumed by later Koreans to be a poetic reference to or an ancient name of the mythic Korean state of Old Chosŏn (traditional dates 2333–194 B.C.E.) in the vicinity of the Liaodong peninsula and southern Manchuria. The *Classic of Mountains and Seas* reports that the nine-tailed fox makes sounds like that of a baby girl; it is able to eat people, but those who eat it cannot be poisoned. In popular Korean lore the nine-tailed fox is able to transform at will into a beautiful and alluring woman; she must kill and consume the livers of a hundred men in order to become a human, but she is usually thwarted after ninety-nine successful attempts.

Yi Kyubo's description of the shaman's practices and shrine for communicating with her familiar spirits bears many similarities to descriptions of shamans in the late Chosŏn period, and even in contemporary Korea. In the process of conversing with her clients she makes a number of statements that may have some bearing on the clients' problems. The shaman's voice, speech, and intonation change when she is in a state of ecstasy, where she is possessed by the gods and spirits. When shamanizing, she dances and jumps, reaching high to the ridgepole, the main support beam of the traditional Korean-style house. The shaman's shrine is located in humble surroundings and is covered with pictures of the celestial deities and spirit officials by whom she claims to have relations and who assist her in diagnosing the problems of her clients. Special shrine niches are located in distinctive places in her house, where she commemorates the household, celestial, and native gods of Korea, some of which have been adopted from the Sinitic and Buddhist pantheons.

Yi suggests that the shaman he describes claims to have a special relationship with the god Chesŏk. The name "Chesŏk" was coined originally to translate the name of the Indian Lord Śakra, or Indra, the thunderbolt-wielding Indo-Aryan king of the gods, into Chinese (*che*, referring to "emperor" or "thearch," and *sŏk*, a transliteration of the first syllable of "Śak[ra]"). Adopted into Buddhism as one of its protector gods, Śakra made his way into Korean religion. In time Lord Śakra was domesticated in Korea and revered as foremost of the indigenous gods in calendrical festivals. By the late Chosŏn period, Chesŏk became so entrenched in shaman ritual associated with childbirth that Korean female shamans explicitly equate Chesŏk with the Birth Grandmother (Samsin Halmoni), the birth spirit. In the mid-Koryŏ period, however, Yi understands Chesŏk to be a celestial deity who is part of the Buddhist pantheon, which perhaps explains one aspect of his condescending suspicion toward shamans. Yi imagines the Chesŏk of Buddhist literature, a resident of the Six Heavens (*yukch'ŏn* in Korean)—not an image pasted on the board of an unlearned shaman. The Six Heavens are celestial abodes experienced by gods possessing sense organs (eyes, ears, nose, tongue, body, and mind) and which are located above the world mountain of Sumeru in between the Brahma realms and the earth. The Six Heavens are (1) the heaven of the four kings, who protect Buddhism and the four directions; (2) Trayastriṃśās, the heaven of the thirty-three gods presided over by Śakra; (3) the heaven of Yama; (4) Tuṣita heaven, the abode of Maitreya, the future buddha; (5) Sunirmita, where all forms of joy are attainable; and (6) the heaven of Māra, the lord of illusion.

The other celestial deities Yi Kyubo mentions as being familiar to the shaman were long worshiped in China as early as the Han period and before. The Seven Primes refer to the sun, the moon, and the five planets of Mars, Mercury, Jupiter, Venus, and Saturn. The Nine Sources of Brightness are the seven stars (Ch'ilsŏng) of the Northern Dipper (Ursa Major) and two attendant stars located nearby. The seven stars of the Northern or Big Dipper enjoyed a prominent place in Korean Buddhist ritual. They were also invoked by Korean shamans for the longevity, fertility, virility, and wealth of their patrons; and shamans possessed by the seven stars were said to be able to predict the future. The Nine Empreans refer to the highest and most glorious heavens. The highest regions of heaven close to the sun were divided into nine fields: the center and the four cardinal directions with their respective subdirections. Yi would have been familiar with these names and other asterisms due to their appearance in the metaphysically speculative writings associated with the "dark learning" (*xuanxue*) tradition of the Northern and Southern Dynasties period (220–589) and the famous Chinese poetry of the Tang period (618–907).

Despite the acidic tone Yi Kyubo takes toward the female shaman who lives to the east of him, his "Lay of the Old Shaman" is the most detailed discussion of shamanic activities and procedures prior to the Chosŏn period. It gives readers insight into the values and moral predispositions of the literati who composed most of the historical records and literature available to us. In conclusion, the blatantly negative interpretation Yi Kyubo presents of the activities of a female shaman in the Koryŏ capital provides compelling evidence that indeed the opposite view of shamans may have been held by many ordinary Koreans of the time. Instead of shamans' being shunned by polite society, as Yi hopes will be the result of the edict expelling shamans from the capital that he celebrates in his poem, he admits that the shaman's clients are so numerous that they gather like clouds and rub shoulders at her door. If normal self-respecting people of the time actually ignored shamans, why would the king need to pass a law forbidding shamanizing and banish shamans from the capital?

The translation is from *Tongguk Yi sangguk chip* (The Collected Works of Minister of State Yi [Kyubo] of the Eastern Country [Korea]) (Seoul: Myŏngmundang, 1982),

2:2b–4b. I have benefited from Korean vernacular translations in Yi Nŭnghwa, *Chosŏn musok ko* (Study of Korean Shamanism), translated by Yi Chaegon (Seoul: Tongmunsŏn, 1991), pp. 45–50; and Yu Tongsik, *Han'guk Mugyo ŭi yŏksa wa kujo* (History and Structure of Korean Shamanism) (Seoul: Yŏnse [Yonsei] Taehakkyo Ch'ulp'anbu, 1975), pp. 154–59.

Further Reading

For translations of accounts of ancient Korean customs and religious practices, and popular beliefs in the Koryŏ period, see Peter H. Lee, ed., *Sourcebook of Korean Civilization, vol. 1, From Early Times to the Sixteenth Century* (New York: Columbia University Press, 1993), or Peter H. Lee and Wm. Theodore de Bary, eds., *Sources of Korean Tradition, vol. 1, From Early Times through the Sixteenth Century* (New York: Columbia University Press, 1997). For a somewhat dated account of shamanism in ancient Korea, see Chang Yun-shik, "Heavenly Beings, Men and the Shaman: Interplay between High and Low Culture in Korean History," in *Papers of the First International Conference on Korean Studies* (Seoul: Academy of Korean Studies, 1979), pp. 1060–74. For an overview of Korean shamanism and its Buddhist accretions, see Hyun-key Kim Hogarth, *Syncretism of Buddhism and Shamanism in Korea* (Seoul: Jimoondang International, 2002). For translations of and commentaries on the shamanic poems of ancient China, see, for instance, Arthur Waley, *The Nine Songs: A Study of Shamanism in Ancient China* (London: George Allen and Unwin, 1955; rpt., San Francisco: City Lights Books, 1973), 29–36. For an interesting study of the River Earl, see Whalen Lai, "Looking for Mr. Ho Po: Unmasking the River God of Ancient China," *History of Religions* 29, no. 4 (May 1990): 335–50. For a study of the Seven Stars, see Henrik H. Sørensen, "The Worship of the Great Dipper in Korean Buddhism," in *Religions in Traditional Korea*, edited by Henrik H. Sørensen (Copenhagen and Aarhus: Seminar for Buddhist Studies, Center for East and Southeast Asian Studies, University of Copenhagen, 1995), 71–105. Though somewhat dated, the best treatment of the textual sources of historical Shamanism in Korea remains Yi Nŭnghwa's (1869–1945) *Chosŏn musok ko* (*Study of Korean Shamanism*), Korean vernacular translation by Yi Chaegon (1927; new edition, Seoul: Tongmunsŏn, 1991).

Lay of the Old Shaman

PREFACE

There is an old shaman who is a neighbor of mine to the east. Men and women visit her daily. I was very displeased due to the licentious songs and absurd chatter I heard, but I had no reason to evict her. Recently, the state issued an edict ordering that all shamans be removed far away and that they must not come near the capital. Not only was I especially overjoyed that the licentiousness of the house to the east would be cleansed and made still, as if swept away, but, moreover, I celebrated the fact that there would be no more licentious sophistry within the capital, that the world would be simple and the people chaste, and that we would return to the customs of high antiquity. Therefore, I wrote this poem to celebrate it.

Now let me illustrate. If those of their ilk had been chaste and simple why would they have been expelled from the royal capital? Conversely, if we look to the licentious shamans to see [why they] have been rejected and repudiated, [we find that] it is self-inflicted. Moreover, who else could be to blame? Ministers are also just like other people. If they are loyal in their service to their lord they will be without fault to the end of their days. If they bewitch in order to delude the masses, then they, without turning the heel (at once), will be defeated. That is a firm principle.

"Lay of the Old Shaman" (Nomu p'yŏn)

Formerly the Shaman Wu Xian, the divine and mystic,
Strove to dwell on grains of pepper and sacrificial rice to see forms and
    solve riddles.
Ever since he ascended to Heaven, who have been her successors?
From the distant past to the present—vast and desolate—
    hundreds of thousands of years have passed.

As for the shamans Fen, Peng, Zhen, Li, Di, Xie, and Luo,
The road to Spirit Mountain is high and difficult to tread
In between the Yuan and Xiang rivers they also believe in ghosts;
Wild and licentious hypocrisy and sophistry—their faults are
    contemptible.

In Korea these customs have not yet been swept away,
Females are witches and males are wizards.
They say of themselves "Spirits descend into my body."
And yet, I hear this, smile, and sigh.

If it is not a thousand-year-old rat in a hole,
It must be a nine-tailed fox inside the forest.
The shaman in the house to the east, by whom the masses
    are deluded—
Her face is rough, the hair on her temples is separated; she is fifty years
    of age.

Men and women [gather around her] like clouds—wooden shoes fill
    the doorway;
Rubbing shoulders as they enter and exit the gate, a row of heads enter.

In her throat delicate words are like the chirping of birds;
There is no order to her mutterings and babble—it is slow and then
   urgent.

Of thousands of words and volumes of speech, if she's lucky to have one
   on target,
Stupid females and idiotic males receive it with respect and as a benefit.
She fills her belly with sour and sweet, tasteless wine;
Jumping and dancing, raising her body, her head touches the ridgepole.

The connecting beam is a shrine niche barely five feet [in length].
She believes her mouth, of itself, speaks the will of the God Chesŏk.
The August Śakra originally dwells up above in the Six Heavens,
[Yet] he willingly enters your chamber,
   which occupies such a desolate, out-of-the-way place?

Paintings fill your walls communicating images of the spirits.
The Seven Primes and the Nine [Sources] of Brightness are marked on a
   board.
The Star Official originally resides among the Nine Empyreans;
How could it be that he would follow you and dwell on your wall?

You absurdly dispense death and life, banes and boons,
How could you probe the unexpected affairs of my life?
You collect the food of the starving men and women of the
   four directions,
And you deprive the clothing of the exhausted husbands and wives in
   the kingdom.

I have a sharp sword [that makes people] tremble with fear, like water.
Many times I desired to go yet I have stopped repeatedly.
The only cause is the three-foot laws [laws and regulations of the state]
   in my ears.
How could that spirit be able to afflict me?

The shaman in the house to the east is approaching the evening of
   her years.
Sunrise and sunset, death stalks—how is she able to live so long?
How could what I am thinking of now be like this?
My intent is to get rid of [these shamans] completely
   and wash clean the shelters of the people.

Have you not seen the edict of Ye District of ancient times?
They drowned the great shamans in the river
   and ceased providing their daughters as brides to the River Earl.
Furthermore, have you not seen Minister Ham of the present day?
Seated, he sweeps away shamans and ghosts
   and does not let tigers near him even for a moment.

After this old crone passes away she will again rise from sleep;
Foul ghosts and old raccoons will fight and gather together again.
I dare to celebrate the fact that the court has a strong plan;
Deliberations have been straightforward about getting rid of the flocks
    of shamans.

Public officials present documents—each has his own opinions.
How could this be for the ministers' benefit?—certainly it is for the
    state's benefit.
Our brilliant Son of Heaven may be memorialized regarding it.
From the end of sunrise extending on to sunset
    it will be as if all traces had been swept away.

If any of you say "My techniques are divine,"
To transformations and ecstasies, I respond without boundaries.
When there is a sound, why won't people shut themselves from
    hearing it?
When there is a form, why won't people keep themselves from
    gazing at it?

Displaying cinnabar and arrayed vermilion, it is still called deception.
How many of you would say it is difficult to make my body disappear?
Lead your followers and associates by the hand and remove yourselves
    far away.
This minor official certainly will be overjoyed for the sake of the country.

When I wander in the royal city by day, conveniently it will be clean
    and pure.
The annoying sound of tiles and drums will not [bruise] my ears.
I think that had any of us ministers [done such things] as this,
Execution or banishment assuredly would have been the rule.

I am now distressed about this—forget and be still!
When I approach the royal capital I will not be startled.
All of the hundred scholar-philosophers wrote that all the gentry,
Comport their bodies carefully and do not approach the licentious
    and strange!

—15—

The Creation of the World
and Human Suffering

Boudewijn Walraven

Historical sources such as *Samguk sagi* (Histories of the Three Kingdoms, compiled in 1145) and *Samguk yusa* (Memorabilia of the Three Kingdoms; comp. 1285), which both draw on older histories that are no longer extant, contain myths about the founders of ancient Korean states, but Korean creation myths are to be found only in the oral tradition of the shamans: in the songs (*muga*) they sing during their rituals. Save for a few short texts or some fragments of longer songs, the *muga* have been recorded only from the twentieth century onward, and none of the narrative songs of the shamans was put into writing before modern times, so we can only conjecture how old these shamanic myths are. The fact that shamanism is supposed to have been the original native religion of the Korean peninsula is sufficient reason for some researchers to assume that the songs the shamans sing nowadays are of equally ancient origin. One should recognize, however, that even if the *origin* of shamanic ritual and shamanic songs goes back to the period of the Three Kingdoms or earlier, both the rituals and the songs have changed considerably in the meantime in response to historical developments. A purely oral genre, as were the *muga* until recently, is always characterized by a certain fluidity. A study of *muga* texts recorded in the twentieth century demonstrates that shaman songs undoubtedly changed in the course of time, because it is obvious that they have absorbed historically datable extraneous influences, including numerous Buddhist elements. The songs also faithfully reflect Confucian values. This combination of Buddhism and Confucianism in the songs is not as curious as it may at first seem and may provide a hint as to their historical development. Conflict between Buddhism and Confucianism arose after the introduction of Neo-Confucianism in the late Koryŏ and early Chosŏn periods, but by the late Chosŏn period Buddhism had adapted to the hegemony of Confucianism by wholeheartedly accepting Confucian values, as Buddhist *kasa* of that period clearly show. One may very well argue, therefore, that the combination of Buddhist and Confucian elements in the *muga* is at least in part due to the amalgamation of Confucian and Buddhist ideas that took place in certain strata of late Chosŏn society. The shamans, eager to add to their own authority by adopting more prestigious forms of religion and social ethics, may have incorporated into their own songs the blend of Buddhism and Confucianism they found in Buddhist *kasa*, for example.

Attention to the historicity of the *muga* may help us understand why some of these narrative, mythical songs are similar in plot to episodes in state-foundation myths or other narratives in the oldest histories, a fact that has been regarded as evidence for the ancient origin of the *muga*. A widely distributed shaman song about the origin of a deity who bestows the blessing of childbirth (best known as the Tale of Tanggŭmaegi), for instance, in some ways resembles the myth about Chumong, the founder of the state of Koguryŏ. We know very little about the roles of shamans in the oldest periods of the Three Kingdoms, but it is likely that at that time they were socially prominent individuals, if not actual leaders of their communities. It would make sense that among the songs they sang there would be a eulogy to the founder of their state. This is a rather bold assumption (since we do not have evidence that they sang any songs at all), but if it is correct, one can imagine what happened once Sinitic culture and the Chinese writing system were introduced into Korea and the social position of the shamans entered a gradual, but inexorable, decline. When the myth of Chumong finally became part of the written history of Koguryŏ (in classical Chinese translation, of course), shamans may have continued to transmit an oral version of the tale in a different social context. In the introduction to his poetic version of the tale of Chumong, the poet and statesman Yi Kyubo (1168–1241) clearly indicates that in his day written and oral versions of the story coexisted, even though he does not specify that shamans took part in the oral transmission. Over time, the oral story will have lost its dynastic, political connotations, and parts of the narrative that were relevant only to the creation of the state of Koguryŏ are likely to have been omitted. The twentieth-century outcome of this process, then, is the story of the origin of a deity of a completely different nature, charged with control over procreation and long life. The chief protagonist of the tale of Tanggŭmaegi, moreover, is a woman, not a man as in the myth of Chumong. In Chumong's myth, the figure corresponding to Tanggŭmaegi is Chumong's mother, who, however, is little more than the passive medium through which the hero enters the world. This shift in gender, which also emerges from a comparison of other ancient myths and modern *muga* with similar plot lines, presumably is related to the fact that modern shamanic ritual is largely performed by women for women.

The fluidity of oral tradition and the historicity of the *muga* and shamanic ritual in general should also be taken into account when the mythical songs translated here are considered. "Ch'angsega," the "Song of the Creation of the World," was recorded in 1923 by the first collector of Korean shaman songs, Son Chint'ae (1900–?). The singer was Kim Ssangdori, a sixty-eight-year old shaman from the northeast of Korea. From a comparative point of view, the "Song of the Creation of the World" belongs to a type of myth that explains the origin of death and suffering and is found over a very large area. At a certain level of abstraction, this type even includes the Greek myth of Pandora's box as it is found in Hesiod (approximately seventh century B.C.E.), which suggests that "Ch'angsega" is related to a mythical complex of ancient date. It undoubtedly is, but it should also not be forgotten that the oral tradition of the shamans is characterized by flexibility and openness; much the same may be said about the nature of myth, for as long as a myth is truly alive, it has to adapt to the circumstances of the lives of those who are guided by it.

"Ch'angsega" is an excellent example of the eclecticism of Korean shamans, who adopt without hesitation bits and parts of other religious traditions to suit their needs. Its account of the creation of this world through the separation of heaven and earth accords with Chinese cosmological representations with which Koreans were very familiar. The Sinitic idea that heaven is round and earth flat and square, with pillars supporting heaven on the corners, was widely accepted, by both those who could read Chinese and those who could not. After this Sinitic overture, however, the song goes its own way almost immediately by suggesting that Maitreya—in the orthodox Buddhist view the Buddha of the Future—was the primordial being and the creator of our world! He is also presented as a culture hero, who introduces the basics of civilization: clothes and cooked food. Consequently, mankind, which Maitreya creates in cooperation with heaven, is able to enjoy the comforts of a civilized lifestyle right from the beginning. In fact, humans live in a kind of paradise that—except for their decently covered bodies and the cooked rice they eat—is not unlike the Garden of Eden.

Of course this paradise, too, cannot last, and, astonishingly, the villain who is responsible for the Fall is the historical Buddha Śākyamuni. When Śākyamuni appears on the scene, he manages to take over from Maitreya as the ruler of our world, but only through deceit. However strange this may seem from a purely Buddhist point of view, there is a certain logic to it. The coming age of Maitreya is described in Buddhist scriptures as a millenarian paradise, whereas the world we live in now—the world in which Śākyamuni was born two and a half millennia ago—is a world in which people get ill, suffer, and die. It is only natural therefore to associate Śākyamuni with our world of suffering and Maitreya with the bliss of paradise, whether that lies in the past or in the future.

The description of the world of Śākyamuni in the song includes many elements that are intrinsically related to the suffering of our postparadisiacal lives. In paradise there is no need for the guardian poles that stood in liminal spaces to protect people against malevolent spirits, no need for shamans who heal the sick and lead the spirits of the dead to the other world, and no place for Buddhist monks who seek liberation from the painful bonds of karmic existence. Also, there are no social classes and no outcasts, such as were shamans and butchers in traditional Korean society. This, the song says, borrowing a Buddhist concept, is the age of the Latter Days of the Law (malse). In fact, in orthodox Buddhist tradition, the Latter Days of the Law begin long after the death of the historical Buddha, according to the one common calculation fifteen hundred years after his entering nirvāṇa. Here there is no such historical distinction: the Latter Days of the Law are simply synonymous with the age of Śākyamuni, which is our own world of human suffering. Thus the at first sight curious roles assigned to Maitreya and Śākyamuni are less absurd than it may seem initially and are not just a consequence of the ignorance of Korean shamans. In fact, variants of this myth found outside Korea sometimes have the same two buddhas as protagonists, no doubt for similar reasons.

As mentioned above, "Ch'angsega" is part of a mythical tradition that extends far beyond the frontiers of Korea, to Central and North Asia, China, Vietnam, and Japan, as well as to Iran, North America, and ancient Greece. In myths from all these regions the origin of death and suffering is held to be the outcome of rivalry between two numinous beings. Pandora's box, for instance, is given to mankind as the final and fatal act in a contest in several stages between Zeus and the Titan Prometheus, who in turn try to outwit each other. At a time when gods and men are still living together, Prometheus first tricks Zeus into accepting the less desirable parts of sacrificial animals, leaving the best parts to humankind. When he realizes he has been duped, Zeus withdraws from man the use of fire. Prometheus's next move is to steal fire from the gods. Zeus retaliates by sending a seductive gift to mankind (up until then all male): a woman, Pandora, who is accepted by the stupid brother of Prometheus, the "one who thinks after he has acted," or Epimetheus, and it is Pandora who finally opens her box (or jar) that contains all the ills of our world.

Part of the fascination of "Ch'angsega" is its position in the dynamics between the generality of a very old and widely distributed mythical complex and its function in the very specific ritual context of shamans from a particular region in Korea, who performed these rituals for particular families or village communities. Both performer and audience were equally unaware of the global tradition to which these myths belonged. Unfortunately, Son Chint'ae has left us only a few details about the context in which "Ch'angsega" was performed, and the shamanic tradition of Hamgyŏng province where this song was recorded seems to have been cut off completely, so that it no longer is possible to conduct further investigations. According to Son, the song was sung only during large-scale rituals and was not known by younger shamans. About its function, he only states that it was used as a kind of prayer. The rather curious ending of the song might confirm this. Following an account of the emergence of everything that brings mankind grief and pain, the song becomes unexpectedly idyllic, providing the note of hope that would fit a prayer. On the other hand, "Ch'angsega" would fit almost any shamanic ritual, in that it highlights the circumstances that make such ritual indispensable. In an unemphatic manner, it even explains the origin of shamans, as shamanic myths like the "Song of Princess Pari" do in a much more sharply focused form.

A narrative shaman song that is in certain ways related to "Ch'angsega" is "Chŏnjiwang ponp'uri" (Origin of the Heavenly King), which was sung by Pak Pongch'un, a male shaman from Cheju Island (where a larger proportion of shamans are men than in most other regions of Korea), and recorded by a Korean collaborator of the Japanese researchers Akamatsu Chijō and Akiba Takashi, who published it in 1937. "Chŏnjiwang ponp'uri" is sung by the leading shaman during the first part (Ch'ogamje) of a major ritual on Cheju Island, to "set the scene." The protagonists of "Chŏnjiwang ponp'uri" are the Heavenly King Ch'ŏnjiwang and his sons, who engage in a struggle with an extremely wicked human being, Sumyŏng changja (in Korean folk narratives changja, "rich man," is often added to the name of the villain of the tale). In other variants of the song, the wickedness of Sumyŏng changja is demonstrated by his flouting of the highest moral imperative of Confucianism: he displays shockingly unfilial behavior toward his father. When in the end Sumyŏng changja is defeated, the pulverized parts of his body turn into all kinds of noxious insects. The motif of an evil person whose body turns into bothersome insects upon his death is not confined to Korea and also appears in folktales from China, Siberia, and North America.

The motif of the contest between two divine figures that we found used in "Ch'angsega" to explain the origin of human sin and suffering is also employed in "Chŏnjiwang ponp'uri," where it takes the shape of rivalry between the twin brothers Taebyŏlwang, "Great Star King," and Sobyŏlwang, "Little Star King" (which is reminiscent of the struggle for similar purposes between the twin brothers Ohrmazd and Ahriman in ancient Iranian mythology). In "Chŏnjiwang ponp'uri," however, the final emphasis of the tale is different. Although it explains the origin of death—inasmuch as it confirms the division between the world of man (with all its imperfections) that the cheating Little Star King controls and the world of the dead ruled by the Great Star King—the younger brother grants luck and happiness and provides the standards for correct moral behavior.

"Chŏnjiwang ponp'uri" also provides a good example of a motif that is frequently seen in shamanic myths, as well as in the myth of the founder of Koguryŏ: the earthly woman who "marries" a deity who has descended from heaven and gives birth to a child or children who will be gods or who will be destined to do great things. In the muga, the children use the technique used by Jack in "Jack and the Beanstalk" to ascend to heaven when they grow up and want to meet their father, who will send them down again, now charged with a divine mission. It is characteristic of the way shamans embraced and adapted Buddhism that in many muga (although not in "Chŏnjiwang ponp'uri") the figure that descends from heaven to father offspring of a union between heaven and earth is depicted as a Buddhist monk. In the popular tradition Buddhism is associated with fertility rather than with sexual abstinence. This, too, has its own logic. Buddhism is positively associated with life in several ways. It stands for the principle of vegetarianism and thus for the production of food resources without resorting to killing—that is, for agriculture, rather than hunting or fishing. The production of crops, in turn, parallels human reproduction. Whether for that reason or not, it is a fact that women wanting to conceive pray to Buddhist figures like the bodhisattva Avalokiteśvara. In the pantheon of the shamans as a whole there is a broad distinction between the vegetarian, nondrinking gods who confer fertility and life—and all of whom are generally gods of Buddhist origin—and the meat-eating, hard-drinking gods, many of them fierce warrior deities, whose boons are limited to such worldly results as success and riches.

Apart from the "Ch'angsega" and "Chŏnjiwang ponp'uri" presented here, there some twenty other variants in the repertoire of the shamans of different regions of myths involving the creation of the world and the origin of human suffering, with considerable variation in their contents. This variation once again confirms that oral traditions are fluid and do not lend themselves to the kind of canonicity a written text like Genesis may acquire. The narratives draw from a rich, but ultimately limited, storehouse of motifs and plots, which may go far back into history, and derive a certain consistency from the fact that they generally follow culturally determined patterns. Within these limits, however, they are like kaleidoscopic images, which may be reconstituted at any moment to make more sense to the performers and their audiences in a concrete social and historical setting.

The texts translated here are from Son Chint'ae, *Chōsen shinka no ihen* (Tokyo: Kyōdō Kenkyūsha, 1930), 1–15, and Akamatsu Chijō and Akiba Takashi, *Chōsen fuzoku no kenkyū*, vol. 1 (Tokyo: Ōsakō Yagō Shoten, 1937), 460–66.

Further Reading

Two articles trace the mythical complex to which "Ch'angsega" belongs: B.C.A. Walraven, "The Root of Evil—as Explained in Korean Shaman Songs," in *Cahiers d'Études Coréennes* 5 (1989): 351–69, takes the Korean myths as its point of departure, whereas Manabu Waida, "The Flower Contest between Two Divine Rivals: A Study in Central and East Asian Mythology," *Anthropos* 86 (1991): 87–109, devotes considerable attention to Ryūkyū Island variants of the myth. The complicated relationship between shamanic myths and other myths and folktales and the historicity of the *muga* are among the themes of Boudewijn Walraven, *Songs of the Shaman: The Ritual Chants of the Korean Mudang* (London: Kegan Paul International, 1994). For the myth of the first shaman, see Seo Dae-seok, comp., and Peter H. Lee, ed., *Myths of Korea* (Seoul: Jimoondang International, 2000); for a discussion of the song, see Michael Pettid, "Late Chosŏn Society as Reflected in a Shamanistic Narrative: An Analysis of the *Pari kongju muga*," *Korean Studies* 24 (2000): 113–41.

The Creation of the World

At the time when heaven and earth came into being,
when Maitreya was born,
heaven and earth were joined together,
not yet separated from each other.
Maitreya saw to it that

heaven became curved like the lid of a cooking pot,
and at the four corners of the earth
he erected copper pillars to support heaven.
At that time there were two suns and two moons.
Maitreya took one moon and with this
created the Northern Dipper and the Southern Dipper.
He took one sun and made big stars out of it.
Of the little stars he made the stars
that govern the life of the people,
of the big stars he made the stars
that govern the life of the monarch and his ministers.
Because there were no clothes,
Maitreya wanted to provide them,
but there was no fabric.
So he dug up the arrowroot that sprawls
over this mountain and over that mountain,
shaved fibers from it, twisted them into threads,
and made them supple.
Under heaven he placed a loom,
from the clouds he hung the warp ties,
with a clatter he lifted the shuttle,
with a clatter he put down the shuttle
and so he wove a coat
made of arrowroot fiber:
one full roll of fabric for the body,
half a roll for the sleeves,
five feet for the outer collar
three feet for the inner collar.
When he made a monk's cap for the head
cutting off one foot and three inches,
the sides did not even come down to his eyes.
When he cut off two feet and three inches,
to make the monk's cap,
the sides did not even come down to under his nose.
When he cut off three feet and three inches
to make the monk's cap,
the sides came down to under his chin.
When Maitreya was born,
in the age of Maitreya,
he ate uncooked food,
without putting it over a fire,
eating uncooked grain.
Maitreya ate one bag of it,
and he ate one measure of it and thought:

"This way it's impossible.
Having thus been born,
only I will be able to find
the origin of water and the origin of fire."
He caught a grasshopper
and put him on the torture rack.
Beating him on the shin bones he asked:
"Hey, you grasshopper, do you know
the origin of water and the origin of fire?"
The grasshopper said:
"In the evening I drink the dew,
during the day I bask in the sun,
how would a living animal know?
Ask the green frog
who has been around one time more than me!"
Maitreya caught the green frog
and beat him on the shin bones:
"Do you know the origin of water, the origin of fire?"
The green frog said:
"In the evening I drink the dew,
during the day I bask in the sun,
how would a living animal know?
Catch the mouse who has been around
twice, thrice as long as me and ask him!"
Maitreya caught the mouse
and beat him on the shin bones:
"Do you know the origin of water, the origin of fire?"
Said the mouse: "What reward will you give me?"
Said Maitreya: "You will have all the rice chests under heaven."
Then the mouse said:
"Go into the Gold-Nugget Mountains;
on one side there is flint
on another side there is iron.
If you strike them strongly against each other,
there will be fire.
When you go to the Soha Mountains,
a spring will gush forth:
that is the origin of water."

Now that Maitreya has learned the origin of water and fire,
let's talk of mankind.
Long, long ago
Maitreya held up a silver platter with one hand
and a golden platter with the other

and prayed to heaven.
Then small creatures like insects fell from heaven,
five on the golden platter
and five on the silver platter.
These creatures he raised
and the golden creatures turned into men
and out of the silver creatures he made women.
Thus raising the silver creatures and the golden creatures
he created husband and wives,
and so mankind appeared in this world.
In the age of Maitreya
people ate rice by the bag, by the measure,
and the days of mankind were peaceful.
But Śākyamuni was born
and wanted to take away this world from Maitreya.
Maitreya said:
"This is still my age, it cannot be yours yet."
Śākyamuni replied:
"The age of Maitreya is all over.
Now I will create my age."
Maitreya said:
"You and me, let's have a wager,
if you want to take away my age,
you dirty rascal Śākyamuni!"
Then he let a golden bottle hang in the East Sea
from a golden cord
and Śākyamuni a silver bottle
from a silver cord
and Maitreya said:
"If the cord of my bottle is broken,
it will not yet be your age."
In the East Sea the cord of Śākyamuni was broken.
Śākyamuni persisted:
"Let's have another wager, once more.
Can you make the water of the Sŏngch'ŏn River
freeze over in summer?"
Maitreya made it freeze
as if it were the time of the winter solstice,
Śākyamuni made it freeze
as if it were the beginning of spring.
With Maitreya the river froze all over,
And so Śākyamuni was the loser.
Śākyamuni proposed a wager once more:
"You and I should lie down in a room

and if a peony flower in full bloom
rises up from my lap, then it is my age.
If it rises up from your lap, it is your age."
With thievish thoughts in his heart
Śākyamuni slept only half,
while Maitreya truly slept.
In the lap of Maitreya
a peony rose up in full bloom.
Śākyamuni broke it off halfway
and put it on his own lap.
Maitreya woke up and said:
"You dirty rascal Śākyamuni!
The peony that bloomed in my lap
you have broken off and put on your lap.
That flower will not bloom for ten days
and when planted will not last for ten years."
Maitreya, sick of being bothered by Śākyamuni,
prepared to cede his age to him:
"You dirty rascal Śākyamuni!
If you want it to be your age,
at every gate there will stand a guardian pole.
If you want it to be your age,
in every household dancing girls will be born,
in every household there will be widows,
in every household shamans will be born,
in every household robbers will be born,
in every household butchers will be born.
If you want it to be your age,
3,000 monks and 3,000 lay Buddhists will appear.
If your age is like this,
these will be the Latter Days of the Law."
And so after three days
3,000 monks and 3,000 lay Buddhists appeared
and then Maitreya escaped.
Śākyamuni with the monks left to look for him
and when they went deep into the mountains
there were deer and roe.
They caught the deer
and put the meat on thirty spits,
cut down old trees in the mountains,
roasted the meat and ate it.
Among the 3,000 monks two got up
and threw the meat on the ground:
"I want to become a Holy One!"

and did not eat the meat.
The other monks died and turned into the rocks
you see at every mountain,
turned into the pine trees
you see at every mountain.
These days, when the third and the fourth month arrive,
the people in the green shade amuse themselves there,
whiling away the time eating flower cakes.

The Origin of the Heavenly King

In the world of mankind
lived Sumyŏng changja:
boundless was his lawlessness.
He possessed nine horses,
nine cows and nine dogs,
and because of their fierceness
mankind was powerless,
even though they were oppressed.
One day Sumyŏng changja
went to the Heavenly King.
"In this world no one can catch me,"
he bragged.
"What impudence!" thought the Heavenly King.
Descending to the world of mankind,
he sat on the branch of a green willow tree,
outside the gate of Sumyŏng changja,
with ten thousand soldiers.
Sending all kinds of calamities,
he made a cow get up on the roof
to create all kinds of mischief,
and let the cooking pots and the winnowing baskets
take a walk outside the gate.
But Sumyŏng changja was not in the least afraid.
Then the Heavenly King wrapped the band
he had worn around his head
around the head of Sumyŏng changja.
Then Sumyŏng changja got a terrible headache
and calling a servant
said full of bravado:
"My head hurts too much,
cut it off with an axe!"
The Heavenly King was astonished:

"This is one tough bastard," he thought
and he took off the headband again.
On his way back he dropped by the house
of old Grandmother Paekchu.
"Tonight I shall lodge here,"
he said and the old crone answered:
"In a house like this
we cannot receive the Heavenly King."
But when he replied that it didn't matter
and entered, there was no rice to cook
and so the old crone worried,
but he told her:
"Go to the house of Sumyŏng changja
and ask for rice.
He will give it to you;
so go there and do it for me."
After she had received the rice
she cooked it
and offered it to the Heavenly King
and fed the ten thousand soldiers.
Then at night, when the Heavenly King was asleep,
there was the sound of hair being combed
with a comb of jade.
"Strange," he thought
and when he asked the old crone,
she said: "That's my little daughter."
When he called her,
she was like the Fairy of the Moon Palace.
The night of that day they became husband and wife,
living together,
but then after three days,
when he was about to ascend to heaven
she said: "If you, Heavenly King,
ascend forever, how shall I live?
And if by any chance a child is born,
what should I do?"
"You, my wife will become Queen Pak
and rule over mankind,
and if you give birth to children,
call them Taebyŏlwang and Sobyŏlwang.
For the time when they want to meet me,
I'll give you a token to know them by.
On the Day of the Ox of the First Month
sow these two seeds of the bottle gourd

and on the Day of the Ox in the Fourth Month
the vines will stretch to heaven
and when the children want to go up,
send them to heaven along the vines."
They parted from each other
and after one year she gave birth to two brothers.
When they turned seven,
they went to their mother
and when they asked: "Where is our father?"
she said: "He is the Heavenly King in heaven."
"How can we go to him?"
Then she told them:
"Plant two gourd seeds
and when the vines reach heaven,
climb up along them
taking this token."
And they planted the gourd seeds
on the Day of the Ox of the First Month
and when on the Day of the Ox of the Fourth Month
the vines stretched up to the skies,
they climbed up to heaven.
When they met their father,
he asked for their family name
and their personal names:
"What is your name,
and who is your mother,
and what token do you bring?"
"Our names are Taebyŏlwang and Sobyŏlwang,
our mother is Queen Pak
and here is our token."
When they showed it to him, he said:
"Clearly you are my sons.
You two brothers should descend
and take charge of good luck and bad luck,
of happiness and calamity in the world of man
and of the measure of long life and premature death
in the underworld.
In a silver basin plant two flowers
and the one whose flower will thrive
shall take charge of the world of man,
and the one whose flower will wilt
shall take charge of the underworld."
When they planted flowers in a silver basin,
the flower Sobyŏlwang took care of

did not grow well,
but the flower Taebyŏlwang took care of thrived.
"Go now to the world of man or the underworld
according to your tasks,"
said their father,
but when they came to the world of man
Sobyŏlwang worried:
"If I myself would take charge
of the world of man
and my brother would take charge
of the underworld,
I would punish Sumyŏng changja
and teach him how to behave,
but my older brother won't be able to do so,"
he thought, and he said:
"Hey, Older Brother, let's sleep!"
and he did as if he lay down and slept.
His older brother's flower he placed
in front of himself
and his own flower he placed
in front of his older brother.
Waking up his older brother he said:
"For some reason, Older Brother,
your flower has wilted
and my flower is in full bloom;
why would that be?"
His older brother understood he was tricked
and said: "If our father comes to know
that you do such things, you will die."
Sobyŏlwang apologized to his younger brother:
"Hey, Older Brother, let's play riddles."
When his older brother agreed he said:
"Why won't the leaves of the camellia fall,
even when winter comes?"
"If the inside is not hollow,
they will not fall."
"If it is like that,
why don't the leaves of the bamboo fall,
even though inside it is hollow?"
And when Sobyŏlwang asked again:
"If grain does not grow well in the hills,
why does it grow well in the fields below?"
Taebyŏlwang answered:
"The earth and water above

flow down to the fields below
and so below the grain grows well."
"Then, what is the reason
that what is above does not succeed,
and that what is below does?"
When the older brother said:
"As I cannot answer,
I have lost to you,"
the younger brother spoke:
"Even if the older brother does not succeed,
won't it be fine if the younger brother does?"
Then Taebyŏlwang said:
"If it is like this,
you should take charge of the world of man.
I will take charge of the underworld!
If by any chance you make a mistake,
You won't be so happy."
Because he exchanged the flowers
the younger brother took charge
of the world of man
and the older brother took charge
of the underworld.
Taking charge of the world of man
Sobyŏlwang called Sumyŏng changja:
"You have committed against mankind
so many violent and lawless deeds
that I cannot forgive you,"
he said and in the field in front
put up an execution rack,
and in the field behind
had the executioner's axe sharpened
and after he had his head cut off
they pulverized his bones and his flesh
and scattered them in the wind
and then they were blown away,
turning into gnats and flies,
lice and mosquitoes.
After he had destroyed his house and his body,
Sobyŏlwang took charge of mankind,
teaching mankind how to behave,
arranging for luck and happiness
distinguishing between good and evil.

—16—

Sending Away the Smallpox Gods

Antonetta Lucia Bruno

The ritual for the gods of smallpox, the *Sonnim kut*, is known throughout Korea under several names, such as *Mama kut*, the ritual for the gods of infection, or *Paesong kut*, the ritual for sending away the gods of infection. The literal meaning of *Sonnim* is "guest," here translated as "visitor," meaning guests on a visit from their place of origin, which is said to be China or Kangnam, literally "south of the [Yangzi] River."

The Visitors are baleful gods because they bring the proliferation of contagious illnesses, including smallpox, which seems to have been introduced into Korea in the fifteenth century. The gods' foreign origin reflects the etiology of the disease itself, but their specific identification with Kangnam still needs more investigation. Nowadays the song for the Visitors is chanted mostly by hereditary shamans (*sesŭp mu*), who are generally not thought to experience trance-possession and whose shamanic prowess is passed down within families.

In the past, this ritual was held periodically during smallpox epidemics, as well as at other times to forestall them. It involved welcoming gods who had arrived from far off, entertaining them as important guests, and begging them to inflict smallpox only superficially on the children of the village. A model of a horse in straw was offered to the gods on their departure.

Few shaman songs (*muga*) of the *Sonnim* ritual were recorded before it disappeared as a religious practice throughout the peninsula. The songs for the Sonnim were characterized by complex regional variants; the texts from the east coast area, one of which is translated here, are considered the richest and most complex, for both their sacred content and their entertainment value.

Comparison of the *Sonnim muga* translated here with other texts not only gives a clear idea of the complexity and variety of the genre but also shows the shaman's competence in adapting *muga* to new contexts. The style and the content suggest that the song was recorded during a ritual. The language used by the shaman is a mixture of the dialect of Kyŏngsang province and the formulaic patterns found in other shaman songs, as well as elements created on the spot to adapt the song to the context of the ritual.

In this ritual context, the shaman ends the *Sonnim muga* with a "love song," which has numerous intertextual links with other genres of oral literature. It is followed by a prayer offered to the gods of smallpox. In the closing section the shaman adds lines highlighting the function and role of the smallpox gods and warning people not to neglect their traditional worship, which can nevertheless be subject to "mistakes," just as is the case with modern medicine.

From both religious and anthropological viewpoints, these oral adaptations are of great interest, as they bridge two different worlds in a harmonious equilibrium, satisfying the wishes of gods and humans. Such adaptations tranform religious songs and myths so they may achieve their full effectiveness; they provide the time-space in which the shaman recontextualizes speech events that occurred outside the ritual into religious speech. Such a process charges such speech with the authorative power of ritual. This occurs also in the case of "hereditary shamans" who lack, according to tradition, the experience of trance-possession and thus do not talk in place of the gods. The characteristic language of charismatic shamans, including such performative utterances as "I will help you" or the switching of personas, is also absent from the prayer for Sonnim. Nevertheless, the ritual language used by "hereditary shamans" is also imbued with authority that lends it efficacy.

A brief summary of the plot is given here of a "complete" version of a *Sonnim muga*. This summary is in fact a synopsis of several texts, and one would never find such a complete song in oral transmission.

According to tradition, every child has three fathers, one the biological father and the other two the gods of delivery and of smallpox. The last is particularly feared because it can cripple a healthy child or even cause death, unless it can be persuaded to cause only a slight infection that leaves no trace of sickness.

Among the gods of smallpox, those from Kangnam are the most feared. Out of the fifty-four Sonnim who live there, only three decide to go to Korea, which is renowned for its superior food, scenery, and clothing. The way the Sonnim are dressed is described in great detail, which varies from region to region and according to the shaman's background.

In the translated text that follows, the shaman has omitted the description of the Literate Sonnim who follows the Monk Sonnim. Riding a horse, the Literate Sonnim carries a book under his arm and a brush to mark the victims of the disease, distinguishing between those who will only be "touched" lightly and those who will die.

In another variant in Chŏlla province, the Sonnim are described in the song as the smallpox gods who follow Chewang. Descending on Korea, Chewang decides who will be born, while Sonnim mark the destiny of each man. Again unlike the text translated here, the Sonnim ask the boatman to lend them a boat after they have failed to cross the river to Korea in boats made of mud, wood, and metal. But as payment for the boat, the boatman demands to spend one night with the female Sonnim, Kak-ssi. She is furious and leaves the spot at once, returning after seven years to exact revenge on the boatman's seven children. All are killed except for the last, thanks to the intercession of the boatman's wife. Once again, this elaborate description of the gods' arrival in Korea differs from the version translated here.

After the Sonnim have asked in vain for hospitality from the rich Mister Kim, they go to the house of a penniless old lady who works in Mister Kim's household. Touched by the kindness of the old lady's hospitality, they ask her permission to inflict the sickness on her nephew lightly. They also give her money to arrange a ritual in their honor, but this angers Mister Kim, who mistreats the old lady because she has spent money on the ritual instead of using it to pay back her debt to him. The Sonnim chastize him by putting the old lady into a trance state and talking to him through her. Mister Kim runs home, hides his son in a Buddhist temple, and spreads all sorts of pollutants in front of his house to bar entrance to the Sonnim. On finding she is unable to enter, Kak-ssi Sonnim disguises herself as the mother of Mister Kim's son and calls him out of the temple to inflict the sickness on him. But, again unlike the version given here, the rich Mister Kim, through his fervid devotion, succeeds in persuading the gods to forgive him, and they stop torturing his son. However, he stops celebrating the incumbent rituals as soon as his son has recovered, and the gods then kill the child. Mister Kim's son begs to become the gods' stable boy and serve them instead of being reborn into a virtuous family. When the gods happen to visit the stable boy's hometown once more during their travels, they are touched by the prayers and misery of his family and decide to forgive them.

The text translated here is from *Tonghaean muga* (Shaman Songs from the East Coast), edited by Ch'oe Chŏngnyŏ and Sŏ Taesŏk (Seoul: Hyŏngsŏl, 1974), pp. 240–406. It was sung by the shaman Pyŏn Yŏnho. Some lines of the song were impossible to interpret, even after comparing them with other texts. For those lines, I have given an approximate translation, where possible, or have simply left them untranslated; in a few cases, I have omitted them, when this does not significantly modify the song.

Further Reading

Two other versions of the *Sonnim kut muga* in Korean from different shamans of the east coast area can be found in *Tonghaean pyŏlsin kut muga*, vol. 2 (Seoul: Kukhak Charyowŏn, 1993), pp. 176–329, and in *Han'gukŭi pyŏlsin kut muga*, vol. 5 (Seoul: Kukhak Charyowŏn, 1999), pp. 265–427, collected by Pak Kyŏngsin. Both texts include annotations and have been recorded during the ritual. This lively atmosphere is absent in shorter texts collected by Kim T'aegon in *Han'guk muga ŭi chip*, vol. 1 (Seoul: Chimmundang, 1989), pp. 345–57. For a very literary rendering of another *Sonnim muga*, see Alan Heyman, "The Ritual Song of the God Sonnim" *Korea Journal* 23 (1983): 50–57. For the story of the smallpox gods, see Kim T'aegon, *Han'guk ŭi musok sinhwa* (Seoul: Chimmundang, 1989), pp. 220–24. For an

English version of the story of Sonnim, also see Seo Dae-seok, comp., and Peter H. Lee, ed., *Myths of Korea* (Seoul: Jimoondang International, 2000). For a detailed regional comparison of the song of Sonnim, see Hong T'aehan, "Sonnim kut muga yŏn'gu," in *Sŏsa muga Tanggŭmaegi yŏn'gu* (Seoul: Minsogwŏn, 2000), pp. 117–37.

The Ritual for Sonnim, the Gods of Smallpox

We welcome [the gods] to the world of human beings,
in the Republic of Korea,
in the district of Ulchin,
in the town of P'yŏnghae in North Kyŏngsang province,
in the street of the big village of Chejŏng!
As for time, at least [every] three years,
to Pyŏlsin on the right, to Todang on the right,
to Pyŏlsin on the left, to Todang on the left,
to Pyŏlsin of the streets, to Pyŏlsin of the crossroads
we playfully offer our devotion.
A thousand people of a thousand families,
a hundred people of a hundred families, ten thousand families,
village chiefs, leaders, and all their representatives [offer the ritual].
If it is night, sleep is light and long,
if it is day, the footsteps are fast [to prepare the ritual].
Few things are displayed, many things are absent [on the altar].
Like [the proverb that says] "the ants accumulate a pile of gold,"
the monk begs,
[following the tradition] handed down since the five hundred years
    of Silla!
Do not give up the tradition, do not start a new divine law.
I offer this devotion according to the tradition transmitted to me from
    the elders,
[for as long as] there will be a Word and a tradition [to transmit] to
    the descendants,
We welcome the gods invoked in this ritual.
[They come] from Kangnam, the country of Great Kings,
they are Visitors, resplendent,
they are entering the district of the big village Chejŏng!
Under the sign of the Rat, Venerable Heaven was created,
under the sign of the Ox, Venerable Earth was created,
under the sign of the Tiger, all men were created,
in the days of Yao, in the time of Shun, when holy governors ensured a
    peaceful reign.
The past is near! Past days are near!
Infinite time! Time of Buddhist sermons!

The time when Sungdŏk-ssi did not know the Gate of Words,
[the state of] Koryŏ was created,
when the relationship [between men] was created
and the interior [with exterior].
In those days Sŏkka Yŏrae [Śākyamuni Tathāgata] created the
    Buddhist Law,
and Maitreya created Confucianism,
Confucius and Mencius created the Scripture.
The Yellow Emperor built the first boats
and when he opened up the way of communicability
he created the net, the net
to fish in clear waters controlled for nine years.
Sillong-ssi regulated agriculture,
dry fields on the upper levels and wet fields on the lower.
It was then, in those days that
resplendent Visitors from Kangnam, the country of Great Kings,
pure Visitors [arrived in Korea],
and the Sun and Moon, however bright they may be said to be,
are they as resplendent as the Visitors?
Although the Stars and Moon are said to be resplendent,
do they shed light like the Visitors?
They are frightening and capricious [but also] benevolent.
Is the place where they come from their origin?
It is the country of Great Kings, Kangnam,
[the country] of *aju* bamboo, of *haejanguk* bamboo,
of purple bamboo, of tall bamboo?
From the Three Heaven Mountain the Visitors have emerged,
how many have emerged? Three, three of them appeared,
although it is said that the country of Great Kings,
Kangnam, is as large as a lotus leaf.
If one takes a look at the prepared food [on the altar]
there are [dishes of] cooked millet to eat,
strong-smelling caterpillars in greens!
Large captured frogs in soup!
White larvae of beetles grilled on the spit.
Though their dress is of silk, it is plain,
and said to be dirty, old, and made from insect husks
[so that the Sonnim] refuse to wear them.
When you arrive in our country, in the Republic of Korea,
glance at our food
and take a look at our prepared dishes:
red beans like plums are mixed in white rice,
its grains as long as cucumber seeds.
If you turn to the vegetable side dishes

you see higher up ferns [to eat] first
and lower down ferns [to eat] later,
pumpkin side dishes, with two, three pumpkins,
eggplants are purple and [tender] as silk,
dishes of tree leaves flutter down,
the harebells turn and turn again,
side dishes of Money Leaves are one coin, two coin,
side dishes of eggplants, two eggplants, three eggplants.
If you have a look at the side dishes,
axes hang from the living ox's head,
knives are thrust in the dead ox's head,
the front trotters [are placed] on front horns,
the back trotters on back horns,
and the skewer of *pana*,
the skewer of lamb meat with the first fruits of the autumn.
[The Visitors] cross the vast Sea of the Orient from the west,
toward the Great Country,
big dried cods' heads with gaping mouths, polyps large and small,
mud eels cry as they swim, the flat fish tails are broad,
black whiting large and small,
squids large and small,
this is how our side dishes are in abundance.
Have a look at our fruits.
We climb mountains for wild plants,
and we descend to the plains for strawberries,
this is how our side dishes are in abundance.
[Fruits from] trees in the mountains, pears, sweet chestnuts, jujube,
and in the mortar even dried persimmons are ground.
When [the Visitors] set out to discover
if there is impurity among human beings, among things,
which of the Visitors will travel?
In the big country of Kangnam, which is said to be as vast as
    lotus leaves,
to be as broad as lotus leaves,
fifty Visitors are conferring, three will travel,
one, at least, they think should remain [in Kangnam].
Which of the Visitors will travel?
Visitor Śākya [monk], Visitor "Noble Official," and Visitor Kak-ssi
    will travel.
Let us have a look at Visitor Śākya,
listen to me, now, if you look at him,
Visitor Śākya is exactly as I am about to say:

T'aryŏng melody

The venerable monk is descending, the holy monk is descending!
Look what that monk does, admire his extravagance!
His face is like the white jade of Mount Hyŏng
and his eyes [like] the wave of the river Sosang!
Over his thick eyebrows the Chinese character *p'al* is drawn!
His ear lobes dangle down,
[on his head] the headgear is one *cha* and one *ch'i* long,
two earlobes dangle down and two waving arms reach to the knees,
the headgear and the hat he wears are so large that they cover his ears,
on top of a large tunic of white cloth he wears a red belt,
on his neck he has a rosary of 108 beads and a small one at his wrist,
a dagger of copper and nickel,
a dagger with silver ornaments is tied loosely to the string of
    his garment.
[Holding] a bamboo stick with twelve knots, from the river Sosang,
leaning on the collarbone, he strolls down leisurely,
swaying in the spring breeze along Mount Śākya.
From whence does this monk come?
[He ascends to the temple] invoking the name of the Buddha,
he descends to the villages invoking the name of the Buddha,
he descends invoking the name of the Buddha:
"*Sinmo Changgun taedarani namora tanadara yayanamma*
aryakbaro kijiya sebaraya motchi sat'ubaya
maha sadubaya mahagaro negaya
oomsalba paiya yesudara nagaraya
tatsamyŏng namagari taba kanadaya
maha harinaya mabart'a isami
sabalt'a sadanam soobanya aheyŏ salba
podanam pabamma pisudagamt'a yat'a oom
arugae arin'ga matchi rogatchi perantchi haee
harema mahamotchi sadaba samara harina."
Listen to me,
he truly descends thanks to accumulated merits by invoking the name
    of the Buddha.
He is followed, I tell you, by two venerable Visitors, "Noble Official"
    and Kak-ssi.
Oh, Visitor Kak-ssi! Let us have a look at her beauty.
Her face is [white like] candid jade from Mount Hyŏng, she has a
    charming face,
her long thick hair is shining with camellia oil,
combed with a dragon comb, gathered and twisted and tied up,
her face is carefully powdered.
Let us have a look at her clothes.
She wears a pair of trousers embroidered with silk,

a pair of trousers of *mulmyŏngju* silk,
a wide skirt of royal silk folded over
and beneath it one of raw silk, of *ilgwangdan* silk.
She grasps the hem of the Tiger-butterfly [skirt],
holds the cord [like] a dragon and the edge of her under skirt.
[The Visitors] have arrived [at the river] Amnok in Ŭiju,
[but] there is no boat!
Looking closer they see one tucked away!
They say: "Boatman! Boatman! Chief Boatman! Loan us your boat."
The boatman replies with the words:
"Listen, venerable Visitors, the boats that were in our country have been
    destroyed
during the disorders that followed the Japanese invasions in the year
    imjin [1592] and only one is left,
the boat to transport the children of the hereditary prince's concubine."
While uttering [these words],
the unkind boatman sees Visitor Kak-ssi opening the shabby door of the
    sedan chair:
"Listen, Visitors, Visitors,
if the Visitor Kak-ssi will spend one single night with me,
then I will carry you across without charging for the journey."
As soon as he uttered these words,
Visitor Kak-ssi, hearing them,
thrusts fire inside the smokestack and a torch into the fire,
seizes the shifty boatman, cutting off his head
and throwing him into the river Amnok in Ŭiju.
She then goes to the boatman's home and, finding his three children,
cuts off the head of the firstborn and prepares to cut off the head of the
    second-born among the last sons,
cuts off the head of the second-born and prepares to cut off the first of
    the last sons,
cuts off the head of the third-born, and prepares a bolted hook
which she drives into the garden gate [to bar the house] and returns
    [inside the house].
"Are you the boatman's wife? What sin do you have?"
She tells her to remarry into a good family,
to have children and to live her life!
She walks again down the road [toward the river] and starts building
    a boat,
having gone down the road she looks for a boat.
[The Visitors] want to take only a wooden boat, but the bottom is
    rotten and they cannot get in,
they want to take only a mud boat, but it dissolves [in the water of the
    river], and they cannot get in,

they want to take only an iron boat, but it sticks to magnets, and they
    cannot get in,
they want to take only a rock boat, but it sinks and they cannot get in.
They reject this boat and that, and when they climb the hill behind the
    house,
they put a silver axe over their shoulder and, having climbed the hill
    behind the house,
[they cut] a leaf [from a tree] to build a boat, they gather leaves [and
    spread them] lengthwise and get on them.
[Over] these twelve rivers, [over] those twelve rivers,
when they cross the river Amnok in Ŭiju,
that boat has neither mast nor anchor nor paddles,
it sails thanks to the merits accumulated invoking the name of the
    Buddha.
When they arrive, crossing the King Dragon River,
they have to invoke the 10,000 dharmas [to overcome] the high tide.
They pray to load the carriage pulled by horse and cow,
it floats lightly as [the Visitors] load it with lapis lazuli,
they mount the sail high on the mast
and in that boat which, like a flying dragon,
comes and goes in the valley of the temples
among this mountain and that,
sailing here and there they make for the Republic of Korea.
[Having] arrived in the Republic of Korea, they hear,
they hear that the scenery is beautiful,
they arrive following the prescribed route,
this is how they get here,
they arrive following the prescribed route!
They travel the length and breadth of the Sŏch'ok,
crossing 500 *li* [one *li* is about 393 meters] in Kwandong, 800 *li* on the
    River Sosang,
600 *li* in Kŭndong, passing Agyangnu Fort, Kosodae,
Mount Sŏl, Mount Ka,
skirting Mount Sobaek, 940 *li* on Mount Kollyun,
[under] the terse winter sky amidst the fog they cross Mat'ae,
a confluent of the East River,
they cross eleven passes of Mounts Sŏl and Ka,
in a small boat they cross the big river of Mount Ka
where the River Ch'ŏngch'ŏn flows.
It is Kija indeed!
They meet him again in the "Castle of a Thousand Mouths" on the
    River Piro.
The men [living in this area] are literate, and the women are
    very beautiful.

In P'yŏngyang there is the white tiger!
[The Visitors] admire [the pavilion] Pubyŏngnu,
[they cross] Mount Moran, which has received "merits and virtues,"
and pass beneath Ŭlmudae
where a tall pine stands erect, hundreds of years old,
[and] they admire it for five, six days
seven months, one month.
It is Mount Pongnae, a place of entertainment,
[perhaps] where Chŏksongja plays?
[The Visitors] look at the temple of Pŏngye from the window [of the
    sedan chair, and hear] the moving sound of the bell,
[people] are admiring the mountains and rivers.
On reaching Mount Songak, [the Visitors] take a good look at the city
    of Kaesŏng,
they want to enter the big village Chejŏng from the right side
where everybody is *yŏkch'ŏnhago tomunhanŭn* [?].
The Visitors have come to our Korea [but] have no definite place to go,
they have heard of the 80,000 families in the crowded capital,
and go up toward Seoul [as] the sun is setting,
the Visitors are not seeking [hospitality] in [just any] family in [any]
    neighborhood,
they are looking for a house to their taste,
and, looking to one side, they see a little shack!
They go up to the shack and ask, "Is the owner there?"
As they say these words a little old woman
comes out who, after a rapid glance, [thinks]:
"These are indeed the pure Visitors!
They are like the portraits of the resplendent gods from the Great
    Country Kangnam."
[She says,] "I beg you to wait here a minute." So saying,
she leaves them waiting and goes into the room,
and in the four corners of the room, and the four corners of the kitchen,
she beats everything,
the dust which is on the ground,
the dust which is on the uprights,
she sweeps everywhere and spreads [carpets]
and although there is only a mat to sit on, she beats it,
sweeps the floor free of all the dirty dust,
washes and lays the clean carpet,
and after beating all the dirty kitchen utensils
and hanging them up again clean,
she receives the Visitors, she welcomes the three Visitors
and as she is receiving them she wonders what she can offer them.
Since there is nothing to offer,

she goes to the house opposite, to the house of rich Mister Kim,
[she would like] to get [at least] one *mal* of rice,
and she gets some leftover rice
which, adding water [and kneading],
she turns into a simple porridge for breakfast and dinner,
in doing so she takes the best of the leftover rice to offer for breakfast
    and dinner.
She cooks some rice in an oxidized copper pot and offers it
    for breakfast.
In this way her sincerity is expressed!
She welcomes the Visitors with devotion
although she has nothing to feed herself,
as she receives them in such a spirit, with such sincerity,
[but] alas,
[the Visitors] do not know how to repay the old woman's kindness;
after two or three days they are to leave
but do not know how to repay her!
So they ask her:
"Grandma, grandma, dear old woman,
do you have a son, a daughter-in-law?
A daughter, a son-in-law?
Do you have nephews? Do you have nieces?
You may have third, fourth, fifth, or sixth degree relatives?"
To the Visitors,
the old woman replies:
"Alas, Visitors! Visitors!
My destiny must be blessed because I lost my husband early
and I have neither children nor daughters-in law,
I have neither daughters nor sons-in-law.
I do not have what are called nephews.
I am quite alone.
If I live in this world,
[it is thanks] to the birth of Kim Ch'ŏrŭng in the family of rich
    Mister Kim.
I have nursed Ch'ŏrŭng and brought him up,
it is thanks to Ch'ŏrŭng that I live.
From Ch'ŏrŭng I have this shack too.
From Ch'ŏrŭng I have what I eat.
I beg you to infect our Ch'ŏrŭng with the first degree [of sickness],
please leave [after] infecting him
and causing the black, the red, and the white rash of the second degree."
The Visitors, hearing her words, saw that she really was very kind,
even though she could barely survive, her life was very honest,
she was indeed a conscientious person, so they said to her:

"Then be it as you wish, dearest old woman."
The old woman went on before the Visitors,
because they walked behind,
and remained outside the gate of Mister Kim's house,
while the old woman,
once inside Mister Kim's house, said to him:
"Master, master,
the famous Visitors from the Great Country Kangnam have arrived.
They will go on their way after infecting our Ch'ŏrŭng with first degree
    [smallpox],
after giving him the second degree with the black, red, and white rash."
As soon as she said these words,
rich Mister Kim shouted at her:
"Curses on you, you insolent old woman!
How dare you [bring] the Visitors into my dignified house?"
So he tells her to leave immediately!
Hearing these words,
hearing these words from outside the main gate,
the Visitors are mortified!
Alas, against [the wishes of Kim they] go back [into his house],
but look what that rich Kim does!
You know, suspecting that the Visitors might come back,
he brings [outside the front gate] all the dirty things
and in each corner scatters hens' droppings
and other putrid things,
upon the gate he hangs branches and sprigs of artemisia
and takes floating feces out of the toilet
and scatters them all over,
he comes and goes in all directions
spreading red hot chili power.
You know, [by so doing] he prevents the Visitors from approaching,
but the Visitors are not to be dissuaded because they are afraid.
Whether he does this or not,
they enter the house of rich Mister Kim.
They cause Kim Ch'ŏrŭng,
who was studying, to stop studying and make him ill.
While he was studying, Kim Ch'ŏrŭng suddenly said:
"*Aigo*, my head! *Aigo*, my legs!
Aigo, my stomach! *Aigo*, what am I to do!"
Breathing causes sharp pain,
and there's no question of eating or drinking,
he feels only sharp pains and a weight.
"*Aigo*, mother, *aigo*, father,

aigo I will die."
Rich Mister Kim, knowing [the symptoms of smallpox, says:]
"*Aigo*, the Visitors have arrived!"
Aware that the Visitors have come,
he takes [his son], alas, on his back
[and goes] to the Yŏnha temple on the hill
behind the house to escape them!
Once there, he says:
"Is the nun inside?
The luminous gods have arrived,
the Visitors from Kangnam, from the Great Country,
they want to infect our Ch'ŏrŭng and have made him ill in this way.
When the Visitors enter by stealth, prevent them from doing so,
make our Ch'ŏrŭng lie down where you sleep and hide him.
I beg you to forbid [the Visitors to enter]
and when they arrive tell them that you do not know [the boy's
    whereabouts]."
[Among] the Visitors, in the meanwhile,
Visitor Kak-ssi took the appearance of Ch'ŏrŭng's mother
and followed him.
Once outside [Ch'ŏrŭng's house], she followed them to the temple,
[and] Ch'ŏrŭng's father, [although] he had hidden him,
knew nothing of the law of Heaven and Earth.
Visitor Kak-ssi took the appearance of Ch'ŏrŭng's mother,
and went up to the temple Yŏnha, calling him from outside.
"Hey, Ch'ŏrŭng! Ch'ŏrŭng!" she calls to Ch'ŏrŭng.
Ch'ŏrŭng, whether he wants to listen or not,
knows that this is really his mother's voice!
He rushes out, *vrrrrr*, to look for her all around,
but there is nowhere his mother might have gone,
only a sinister and desolate wind blowing!
After looking around carefully, Ch'ŏrŭng does not see her,
and is about to go back into the temple.
How can Visitor Kak-ssi, who is a divinity,
become visible to human beings?
As Ch'ŏrŭng is going inside, she catches him and inflicts a first stab,
she catches him, and as she inflicts one stab at time,
[Ch'ŏrŭng says], "*Aigo*, what pain in my legs,"
as she inflicts the second stab on the head, his head hurts,
as she inflicts a stab in the stomach, his stomach hurts,
and inflicts further sharp pains inside the temple.
"*Aigo*, my head! *Aigo*, my legs!
Aigo, my stomach! I am dying!

Is the nun inside?
Please inform my father!
If I must die, I will go home to die,
and if I must live, I will certainly go home to live.
I am going, I am going.
I go where my mother is,
I go where my father is."
Since this is what he wishes, [the nun],
after informing the family of rich Mister Kim,
takes sick Ch'ŏrŭng who finds a warm welcome.
In the meantime, the Visitors sit on his pillow
and submit him to all sorts of illnesses!

Nowadays civilization is greatly developed,
there are good medicines, there are injections,
but at that time, in those days, if children were infected with smallpox
      or measles,
at that time there were neither medicines nor injections,
we worshiped the Visitors
wondering if [the child] would die or live
and we offered pure water and prayed,
we protected [the child] from the wind,
wondering if [the child] would die or live.
Nevertheless things worked at that time,
So why shouldn't they do so [nowadays as well]?
Things worked without any mistakes.
Nowadays there is medicine, there are also injections,
yet many mistakes are made.
All the same, still [today] we should offer pure water
to the Visitors, and pray and abstain from impure acts.
If you do this, you will induce the Visitors,
[smallpox] and even measles, [to go away],
but look, [that] meaningless fellow, that cur, the rich Mister Kim!
When you have a child so ill,
you should pray to the Visitors more than once, repeatedly,
but he does not do so, and tries in every way,
ever pigheaded and whining, to outwit the Visitors.
Well,
although the Visitors hope that rich Mister Kim will submit today
      or tomorrow,
he does not do so, he holds out stubbornly cursing.
Meanwhile, [the Visitors] force Ch'ŏrŭng to say:
"*Aigo*, father, *aigo*, mother!
I am dying, I beg you to let me live a little longer.

Father! Please let me live.
Mother! Please let me live.
I am going, going away,
going away following the Visitors.
The supplies in store, behind, who will eat them after my death?
The goods in store, in front, who will you give them to after my death?
Aigo, my father, I am leaving.
My teacher [who lives] on the other side of the hill, [from whom] I
    learned to write,
greet him and tell him that I have to leave without seeing him.
Please let me live longer!"
In spite of his bitter pleas, look what stupid rich Mister Kim does.
The wicked rich Mister Kim feels no regrets and remains impassive.
As [his son] is saying these words,
the Visitors pierce his throat with a metal staple
and his mouth with an iron gag,
so that he may say no more.
And yet the rich Mister Kim does not give, but only fumes.
So let me tell you about Ch'ŏrŭng,
he is the only son in three generations,
nevertheless [you], rich Mister Kim, fume in vain and remain
    pigheaded,
you, who were not even a human being in your previous life,
who were even lower than a horse or a cow,
a son like him is too much for a fellow like you.
Alas, they are taking Ch'ŏrŭng with them, now,
they go away taking Ch'ŏrŭng with them, now.
How is all this possible?
All the elders who have held office in the world,
[between] heaven and earth, they know.
I tell you, before, in those days, in their villages,
[fearing lest their children] be possessed by smallpox or measles,
that they might die of smallpox or measles,
before departing from the village,
they moved *ttŏktae* [a rectangular wooden board used to prevent pans
    from falling] to the hill behind the house,
and laid the corpse on top of *ttŏktae*,
so that everybody, whether adults or children,
kept watch over it night and day, day and night,
it seems that sometimes [the dead] returned to life.
However, Ch'ŏrŭng was dying!
Rich Mister Kim wondered if the Visitors really intended to take
    Ch'ŏrŭng with them forever.
And in the meanwhile, as Ch'ŏrŭng was dying,

[he was] confronted by moments of darkness, beyond all imagining!
The Master named Yŏng, how can he possess such deep knowledge?
It is Master Yŏng who divines:
"Kim Ch'ŏrŭng who is without sin is following the Visitors!
In truth it is because of mistakes committed by his mother and father,
because of mistakes they have committed that Ch'ŏrŭng,
without sin, is following the Visitors.
His life is too precious,
the [family] line of rich Mister Kim is about to break,
so I must go myself to bring Ch'ŏrŭng back to life."
Master Yŏng loses no time in presenting himself to the Visitors
and humbly begs them, saying:
"Please listen, Visitors,
do not torture that stupid rich Mister Kim,
Ch'ŏrŭng is an only son, an only son in three generations,
it is his mother who has made mistakes [by not worshiping you],
it is his father who has made mistakes,
since he who is dying is innocent, I beg you to give him back his life!"
[Master Yŏng] asks them not to torture that cur, rich Mister Kim,
and to let Ch'ŏrŭng live again,
he prays and implores them.
At this, the Visitors, who, you know, are intelligent and ready to
    concur, [say]:
"If we consider rich Mister Kim,
there is no doubt that we should take Ch'ŏrŭng with us,
but you have come and implored us in this way; well then,
we will let him live again.
We will let him live again, so don't bury his corpse,
set up *ttŏktae* on the hill behind the house and lay out his corpse
and tell rich Mister Kim to go there to keep watch!
Tell him to stay awake night and day,
to keep watch [over his son's body]." These were their orders.
In the meantime rich Mister Kim had been convinced that Ch'ŏrŭng
    would not die on any account,
but instead he died, [and Mister Kim] was utterly distraught!
He laid out Ch'ŏrŭng's body on *ttŏktae* on top of the hill behind the
    house,
and rich Mister Kim, oblivious to whether it was day or night,
went there to keep watch [over his son]!
When the Visitors are no longer angry, I mean,
when they are truly pacified, they let Ch'ŏrŭng live again!
They bring Ch'ŏrŭng back to life.
Because they bring Ch'ŏrŭng back to life again,
how happy Ch'ŏrŭng's mother was, and rich Mister Kim!

In the meantime, after considering everything,
rich Mister Kim celebrates the ritual [for the Visitors],
he prepares the ceremony and makes a [straw] horse,
he takes [rice] from the store, in front, and steams a rice cake in a
    big pot,
and takes [grain] from the store, behind, to ferment it and make liquor,
    no less.
[In the yard] under a tent made up from thirty-three pieces of fabric,
under the pole *kojit* and the banners,
the ritual in honor of the Visitors is held.
[To celebrate the ritual] he summons all the shamans,
fairy shamans, from heaven,
women shamans, from earth,
lady-in-waiting shamans, from the royal palace,
from each district, the local shaman,
he summons all in order to celebrate the ritual for the Visitors,
so that the ritual will be wonderful!
Parasols are prepared, everything is made, even the [straw] horse,
calling first the artists and then the stable boys,
[shamans] perform the ritual for the Visitors,
the ritual is celebrated magnificently.
How happy is Ch'ŏrŭng's mother!
How happy she is because her dead son has come back to life!
She hugs her son and expresses her happiness thus
[singing the following love song].
"*Tung tung tung turidung tung tung tung*
turidu tung tung tung my puppy!
Where have you been that you return only now?
Where have you been that you return only now?
Have you fallen down, *pluf*, from the heaven,
have you come out of the earth with an eruption?
Summer clouds are numerous [around] the strangely shaped
    mountaintops,
have you come perhaps in a cloud whipped by the wind?
tung tung tung turidung tung tung tung
turidu tung tung tung my puppy!
You have had bad parents, whether they are living or dead!
And you, a dead child, have been born again!
Even if gold is offered, can you be bought?
Even if jade is offered, can you be bought?
Even if the yard in front of the house were fertile,
this would not make me as happy [as I am having you back],
even [if I received] pearls and corals,
would I be happier then?

Tung tung tung turidung tung tung tung
turidu tung tung tung my puppy!
If one does not possess wealth or whatever, accumulating with diligence
one can have money,
but one cannot have a son like this just by wishing,
one cannot have [a son] like this!
When one has no son, what a great woe it is!
[When one] has no son, alas,
nor even a daughter, what a great woe it is!
[When one] has no daughter, alas,
even if there is much wealth,
there is great woe because there are no children,
[when one] has no son or daughter.
Tung tung tung turidung tung tung tung
turidu tung tung tung my puppy!
turidu tung tung tung my puppy!
[A son is as precious as] a single cane for ten blind men,
Ch'ŏrŭng returns after having been who knows where,
you return after having been who knows where.
Have you come back to life transformed into Chingnyŏ
who meets her lover on the Bridge of Magpies above the Silver River?
Have you come back to life transformed
into Suyang, [who fell] into the River Soji?
Tung tung tung turidung tung tung tung
turidu tung tung tung my puppy!
Tung tung tung tung tung tung tung
turidu tung tung tung my puppy!
The Black Dragon of the Black Sea
with a pearl in its mouth turns somersaults
among the colored clouds,
and yet is not faster than our Ch'ŏrŭng.
The phoenix of Mount Tan
with a bamboo flower seed in its beak
may jump back and forth in the heart of the Paulownia forest,
and yet it is not as agile as my son.
Not even the sound of the Paulownia cithara
is like the cry of our son.
Turi tung tung tung tung tung turi tungdung tungdung
tung tung tung tung tung my puppy!
On the stove a saucepan lid in the form of a whole turtle,
my son, you who shine like gold!
Turidu tung tung tung my puppy!
Turidu tung tung tung my puppy!
The jewel lying beneath the water in a cave,

even if green with moss,
is beautiful by its nature.
The wild roses which [grow] under the shrubs,
even if there are thorns,
are beautiful by nature!
Pearls are [attached] to the ribbons [in his] hair,
and amber pendants to the coat strings!
Tung tung tung tung turidung
tung tung tung my puppy!
Whatever your age and gender,
give no heed to any words other than these:
Young wives and young [husbands],
do not forget filial devotion toward parents
before you fall asleep!
If you are devoted to your parents,
you will have devoted children.
If you lack filial devotion then
you will have children lacking in devotion toward you.
Among the devoted, devotion is born,
among the honest, honesty is born,
among the virtuous, virtue is born,
from wealth, [comes] someone who is rich.
Although each valley has its dead devoted children,
there are all too few devoted children alive.
After death, delicious dishes
of a thousand delicacies have been prepared,
[the deceased] leave after eating, [they leave] after taking their rest.
Truly this is nonsense.
[The altar] is prepared for the others to look on,
why have you prepared [the delicacies]?
If just once in a lifetime a glass of strong wine
is offered with deep devotion, [that person] is a devoted child.
Tung tung tung tung turidung tung tung
tung tung tung tung tung
tung tung turidung tung my puppy!
Consider all the love of parents.
Even if you picked the mushrooms of longevity that grow on the
    mountains
and [along the] rivers by virtue of the tiger to give [to them],
this would not suffice to pay back the love of parents.
If you tear out your hair and use it to sew up [your parents'] shoes,
if you tear out your tongue and use it to sole [your parents'] shoes,
if you tear out your teeth and use them to make [ornaments] for their
    shoes and let them wear them,

[all this] does not suffice to pay back the love of parents.
All the regrets [parents feel] at [being unable] to nurture [their
    children] during their life,
because they could not provide food,
because they could not provide clothing,
don't let them die with [such regrets] in their heart!
The parents' hearts harbor the Buddha, the children's hearts harbor the
    tiger.
Parents, when they die, are buried in the ground,
children, when they die, are buried in their parents' hearts,
and become [a cause of] anxiety before sleep prevails.
Tung tung tung tung my daughter!
Tung tung tung tung my son!
In bringing up children, once they have come into the world,
they are laid in a dry [place]
and the mother lies down in damp places,
[they] are brought up with attention and love, and their education [is
    taken care of]."

Spoken:
   He says that he is adult, that he's grown up just because he came into the
world. When there is good food, he gives it to his wife and his children, not
caring about his parents. Nowadays it is like this.

Sung:
      Turi tung tung tung tung my puppy!
      tung tung tung my children!
      There is an old saying:
      "Yes, there are wives and children in every valley,
      but if parents and siblings once die, when will you ever get them back?"

Spoken:
   Parents are precious, they are precious indeed; merely because I say these
words, tears start to roll down my face. Things are getting worse these days. . . .
   In the past, when I grew up, it was certainly different from the way things are
now; and do you know why? Nowadays, truly, things have become too easy. I
mean, after bearing a son you do everything to feed him properly, dress him well,
you work hard because you want to give him a good education, and after you
have done your best and given him an education, do you think your son and his
family still acknowledge his parents? I have heard that there are bad offspring
who answer back, beat and banish their own parents. In truth there are also filial
offspring, I mean, dutiful sons and daughters-in-law, but taken as a whole, disre-
spectful offspring cannot be considered human beings. I saved money by going
around, living frugally, but once I had raised my children, do you think they respected me? Not at all, starting from my own children! Therefore [they say to

me]: "Grandpa! During your lifetime eat well, dress well and go around, make the most of it." "Hey! Eat abundantly." "Hey, eat often. If the offspring live well, that's that, if they do not live well, that's that. Grandma, eat well."

Song:

Listen to me, you know, our Visitors have arrived.
In the big village of Chejŏng I offer a prayer.
Hey, Visitors! This is a prayer, a prayer!
It is [offered] in the big village of Chejŏng!
The Visitors have really come 10,000 *li*
and I heard [they possess] miraculous virtues.
Please listen carefully.
Listen how miraculous the Visitors are!
Grandmother Samsin is exhausted, and also
step-grandfather is exhausted by the one-day ritual,
everybody is exhausted.
Why is everybody exhausted?
Even those who go often to one- and two-day rituals
have a rest for one day and [then] go again,
it is exhausting and even Grandmother Samsin is exhausted!
[They] equally give [offspring to] families without children,
distribute [food] to families without food,
and [clothes] to families without clothes.
If they often distributed them then
there would be a lot of money, and
families who live comfortably and in luxury
petition because they are without offspring.
[When they] do not stay in families [of believers]
and so there are no miraculous virtues, but
[people have to] experience [the visit of] the benevolent Visitors once,
and then, whether you present them with offerings large or small
if they have gone to a person once
they don't go there again.
That's what the Visitors are like!
If they infect only with the first degree, they do not depart.
Visitors! Visitors! This is the big village of Chejŏng!
Descendants of different surnames, descendants of the six surnames,
Crawling children, toddlers, [the Visitors infect them] all.
If not, they really infect adults too.
If they do not infect adults once, it is said they will infect again.
Everybody, at least once a year, two or three years,
when spring begins the Visitors [must be worshiped] in each village
and although there is effective medicine,
even though there are said to be good injections,

this year too, here and there,
the Visitors have arrived and left often.
One by one, to inspect the purity in the houses,
of the people, to check the level of civilization,
in one day the Visitors come and go [visiting] all families, one by one.
If the Visitors should happen to come to the village of Chejŏng,
please [infect] children, the children gently,
please [infect them] gently, gently.
If measles comes too, please infect [the children] gently.
However, it is only after the first degree infection [of smallpox]
and after the second degree that the white and red rashes form
and after the third degree the black rash [appears].
In any case please do it well.
If [the Visitors] wish to make the deformed offspring handsome, [they]
    do so,
if they wish to deform those who are healthy, [they] do so.
The Visitors can do whatever they wish!
Wherever you are, Visitors,
enjoy yourselves and have a good time
and in the village, in the village not only smallpox
but also all kinds of sickness, [make them] disappear.
It is said that recently there is really so much sickness!
Although all kinds of frightening sicknesses arrive,
Visitors, please block them all, front and back!
[We] receive you, prostrated with respect.
When the Visitors come and infect even children in the first degree,
and do it gently, they bring blessings.
If the Visitors are well welcomed there will be more luck,
when the Visitors enter fortune increases
silver treasure—a thousand pieces of gold,
gold treasure—a thousand pieces of gold,
please increase fast, fast.
Please bless with all kinds of fortune!
Bless with the Five Fortunes
so they are distributed equally in the Five Directions
and lengthen the short life so that long life gathers in coils,
eighty, eighty, twice eighty,
please make it as long as [the life of] the Chinese phoenix
on the highest tip of the Paulownia tree.
And to children, children,
please give their eyes the power of reading,
their ears the power of listening.
Distribute all sorts of [skill to] talk,
distribute all sorts of [skill to] write

so that they carry books in their bosom.
Give ability also to children
who study in front of their teacher, [fearful] as a tiger,
and give their eyes power in order to win a scholarship,
[to be] an honored student,
to be exempted from university taxes
or as a middle school student or elementary student.
In any case, please bless them with lots of money
and bless them in front, grain stored in front,
and behind, grain stored at the back,
a mountain of stored grain [for] government tax,
stored grain for the military,
bless with [food] to eat while it lasts, to use while it lasts,
bless with goods and money to live.
Let all kinds of fortune increase!
Human luck enters on foot,
and only if goblin luck enters in a boat,
you know, a thick cloud of luck will rise up.
Please bless with flowing water bringing luck so that
human luck will enter on foot.
This year, you know [because of the] luck of the year *imja*
I with my [spiritual] children serve the Visitors, serve the elders in the
    temple and
[every] three years I offer devotion in this way; and
when devotion is offered with a sincere heart
please bless [us] making our reputation widely known.
Please bless [our] families.
In the world we are already dead flowers.
From now on we are no use but
my [spiritual] children will be known in the future,
known to families [living] 1,000 and 10,000 *li* [off].
In the future in order to celebrate many rituals
[we will] take charge of Pyŏlsin in villages and
take charge of many things, all,
please give the blessing!
All, everybody in the big village of Chejŏng,
in the big village of Chejŏng, I mean in the past, really,
because of human feelings [you feel for the] grandmother Ch'uri who
    died,
you have entrusted in this year of good luck
the ritual to these youngsters who don't know anything yet, this time,
and even if all kinds of things
are done the wrong way [by the inexperienced new team]
the [village] elders will regard that with indulgence,

will regard that with benevolence
we will be extremely grateful when we return.
How wonderful that will be!
If they were strangers [I] might still react in that way but
because they are my [spiritual] children, my own children, I let things
    go as they are,
I am concerned for them
and wonder if they have bought a rice paddy or a dry field
let's see [how] it goes!
Please make things well in the big village of Chejŏng,
please help to make things well!
Because with an open mind [I] offer the prayer.
Let the elders also love my children dearly and assist them!
Please let this village be in peace.
The village is in peace and [luck] enters Chejŏng,
all who are fishing with nets as [their] job
will earn a lot of money.
Help in the plant, too, so no accident
befalls the boiler technician and the diver,
[help] so that food does not harden, producing much seaweed,
and then we shall be happy, won't we?
Offspring who have gone far off, even those
who live 1,000 *li* away in foreign countries,
let them make an easy, safe return home, then we shall be happy.
[I] prostrate myself to receive [your] approval.
Everybody, in this year of *imja*, in the big village of Chejŏng
with elders, with gods and all together with the children
everybody is concerned with wishes and destinies.
We welcome you sincerely,
we welcome gods and [also] ancestors
[we] make [you] known to families 1,000 and 10,000 *li* [away]
[we] make [you] known to families 1,000 and 10,000 *li* [away].
However dangerous this time, [in the future] we will, I mean,
Chonho-nim should drink and enjoy so that
neither alcohol nor ugly windy sickness will come.
Bless [us] so the wine will be abundant
so there will be no worry or anxiety [for those] with offspring.
Grandmother, in this year on the 3rd of March
because [you] have made the offering to the gods,
in future don't do so much.
Please live a hundred times more,
live until then!
Commanders in chief, village headman, everybody
I mean, in front of the family like a tiger,

although you go backward and forward doing things for the village
for the fishermen's union, there everybody
or the government office, for everybody;
In families large and small
although you go backward and forward in Chejŏng village,
the commander in chief is intelligent! The village headman also
    works well!
Such reputation will spread wide,
the village headman works very well!
The leading men also do very well.
Please grant that for all kinds of work, you know,
"New Village Projects" to get done, you know,
the money that is lacking will come in aplenty,
grant that what you have set out to do goes well!
Other villages will fall on their faces like falling off a high mountain,
a big mountain,
while we in this village, my son-in-law and my daughter,
have taken charge of this Pyŏlsin [ritual]
and [pray to the gods that] if we go now after doing this,
they will give you the resources to farm, the resources for mining.

Two years [is made up of] twelve months, 360 days, last year 10th, 11th,
and 12th
This year 1st, 7th months, 2nd, 8th months, 3rd and 9th months, 5th and
11th months, 6th month and 11th and 12th, one month 30 days, one day 12
[Asian] hours; at any time, please load us with luck!

—— 17 ——

Village Deities of Cheju Island

Boudewijn Walraven

Korean shamans have always served communities rather than individuals, whether these consisted of a nation, a town, a village, or a family. Over time, however, there has been a gradual reduction of the role of the shamans in this respect. Although early rulers of Silla may have had the status of shamans, the power of the shamans, based as it was on the very personal inspiration of an initiatory experience, did not fit the regulated procedures of the bureaucratic state that developed over time, and the prestige of Buddhism and Confucianism, with their sacred books, encouraged skepticism among the elite as to the shaman's claims of authority. In Koryŏ, the Confucian scholar-statesman Yi Kyubo (1168–1241) expressed this forcefully in his long descriptive poem "Nomu p'yŏn" (Lay of the Old Shaman), which depicts an ignorant, wildly dancing old crone. Yet even at the beginning of the Chosŏn dynasty, there still was a national or royal *mudang* (*kungmu* or *nara-mudang*). From that time onward, however, the government made concerted efforts to remove shamans from any role in official rituals. The last official rituals performed for the central government in which *mudang* took part were probably rain rituals, but by the mid–seventeenth century, that role too came to an end. In the countryside, government officials at the prefectural level also strove hard to Confucianize the rituals for which they were responsible, removing offensive images of the local deities and forbidding shamans from taking part. At the village level, however, shamans continued to work for both the community and individual families. From twentieth-century evidence, we may presume in the second half of the Chosŏn period shamans also performed communal rituals for neighborhoods in the mercantile satellite towns of the capital, such as Map'o, which sprung up on the banks of the Han River, outside the city walls. Thus the lowest community level at which the shamans were still active was that of the village or neighborhood, but even there their position was at risk. The Confucianization of Chosŏn society was a continuous process, which by the end of the nineteenth century also had reached into many rural communities. The pressure to Confucianize, however, lessened as the distance from the capital increased.

Although early in its history, when it was known as T'amna, Cheju Island had recognized the suzerainty of the states on the Korean peninsula, because of its geographic remoteness it long remained an area with its own traditions. There, the Confucianization of society came quite late and never was as thorough as in other regions. In the early eighteenth century, a zealous official from the capital, who wanted to stamp out illicit cults on the island, found 129 shamanic shrines to be destroyed. On the mainland, such violent repression had taken place much earlier. The destruction of the shrines of Cheju Island is described in shaman songs, which nevertheless conclude, in full agreement with the facts, that this attempt to suppress the cults was unsuccessful. Even in the twentieth century the islanders maintained vigorous shamanic cults in almost every village.

Cheju Island not only has maintained a large number of shamanic shrines, but its shamanic practices are also qualitatively different and in some ways may have retained archaic characteristics. The most common term on the island for a shaman, *simbang*, is found in an early *han'gŭl* text, a 1461 vernacular-Korean translation of the *Śūraṃgama-sūtra* (*Nŭngŏmgyŏng ŏnhae*), and apparently at that time was in use on the mainland as well. The special character of the rituals of the island also is reflected in several ways in the shaman songs of Cheju Island. Whereas on the mainland the number of narrative shaman songs is limited, on Cheju they are very common and most village deities have songs explaining their origin (*ponp'uri*). One even finds songs devoted to the deified ancestors of certain families of nonshamans. The contents of Cheju *ponp'uri* and mainland narrative songs differ, moreover, in that the former depict the deities as freely interacting with each other, while in the latter certain deities may appear together in the one song (e.g., Sŏngju the god of the house and Chisin, the goddess of the earth, his wife), but most of them seem to lead independent, parallel existences. By contrast, Cheju Island deities interact with each other very much like the Olympian gods, or even like characters in a soap opera, quarreling with their relatives, having extramarital affairs, or changing jobs in their search for a position that really suits them.

Both songs translated here were collected in the 1930s by Korean assistants of the Japanese researchers Akamatsu Chijō and Akiba Takashi. The nationality of the researchers for whom the work was done may have prompted an alteration to the text. In the first song, a young girl is raped by sailors from a "foreign" ship. Other versions of the song state that she is violated by "Japanese pirates." If so, this is but one instance of the changes to the text that are almost inevitable in oral narratives, because these are never completely rigid and are in every case influenced by the context in which they are performed.

The first translation is of "T'osandang ponp'uri," the story of the origin of the deity of a shrine in T'osan (not the main village shrine). She is a snake goddess, who according to tradition is also worshiped at home and will follow girls from T'osan when they marry, in a matrilineal pattern of veneration. Several Chosŏn-period sources testify that this cult already existed in this region at that time. It overlaps with a general cult on the island of the snake as a protector of all aspects of human life. Snakes are also worshiped in some other shrines on the island. This precise form of such cults is unknown on the mainland, but there is ample evidence of snake worship there, too, in both historical sources and surviving folk customs, particularly if one keeps in mind that there was no clear dividing line between snake and dragon worship. The snake was one of the "lucky animals" (ŏp) worshiped in many families until the mid–twentieth century.

In recent decades, the T'osan tradition of snake worship in family homes has come to be felt as something of burden in the village, because people of other areas are afraid of women from T'osan and shun contact with them. T'osan girls who go to Cheju City to study, for instance, may find no one willing to rent a room to them. When I visited the village in 1988, initially no one wanted even to talk about the cult. The song, however, allots a much more positive significance to the worship of the snake goddess: it is thanks to her that the women of the village are so virtuous and beautiful.

One aspect of the tale that is of particular interest is that it reflects the tension between popular beliefs and the convictions of the Confucian elite, who looked down on shamans and their gods. Thus in a way it records a crucial part of the historical development of shamanism. The first section of "T'osandang ponp'uri" is a version of a well-known legend about a Chosŏn-period Confucian magistrate, Hong Yunsŏng (1425–75), which was put into writing by several Confucian scholars who opposed "uncivilized" rituals. The legend relates how Hong resolutely deals with a local deity near Naju in Chŏlla province, who does not show appropriate respect to His Majesty's officials. In the muga (where the official is called Yi), the deity is held responsible for the dismissal of all the hapless individuals appointed to serve as magistrate of Naju. The official's attitude toward the deity, who is considered to be a kind of supernatural counterpart to himself, is typical for Confucians of his age. While he does not deny the existence of such beings, he firmly believes that even deities of this kind should recognize royal authority and be sternly dealt with if they refuse to do so. In the shaman song, the official has the deity, who turns out to be a female dragon god, cut up into small pieces when he finds that she falls short of his standards. In contrast to the legend as told by Confucians, however, for the shamans this is not the end of the matter, for the deity merely changes shape and in the end is reincarnated as the snake god of T'osan, where she becomes both the shrine deity and simultaneously, as the "sun-and-moon ancestor," a guardian deity of individual families. Thus she represents a phenomenon that is common in Korean popular beliefs: the deity is singular and plural at the same time. As the heroine of the ponp'uri and the goddess worshiped by the village as a whole she is one, but at the same time each family has its own snake deity. House gods like the birth goddess Samsin have the same characteristic.

Cheju Island is famous for the strength of its women, who traditionally have more power in the family than do women on the mainland, probably because of their economic prowess as divers and possibly also because the hold of Confucianization of Cheju society has been less deep-seated. The number of female deities is also remarkable. Even on Cheju, though, women have been bound by all kinds of restrictions on their freedom, and it is striking how much attention "T'osandang ponp'uri" devotes to violence against women, whether perpetrated by indigenous men or foreign sailors.

Near the end of the song two young women become ill because of the anger of a deity. It is a common assumption that this is a kind of possession, which means that the sick person may lend her mouth to the possessing spirit to transmit a message. This is what happens in the song. The way in which this is described is potentially confusing, however, although the pattern seen in this song is typical for such verbal exchanges in Korean shamanic ritual. The person who is possessed will at one moment speak as the deity or spirit and then suddenly shift back to her own persona. In this song in one and the same speech event the two women say "I" when they speak as the goddess and "we" when they speak as themselves.

A recurring motif in the ponp'uri, which is also seen in this song, is the search for a right place for the god to settle. Invariably the deity first comes to a place that is either already occupied or somehow unsuitable, before a spot is located that is satisfactory in all respects. Indirectly this emphasizes the strong affinity between the deity and the villagers who worship him or her. Sometimes the arrival of the newcomer leads to a redistribution of tasks. This happens in the second song translated here, "Sŏgwi ponhyangdang ponp'uri," where the story explains a divine distribution that is very common on the island, with a main shrine, the ponhyangdang, for the most important deity of the village and a second shrine for a deity with more specific tasks.

"Sŏgwi ponhyangdang ponp'uri" might be called the romance among the ponp'uri and explains the origin of the guardian deities of Sŏgwi-p'o, Ilmun (or Ilmun'gwan) Paramun and Chi San'guk, who are respectively associated with wind and rain. To demarcate their territory Paramun and a female deity, his estranged lover, shoot arrows, a motif that is also seen in the myth of the origin of the three most prominent clans of the island, which was recorded in writing in the fifteenth century. Here this motif explains the strict division, if not the antagonism, between two villages. Additionally, the song explains how an ancestor of the shrine keeper who by heredity is in charge of the shrine came to assume this function and how the most important rituals came to be performed. The rituals mentioned are in fact the main rituals of all shrines on the island. The New Year's ritual is the annual village ritual and the most indispensable and largest in scale. The ritual on the fifteenth of the second lunar month in this song is called Yŏngson maji, but it is better known as the Yŏngdŭng ritual. It is performed particularly for the benefit of the female divers who collect all kinds of shellfish and seaweed, but has acquired a wider meaning as a ritual for success in fishing in general, good harvests, and the prevention of natural disasters. When on the thirteenth of the seventh lunar month the Mappullim ritual is held, the robes of the deities are aired to prevent molding. Because it was combined with an agricultural festival (Paekchung) that in the past was celebrated nationwide in the middle of this month, an added purpose of the ritual is to ensure the well-being of horses and cows.

In spite of the unrealistic, wildly romantic love story of its protagonists, taken in its entirety "Sŏgwi ponhyangdang ponp'uri" is directly connected to the essentials of the villagers' daily lives. Apart from the sacred calendar that structures their sense of time, it furnishes an affirmation of their identity vis-à-vis the neighboring village, which is reinforced by special ties to their own village deities. One of these is, as the song describes, a goddess called "the wife of the Present Emperor," who assists them in their daily tasks of fishing and diving for shellfish, the mainstay of their livelihood.

The translated texts are from Akamatsu Chijō and Akiba Takashi, *Chōsen fuzoku no kenkyū* vol. 1 (Tokyo:Ōsaka Yagō Shoten, 1937), 357–69, 341–57.

Further Reading

B.C.A. Walraven, "The Deity of the Seventh Day—and Other Narrative *Muga* from Cheju Island," *Bruno Lewin zu Ehren: Festschrift aus Anlass seines 65. Geburtstages*, Band III, (Bochum, 1992), 309–28, contains another *ponp'uri* in translation and discusses motifs and themes that are frequent in Cheju *muga*. Seong Nae Kim, "Lamentations of the Dead: The Historical Imagery of Violence on Cheju Island, South Korea," *Journal of Ritual Studies* 3, no. 1 (1989): 251–85, shows that the shamanic rites of the island, while representing an ancient tradition, also reflect contemporary concerns and preserve local memories, such as those of the April Third Communist Uprising in 1948, the memory of which successive authoritarian governments have tried to suppress. The intricate shifts of speaker in the oracles of the shamans are analyzed in Antonetta L. Bruno, *The Gate of Words: Language in the Rituals of Korean Shamans* (Leiden: CNWS, 2002). The myth of the Three Clans of Cheju Island is translated in James H. Grayson, *Myths and Legends from Korea: An Annotated Compendium of Ancient and Modern Materials* (Richmond, Surrey: Curzon, 2001), 118–23, and discussed in greater detail in Michael Pettid, "Reshaping History: The Creation of the Myth of the Three Surnames, the Foundation Myth of the T'amna Kingdom," *Review of Korean Studies* 3 (July 2000): 157–77.

Song of the Origin of the Local Shrine of T'osan

Year after year the magistrates of Naju
suffered dismissal from office.
Everyone thought it strange
and whoever it was
feared being appointed to Naju.

Then Magistrate Yi, who lived in Yŏngju,
said that if he would become magistrate of Naju
he would complete the full term of three years,
and volunteered for the said post.
Before long the king granted his appointment
And so his wish was fulfilled.
On the journey to his destination
he passed in front of Mount Yŏng near Naju
when unexpectedly, with thunder and lightning,
there was a downpour of rain
that stretched for a hundred *li*;
east, west, south, and north
became difficult to discern.
When he asked: "What is going on?"
to the clerk in charge of punishments of that area,
the clerk answered:
"There is an Official who rules over this district."
"Is there an official ruling over this district
who is superior to me?"
"Yes, there is the Official in the shrine."
"What then should we do?"
"You should descend from your horse."
When he descended from his horse,
suddenly the clouds lifted
and there was a blazing sun in a blue sky
and so, without mishap, he assumed his office.
Three days later he spoke:
"They say the spirit in the shrine is beautiful;
let's go and have a look at the deity."
When they came to the mountain
there was fog on all sides
and it was all darkness before their eyes.
The clerk in charge of punishments said:
"Sir, please recite some scriptures!"
The magistrate said:
"If there is a spirit,
please lift this fog for us!"
and then it was immediately swept away on all sides
and their view widened.
When he looked around on Mount Yŏng,
wind bells dangled from the four corners
of an eight-story pavilion,
the view of a huge palace enraptured
all those who saw it!

When he called the hereditary keeper and asked:
"Who is the spirit?" the man answered:
"If you want to see spirits,
you have to conduct a ritual."
When he conducted a ritual,
a dragon deity with three heads and nine tails,
whose upper jaw touched heaven,
whose lower jaw touched the earth,
manifested itself and then the shaman spoke:
"That is the spirit."
"If so, does it have a treasure,
a jewel in its beak that lights up the night?"
"It has, but it is not visible."
"What kind of divinity does a being like that possess,
that year after year it causes
the dismissal of the magistrates of Naju?"
the magistrate said
and ordered an assassin with a yellow headscarf
to cut the dragon deity in pieces;
and when he burned the pieces in a dust basket,
without the slightest mercy,
the dragon was reborn as a jade *go* stone
and floated away through the air
like a crane over the green mountains.
At that time Mr. Kang, the clerk in charge of punishments,
and Mr. Han, the clerk in charge of personnel, of Cheju Island
on their way to the capital to deliver local tribute
had moored their boat on the Han River
and had set foot on the shore,
when from nowhere a jade *go* stone fell down.
Because it was so shiny
they thought it was a kind of metal object
and put it away in a travel basket.
When thereupon they entered the capital
the local tribute of the Eight Provinces
was rejected in its entirety,
but Mr. Kang the clerk in charge of punishments
and Mr. Han the clerk in charge of personnel
from T'osan on Cheju succeeded in delivering the tribute
and receiving thousand-fold, ten-thousand-fold profit,
they earned a tidy sum.
When filled with jubilation they left the capital,
on the way they thought:
"This *go* stone is definitely the metamorphosis of a deity

and that this time we have been successful
has been due to his invisible support,
but if we take it back to Cheju Island
where the land is rugged
and the people are ignorant,
there will be a danger
that something inauspicious will happen."
They left the jade *go* stone at its original place,
but when they reached the Han River
and wanted to set sail,
the weather changed abruptly
and because the violence of the wind and the waves
for three months and ten days, for a hundred days
they suffered hardships, far away from home.
In the end, when they asked for advice
to the great master of a certain temple, he said:
"There is a deity you have to accompany to Cheju.
You must accompany that deity.
If you don't, you will turn into spirits of the dead."
And thus, in the severe cold
of the month of the winter solstice,
they took off their clothes
and lustrated themselves in the Han River
and after they had found the jade *go* stone
they respectfully enshrined it on the ship's altar,
and prepared all kinds of offerings.
Then, while they gazed at the white sandy shore,
while the blue waves were calm,
a light, favorable breeze blew softly.
They were as happy
as if they had been revived from the dead.
They hoisted high the great sail
and in an instant approached Cheju,
when the sailors spoke:
"This is definitely a spirit;
if it enters Cheju,
nothing much has to happen
or it will inflict damage and death
and therefore the complaints of the people of Cheju
will be most severe."
"It's right," "It's wrong,"
contrary opinions clashed
until in the end it was decided
to throw the jade *go* stone

into the deep waters of the ocean.
Then, suddenly, a gale raged:
it was as if the hulk of the ship
would be turned over,
as if it would be torn apart.
The whole crew, in mortal fear,
with desperate efforts tried to reach Sanji,
but they couldn't,
neither could they reach Choch'ŏn
nor could they reach Kŭmnyŏng.
When they were thrown hither and thither,
buffeted by the waves,
one vicious breaker enveloped them
and pitched them on the stony beach
of Ishindi near Yŏruni in Chŏngŭi.
With their bodies exhausted, their minds dazed
the men collapsed, as if they had died,
as if they were sleeping.
Then a woman as beautiful
as a maiden of the Moon Palace appeared:
"Mr. Kang, the clerk in charge of punishments
and Mr. Han, the clerk in charge of personnel
have acquired merit, but . . ."
Before she had finished her words
they abruptly awoke
and wondered if it had been a dream.
When that deity presented herself
to the goddess Lady Myŏngwi from the Southern Field
in the village of Yŏruni, the latter asked:
"What kind of divinity are you?"
"I am the guardian deity,
in charge of the land of Mount Yŏng near Naju."
"For what reason have you come here?"
"I have come to take a look at the land,
to take a look at the water,
to take a look at the people."
"Here the land is my land,
the water is my water
and the people, too, are my people."
"Isn't there an empty place somewhere?"
"A place they call the Lower Shrine of T'osan is empty."
"In this case, if it is like that,
I beg you to show me the way right now."
Thus the Senior Official Sir Yi

was made to guide the way
and following her guide
the deity entered T'osan.
At that time a deity titled
Military Commander of Yŏngsan at Unnaekki
with an entourage of ten thousand,
accompanied by musicians, was enjoying himself.
Seeing a beautiful woman pass he called out:
"That there is not a person from Cheju!
Let's go after her!"
When he followed her,
the deity noticed him and quickly ran off.
When she reached the Kŏsin pond of T'osan
she scooped up some water with her hand
and found that that place was fine
as a place to settle down
and so she settled down there.
Then the Military Commander of Yŏngsan at Unnaekki
suddenly rushed at her and gripped her by the wrist.
Angrily he scolded her:
"Evil bitch! Are you the child of a nobleman,
or the child of a technical specialist from the mainland?
Cheju is a place where women don't walk around alone!"
With a silver decorative knife she cut off
the wrist he had grabbed
and while she wound a silken handkerchief around it
she threw herself down, with a big splash,
into the sea near the Dragon Hall Cape.
   The Military Commander of Yŏngsan
   could not but feel ashamed:
"I have been lacking in respect
because I didn't know she was a deity,"
he spoke while he withdrew
and he enshrined this deity
in the Lower Hall near Dragon Hall Cape.
But there was no one who prayed to her
and no one offered her even a cup of sweet wine.
One day the daughter of Village Elder O
accompanied by her servant girl Cho
went to do her laundry in the pool of Sanmanŭl Village.
At that time the deity was looking out over the southern sea.
when a huge foreign ship appeared.
Making a furious wind blow, she caused it to suffer shipwreck
and clambering to the shore

the sailors barely escaped with their lives.
Those fellows discovered the pool of Sanmanŭl Village
and when they went there to quench their thirst,
there was a lovely young girl;
like venomous beasts they rushed at her.
The servant girl Cho hid like lightning and escaped,
but eventually they caught the daughter of Village Elder O.
She adamantly resisted the villains
whose eyes were bloodshot with animal lust,
but in the end, after a final battle,
this bold beauty perished.
The band of cowardly villains ran away
as fast as a raging gale.
When the servant girl Cho came to take a look,
the untainted beauty who until a moment ago
had been like a lady-in-waiting of the Jade Emperor
had disappeared, only a corpse covered in blood
lay on the earth, looking up to heaven.
When she went to her side and shook her,
tears obscured what was in front of her eyes
and she could not bear to look at her in detail,
but from the lips that had been so beautiful
fresh blood had flown,
coloring her fair complexion and her clothes.
The servant lamented even louder:
"Oh, my mistress! Return to life,
even if it is just for one moment!
My poor mistress! My compassionate mistress!"
But on all sides it remained quiet,
there was not the slightest response.
The despair of her parents was bottomless.
They buried their daughter
and spent day and night in sorrowful tears.
Mr. Kang the clerk in charge of punishments
and Mr. Han the clerk in charge of personnel of T'osan
had exchanged sisters and each of them
had a beloved only daughter,
and both had married.
In the scorching heat of the sixth month
the two daughters were grinding barley
when suddenly they fell ill:
their bodies became completely paralyzed.
"What kind of sudden illness is this?"
they wondered and called a doctor

who treated them with acupuncture.
Then the daughters suddenly became crazy
and no longer recognized their parents,
their relatives, or the people of the village.
They called a shaman who prayed and held a ritual.
When she was taking away the pollution
the two daughters shouted,
and told in lavish detail the story
of the time when their fathers had gone
to offer tribute in Seoul
and also the story of the death
of the daughter of Village Elder O.
"I now live in the Lower Hall in T'osan
and stand guard over that place.
The daughter of Village Elder O
at this moment, under my supervision,
is keeping the records of the people.
The silk I haven given you
you have used for the letters requesting marriage,
but when you married,
you did not even present me with a sacrifice
of newly harvested rice
and disregarded me.
This is infinitely hateful
and therefore I've sent you a divine illness!
In the box next to our pillow
there is shiny satin and dark-blue 'water satin.'
Take that and hold a ritual
twice monthly, on the seventh and fourteenth day
and in that way save us!"
When they looked in the box
indeed there were water satin and shiny satin!
When they took the satin out,
inside there was a snake.
Astounded they held a ritual
and then, after ten days
the illness of the daughters was healed.
And so we worship that deity
as the main deity of the shrine
and at home we worship her
as our sun-and-moon ancestor
and therefore all people praise
the women of the village,
as dutiful daughters and chaste wives,

beautiful as the radiant harvest moon.
That is why the people of the village
vie with each other in worship of this deity
and for three, four, five *li*
within Upper T'osan and Lower T'osan
all the people of Chŏngŭi,
serve her full of devotion
in the shrine of Lower T'osan.

Song of the Origin of the Deity of the Shrine of Sŏgwi

In the land of Cheju, in Sŏlmaeguk
arose Ilmun'gwan Paramun
with a topknot as big as a fist,
a headband woven from a single thread,
with a cord of brass,
a black felt officers' hat made of the hair of wild animals,
lined with sun-patterned Chinese silk,
with a chin band made of an abundance of heavy silk
and a loose-hanging string of a small bit of heavy silk
and enormous amber beads on the string,
with egret's tail feathers adorning his hat,
with wide trousers made of silk from the east,
with a wide jacket made of silk from the north,
with a dark-blue military coat and sleeveless overcoat
and a waistband of *sura* silk,
holding a bow so big that it filled his arms,
his eyes bulging like those of a goldfish,
and a triangular beard curved upward.
If he shot one arrow,
three thousand soldiers would come forth.
If he shot another arrow,
three thousand soldiers would retreat.
He was conversant with the heavenly signs above
and understood the principles of the earth below.
There was a whisper in the wind
that over the mountains, across the sea
ten thousand miles away,
—"rain fall!": five thousand miles of rain,
"red dust come forth!": a thousand miles of red dust—
there was a beauty called Ko San'guk.
When surrounded by a blue cloud
he arrived there in just a moment,

it turned out she was a real beauty indeed.
When he greeted her, she asked:
"From where do you come?"
"I am Ilmun Paramun
who has arisen in Sŏlmaeguk
on Mount Halla in Cheju."
"I am Ko San'guk."
After they had exchanged greetings
they looked at each other's faces
and fell in love.
"Longing for you I having come here
in spite of the long voyage."
"Last night I had a very special dream,
and today I have the good luck to meet you."
They were joined together
and became husband and wife.
Two, three days passed in bliss,
when unexpectedly another beautiful woman appeared.
This was an absolute beauty, unsurpassed in the world
many times more ravishing than Ko San'guk.
When he asked who she was,
Ko San'guk said: "This is my younger sister"
and they exchanged greetings.
Calling each other sister-in-law and brother-in-law
they were most friendly with each other,
but from that time in Ilmun'gwan's heart
it was as if the bliss of two, three days had been shattered,
and it turned dark in his soul.
Not for a moment could he forget
the younger sister of Ko San'guk.
Where had the bravado gone of such a bold hero?
If he did not see her, he pined for her,
if he met her, he was dazed,
neither his body nor his heart knew rest.
In front of Ko San'guk he was frightened
and didn't know what to do,
as if he had become a great criminal.
But the younger sister of Ko San'guk, too,
in her heart felt a limitless love for Ilmun'gwan:
her torment was in no way different
from what Ilmun'gwan felt.
Yet, the girl was unaware of the torment of Ilmun'gwan
and Ilmun'gwan was unaware of the torment of the girl.
While they longed for each other,

every time when they met
their facial expression was uneasy
and in the end they seemed coldhearted.
In such torment they passed a good twenty days,
when Ilmun'gwan finally took a decision:
in the third wake of the moonlit night
he took firm hold of the tender wrist of the girl.
But the words Ilmun'gwan wanted to speak
stuck in his throat,
only big tears dropped from his eyes.
Also from the face of the girl tears streamed down,
but because they could not cry loudly,
they felt even more frustrated.
After several scores of days
a secret plan to run away was formed.
Enveloped by a blue cloud
they reached the numinous mountain of Cheju.
When day dawned and Ko San'guk woke up,
there was no trace of Ilmun'gwan Paramun.
Wondering if he was sleeping late
she looked in Ilmun'gwan's room,
but he wasn't there.
Asking herself if he might have gone to the back garden
to breathe some cold, fresh air
she went there to look for him,
but there was no trace of even his shadow.
But what startled her
was that his travel gear
had vanished into thin air.
Ko San'guk was at the end of her wits.
Because there was nothing else to do,
she went to look for her younger sister
to discuss where Ilmun'gwan might have gone,
but even her sister had disappeared,
and her travel gear, too!
Ko San'guk could not find Ilmun'gwan,
but she was conversant with the heavenly signs above
and understood the principles of the earth below,
and so she wondered:
"Wouldn't these two have become crazy
and run away together?"
and as a last resort prayed to bright heaven,
putting up an official banner
and then in spite of a strong adverse wind

the flag flew vigorously to Mount Halla.
When Ko San'guk, hanging on to the flag,
reached numinous Mount Halla,
her younger sister and Paramun had indeed fled there
and become man and wife:
they were intoxicated with first love!
Exploding with anger
she wanted to shoot them both at the same time
with an arrow shot from a sling,
when the younger sister "Ko San'guk" practiced fog magic:
ink-black night descended
and the elder sister "Ko San'guk" became confused.
Employing all kinds of magic
the elder sister prayed several times to the Lord of Heaven,
but by nature the younger sister's magic was superior
and thus the elder sister failed
to find her way through the black fog
and could not think of a subtle plan
to extricate herself from the mist
and so, instead, she was vanquished.
Thus she said to her younger sister:
"You cruel, malicious bitch!
Even though I have taken a shot at you with my sling,
I could not bear to kill you.
And even if I wanted to kill you,
how can you, who has committed a crime
for which you deserve to die,
let your elder sister wither to death
in this abominable situation!
Won't you even apologize?
But you, you evil wench,
I cannot bear to kill you!
Let's not harm each other!
Now you make this fog lift!"
And so Ilmun'gwan Paramun broke off
the south-facing branch of a juniper tree
and when he stuck it between some steep crags,
it turned into an enormous rooster
which crowed with a loud voice
and then the night came to an end
and in the east a pretty moon rose up.
Only then it became possible to distinguish faces.
Ko San'guk was very angry: "You damned bitch,
you deserve to be slaughtered.

You scoundrel, you deserve
to be put on the chopping board.
You, Paramun, you are like a beast.
Though it was my first thought
to kill you both together,
I cannot bear to kill you
even if, to tell you the truth,
my indignation won't disappear.
But you, devilish creature,
are not my younger sister.
You should change your family name
and adopt the name of Chi.
I want to go back to my own place,
but because I feel ashamed,
I'll just go where my feet take me.
You go where you want to go.
I'll go wherever I feel like going."
In this way Ko San'guk cut off all ties.
When she descended from Mount Halla,
Chi San'guk and Paramun
roamed through the mountains
at Haegŭmuni and Talgŭmuni
near the White Deer Lake on Mount Halla
and in search of a place to settle
looked around using a telescope and a compass.
The Upper Hall of Hogŭn-ni seemed fine
and so they went there and looked,
but because it was unsuitable
they again used the compass
and the top of Rice Hill was appropriate
and therefore they went there to settle
and put up a white awning.
A man from Upper West Village
called Kim Pongt'ae
with a jacket of mole skin
and trousers of marten skin
a long coat of yellow-dog skin
and on his belt a hunting bag with a narrow opening
and an ornamented knife, with his four dogs:
Four-Eyes, Shepherd, Horse-Manes, and Long-Hair,
wanted to go hunting for pleasure.
When he got up to the lowest watchtower
he saw a white awning
on the highest peak of Rice Ridge.

Because a white awning is something
only an immortal or a divine being will put up,
he thought it strange
and so he ascended the middle watchtower
and saw that it still was there.
When he then got up on the upper watchtower
he again saw it still was there,
so definitely they would be divinities.
He approached them to a distance of a hundred paces
and respectfully greeted them with folded hands.
"What kind of person are you?" they asked
"I am Kim Pongt'ae of Upper West Village."
"Why have you come?"
"I have come to hunt for pleasure.
What kind of divinities are you?"
"I am Ilmun Paramun
who has arisen from Sŏlmaeguk
and this is Chi San'guk
—'rain fall!': five thousand miles of rain,
'red dust come forth!': a thousand miles of red dust—."
"For what reason have you descended to this place?"
"Receiving orders from His Highness the Jade Emperor
I have descended to look at the affairs of mankind
and to take charge of their affairs."
"Ah, is it like that?"
"Because you are a person entrusted to us,
you should show us the way."
"Aye, filled with trepidation I obey."
"Which village is the place
that from here seems nearest?"
"That's Upper Sŏgwi.
Down there, that's Lower Sŏgwi."
"And what village is that again,
there to the west?"
"That is West Hong Village."
"Show us the way then to Upper Sŏgwi!"
But when they came to Upper Sŏgwi
there was no proper place to settle
and so they said.
"What would you think
if we live together in your house
and stay there for three months?"
"I am filled with the utmost trepidation.
Because it is a human dwelling,

It's extremely dirty and messy.
There is the smell of dust
and there is the smell of soot.
There is the smell of cooked food
and there is the smell of human beings.
I would feel too embarrassed
when divinities stay there."
"In spite of all that it's fine;
let's go to your house!"
Because there was nothing to be done,
he cut short his objections
and accompanied them
and while they lived together,
in spite of his embarrassment,
he felled a tree in the thicket of the Upper Shrine
and built a small house.
"I'm sorry, but please live here for the time being."
When the two divinities stayed there for three months,
they no longer could bear the sight of people on horseback,
they no longer could bear the sight of dogs
and said: "We can no longer live here."
They called Kim Pongt'ae: "We feel sorry,
because we are so much indebted to you,
but know that after a few months
you will hear from us."
Saying this they left.
Then they came to a grotto called Mŏkkohol
and settled in that place.
After spending three months there,
because of the sound of the river that flowed nearby
and the loneliness of the lush forest on one side,
it happened that the two divinities talked once more
about moving to another place to settle.
"In the end we parted in disharmony from Ko San'guk,
but for us it would be fitting to meet once more
and then it would be good, after we've met,
to determine the place where we should settle."
So they decided
and because Ko San'guk was in charge
of human affairs in West Hong Village,
they sent a message to her
and agreed to meet at Kasimŏri Mettol.
When they thus met on the agreed day
and in the agreed place,

Ko San'guk's anger had not dissolved:
"Why have you called me
proposing to meet again?"
"Wouldn't it be fitting,
rather than to go in this way forever,
to discuss everything to our hearts' content,
dividing the territory,
and then to take charge of the land,
taking charge of human affairs?"
"What is the meaning of 'to our hearts' content,'
what is the meaning of 'discuss,'
once we have completely cut off our relationship?"
Because Ilmun Paramun so forcefully pleaded
as if he wanted her to bow for the inevitable,
Ko San'guk became angry
and took a shot with her sling
which reached Hangnam.
Then Ilmun Paramun shot with his bow
and the arrow reached the Big Rock of Mun Island.
And so Ko San'guk spoke: "It is inevitable:
I will make Hangnam the border
and as before shall take charge of West Hong Village.
You will take charge of Higher and Lower Sŏgwi
north of Mosquito Island,
but the people of West Hong Village
will not be able to marry in East Hong Village,
and the people in East Hong Village
will not be able to marry in West Hong Village.
The shrine keeper of East Hong Village
will not be able to go to West Hong Village
and the shrine keeper of West Hong Village
will not be able to go to East Hong Village;
please be aware of that!"
So Ko San'guk went for good to West Hong Village.
When Paramun looked at his compass and its magnetic needle,
around the upper branches of the holy tree of Lower Sŏgwi
there was an auspicious aura
and so he went down there to settle,
but then there was not a single human being
to take notice of him.
One day the grandchild of the O family of Upper Sŏgwi
fell ill and the illness was very severe.
At great length they talked about Paramun and Chi San'guk:
"Now they have come to the upper branches of our holy tree,

but because we do as if we hardly see them,
as if we are not aware of them,
they consider this an unrivaled insolence
and therefore have given our grandchild such an illness."
And so someone from the O family
went down to Lower Sŏgwi
and put their case first of all to the Song family.
Thus the Song family came to take the lead.
The villagers of Lower Sŏgwi joined forces
and decided to build a shrine.
After they had felled countless trees
they built the shrine.
Then they designated a shrine keeper
and went up to the capital
and bought lunar-splendor silk, solar-splendor silk,
heavy silk, Chinese silk and green satin
silver rings, golden rings, big beads,
and a string of amber.
Then they put up spirit flags
and held the great ritual for the beginning of the new year
on the first day of the first month,
the great ritual to welcome the dragon god
on the fifteenth day of the second month,
the great ritual of Mappullim
on the thirteenth day of the seventh month
and the birthday ritual for the god
on the first day of the eleventh month.
Later Kim Pongt'ae was called
to become the "purveyor"
of Paramun and Chi San'guk.
Becoming the servant of the two divinities
he came to receive the offerings of mankind.
Thus the two divinities became the village protectors
of Upper and Lower Sŏgwi, where they lived.
Before that, the wife of the Present Emperor
of Sujinp'o at Sonam Cape looked from afar
at the holy tree of Upper Sŏgwi,
when unexpectedly some divinities settled there.
She thought it strange and asked:
"What kind of divinities are you?"
"We are Paramun and Chi San'guk."
"For what purpose have you come to this place?"
"We have come to take charge of the human affairs
of Upper and Lower Sŏgwi."

"I, too, am in charge of Lower Sŏgwi."
"Ah, we have made a mistake.
If we had known that you are in charge
of the human affairs of Lower Sŏgwi
we would not have done like this,
but we didn't. Please forgive us."
But the wife of the Emperor spoke
with even greater friendliness:
"Because my forces are weak
I cannot block the dangers
that come from the east and the west
and I cannot save all the people
of the east and the west.
If you take care of the people
of the mainland of Upper and Lower Sŏgwi
and rule over them,
I will take care of the Dragon Palace
and take care of ships that come
and ships that go,
of diving women that come
and diving women that go,
of divers that come
and divers that go,
and rule over them."
The wife of the Emperor went into the Dragon Palace
and Ilmun'gwan and Chi San'guk entered the shrine
to take charge of Upper and Lower Sŏgwi,
and there receive offerings from mankind.

—18—

Shamans, the Family, and Women

Boudewijn Walraven

Although shamans may have had considerable influence in public life during the early history of Korea, in the course of time their rituals were increasingly relegated to the private sphere. By the second half of the Chosŏn period, under the influence of the Confucian transformation of Korea, shamans no longer performed in any of the central state rituals. The only public rituals they still enacted were for village communities, and even there they lost ground as more and more villagers preferred rites performed in Confucian style. Continuing their activities within the private sphere, shamans worked on behalf of families (which still included some of the most powerful in the land) rather than individuals, and consequently family affairs occupy an important place in the rituals.

Because men of almost all classes increasingly turned toward Confucian-style rituals, the clients seeking the help of the shamans in the private domain have long been predominantly women, for whom Confucianism was not particularly attractive. Confucianism demanded much of women but offered them little in return. Women could derive no consolation from it when they were faced with problems like childlessness (a grave sin from the Confucian point of view) or the tragedies of widowhood (aggravated by the Confucian ban on remarriage, which was absolute even when widows were still very young) and the loss of children. Nor was there any Confucian solace for women when it came to the worries and difficulties that come with childbearing and child rearing. It is not surprising, therefore, that women sought refuge in Buddhism and shamanic ritual and that female concerns are reflected in shamanic ritual and shaman songs in all kinds of ways. It was only to the shamans, for instance, that women could turn for a prayer for smooth lactation. The strong ties between women and shamanic ritual have been reinforced by the fact that the shamans themselves have been predominantly female for many centuries. Why this happened is not easily explained. One crucial factor is that men, who had exclusive access to the public domain, turned to the written traditions of Buddhism and Confucianism, which led to more and more shamanic rituals being held for female believers. This change must have made it more difficult for male shamans to act on their behalf, particularly when the Confucianization of the country demanded strict gender separation in most public activities. There may be still other factors involved. It has been suggested that becoming an inspired shaman is "a pathway out of impasse," a way of coping with unbearable existential problems of whatever nature, whether psychological or economic. The enumeration of all kinds of afflictions sent by the gods to force a candidate shaman to accept the calling, which is a standard ingredient in accounts of the process of becoming a shaman, corroborates this argument. Because women were (and, to a lesser degree, are) subject to more restrictions than men, and therefore more likely to find themselves in desperate situations, it is possible that their numerical predominance in the shamanic profession may be related to this as well. An emic explanation might also be that spirits represent *yin* (in Korean, *ŭm*), the female principle, and that for that reason women have a greater affinity with them and are more likely to become possessed. Whatever the confluence of causes, it is a fact that the typical shaman is a woman, to the point that male shamans will wear women's clothes during a ritual (in Hwanghae province) or don a skirt underneath the most commonly male garb of a particular spirit's clothes before they perform a section of a ritual (in Seoul).

The first two texts translated here are chanted prayers that directly address the concerns of women: "Prayer after Childbirth" and "Prayer Offered When a Child Cries Too Much." Both were collected in the 1920s by Son Chint'ae in the South, in Tongnae, from a female shaman. The "singing" mentioned in the second song is of course a euphemism for the bawling of the baby. The third text, "Hwangch'ŏn honshi" (Song of the Ritual of the Yellow Springs), is a narrative song sung when children were ill. Yellow Springs is a common term of Sinitic origin used to refer to the world of the dead. The name of the song is related to one of its main themes, the prevention of the premature death of the brothers who are the protagonists of the story. Additionally, the song emphasizes the importance of caring well for the dead as a key to a long and happy life. Support granted to the living from beyond the grave in exchange for sacrifices of food, drink, and clothes is a key concept in every shamanic ritual. The depiction of the Underworld in the story reflects a Sinicized version of Buddhist representations of death, with Yama as the main judge who sends his messengers to our world to "arrest" those who are fated to die and judges the good and evil acts of the dead in order to decide in what form they will be reincarnated. In the end the terrifying messengers of the Underworld, who manifest extremely rough and frightening behavior when they enter the body of a shaman during rituals, are persuaded to take substitutes for the children to Yama. The choice of these substitutes, which in translation sounds completely arbitrary, can at least in part be explained by similarity between their Korean names and the names of the boys. "Hwangch'ŏn honshi" is a song from the repertoire of Kim Ssangdori, which Son Chint'ae recorded in northeast Korea in 1926.

Shamanic ritual and the family are also linked through a number of house gods with specific tasks. First of all, there is a deity who is responsible for fertility, both of crops and of humans, as well as for a long and healthy life, and who is worshiped in the form of a jar filled with grain. The name of this deity differs according to the region: Chesŏk (Indra), Sejon (the World-Honored One, viz., the Buddha) and Grandmother Samsin are common appellations; Chiyang is another. This deity is closely related to the sphere of women, but Sŏngju, the god of the house, as the protector of the master of the house, is a "man's god." His place of worship is the most important roof beam of the house, which is considered to be the mainstay of the house and the family that inhabits it. In the last song translated in this chapter, "Sŏngju" is also used to refer to this roof beam. Other house gods of lesser importance are the Kitchen God and the gods of the house site, the outhouse, and the gate.

"Sŏngju pon'ga," the "Song of the Origin of Sŏngju" translated here, belonged to the repertoire of a female shaman from Ahyŏn (presently part of Seoul) and was published in 1937 in the collection of Akamatsu Chijō and Akiba Takashi. Its most striking feature is the portrayal of Hwang Uyang, the man who is to become Sŏngju, and his wife. Although the song is dedicated to the male deity par excellence, Sŏngju is represented in songs of this type as a male chauvinist who is ready to speak disparagingly to his wife but is helpless whenever a (self-inflicted) crisis occurs. It is his wife who, through her resourcefulness and wit, pulls him through all kinds of difficulties and finally provides a happy ending to the myth. This can only be understood when one thinks of the predominantly female context of shamanic ritual, which in this case transforms a eulogy to a male deity into a demonstration of the indispensable services wives offer (in conformity with the best Confucian traditions!) to their grandiloquent but ultimately feeble husbands. In one scene, the husband literally hides under his wife's skirts. The myth is as much about domestic power relations as about theogony. The unflattering portrayal of the husband corresponds to the equally negative description of the other man in the story, who displays similar male weaknesses. He is so gullible that he believes Hwang Uyang's wife when she says "a woman's life with her in-laws is as fine as the life of a governor," an outrageous inversion of reality. In the end the wife uses his typically male proclivities for sex and alcohol to undo him. The way he gets his comeuppance is narrated tongue in cheek. He, too, becomes a deity of sorts: a local guardian spirit, a Sŏnang, who used to be represented in the form of a heap of stones at which passersby might spit.

The end of this song also merits attention because it ties the song to the actual situation of the ritual. The prayer that, as Hwang Uyang proclaims, people henceforth will address to him and his wife, simultaneously becomes a prayer for the family for whom the ritual is performed. The myth flows over into the reality of the believers for whom the song is sung.

Descriptions of clever, quick-witted women can be found in many other shaman songs. By accentuating female resourcefulness and ridiculing typical male arrogance, such songs boost morale and relativize macho behavior that is otherwise hard to bear. Other songs may be regarded as cathartic dramatizations of common episodes in women's lives, like the transition from chaste virgin to fertile mother, the "rejection" of women by their natal family upon marriage, or the difficult process of settling down in the household of the in-laws. It should be pointed out, however, that as time progresses the number of narrative songs in the rituals decreases and the social context changes to such an extent that, although the clientele of the shamans continues to be predominantly female, these functions of the songs—if they are still sung at all—are on the wane.

The translated texts are from Son Chint'ae, *Chōsen shinka no ihen* (Tokyo: Kyōdō Kenkyūsha, 1930), 205–6, 207, 28–38, and Akamatsu Chijō and Akiba Takashi, *Chōsen fuzoku no kenkyū*, vol. 1 (Tokyo: Ōsaka Yagō Shoten, 1937), 205–22.

Further Reading

For the Confucianization of Korean society in the Chosŏn period, see Martina Deuchler, *The Confucian Transformation of Korea: A Study of Society and Ideology* (Cambridge, Mass.: Council on East Asian Studies, Harvard University, 1992). The changing place of shamanic ritual in the Chosŏn period is traced in Boudewijn Walraven, "Popular Religion in a Confucianized Society," in *Culture and the State in Chosŏn Korea*, edited by Martina Deuchler and Jahyun Kim Haboush (Cambridge, Mass.: Harvard University Asia Center, 1999), pp. 160–98. Laurel Kendall's *Shamans, Housewives and Other Restless Spirits: Women in Korean Ritual Life* (Honolulu: University of Hawaii Press, 1985) focuses on the role of women in shamanic rituals in the 1970s and 1980s. The concept of the career of the shaman as a "pathway out of impasse" is introduced in Youngsook Kim Harvey, *Six Korean Woman: The Socialization of Shamans* (St. Paul, Minn.: West Publishing, 1979). For the depiction of gender in shaman songs, see Boudewijn Walraven, "True Grit: Gender in Korean Shamanic Songs," *Review of Korean Studies* 1 (1998). 126–46. Clark W. Sorensen, "The Myth of Princess Pari and the Self-Image of Korean Women," *Anthropos* 83 (1988): 409–19, demonstrates how women might identify with the heroine of the myth of the "First Shaman." Boudewijn Walraven, *Songs of the Shaman: The Ritual Chants of the Korean Mudang* (London: Kegan Paul International, 1994) contains the translation of a more male-oriented Sŏngju song.

Prayer after Childbirth

Birth Goddess Chiyang,
ensure that the mother of the baby
eats her soup properly,
eats her rice properly,
and that if she takes medicine,
the medicine will have effect,
so that the weariness of her body disappears
melts away like ice,

melts away like snow.
Take it away, please,
as one uses pincers to remove
a splinter from the wooden floorboards.
Purify this household with light,
as if a jade lantern has been lit,
purify it with water,
make flowers of laughter
bloom in this household.

Prayer Offered When a Child Cries Too Much

Wise Chiyang, gentle Chiyang,
when you grant life,
take away the sound of singing
to make the baby sweet and obedient,
to make it drink its mother's milk properly,
take it away at all hours
and at all times,
to make the baby eat and sleep,
sleep and eat.

Song of the Ritual of the Yellow Springs

Songnimdongi, Idongi, and Samadongi
were three brothers.
Their father in his time had gathered a fortune,
but when they came into the world,
they had just enough to subsist.
When one day Samadongi
on the seventh of the seventh month thought:
"Let me have a look at the fields,"
he went out and on all sides
the ears of the grain were fine,
and well-developed.
The three brothers cut off the ears
of all the different kinds of grain,
but they could not eat the grain just like that.
"Let's grind this and make rice cake
to worship the Deity of the Earth,
worship the Mountain God,
worship the Kitchen God,

and then start our farmer's work again,"
said Samadongi, and his older brothers agreed.
Songnimdongi became the plowman,
Idongi spread the ash to fertilize the field
Holding half a dried calabash with seeds in his hand,
Samadongi became the sower.
When they had plowed about half the field
and went up again,
white bones, green bones, emerged
and the three brothers said:
"Without us three brothers
wouldn't our Father and our Mother become like this?"
The three brothers took off their inner jackets,
wrapped the white bones in them
and put up an altar in front of their room
and offered them a morning meal in the morning,
lunch at noon, an evening meal in the evening.
Then a flame rose up from the food bowls,
after five or six years the white bones cried in the night.
Long ago the trees and the stones spoke,
pythons and snakes wagged their tongues
and because it happened in those times,
the white bones cried.
Songnimdongi, Idongi, and Samadongi
woke up and changed their clothes to pay them homage
and stepping back they bowed thrice
and stepping forward they bowed thrice:
"White Bones, why do you cry so much,
while we haven't done anything wrong?"
White Bones spoke:
"Because I met you I live in luxury,
but the Great King Yama, the Judge of the Underworld,
will take you three brothers away.
In three days his messengers will come to take you."
"White Bones, up till now
we have given you a fortune in offerings;
please find a way for us to escape."
"Do you have a black cow at home?
You make it lie down, bridle it,
make it stand up, make it submit,
and slaughter the cow,
placing the meat on thirty-three trays.
Place a food table at the end of the bridge
in the Kŭngwang Mountains,

and fill it with all kinds of food.
You three brothers must hide under the bridge.
Then, if the three messengers that come for you
will hungrily eat from that
and then sit back and put on their straw shoes,
come out from under the bridge
bow thrice stepping back,
bow thrice stepping forth,
offering twice three bows,
and beg to let you live!"
The messengers went on their way,
and when they crossed the bridge
in the Kŭngwang Mountains
they felt hungry.
"At a moment like this it would be great
even to have some rice left over by kids."
The messenger in the rear said:
"Having spoken the first word, don't say another word.
Even if you go to take one person, you cannot speak that way.
How can you do so now that we go to catch three people?
Let's go quickly, let's go swiftly!"
When they crossed the end of the bridge,
the brothers had placed a table there,
and filled it with food.
The three messengers said:
"Mice hear what is said at night,
birds hear what is said in the daytime.
Even if we eat this food, how can they escape?"
Seeing the food, they could not retreat,
seeing the food they could not just pass by.
When the three messengers had eaten all,
Songnimi and his brothers appeared
and made bows to the three messengers.
"What kind of people are you?"
"I'm Songnimdongi."
"I'm Idongi."
"I'm Samadongi."
"How, having eaten your food,
could we just go and take you?
Songnimdongi, quickly bring your yellow cow!
Idongi, bring a rain cape of oiled paper!
Samadongi, bring a brass basin!"
The messengers took the cow, the cape, and the brass basin
and through the great gate entered the realm of Yama.

"Why haven't you been able to catch Songnimdongi?"
"We looked in all nooks and crannies,
but the name of Songnimdongi was nowhere to be found.
Because there was a yellow cow in that place
we undid the rope with which it was tied up
and brought it with us instead."
"Don't you have Idongi either?"
"Because he wasn't there, we pinched a rain cape from that place."
"Don't you even have Samadongi?"
"We looked in all kinds of nooks and crannies,
but the name of Samadongi was nowhere to be found
and so we took a brass basin from that place."
Long ago, doing like this,
the brothers lived until the age of eighty
and after they had died
as holy ones they received ritual offerings
and the people invited them as holy ones,
invited them for ritual offerings.

Song of the Origin of Sŏngju

. . .

We want to recite the story
of the origin of Sŏngju
and while we respectfully offer candles and lanterns,
a container filled with one measure of rice,
long-life coins and longevity coins, and a live chicken
we recite the story of Sŏngju's origin.
The origin of Sŏngju?
His origin is the Palace under Heaven.
The Great Heavenly Tree God of the Palace under Heaven
and Lady Chit'al of the Palace under the Earth,
concluded a marital agreement
to last for a hundred years,
and so a child was conceived:
after three months the blood gathered,
after five months it became half a load,
when it was six, seven months,
the expectant mother didn't eat
what was not cut properly,
she didn't sit when the seat was not right,
her ears didn't listen to lewd talk,
her eyes didn't look at evil sights,

without change in her eating and sleeping,
she reached the tenth month
and gave birth to an adorable baby.
Look at that child!
Its face is as beautiful as the jade
that adorns an official's cap,
its demeanor lofty like that of Du Mu,
its words are as eloquent as those of Su Qin!
Even trees open their eyes,
even stones open their eyes.
He became conversant with the heavenly bodies above,
he penetrated the principles of the earth below.
The *Six Quivers* and the *Three Strategies*,
the Nine Directions and the Eight Trigrams,
the art of making oneself invisible . . .
when he was able to make use of everything at will,
to the pavilion with a thousand balustrades
of the Palace under Heaven
a strange wind from the East
came blowing ceaselessly.
The pavilion inclined to the East
and fell into ruins toward the South,
and ruined was Sŏngju's roof beam,
but in the Palace under Heaven there was no one
who could put up Sŏngju's roof beam
except for Hwang Uyang
who lived under Hwang Mountain
in the land of the Palace under the Earth.
A special envoy was called in
and he was given special authority,
to have Hwang Uyang present himself
as fast as a shooting star.
When this order, severe as frost, is given,
look what the envoy does!
Affixing the character *chŏng*, "official business,"
firmly to his felt hat made of animal hair,
with a sleeveless coat of heavy hemp cloth
tied tightly over his breast with a dark blue band,
with socks of heavy hemp cloth
and leggings out of one piece of cloth,
with a six-sided stick over his shoulder
he came down, fast like a shooting star,
and when for the first time he rushed up to Hwang Uyang
to catch him, he couldn't,

because Hwang was too portly.
He assaulted him for a second time,
but again he could not catch him.
When, lost in thought, he stood at the side of the road,
Grandfather Kitchen God of Hwang Uyang's house asked him
of which palace he was a messenger,
and the messenger of the Palace under Heaven said:
"The pavilion with the thousand balustrades of the Palace
    under Heaven
has collapsed because of the East wind,
the country is ruined, its Sŏngju roof beam is ruined.
All the officials of the whole court deliberated
and told me to bring Hwang Uyang,
but because he is too portly,
I cannot catch him."
"In that case, go to the outhouse tomorrow,
when the light fades.
Then you must catch him
By binding him with a cord."
Having heard these words the messenger stood alone
within the dank walls surrounding the yard of the house
and waited for Hwang Uyang to come out.
The next day, when the light faded,
when Hwang Uyang went out to the outhouse,
the messenger ran up to him, caught him and tied him up,
and handed him the special summons.
There was nothing Hwang Uyang could do about it,
even a summons of the King of the Underworld of the Land of Yama
would not have carried as much weight.
But he did no longer have the tools he had used before
and thus asked for three months of respite.
The messenger did not give it because it was too long,
but left giving him three days respite only.
Hwang Uyang was baffled, passed his time worrying,
And couldn't eat the rice, of which he used to eat so much,
passing his time in distress.
Then Hwang Uyang's wife said:
"My husband, why have you stopped eating completely?"
Hwang Uyang answered: "Woman, don't you have eyes or ears?
The pavilion with the thousand balustrades of the Palace under Heaven
has collapsed because of the East wind,
the country is ruined, its Sŏngju is ruined.
There is no one to restore the Sŏngju
and I was served with a summons to present myself.

Now I don't have the tools I used before,
and I don't have even one suit of clothes,
what should I do?"
His wife spoke:
"Does a man of your caliber
completely stop eating for something like that?
Don't worry, eat your meal!"
She let Hwang Uyang go to bed,
prepared one sheet of paper to be burned in sacrifice
and sent it up to the Palace under the Earth.
Five measures of iron powder,
five measures of brass,
five measures of scrap iron
she made come down.
Big bellows at the Big Mountain
small bellows at the Small Mountain
a big axe and a small axe
a big saw and a small saw,
a trimming axe and an instrument to draw ink lines,
planes and a drawing hook she made
and after she had made clothes for the four seasons,
socks and shoes, exactly as they should be,
she made a mule ready,
loaded it with a box for half a load,
and called: "My husband, get up!
The hour is late, the hour has passed
Quickly, swiftly leave!"
Startled Hwang Uyang got up
and when he looked carefully
there was his travel kit, no mistake about it.
When he went on his way in haste,
and cried: "Go, my horse!" and gave it the spurs,
his love held him back and shed tears.
The wife of Hwang Uyang spoke:
"Whoever asks something on the way you go,
don't give him an answer.
If you give an answer, you will give me,
your beloved wife, to another.
I beg you, don't answer!"
Hwang Uyang took leave of her,
lifted the whip and when he cracked it once,
the running horse was like an arrow.
In the flicker of an eye
he passed the plain of Hwang Mountain,

and arrived at Sojin Plain.
Then Sojin of Sojin Plain
came down to Sojin Plain
riding a mangy horse, sitting on a moth-eaten saddle.
Seeing Hwang Uyang he said:
"Who is the gentleman riding there?"
He asked once and there was no answer.
He asked twice and there was no answer,
and thus he followed him on purpose
and called: "Fatherless boor!"
Hwang Uyang thought by himself:
"I suffer such ignominy
because I heed the words of my wife."
He turned and said:
"Someone who wants to talk to a man
who goes on a long journey
is himself a fatherless boor."
"You there, who are you?"
"I'm Hwang Uyang who lives
at the foot of Hwang Mountain.
Who are you?"
"I am Sojin of Sojin Plain.
And you, where do you go?"
"I have been called from the Palace under Heaven
and go to do building work,
to the Palace under the Earth.
It's my turn for a three-year corvée,
It's my turn for three times three years."
"Have you looked at the geomantic qualities of the spot?
If you build a house on a silkworm spot,
you are bound to die,
because it is a silkworm spot.
If the direction is One: Heavenly Boon, Two: Eye Loss,
Three: Food Deities, Four: Call and Break, Five: Ghosts,
Six: Combined Food, Seven: Advancing Ghosts,
That means that even though there will be a trace of you going,
there will be no trace of you coming back."
Hwang Uyang said: "What should I do?"
"Let's change clothes."
Hwang Uyang and Sojin put on each other's garb
and Hwang Uyang went on to the Palace under Heaven.
When Sojin, because he had heard
that the wife of Hwang Uyang was an outstanding beauty,
went to the plain of Hwang Mountain,

the wife of Hwang Uyang, because she felt restless,
had just gone out to the back garden
to enjoy the flowers, to enjoy the leaves,
to look at the blossoms and willows.
When she went up into the garden
with Oktanch'un and Tandanch'un,
the front maid and the back maid, fore and aft,
the peach blossoms were in full bloom,
coloring the mountain red,
the plum blossoms were in full bloom
coloring the mountain white.
The golden oriole sang between the willows,
butterflies white as snow
went up and down between the flowers.
Strolling here and there,
she delighted in the spring scene,
when outside the garden wall
there was the loud sound of a horse's hoofs
and the bells of a horse's bridle could be heard.
"That fellow that comes there clearly is a robber.
Let's go in quickly!
Gatekeeper close the gate,
keeper of the key, lock it up!
If you open it without my command,
you will be beheaded according to martial law
after the master's journey."
"Open the gate," Sojin shouted,
"When the master returns home,
you open even a closed gate.
How for heaven's sake is it possible
that you close the open gate again!"
The wife of Hwang Uyang said:
"My husband has gone away the day before yesterday
Because it is out of the question that he returns now,
I beg you to go home quickly."
Sojin thought a good while,
then took off the undershirt Hwang Uyang had worn
and threw it over the wall that was a hundred meters high:
"Look at this and open up!"
She picked up the shirt and took a look:
"The needlework is mine,
but the smell of sweat is different.
Quickly, swiftly go away!"
Look what Sojin does!

"Would a real man be unable to open a gate
a mere woman has closed?
Demons, demons all!"
Thus he called thrice three times,
and then, without a key, without sound,
the main gate and the middle gate opened.
He rushed into the house, a sword in one hand,
grasping her by the throat with the other.
"However much you try to fly or crawl away
will you fly to heaven like a whippoorwill,
or creep into the ground like a mole?"
The wife of Hwang Uyang is like a pheasant
caught by a falcon,
a chicken between the jaws of a dog.
There was nothing to be done about it,
but she thought of a ruse and said to Sojin:
"A new love is fine, but how can I forget my old love?
If the sun sets and night comes,
there will be the sacrifice to my father-in-law.
Let's sleep together after the sacrifice.
A man's life with his in-laws
is like life in exile,
a woman's life with her in-laws
is as fine as the life of a governor.
Let's go to your palace."
He agreed with her words
and after gathering together pots and pans
they went to Sojin Plain,
she tore a piece of the sleeve of her silken undershirt
bit her middle finger
and with the running blood wrote a letter:
"If you return dead, let's meet in the Underworld,
if you return alive, come to Sojin Plain."
After she had written the whole story,
she put it under a cornerstone of the house
and when they went to Sojin Plain,
she thought of another ploy.
"Let's have a look at the direction!
One: Heavenly Door, Two: Eye Loss,
Three: Food Deities, Four: Call and Break, Five: Ghosts,
Six: Combined Food, Seven: Advancing Ghosts,
the direction is west-south-west.
Seven spirits have attached themselves to my body
and so we should sleep together

after you have dug a hole for me in Dog-Dung Field
and fed me sacrificial rice for three years.
If I give you my body now
not only your paternal and maternal relatives
and the in-laws will be ruined,
but all our relatives, of past and future generations,
will despise us.
So feed me sacrificial rice for three years."
"That's agreed."
He dug a hole in Dog-Dung Field
and while she ate sacrificial rice for three years,
Hwang Uyang dreamt a strange dream
and he felt confused,
so he asked around:
"Is there a fortune-teller here?"
"There is one at a distance of ten *li*."
Giving him three *toe* of pure gold,
he asked him to tell his fortune.
Look what the fortune-teller does!
He took out a little round table,
shook a divination box of tortoiseshell
and intoned: "What words does heaven speak?
What words does the earth speak?
Spring or autumn, every day,
it is through events they speak.
For beneficial influences there is a division between heaven and earth,
for brightness there is a division between sun and moon,
for good and bad fortune there is a division between the four seasons.
The great Sages, Fu Xi, Shenneng, the Yellow Emperor,
the Heavenly King of the Nine Heavens, King Wen,
Master Guigu, Master Sun Bin, Master Guo Po,
Li Chunfeng, and Shao Kangjie,
the meaning of the eight times eight,
that is sixty-four hexagrams
posed no problems to them.
If it is auspicious, auspicious spirits flourish,
if it is inauspicious, inauspicious spirits follow the commands.
Please provide a clear judgement at once!"
He turned the box and with a clatter
threw the divination sticks down:
what came out was a jumble!
Once more he threw them down:
what came out was a mess!
"I cannot do this divination at all!"

"Who wants to ask asks the fortune-teller,
who wants to know relies on the celestial bodies.
Tell me as much as you know!"
"The site of your house has turned into a parsley field,
your wife has gone to someone else's house to marry.
Quickly, swiftly go and take a look!"
Hwang Uyang was stunned,
in a rush, impatiently he came out,
and wanted to do the work fast:
the work for three years he did in one year,
the work for one year he did in one month,
the work for one month he did in one day.
In a rush he went down
and when he came to the house where he had lived,
the site of the house had turned into a parsley field;
only the cornerstones were left,
the well from which they drew their drinking water
was overgrown with green moss,
the creeper that had grown below the road
had spread over the road.
Hwang Uyang sighed and lamented to heaven
and when with his head on a cornerstone
he fell asleep with exhaustion,
a gull from the T'aebaek Mountains
who had not even had a pebble or a stone to eat,
flew past crying *kalgok chilgok*,
flew past crying *hasŏkp 'il*.
Hwang Uyang woke up startled,
"Gull that flies away there, do you want to tell me something?
Ha is clearly the character *ha* that means 'under,'
sŏk is clearly the character *sŏk* that means stone.
It seems there is something under the stone."
When he lifted the cornerstone,
there was his wife's shirt!
When he unfolded it carefully,
there was a letter written in blood:
"If you return dead, let's meet in the Underworld,
if you return alive, come to Sojin Plain."
So she had written the whole story.
After reading the message written in blood
he went down like a shooting star to Sojin Plain
and sat in an old pine tree
at the side of a well with a leafy roof.
His wife had a confusing portentous dream

but she guessed its meaning,
and carrying a silver jar on her head
went out to the well and sat down.
When she stirred the water once,
the shadow of Hwang Uyang was reflected in the water.
The wife of Hwang Uyang spoke:
"If you have died, come down crying,
if you are alive, come down laughing!"
Happy, Hwang Uyang came down, laughing loudly:
"Couldn't you stand it in the meantime?
That's why you became someone else's wife?"
His wife spoke: "What did I tell you?
Because you replied to the question,
even I had to suffer,
but with that fellow I have not had any relations.
I have avoided him all the time
up to the present moment.
Let's take revenge on our mortal enemy,
leave together and live in happiness."
Hwang Uyang used magic
to turn himself into a blue bird, a red bird,
and went into the house of Sojin
wrapped in the folds of his wife's wide skirt
made with nine lengths of cloth.
He took out big thongs and small thongs
and attached the skin of Sojin's crane to his heels,
so that he could use none of the thirty-six thousand parts of his body,
and beat him mercilessly with an ash-tree switch.
Sojin was frightened out of his wits
and kowtowing a hundred times said:
"I haven't done anything wrong!
Except that I dug a hole in Dog-Dung Field
and fed her sacrificial rice for three years.
Please save my life!"
Hwang Uyang spoke:
"I should shed your blood and kill you,
but you are the grandson of a duke.
Though I can't kill you,
I will put you in a box of stone
and make sure that you cannot drink even a sip of water.
You and all the members of your family
will become Sŏnang everywhere along the roads.
I will see to it that you drink the spit
of peddlers going up and travelers going down,

I'll see to it that your chickens and your animals
are chased to the mountain garden behind the house,
turn into pheasants, pigeons, and deer,
and will be shot, bang bang, with a gun, to be eaten."
Hwang Uyang and his wife, both, went up to Hwangsan Plain,
and when they spent the night on the way,
they took this end of a stalk of pampa grass
and joined it to that end of a stalk of pampa grass,
joined this end to that end
and put up her skirt made of five lengths of cloth
left and right around them by way of a tent.
Thus they spent that night on the way
and he asked:
"My wife, what skill have you acquired in the meantime?"
"After Your Excellency had left, I spent my days in tears.
I wrote a request on a sheet of paper
and by burning it sent it up to the Palace under Heaven
and so I received one dish with baby silkworms.
I fed them and put them to sleep for ten nights
and when I put them on a bed of leaves
they produced five measures of green, white, and yellow cocoons.
When, behind the loom, I took the shuttle
and once moved it in and out,
I produced strangers' silk and outside silk,
when I took the shuttle and moved it in and out twice,
I produced owner's silk and inside silk.
Fifty-five feet and forty-five feet I wove,
and I made one set of clothes for Your Excellency
and when I opened the eastern window,
I noticed that the basket with lunch had just been brought.
Is such skill something ordinary?"
Hwang Uyang spoke:
"How great are our talents,
but in order that when we die, after death,
we shall receive offerings of sacrificial wine
and that even though ten thousand springs and autumns pass
we shall receive prayers and blessings
I will become Sŏngju, the God of the House
and you will become Chisin, the Goddess of the Earth.
When in every house, in every village,
in every district, in every region
we become Sŏngju and Chisin,
when we become the Sŏngju and Chisin
of Family X in neighborhood Y

they worship Sŏngju,
they offer rice cake steamed especially for Sŏngju
a cow's head especially for Sŏngju,
an offering table with big bowls,
old-age cloth and longevity cloth
a living chicken they offer, worshiping him.
And they pray:
'Please partake of the sacrifices
bestow the ten thousand benefits and blessings,
please grant that even if Family X does this or does that,
on behalf of the family that has worshiped you
during one year, during twelve months,
even if there is an intercalary month and thirteen months pass,
you will destroy and put at a distance of a thousand miles
the Three Misfortunes and the Eight Hardships,
that the ten thousand things are accomplished smoothly
that Luck will find the doors wide open,
that the things they want to do go as they wish.
When Sŏngju is apprehensive, Chisin is steady,
when Chisin is apprehensive, Sŏngju puts her at ease.
When the master of the house is apprehensive,
the mistress of the house puts him at ease.
Sŏngju is the ruler of the house
and Chisin is ruler of the house, too.
The master of the house is the ruler of the house,
and the mistress of the house is the ruler of the house, too!
Please make the four rulers of the house as one,
as the single tip of a tree sways up and down.
After this shaman has entertained the gods here,
bestow happiness on the first three days
and long life on the latter three days,
grant on a mountain of the Seven Treasures
an infinite number of sheaves of grain.' "

——19——

A Shamanic Ritual for Sending

On the Dead

Antonetta Lucia Bruno

Ssikkim kut, the shamanic ritual of purification, is performed on Chindo, the fourth-biggest island of Korea, situated off the southwest coast of South Chŏlla province. *Ssikkim kut* belongs to the rituals and religious practices related to death, which involves sending the deceased on to a "good place."

The structure, function, and name of the ritual of purification, known also by the names *Chinogi* in the province of Kyŏnggi and *Ogu kut* elsewhere on the island of Chin, vary according to the modality of death. Among the various versions, the one performed in front of a grass tomb, or *ch'obun*, is the most interesting, although it is no longer in use after the 1980s. The term *ch'obun* indicates a bridge between life and death and is associated with the custom of double burials, which goes back to the first century B.C.E. This practice involves a bone-washing ritual performed in front of the "grass-roofed tomb" after the purification ritual in order to move the bones of the deceased from the temporary tomb to the permanent one.

The wide distribution of this custom along the rivers and seacoasts of Southeast Asia suggests that the temporary grass tomb originated there. People on Chindo explain the practice of temporary burial from a hygienic point of view, referring to the shorter time required in this way to get rid of the flesh of the deceased. This simple explanation stands in stark contrast to the extraordinarily elaborate purification rituals that are performed after the corpse's stay in the *ch'obun* comes to an end, rituals that betray the fear of the dangerous consequences if one were to neglect to take proper care of the deceased.

The ritual of washing the bones began after a geomancer had chosen an auspicious day. The body was exhumed, cleaned, and washed with a bamboo knife, a brush made of pine leaves, and three different kinds of water. The washed bones were placed in a white cloth and placed with extreme care following the order of the skeleton, which was assembled piece by piece. Even one piece missing meant that the deceased would not gain access to the "other world."

There were seven different *ch'obun* burial customs according to the modes of disposition of the corpse: Surface Burial, Stone-Platform Burial, Scaffold Burial, Y-Shaped Burial, Tree Burial, Sand Burial, and Beneath the Floor Burial. *Ch'obun* was performed only for an old person who died a natural death; for two or three years, until the flesh disappeared, the deceased was taken good care of by his descendants, who held ceremonies on the memorial day and on all holidays, and renewed the tomb's grass roof on the last day of the year.

The sequences followed in the purification ritual are celebrated in different places according to the manner of death: *Honmaji Ssikkim kut* is celebrated in the street in order to receive the soul of a person who died far from home; *Hon'gŏnji Ssikkim kut* is celebrated at the water's edge in order to rescue the soul of a person who drowned; *Hojebi Ssikkim kut* is performed in the house, to placate the restless souls of a bachelor and bachelorette celebrating the marriage they had missed during their lives.

I here describe a ritual that I witnessed on the evening of July 5, 1988. It was performed in the Cho family house for their deceased mother, who died at the age of seventy-five. Following a month of illness, she had died a year before the ceremony, on a day regarded as inauspicious. Thus one year later her son had decided to have the ritual performed in order to purify her death and ensure that her soul would enter into a "good place," whereby he would receive beneficial effects from his mother on his own family.

The ritual was performed by the shamaness Kim Taerye with the assistance of the musician Kim Kwibong.

The text given here is the only complete *Ssikkim kut* from the area of Chindo, as chanted by the shamaness Chŏngnye, and published in *Chindo musok hyŏnji chosa* (Kwangju: Kungnip Minsok Pangmulgwan, 1988). I describe here only the most significant sequences in the ritual. The first sequence is *Anttang*, when the shamaness, inside the tent, in the darkness of the night, informs the gods of the reason for the ritual and invites them to participate. In the yard all the lower supernatural entities attracted by the feast are welcomed with libations by the shamaness's assistant, while in a small room, off the central one, a table with offerings is prepared. The Messengers of Death are welcomed with a cup of water in the yard.

Further Reading

For a general introduction to shamanic rituals on Chindo see Keith Howard, *Bands, Songs and Shamanistic Rituals: Folk Music in Korean Society* (Seoul: Korea Branch of the Royal Asiatic Society, 1989); and Antonetta L. Bruno, "Sosang Nalbaji Ssikkim kut in Chin-do," in *Korean Cultural Roots, Religion and Social Thought*, edited by Kwon Ho-youn (Chicago: North Park College and Theological Seminary,

1995), pp. 45–67, for the religious meanings of the rituals. For further reading from an ethnographic perspective, see Pak Chuŏn, *"Ei tchanhan saram!" Naega nabogo kŭrayo?* (Seoul: Ppuri Kip'ŭn Namu, 1992). This book is based on the oral history of the shamaness Ch'ae Chŏngrye in Chindo dialect, mixed with Japanese terms and special shamans' language. For Korean shamanism in general, see Laurel Kendall, *Shamans, Housewives and Other Restless Spirits: Women in Korean Ritual Life* (Honolulu: University of Hawaii Press, 1985); for Korean shamanic songs and literature, see Boudewijn Walraven, *Songs of the Shaman: The Ritual Chants of the Korean Mudang* (London: Kegan Paul International, 1994); and for the language behavior and social interaction of the shamans inside and outside of the ritual from the point of view of linguistic anthropology, see Antonetta L. Bruno, *The Gate of Words: Language in the Rituals of Korean Shamans* (Leiden: CNWS Press of the Research School for Asian, African and Amerindian Studies, 2002). For further reading, see Chai-shin Yu and R. Guisso, eds., *Shamanism: The Spirit World of Korea* (Berkeley: Asian Humanities Press, 1988), and Keith Howard, ed., *Korean Shamanism: Revivals, Survivals, and Change* (Seoul: Royal Asiatic Society, 1998).

Anttang

Sovereign! Sovereign!
For acquired merits [you] build the temple,
[its] origin is Mount Namunam!
Korea is the nation,
With eighty thousand inhabitants in the Western Capital,
Sŏgyŏng too is a capital.
Hanyang too is a capital.
Kaesŏng too is a major capital.
Build the residence in the Heaven of the Thirty-three,
the Twenty-eight Constellations rotate, descending,
the *Hŏgung* Heavens, the *Pibi* Heavens
Samhwa and the *Tori* Heavens.
When the Ten Kings,
when [the Kings] prepared to rule,
they took control of the seventy-seven offices of government
in the province of Kyŏngsang,
[in the] seventy-seven districts of the province,
they took command of the Tojuwŏl
and the fifty-three offices of government in the province of Chŏlla,
they took control of the fifty-three districts in the province.
In the hour of the Rat, when the sky was created,
the heaven was created
and in the hour of the Ox, when the earth was created,

the earth was created
and in the hour of the Tiger, human beings were created.
T'aewŏl! Ch'ŏnhwang-ssi!
[They] lived for eighteen thousand years
when Inhwang, living for eighteen thousand years
near the River Yŏk,
created a host of men and then
rectitude, sense of justice,
love, altruism, moral principles for ten thousand years,
the Three Relations and the Five Constant Bonds,
created family names [for men],
and Yŏmje Shennong
cut down the tree and carved it,
and created all tools,
teaching men to cultivate the fields.
Suin lent fire [to men]
so that they could invent a way of cooking food.
Hŭnhwŏn built the boat
that made communications possible.
To the East *kap, ŭl* and then 3, 8, wood,
the Blue Dragon was deputed,
to the South *pyŏng, chŏng* and then 2, 7, fire,
the Red Dragon was deputed,
to the West *mu, ki* and then 4, 9, gold,
the White Dragon was deputed,
to the North *kyŏng, sin* and then 1, 6, water,
the Black Dragon was deputed,
to the Center *im, kye* and then 5, 10, earth,
the Yellow Dragon was deputed.
To the East, T'aeho Pokhŭi,
to the South, Yŏmje Sinnong,
to the West, Chŏnuk Koyang,
to the North, Soyu Kŭmjŏn
and to the Center, Hwangje Hŭnhwŏn.
When [the divinities], the Sun and the Moon, receive the offerings
[in] Korea, in the province of South Chŏlla,
in the district of Chindo, in the municipal area of Ŭisin,
the village Wŏndu, where they took up residence,
is an ideal site with good auspices.
If we inquire into the family [of the husband]
and we inquire into the family [of the wife],
the family [of the husband comprises]
"old" rulers who ascend [in rank]
and "new" rulers who descend,

after the state examinations becoming academics, high-ranking officials,
doctors and officials.
Alongside the family of Master Ham,
which is as charming as the family of a prince,
there is the family of the precious daughter [the daughter-in-law of
    Master Ham],
the head of the family, Mistress Ch'ae,
is like silver and the crane.
If you distinguish the month and the year,
the year is *chŏngmyo*,
the month and the position of the moon in the sky [correspond] to the
    tenth month,
and the day is the third of the month.
Sŏngju is the greatest authority,
he takes his place as the master of the house.
Chisin is the "guest" authority
and Chowang is the mistress.
Doesn't the head [of this family] know that in this house
an important rite is being performed?
Hey! Forty-five-year-old [man]!
Let's give a welcome to the God Sŏngju
who received the rite [in the] Palace of the Middle, the Grand Palace.
On the ninth day of the month the God Hagye Chowang,
on the nineteenh day of the month the God Chingye Chowang,
on the twenty-ninth day of the month the eighty-four thousand
    [divinities],
around the great Kyŏngdŏk Palace, a vast and roomy place,
Chidae Chowang who sees to the construction,
we receive you.
Let's give a welcome to the ancestors,
the motive for our devotion
is none other than this:
[we ask that] parents, worthy of piety,
[be] purified and accompanied to the other world.
I beg you to go and be reborn in paradise!
[In the courtyard] the energy of the courtyard, the energy of the garden!
Let us raise up the tent, supporting it with bamboo poles.
When we perform the ritual during the night,
[why is it that] the God Sŏngju
[does not know] the master of this house?
[The master of the house] gives a welcome to the God Sŏngju
and wishes to offer this rite,
[hence] the man's vitality [is reinvigorated, and this will be]
    good fortune for the woman,

the vitality of the woman, good fortune for the man.
Let's make the most of the days of good auspices and vital energy!
To the West the Blue Spring,
to the South the Red Spring,
to the East the White Spring,
to the North the Black Spring,
the Odong Spring and the Kamdong Spring!
Water which flows and water which overflows
carries it away silently,
in the upper baths to wash the hair,
in the central baths to bathe,
in the lower baths for the hands and feet,
the hair shaved off, and [after] abstaining from alcohol—
a white turnip [like the head of] a sister monk—there,
the terracotta jug is filled up with the liquor
that over the years becomes thick
and as it ages becomes [dark like] soy sauce,
the seasoned vegetable dishes,
cooked rice and soup,
ten thousand delicious things,
I turn my back [on the public] and prepare the delicacies.
I beg you to help yourselves abundantly.
The Han family, *pyŏlsang* of the head of the family,
if you ask how old he is this year,
he is sixty-one!
Life [is] three thousand sexagesimal cycles long,
as long as the life of Tong Pangsak,
a fortune [equal to the] fortune
that Sŏk Sung possessed,
I beg you to bless him [with longevity and good fortune].
A year is made up of twelve months.
One year and more has thirteen months.
The little month has twenty-nine days,
the big month has thirty days:
1st 7th, 2nd 8th,
3rd 9th, 4th 10th,
5th 12th, 6th 11th months.
Even if the 365 days
speed past like lightning,
the evil darts of misfortune brought on by the authorities and by gossip
passed from mouth to mouth by all
are forestalled [by the divinities],
even the invisible darts of the chill that others receive
in cold weather, which strike home,

are diverted in advance.
Even if among the twelve worlds of East, West, South, and North
[the darts] fly hither and thither from the four corners of the world,
the Hoe darts, whose approach is hidden, are blocked,
and also [the darts of the virgin] Kaekkwi that come from behind
are forestalled,
as are the terrible Taesin darts [of death by dangers] that come in from
    the East,
the Chomun darts [of funerals] that come in from the South,
the evil darts of discord between couples,
the evil darts that create a bad reputation among descendants,
the evil darts of loss of one's goods,
the evil darts of house fires,
the evil darts of the peasants' millet crops,
the evil darts of illnesses,
and the evil darts of a sudden fall,
are forestalled.
We beseech you, grant our wishes,
the fortune that we desire
[we beseech you] to grant us what we wish,
the fortune that we ask you for.
We beseech you to ensure that, wherever hands reach out,
wherever footsteps are bent,
[there is] fortune in whatever the hands grasp,
and fortune for the feet wherever they tread the earth.
I beg you to grant longevity [to the members of the family]!
Mistress Ch'ae is the head of the family.
If you ask how old she is this year
she is sixty-three!
We beseech you to grant [to this lady]
a long life, as long as an anchor chain with iron links,
and an incalculable fortune!
A year is made up of twelve months.
One year and more has thirteen months.
The little month has twenty-nine days,
the big month has thirty days:
1st 7th, 2nd 8th,
3rd 9th, 4th 10th,
5th 12th, 6th 11th months.
Even if the 365 days
speed past like lightning,
the evil darts of misfortune brought on by the authorities and by gossip
passed from mouth to mouth by all
are forestalled [by the divinities],

even the invisible darts of the chill that others receive
in cold weather, which strike home,
are diverted in advance.
Even if among the twelve worlds of East, West, South, and North
[the darts] fly hither and thither from the four corners of the world,
the Hoe darts, whose approach is hidden, are blocked,
and also [the darts of the virgin] Kaekkwi that come from behind.
We beseech you to grant long life,
and that [for Mistress Ch'ae], in her last years, the stars may be
    favorable,
that in her last years the stars may be favorable.
[The master of the house] has accumulated a thousand gold pieces,
while still young the master of the house is an official.
If you ask how old he is this year
he is thirty-nine!
I beg you to bless him
with a life three thousand *kapcha* long
as long as the life of Tong Pangsak,
with the fortune, the fortune
which Sŏk Sung possessed.
A year is made up of twelve months.
One year and more has thirteen months.
The little month has twenty-nine days,
the big month has thirty days.
Even if they speed as fast as lightning,
I beg you, block
the evil darts of misfortune brought on by the authorities and by gossip
passed from mouth to mouth by all,
[the darts] are forestalled [by the divinities],
even the invisible darts of the chill that others receive
in cold weather, which strike home,
are diverted in advance.
Even if among the twelve worlds of East, West, South, and North
[the darts] fly hither and thither from the four corners of the world,
the hoe darts, whose approach is hidden, are blocked,
and also [the darts of] Kaekkwi which come from behind.
The evil darts among parents,
the evil darts of discord between couples,
the evil darts of loss of one's goods,
the evil darts of house fires,
and the evil darts of a sudden fall
are forestalled.
We beseech you that all our wishes may be scrupulously fulfilled,
as they were conceived,

just [as if their realization] was here before our eyes,
that wherever hands reach out,
wherever footsteps are bent,
all fortune will take hold there.
We beseech you to grant longevity and good fortune.
The young Master Kim is the master of the house.
If you ask how old he is this year
he is thirty-five.
[. . . omission in the manuscript]
The fortune to have descendants, to embrace them,
good fortune in raising them, grant this to him.
Make sure that his male issue
increase in prosperity
and that his female issue
have a long life.
The male descendant
is as precious [as a] heap of a thousand gold pieces and ten thousand
    gold pieces.
If you ask how old he is this year
he is twenty-three!
We pray to the Ch'ilsŏng-nim [Seven Stars] for long life,
we pray to Chesŏk-nim [Indra] for good fortune,
that they may entwine the long life
and lengthen the short life.
Grant him a long life,
as long as that of Tong Pangsak,
and the fortune, the fortune
that Sŏk Sung possessed!
Mount Ch'ŏllyung was his father,
Mount Pŏmnyung was his mother.
An official from a foreign land, a famous official,
crossed rivers, crossed the great rivers
and is said to have gone to a foreign land a thousand li off.
The foreign nation possesses a thousand family names,
Korea has ten thousand.
The thousand and ten thousand family names
blossom as flowers
in the sight of many officials,
in the sight of a thousand soldiers
who built the castle of Tŏhwa,
and [although this was] a time of war,
tumultuous times
which came on like flashes of lightning,
the ten thousand people

in brilliant silk garments, with shiny hats
and their feet shod,
[to] East, West, South, and North, in the twelve worlds
roam hither and thither in this world.
[. . . *omission in the manuscript*]
Make sure that
the ten thousand people are virtuous,
and that they may enjoy longevity.
The male descendant
is as precious [as a] heap of a thousand gold pieces and ten thousand
    gold pieces.
If you ask how old he is this year
he is nineteen.
[. . . *omission in the manuscript*]
[I beg you to grant] to his eyes the gift of being able to read,
to his hands the gift of art,
that he may excel in his talents,
[that he may compose] phrases both written and oral,
the gift of reading and the gift of speaking.
Open to them the way
[to equal] the eloquence of Sojungnyang,
the thought of Chegal Yang.
A year is made up of twelve months,
one year and more has thirteen months,
spring, summer, autumn, and winter, the four seasons
even if they speed by like lightning
[. . . *omission in the manuscript*]
avert in advance
coughing, sneezes
and bloodshot eyes.
Even if in the twelve worlds to East, West, South, and North
[the evil darts] fly among schools and public buildings
[. . . *omission in the manuscript*]
The ancestors and Puru Chesŏk-nim
are like a single entity in the heart
indivisible like the course of the Yellow River.
The noxious influences of the Heaven and the Earth,
the Moon, the Sun, and the Stars control them.
The noxious influences beneath the earth,
the divinities of the four seas control them.
The noxious influences above the water,
the Dragon God controls them.
The noxious influences above the fire,

the God of the fire controls them.
The noxious influences above the stone,
the God of the stone controls them.
The noxious influences above the earth,
the God of the earth controls them,
The noxious influences of the wood,
the God of the wood controls them.
Please take note that
if that descendant becomes adult,
he will be devoted to the nation,
he will be a virtuous son,
peace will reign within the domestic walls,
fraternal love [will reign] among brothers,
[fraternal] trust among friends,
make sure that ten thousand people are virtuous,
grant us longevity.
The ancestors and Puru Chesŏk-nim
are like a single entity in the heart
indivisible like the course of the Yellow River,
uproot and destroy
the twelve impurities, the twelve evil darts,
the serious illnesses,
the cold, the cold, the cold
as soon as [the darts] arrive in this house,
[the darts which] enter following men,
getting into the food,
clinging on to the life of the living.
It is a prayer [to obtain] fortune,
wealth, and honor
we beseech you to grant longevity and merits in abundance.

As the song ends, the relatives of the deceased take off their funeral costumes and, together with their shoes and some money, these are shaken over a fire in the yard. In the tent the table of misfortunes is set up. The table is laid with five bowls known as the "bowls of misfortune," in which a candle and a spoon are stuck into uncooked rice. Each spoon has a white thread around it, tied with loops corresponding to the age of the relative it represents. After sitting down in front of them, the shamaness sings the song that wards off misfortunes for the family.

At the end of the song, the shamaness goes into the courtyard and, after invoking all the divinities, the deceased, the ancestors, and the souls of the deceased's friends, she sings another song in which she urges the supernatural beings to cross the numerous hills on the way to the feast. Musicians accompany the song with a gong while an assistant beats a drum and sings the refrain.

Ch'ogamangsök

To become old, old, the elderly should give us ten thousand years,
once the ten thousand years have passed and we have become old
it is difficult to become young again!
[*musical refrain*]
It's the God, Mayajangch'ŏn,
today is [the day of the rite]!
He-heya-heiyo
In the shadow of Mount Unhang
the cuckoo sings mournfully!
"Why are you crying so sadly?"
"Because a dead tree has come into bud,
because flowers have blossomed on all the branches,
but my heart is sad."
[*musical refrain*]
The letter "Heaven" is written on high
and looks down on the letter "Earth,"
Confucius and Mencius,
their names are in all books,
but in which book will be recorded
the [name of the] poor deceased, Master Ham?
[*musical refrain*]
"The teaching that transforms [man] has been made manifest,"
"the teaching that transforms [man] has been made manifest"
in the presence of the Lord of the Heavens!
That water flows and ebbs
is the law of the Dragon-King of the Seven Seas,
that wind blows and it rains
is the law of the God of the Heavens,
that man is born and dies
is the law of the Ten Kings of Hell.
[*musical refrain*]
The Mountain!
When the [noxious influences] go on after resting on this mountain,
and go on after resting on this mountain,
resting on this or that mountain,
[when] the noxious influences of the villages enter the villages,
the noxious influences of the rooms enter the rooms,
let them go on after they have rested!

Sovereign! Sovereign!
For acquired merits [you] build the temple,
[its] origin is Mount Namunam!
Korea is the nation,

With eighty thousand inhabitants in the western capital,
Sŏgyŏng too is a capital.
Hanyang too is a capital.
Kaesŏng too is a major capital.
Build the residence in the Heaven of the Thirty-three,
The Twenty-eight Constellations rotate descending,
the *Hŏgung* Heavens, the *Pibi* Heavens
Samhwa and the *Tori* Heavens.
When the Ten Kings,
when [the Kings] prepared to rule,
they took control of the seventy-seven offices of government
in the province of Kyŏngsang,
[in the] seventy-seven districts of the province,
they took command of the Tojuwŏl
and the fifty-three offices of government in the province of Chŏlla,
they took control of the fifty-three districts in the province.
In the hour of the Rat, when the sky was created,
the Heaven was created
and in the hour of the Ox, when the earth was created,
the Earth was created
and in the hour of the Tiger human beings were created.
T'aewŏl! Ch'ŏnhwang-ssi!
[They] lived for eighteen thousand years
when Inhwang, living for eighteen thousand years
near the River Yŏk,
created a host of men and then
rectitude, sense of justice,
love, altruism, moral principles for ten thousand years,
the Three Relations and the Five Constant Bonds,
created family names [for men],
and Yŏmje Shennong
cut down the tree and carved it,
and created all tools,
teaching men to cultivate the fields.
Suin lent fire [to men]
so that they could invent a way of cooking food.
Hŭnhwŏn built the boat
that made communications possible.
To the East *kup, ŭl* and then 3, 8, wood,
the Blue Dragon was assigned,
To the South *pyŏng, chŏng* and then 2, 7, fire,
the Red Dragon was assigned,
To the West *mu, ki* and then 4, 9, gold,
the White Dragon was assigned,

To the North *kyŏng*, *sin* and then 1, 6, water,
the Black Dragon was assigned,
To the Center *im*, *kye* and then 5, 10, earth,
the Yellow Dragon was assigned.
To the East, T'aeho Pokhŭi,
to the South, Yŏmje Sinnong,
to the West, Chŏnuk Koyang,
to the North, Soyu Kŭmjŏn
and to the Center, Hwangje Hŭnhwŏn.
When [the divinities], the Sun and the Moon, receive the offerings
[in] Korea, in the province of South Chŏlla,
in the district of Chindo, in the municipal area of Ŭisin,
the village Wŏndu, where they took up residence,
is an ideal site with good auspices.
If we inquire into the family [of the husband]
and we inquire into the family [of the wife],
the family [of the husband comprises]
"old" rulers who ascend [in rank]
and "new" rulers who descend,
after the state examinations becoming academics, high-ranking officials,
doctors and officials.
Alongside the family of Master Ham,
which is as charming as the family of a prince,
there is the family of the precious daughter [daughter-in-law of Master
    Ham],
the head of the family, Mistress Ch'ae,
is like silver and the crane.
If you distinguish the month and the year,
the year is *chŏngmyo*,
the month and the position of the moon in the sky [correspond] to the
    tenth month,
and the day is the third of the month.
Sŏngju is the greatest authority,
he takes his place as the master of the house.
Chisin is the "guest" authority
and Chowang is the mistress.
Doesn't the head [of this family] know that in this house
an important rite is being performed?
Hey! Forty-five-year-old [man]!
Let's give a welcome to the God Sŏngju
who received the rite [in the] Palace of the Middle, the Grand Palace.
On the ninth day of the month the God Hagye Chowang,
on the nineteenh day of the month the God Chingye Chowang,
on the twenty-ninth day of the month the eighty-four thousand
    [divinities],

around the great Kyŏngdŏk Palace, a vast and roomy place
Chidae Chowang who sees to the construction,
we receive you.
Let's give a welcome to the ancestors,
the motive for our devotion
is none other than this:
[we ask that] parents, worthy of piety,
[be] purified and accompanied to the other world.
I beg you to go and be reborn in paradise!
[In the courtyard] the energy of the courtyard, the energy of the garden!
Let us raise up the tent, supporting it with bamboo poles.
When we perform the *kut* during the night,
[why is it that] the God Sŏngju
[does not know] the master of this house?
[The master of the house] gives a welcome to the God Sŏngju
and wishes to offer this rite,
[hence] the man's Vitality [is reinvigorated, and this will be] good
    fortune for the woman,
the vitality of the woman, good fortune for the man.
Let's make the most of the days of good auspices and vital energy!
To the West the Blue Spring,
to the South the Red Spring,
to the East the White Spring,
to the West the Black Spring,
the Odong Spring and the Kamdong Spring!
Water that flows and water that overflows
carries it away silently,
in the upper baths to wash your hair,
in the central baths to bathe,
in the lower baths for hands and feet,
the hair shaved off, and [after] abstaining from alcohol—
a white turnip [like the head of] a sister monk—there,
the terracotta jug is filling up [with the] liquor
that over the years becomes thick
and as it ages becomes [dark like] soy sauce,
the seasoned vegetable dishes,
cooked rice and soup,
ten thousand delicious things,
I turn my back [on the public] and prepare the delicacies.
I beg you to help yourselves abundantly.
Since you have come to receive purification,
I beg you to accept the offerings,
and escape from the Ten Hells,
and free yourselves too from the sins [accumulated in life],
escape also from the anxieties of your parents,

free yourselves from wet clothes and put on dry ones
and when you are reborn in paradise
free yourselves
from the problems of the domestic walls,
of illnesses and malignant darts.
I beg you to open the way for us,
that the descendants may have good fortune,
that they may excel in cultivating the fields,
that they may become rich and famous.
I beseech you to go and become a Buddha
and be reborn in paradise,
in the Hall of the Lotus Flower [adorned] with jade bells
in one of the [Buddhist] nine degrees of merit.

At the end of the song, the shamaness vigorously shakes the "money tree," a bamboo stick with strips of white paper attached, to indicate the change of music. She then starts to dance the "Flower Dance," holding the "money tree" very gently in her arms.

Mourners offer money to the spirits to secure their collaboration for the voyage of the deceased toward "the other world." When the music stops, the shamaness continues to dance, and then she sits and sings a long song for the Gods of Smallpox, who descend in a cane of bamboo that starts to tremble. The shamaness prays that the gods will not spread contagious illness in the village. The songs of the sequences dedicated to the Gods of Smallpox, to the god who protects children, Chesŏk, to the ancestors and to the tutelary House god, Sŏngju, are omitted here.

After a pause we come to the most significant sequences of the Ritual of Purification.

Ko p'uri, *"Untie the Hardships"*

This is the moment at which the soul of the deceased is appeased by loosening its hardships one by one, represented by five knots in a long strip of cloth. The shamaness unties the knots that symbolize all the hardships, pain, and affliction that cannot be untied in this world. She invites the deceased to free herself from all the mundane afflictions, because this release is just the beginning of the steps that will bring the soul to final purification, a condition indispensable to entering a superior level. Success is ensured through the knots that the shamaness unties one by one with a decisive and vigorous movement: when a knot does not come undone, the shamaness repeats the song and the religious acts.

Here's to longevity, long live Taesin!
Open the cloth and tear it into strips [to get rid of the impurities]!
Brilliant green strips,
Virgin Sŏwang, I beg you, undo
delicately [the knots] before the Great Sovereign!
Poor departed one,

in which knot are you tied up?
Have you got caught up in the knots of the other world?
Are you tied up in the knots of the Mountain God?
If you have got caught up in the knots of the other world
and are tied up in the knots of the Mountain God,
you cannot go on toward paradise,
and hovering outside the house
you are a source of anxiety for your descendants.
If you have got caught up in the knots of grievances and chagrin,
if you have got caught up in the knots of afflictions,
you cannot go on toward paradise where you are supposed to go,
and hovering outside the house,
you cause illnesses among your descendants.
A thousand knots, ten thousand knots, knots which are tied,
undo them now, this very moment,
[the knots of] apprehension and anxiety for domestic matters,
[the darts] of illnesses and the evil darts,
uproot them and go into the Western Paradise [of Amitābha]!
Open the cloth and tear it to strips!
Brilliant green strips, Virgin Saewang,
delicately before the Great Sovereign,
I beg you, undo [the knots]!

Ssikkim, "Washing"

We are finally in the most delicate and important phase of the ritual, in which the soul is "washed." First of all, a structure called a yŏngdon is prepared. Imagining that the deceased lies on the straw mat, the shamaness dresses her in traditional Korean dress and puts some money in it and then she rolls up the mat. The mat symbolizes the bones of the deceased. The shamaness prepares the second mat in the same way, this time putting two dresses and items of underwear in it. Meanwhile, the shamaness has prepared the "soul receptacle," which symbolizes the head of the deceased and consists of a rice bowl with a few grains of rice, money, and the soul inside. One of the mats is placed in a vertical position and on top of it is laid a ring of glutinous rice, a ring made of straw, and a big brass lid.

In the meantime the Messengers of the Dead arrive. They are welcomed at a small table in the yard near the main entrance, which is laid with three bowls of water and some fruit.

The shamaness holds a spoon with the "money tree," and the mat is held by female members of the family. A brief dance by the shamaness takes place before she starts to wash the mat, immersing the brush first in the water with incense ash which cleans the soul, then in the water with artemisia for the physical body, and then in clean water to complete the washing.

In this way, the shamaness has wet, washed, and brushed dew upon the deceased. She repeats this operation three times, and then dries with a cloth first the hat of the de-ceased, followed by the soul receptacle. All these operations are accompanied by the song that follows.

'Tis the soul! 'Tis the soul!
I knew not it was the soul,
but now I know it is the soul!
'Tis the divinity! 'Tis the divinity!
I knew not it was the divinity,
but now I know it is the divinity!
If the soul arrives,
we shall lodge it in its casket,
if the divinity arrives,
we shall invite it to take its place on the altar,
if soul and divinity arrive,
we shall welcome them in a silk gown and with silver dishes!
When it arrives, this soul
passes through the city of Seoul,
carrying with it a silver knife.
Hey! Look how it cuts—snip, snip!
When we guide the casket of the soul [along the bridge toward the
    other world],
darkness seems to come toward us,
we light the silk-covered lamps,
lamps colored red and lamps colored pink,
and the great groom and the little groom
come to meet us with the casket of the soul.
Hey! You who live on this earth!
Be not proud when you are alive
nor sad when you are dead!
I too lived until yesterday
and would have wished to live for a hundred years,
but perhaps it is my destiny [to die now].
There is a time to be born and to die,
Alas! Once you die
it is difficult to return [to life].
The guards have fled from the military camps
leaving the garrisons deserted.
When the Sovereign Ch'o P'ae was captured
because he grasped the knife and raised it
for the sake of brothers, husbands, and wives
[what should he do?]
At the third step he hesitated,
the four directions cried and sobbed

and [among] the five directions he did not know what to do
Poor departed one,
come and receive purification,
the receptacle for the soul has been prepared.
When man was created,
[even if] it was decided he would live for eighty years,
yet oh, my life, it is no good,
if once it goes away, it cannot come back.
When the Sun sets over the mountains in the west,
and it is tied to the tall branch [of the tree Pusang, the tree that stands
    in the East Sea where the sun rises],
the Moon that rises in the East Capital
[seems like] the lamp illuminating the River Ch'osang.
Wonderful landscape of roses and dunes!
My flower that is fading away, do not be sad!
Even if it wilts,
in March next year, when spring is here once more,
the flower will bloom again,
but even if the leaves sprout,
once you have left life behind,
it is difficult to come back.
Hey, you on earth!
Listen to what I have to say!
By whose merit did you come into the world?
By whose merit did you come into the world?
From your father you received your bones,
from your mother you received your life,
from Ch'ilsŏng-nim you received life,
from Chesŏk-nim you received fortune.
You come into the world of men
and in the first two years of life you ignore wisdom,
you do not know the merits of your parents, then,
having lived more than twenty or thirty years,
and reached the age of seventy,
in the morning the body is sound
but in the evening it is ill.
This body of mine, hanging by a thread,
gets terribly ill,
even though I have taken medicine, ginseng, and stag's antlers,
will the medicine do any good?
Although I have consulted the soothsayers for a reading of the sacred
    texts,
have I received any merits [positive results] from the sacred texts or the
    lips [of the soothsayers]?

Even if you say you have many friends,
when you go to the other world
what friend will go in your stead?
Even if you say you have many relatives,
which relative will go in your stead?
The person you invoke will be your mother,
the thing you wish for will be a little cold water.
Even if I wanted to go to paradise, giving as a bribe
the money I saved by halving my cigarettes
to that Messenger [of Death], will he take it?
Poor departed one,
even if you sent someone to fetch
the elixir of immortality on Mount Samsin,
when you die a sudden death
all communications are abruptly broken off.
On the day in which darkness encroaches,
the wooden pallet [becomes] the deceased's companion,
you will feel like a mere wanderer!
Alas, for the one who died today,
when you meet sudden death,
you become a soul, an unforgettable skeleton,
your sad soul weeps
and when it weeps like rain falling,
we wash it, and purify it with water!
Poor departed one,
today we purify you.
Poor departed one,
today we purify you.
We perform the rite so that you can go to paradise, on the road of
    the sun,
go to be reborn in paradise!
If we wash you with water and artemisia,
you will escape the hell Aksa,
you will escape the hell Tot'an,
and so that you can go to be reborn in paradise
we wash you with water and artemisia!
Wonderful landscape of roses and dunes!
You, flower who are fading, do not be sad!
You, flower, even if you are fading,
when spring comes again next year in March,
even the leaves will sprout again, and the roots too.
Poor departed one,
if you should happen to die a sudden death,
even though there is a road for you to take

I see no promise of your return!
Since you have been washed with water and artemisia,
if we wash you with scented water,
you will escape the hell Hat'an,
you will escape the hell T'aesan,
you will escape the hell P'yŏngdŭng,
that's why we wash you with scented water!
If we wash you with scented water,
you will escape the hells
and go to be reborn in paradise,
so, since you have been washed with scented water,
now we wash you with pure water!
If we wash you with pure water,
you will escape the Ten Hells,
you will escape the sins committed during your life
you will also avoid the *chungbok*,
and go to be reborn in paradise,
purify yourself in the pure water,
in the upper baths to wash your hair,
in the central baths have a bath,
in the lower baths for hands and feet,
purify yourself with care,
then shed your wet clothes
and put on dry ones.
I beseech you to go and become a Buddha
and be reborn in paradise, in the Hall of the Lotus Flower [adorned]
    with jade bells
in one of the nine degrees of merit,
go transformed into clear water.

The shamaness embraces the mat and dances in order to console the deceased. Then she orders the family to sit near the displayed mat and puts the "soul" of the deceased, represented by a white paper mannekin, on top of the descendants' head, trying to lift it with the "money tree." This time the soul rises immediately so that the shamaness can shake the "soul," "money tree," and the spoon, holding all together above each family member in order to transmit to them purification, luck, and prosperity.

Nŏk olligi, *"The Soul Is Risen"*

'Tis the soul! 'Tis the soul!
I knew not it was the soul,
but now I know it is the soul!
'Tis the divinity! 'Tis the divinity!
I knew not it was the divinity,

but now I know it is the divinity!
If the soul arrives,
we shall lodge it in its casket,
if the divinity arrives,
we shall invite it to take its place on the altar,
if soul and divinity arrive,
we shall welcome them in a silk gown and with silver dishes!
When it arrives, this soul
Passes through the city of Seoul,
carrying with it a silver knife.
Hey! Look how it cuts—snip, snip!
When we guide the casket of the soul [along the bridge toward the
    other world],
darkness seems to come toward us,
we light the silk-covered lamps,
lamps colored red and lamps colored pink,
and the great groom and the little groom
come to meet us with the casket of the soul.
It is said you cannot escape death!
The Kings of Heaven, of Earth and of Man are the Emperors Sinnong,
    Hwangje, and Pokhŭi.
Yo, Sun, U, T'ang, Mun, Mu, Chugong
who created the moral virtues
without once pausing to rest,
they are the Sages!
The First Emperor of Chin
takes his place in the upper part of the Abang palace
after [ordering] the erection of the Great Wall,
these heroes
[although] they have left historical records,
are [like] dew on the grass, as we are,
and once they die,
seven knots are tied with a strip of silk
[round their bodies] from top to bottom,
[the body is laid] on a large bier, [inside] a little coffin,
it is carried on shoulders, elegantly upraised,
and all go toward the Mount of the Dead,
a house is built out of the mud of the mountain,
the enclosure is barred with bamboo and pine,
and the age-old cuckoo becomes his companion.
In the depths of night, among the never-ending mountain ranges,
the soul is a paltry thing!
The cuckoo cries during the day,
when the cuckoo cries at night,

the cry of that bird, grating on the ear,
can be heard from every branch
and the water, unpleasant to the eye,
is flowing in every valley!
The Celestial Emperor, the Human Emperor,
even if they lived for eighty-four thousand years,
did not succeed in placating the Great King Yŏmna [Yama, King of
    the Dead],
King Yi of our country,
even if he saw to [offerings] in the festivities of spring and autumn,
he could not placate the Great King Yŏmna,
Did [the doctors] Hwa T'a and P'yŏn Chak
die for want of medicine,
or Confucius and Mencius
because they could not write?
Hey, you youngsters who are listening to me!
Do not mock when you see gray hairs,
young yesterday, gray-haired today,
it's a sad matter.
Oh splendid [young girl] of the Tang dynasty,
do not boast because you are beautiful!
Has someone [perhaps] forbidden
the sun to set behind West Mountain?
The water which flows toward the vast azure sea
is unlikely to be seen again.
Poor departed Ham,
even if you sent someone to fetch
the elixir of immortality on Mount Samsin,
when you die a sudden death,
all communications are broken off abruptly.
On the day in which darkness encroaches,
the wooden pallet [becomes] the deceased's companion,
you will feel a mere wanderer!
'Tis the soul! 'Tis the soul!
Who knows whose soul it is?
Can it be the soul of the [concubine] Wang Sogun who
had liaisons with everyone?
Can it be the soul of the departed [devout daughter] Sim
who lit up the blindness [of her father]
offering 300 sŏk of rice?
It is the soul of the departed Ham,
pitiable and worthy of mourning!
I beg you, go up, go up!
Go up, [you who are called] "soul."

Go up, [you who are called] "divinity."
Go up, [attaching yourselves] to the divine knife,
if you go up, [attaching yourselves] to the divine knife,
you will escape the Ten Hells
and will free yourselves from the sins committed during your life,
cleanse yourselves from *chungbok*.
We accompany you to paradise, purified, on the road of the sun,
we open the way invoking the name of Buddha,
go, I beg you, toward paradise
and go up, I implore you, with the divine knife!
Do not hesitate and go up.
He is sad, he is sad.
The departed Ham is sad.
When night fell a *may ŏkch'a* [?],
the young girl Sun was sad too,
when she had to say farewell to her relatives,
did she feel as sad as the deceased?
Even if [the *kisaeng* heroine] Ayami was sad,
the one who died throwing herself into the River Nam at Chinju
clinging round the neck of [the Japanese general Katō] Kiyomasa,
can she be as sad as the deceased?
Do not be sad, go up!

This time the "soul" rises immediately, so the shamaness shakes it over the family members, conferring on them luck and prosperity. She then sings a Buddhist prayer advising the soul how to go toward the "good place" and surmount obstacles and difficulties along the way. The shamaness also lights candles for the soul's journey. After the prayer is sung, she ties a long strip of cloth around a pole situated near the main room. This cloth represents a road toward the "other world." She crosses the space under the tent where the ritual has been held and a descendant holds one end near the outer gate. This is the road by which the shamaness will exhort the soul to leave, so she cleans and smooths the road to make its journey easier.

   The container of the "soul" is sometimes moved in a zigzag manner by the shamaness. Often it is halted to let the soul rest, or it is moved backward in front of obstacles. Along the road, the bereaved put in money, which serves to buy the cooperation of the spirits. The shamaness puts all the belongings of the deceased on the "road," moving them along as described above.

Kilttaggŭm, *"Smoothing the Way"*

All bodhisattvas!
All bodhisattvas!
Namu ŭ ŭŭŭ
ŏya na—hee

ŏyanamu namuyŏ
We ask for the protection of Amitābha Buddha.
Hey seagull! Seize the fish!
Let the boat float on the clear river with the green willows!
Poor departed one today,
I beg you, go to be reborn in paradise!
[*musical interlude*]
If you wish to smooth the way in this world,
smooth it with a metal rake,
smooth it by leveling the high part,
smooth it by raising the low part!
Poor departed one today,
I beg you, go to be reborn in paradise!
[*musical interlude*]
When you smooth the way to the other world,
smoothing the way, invoking the Buddha incessantly,
the dark road is lit up
and the narrow road is made wide!
Poor departed one today,
I beg you, go to be reborn in paradise!
[*musical interlude*]
Namuya Namuya
namu namuya
We ask for protection from Amitābha Buddha.
Smooth the way!
In the spring days [the earth] is a wasteland,
in the summer days it is a tundra,
the green trees and the blue leaves are in full bloom,
look for a place to rest and then go on!
[*musical interlude*]
Once you have gone beyond a peak,
If there happens to be a white egret on the green waters of the Red River
and a pair of mallards,
ask about the road for paradise and go on!
[*musical interlude*]
After another peak,
the bees, butterflies, and camellias all swarm together,
if there happens to be a bluebird,
ask about the road for paradise and go on!
[*musical interlude*]
An old man with gray hairs seated in front of a monk
has a *paduk* [chess] set in front of him,
he seems to be putting black and white points in front of him,
here and there.

It is clear that it is Mount Samsin,
so find the beautiful view,
rest and then go on!
[*musical interlude*]
After another peak,
white clouds above the shrine,
if there happens to be a monk there,
[ask him] to accompany you
on the road to paradise which is far, so far away!
[*musical interlude*]
After another peak,
on Mount Pongnae, within the clouds
two children in blue jackets are sitting
and playing mournfully on a jade flute,
once you find the beautiful view, rest and then go on.
[*musical interlude*]
After another peak,
on Mount Pongnae, among the clouds,
beneath an old pine on the steep and rocky mountainside,
the children are digging for medicinal plants,
[but] if you are full of grief and greatly indignant,
ask for the immortal herb, eat it
and be reborn!
[*musical interlude*]
O you, all buddhas and all bodhisattvas,
all buddhas and all bodhisattvas,
we ask for protection from Amitābha Buddha.
The road for this world [measures] 480 *li*.
[*musical interlude*]
We ask for protection from Amitābha Buddha.
the road to that world [measures] 480 *li*!
[*musical interlude*]
[the road] of the "middle way" [measures] 960 *li*!
[*musical interlude*]
just one bridge has been built from a single tree
[*musical interlude*]
the deceased who lack money for bribes
[*musical interlude*]
may not cross that bridge
[*musical interlude*]
and remain hovering here and there.
[*musical interlude*]
Poor departed one today,

[*musical interlude*]
cross the bridge and go to King Sae!
[*musical interlude*]
The boat running up its sails is the boat of the White Cloud
[*musical interlude*]
and on the sail is written: one-way passage [to the other world]
[*musical interlude*]
On the Blue River, blue
[*musical interlude*]
there is just one bridge built from a single tree.
[*musical interlude*]
Life and death are sacred things.
[*musical interlude*]
Poor departed one today
[*musical interlude*]
I beg you to cross the bridge to go to paradise
[*musical interlude*]
paying your way with bribes and the cloth.
[. . .]

At the end of the song the shamaness takes everything into her arms and performs a brief dance to convince the soul to stay in her new world.

Bidding the Deceased Farewell

Long live Taesin!
Be generous with your offerings!
I beg you, go to paradise.
To the East, General Blue
wears the blue uniform and helmet
and flees those who, finding death by water or at the end of a rope,
return from the South, arriving with a commotion.

To the South, General Red
wears the red uniform and helmet
and flees those who, finding death by water or at the end of a rope,
return from the East, arriving with a commotion.

To the West, General White
wears the white uniform and helmet
and flees those who, finding death by water or at the end of a rope,
return from the North, arriving with a commotion.

To the North, General Black
wears the black uniform and helmet

and flees those who, finding death by water or at the end of a rope,
return from the West, arriving with a commotion.

The ritual is almost over. It is dawn. Outside the main entrance, a small table is prepared for the final sequence, when all the paraphernalia is burned and all the spirits are invited to leave.

Christianity

20

Martyrdom and Social Activism:
The Korean Practice
of Catholicism

Inshil Choe Yoon

Catholicism has existed for more than two centuries in Korea and is Korea's longest practiced denomination of Christianity. Rather than having been imported by foreign missionaries, Catholicism grew initially in Korea through the interest of scholars in the late Chosŏn dynasty, who established the first Catholic communities on the peninsula. Catholicism thus became deeply intertwined in Korean history. Korean Catholicism progressed in three stages: (1) a century-long underground practice of the religion during the late Chosŏn dynasty until 1884, when the Court officially permitted Catholic activity; (2) open practice through the Japanese colonial period until liberation in 1945; and (3) active practice in South Korea and curtailed practice in North Korea during the cold war division of the peninsula up through the present.

The Underground Practice of Catholicism (1784–1884)

The development of the Catholic community in Korea grew gradually out of a scholarly interest in Catholicism during the Chosŏn dynasty. Although there are records that the Jesuit priest Gregorio de Cespedes was sent to Korea during the Japanese Hideyoshi invasion (1592–98) to minister to Japanese soldiers (where he is claimed to have baptized more than two hundred abandoned children), his putative presence had no effect on the subsequent practice of Catholicism in Korea. Instead, Korean scholars in the seventeenth and eighteenth centuries were first introduced to Western science, geography, and Catholicism through books that Jesuit missionaries wrote in China. Among the books that Korean emissaries brought back from Beijing were Matteo Ricci's (1552–1610) *Tianzhu shiyi* (The True Meaning of the Lord of Heaven) and Didacus de Pantoja's *Chike* (Seven

Overcomings), which became popular especially among *namin* (Southern Faction) scholars. Thus, prior to the arrival of Christian missionaries, there were already Koreans with strong personal interest in Catholicism.

By the 1780s, this interest in and willingness to accept knowledge from the West became more focused on religious practice. In 1784 a young Confucian scholar traveled to Beijing, met a French priest there, and was convinced by him that what those Catholics books said should be taken seriously. Yi Sŭnghun (1756–1801), now baptized as Peter, returned to Korea to share what he had learned with friends and relatives. He brought several Catholic books with him and even performed baptisms for fellow scholars. Soon there was a small but growing Catholic community on the Korean peninsula. There were no foreign missionaries in Korea at that time, so there was no one to explain to Korea's first Catholics how different Catholicism and Confucianism were. Apparently, most of them believed that Catholicism and Confucianism were compatible. However, in 1790, they discovered that was not the case. A letter from the French bishop of Beijing informed the fledgling Korean church that Catholics were forbidden to use the ancestral tablets that played such a central role in Confucian memorial services. When the mother of one of those Catholics died the next year, the stage was set for confrontation.

In 1791, Paul Yun Chich'ung (1759–91) and his cousin James Kwŏn Sangyŏn (1751–91) were arrested when it was discovered that they had not followed proper Confucian ritual procedure in mourning Yun's recently deceased mother. The authorities found that food was not laid out properly and that liquor had not been offered to the deceased. They also discovered that Yun had not set up a memorial tablet for his deceased mother and that the tablets of Yun's ancestors had previously been burned. (Other Catholics instead chose to bury their ancestors' tablets next to their graves.) When the Catholics justified their refusal to perform the ancestor memorial service in the prescribed manner by saying their duty to obey God's laws overrode their duty to obey their king, they were beheaded. That persecution drove the remaining Korean Catholics either into apostasy or underground.

The underground church, remarkably, continued to grow. In 1794 a Chinese priest slipped into Korea undetected by the government and began secretly ministering to this infant church. When a relatively tolerant king died in 1800, the government that replaced him decided to find the priest and kill him and the members of his flock. This was the dragnet that caught Lutgarda Yi Suni (1782–1802) and led to her imprisonment, where she wrote the letter translated here in which she anticipated her death. The Korean Catholic church was less than twenty years old at that point. Though she and hundreds of other Catholics, including most of the leadership, were executed in 1801 and 1802, enough members survived to keep the Korean Catholic community alive. There were sporadic persecutions over the next seventy years, including major persecutions in 1839 and 1866 that took the lives of French missionaries as well as Korean believers. A smaller persecution in 1827 caught Yi Kyŏngŏn (1792–1827). A portion of his interrogation is translated later in this chapter.

God as the Great King and Father

The emergence of Catholicism on the peninsula marked the first time Koreans accepted a personal and loving God as the creator of the universe, who incarnated and suffered for humanity's salvation. Their reverence of God above as the Great King and Father (*taegun taebu*) and the Great Parent (*taebumo*), superior even to king and family, clashed with the principles of loyalty and filial piety that are so central to Neo-Confucianism. In addition, it challenged the political authority of the Court. For example, in his interrogation, Yun Chich'ung states, "Once one accepts the Heavenly Lord as the Great Parent one is bound to revere Him by following His order. The Catholic Church bans the use of wooden tablets [on which the name of the deceased is written and which is used for ancestral rites] kept in scholar-gentry households. I would rather commit a crime against the scholar-gentry than commit a sin against the Heavenly Lord. That's why I burned the tablets and buried them. . . . The Church also bans offering food and wine to the deceased" (*Chŏngjo Sillok* [The Annals of King Chŏngjo], *muin* day, eleventh moon, fifteenth reign year [1791]). This was seen by the Court as a pernicious example of abandoning the norm of filial piety that was the foundation of a stable society. Because Yun Chich'ung refused to perform ancestral rites, he was beheaded in 1791. Ironically, filial piety was in fact emphasized and practiced among Catholics not only toward their own parents but also toward their parents-in-law, as seen in Yi Suni's letters.

The Equality of Humankind

Chosŏn society was characterized by a rigid social hierarchy of *yangban* (an upper class of scholars and military officials), *chungin* (clerks and technicians), *yangin* (freeborn commoners), and *chŏnmin* (lowborn). The Catholic teaching of a Creator who loves human beings equally and exhorts them to love one another prompted an egalitarian movement within Chosŏn Catholicism and prompted the church to embrace people of every social status. This practice is demonstrated in four ways: (1) in choosing leaders during the initial formation of the church, (2) the acceptance of members from all classes, (3) the egalitarian nature of their gatherings, and (4) the slaves they released.

Thus, while the church was established by the scholar-gentry class, the first leaders included members from the middle people and commoners. An early Catholic adherent, the butcher Hwang Ilgwang, was of the lowest class and hence despised in society. When he became a member of the Catholic community, he was overwhelmed with emotion for being treated as a peer and said he found two paradises: one in this world, and the other after death. Other members of the community released their slaves. Releasing slaves was revolutionary in Chosŏn society, because the upper class depended on them to perform their household chores and to maintain their wealth. A translation of Yi Kyŏngŏn's (1792–1827) journal excerpts, included later in this chapter, illustrates the basic Catholic mentality regarding the equality of humankind as well as the Korean Catholic penchant to revere God as the Great Parent.

Korean Catholics embraced the notion of promoting faith and righteousness between husband and wife and prohibiting the practice of polygamy. This view was groundbreaking as it was perfectly acceptable in Chosŏn society for husbands to keep concubines, and women were expected to obey their husbands and fulfill their duties required by the Neo-Confucian value system. In a society where arranged marriages were the norm, it was also radical that Catholics allowed young people to choose whether or not to marry. Up until this time, it had been unacceptable in Chosŏn society for people to remain unmarried, since it was regarded as unfilial if people failed to perform their duty to produce offspring.

Serving the Lord and Saving Souls

Korean Catholics during the persecution period showed more interest in life after death than in life before death. This is seen in the eagerness (albeit mingled with trepidation) with which Yi Suni awaits her martyrdom, as her letters so eloquently describe, and in the way in which Ch'oe Yangŏp dismisses this world as a "fleeting world [that is] not the place for us to settle down" and insists that heaven is our true home.

In the letters of Yi Suni and Yi Kyŏngŏn, as well as in the "Sahyangga," a mid-nineteenth-century hymn by Ch'oe Yangŏp (the second Korean in history to be ordained as a priest), which is translated in this chapter, we can see a distinctive abstemious trait that characterizes Korean Catholicism. The first Korean Catholics were already exposed to the self-discipline that was inherent to Neo-Confucianism, and this temperance was reinforced in Catholic circles by the ascetic strain of Catholicism preached by the Paris Foreign Missions Society, which had replaced Jesuit missionaries in China in the last quarter of the eighteenth century and became responsible for dispatching priests to Korea in the nineteenth century. Another reason for this abstemiousness was so that Catholics could find the spiritual strength they needed to survive the poverty caused by maintaining their faith.

Catholic valorization of the soul over the body and the life in the later world over that of this world is articulated in the phrase *saju kuryŏng* (serving the Lord and saving souls). In response to continuing persecution by the government, Catholics embraced the suffering of this world while simultaneously working toward the salvation of their souls in heaven. Reminding each other of *saju kuryŏng*, they aspired to maintain their faith and be martyred. Martyrdom was regarded as an honor and heaven as one's true home. Their faith was also enriched by such manuscripts as Chŏng Yakchong's (1760–1801) *Chugyo yoji* (The Essentials of Catholicism), the records of Yun Chich'ung, and the letters of Yi Suni. They also read works by the martyrs Saint Agatha and Saint Victoria and reflected on the passion of Jesus. They had a deep devotion to the Sacred Heart of Jesus, Mary, and the Korean martyrs. "Sahyangga," Hymn of Longing for Home, a typical song of the period, asserts the way to heaven as its main theme. (A portion of "Sahyangga" is translated later in this chapter.)

A unique case of pursuing the ideal of "serving the lord and saving souls" during this period involves Yi Suni (1782–1802) and Yu Chungch'ŏl (1779–1801), who maintained celibacy even after marriage. Yi Suni learned that Catholics in the West sometimes led celibate lives and decided she would emulate Saint Agatha (?–251), a virgin and martyr during the Roman Empire. She told the Chinese Father Jacobo Zhou Wenmo (Korean, Chu Munmo), who had arrived in Korea in 1794, that she wanted to lead a celibate life devoted to God. However, remaining unmarried was not an option in upper-class Chosŏn society, since this would have been viewed as unfilial. Since there was no Catholic convent or monastery in Korea for Yi Suni to enter, Father Zhou arranged a marriage for her with Yu Chungch'ŏl, who had also expressed the aspiration to live a similar way of life. One year after their marriage ceremony in Yi Suni's house, they moved into Yu Chungch'ŏl's parents' home and held a ceremony there declaring their commitment to celibacy. Their mutual trust and affection and their struggle to maintain their commitment to celibacy are well described in Yi Suni's prison letters to her mother and sisters. In these letters, excerpts of which are translated later in this chapter, one sees how Catholic women were simultaneously still able to satisfy Confucian virtues by taking care of parents and parents-in-laws, husbands, and relatives.

Members of the Catholic Church, such as Yi Suni and Yu Chungch'ŏl, overcame their own difficulties in maintaining their faith. Nonetheless, many failed to retain their faith under the threat of torture and death by the Court. Throughout the nearly century-long period of persecution, about 10,000 people were killed for their beliefs. Not all Korean Catholics were able to maintain their faith during their torture. A record from 1866, for example, notes that of 408 Catholics brought in for interrogation to the police station in Seoul, the majority denounced their faith at some stage during torture, and only 35 percent of them professed their commitment to their faith consistently.

The Propagation of Catholicism

Catholics during this underground period were restricted in their social activities because of constant surveillance by the government. Even so, many Koreans were attracted to Catholicism because of its accessibility. Right after the community was formed, Catholic books including parts of the four Gospels were translated into han'gŭl (the Korean alphabet), so that people of lower social classes, who were not adept in literary Chinese, could read the texts. Common practices during the Chosŏn included saying private and public prayers, and emulating the Gospel message of a charitable life. Catholics started the day with prayers and said the Angelus in the morning, at noon, and in the evening. The rosary was also typically said before evening prayer. On Sundays and days of celebration, Catholics gathered in secret to pray. Those who could not join in the prayers said the Lord's Prayer sixty-six times, the Hail Mary ninety-nine times, or the Stations of the Cross. They often reflected on their lives as they recited the Ten Commandments. They practiced charity by looking after orphans and treating people of all classes equally, and in some cases, releasing their own slaves.

Dissemination developed in fits and starts. Two years after the establishment of the church, Catholics formed a quasi-hierarchical system to minister to the congregation. The majority of leaders were *yangban* (upper class) in their thirties, who led economically comfortable lives. After learning that the bishop in Beijing had declared such a system to be inappropriate, the practice was stopped. From that point on, congregations grew not only in Seoul but also in Kyŏnggi province, Ch'ungch'ŏng province, and Chŏlla province, reaching one thousand members by 1790.

However, the executions of Yun Chich'ung and Kwŏn Sangyŏn resulted in an attrition of *yangban* church leaders. Under increasing danger and with few leaders, Catholics fled either to Seoul, where their presence would not have been noticed as much as in the countryside, or to isolated, mountainous areas in Kyŏngsang and Kangwŏn provinces. Those who fled to the mountains formed Catholic settlements (*kyoch'on*), the largest of which boasted around fifty residents, but most of which were much smaller. The villagers' life was poor, eking out a living in subsistence farming or making pottery for sale. They had to be watchful and ready to leave their village at any time to flee from Court officers who suspected they might be bandits. Through peddling pottery or paper, brushes, and ink sticks, however, Catholics were able to contact members in other areas and thus maintain their faith. Ironically, in this way Catholicism also spread to other regions of the peninsula.

Catholicism's resilience was viewed as a sign of its egalitarian nature and as a result, the community grew to 4,000 in 1794, especially among the middle people, commoners, and lower class, and to 10,000 in 1800. This growth is remarkable, considering that it occurred during a quarter-century-long ban by the court. There are no reliable statistics regarding membership during the persecution period; however, government arrest records offer clues. The Court records that, of the 672 Catholics arrested in 1801, more than half resided in Seoul and the rest in either Kyŏnggi, Ch'ungch'ŏng, or Chŏlla provinces.

In Seoul, the majority of the members were *yangin* commoners doing manual labor and *chungin* "middle people" working as translators or herbal medicine doctors. In Kyŏnggi and Chŏlla provinces, the majority of members were from the *yangban* class, while in Ch'ungch'ŏng province *yangin* commoners were the majority. In all, 7.69 percent of the identified Catholics were *ch'ŏnin* (the low class). The records confirm that Seoul was the center of Catholic activity and that not only *yangban* but people from all four social classes practiced Catholicism.

There is no mention of women during the early stages of development. Court records of 1801 do reveal that women made up a quarter of the 672 total members, and that in Seoul more than one-third of the members were women. These figures suggest that Seoul was also the center of a growing cadre of Catholic women. One woman, Kang Wansuk (1761–1801), played a key role in proselytizing to women and making possible the pastoral activities of the Chinese Father Zhou, who arrived in Korea on December 23, 1794, by hiding him in her house. Furthermore, the record in Kihae ilgi (Diary of the Kihae Year) during the persecution of 1839 indicates that, of a total of eighty martyrs, fifty-one were women, a figure far outnumbering that of men.

The Catholic community did not have priests from 1800 through 1830, yet its members still maintained and propagated Catholicism successfully. Chŏng Hasang (1795–1839) wrote to Beijing and Rome, calling on the church to send priests to Korea. In response, the Vatican established the Korean church in 1831 as an apostolic vicar separate from the Beijing diocese and in 1835 sent priests to Korea from the Foreign Mission Society of Paris. After the arrival of foreign missionaries, the Court implemented another large-scale persecution in 1839 and executed Bishop Imbert and Fathers Maubant and Chastan. Chŏng Hasang defended his beliefs in his Sangjaesangsŏ (Letter to the Prime Minister), but he was also executed.

During this time, the foreign missionaries adopted Korean customs, ate local food, wore Korean dress, and lived in Korean houses, which also substituted for churches. When they went outside, they disguised themselves as Korean mourners wearing shoes made of straw and deep straw hats to cover their faces because they were the main target of the Court. As devoted pastors working in a limited environment, missionaries were assisted by lay Koreans. One missionary, Father Zhou Wenmo, escaped arrest in 1795 because of the efforts by Korean Catholic laywomen.

In the persecution of 1846, around three hundred Catholics were executed, including the first Korean priest, Kim Taegŏn, who was killed after only a seven-month-long ministry in Korea. Father Ch'oe Yangŏp succeeded in entering Korea in 1849 and devoted his life to ministering to people until his death in 1861. He spent most of his time visiting the 127 Catholic settlements scattered in five provinces. He wrote Catholic verses (Ch'ŏnju kasa), including "Sahyangga" (Hymn of Longing for Home), using the traditional kasa form, in which each unit of verse is arranged into four groups of mainly four syllables. Reciting verses proved to be an easy method of indoctrination, and the recitation of Ch'ŏnju kasa was handed down to younger generations and served as a tool for educating children at home.

From 1866 to 1869, Korean Catholics endured another broad persecution. Initiated by the Taewŏn'gun, the regent and father of King Kojong (r. 1865–1907), the persecution ultimately claimed thousands of lives, including all but three foreign missionaries active in the country, and prompted French retaliation. The French navy's attack on, and looting of, Kanghwa island, which involved some Korean sympathizers as well, prompted an even more severe persecution. Catholics were further oppressed because the Court suspected them of being connected with the invasion of the island by the United States navy in 1871. With the signing of the treaty with Japan in 1876, Korean society changed drastically. Still,

while foreign missionaries in prison were then being deported instead of executed, Korean Catholics were still subject to arrest and execution.

The Open Practice of Catholicism (1884–1945)

Catholics observed remarkable changes in the Court's attitude in 1884, when the
Court tolerated the opening of the first Catholic school. Full freedom of the faith
was confirmed during Bishop Mutel's meeting with King Kojong in 1895, at
which time the king expressed his regret for the 1866 persecution. Catholics began actively propagating Catholicism by reopening the seminary and building the
Myŏngdong cathedral in Seoul and churches across the peninsula. The increased
proselytization and the growing number of converts led to conflict in some areas,
such as in Chejudo Island in 1901, where several hundred lives were lost. The
conflict between Catholics and Protestants, such as in Hwanghae province, resulted in an uneasy relationship between the two main branches of Christianity,
which lasted until the 1960s. In the Kando area, however, Korean Catholics and
Protestants cooperated in establishing schools and financial companies, and participated in the independence movement against the Japanese colonial government in Korea (1910–45).

Catholics actively participated in the modernization of Korea and in the anti-
colonial movement against Japan. They organized prayer meetings in Myŏngdong
cathedral to denounce the Japanese occupation of the Korean peninsula. In an effort to resist the growing Japanese encroachments in Korea, Sŏ Sangdon, a
Catholic, initiated a collection to redeem the national debt and received nationwide support until 1910, when Japan formally annexed Korea. Some individual
Catholics showed their nationalism in force. Many joined an army of independent guerrilla fighters after the disbandment of the Korean national army in
1907. In 1909, An Chunggŭn, who was a catechist and teacher, assassinated Ito
Hirobumi, who had become the resident general in Korea after making Korea a
virtual protectorate of Japan.

Under the oppression of the Japanese colonial government, Catholics endured
another period of hardship, especially in their involvement with social activities.
Their freedom of speech was revoked with the closure of the *Kyŏnghyang Sinmum*
(Kyŏnghyang Newspaper), and more than half of the 124 Catholic schools then
operating in Korea were closed in 1910. From 1915, Catholics had to receive
permission from the colonial Government General to engage in evangelism.

The Catholic Church did not officially take an active role in the resistance
against Japanese colonialism. However, individual Catholics expressed their defi-
ance by joining the March First Independence Movement of 1919, the independent Korean armies that formed in Manchuria, and the provisional government
of Korea in Shanghai.

Moreover, according to catechism guidelines published in 1925, the church
prohibited participation in the Japanese Shintō worship ceremony, and some

Catholic students were expelled from the public schools for not participating. After the Japanese government declared Shintō worship to be a public, not a religious, ceremony, the church allowed believers to participate in it. Some Catholic priests and laity, however, strongly refused to participate in such observances, at the cost of their employment or the closure of their churches.

Active Practice and Renewal in South Korea
(1945–Present)

After liberation from Japanese colonization on August 15, 1945, Catholics in the South resumed their religious, educational, and social activities. Northern Korea was disarmed by the army of the Soviet Union, and Koreans there came under Communist rule, which was antipathetic to religion. After the division of the peninsula into North and South Korea in 1948, Catholics in the North struggled to retain religious freedom.

The Korean War (1950–53) resulted in heavy casualties on the peninsula, and Catholic activities in North Korea became severely curtailed, while many clergy, religious, and laity were killed during the war. In South Korea, however, the church actively participated in relief work, with aid from abroad. After the war, membership in the South Korean church grew by an average rate of 16.5 percent annually through the 1950s. This marked the highest annual growth rate ever recorded for Catholic membership in Korea. Laity joined such organized movements as the Legion of Mary, which ministered to the sudden influx of members.

Renewal after the Second Vatican Council and Lay Movements

With the opening of the Second Vatican Council (1962–65) and the Korean church becoming an autonomous hierarchy in 1962, Korean Catholics sought to adjust to contemporary needs. Among the reforms were these radical changes: the Koreanization of rituals, including saying mass in Korean; the active participation of laity in proselytizing; communication with Protestant churches and other religions; and engagement in social and political causes.

In the spirit of the Second Vatican Council, lay Catholics started to participate actively in the leadership of their parishes by forming the lay Apostolate Councils. They also joined in lay movements such as the Cursilio, a short intensive program for lay leaders, and the Charismatic and Focolare movements, which were introduced to Korea in the 1970s. The most noteworthy was Kat'ollik Sŏngsŏmoim (The Catholic Bible Life Movement), which originated in Seoul 1972.

University students eager to study and live the message of the Bible as interpreted by the Catholic Church were supported by the Sisters of Mary of Perpetual Help, who created a Bible program for reading the books of Genesis, Exodus,

Mark, or John. This was a creative response to the need for "religious education of the youth," which both Korean clergy and students themselves ranked as the most serious problem of the church in a 1971 survey. The program soon grew to include all age-groups and became an established lay program in parishes. Inspired by this movement, a variety of other Bible study programs were formed in later years, and many Catholics have rediscovered the importance of leading their lives according to the message of the Bible.

Catholics continue to renew their faith through various creative programs offered by both lay and religious communities. To cater to the needs of a growing membership and overly large parishes (some with more than ten thousand parishioners), lay Catholics lead parish-based "small-scale community" projects, which were adopted by the dioceses. They also participate in evangelizing abroad by supporting Korean missionaries working through such organizations as the Korean Foreign Mission Society, which is active in Papua New Guinea, Taiwan, China, Cambodia, Russia, Africa, and Latin America.

Embracing Korean Tradition and Other Religions

The most visible innovation in the Koreanization of Catholicism is the performance of ancestor worship. Catholicism's failure to perform the rites, which were denounced and prohibited by the church, was the main cause of the nascent church's persecution in the late eighteenth century. As part of the effort to restore Korean heritage, the church now accepts such rites as an indigenous way of promoting family bonds. Freed from church officials' rigid interpretation of the rites, Korean Catholics now express their filial piety through rites and prayers for the deceased.

The belief that living members can pray to God for mercy for the dead encourages families and friends to gather to pray in the home of the deceased until the funeral. Called *yŏndo* (prayer for the souls in purgatory), this practice is a combination of psalms, prayers of convocation, and other observances. Even after the funeral, they continue to pray for the deceased, but especially on the 3rd, 7th, 49th, and 100th days after death, which the prayer guidelines state are particularly memorable days. By saying prayers on or during these traditionally auspicious dates, Korean Catholics honor the traditional Korean values that other religions, especially Buddhism and Confucianism, have implanted in Korea.

Since the 1960s, Catholics have taken the initiative in communicating with members of other religions. This effort has continued through the human rights and democracy movements of today. Catholics also reportedly maintain an open attitude toward other religions. In the 1983 Gallup survey on religion and religious consciousness among Koreans, Catholics were most open to other religions: 86.4 percent of the Catholics surveyed agreed with the statement "The doctrines of various religions at a glance look different, but in the end they are the same"; 80.1 percent of Buddhists and 64.6 percent of Protestants agreed with this statement. This inclusive mentality of Korean Catholics has been maintained:

the 1997 survey revealed that 85.4 percent of Catholics agreed with the statement, whereas 87.0 percent of Buddhists and 61.7 percent of Protestants agreed with it.

Active Participation in Social Causes

With urbanization and industrialization during the 1960s, Catholics committed themselves to social justice through such organizations as the Association of Catholic Farmers. Under the *Yusin* dictatorship, which started in 1972 and deprived citizens of their freedom of speech and assembly, the Priests' Association for the Realization of Justice played a major role in democratization by calling for the restoration of human rights and political freedom in several declarations since 1974. (A part of the first declaration is translated later in this chapter.) In the democratization movement, the Catholic clergy joined forces with the clergy of other Christian churches. The Declaration for Saving the Nation, which was read in 1976 at Myŏngdong cathedral, was one of the outcomes of this joint effort. Myŏngdong cathedral, built on the site of the first Catholic gathering in Korea in 1785, became the center of the modern democracy movement. The area surrounding the cathedral has provided a venue for the needy and for protests by those making desperate appeals to the broader society, such as displaced slum dwellers and, more recently, foreign workers who have overstayed their visas.

Catholics have engaged the educational and social service sectors. They have established many schools and universities, such as the Catholic University of Korea, the Catholic University of Taegu, and Sŏgang University, as well as hospitals and various social facilities for the handicapped, elderly, youth, children, and women.

Immediately following the International Monetary Fund financial crisis of 1997, Catholics initiated a national campaign to collect personal gold jewelry to alleviate the shortage of foreign currency at the time. Two thousand tons of gold jewelry, worth some US$20 billion, were collected during the campaign. In 1998, Catholics were reported to be the most active religious denomination in providing overall social services, including programs for those who lost their jobs after the economic crisis. (The translations include an interview with a Catholic layperson to provide a glimpse into the life of a Korean Catholic who had gone through the economic crisis.)

Catholics have also supported the church's initiatives to dialogue with North Koreans. After several visits made by priests, Bishop Andrew Choi Changmu (Ch'oe Ch'angmu) made a pastoral visit to North Korea in 1998 and said mass at the newly constructed Changch'ung Church in P'yŏngyang, which has no clergy but has around six hundred parishioners. It is estimated that there are six to eight thousand Catholics in the whole of North Korea. Visits to North Korea by South Korean Catholics, and support of their northern brethren, continue. Indeed, Catholics made the largest financial contributions to North Korea in 1998 of any religious denomination.

Conclusion

Korean Catholicism has been practiced over the last two centuries, during which time it encountered a series of obstacles in a changing Korean society. It began primarily as a *yangban* literati religion, which then became accepted by people of all social classes. Through its myriad tribulations, Korean Catholicism has established a strong identity as a Korean religion fully engaged in society. The canonization of 103 Korean Catholic martyrs, more than all but four other nations, further points to the maturity of present-day Catholicism in Korea.

With the church's present oversized parishes, Catholics are striving for an ongoing renewal, aiming at restoring human dignity and social justice by living as "salt" in a society plagued by rampant materialism. Challenges that Catholics face include the increasing numbers of inactive Catholics, the need for diverse programs for Catholic spirituality, the laity's dependence on the clergy, and the gender imbalance in leadership positions. As members of one of the fastest-growing churches in Asia, Catholics in Korea endeavor to serve a major role in evangelizing Asia and other continents. They are also committed to building closer relationships with Catholics in North Korea and encouraging peace and unification on the Korean peninsula.

Excerpts from Yi Suni's "Letter to Her Sisters" are translated from Kim Jinso, ed., *Yi Suni Nugalta Nammae Okchung P'yŏnji* (Yi Suni Lugartha and Her Brothers' Letters Written in Prison) (Wanjugun: Ch'ŏnjugyo Honam Kyohoesa Yŏn'guso, 2002), pp. 41–65. Yi Kyŏngŏn's "Prison Journal" is translated from the same book (pp. 69–84). Ch'oe Yangŏp's "Sahyangga" is translated from Kim Ok-hy, ed., *Ch'oe Yangŏp Shinu ŭi Ch'ŏnju kasa I* (Catholic Verses by Father Ch'oe Yangŏp) (Seoul: Kyesŏng Ch'ulp'ansa, 1986), pp. 89–136. The First Declaration by the Priests' Association for the Realization of Justice, on September 26, 1974, is translated from the document provided by the association. "An Interview with Simon Kim" is translated from an article that appeared in *Pyŏnghwa Sinmun* (Peace Newspaper) on November 15, 1998. I wish to thank Professor Cho Kwang of Korea University for his valuable comments and suggestions on an earlier draft of this manuscript.

Further Reading

There is very little literature in Western languages on the history of the Catholic Church in Korea. A classic study is Charles Dallet, *Histoire de l'Eglise de Corée* (Paris: Victore Palme, 1874); this has been translated into Korean, with annotation, by An Ŭngyŏl and Choi Suk-Woo (Ch'oe Sŏgu) as *Han'guk Ch'ŏnjugyohoesa*, 3 vols. (Seoul: Han'guk Kyohoesa Yŏn'guso, 1980). A brief sketch of Catholic history can be found in Choi Suk-Woo, "Korean Catholicism Yesterday and Today," *Korea Journal* 24, no. 8 (1984): 4–13, which also appears in Chai-Shin Yu, ed., *The Founding of Catholic Tradition in Korea* (Mississauga, Ontario: Korea and Related

Studies Press, 1996), pp. 141–60. The Web site of the Catholic Bishops' Conference of Korea (www.cbck.or.kr) contains information on the Catholic Church and its history in both Korean and English. One of the most authoritative monographs in Korean on the history of the Catholic Church in Korea is Yu Hongnyŏl, *Han'guk Ch'ŏnju kyohoe sa* (A History of Catholicism in Korea), 2 vols. (Seoul: K'at'ollik Ch'ulp'ansa, 1994). First published in 1962, this book has been revised several times and has extended its coverage to the early 1970s. For a concise history see especially Cho Kwang, *Han'guk Ch'ŏnju kyohoe sa* (The History of the Catholic Church in Korea), 2 vols. (Seoul: K'ŭrisuch'an, 1990). For claims of the formation of the Catholic Church in Korea during the Hideyoshi Invasion, see Juan Ruiz de Medina, *The Catholic Church in Korea* (Rome: Istituto Storico, 1991); this is John Bridges's translation of Medina's *Origenes de la Iglesia Catolica Coreana* (Rome: Istituto Storico, 1987). See also the several chapters on Korean Catholicism appearing in Robert E. Buswell Jr. and Timothy S. Lee, eds., *Christianity in Korea* (Honolulu: University of Hawaii Press, 2005).

The social upheaval in Chosŏn society prompted by the reception of Catholicism is one of the best-researched areas in Korean Catholicism. See Kŭm Chang-t'ae, "The Doctrinal Disputes between Confucian and Western Thought in the Late Chosŏn Period," in *The Founding of Catholic Tradition in Korea*, edited by Chai-Shin Yu (Mississauga, Ontario: Korea and Related Studies Press, 1996), pp. 7–44. See also the several articles by Donald Baker: "The Martyrdom of Paul Yun: Western Religion and Eastern Ritual in Eighteenth-Century Korea," *Transactions of the Royal Asiatic Society, Korea Branch*, no. 54 (1979): 33–58; "A Confucian Confronts Catholicism: Truth Collides with Morality in Eighteenth-Century Korea," *Korean Studies Forum*, no. 6 (1979–80): 1–44; "Neo-Confucians Confront Theism: Korean Reactions to Matteo Ricci's Arguments for the Existence of God," *Tonga yŏn'gu*, no. 3 (1983): 157–83, and reprinted in *Inculturation* 5, no. 3 (Fall 1990): 43–46.

On the characteristics of Catholic practice in premodern Korea, see Cho Kwang, "The Meaning of Catholicism in Korean History," *Korea Journal* 24, no. 8 (1984): 14–27, which also appears in *The Founding of Catholic Tradition in Korea*, edited by Chai-Shin Yu (Mississauga, Ontario: Korea and Related Studies Press, 1996), pp. 115–40; Ch'oe Ki-Bok, "The Abolition of Ancestral Rites and Tablets by Catholicism in the Chosŏn Dynasty and the Basic Meaning of Confucian Ancestral Rites," *Korea Journal* 24, no. 8 (1984): 41–52; Kim Ok-Hy, "Women in the History of Catholicism in Korea," *Korea Journal* 24, no. 8 (1984): 28–40. For the general characteristics of Catholicism in contemporary Korea, see O Kyŏng-hwan, "Korean Catholicism since 1945," in *The Founding of Catholic Tradition in Korea*, edited by Chai Shin Yu (Mississauga, Ontario. Korea and Related Studies Press, 1996), pp. 161–86. For an overview of the changes in the social participation of Catholics in Korean society, see Donald Baker, "From Pottery to Politics: The Transformation of Korean Catholicism," in *Religion and Contemporary Society in Korea*, edited by Lewis Lancaster and Richard Payne (Berkeley: Institute of East Asian Studies, Korean Monograph Series, University of California, 1997), pp. 127–68.

Several publications have analyzed contemporary Catholic practice based on social science surveys, including William E. Biernatzki et al., *Korean Catholicism in the 1970's* (New York: Orbis Book, 1975). An in-depth and interdisciplinary analysis of Catholic practice seen from both inside and outside the church can be found in Kim Chaedŭk, Pak Munsu, Pak Iryŏng, et al., *Ch'ŏnjugyo wa Han'guk Kŭn-Hyŏndae ŭi sahoemunhwajŏk pyŏndong* (A Study on the Sociocultural Influences of the Korean Catholic Church during the Twentieth Century) (P'aju: Hanul Akademi, 2004). Catholic practice can be compared with that of Buddhists, Protestants, and nonreligious in the surveys collected in *Han'gugin ŭi chonggyo wa chonggyo ŭisik* (The Religions and Religious Consciousness of the Korea People) (Seoul: Korea Survey [Gallup] Polls, 1984, 1990, 1998, 2004).

Yi Suni's "Letter to Her Sisters"

To my sisters,

I would like to say a brief good-bye by writing what I had in my heart during the four years of my marriage, during which time I lived away from you. From the beginning of this year, things became worse and we have been helpless in agony. In the end, my father-in-law was executed. At this point, I no longer strive to live but have decided to offer my life to the Lord at the right time and have prepared myself for this in my heart.

One day several policemen and officers broke into our house and arrested me. This was an opportunity for my wish to be fulfilled, which I had not found earlier. I thanked the Lord for his grace and lost myself in happiness. At the same time, I was at a loss at this sudden intrusion. Desperate cries resounded as they pushed and thrashed people around me. I had to say good-bye to my widowed mother, friends, neighbors and hometown without knowing when I would return. As I had failed to sever my ties with them, I turned my back in a hurry with tears in my eyes. All I hoped was to live a good life with a blessed death.

After staying in [a prison in] the Sugŭpch'ŏng (Receiving Bureau) [in Chŏnju], I was later transferred to a place called the Changgwanch'ŏng (General Officer's Bureau), where I found my mother-in-law, my husband's aunt, and two brothers-in-law [one of them a cousin]. Without speaking, we looked at each other tearfully till night. Because it was the 15th of the Ninth Month, the sky was brightly lit by the full moon. As the moon shone through the window, the thoughts of the people in the prison cell seemed to be revealed. Whether sitting up or lying down, what we all sought was the grace of martyrdom. Full of this hope in our heart, we said the same thing. Five of us promised that we would die for the Lord and each of our wills were as solid as metal and stone. . . . As the days went by, our souls rejoiced in the grace of the Lord, with few worries or worldly concerns.

My only concern, however, was of one person, John, who was in another prison. The reason why I thought of him was that I wanted to pass him a note saying "Let's die together at the same time on the same day," the wish I had had while we were living at home. I hesitated because I could not find the right person to run the errand. When they prohibited altogether communications between prisoners, I lost the opportunity to pass a note to him. . . . My younger brother-in-law was taken out of prison on October 9 without explanation. "Where are you taking him?" "I was told to take him to the bigger prison so that the brothers could stay together." When they abruptly tried to take him, I was ready to accept the sudden separation and said, "Go and stay with your brother. . . . Tell your brother that I wish for us to die at the same time." . . .

Rather than being sorry for the death of these two people, I rejoiced over John's blessedness. However, when my thoughts touched upon "how he faced death," I felt like my heart was being stabbed with a billion knives and my mind was running in many directions. In the afternoon, however, I settled down, possibly thanks to his grace, and was relieved at the thought that the Lord would not abandon him, considering John's achievements over his lifetime. I still kept thinking about him and asked his cousin about him. He said that John had firmly made up his mind for martyrdom from an early stage.

A message arrived from home. When they brought John's corpse home and looked through his clothes, they found a letter to me. In his letter he advised me to keep my faith and consoled me, saying, "My dear sister, let's meet again in heaven." I realized that I worried unnecessarily! . . .

The wish that I had for several years has now come true: when I revealed my wish to him he also told me that he had had the same idea since his youth. As we met each other thanks to a special grace of the Lord, the way to thank Him is to keep our faith even at the cost of our lives. We made a pact: if our parents left us with their property and businesses, we would divide them into three or four and give a portion to the poor, another to his brother so that he could look after his parents, and when we had the freedom of faith, we would lead separate lives.

In the Twelfth Month of last year we were so troubled with sensual temptations that it felt like walking on thin ice or standing at the edge of deep water. We prayed earnestly to the Lord so that we would overcome this temptation. Thanks to his graceful help, we were able to overcome the temptation and keep our celibacy. Our faith became firm and our trust and love for each other became unmovable like a big mountain.

Promising to live as a brother and sister, we lived together for four years until this spring, when he was arrested. For the last four seasons, he has had to wear the same clothes that he wore at the time of his arrest. He had been put in a pillory for eight months and was released from it only before he was to die. I had been worried that he might denounce the Lord and had prayed in tears to die together with him. Who would have known my wish and his earlier death? It is the ultimate grace that he died without denouncing the Lord. There is nowhere in the world that I can find rest: the only place that I long for is heaven.

On the 13th of the Tenth Month, I received the sentence of exile to Pyŏk-tong [in P'yŏngan province] as a public slave. I went to the director of the bureau and said, "Because we revere the Lord, we are willing to be executed as prescribed by law." The director growled at me to depart into exile. . . . As we departed, we prayed even harder that our wish would come true. After a walk of over 100 *ri* [40 kilometers], we were taken back to the prison. How can I thank the Lord enough for this ultimate grace? Even after my death, please thank the Lord for this.

In the first inquisition, I revealed my will to die while revering the Lord. Having quickly reported to their superior, they received the order and called me out of the prison. They reviewed the second sentence, the death penalty, and confirmed my will. I was tortured, put in a pillory, and then put back into a prison cell. . . .

My dear sister-in-law, even if my brother is executed, please do not worry too much. Settle your heart without feeling sorry unnecessarily, but thank the Lord for his grace. Please look after the parents of both houses and your household despite your destitution. . . . Although other virtues are worth acquiring, faith, hope, and love are the most important, above all other virtues. If you practice the three virtues, others will naturally follow. . . .

Having lived with my parents-in-law, I found that they were most happy when I honored their wishes. Being destitute, you may find it hard to support our mother as you wish. If you look after her by obeying and consoling her, her hazy mind will soon be cleared. . . . No matter how sorrowful you may be, conceal your sorrow while thinking of our mother. Please take good care of her by joking with her even if you have to force yourself. . . .

My affection toward my brother John is unforgettable even now when I face my death. I do not have anybody whom I disobey. However, the person that I obey and like the most is my brother John; among woman, it is Saint Agatha. People call him my husband, but I regard him as my true friend. If he went to heaven, he will certainly remember me. When he was in this world living with me, he had the deepest affection for me. If he lives in heaven enjoying all the blessings, he would hear my voice when I call to him secretly in pain. If I keep the promise that we are always reminded of each other, this time we will not live apart. When can I get out of this prison and share the joy of meeting God, our Great King and Great Father, Mary, the Queen of Heaven, my beloved father-in-law, my younger brother-in-law, and my true friend John? . . .

As for my sister-in-law, who was brought up in luxury, she has now lost her parents and brothers. Being deprived of all her property by the Court, she had to leave that big mansion and now lives in an old hut relying on her poor aunt and aged grandmother. Although she was married she could not go to her in-law's house: they still have not decided whether they will take her or not. How can I describe all of her poor and miserable situation? My three brothers-in-law of nine years, six years, and three years old were sent into exile to Hŭksan

Island, Shinji Island, and Kŏje Island, respectively. How heartbreaking and sorrowful is their situation? . . .

From now on till our death, let's accumulate merits through good deeds and all go to heaven by keeping our bodies and souls clean. I wish that we will live happily with God, our Great Father and Mother, and our parents and brothers and sisters. I will constantly plead this to the Lord even after my death. . . .

Yi Kyŏngŏn's "Prison Journal"

. . . In the middle of the night I was taken out to the Changgwanch'ŏng. I thought of my elder sister [the martyr Yi Suni]. "Right! I will follow her footsteps." . . . Before long, the governor called and interrogated me as the Divisional Commander did yesterday. "What is the Heavenly Lord?" "He is the Great King and Great Father who created heaven and earth, angels, human beings and every creature. . . ." "Have you seen him?" "One does not believe in him only after seeing him. Have you seen the builder who built this Sŏnhwadang? We sense sounds, colors, smells, tastes, etc., with our five sense faculties but we distinguish formless principles through our minds." "Tell me all that you have learned." "I know the Ten Commandments, the Seven Overcomings, and the morning and evening prayers." "I have already heard about them all. Can you not denounce your faith?" "I cannot. If children do not serve their father and subjects do not serve their King, it is against filial piety and loyalty. How can I as a human being not serve the Heavenly Lord?" . . .

The following day, I was called to where the governors of Chŏnju, Kosan, Koksŏng, Tongbok, and Chŏngŭp gathered. There I was questioned by the governor of Chŏnju. "You, from a *yangban* family, are different from ignorant commoners. How could you be committed to Catholicism?" "Catholicism does not make distinctions between high and low status, noble and common birth, and fine and ugly appearances. It is concerned only in the distinctions of right and wrong with wisdom and intelligence." . . . I explained the existence of the Heavenly Lord, human nature, the gist of reward and punishment after death, and the Ten Commandments. He said, "These are fallacies: there are no souls, no heaven and hell, no Heavenly Lord. I was told that Catholics refuse to offer ancestral rites and own goods and wives in common. Catholicism is a false teaching that goes against morals and virtues." I replied, "It is true that we do not offer ancestral rites but we do not own either goods or wives in common. . . . We share our goods to support the poor. As for the wives, it is prohibited . . . even to covet another's wife. . . . The governor continued, "Your mother is eighty years old and you have a wife and children. Wouldn't it be better simply to denounce your faith and get out of this prison and see your aged mother and your family?" "In order to see my parents, I would have to betray the Heavenly Lord. Since the Heavenly Lord, the Great Parent, created my mother, how can I forget his grace and betray him? . . ."

Ch'oe Yangŏp's "Hymn of Longing for Home (Sahyangga)"

Hello, my dear friends,
Let us go to find our true hometown [in heaven].
East, West, South, and North, in the four seas and eight directions,
Where is our true hometown?

As for the Blessed Land,
Moses, the saint did not get there.
As for the Garden of Eden,
Adam, the forefather, was banished from there.

Even if you are rich and noble, with glory and prosperity,
For how long would you enjoy it?
Even if you are poor and unfortunate
For how long would you be worried?

The fleeting world as such is
Not the place for us to settle down. . . .

As I observe the profound law
Of creation in the universe,
Neither the valley of weeping nor the place of banishment
Is the right place for us.

Perhaps our paradise is in
Heaven alone and nowhere else,
Where the blessings and pleasures are pure and perfect,
Full of auspiciousness and happiness.
What else would be greater than
Earning the life of eternity? . . .
There is certainly a way to heaven.
But it is hard to get there.

Numerous thieves powerful and thriving
Hide themselves here and there.
As they ambush us on the narrow road
Our journey is far from easy.
Three enemies attack us from outside and
Seven thieves attack us from within.
How can we defeat them,
Empty handed by ourselves? . . .

Let's not use the strategies of Taigong
Nor those of Sunzi.
Let's model ourselves on our Lord Jesus
And King David.

Let's accept the difficulties in the world as our battlefield
Build a castle with perseverance through suffering and
Build the general's podium with the Ten Commandments.
Make the gates with the virtue of wisdom,
The soldiers, with the virtue of charity, and
The horsemen, with the virtue of humility.

Reflection is our manual of strategy,
The Bible is our shield.
The virtue of control is our flag,
The virtue of righteousness, our armor,
The virtue of courage, our horses,
The virtue of faith, our spearhead,
The virtue of hope, our ambush,
The statue of the Lord's suffering, our axes,
The cross, our spears and swords.

After we complete the preparation and
Decide on the strategy of the battle,
Align the seven stands and
Select the eight generals.

As for the enemy of pride,
Defend against it with humility. . . .
As for the enemy of jealousy,
Defend against it with benevolence and love.
As for the enemy of laziness,
Defend against them with diligence. . . .

When we encounter the camp of greed
Let divine poverty take charge of this.
When we encounter the camp of violence
Let goodness take charge of this. . . .

When we are short of strength
While we fight along
On our knees to the Lord,
We will plead for help from heaven.

When we receive the reinforcements
Thanks to the grace of the Father,
We will fight with great ease and
Also gain victory in ease.

Having defeated these thieves
Together with our combined strength
When we complete our journey through the narrow path
There! Awaits the gate to heaven!

The First Declaration by the Priests' Association
for the Realization of Justice

We believe in the importance of human dignity and its vocation. Human beings
are precious because we are created by God in his image and saved by Jesus
Christ, the only Son of God. Hence, human beings have the right to have our
dignity respected in this world, and also have the right and duty to develop and
create an environment which can flower and bear fruit for our call to enjoy perfect and everlasting happiness with God in heaven, which will be fulfilled. . . .

The [Catholic] Church has the right and duty to safeguard human dignity,
vocation, rights of survival, and basic human rights. Therefore, whenever and
wherever such basic rights are infringed, the Church has the right and duty to
protest, resist, and fight against the culprit by speaking for the victims, whoever they might be, to restore their rights.

What is our present situation like? . . . The laws of the so-called *Yusin* constitution destroyed the democratic constitution on November 17, 1972. Through
such meaningless legal procedures as "emergency order" and the abuse of
power, an autocratic ruler is trampling on the basic human rights and dignity of
our citizens. Granting legitimacy to such an abuse of power, the *Yusin* constitution prolongs the rule of the autocrat and allows the governing powers of legis-
lation, administration, and adjudication to be handled by one man. . . . The
government also misleads public opinion by ignoring citizens' right to be informed, prohibiting any type of criticism, and suppressing the media. . . .

We have been expressing and declaring our beliefs through open prayer
meetings held all over the country. The government, however, has so far not
shown any change in its policy in earnest response to this entreaty. Therefore,
as we again confirm our resolutions as follows we urge the government to
awaken and respond earnestly. We declare we will stage a peaceful march as a
rightful and legitimate way of expressing the wish of many citizens.

Our resolution:

1. Abolish the *Yusin* constitution and restore the democratic constitution.
2. Nullify all aspects of the "emergency measures" and release the clergy at
    once, including Bishop Chi Haksun, professors, students, and fighters
    for democracy.
3. Respect citizens' rights of survival and basic human rights and guarantee
    freedom of speech, report, assembly, and association.
4. Establish an economic policy that guarantees a minimum living standard
    and the well-being of the people.

An Interview with Simon Kim

. . . His company has also gone through a massive restructuring. Compared
with June 1997, as many as 50 percent of his company's employees were made

superfluous The cruel waves resulting from the economic crisis of 1997 naturally did not spare Catholics, who make up of 7.9 percent of the whole population. . . .

"As a Catholic, I expected to see something different from me, but I don't. Any layman would feel the gap between what they believe and how they live." Five years ago, as the head of a branch office, he occasionally received private requests from customers for loans. He rejected all of them but one. He kept one million *won* in cash, which a customer left [as a bribe], in his drawer for half a day, but deposited 908,000 *won* back into the customer's account. He then telephoned him, "I spent twenty thousand *won* for a taxi. I have certainly received your money."

In the mid-1980s, when property speculation was at its height, a colleague asked him what he was doing in the weekends. "I play tennis on Saturday afternoons and spend the whole day on Sunday in my parish church." "You are out of your mind! If you worked a little on the weekends you could see a lot of money pouring in." Thanks to his usual weekend trips to nearby Kyŏnggi province in search of land, his colleague now enjoys much wealth. "If I indulged in property speculation, would I have been as faithful even as much as I am now? Salary men are supposed to live on their salaries and not on other extra things." . . .

He and his wife have two daughters, who are preparing for their imminent university entrance exams. Nowadays, he can hardly see his daughters because they come home at 2 o'clock in the morning from "reading rooms" [privately run businesses that provide a space for studying]. He feels sorry for not being of any help to them, exhausted as they are from their studies. . . . "My prayers for my two daughters can be labeled a 'prayer of seeking worldly interest.' However, as I will have a daughter sitting for exams two years in a row, how can I not pray to God for their successful admission?"

He has served in most of the activities in his parish. "Laypeople are supposed to be the agents of a parish but we are too passive and weak in autonomy. Because we do not fulfill our responsibility, we cannot claim our prerogatives. We must consciously be more active and positive, not as 'visitors' to the community but as its 'owners.' The world is changing drastically but we are reluctant to change. Let's reflect on how actively laymen participate in the change and renewal that are taking place in the Catholic Church upon entering the Jubilee of the third millennium."

21

Catholic Rites and Liturgy

Franklin Rausch and Don Baker

The Roman Catholic Church wears the self-assigned label "catholic" with pride. "Catholic" with a small *c* means "universal," and that is how the Roman Catholic Church sees itself. The Catholic Church may be based in Rome, but it boasts that its global hierarchy, with local priests reporting to bishops who report to Rome, ensures a universal uniformity of doctrine and ritual. Catholics expect that, in whatever city in whatever country they find themselves on any given Sunday, they can attend a mass that is essentially just like the mass they would attend anywhere else on earth. The only difference, and one that has appeared only since the 1960s, is the language in which the mass is said. Whereas masses once were said everywhere in Latin, now the mass is said in the vernacular, the language spoken by the congregation that attends that mass.

While it is true that the fundamental doctrines taught in Catholic churches as well as the basic structure of such core rituals as the mass are the same from country to country, an institution as old and as large as the Catholic Church will inevitably exhibit local variations. Catholic leaders themselves recognize not only the existence of such variations but their importance as well. They encourage "inculturation," by which they mean the process by which the universal truths and practices of the Roman Catholic Church are dressed in local costume. That might mean that a Korean priest wears ritual clothing that more closely resembles the clothing his *yangban* aristocratic ancestors wore than it does vestments based on ancient Roman wear. Or it might mean that Korean traditional musical instruments such as the *kayagŭm* zither and the *p'iri* flute are used for the hymns sung during the mass, rather than the organ, the piano, or the guitar. Such adaptation of the nonessentials of Catholic ritual to local traditions is encouraged in the belief that local believers will feel more comfortable with music and clothing that are familiar to them.

Such inculturation is seen occasionally in Korean churches, particularly in masses said on Korean national holidays. However, Koreans normally prefer their priests to wear the same sort of vestments priests wear elsewhere. And they prefer to hear the sort of sacred music they would hear in Catholic churches in other countries (even if the words are sung in a different language). In other words, Korean Catholics are proud to be part of a catholic church, since that means they are part of a global community that constitutes the single largest religious denomination on the face of the earth. They are a minority in South Korea (where only about 8 percent of the population is Catholic), and therefore sometimes need reassurance that they are not alone, that hundreds of millions of other human beings believe the same things they believe and worship God the same way they worship God.

Localization of ritual dress and ritual music is conscious inculturation. This process requires a deliberate decision to differentiate local practices from those of fellow believers from a different cultural background. More common in Korea is unconscious inculturation, in which the broader culture in which Koreans are immersed influences the way they worship, pray, and talk about their faith. Such inculturation appears, for example, in the Korean Catholic emphasis on filial piety, and in ritual displays of love and respect for departed parents and grandparents. Unconscious inculturation also appears in the pride Korean Catholics show in the history of their local church, and in the prayers they pray to, and the shrines they erect for, the martyrs who laid the foundations of the Korean church.

Koreans are proud that 103 of their predecessors in the Korean Catholic Church have been given the highest order the Roman Catholic Church can bestow: they have been canonized as saints, which means that church authorities formally certify that those martyrs, who were tortured and executed during the nineteenth-century persecution of the Catholic Church in Korea, now enjoy eternal life in heaven. That gives Korea more official recognized saints than all but four other nations on the face of the earth. Moreover, Koreans know that there were many more martyrs than that. It is estimated that around ten thousand Koreans were killed by their government between 1791 and 1871 simply for the crime of believing in and practicing Catholicism. First-person accounts by two of those as yet uncanonized martyrs, Yi Suni (1782–1801) and Yi Kyŏngŏn (1792–1827), were translated in the previous chapter.

Korea's Catholics have also traditionally expressed disdain for the things of this world and have shown more interest in life after death than life before death. Korean Catholicism maintained its otherworldly orientation long after the persecution that forced it out of the public realm had ended. Korean Catholics congregated in remote villages, where they supported themselves producing earthenware pots and growing tobacco, unlike Protestants, who began building modern schools and medical facilities soon after they arrived in Korea in 1884. It was not until after the Korean War, in the 1950s, that the Korean Catholic community began to have a significant urban presence. The move from villages to cities, along with enough of an increase in local clergy that Korean priests and bishops finally outnumbered Western missionaries both in parish churches and in bishops' chanceries, brought dramatic change to Catholicism in Korea. A church that had once been persecuted for refusing to use ancestral tablets in ancestor memorial services now devised its own ritual for honoring ancestors, a ritual that can include a plaque on which the name of the ancestor being honored is written. (A suggested script for that ritual is translated in this chapter.) And a church that once fled from the political arena in fear of its life now speaks out boldly on political issues, if it believes those issues have moral implications. In fact, the Catholic clergy provided many of the leaders of Korea's long but eventually successful fight for democracy, from the 1960s through the 1990s. Myŏngdong Cathedral was once a favorite gathering place for pro-democracy activists. It is not surprising that, when Korea had its first peaceful transfer of power in 1997, the man who moved into the presidential offices, Nobel Prize–winning Kim Dae Jung, was a Catholic. His path to the presidency was partially paved by the demands for democratization made by his coreligionists.

Though Korean Catholicism has modernized over the last few decades, it has not abandoned its past. For example, the otherworldly orientation characteristic of premodern Catholicism lingers today, as can be seen in the statements by the modern lay Catholic Simon Kim, which were translated in the preceding chapter. Kim appears to feel slightly guilty about praying for his daughter to get into a good university, and he proudly declares that he is less interested than are his fellow workers in getting rich. In another sign that Korean Catholics have not forgotten their Korean roots, they remain proud of their heritage of martyrs, as can be seen in the prayer to the martyrs (translated later in this chapter) that is said in Korean Catholic churches every September, the month designated in Korea as the month of the martyrs. The Catholic ancestor memorial service is further evidence that Korean Catholics remain Korean. They share with their fellow Koreans a recognition that they are not brought into this world as isolated individuals but are members of families and as such need to show through ritual that they respect and love those who raised them. Catholics all over the world love and honor their parents, of course. Not only is that a normal human emotion, it is also the Fourth Commandment Catholics must obey. However, Koreans go farther than Catholics elsewhere in expressing that love and respect through a specific religious ritual. That is just one aspect of the inculturation that keeps Korean Catholics Korean. Although the Korean Catholic Church is a proud member of a global religious community, it is also proud of its Korean heritage and continues to be both Korean and Catholic.

Catholic Liturgy and Rituals

Other aspects of Korean Catholic practice also show the influence of Korean culture. A similar process of inculturation is seen in the Latin rites used in Korean Catholicism. Though practicing Western Catholics would no doubt have a general idea of what is happening, since the order of the mass is essentially the same, they would notice differences between the way things are done in Korea and in their home parishes. They also may note certain differences in Korean devotional life as well, and although the doctrine may be the same, the emphasis might be very different.

The Mass

The parish is the center of Catholic liturgical life in Korea. However, the way that parishes are named is distinctively Korean. In the West, parish churches are usually dedicated to a saint (such as Saint Paul or John the Baptist) or to a specific devotion (such as Sacred Heart). In Korea, however, parishes are simply named after the areas in which they are located.

Except for some of the older churches, which are built in the traditional cross shape, most of the parish churches in Korea are rectangular and have multiple stories (so as to have space for offices and classrooms, as well as the actual chapel). On the outside of the church, there is usually a cross or a statue of Jesus mounted on the roof. Stained glass is also popular. At one church in Iksan, for example, the stained glass window depicted a number of Koreans in traditional dress (presumably martyrs) surrounding a cross. Many parish churches have some sort of art object depicting Koreans in this way.

On the church grounds, there is often some sort of stone monument with a saying on it. For instance, the stone monument at the same church in Iksan declares, "Go and Proclaim the Gospel." There is also often a large statue of Mary. At another church, in Pusan, this statue had a blue neon halo that was lit on certain occasions. Some Koreans will stop in front of statues, make the sign of the cross, and bow toward the statue. This same act was performed in front of crucifixes as well.

The inside of the typical parish church, like the exterior of the building, is usually rectangular. In addition to some stained glass, there are typically several statues, and the hangings marking the Stations of the Cross. Behind the altar, there is almost always a crucifix. Most of the art resembles what can be seen in a Western parish, though there are occasional differences. For instance, at the Iksan church, sometimes a Korean-style hanging scroll showing the pietà hangs behind the altar.

When entering the chapel itself, Korean Catholics typically cross themselves, using holy water found in a small font. Sometimes during the summer months, sponges soaked in holy water are placed in the font, rather than the usual standing water. Some Korean Catholics also bow toward the altar. Unlike Western Catholics, Korean Catholics do not normally genuflect before sitting down.

Seating is typically in pews, though at the heavily attended masses at Chŏltusan, a holy site famous as a place of mass martyrdom during the nineteenth-century persecutions, mats were available so that people could sit on the floor when the pews filled. The pews almost always have kneelers.

There is a strong tendency among Korean Catholics to choose seats near people of the same age and gender. The emphasis on age difference can also be seen in the schedule of masses: Sunday morning mass is generally attended by older people, and Sunday evening mass is sometimes a sort of folk mass (complete with guitar music) aimed at the youth. Differences in gender are also clearly seen in the seating pattern. For example, women often sit in the pews on the left as you enter the church, and men sit on the right. The center is the most mixed. Women usually outnumber men, a fact that is clearly seen at mass because many Korean women continue the practice of wearing white veils to mass. Thus, a visitor is often confronted with a sea of white veils, with a few islands of the black hair of men and the few women who do not wear veils.

Korean Catholics typically arrive early at mass, and a parish church can be fairly full even ten minutes before mass starts. This time is often used to practice the hymns for the mass. Sometimes, especially at holy sites, people come early to pray to the Stations of the Cross. In Canada and the United States, this devotion is usually practiced during Lent (usually in February until March or April), but in Korea it can occur during the summer as well.

The actual mass, though essentially the same in its order and components as that found in Western countries, does show some liturgical differences. For example, during the entrance song, it is unusual to witness a crucifix carried in procession to the altar as is often the case in North America.

The responses during the mass are also of interest. Firstly, both the priest's part and the responses from the audience are usually chanted in a rather flat style, similar to a chant. Special care is taken during the responses. They are usually not rushed but are said slowly and clearly, especially the Gloria and the Apostle's Creed (which is typically used instead of the Nicene Creed employed by American Catholics during their profession of faith). One interesting characteristic is that there is a line in the Apostle's Creed during which everyone is expected to bow, a practice generally unknown in the United States and Canada.

Another difference occurs while performing the penitential rite. Korean Catholics continue to use the line "my fault, my fault, my great fault," striking their chests lightly three times as they say it. This practice has been discontinued in many areas in the United States and Canada.

Just as the responses often have a flat and chantlike quality to them, Catholic preaching is usually fairly subdued. During the homily, the priest rarely raises his voice, and his body movements and gestures are usually simple.

Korean Catholics excel at singing, often accompanied by an organ. A great deal of time and effort is spent on making quality music. There is even a program on the Catholic broadcasting network showing a music director teaching a choir, complete with sheet music and words on the bottom of the television screen. The music, though often quite simple, has a profound quality to it. There has been some effort to develop and use Korean-style music, though it is not often performed at mass in Korea.

The Eucharist is given special attention in Korean Catholicism. For example, the laypeople who bring the bread and wine to the priest usually wear a white robe, a stole, and white gloves. During the consecration of the Eucharist, at those parts in which a bell would sometimes be rung in the West, a gong is struck instead in Korea. The first time it is struck, the parishioners bow, and the second time it is struck, they stop bowing. This is usually done twice, once for the bread, and once for the wine. Unlike in North America, where both types of communion are usually taken, Koreans usually take only the bread, reserving wine for special occasions. The practice of bowing when there are only one or two people ahead of oneself while waiting for communion, a phenomenon that has just recently started in some areas of the United States, is often practiced in Korea, and was apparently practiced there first.

There are several other differences as well. During the offering, instead of passing a plate or having ushers come with baskets, Korean Catholics usually walk to the basket, pew by pew, and deposit their money in a covered box with a small slot. In addition, during the sign of peace, instead of shaking hands, as is usual in the United States and Canada, Korean Catholics place their palms together and bow toward one another. Kneeling is practiced in most areas in Korea during certain times, such as the consecration, though where kneelers are unavailable, standing and bowing are practiced.

Oftentimes, right after the closing song, when Catholics in North America typically leave, Koreans perform an extra blessing led by a lay Catholic. Mass is typically about an hour long but sometimes can stretch to an hour and a half; on special feast days such as Easter, it may be several hours in length.

One interesting practice is that many people come to the priest after mass to ask him to bless some religious item for them. It is not unusual to see a line formed to ask for the priest's blessing.

Devotional Life

One characteristic of Korean Catholicism, which is however by no means unique to the peninsula, is devotion to the Virgin Mary. The rosary is quite popular, and there are often large statues of Mary at parish churches and even in the homes of Catholics. Catholic paintings and statues frequently depict Mary, often with the child Jesus, as Koreans, wearing traditional Korean dress. Jesus is sometimes dressed as a prince, and in the church at Saenamto in Seoul is shown as a Korean king. Curiously, though this style of art can be seen in Catholic shops and parishes, it is not particularly common in Catholics' homes. There, Western crucifixes and the image of Our Lady of Lourdes are much more popular.

Owing to the martyrdoms from the late eighteenth century (carried out by the Chosŏn dynasty government) into the middle of the twentieth (mostly arising from Communist persecutions during the Korean War), Korea has many holy sites where Koreans will go on pilgrimage. These sites often contain Stations of the Cross, statues of Jesus, Mary, Joseph, and various Korean martyrs, museums, and instruments of torture used on Catholics during the persecutions. The centerpiece is usually the graves of several martyrs, often set up in Korean fashion with a large, grass-covered, earthen mound. Korean Catholics often make a deep bow (*sebae*) toward these graves. In addition, while praying in front of the tabernacle, where the consecrated hosts are kept (in Catholic belief, the consecrated bread is believed truly to be the body of Jesus), Korean Catholics perform a *sebae*. Special respect is also given to parents, and a prayer book may include have a prayer specifically for parents, something that is often not present in American prayer books.

The way in which the dead are treated in Korea shows important cultural characteristics. In Korean Catholic funerals, for example, mourners related to the deceased wear white robes and rope belts. Other mourners are led into a small room where a picture of the deceased, various fruits, and crosses are set up on a table. There prayers are chanted for the deceased.

Koreans not only carry out the traditional practice of having masses said for the dead but may have a group mass, followed by a trip to the cemetery to clean the graves. Korean Catholics are allowed to carry out a variation of traditional Confucian ancestral rites, provided that they do not believe in certain things inconsistent with Catholic doctrine, such as that the spirits need to be fed.

Finally, it should be noted that Korean Catholics produce and appear to read a great many books. There are several large Catholic bookstores in Korea, with the majority of titles written by Koreans. There are even Korean Catholic comics. One specific comic, "*Sabunim, Sabunim,*" about the adventures of several Western monks in the Middle Ages, is even being made into a cartoon for the Catholic Peace Broadcasting Station.

Thus, although Korean Catholicism is firmly within the bounds of orthodoxy established by the Catholic Church, it shows its own unique cultural characteristics. The emphasis on singing, variations in the liturgy, and the presence of the Korean martyrs make for a distinctly Korean variety of Catholic culture.

The script for the Catholic ancestor memorial service is translated from *K'at'ollik kidosŏ* (A Catholic Prayer Manual) (Seoul: Han'guk Ch'ŏnjugyo Chungang Hyŭbŭihoe, 2004), pp. 33–35. The text can also be found on the Web, at http://fr.catholic.or.kr/jhs/liturgy/sacrifice.htm (accessed April 15, 2005). The prayer to the Korean martyrs was published in *Meil Misa* (Daily Mass), September 2004, published by the Catholic Conference of the Republic of Korea.

Further Reading

Joseph Chang-mun Kim and John Jae-sun Chung, eds., *Catholic Korea Yesterday and Today* (Seoul: Catholic Press, 1964), offers a comprehensive history of Catholicism in Korea up to the 1950s. More accessible are the various articles translated in Chai-shin Yu, ed., *The Founding of Catholic Tradition in Korea* (Mississauga, Ontario: Korean and Related Studies Press, 1996), though this book is marred by the uneven quality of the translations. There are also a number of articles in the August 1984 issue of *Korea Journal* (24:8), which was dedicated to an examination of Korean Catholicism. Those articles include Kwang Cho, "The Meaning of Catholicism in Korean History," 14–27; Suk-woo Choi, "Korean Catholicism Yesterday and Today," 4–13; Ok-hy Kim, "Women in the History of Catholicism in Korea," 28–40; and Ki-Bok Ch'oe, "The Abolition of Ancestral Rites and Tablets by Catholicism in the Chosŏn Dynasty and the Basic Meaning of Confucian Ancestral Rites," 41–52. For a short summary of the history of Korean Catholicism from its beginnings to the present day, see Don Baker, "From Pottery to Politics: The Transformation of Korean Catholicism," in *Religion and Society in Contemporary Korea*, edited by Lewis R. Lancaster and Richard K. Payne (Berkeley: Institute of East Asian Studies, University of California, Berkeley, Center for Korean Studies, 1997).

Ancestor Memorial Rites

This manual outlines three different types of ancestor memorial rites. It is provided for those Catholics who wish to perform such rituals. Catholics are not obligated to do so.

I. ANCESTOR MEMORIAL SERVICES FOR IMMEDIATE FAMILY MEMBERS

This type of ancestor rite can be used on the anniversary of the death of the ancestor who is to be honored, either on New Year's Day, during the Harvest Moon Festival, or on Hansik (the day in spring designated for visits to the graves of ancestors).

Preparation

1. Mental Preparation: Ask yourself if you have any neighbors with whom you are not getting along. If there are any such neighbors, promise yourself that you will reconcile with them. Also, purify your heart through the sacrament of confession.

2. Physical Preparation: In the days preceding the ancestor memorial rite, make sure that you do not drink so much alcohol that you become inebriated. Also, make sure you do not give into gluttony and overeat. If possible, you and members of your family should look around your neighborhood to see if there is anyone who may need assistance. If there is, offer to help them. The day before the ancestor memorial service, take a bath. The day you are to perform this ritual, put on somber clothing appropriate for a ritual of remembrance.

3. Preparation of the Table: The day before conducting the ancestor rites, tidy up your house inside and out. Inspect the table to be used for holding the food

for the ancestor rites to ensure that nothing is wrong with it. Clean and polish the utensils that will be used for the ancestor rites.

Order of the Ceremony Itself

4. Once everything is ready and the portrait of the ancestor (or an ancestral table) has been placed on the ritual table, the chief mourner calls for the start of the ancestor memorial service and makes the sign of the cross.

5. All those attending bow twice in unison.

6. Next, the chief mourner steps forward and kneels down in front of the portrait (or the ancestral table). He lights incense. He then takes a cup and pours wine three times into a ritual vessel prepared for just that purpose. After that, he gives the cup to his assistant, who places that cup on the ritual table and then takes the top off a bowl of white rice. The chief mourner bows twice and retires. The others in attendance approach the ritual table one by one and offer wine as well. However, they offer wine only once. The chief mourner is the only one who offers wine three times.

7. When this part of the ritual is over, the chief mourner reports to the ancestor:

> Through the grace of God,
> Today we are able once again to pay you ritual respect.
> Please accept this clear wine and these various foods
> As an expression of our sincerity and our respect for you.
> Because you are always in our hearts,
> We are performing this ritual today.
> We ask you to please pray for us
> That we will act in accordance with the will of the Lord
> And will love one another and live together harmoniously.

8. The chief mourner asks those in attendance to think about the ancestor while listening to the following words:
The apostle Paul, quoting the words of the prophet Isaiah, says to us thusly: "But as it is written: 'What eye has not seen, and ear has not heard, and what has not entered the human heart, what God has prepared for those who love him'"
(1 Corinthians 2, 9); in addition, he also says: "None of us lives for oneself, and no one dies for oneself. For if we live, we live for the Lord, and if we die, we die for the Lord; so then, whether we live or die, we are the Lord's. For this is why Christ died and came to life, that he might be Lord of both the dead and the living" (Romans 14, 7–9).
Believing what the Bible says, we know that (insert ancestor's name here) is enjoying eternal happiness in heaven and is one with us in the Lord. We also believe that he (she) is praying for us. We are all one people in the Lord.
(The chief mourner may read a different passage from the Bible, if he so desires.)

9. Next, the lady of the house steps forward to the ritual table and places a spoon on top of the rice in the open bowl. The chief mourner and all those in attendance bow twice. After bowing, those present should quietly think about the ancestor for a short while.

10. Then the chief mourner (who is the head of the family) and the lady of the house fill a soup bowl with cold water or scorched rice tea and place it on the ritual table.

11. As the chief mourner and all those in attendance bow twice in unison, they say their good-byes. At the close of this ancestor memorial service, the ancestor's family and close relatives resolve to strengthen their familial ties, and then sing a song of thanksgiving to the Lord.

12. After putting away the portrait (or ancestor tablet), those in attendance share the wine and the food. This shared meal is important because it is a meal of love and harmony that will deepen the familial ties uniting the departed and the living.

II. ANCESTOR MEMORIAL SERVICES ON HOLIDAYS

Preparation

1. Clean every part of the house and make sure that the room where the ancestor memorial service will be conducted is properly prepared for the ceremony.

2. Take a bath and wear appropriate clothing.

3. Purify the heart through the sacrament of confession.

4. Putting all pretensions aside, place on the ritual table food that the family likes, rather than fancy dishes.

5. On the ritual table place two candles and some flowers; it is also acceptable to light incense.

6. Hang a crucifix on the wall behind that table and place a picture of the ancestor below the crucifix. If you do not have a picture to place there, neatly write the ancestor's name and respectfully place it below that crucifix.

7. Place a clean mat or cushion in front of the ritual table.

Mass

If it is at all possible, have the entire family attend mass together that morning. In church, join with everyone present there to pray for ancestors and their descendants and offer thanks and praise to God.

The Ancestor Memorial Rite

8. Make the sign of the cross.

9. Hymn: Choose a song from the Catholic hymnal to sing (for example, no. 28, no. 423, no. 480, no. 50, or another such hymn).

10. Reading: Choose from among the verses listed below and read them aloud reverently: John 14, 1–14; John 15, 1–12; John 17, 1–26; Luke 2, 41–52; Matthew 5, 1–12; Romans 9, 1–18; Romans 12, 1–21; 1 Corinthians 13, 1–13; Ephesians 5, 6–20.

11. Address by the Head of the Family.

   A. He introduces the ancestor and talks about the family's precepts and traditions, and things the ancestor said.

   B. He talks about the family's situation at the present time and prospects for the future.

   C. He talks about living sincerely in accordance with God's word, and in accordance with the final injunctions of the ancestor. He urges family members to vow to maintain love and unity among themselves through dialogue.

12. Deep Bow: The mourners, one by one, make a full bow before the portrait of the deceased (do not differentiate between men and women when determining the order in which they offer their bows).

13. *The Apostle's Creed*:

   I believe in God,
   The Father almighty, creator of heaven and earth.
   I believe in Jesus Christ,
   his only Son, our Lord.
   (All bow during the two lines below)
   He was conceived by the power of the Holy Spirit,
   and born of the Virgin Mary.
   He suffered under Pontius Pilate,
   Was crucified, died, and was buried.
   He descended to the dead.
   On the third day he rose again.
   He ascended into heaven,
   and is seated at the right hand of the Father.
   He will come again to judge
   The living and the dead.
   I believe in the Holy Spirit,
   The holy catholic church,

The communion of saints,
The forgiveness of sins,
The resurrection of the body,
And the life everlasting.
Amen.

A Prayer for Parents

Oh Merciful God,
You have commanded us to love and respect our parents,
And to be grateful to them for all they have done for us.
We will obey, and will serve our parents with complete filial piety.
Our parents brought us into this world and raised us,
Cheerfully overcoming many obstacles along the way.
We now understand how much they have done for us
And pray that you will let them pass their remaining days peacefully.
Lord, by your grace, protect our parents and
When they have passed on, let them enjoy eternal happiness.
We ask this through our Lord, Christ.
Amen.

A Prayer for One's Children

God, who created this world in which we live,
You also have created precious sons and daughters for us.
We pray that we may raise our children in the love of the Lord
and have them manifest the glory of the Lord.
Lord, may our beloved sons and daughters
be protected by your Divine Providence.
Do not let them be stained by the corruption of this world.
Shield them against the many temptations to evil this world contains.
Taking Jesus as our example,
Let us become workers accomplishing the will of the Lord.
We ask this through our Lord Christ.
Amen.

A Prayer for Married Couples

Benevolent God the Father,
For bringing us together as man and wife
Through the sacrament of marriage,

And for watching over us, we thank you.
As we renew our marriage vows today,
Help us to remain faithful to that vow
Whether we are happy or troubled,
Whether we are rich or poor,
Whether we are healthy or ill.
Through good times and bad,
Help us preserve mutual love and respect
And help us continue to be trustworthy and loyal.
We also pray that our life together,
In which we always glorify you,
Will become a sacramental manifestation of your love for us.
We ask this through Christ Our Lord. Amen.

A Prayer for the Family

Jesus, you who sanctified family life
By living a life of obedience to Mary and Joseph,
Please bless our family as well.
Help us model our family on the Holy Family
And live in accordance with the will of the Lord.
Saint Mary and Saint Joseph, we pray to you
Keep our family members healthy and happy,
Help us serve the Lord at all times,
Help us love our neighbors,
And help us through the grace of the Lord
Join the Family that lives forever in heaven.

14. Those present offer prayers for universal intentions.

15. Hymn: Choose one of the hymns in the Catholic hymnal (such as no. 50).

16. *The Lord's Prayer*: said aloud in unison.

Our Father, who art in heaven,
Hallowed be thy name,
Thy kingdom come,
Thy will be done on earth as it is in heaven.
Give us this day our daily bread,
And forgive us our trespasses
As we forgive those who trespass against us,
And lead us not into temptation,
But deliver us from evil.
Amen.

17. Meal: Share the food offered in the ancestor memorial service as a meal of love and harmony.

18. Finish the ceremony by making the sign of the cross.

It is possible to reverse the order of the mass and the ancestor memorial service according to the schedule of the church in which it is held.

III. ANCESTOR MEMORIAL SERVICES FOR THE GENERAL PUBLIC

Preparations

1. In order to prepare yourself spiritually, go to confession and purify your mind. Then recall memories of the deceased ancestor.

2. To prepare yourself physically, cleanse your body with a bath, make sure you behave in a fashion appropriate for a day in which such a ritual of remembrance will be held, and put on clothes that are the most appropriate for such a somber rite.

3. Clean your house inside and outside, being especially careful to make sure that everything in is order in the room where the ritual will be held. Place a crucifix on the wall and then place a picture of the ancestor beneath the crucifix. Also, place candles and incense on the ritual table. At that time, you may also place on the ritual table the ritual food you have painstakingly prepared and decorate the ritual table with flowers.

The Memorial Service on the Anniversary of a Death

4. When announcing that the ceremony is about to begin, explain for whom the ancestor memorial service that day is being held.

5. You may bring in a portrait of the deceased while a hymn is sung.

6. The chief mourner offers incense; all present join with the chief mourner in bowing twice.

7. Say an opening prayer.

8. Read a Psalm of Condolence (for example, Psalm 130 or Psalm 51).

9. Bible Reading: Sirach 3, 1–16; John 15, 1–17; 1 John 3, 14–18, Ephesians 5, 5–20, or other similar readings.

10. The chief mourner speaks briefly: Drawing on the words just read from the Bible, the chief mourner discusses the meaning of this memorial service, the dying injunctions of the ancestor, family traditions, or similar appropriate matters.

11. *The Apostle's Creed*:

> I believe in God,
> The Father almighty, creator of heaven and earth.
> I believe in Jesus Christ,
> His only Son, our Lord.
> (Everyone bows while the two lines below are said.)

He was conceived by the power of the Holy Spirit,
and born of the Virgin Mary.
He suffered under Pontius Pilate,
Was crucified, died, and was buried.
He descended to the dead.
On the third day he rose again.
He ascended into heaven,
And is seated at the right hand of the Father.
He will come again to judge
The living and the dead.
I believe in the Holy Spirit,
The holy catholic church,
The communion of saints,
The forgiveness of sins,
The resurrection of the body,
And the life everlasting.
Amen.

12. Pray for Universal Intentions: At this time, when you pray for universal intentions, you may offer an ad hoc prayer or offer a standard prayer instead.

13. Light the Incense and Pay Your Respects to the Departed: At this time, you may present wine, fruit, food, flowers, and other such objects. When there are many people participating in this memorial service, you may have representatives present such offerings instead of having each person do so individually.

14. Say a few words in memory of the departed.

15. Meditation: Remain silent for a while, reminding yourself how grateful you are to the deceased for all he did for you while asking at the same time that he forgive you for all your transgressions against him. Resolve to live a better life from now on and ask your ancestor to intercede on your behalf that you may receive the grace necessary to do so.

16. Everyone bows to those around them in a greeting of love and reconciliation.

17. *The Lord's Prayer*:

Our Father, who art in heaven,
Hallowed be thy name,
thy kingdom come,
Thy will be done on earth as it is in heaven.
Give us this day our daily bread,
And forgive us our trespasses

As we forgive those who trespass against us,
And lead us not into temptation,
But deliver us from evil.
Amen.

18. The Doxology
(Everyone bows while saying the first line)

Glory be to the Father, and to the Son, and to the Holy Spirit.
As it was in the beginning,
is now, and ever shall be, world without end.
Amen.

19. Bow to those around you before you take your leave.

20. Closing Hymn: You may return the portrait of the departed to its usual location while the closing hymn is being sung.

21. Sharing the Ritual Offerings: This banquet of love and harmony strengthens good relations with the ancestors and harmony among family members.

Communal Prayer to the Korean Martyrs to Be Used during September, the Month of the Martyrs

LEADER: All ye martyrs of this land, because of the strength you gained through the grace bestowed by God, with your firm faith you shed your blood for the Gospel, the Church, and your love of Jesus Christ.

ALL: While we are engaged in a fierce battle with the evils of this world, you sing the glory of the victory you have won and praise God, who is the origin of all there is. Please pray to God for us.

LEADER: Great martyrs, please join with Holy Mary, the Queen Mother in Heaven above, to pray for us and obtain God's mercy for us.

ALL: We pray even now, when there are forces of darkness persecuting our church, that God will envelop our church with his almighty arms and protect it. We ask God to extend his saving grace even into those corners of the world that still lie in darkness.

LEADER: Brave martyrs, we have a special request for you. Please pray to God for our country.

ALL: You suffered so much while you were alive in this world and even ended up sacrificing your lives.

LEADER: Please pray to Almighty God for us that the church in Korea will continue to grow larger every day and will produce more priests.

ALL: Also, ask God on our behalf to help the faithful keep his commandments, to help those whose fervor has cooled to become devout again, to help our divided Christian community become one in the same faith, and to help nonbelievers awaken to the true faith so that they can find God and come to know that he is the Savior of humanity and the creator of heaven and earth.

LEADER: Truly glorious martyrs, when we think of that glorious crown you now wear, we rejoice. We sincerely entreat you to intercede with God, our merciful Father, on our behalf that he may grant us, our relatives, and our benefactors the grace we need to follow your example of fidelity to our faith.

ALL: In addition, ask God to help us consistently confess our steadfast faith in Christ as long as we live on this earth, so that even if we have not had to shed our blood for our faith, with the grace of the Lord supporting us, we will nevertheless be welcome in heaven after we die.

LEADER: Saint Andrew Kim Daegun, Saint Paul Chong Hasang, and your fellow martyrs.

ALL: Please pray for us.

22

Conversion Narratives in

Korean Evangelicalism

Timothy S. Lee

A hallmark of Evangelicalism is conversion experience. In his landmark work, *Encyclopedia of Evangelicalism*, Randall Balmer states, "Conversion, from the Latin *conversio* (meaning 'turning toward'), is the centerpiece of evangelical faith and piety, a definite and decisive transformation from sinfulness to 'salvation.'" In another important work, *The Westminster Handbook of Evangelical Theology*, Roger E. Olson states:

> If the evangelical movement is about anything, it is about the call to conversion to Christ. The best-known example of this to the modern mind is evangelist Billy Graham's mass appeal and the responses of thousands who stream forward at his evangelistic crusades to "receive Christ as their personal savior" . . . and conversion is salvation's initial or crucial event. It is the event . . . in which an individual responds to the call of God with repentance and faith and receives from God regeneration (being 'born again') and justification (forgiveness and declaration of righteousness). . . . For evangelicals, conversion to Christ may be part of a process, but it is not identical with baptism nor is it merely turning over a new leaf. . . . Without eschewing sacraments or Christian education, evangelicals insist that authentic Christian life comes into existence through personal conversion, even if that is the culmination of a process that begins with infant baptism and/or Christian nurture. (pp. 160–61)

Given these attestations, it is not surprising that conversions have occurred regularly in Korean Evangelicalism—or that Korean evangelicals, when narrating their faith journeys, almost invariably reflect on their conversion experiences. This chapter contains four such narratives, all of them classic. Three of these—those of Kil Sŏnju, Ch'oe Chasil, and Han Kyŏngjik—were translated from their Korean originals; the fourth—that of the Great Revival of 1907—is in its original English text.

The Great Revival of 1907

This narrative was authored not by a Korean but by an American Presbyterian missionary to Korea, Graham Lee (1861–1916), who witnessed the collective conversion event that occurred three years before Korea was annexed by Japan. A watershed event in Korean Protestantism, the revival indelibly marked the Korean Protestant church as evangelical, just as the Great Awakening of the eighteenth century did for the American Protestant church. In January 1907, Lee participated in one of the key events of the revival. Two months later, he had his recollection of that event published as an article, reproduced here, entitled "How the Spirit Came to Pyeng Yang," in *Korea Mission Field*, the leading missionary journal in Korea at the time.

Kil Sŏnju (1869–1935)

The second narrative comes from the biography *Yŏnggye Kil Sŏnju* (*Kil Sŏnju, the Spiritual Stream*). Kil Sŏnju was a pivotal figure among the first generation of Korean Protestants and appears in Lee's account mentioned earlier. In September 1907 in P'yŏngyang, where the spirit of the revival still lingered, Kil was ordained into the ministry of the newly established Presbytery of Korea, one of the first to be so ordained. Thereafter, until his death, Kil was a highly revered churchman and revivalist of the Korean church. He was especially renowned as an initiator of the *saebyŏk kidohoe* (daybreak prayer devotional), for his relentless premillenarian preaching, and as a signatory to the declaration of independence that unleashed the 1919 March First Independence Movement, a pivotal event in modern Korean history.

In his late teens, Kil set upon an intensive spiritual quest. This quest immersed him in Sŏndo—a native occultism that blended elements of shamanism, Buddhism, Confucianism, and Daoism—becoming quite proficient at it in his late twenties, endowing him with extraordinary abilities, such as the ability to break a stone with his bare fist. Even so, he was not satisfied; he yearned for something more. At this point, a friend, Kim Chongsŏp, handed him a Korean translation of John Bunyan's *Pilgrim's Progress*. Earlier Kim had urged Kil to pray to Hananim, the native Korean term for God; Kil rebuffed him, insisting that Samnyŏng Sin'gun (Kingly Spirit of the Three Spiritual Realms), to whom he had been accustomed to praying, was just as worthy as Hananim. Kim then suggested to him to pray continually to Samnyŏng sin'gun—asking the deity to reveal to him whose is the true Way (*to*), Jesus' or that of Samnyŏng Sin'gun. The excerpt begins with Kil reading the Puritan classic, which eventually led to his dramatic conversion experience.

Ch'oe Chasil (Choi Ja Shil) (1915–89)

Ch'oe is another remarkable leader of Korean Evangelicalism. She is often discussed in the same breath as the Yŏido Full Gospel Church, which at the start of the twenty-first century is regarded as having the world's largest congregational membership, with more than seven hundred thousand members. This tendency is not surprising, since Ch'oe was a cofounder of this church, along with Cho Yonggi, the senior minister of the church, who eventually became her son-in-law. Ch'oe, twenty-one years older than Cho, met the latter at Full Gospel Bible Institute in Seoul, where she was the most fervent evangelist, he the top student. After graduation, in May 1958, they collaborated to found a tent church in an impoverished section of Seoul known as Pulgwangdong. In time the church grew by leaps and bounds—many of the parishioners reported experiencing healing and changed lives. In 1961, with the help of Pentecostal missionaries from the United States, the congregation moved to another section of the city, Sŏdaemun, to worship in a structure made of prefabricated building materials. The structure was large enough to accommodate fifteen hundred people. By 1966, the attendance increased to five thousand compelling Cho and Ch'oe to hold three services each Sunday; two years later, three thousand more were added to the church, and more were coming. Then in April 1969, the church held a groundbreaking service at Yŏido, a man-made islet in the middle of the Han River, then largely undeveloped and unoccupied; in 1973, the church held its first service in the new Yŏido Sanctuary, having already passed the ten thousand membership mark in the previous year.

Throughout this period, Ch'oe served in tandem with Cho as the top leader of the church. In deference to Korea's patriarchal culture, she did not contest her son-in-law's paramountcy in the church. She was content to remain as an evangelist, traveling throughout Korea and other countries to disseminate the gospel of Pentecostalism, all the while modeling a prayerful life; in 1972 she was formally ordained into the ministry by Japanese Assemblies of God, whereupon she became a collaborating minister at Yŏido Full Gospel Church. She died while visiting Los Angeles in 1989.

The excerpt in this chapter is taken from a section of her autobiography, Nanŭn Halleluya ajumma yŏtta (I Was a Hallelujah Mama), published in 1978. The book relates Ch'oe's life from childhood to her heyday as a leader in Yŏido Full Gospel Church. The excerpted portion is preceded by an account of Ch'oe's life as daughter of an impoverished single-parent household (her father died when she was six), led by a mother who eked out a living as a seamstress but who was devout in the Holiness tradition of the Protestant church. It tells of Ch'oe's efforts to break away from poverty, becoming a nurse, and marriage. It also tells of her backsliding in faith, success as a businesswoman, and estrangement from her husband. It then describes the bereavement of her daughter, the bankruptcy of her business, and her descent into despair.

Seeing no way out of the despair, Ch'oe resolved to die by starvation in Seoul's Samgak Mountain. On that mountain, she unexpectedly encountered an old friend, who, upon learning of Ch'oe's plan, insisted that she participate in a revival that was going on nearby. Ch'oe at first rebuffed the suggestion but then allowed herself to be taken to the revival, where she underwent a chungsaeng ŭi ch'ehŏm (experience of rebirth), the title of the section from which the excerpt was taken.

Han Kyŏngjik (Han Kyung Jik) (1902–2000)

Han was arguably the most influential Protestant minister in Korea in the second half of the twentieth century. Born in northern Korea, he attended mission schools there before going to the United States to receive further education. In the United States, he earned a bachelor's degree from Emporia College in Kansas and a divinity degree from Princeton Theological Seminary, graduating from the latter in 1929. Ordained in 1933 by the Presbyterian Church of Korea, he served Second Presbyterian Church of Sinŭiju for nine years. In December 1945, due to Communist repression of Christians in the North, Han migrated to the South. In Seoul he founded Yŏngnak (Youngnak) Presbyterian Church. Initially the church consisted largely of northern refugees; in time, southerners also joined, and it grew rapidly. By the time of his death in 2000, Yŏngnak was one of the largest Presbyterian churches in the world, with sixty thousand members.

Han was a moderate evangelical who embraced ecumenism and guided Korea's mainstream Presbyterianism away from extreme fundamentalism. In his lifetime, he founded more than five hundred churches around the world and established numerous schools and social service institutions. He provided leadership for many national and international bodies, including the Korean National Council of Churches and the World Vision of Korea. He also received many accolades, including the 1992 Templeton Award.

The excerpt here is a translation of a sermon he delivered in July 1955, entitled "Yŏngsaeng ŭi hwaksin" (The Certainty of Eternal Life). In it, Han redefines "rebirth," or "being born again" (chungsaeng), as when one's old sinful life is transformed into a new spirit-filled life. Along the way he stresses an evangelical refrain that merely going through the rituals of Christianity does not lead to salvation: salvation, he insists, must accompany a personal experience of conversion, even if it is not an instantaneous and dramatic experience but the culmination of many years of Christian nurturing. In making this point, he adduces his own experience of conversion.

Graham Lee's report, "How the Spirit Came to Pyeng Yang," is reprinted from the *Korea Mission Field* 3, no. 3 (March 1907): 33–37. The account of Kil Sŏnju's conversion experience appears in Kil Chin'gyŏng, *Yŏnggye Kil Sŏnju* (Kil Sŏnju, the Spiritual Stream) (Seoul: Chongno Sŏjŏk, 1980), pp. 70–72; Yŏnggye (Spiritual Stream) is Kil's pen name; the author is Kil Sŏnju's son. Ch'oe Chasil's conversion experience appears in her autobiography, *Nanŭn Halleluya ajumma yŏtta* (I Was a Hallelujah Mama) (Seoul: Sŏul Sŏjŏk, 1978), pp. 121–26. Han Kyŏngjik's sermon "Yŏngsaeng ŭi hwaksin" (The Certainty of Eternal Life) about the experience of "rebirth" is translated from *Han Kyŏngjik moksa sŏlgyo chŏnjip* (Anthology of the Sermons of Rev. Han Kyŏngjik) (Seoul: Kidokkyo Munsa, 1987), vol. 2, pp. 61–66.

Further Reading

Randall Balmer, *Encyclopedia of Evangelicalism*, revised and expanded edition (Waco, Tex.: Baylor University Press, 2004); William N. Blair and Bruce Hunt, *The Korean Pentecost and the Suffering Which Followed* (Carlisle, Pa.: Banner of Trust, 1977); Robert E. Buswell Jr. and Timothy S. Lee, eds., *Christianity in Korea* (Honolulu: University of Hawaii Press, 2005); Kim Ig-jin, *History and Theology of Korean Pentecostalism: Sunbogeum (Pure Gospel) Pentecostalism* (Zoetermeer: Uitgeverij Boekencentrum, 2003); Timothy S. Lee, "Born-Again in Korea: The Rise and Character of Revivalism in (South) Korea, 1885–1988" (Ph.D. diss., University of Chicago, 1996); Timothy S. Lee, "The Great Revival of 1907 in Korea: Its Evangelical and Political Background," *Criterion* 40, no. 2 (2001): 10–17; L. George Paik, *The History of Protestant Missions in Korea: 1832–1910* (1927; repr., Seoul: Yonsei University Press, 1987); Roger E. Olson, *The Westminster Handbook to Evangelical Theology* (Louisville: Westminster John Knox Press, 2004).

The Great Revival of 1907

In August, 1906, we Pyeng Yang [P'yŏngyang] missionaries had a Bible Conference which lasted one week, and the object of which was the deepening of our own spiritual life. Dr. Hardie of Won San came and helped us greatly. At that meeting was born the desire in our hearts that God's Spirit would take complete control of our lives and use us mightily in His service. Immediately after our conference we went to Seoul to attend our Annual Meeting, and there met Dr. Howard Agnew Johnston, from whom the Seoul missionaries had received a great blessing. Dr. Johnston came to Pyeng Yang and while here spoke to our Korean Christians, telling of the wonderful manifestations of the Spirit in India, and his telling of it gave some of our people a great desire to have the same blessing. From that time until the blessing came Koreans and missionaries have been praying that it might come.

We returned from Annual Meeting and held some special services, praying for an outpouring of God's Spirit, but at that time did not receive the answer. The Koreans enjoyed the meetings, but the Spirit was not with us in power. We kept on praying however, and at Christmas time there was born in the hearts of us missionaries a desire to have a special week of prayer. This we had with great benefit to us all. Before these meetings closed out Winter Training Class for men had begun and about seven hundred men spent two weeks here in Bible study. God gave us a great desire in our hearts to have a special blessing on this class, so we Presbyterian missionaries agreed to meet every day at noon and pray for the class. This we did with great profit to ourselves, for those noon prayer meetings were a very Bethel to us.

On January 6th, we began evening meetings for the class and the people of the city in the Central Church, the four Presbyterian churches uniting.

Knowing the building would be too small if we had a mixed audience, we arranged the meeting for men only, asking the women to meet separately in four different places and the school boys to meet in the Academy chapel. The Central Church will hold about fifteen hundred people and it was full every night. The meetings grew in power each evening until Saturday evening, and that meeting was the best of all the week. On Sunday we had the regular services in all the churches, and then Sunday evening we gathered again at the Central Church in a continuation of the union meetings. We expected great things from that Sunday evening meeting, but instead of receiving a great blessing we had a most peculiar experience. The meeting seemed dead and God's Spirit seemed to have departed from us. After an address and a few perfunctory testimonies, which testified to nothing, we went home with heavy hearts, wondering where the trouble lay. During the meetings before there had been testimonies which had life in them and confessions of sin which were real and earnest, but Sunday night everything seemed blocked and the meeting a dead formal meeting. The Korean brethren felt just the same as we missionaries, and Sunday night was a night of gloom. At our noon meeting on Monday we cried to God for help, and God heard us, for on Monday evening the blessing came.

We went to that Monday evening service, not knowing what would happen, but praying all the time that God would hear and answer. When we reached the building I think we all felt that something was coming. After a short address we had audible prayer together, all the audience joining in, and this audible prayer, by the way, has been one of the features of these meetings. After the prayer there were a few testimonies, and then the leader announced a song, asking the audience to rise and stating that all those who wished to go home could do so, as we intended to stay until morning, if there were men who wished to remain that long and confess their sins. A great many went, but between five and six hundred remained. These we gathered into one ell of the building, and then began a meeting the like of which none of us had ever seen. After prayer, confessions were called for, and immediately the Spirit of God seemed to descend on that audience. Man after man would rise, confess his sins, break down and weep, and then throw himself to the floor and beat the floor with his fists in a perfect agony of conviction. My own cook tried to make a confession, broke down in the midst of it, and cried to me across the room "Pastor tell me, is there any hope for me, can I be forgiven?" and then he threw himself to the floor and wept and wept, and almost screamed in agony. Sometimes after a confession the whole audience would break out in audible prayer, and the effect of that audience of hundreds of men praying together in audible prayer was something indescribable. Again after another confession they would break out in uncontrollable weeping, and we would all weep, we couldn't help it. And so the meeting went on until two o'clock A.M. with confession and weeping and praying. A few of us knew that there had been hatred in the hearts of some of the prominent men of the church, especially between a Mr. Kang and Mr. Kim, and we hoped that it would all come out and be confessed during these meetings. Monday night Mr. Kang got the strength and told how he had hated Mr. Kim and asked to be forgiven. It was wonderful to see that proud, strong man break down and then control himself and then break down again as he tried to tell how he had hated Mr. Kim. When two o'clock came there were still men who wished to confess, but as the building was growing cold, and as we had still another evening, we thought it best to close.

Tuesday noon at our prayer meeting we missionaries met with hearts full of thanksgiving for the wonderful meeting of the evening before, and again we asked God for greater blessings on the Tuesday evening meeting. We conducted the service in the same way as on Monday. After an address by Mr. Kil, our most gifted Korean preacher, we dismissed all those who wished to go home, and again nearly six hundred remained. The meeting was much the same as the Monday evening meeting, but the manifestation was greater. Some of us were praying for two men especially, Mr. Kim and Mr. Chu, for we felt that these two men had things in their lives that needed to be confessed. The climax came when Mr. Kim gained the needed strength. He was sitting on the platform and suddenly he arose and came forward and was immediately given an opportunity. He confessed to hatred in his heart for the other brethren and especially for Mr. Blair, and then he went all to pieces. It was terrible beyond description, the agony that man went through. He fell to the floor and acted like a man in a fit. When he broke down the whole audience broke out in a perfect storm of weeping and they wept and wept and wept. We missionaries were weeping like the rest, and we simply couldn't keep from it. While they were weeping Mr. Kang got up to pray, and that poor man agonized in prayer, and then he broke down completely and wept as if his heart would break. The brethren gathered around, put their arms about him, and soon he became quiet, then it was beautiful to see him go to Mr. Kim, put his arms lovingly about him, and weep with him. When Mr. Kim broke he turned to Mr. Blair and said, "Pastor Blair, can you forgive me, can you forgive me?" Mr. Blair got up to pray, said the word "Father" twice and he could go no further, he was beyond words. The audience kept on weeping and it seemed as if they could not stop. At last we had to sing a hymn to quiet them, for we feared that some might lose control of themselves. During the singing they quieted down and then the confessions began again and so it went on until two o'clock.

One of the most striking things of the evening was a prayer by one of the college students. He asked that he might be allowed to make a public confession to God and was given the opportunity. In a broken voice he began to pray, and such a prayer I never heard before. We had a vision of a human heart laid bare before its God. He confessed to adultery, hatred, lack of love for his wife, and several other sins that I do not remember. As he prayed he wept, in fact he could hardly control himself, and as he wept the audience wept with him. We all felt as if we were in the presence of the living God.

With that meeting the class closed, and we wondered if these manifestations would now cease. What a joy it was to find that in our four prayer meetings Wednesday evening was manifested the same mighty power. I had announced that two elders would be elected at the Central Church on Wednesday evening, and on the way to the service I was wondering if it would be best to try and have an election that evening. As soon as I entered the building I felt that there would be no elders elected that night. One could feel that God's Spirit was present.

After a short address all who wished to go home were dismissed. As soon as the audience was quiet we had audible prayer together, and immediately after a number of men jumped to their feet, signifying an intense desire to confess their sins. After a few confessions the climax came when Elder Chu got the strength to make his confession. All through that wonderful Tuesday evening meeting he sat and looked like a man who has received his death sentence. We felt sure he had some terrible sin to confess, and we prayed that God would give him strength. He had been sitting on the platform, and suddenly I found him standing beside me, and then my heart gave a bound of joy, for I knew he had surrendered and that God's Spirit was now able to cleanse him. He began in a broken voice and could hardly articulate, so moved was he. As he went on his words grew clearer, and then it all came out. He confessed to adultery and misuse of funds, and as he told of it he was in the most fearful agony I have ever seen expressed by any mortal being. He was trembling from head to foot and I was afraid he would fall, so I put my arm about him to hold him up. In fearful distress of mind he cried out "Was there ever such a terrible sinner as I am?" and then he beat the pulpit with his hands with all his strength. At last he sank to the floor and writhed and writhed in agony, crying for forgiveness. He looked as though he would die if he did not get relief. It was terrible to witness, but oh! It was so beautiful to see the Korean brethren gather about him, put their arms around him, and comfort him in his time of anguish. As soon as Mr. Chu broke down the whole audience broke out in weeping, and they wept and wailed and wailed and it seemed as if they couldn't stop. I had to begin a song to quiet them. We held the meeting a little longer and then dismissed the audience, thankful that God's Spirit was still manifest among us, and more than thankful that Elder Chu had obtained the strength to make his confession.

Wednesday morning there was the same manifestation at the Advance School for Girls and Women. Miss Snook went as usual, and the first classes were held, and then chapel began at ten o'clock, but there was no regulation chapel exercises that morning. After a few remarks and prayer the girls broke down and began to weep and confess their sins, and until after twelve o'clock the meeting went on with nothing but prayer, tears, and confession of sin. Thursday morning was a repetition of Wednesday, and chapel lasted until noon. On Friday all recitations were laid aside, and the whole morning was spent as the two previous days. On Wednesday morning at the Central Church boy's school the same manifestation was present. The school was opened as usual, but no lessons were heard, and until one o'clock they remained weeping and confessing their sins. Three boys lost control of themselves and became unconscious from the strain of the meeting. Evidently the Korean in charge did not know how to relieve the strain when necessary.

On Thursday morning the Spirit fell on the primary school for girls. As some of us were going by the school room we heard the sound of wailing and knew the same power was there. Miss Best went down immediately to look after them. Hearing of what was going on at this school, Mrs. Bernheisel went down to the girls' school in the city to see how matters were there. She said a few words to the girls, and immediately they began to weep and confess their sins. At our own prayer meeting on Wednesday noon was manifested this same power. Instead of a half hour prayer meeting, we stayed until two o'clock, weeping and making confession of our sins. I never attended a prayer meeting like that before. The Spirit of God literally fell upon us, and we couldn't help but weep and confess our sins. It seemed as if God was trying to cleanse from our community everything that would hinder or cause offense.

All through the class the women of the church had been meeting separately, but there had been no special manifestation among them. We determined to hold meetings for them in the Central Church on Thursday, Friday, and Saturday evenings. Thursday and Friday evenings there was no special manifestation, for the women were not ready; there were a few confessions and few rambling talks by some self-righteous old women, but the Spirit was not there in power. Saturday night the power came, and then the women confessed and agonized just as the men had. We all rejoiced in the confession of one young girl, who has been a cause of grief and sorrow to us. We wished to help her, but could find no way to do so. Saturday night she broke down, made a confession, and wept as if her heart would break.

Sunday morning at the Central Church we had our usual classes for Bible study, and then in the afternoon service was another manifestation of great power. Mr. Kil preached, and ended his sermon with a most graphic illustration. He had a band attached to a rope, and the band he fastened about his waist, asking one of the Leaders to hold the rope while Mr. McCune stood at the pulpit beckoning him to come. Mr. Kil explained how it was to represent a sinner bound by sin, trying to break away and get to God; then he began to pull and writhe just as some of the men had done while under conviction, and at last the band broke, and then he rushed across the platform and he and Mr. McCune threw their arms around each other. I was not at the service, was in the country holding a country class with Mr. Blair. Mr. McCune said that while Mr. Kil was trying to break away the audience was breathless, but when the band broke and he and Mr. Kil threw their arms around each other the effect was indescribable. A number of men were on their feet at once, crying out with a desire to confess their sins, while others threw themselves to the floor in a perfect agony of weeping. Mr. Kil told them to go home, confess their sins to men, and come back to the evening meeting.

On Monday and Tuesday evenings were held meetings for women only, and again was manifested God's mighty power. So great was the strain that one woman became unconscious and others nearly lost control of themselves.

The meetings have closed, and the people are rejoicing with a great joy, but out in the country district the work goes on. Mr. Blair and I have just returned from a country class and at that class the manifestations were exactly the same, terrible agony on account of sin and great joy and peace resulting from confession of it.

And thus has begun in our city a work of grace for which we give to God our most grateful thanks, praying that what we have seen may simply be the earnest of the greater blessing that God has yet in store for us, and not for us only but for this whole land. To God be all the praise, to whose name be glory for ever and for ever.

Kil Sŏnju's Conversion Experience

Kil began reading *The Pilgrim's Progress*. While reading, his heart was greatly moved and he wetted the pages with tears. But he could not understand who God was and did not have the desire to completely believe in Jesus. As a result, his agony intensified, his distress deepened. When he finished reading *The Pilgrim's Progress*, Kim Chongsŏp once again visited him.

KIM: How do you feel now that you've prayed to Samnyŏng Sin'gun?
KIL: By praying, I've only gained agony.
KIM: Then you should pray to Heavenly Father [*Ch'ŏnbu*].
KIL: What? Look here! How could one dare to refer to the Majestic and Supreme Lord of Heaven [*Sangje*] as father?
KIM: If that is how you see it, just refer to him as the Heavenly Lord [*Sangje*] and pray to the Heavenly Lord.
KIL: Very well, I will do so.

Kil began praying to the Heavenly Lord. The substance of the prayer that he rendered to the Lord late into the night and early in dawn went something like this:

Dear Heavenly Lord, take pity on me. I have come to have doubts about Sŏndo, which I have devotedly believed in and studied for many years; yet I do not understand whether that seemingly righteous teaching of Christianity is indeed the truth leading to eternal life; I am so distraught I am at the edge of death. Please take pity and give me peace in my heart.

For several days, Kil continued to pray in such a way. One time it was deep in the night, near one o'clock in the morning; human traffic had ceased and the world was quiet, asleep amid the darkness; it was the kind of autumn night when the nippy dawn air bites and the mind gets particularly clear by the clear and ubiquitous cries of the crickets. In the upper room, Yi Chŏngsik was in deep sleep, snoring; Kil was on his knees, hunched over and alone, earnestly in prayer. He was engaged in a wrestling—the wrestling of life and death to seek God, just like the wrestling of life-and-death that Jacob had engaged in with God to be confirmed of an answer to his prayer. Before Kil—in earnest with sweat streaming down his face—had uttered, "Tell me whether Jesus is the true savior of humankind," inside of the room reverberated with a ringing sound of a jade flute, followed by thunderous gun noises that seemed to shake the room. In the instant when Kil was startled and astonished, he heard above the din three times—"Kil Sŏnju, Kil Sŏnju, Kil Sŏnju"—which so terrified and shook him up he did not dare raise his head; in prostration he prayed, "My father who loves me, please forgive my sins and save me." In that moment, his heart finally burst forth and his mouth opened, enabling him to call God father. On his own, Kil realized he was a sinner and wailed loudly. His body grew hot like a ball of fire; he prayed the harder and the louder. Yi Chŏngsik, who had been deep asleep, was awakened by Kil's wailing and loud prayer; getting down on his knees, he began chanting a formula of nine spirits and three souls (kuryŏng samjŏng) that Kil had taught him. For a long time, Kil's prayer continued. Kil reached a state of ecstasy. Joy gushed forth from his heart; tears of gratitude overflowed like spring water. As if in a state of frenzy or intoxication, he felt nothing but joy filling up his heart. His mind was peaceful. His pessimism toward the world was overcome by joy; his nickname the Hercules would be replaced by another, the "Madman of the Gospel." The moment he prayed to the Heavenly Lord seeking enlightenment as to whether Jesus was the savior, calling God father, Kil himself had become a captive of Christ.

Ch'oe Chasil (Choi Ja Shil)

But the God on whom I nightly vented my rancor was not as remote as I had thought. Going down by a brook to buy something to eat, holding my famished stomach, I encountered at the foot of the mountain a friend I had parted with thirty years ago. At first we did not recognize each other, but both of us thought there was something familiar in the other, so we kept glimpsing at each other, till we recalled our past memories and were beside ourselves with gladness. Sitting by the brook, my friend and I exchanged stories about our pasts. Oblivious to the passing time, laughing and crying amid complaints and regrets, I divulged my past years. [I said to myself,] "Well, I'll never see you again after tonight; so for the last time, I'll just tell you all the stories I've wanted to tell."

Regarding this as my last opportunity to bewail my ill fortunes, I told her every word that was in my heart. After listening for a time, my friend tightly held my hand and said, "Chasil, you should receive the Holy Spirit." I was startled enough to jump. "It should be enough to believe in Jesus. What need is there of the Holy Spirit? Since twelve, I've believed in Jesus and twice I was the first chair of women's fellowship associations; yet this, as you can see, is all I have to show for." [The friend replied,] "So even after believing in Jesus for twelve years, you've come to the mountain in such a pathetic shape only to die?"

Upon reflection, I had nothing to say. As the friend pointed out, if I died this way, the only conclusion that could be drawn is that I believed in Jesus wrongly. [She said,] "Over that hill, preachers are now gathered and are leading a revival; let's go and get some blessings. If you have to die, die afterward. Stand up. Let's go! You are now possessed by a suicide demon. Unless you kick it out, you'll go to hell." [I replied,] "I don't care for it. No, I am not going. Let go of this hand! You go ahead and get the Holy Spirit and prosper. I don't want to have anything to do with it!"

Put off by hearing that I was possessed by a suicide demon, I let out desperate shouts and screams, but on the other hand, in another part of my mind, I was saying something totally opposite: "If you let go of this hand, I am going to die tonight. Please, I beg of you to not let it go and take me to that place, by force if you have to." In the end, I was forcibly led by my friend to the revival site. There, inside a tent with straw coverings on the floor, five hundred or so people sat clapping and singing hymns: "The Holy Spirit has come, the Holy Spirit Has Come. The Holy Spirit that my Lord has sent has come."

Sitting next to my friend and glancing around, I muttered, "Good grief! They all have gone mad in this mountain valley." It was captivating to see all these folk shake their bodies back and forth, side to side, clapping and singing hymns, as if they were possessed; on the other hand, the sight was off-putting. Still, in a corner of my mind, from whence I don't know, there was a resounding desire: I, too, wanted to be possessed like them, if only I could. Then right there that night, I was able to hear a sermon by Reverend Yi Sŏngbong that I had heard thirty years ago. It was something unexpected. What was even more surprising was that the content of the sermon he preached that night was the same one that I had heard thirty years ago in Haeju.

[He shouted,] "Friends, what do people live for? Is it to have children? Dogs and pigs bear more offspring than people. Then is it to work? Surely not! Have you seen anyone who has worked more than a cow? Let us know who you are if you did. But then what is the end of the cow?" I was reminded of my childhood in Haeju. It is this sermon that led my mother to the church, and it is upon hearing this sermon that my faith had begun. Yet today, thirty years hence, I am here on this mountain to commit suicide; what on earth has gone wrong? [I then thought,] "Yes, in the past thirty years, I lived exactly like that cow and pig. Thinking only of money, I killed my daughter and drove a nail into the heart of my mother. How could I have walked on such a vain path, having heard the pastor's sermon, thirty years ago? Why did I live in such a way, with my mind off the road?"

After the sermon, a loud prayer (*t'ongsŏng kido*) began. In the heat of the prayer that seemed to shake the world, my heart gradually moved toward repentance. Unashamedly, I began to weep. I was no longer shedding tears of rancor, nor was it of regrets. Nor was I weeping because of some vague sense of sorrow. It was not the sort of crying I did yesterday. It was the kind of crying a child might cry in her mother's bosom—that was the kind of crying I was crying.

On the third day of the revival, the process of repentance that began thus erupted like a volcano. Around eleven o'clock in the night, in a corner of a tent under which everyone was asleep, an unbearably sorrowful repentance flowed out; in the process, I repented of all the sins I could remember, beginning with my badmouthing of my five cousins' wives. Once I opened my heart and started to repent, there was so much to repent of—why was I such a sinner?—even as the daybreak approached, there seemed to be no end to my prayer of repentance. Moreover, the past wrongs I had committed that I had forgotten about reappeared like stars in the sky, wrongs I could hardly have recollected. Had there not been the Holy Spirit, I could never have repented in such a thorough and perfect way.

It was around three o'clock in the morning. All of a sudden, with a thump, something like a heavy steel ball struck my chest, and my entire body vibrated like a ball of fire that was vigorously burning, and some strange sound that I had never heard in my entire life was coming out of my mouth; I was speaking neither English nor Japanese, but some strange language. I mistook this to be the work of the devil and prayed for repentance even more vigorously. [I thought to myself,] "Alas, because I haven't eaten anything in this mountain for two weeks, the mountain spirit must have come into me." My deceased mother always used to say that it is difficult for neophyte believers to discriminate between the work of the Holy Spirit and that of the devil and that one must be the more cautious the more deeply one enters into the realm of grace. Mother also said that the work of the Holy Spirit leads to a sense of peace and joy, whereas the work of the devil leads to uneasiness, terror, and fear. Curiously, my mind was at peace, was joyous, and was exuding a prayer of gratitude. "Is this the work of the Holy Spirit? Is this the work of the devil?" Not in the least could I tell. But no sooner had I started to pray than this strange sound flowed out of my mouth; and no matter how much I tried, I could not stop it. Through the night, I had knocked my head so much against the ground that my body was a mess, covered with sweat and dust.

"Hallelujah!"—that was the sound which came out of my mouth unwittingly. As I opened my eyes and looked up, the refreshing and invigorating air of the early morning permeated inside the tent. The dawning sky could be seen from a rip in the tent, and from this and that corner of the tent, people came toward me; patting on my back, they greeted me, "Sister, you were abundantly filled with the Holy Spirit last night." "You spoke in *pangŏn* [glossolalia] quite fluently as well." "Congratulations, Sister!" What is more, the friend who had led me to that place told me that all through the night she had prayed for me, and upon hearing that I had received blessings—even though it was I who was blessed—she was beside herself with joy as if it was she who was blessed. I was also joyous.

Having done the daybreak prayer, I went up following the valley. My steps were light as if I could fly. The sound of the water that flowed in the valley was not that of yesterday's. The murmuring and rushing sound of the water had a rhythm, and it seemed as if the rocks were dancing to it. The weeds that grew between the rocks seemed to be singing in unison, and the fog that was rising on top of them seemed like the glory of God. The pine trees that till just yesterday looked dreary seemed especially green that morning. When I got on a rock and breathed deeply, it felt as if the Samgak Mountain was being absorbed into my stomach and all creation was rendering praise and glory to God.

Looking around the natural scenery, I once again gave a prayer of repentance. Trees and grass were growing upward toward the sky, and the water of the valley flowed from top to bottom following the natural order of things; but I, disobeying mother and servants of the Lord, had been going up against the grain of all things. Here, once again, I became aware of the mercifulness and loving-forgiveness of our God. And I gave thanks as I felt deep in the marrow of my bones the boundless, loving truth that God never abandons a people God had once chosen.

Han Kyŏngjik (Han Kyung Jik) and Gradual "Rebirth"

Finally Jesus himself came, having put on the human flesh, and showed us what the life of God is like. As a result, eternal life is gained through faith . . . in Jesus who came to the world . . . as the life of God. . . . Here faith has two meanings. [For one it means] admitting, believing, and acknowledging. . . . It is generally regarded as believing simply to think in one's head as to who Jesus is, who God is, how Jesus came and died nailed to the cross, and how he returned to life and ascended to heaven. But this is only the first step of faith. If faith stops there, eternal life cannot be attained. In the Bible it is said even the devil has such faith. The devil knows more about God and Jesus than us. Simply knowing alone is not faith but is the first step of faith.

There is a second meaning of faith. It is trusting. . . . It means believing and depending [on someone]. Jesus is the being who is the life of God dwelling in us humans. . . . When we know who Jesus Christ is and entrust our souls to him, we will naturally repent of our past sins . . . and when that happens, our past lives will be transformed in their entirety—that is called spiritual resurrection. Thereafter . . . Jesus comes to the center of our hearts, and that is called rebirth [chungsaeng]. . . .

This experience of rebirth varies according to persons. To some, it will come suddenly. Such persons are well aware of their experiences. They know when they repented and say that it is from that point that they have received eternal life. For instance, Apostle Paul had such an experience suddenly on his way to Damascus. . . . But to other people, such experiences come slowly. It does not appear that the faith of the twelve apostles came suddenly; it came gradually through their contact with Jesus. Now, even today, such an experience would not come suddenly to a person who grew up in an especially devout household, learning the Bible since childhood and being exposed to religious education. As a result, the person does not know whether such an experience has been had. To use a metaphor, a pupa inside a cocoon gradually transforms and becomes a butterfly—it gradually develops wings, grows antennae, and becomes a butterfly. But upon becoming a butterfly it has to—at least once—bore through the cocoon to come out. . . . Likewise, there comes a time when even the youth who grow up in our devout families [must] undergo gradual transformation from pupas to butterflies—boring a hole through the cocoon and coming out. Thus there is a step by which their lives are thoroughly transformed, even if it does not happen suddenly while they are steeped in sin.

I apologize for bringing up my own experience, but since I was nine years old, I have been a believer. I attended a Christian elementary school, a Christian middle school, and a Christian college. From my own experience, you can tell that Christian education has matured [in Korea]. One time, when I was twenty-two years old, it occurred to me to go to Kumi port and take a walk in a moonlit night. That night, while walking alone on the shore, I received a special blessing, which caused me to fall on my knees on the sand and to pray earnestly before God—I will never forget that hour so long as I live. Friends, if there has been an experience in your life in which you wholly entrusted yourself to Christ, you—whoever you are—have received eternal life. There is no need to doubt.

There are some people who, despite having had such an experience, often doubt and worry, but that is misguided. Such are the people who still hold on to the old legalistic idea that salvation is attained through works—even after being instructed in the Bible in our Protestant tradition, and being taught numerous times that righteousness is attained through faith and that the righteous shall live by faith. Such persons say it scarcely seems possible that they had received eternal salvation since they continue to commit sins, since even now they sin repeatedly. Heed this without fail! It is by believing in the Lord Jesus Christ that you become righteous and receive eternal life—not by works. Given that the Bible says that there is no one in the world who can be called righteous through works, do you think you could be so called? So do not misunderstand! [Salvation] is not attained through works. It is not obtained through good deeds. It is not gained by living a virtuous life.

Secondly, there are people who mistakenly think that an extraordinary experience must accompany a rebirth. Some have such an experience, but more do not. Some think that to be born again, they must see some strange thing in a dream—a vision in some dreamy state—or experience a burning bodily sensation. Such is absolutely not the case. Do not rely too much on emotion. . . . We do not go to heaven by how we feel. So long as we know Jesus Christ to be our savior and have entrusted our lives to him, we will go to heaven whether we feel good or bad. This must be clear to us.

— 23 —

A New Moral Order: Gender Equality
in Korean Christianity

Hyaeweol Choi

After the open-door policy of 1876, Korea experienced a sudden influx of new ideas from other countries, and "civilization and enlightenment" (*munmyŏng kaehwa*) was regarded as an urgent mandate to ensure national sovereignty and prosperity. Under this mandate, traditional values and customs were critically evaluated against foreign examples, and a new moral order governing human relations began to gain legitimacy for the modern nation-state. One of the most prominent social issues to illustrate a major shift from the old/traditional orientation to the new/modern one was the role and status of women as an important measure of civilization. In the social Darwinian discourse of civilization and enlightenment, the "backwardness" of Korean women had to be remedied in order to move forward along the universal, linear path of history. Women were expected to come out of the inner chambers, to become educated, to be well versed in domestic and world affairs, and to play a role in building an independent nation-state. A group of enlightenment-oriented intellectuals and national leaders championed these new roles for women in the public sphere. The emerging print media, such as *Tongnip sinmun*, *Cheguk sinmun*, *Hwangsŏng sinmun*, and *Taehan maeil sinbo*, served as an important vehicle in challenging the hierarchical gender relations of old Korea and advocating gender equality. By 1898 upper-class women had distributed a public circular (*t'ongmun*), calling for recognition that women were endowed with the same rights as men. This call marked the beginning of the women's movement in Korean history.

In this historical context, Protestant Christian missionaries also played a significant role in introducing and distributing a new configuration governing gender relations in Korea. Coming from the West—largely the United States, the United Kingdom, Canada, and Australia—these missionaries represented themselves, and also were perceived by Koreans, as the bearers of Western civilization, whose core values were presumed to be based in Christianity. In the minds of missionaries, civilization and Christianity were not merely inseparable, they constituted each other. Thus, the missionaries' primary goal of spreading the gospel went hand in hand with their "civilizing mission" in the sociocultural domain.

Of the many sociocultural issues that generated debate among missionaries, gender relations proved to be one of the most challenging for missionaries to tackle. George Heber Jones, an early Methodist missionary from the United States, succinctly represents a missionary understanding of Korean gender ideology when he reports in *The Gospel in All Lands* (September 1893) as follows:

> The sages of Korea taught the nation that woman is inferior to man. Christianity flatly contradicts this, and there is a clash. . . . Viewed as inferior to the man, her lot is one of subjection. From the father she passes under the control of the husband; after whose death she is virtually subject to the eldest son. She enters the marriage state during the age of fourteen to seventeen, this being absolutely obligatory if she would retain the respect of her people. Ancestral worship being based on the possession of male posterity, places its sanction on plurality of wives, and in thus destroying the true home life opens the way for great immorality. The true wife is often deserted for some favorite concubine or mistress, and no stigma of disrepute occurred.

The missionary representation of Korean women foregrounded this cultural clash over the status of women. Korea and the Christian West are often presented as binary opposites in which "heathen sisters" of Korea had to be rescued by Christian teachings that were presumed to offer new moral values. Although women in the West were experiencing gender discrimination in life and work at the time, the fact that they had more freedom and opportunities than their "heathen sisters" was a basis for the claim that Western women held the superior position to their counterparts, and Christian ethics were supposed to be responsible for the idealized Western womanhood. Emphasizing that women and men were created equal under God, the missionary discourse on gender tried to set a new standard for gender relations that moved away from the Confucian-prescribed sociocultural arrangements and that would seek to ensure the success of evangelical endeavors.

From the missionaries' point of view, such Korean customs as the "Inside-Outside Rule" (naewoebŏp) prohibiting women in the public space, the nearly complete denial of education to women, the practice of early marriage, and the continuation of the concubine system demanded special attention because they significantly hindered the prospect of expanding and consolidating a new Christian community in Korea. For example, early missionaries were intrigued by the scarcity of girls and women in the streets. They came to learn that boys and girls were segregated from each other after age seven, and older girls and women were not allowed to be seen in public. The confinement of women to the inner chambers posed impediments for the missionary endeavor. This rule of separation was particularly strict for women of the *yangban* upper class, which resulted in mission policy that focused more on the lower classes largely because it was much easier to gain access to this segment of the population. The widespread lack of education for women was a major barrier to introducing the Bible, because most women were illiterate. Founding girls' schools and promoting literacy were indispensable mission policies to enable the introduction of the gospel to women. Furthermore, the custom of early marriage arranged by parents caused serious problems for the success of the mission in that youngsters often quit school and never returned to church, which was detrimental to the growth of the Christian community. In general, missionaries tried hard to assert fundamental Christian principles; however, to gain access to the Korean population, they needed to remain sensitive to centuries-old customs. Missionaries' reform efforts in gender relations adopted strategies that ensured their goals of spreading the gospel by adjusting their own Christian practices to accommodate some traditional customs of Korea.

Newly converted Korean Christians actively participated in the discussion on the role and status of women in the modern era. At one level, their gender discourse often pointed to issues similar to those that missionaries wanted to reform or totally eradicate, but it significantly extended the missionary debate by scrutinizing centuries-old traditional practices in great detail. Located at the intersection of cultural and religious encounters, Korean converts worked with missionaries, negotiating between the old customs and religious practices of Korea and the new worldview presented by Western Christianity. Their reconfiguration of gender relations demonstrated the ways in which they tried to overcome problematic aspects of the old practices and embrace new human relations based on Christian morality.

At another level, the gender discourse of Korean Protestant converts significantly intersected with the discourse of civilization and enlightenment, in which Korean intellectuals championed a new role for women. Indeed, many prominent intellectuals, such as Sŏ Chaep'il, Yun Ch'iho, and Yi Sŭngman (aka Syngman Rhee), became Christians early on and were significantly influenced by Western civilization and Christian faith. In their leadership capacities, they advocated Christian civilization and the role it could play in creating a new, modern Korea. Yun Ch'iho wrote in his diary (February 19, 1893) that "Christianity is the salvation and hope of Corea [Korea]." Yi Sŭngman, who became the first president of the Republic of Korea in 1948, explicitly claimed in Sinhak wŏlbo (1903) that "Christianity is the foundation of the future of Korea." Assuming that Christian ethics would be the basis for advanced civilization and enlightenment, these converted Korean intellectuals advocated new gender relations that were not only faithful to Christian ways but also in keeping with the nationalist project toward modernity.

The essays translated in this chapter center on the theme of gender equality as a marker of civilization and Christian moral ethics. Each essay touches on a specific topic—separation of genders, problems in wedding rituals, the ill-treatment of women in Korea, the importance of women's education, or the vice of the concubine system—offering strong criticism of the old cultural practices that privileged men and oppressed women. In advocating higher status for women in the family and society, the authors took the example of Western women, whose education, knowledge, and participation in the public sphere were indicative of a better, more advanced civilization. These examples are often oversimplified and exaggerated. By the same token, the portrayal of traditional womanhood in Korea tends to ignore the agency that Korean women had even within the strictures of traditional gender roles. In other words, an overly idealized image of Western women is juxtaposed with an exaggerated description of the downgraded status of Korean women. In addition, there is a significant gap between the rhetoric and the reality for women in both the Christian and the non-Christian communities of the time. Although missionaries and Korean converts advocated gender equality, mission organizations and Korean churches were highly patriarchal and continued to regard women's roles as secondary. Even the widely publicized rhetoric in favor of women's education ultimately derived from the roles of women as wives and mothers, refashioning traditional Confucian gender ideology under the strong influence of the Meiji gender ideology that emphasized "good wife, wise mother" (ryosai kenbo) and also the Victorian notion of "true" womanhood that privileged domesticity. Nonetheless, these writings on the necessity of changing the role and status of women as a prerequisite for civilization and enlightenment shed light on the ways in which Protestant Christianity as a new religion in Korea offered a platform to critique and reinterpret traditional practices involving gender. They also provide an insight into the process of negotiation and readjustment between centuries-old customs and newly introduced moral values based on Christianity.

The essays were published in Sinhak wŏlbo (Monthly Magazine on Christian Theology) and Kŭrisdo sinmun (Christian News)—two early Christian periodicals published in Korea. Sinhak wŏlbo was founded in December 1900, with George Heber Jones, a missionary sent by the U.S. Methodist Church, serving as its first editor. After a brief hiatus in 1904, it restarted publication under the name Kamnigyo hoebo (Bulletin of the Methodist Church) and survived until 1910. Kŭrisdo sinmun was founded in 1897 with Horace Underwood, a missionary sent by the U.S. Presbyterian Church, as its first editor. It changed its name to Yesugyo sinbo (Christian Newspaper) in 1907 and later on to Yesugyo hoebo (Bulletin of Christianity) in 1910. These magazines and newspapers touched on a variety of issues, ranging from theological to cultural and societal topics. There were comparatively few items focusing on gender, but the following pieces represent some of the most important documents, offering a glimpse of the emergence of a new gender ideology and reform efforts in a transcultural and transreligious context.

"The Custom of the 'Inside-Outside Rule'" was written by the evangelist Mun Kyŏngho and published in Sinhak wŏlbo 3, no. 7 (1903): 187–90. "Education for Women" is translated from Kŭrisdo sinmun, February 28, 1901. "Questions and Answers about Marriage" appeared in Kŭrisdo sinmun, August 8, 1901. "The Way of Husband and Wife" was published in Sinhak wŏlbo 1, no. 3 (1901): 101–4. "The Vice of the Concubine System" is translated from Sinhak wŏlbo 1, no. 11 (1901): 437–41.

Further Reading

For the limitations of the discourse on gender equality in Christianity, see Kim Yunsŏng, "The Predicament of Modern Discourses on Gender and Religion in Korean Society," *Korea Journal* 41, no. 1 (Spring 2001): 114–36. On marriage for Christians, see Han Kyumu, "Ch'ogi Han'guk Changno kyohoe ŭi kyŏrhon munje insik" (A Perspective on Marriage Issues in the Early Korean Presbyterian Church), *Han'guk Kidokkyo wa yŏksa* 10 (1999): 67–100. On polygamy, see William M. Baird, "Should Polygamists Be Admitted to the Christian Church?" paper prepared for the consideration of the Presbyterian Council of Korea and printed in *The Korean Repository, 1896* (Seoul: Trilingual Press, 1896); W. L. Swallen, "Polygamy and the Church," *Korean Repository* (August 1895): 289–94; and Ok Sŏngdŭk, "Ch'ogi Han'guk kyohoe ŭi ilbudach'ŏje nonjaeng" (Debates on Polygamy in Early Korean Church), *Han'guk Kidokkyo wa yŏksa* 16 (2002): 7–34. Regarding Confucian gender ideology, see Martina Deuchler, *The Confucian Transformation of Korea* (Cambridge, Mass.: Harvard University Press, 1992). See also two chapters in *Women and Confucian Cultures in Premodern China, Korea and Japan*, edited by Dorothy Ko, JaHyun Kim Haboush, and Joan Piggott (Berkeley: University of California Press, 2003): Martina Deuchler, "Propagating Female Virtues in Chosŏn Korea" (pp. 142–69), and JaHyun Kim Haboush, "Versions and Subversions: Patriarchy and Polygamy in Korean Narratives" (pp. 279–303). For the issue of Christianity and discourse of modernity, see Cho Hyŏnbŏm, "Hanmal Kaesingyo ŭi munmyŏnghwa tamnon e kwanhan yŏngu" (A Study of the Discourse of Civilization in Protestant Christianity in Late-Chosŏn Korea), *Chonggyo munhwa pip'yŏng* 1 (2002): 1–14. For the history of Christian literature in Korea, see Kim Ponghŭi, *Han'guk Kidokkyo munsŏ kanhaengsa yŏn'gu, 1882–1945* (A Study of the Publishing History of Christian Literature in Korea, 1882–1945) (Seoul: Ewha Womans University Press, 1987).

The Custom of the "Inside-Outside Rule"

Regardless of the level of civilization or the size of their territories, all nations have their own customs, some of which are good and others bad. In the next hundred years many countries on earth will engage in reforming their customs, making good customs better and eliminating bad ones so that they can save people from ignorance. It would be impossible to list all the customs of all nations, but let us take as evidence of the movement toward civilization the examples of the countries that have abolished evil customs and joined the league of advanced countries. [Among the old harmful customs, one can cite the following.] Intending to make their babies beautiful, people in the United States press the head of a new baby with their rough hands so that its occiput will be round [instead of being flat]. Black people in Africa have piercings in their ears, noses, and lips, and they go around naked without feeling any shame. People in India burn widows and drown babies in the river. The Japanese put on permanent tattoos of dragons, black lions, and other ferocious animals over their entire bodies. Russians grow beards and mustaches because they believe they cannot go to heaven without wearing them. In China, in order to confine women to the inner chambers, men have the feet of the women bound from childhood. As a result, women need to use canes in order to go anywhere. However, from last year the Chinese decided to abandon this awful custom, and these other countries have been reforming their traditional practices.

But in our own country, we have not even begun to change the custom of the "Inside-Outside Rule" (naewoebŏp). Treated like material objects, women in Korea have been confined to the inner chambers, prevented from going anywhere. Men have their women make clothes, prepare food, and do all kinds of odds jobs as if they were slaves. And if a wife does not prepare food or clothing in a timely manner, her husband harshly criticizes her. While men enjoy drinking and eating fine food, they do not even consider sharing these pleasures with their wives. While they go on picnics to scenic places, they prohibit their wives from moving even one step outside the house. While men would never consider criticizing a fellow for destroying his family through profligacy, gambling and drinking, they cannot forgive the slightest mistake made by their wives and beat them half to death or kick them out of the house. They never let their wives know what they are doing. As a result of the treatment they receive from their husbands, many women drown or hang themselves. Some run away or take opium or poison to kill themselves. Even a slave that costs hundreds of nyang [old Korean currency] and would be willing to work to death could not endure a more harsh life than this. Korean wives are the most miserable of the miserable. Alas, how sad it is!

When God created man and woman, he planned for them to live in perfect harmony and love each other as equals. So how could Korean women not have any rights? There is no reason other than ignorance. It is reported that the population of our country is now twenty million, and women, fully half of the population, have been oppressed and treated like prisoners by their husbands. They have been confined to the inner chambers and have never had a chance to see the outside world if they desired. This is a truly lamentable situation. Once when I visited a prison on an evangelical mission, I saw a man who had been caught during a riot and put in jail a few years prior. Many other prisoners had been granted leniency at major celebratory events for the nation, but since this man was a widower and an easy mark, he was never released. Instead, he was kept on in the jail to do all kinds of odds and ends with a meager wage. He was never allowed to see the outside world and spent the remainder of his life with prisoners. The life of this man was an endless misery, and yet could we say the lives of Korean women are any better than his?

Regardless of whether we are satisfied with them or not, we Christian men will love and protect our wives, chosen for us by God, and we will give them freedom so that they can go anywhere that they wish. In addition, the husband and wife must act together for the good of both. For example, if the husband practices Christianity, but he does not allow his wife to go to church because he is concerned about her walking openly in the street, then her soul will be plunged into hell because she did not go to church. If we Christians do not give up this evil custom of the "Inside-Outside Rule," how can we win and save the world?

Education for Women

People in enlightened countries believe that the prosperity or adversity of the nation depends on whether they educate women, or not. In the past the United States was not that different from Asian countries in that it did not make any particular effort to educate women. However, about fifty years ago people became enlightened, and women began to receive education. The result of this change has been the emergence of women scholars of international reputation whose record of distinguished achievement is equal to that of male scholars. In the United States, almost three-fourths of teachers are women. In the past, women did not have any particular occupation, but now they take part in business along with men. Thus the nation has doubled its workforce, which must be seen as the foundation of national prosperity.

The American example demonstrates that educating women is the most important matter for a nation. But in Korea this has not happened yet. We all need to turn our energy to changing the current state of affairs in women's education. We should make efforts to establish girls' schools. Our churches founded girls' schools early on, and those who are educated in our mission schools gain knowledge and new perspectives that are not available to other women.

If we want to civilize our country, Korean men should respect women and avoid all of the absurd behaviors that oppress women. I believe there is no shortage of women who wish to see abolished the old custom of imprisoning women in the inner quarters throughout their lives. One cannot simply hope that things will improve. People must make conscious efforts to realize their wishes. The first thing to do is to educate women. Only when women are educated, can they be respected. And if women are knowledgeable but men are unenlightened, our goal cannot be realized. Therefore, along with women's education, we should also emphasize men's education. Those who understand the importance of education for both men and women ought to turn their efforts to founding churches and schools. None of this can be accomplished in just a few days, but as long as we make sincere efforts, there is nothing we cannot do. If there is anything that is not realized, it is largely because of a lack of sincerity, not a lack of money. Good faith will attract money; therefore, the true danger is lack of faith and sincerity. If we observe people who have great accomplishments in big business in other countries, their earnest efforts always enable them to deploy resources successfully. We do have wealthy people in Korea. If they realize how important it is to educate our people, how could they withhold their financial support? However, it ultimately depends on how many people are really engaged in this task with heartfelt effort.

Questions and Answers about Marriage

QUESTION: *What is marriage?*

ANSWER: Marriage is the most important affair in human life in which a man and a woman vow eternal love.

QUESTION: *Are the customs of marriage the same for the different races on earth?*

ANSWER: They are different. In the West, a man and a woman meet, try to understand each other and to check if they are compatible on their own. If they like each other, then they tell their parents about their relationship. In contrast, in the East, parents choose spouses for their children with the assistance of a go-between.

QUESTION: *Setting aside the different practices of the East and the West, what is the best foundation for a marriage?*

ANSWER: To be brief, it is best for a man and a woman to marry after they understand each other.

QUESTION: *Why is that so?*

ANSWER: Marriage should not be imposed on children by parents. It should be a mutual union between two people, agreed upon by the couple themselves. Thus the marriage will be at risk if their minds are forced to be united and they have not found harmony.

QUESTION: *Would there be any problem if young people are allowed to choose their partners as they do in the West?*

ANSWER: Yes. Many young men and women may not find compatible partners. So there is a risk that many of them will never marry.

QUESTION: *Would there be any problem if parents arrange the marriage of their children as we do in the East?*

ANSWER: Yes. Because parents choose the spouse, the young couple gets married without even knowing what their companion looks like or what personality he or she has. As a result, the husband is likely to take concubines.

QUESTION: *When should people marry?*

ANSWER: Marriage most importantly involves governing the household and taking care of the family; thus, people should marry after they have grown up, finished their studies, and acquired the knowledge of an adult.

QUESTION: *What kind of wedding rituals should be used?*

ANSWER: People should follow the will of God, so wedding rituals should conform to what the Old and New Testaments specify.

The Way of Husband and Wife

When God created the universe, he created a man and a woman. Rather than leaving them to live alone, he paired them as a couple and established the law of family. With this, the practice of marriage becomes the law of heaven. When one looks at the secular law of earth, the way of a married couple is the third of the five ethical codes governing of human relations, and therefore everyone should assume its importance.

Just as the calendar is marked by seasons, our lives are marked by rituals that provide us with order based on the rule of heaven and the law of human relations. Of all rituals, the wedding ritual is the most precious. If a man and a woman live together without the marriage ceremony, they are no different from animals. The extent to which people regard the way of married life as either important or trivial is indicative of the level of enlightenment they have achieved. If a people regard and preserve the way well, we think of them as being enlightened. On the other hand, a people who hold the opposite view should be called barbaric.

In Korea, a wedding ceremony is one of the four rituals. For the wedding, the concerned parties exchange gifts through a go-between. When a bridegroom goes to the house of a bride for the initial ceremony, her family sets up a table between the couple. On the table, one can find a bottle of wine and cups, a hen and a rooster, and colorful fruits and cakes. The bride first bows to the groom, and he returns a bow to her. A female servant pours wine into a cup and gives it to the groom. He drinks half, and the servant brings it to the bride, who drinks the rest. They repeat this, and then on the third sharing the cup is wrapped with a red thread and a blue thread. After this, the bride bows to him four times, and he does three and a half bows to her. According to an old adage, this is the rule of heaven. After the groom stays at his in-laws' house for three days, he brings his bride to his house, where the bride presents herself to her parents-in-law and also participates in rituals to honor her new husband's ancestors. This is a Korean-style wedding ceremony.

If a man has followed it properly, no one would dare to say he did not marry and form a proper union with his wife. This wedding ritual distinguishes marriage from nonmarriage. It is the beginning of new life and the foundation of all fortunes. The traditional wedding ceremony should be recognized as legitimate even if the couple later discovers a better, more Christian wedding ritual. As long as they have followed the proper manners and customs of the nation, the couple does not need to have another ceremony following the new wedding sacrament.

The first item in the revised regulations for virtuous conduct suggests that any couple who has been married in our traditional Korean wedding style before they received baptism does not have to hold a Christian wedding ceremony unless they volunteer to do so. As we interpret this new regulation, there is no need to feel ashamed of having the traditional wedding instead of a Christian wedding because one had simply followed a custom before joining the church. In our traditional wedding rituals in Korea, people choose a date for the wedding based on the reading of the "four pillars" (*saju*), a bride and groom drink wine during the initial ceremony, and they perform a sacrificial rite for ancestors, all of which violate the rule of God. As a result, there are many believers who are concerned about the validity of the practices in their earlier life. If we do not explain and suggest what is acceptable, they will continue to worry. Thus, here is the suggestion: those who had properly followed the traditional Korean wedding rituals before they became Christian will be forgiven by God because they did not know God yet, and there is no need for them to perform a Christian wedding ceremony.

The Vice of the Concubine System

In the beginning God created a man and then a woman and thus established the model of husband and wife. In Mark 10:7–8, we are told that one leaves his parents and joins with his wife, and thus two bodies become one. The union of a husband and wife is the beginning of human ethics and the foundation of new life. God designed the way of husband and wife with the intention of preventing adultery and having each help the other.

Just as it is a sin for a man to take two wives, it is a sin for a woman to take two husbands. Therefore, it is absurd if a woman is punished for this sinful behavior, but a man is forgiven for the same sin. Men confine their wives to the house, force them to make clothing and food, and treat them like slaves, while they indulge themselves with sensual pleasures and vicious emotion and take two or even three concubines. Some wealthy houses are full of concubines. People even refer to the practice as having "three wives and eight mistresses." In this practice, men defy the rule of monogamy given by God. How is it that people do not find this old custom appalling and terrifying?

In the beginning one man married one woman; nonetheless, the vice of the concubine system began early on. As Genesis 40:19 indicates, even the people of God were infected by this evil practice so that Abraham took Hagab because he did not have a son, and Jacob took Bilhah and Zilpah. Ultimately this led to catastrophe. However, since it happened before the Commandments were delivered, they could be forgiven.

In the East, after the Chinese emperor Yao [Kor. Yo] gave his two daughters to Emperor Shun [Kor. Sun] as wives, people took this custom of plural wives for granted. Because of this custom, Emperor Jie of Xia [Kor. Ha Kŏl] was destroyed by Chuhŭi [sic; the author probably intended to write Malhŭi, Ch. Moxi], and Emperor Zhou of Shang [Kor. Sang Ju] lost his country because of Daji [Talgi]. Since then, innumerable people and countries have been ruined by concubines.

An old adage says that only after a husband and wife live in harmony can they create a family in the right way. It is impossible to overemphasize the importance of the truthful way of husband and wife. How can we continue to damage the life of the family by allowing men to keep concubines?

The custom of concubinage started from ancient times, and regardless of rank, descendants have followed the custom, almost taking it for granted. Eager to please their concubines, men compete with each other to make the house of their concubines more luxurious than that of others. Counting on the affection of her man, the concubine becomes more arrogant. But since the foolish man is intoxicated by the coquettish concubine and simply trusts her, he ends up disfavoring his own family. Worse yet, he mistreats his parents and regards his own wife as an enemy. Jealousy between a wife and a concubine sometimes leads them to kill each other, resulting in the ruin of the family and the destruction of well-being. Lives are ruined by a mere concubine, and the man does not feel any shame about this evil custom, showing no sign of regret. Alas, this kind of person is doomed to endure not only the calamity of hell but also misfortune in this world.

Some say that they take concubines because their wives have not given birth to a son. They argue that, according to Mencius, having a son is the greatest of the three filial obligations one must perform to show respect to one's parents; therefore, a man has no choice but to seek a concubine. [But this reasoning is faulty.] The responsibility for the birth of a son does not fall entirely on the woman. Men bear half the responsibility. So, if the marriage does not produce any male offspring, and the husband seeks a concubine in an effort to produce a son, then the wife should be entitled to take a male concubine toward the same end. The argument ignores the truth that having a son is not controlled by the intentions of human beings but rather by the will of God.

How can we find the true way of husband and wife if people live in this manner? The real concern about the lack of a male heir has to do with the worry that there will be no one to hold ancestor worship rituals. But even if there is such a thing as a messenger of the ancestors who comes to the worship ritual, would he gladly receive a ceremony prepared by the son of a concubine who came to this world out of lascivious desire? Wouldn't this be a greater offense? Some argue that since there are too many things to do in the house, a concubine could be a help to the primary wife. But with the money spent for the support of a concubine, one could instead hire a hardworking maid who would be of much greater help.

In essence, having a concubine is against the rule of God, who teaches monogamy, and there should not be any excuse or exception to this rule. Some conscientious men know how harmful it is to have a concubine, but unfortunately they cannot resist the impulses of their lewd desire and end up going down the deadly path. How dreadful is it? When I try to spread the gospel to people, they understand the logic and propriety of monogamy and admit that Christianity will win over the world. But they are often tied to their concubines, so they cannot resolve the problem. How foolish are these people? Their behavior will cause misfortune not only for themselves but also for their descendants. Even if someone has an incredible talent and he is more powerful than the president of the country, if he is in conflict with his wife and is seduced by a concubine, he will not be able to escape the ridicule of the people. In those civilized countries of the West, even someone whose status may be higher than that of the president has only one wife, and it is needless to say that those who are below him naturally follow his example. Our Savior says that there is no meaning for all the material benefit of the world if one forsakes his soul. There is nothing that can replace the soul. In relation to the message in Matthew 16:26, a question should be raised: would anyone forfeit his soul because of a mere concubine? Our Savior says that he who looks at a woman with sexual longing has already committed adultery in his mind, and the lesson in Matthew 5:28 is that adultery is a sin. If a man follows this lesson, gives up all the sensual desire in this world, and becomes a true human being, he will act firmly with conviction even when the whole world gets in the way. If he does not, he will easily be seduced.

I sincerely wish that we conform to the will of God, and that a husband and wife love each other and make the family felicitous, so that we will all be blessed by God and enjoy unlimited fortune and happiness all the way to the eternal world.

——24——

Indigenized Devotional Practices
in Korean Evangelicalism

Timothy S. Lee

Since its dissemination in the late 1870s, Protestantism grew apace in Korea, adapting to the native soil in the waning years of the Chosŏn dynasty (1392–1910) and persisting through the harsh period of Japanese occupation (1910–45). The Korean War (1950–53) severely challenged the religion, reducing the number of its adherents in the North from about three hundred thousand in 1945 to fifteen thousand at the end of the century. But in the South, the religion thrived to such an extent that a Gallup survey found that by 1997 every fifth South Korean was a Protestant.

Though this survey does not show it, the vast majority of Korean Protestants adhere to Evangelicalism—a species of Protestantism characterized by a literalist bent in biblical interpretation, a soteriology that values the individual over society, an emphasis on conversion experience, and evangelism—relegating rituals such as baptism and Communion to a secondary place. Many Protestants, to be sure, identify themselves as nonevangelicals, and they have performed vital roles in Korean society, taking the lead in the 1970s and 1980s, for example, in opposing political dictatorships. Even so, there is no denying that in numbers and church influence, evangelicals dominate the Protestant church, constituting upwards of 90 percent of the Korean Protestant population and cutting across denominational lines.

It is well known that modern Korean society has been deeply influenced by Protestantism, especially in its evangelical form. The reverse is also true: Korean society has deeply influenced evangelicalism to the extent that evangelicalism has become indigenized in Korean society. However, one would be hard put to find evidence for such indigenization in the theology of Korean evangelicalism, given the movement's conservative hermeneutics and its suspicion toward theological innovation. True, prosperity prophets such as Cho Yonggi have been accused of preaching innovative—or shamanistic—gospels. Yet their innovation is more in style than in substance; their theology's central thrust remains squarely in the Pentecostal tradition of Evangelicalism.

In devotional practices, however, one can readily find evidence of indigenization. Korean Evangelicalism practices several devotionals that are peculiar to it—peculiar not in the sense that there are no analogues outside Korea but in the sense that it is only in Korea that they are practiced widely and regularly. This chapter discusses three of the most distinctive types of such devotionals: the daybreak prayer devotional (*saebyŏk kidohoe*), the nightlong prayer meeting (*ch'ŏrya kidohoe*), and the fasting-prayer (*kŭmsik kido*).

Daybreak Prayer Devotional (*Saebyŏk kidohoe*)

Of all its devotional practices, Korean evangelicalism is probably best known for its *saebyŏk kidohoe* (literally, "daybreak prayer gathering"). Its origin dates back to 1906, a year before the eruption of a great evangelical revival that swept the churches, leaving an indelibly evangelical mark on them. The persons credited with instigating it are the Presbyterian elders Kil Sŏnju (1869–1935) and Pak Ch'irok (d.u.; ca. 1865–1935). In a charged atmosphere, due to large revivals planned for the following year, the two men met daily for prayer at 4:00 A.M. in their church. Soon their prayer activity became known, and others joined them. During the Korean War, the exigencies of life and death prompted the churches to engage in this devotional daily. By the time the war ended, the daybreak devotional had become routinized in Korean evangelicalism.

Nowadays, the daybreak devotional is a regular feature of most Protestant churches in Korea. Some of them hold it once or twice a week, but the majority hold it daily, usually at 5:00 or 5:30 A.M. The structure of the devotional is simple. Its main part is the corporate worship—which typically consists of hymn singing, scriptural reading, short preaching, more hymn singing, and *t'ongsŏng kido*, a loud simultaneous prayer. All this typically lasts about thirty minutes. Thereafter the participants may remain as long as they wish for private prayer. During private prayer, participants—especially those suffering from illness or stress—may request the pastor for an *ansu kido*, laying-on-of-hands prayer, which is believed to be especially effective.

In an average Protestant church in Korea, attendance at the daybreak devotional draws about 10 percent of its typical Sunday attendance. But occasionally it can equal or even surpass Sunday attendance, especially at times set aside for special daybreak devotionals. Such events are often given names—such as Forty-Day Daybreak Prayer Meeting or Seven-Day Daybreak Prayer Meeting to Conquer the Walls of Jericho—and are usually preceded by weeks or months of preparation. During this preparatory period, the minister impresses upon the congregation the importance of attending the devotional and exhorts them to invite guests. It is not surprising, then that this kind of gathering usually engenders a revivalistic atmosphere.

In Seoul, there is a church famous for its unusually fervent daybreak devotion als: Myŏngsŏng (Presbyterian) Church. Every day, Myŏngsŏng Church holds two daybreak devotionals, one at 4:30 A.M. and the other at 5:30 A.M., each of which is attended by thousands. Furthermore, every March and September, Myŏngsŏng Church holds special monthlong daybreak services, during which time even greater numbers of people come. In late March 1989, for example, the church caused a stir by successfully drawing ten thousand people a day to its special daybreak devotionals.

Nightlong Devotional (*Ch'ŏrya kido*)

Though not as well known as the daybreak devotional, the nightlong devotional is another ritual that is commonly practiced in Korean evangelical churches. This practice also has its origin in the Great Revival of 1907 and seemed to have become a fixed practice sometime after the Korean War. Unlike the daybreak prayer, a nightlong devotional is normally not a daily practice. In some churches, it is held once a month, though holding it weekly seems to be the norm. Usually held on Fridays, the devotional starts any time from 9:30 P.M. to 11:30 P.M. and lasts until between 2:00 A.M. to 4:00 A.M. The excerpt translated here describes how this devotional was practiced at three well-known churches in Seoul in the 1980s: Sungŭi (Methodist) Church, Yŏido Sunbogŭm (Pentecostal) Church, and Chunghyŏn (Presbyterian) Church.

Fasting-Prayer (*Kŭmsik kido*)

Fasting-prayer is another of the widely practiced devotionals in Korea, one that points to the ascetic strain in Korean evangelicalism. In *San'gortchak esŏ on p'yŏnji* (*Letters from a Mountain Valley*; vol. 2 [Seoul: Kungmin Ilbo, 1985], p. 261), the following comment is made by author Reuben A. Torrey (Tae Chŏndŏk in Ko rean), a respected Western Episcopalian priest who resided in Korea for four decades until his death in 2002 and who wrote numerous books in Korean on spirituality:

> Among the spiritual practices observed of the Korean church, yet another that shocks foreigners is fasting. Jesus taught us specifically that a fast should be done secretly so that no one could detect our doing it. I have frequently had Korean ministers ask me, "Father, what was the maximum number of days that you fasted?" I was shocked that they, by asking such a question, not only sought to show off their own experiences of fasting but also disdained Jesus' warning by trying to dig out the secret that should lie only between Jesus and me. I do not believe the missionaries had engaged in such behavior. I tend to think that this is a small piece of influence coming from shamanism. As I think about it, I am shocked as to how the Korean

church could have fallen into such a snare. In other words, the assumption is that if one applies pain to oneself, God will sympathize with him—if only reluctantly—and that if that pain is made known to others so that one could be praised, that in itself could prove to be a great consolation.

Torrey's observation is problematic yet suggestive. It is problematic because it gives the impression that Korean ministers in general are ostentatious about their fasting. This is not the case, as attested by articles in journals such as *Kido* and *Mokhoe wŏlgan* (Pastoral Monthly), where such behavior is routinely denounced—though, of course, the very existence of these articles implies that at least some of them do engage in such behavior. Also, Torrey's conjecture that the alleged problem of ostentatious fasting derives from shamanism is invidious; it reflects a common tendency that has prevailed among evangelicals in Korea, that of caricaturing shamanism and attributing to it just about everything bad and "unsophisticated" about their religion, a tendency that is directly linked to the early missionaries' haughty contempt toward native religion.

These caveats aside, however, Torrey's comment is still suggestive. For one, it rightly suggests that Korean evangelicals are less prudish about fasting (than fastidious Episcopalians, at least, to invoke another stereotype!)—that Korean evangelicals fast commonly and, sometimes, quite openly. All this, in turn, presupposes that among Korean evangelicals there is a belief that fasting-prayer is an especially effective means of approaching the divine. For unless this is presupposed, it is difficult to understand their ardent practice of it, not to mention the reams of writing recommending the virtues of fasting.

The excerpt on fasting-prayer included here was written by a premier practitioner of fasting-prayer, Ch'oe Chasil (Choi Ja Shil) (1915–89), cofounder of Yŏido Full Gospel Church. During her life, Ch'oe was renowned for her intensive prayer life—fasting in particular—such that after her death, the largest prayer center in Korea, belonging to Yŏido Full Gospel Church and located in Osanni, was named after her and her passion: Osanni Ch'oe Chasil kinyŏm kumsik kidowŏn (Osanri Choi Ja Shil Memorial Fasting-Prayer Mountain). Ch'oe's discussion here belies much of the impressions Torrey made about fasting in Korea.

The informal survey of Korean prayer practices is translated from Kim Myŏnghyŏk, "Han'guk kyohoe ŭi kido sŭpkwan" (Prayer Habits of the Korean [Protestant] Church), *Kido* (Prayer), February 1987, pp. 46–47. "The Korean Church and the Daybreak Prayer" is a translation of Im Taekchin, "Han'guk kyohoe wa saebyŏk kido," *Kido* (Prayer), January 1986, pp. 20–21. Im Taekchin is a minister and former moderator of Yejang t'onghap, one of the largest Presbyterian bodies in Korea. The article discusses the historical background and religious significance of this early morning devotional. "A Story of Korean Prayer" was written by the Presbyterian missionary William L. Swallen and appeared in *Korea Mission Field* 5, no. 11 (November 15, 1909): 182, an influential missionary journal published in Korea from 1905 to 1941, Swallen's account may very well be the earliest account available of the prayer gathering involving Kil Sŏnju that eventually became the *saebyŏk kidohoe.* "In Search of the Nightlong Prayer Meeting" translates the article "Chŏrya kidohoe rŭl ch'ajasŏ," *Kido* (Prayer), February 1987, pp. 26–27, written by the staff of the journal. "The Method of Fasting-Prayer" is translated from Ch'oe Chasil, *Kumsik kido ŭi nungnyŏk* (The Power of Fasting-Prayer) (Seoul: Seoul Sŏjŏk, 1977), pp. 64–70.

Further Reading

Jashil Choi, *Korean Miracles* (Seoul: Seoul Books, 1978); Karen Hurston, *Growing the World's Largest Church* (Springfield, Mo.: Chrism, 1994); Laurel Kendall and Griffin Dix, *Religion and Ritual in Korean Society*, Korea Research Monographs (Berkeley: Institute of East Asian Studies, 1987); Ki-Woon Kim, "A Critical Study of the Tradition of Early Morning Prayer Meetings in the Korean Church with an Accompanying Guideline for Pastors" (Doctor of Ministry thesis, San Francisco Theological Seminary, 1993); Sung C. Kim, "The Early Morning Prayer Meeting in the Korean-American Church" (Doctor of Ministry thesis, Boston University, 1995); Jung Young Lee, ed., *Ancestor Worship and Christianity in Korea* (Lewiston, N.Y.: Edwin Mellen, 1988); Timothy S. Lee, "Born-Again in Korea: The Rise and Character of Revivalism in (South) Korea, 1885–1988" (Ph.D. diss., University of Chicago, 1996); Seong-Won Park, *Worship in the Presbyterian Church in Korea: Its History and Implications* (Frankfurt am Main: Peter Lang, 1999).

Informal Survey on Korean Prayer Practices

Below I present prayer characteristics of Korean clergy and laity. For this presentation I sent a survey to 300 ministers; 100 responded. This presentation is based on the latter responses.

1. DAYBREAK PRAYER (*SAEBYŎK KIDO*)

One hundred percent of the ministers who responded regularly practiced the daybreak prayer, and 80 percent of them prayed individually in the church for thirty minutes to an hour after the daybreak prayer meeting ended. In most cases, the senior minister led the daybreak prayer, although on occasion an associate minister led it as well. Of the laity, about 10 percent [of the church membership] regularly participated in a daybreak prayer meeting held at 4:30 A.M. or 5:00 A.M. After about twenty minutes of the devotional, they engaged in about thirty minutes of individual prayer. At this time, they prayed as they wished, whether or not making loud sounds; occasionally they prayed making loud sounds. Some ministers strongly emphasized the importance of the daybreak prayer and stated that the success or failure of their ministry depended on it.

2. NIGHTLONG PRAYER (*CH'ŎRYA KIDO*)

Fifty percent of the responding ministers stated that they hold a nightlong prayer meeting once a week. Most of the churches gathered on Friday nights for a nightlong prayer meeting. Some churches met at 10:00 P.M. and prayed till 4:00 A.M. in the following morning; some churches met at 10:00 P.M. and prayed till 2:00 A.M. in the morning; and some churches held a nightlong prayer meeting from 12:00 midnight till 4:00 A.M. in the morning. About 10 to 20 percent of the congregation participated in these prayer meetings. Most of the time, a minister led these prayer meetings, though a group leader occasionally led them. In these meetings, participants hear simple messages or testimonies and pray individually; or they loudly pray together about several topics. Some congregational groups hold their nightlong devotionals at a prayer center in the mountains.

With regard to the benefits of the nightlong prayer meeting, the respondents stated that it adds vigor to their spiritual life, instills a prayer habit in them, and provides opportunities for close fellowship among the participants. They testified that many have received answers to their prayers through the nightlong prayer. As to the problems of the nightlong prayer, they indicated that there is the risk that the participants could lapse into spiritual pride and self-satisfaction. Another problem is that because the nightlong prayer causes one to be fatigued physically, participants cannot do anything the following day unless they take a nap at home or at the office.

3. FASTING [PRAYER] (*KŬMSIK [KIDO]*)

Quite a few of the ministers and the laity had experienced fasting from time to time. A small number of the ministers even had the experience of fasting ten or forty days. As to the main reasons for fasting, the clergy gave the following responses: (1) to cultivate a deeper spirituality, (2) to resolve one's family problems, (3) to cure illness, (4) to resolve business problems, and (5) to resolve church problems.

With regard to the benefits of fasting, the respondents stated that by affording intensive prayer and deep self-reflection, it enables them to have an experience of assurance. And it allows one to look up to Jesus by enabling one to overcome the passions of the body. But problems of fasting were also pointed out. That is, like the nightlong prayer, it can easily cause one to have spiritual pride, self-satisfaction, and even a sense of superiority over other believers. Sometimes fasting is misunderstood as a panacea for illness and problems.

The Korean Church and the Daybreak Prayer

The Korean church's daybreak prayer meeting is a peculiar type [of devotion] not found in churches of the West or of other parts of the East. The daybreak prayer meeting designates an assembly where believers gather at church every day before daybreak to pray. Though it is called a prayer meeting, its content consists of a collective worship comprising hymn singing, prayer, and scriptural instruction or sermon, followed by individual or collective prayer.

Time should be set aside for prayer but why pray at daybreak? Daybreak is a time that holds immense significance for religious mystery. Even in shamanism, aside from its significance as the start of a day, daybreak is highly valued as a sacred time belonging to deities, the time whose importance is no less than that of a place where supplications to deities are realized. . . .

Bible study and daybreak prayer meetings have also permanently influenced the Korean church's revival movement. The start of the Korean church's revival movement was in Wŏnsan in 1903. In Wŏnsan the missionaries engaged in weeklong Bible study and prayer meetings, and they repented of their sins and experienced the Holy Spirit, thus initiating the revival of the church.

In 1907, as a great revival occurred while holding Bible study conferences, daybreak prayer meetings occurred simultaneously. The daybreak prayer that Reverend Kil Sŏnju started was held not only during Bible study conferences but at church every Sunday; and even on days other than Sunday believers came to church to pray, a practice that eventually became a permanent custom. At every Bible study conference or retreat, a daybreak prayer meeting was held as a matter of course; this was also the case whenever a presbytery or assembly met to carry out its business. After liberation [from Japanese occupation in 1945] and the Korean War, the churches came to hold daybreak prayer meetings not only on Sundays but every day. The Korean church has made the daybreak prayer its own, and the devotional has now become an essential element of the [church's] revival movement.

A Story of Korean Prayer

Mr. Kill [Kil Sŏnju,] the Korean pastor of the large Central Church in Pyeng Yang [P'yŏngyang], having felt some time that a kind of coldness had come over the Christians in the city, resolved with one of his elders to go to the church every morning at dawn to pray. These two men with humble trustful faith thus continued in prayer every morning at a little after four for about two months, without having spoken to anyone about it—in fact I think no one knew of it. But somehow when it gradually became known to a few, some score or more united with them in these morning prayers. Then the pastor, seeing there was a desire on the part of others to join him, announced to the church on Sunday morning that any who *wished* to pray with them at this time might do so, and that the bell would be rung at 4:30 A.M. The next morning at 1 A.M. the people began coming, and by two o'clock several hundred had gathered. When the bell was rung there were some four or five hundred Christians present, and after a few days the number who met at this early hour was between six and seven hundred. On the fourth morning while praying, suddenly the whole congregation broke down weeping for their sins of indifference, coldness, and lack of love and energy for work. Then came the joy of forgiveness and a strong desire to be shown ways and means to work for God. Four more mornings were thus spent in prayer, singing praises and asking God's direction, when the pastor thinking that it was now time to do something, asked how many would give a whole day to go out and preach to the unbelieving souls and lead them to Christ. *All* hands went up. Then he asked how many will go two days. Again nearly all hands were raised. At the request of three days fewer hands went up but still many, and so on through four, five, and six days, the number gradually lessening, but even for seven days there were quite a number.

That was a blessed communion which they partook of on the following Lord's day, and since then the whole church is eagerly going out and leading others to Christ.

In Search of the Nightlong Prayer Meeting

SUNGŬI CHURCH

Located in Inch'ŏn, Sungŭi Church (Korean Methodist Church) has held nightly prayer meetings for the last decade, and it is among several churches that have actively engaged in the practice. From 10:00 P.M. to 11:00 P.M. the participants prepare for the service by singing hymns and gospel songs, and the leader leads the praise as a team, along with a trio of guitarists and a pianist. From 11:00 P.M. to midnight a service is held, minus offertory. After the service, participants pray loudly and simultaneously about their individual problems. At the end of the prayer, Reverend Yi Homun, the senior minister, appears and gives a report of the past week. It is followed by a coffee break.

About 2,000 meet weekly for a nightlong prayer service, and the service is held at Bethlehem chapel, which was made specifically for this purpose. The coffee time lasts from thirty to forty minutes, with coffee provided freely. Before the start of the second part, participants prepare the mood by engaging in twenty minutes of hymn singing. Then around 1:00 A.M., the body-rhythm singers appear, leading the participants to twenty minutes of body-rhythm worship, with the wife of Rev. Yi Homun as the leader of the team. Next appears a twelve-member band that performs gospel music, and then the prayer service starts under the leadership of Rev. Yi Homun. At this time, prayers are made for designated topics, and prayers are said for the country, the church, and topics requested by church members. These requests are mainly for concerted prayers for healing of the ill—and there have been many answered prayers. Next, a male or a female vocal ensemble performs—they alternate weekly; then there is a short prayer meeting. Afterward, from 2:00 A.M., a guest testifier shares a testimony for about two hours.

This meeting has been held for the past ten years without a week having been skipped, and countless testifiers have visited. Testifiers are selected mainly from the laity. After the testimony, it is about 4:00 A.M.; thereafter, Rev. Yi Homun and associate ministers round off the prayer meeting, and the members return home after praying as they desire. Rev. Yi Homun does all the presiding, and the occasional display of wit on his part to stave off tedium meshes well with the efforts of the participants to make this nightlong devotional shine.

YŎIDO FULL GOSPEL CHURCH (YŎIDO SUNBOGŬM KYOHOE)

Yŏido Full Gospel Church ([led by] Rev. Cho Yonggi) has held the nightlong prayer service for a long time. From 10:30 P.M., the participants engage in 30 minutes of preparatory hymn singing. From 11:00 P.M., there is a sermon and hymn sing; this is followed by a prayer seeking the arrival of the Holy Spirit. Concentrated prayers are said for those who have not received the baptism of the Holy Spirit. At 1:30 A.M., body-rhythm singing is done to refresh the atmosphere. Then the members give testimonies, usually five to seven minutes of testimonies regarding changes they have experienced—healing or some special changes they experienced during worship or nightlong prayer. . . . The testimonies last for about an hour; afterward, topical prayers are held. Prayers are said for topics such as the state, the nation, and the church; thereafter, participants freely return home. About 20,000 participate in the service.

CH'UNGHYŎN [PRESBYTERIAN] CHURCH (CH'UNGHYŎN KYOHOE)

Ch'unghyŏn Church ([led by] Rev. Kim Ch'angin) holds its nightlong prayer service at the church and its North Korean Missionary Institute. At the church itself, about 1,000 gather; and from 11:30 P.M. to 1:00 A.M., worship, which includes preaching, is held; this is followed by thirty minutes of snack time. From 1:30 A.M. to 3:00 A.M. or 3:30 A.M., a prayer service is held, which ends with topical prayers. At North Korean Missionary Institute ([at] Mount Sinae prayer house), preparatory hymn singing is held till 11:30 P.M., and worship is held till 12:30 A.M., which includes hymns and body rhythm, with a band providing accompaniment. After having some enjoyable time, a topical prayer session is held till 3:00 A.M.; then with a sermon till 4:00 A.M., the service is over. One thousand people participate in the nightlong prayer meeting.

The Method of Fasting-Prayer

1. PREPARATION FOR FASTING-PRAYER

Up to this point, we have learned that fasting-prayer bears amazing efficacy and blessings. From now on, let us investigate specifically how to do fasting-prayer. For however much efficacy fasting-prayer has, we cannot attain the desired results if we do not have adequate preliminary knowledge about fasting-prayer.

From days of old, people have known that fasting-prayer is a way to experience spiritual blessing and God's great ability for healing incurable diseases, but they have not practiced it widely because of the misconception that it is difficult and painful to undertake. In past days, in undertaking fasting-prayer, one would go into a tall mountain or a deep valley and blindly engage in the asceticism of fasting-prayer, without any preparation, relying solely on one's mental power. Consequently, it was unimaginable for ordinary persons—or the sick and the weak—to engage in fasting-prayer.

It is true that fasting-prayer requires a total abstinence from food, but it differs from physical starvation. It avails itself of the nutrients that have been accumulated in the body; consequently, if we properly manage the initial transitional reactions and if there is a guide who, in faith, ensures that the faster is at a physiologically sound state, anybody can easily engage in fasting-prayer for a week or two without much pain—and if they persist with effort and patience, they can continue even longer, to thirty or forty days. But if we follow others into fasting-prayer simply because they have vaguely said it is desirable, without sufficient preliminary knowledge, we will not only fail to experience the amazing power of fasting-prayer, but won't be able to endure even three days—and may even incur unexpected injury.

In doing fasting-prayer, the biggest temptation is the thought that "I should fast longer than anybody else." This is called hubris. Consequently, if we do not think of our physical limits and force ourselves unreasonably, driven by physical and carnal thought, we will instead diminish life and inflict huge injury on our faith. Therefore whoever wants to engage in fasting-prayer should properly understand their circumstances and undertake it with firm conviction and a clear goal.

2. MATTERS TO BE AWARE OF BEFORE FASTING

It is paramount that those who wish to undertake fasting-prayer should know that conduct before and after fasting is more important than during the actual fasting. The preparatory period before fasting is known as the preliminary fasting period. During this period, the faster should start limiting food intake beforehand. Over two to three days, food intake should be reduced step by step from three meals a day to two meals a day and from two meals to one meal, till entering the actual, complete fasting. And during preliminary fasting, it is even better to take vermicide to eliminate mawworms and parasites and to take a laxative to eliminate feces in the large intestine and to keep the stomach and the intestine clean.

3. MATTERS TO BE AWARE OF WHILE FASTING

Those who have gone through the preliminary fasting stage, have completed the preparation, and have entered fasting-prayer in earnest should take special note of and carry out the following points. First, they should take unfailing care to drink water. According to *Webster's* dictionary and a Bible dictionary, fasting is defined as "abstaining from food, especially as a religious discipline." Food is defined as "nutrients that have solid forms." Therefore cold water that has nothing added to it is not food.

Therefore since it absolutely does not contravene faith to drink water, which promotes the cleansing in the body, a faster must drink water. And it should not be forgotten that the liquid must be cold water. Cola, cider, or any kinds of fruit nectar that have sweeteners added to them are not acceptable. It is all right to drink water from a well or a tap as it is, but boiled water is not good. As those of us who keep goldfish know, a goldfish that lives in cooled boiled water will not live for long. Similarly, it is also difficult for people who are fasting to maintain their energy on boiled water. Cold water should not be drunk a lot at once but a cup at a time—six or seven times a day. If fasting is undertaken without drinking any water at all, an ordinary person will become exhausted in less than ten days. (It is all right for a person who fasts over ten days to take some salt.) As long as water is drunk, anyone can fast for three to four weeks without a problem—even to 120 or more days. Therefore when fasting, we must drink water without fail.

Second, while undertaking fasting-prayer, we should not take a hot bath. If we take a hot bath, we will feel dizzy and find it difficult to remain standing. Therefore rather than taking a bath in hot water, it is better to wipe the entire body clean with a wet lukewarm towel. We should do this without fail. For toxins that remain in the body while fasting will extrude in a powerful way, causing the skin to smell very stinky. (The teeth should be brushed often.)

Third, while undertaking fasting-prayer, one should, of course, not engage in excessive exercise or excessive work; one should not even engage in intensive reading for a long time. Since intensive activities greatly tire the body and the mind, they are big obstacles in achieving the effects of fasting. On the other hand, light exercise, work, or reading hinders fasting little. Quite the contrary, it is very good to read the Bible while engaged in fasting-prayer. Since inside the Bible are 32,500 promises that God has made, reading the Bible gives the faster faith, conviction, courage, and the blessings of heaven, as well as the springing of gratitude from within. Moreover, it is possible to read through the entire Bible during a set period of fasting-prayer.

Fourth, I mentioned above that during preliminary fasting, a laxative should be taken to cleanse the intestine. If even after taking laxatives daily, there is no bowel movement after two or three days due to constipation, it is desirable to empty the bowels using an enema. Do not fail to resort to an enema. (The exception here is in the case of rectal cancer.)

These are the four matters that must be kept in mind while engaged in fasting. The Bible says that one person undertaking fasting-prayer can drive away a thousand enemies; two, ten thousand enemies; and when two or three beseech, I [God] will be with you—consequently, (assuming it is possible) it will be all the more helpful in receiving large blessings if the more people fast together. If we engage in fasting-prayer, we will receive a gift of love, which will cause our hearts to be generous—removing from them anyone to hate—and will enable us to forbear for a long time and persevere till the end. For we destroy carnal thoughts that are within us and become persons of spirit.

4. MATTERS TO BE AWARE OF AFTER FASTING, WHILE ENGAGED IN CONSERVATIVE EATING

The most difficult stage in fasting-prayer discipline is resuming eating right after fasting. Indeed it is not an exaggeration to say that the success or failure of fasting-prayer depends on how much care is taken during this stage.

Put differently, fasting is like laying the foundation when building a house. Adjusting how one eats after fasting is like building a house on top of that foundation. Unless we are careful about this point, we may not only fail to reap the efficacy of fasting but might instead have to face the possibility of causing great harm to our body. Consequently, after fasting, what we must be most careful about is not to eat solid food and not to overeat. When we finish fasting, the temptation to eat food will be overwhelming. Should we regard this lightly as a sort of instinct and eat to our fill—as demanded by our mouths—we might even run the risk of losing our lives. I know of an instance in which a person lost her life after thirty days of fasting because she fell into the temptation of appetite and did not follow the warnings and ate solid foods such as rice and meat. Therefore upon completing a fast, we must overcome this fearsome challenge of our instincts and only slowly increase our food intake.

There is no set regulation, but the following generally addresses how much to eat when resuming eating and how to manage it. On the first day, it is good to start off by drinking *kimch'i* juice (continually drink watery radish kimchi [*tongch'imi*]), and it is good to take thin gruel in the morning and in the evening. The quantity should normally be about a cupful. In some cases, it would be all right to drink a mixture of a half cup of apple juice and a half cup of gruel. If possible, it would be good to consume a thin porridge made of rice powder and ripe squash or a thin porridge made of bean sprouts. On the second day, drink a slightly thickened gruel. On the third day, we should normally eat a bowl of porridge and a piece of tomato or apple or a piece of preserved peach. Hereafter, though it varies depending on the length of fasting, the aim is gradually to increase the quantity of porridge and to transition into small portions of cooked rice, as well as increasing the variety of side dishes. When eating again, we should, as far as possible, chew thoroughly and for a long time, to ensure that our food is well mixed with saliva. Generally the period we eat like this should be directly proportional to the period we have fasted. In other words, if we have fasted one week, we should be careful about eating for one week.

When we have resumed eating, from the start, we will be powerfully tempted by a strong appetite. At this time, we need to forbear with patience and limit our eating. When resuming eating, this is the most difficult time. We need to be alert and transition through this time. We must be cautious, for if we eat according to our appetite's inclination, we will have a big disaster at our hands. That is because in the second or third week after fasting, our liver is not yet able to function normally. Even if we have fasted for a long time, if two weeks have lapsed since fasting, we can eat whatever we wish, so long as it is not too much. And after three weeks, we can return to a normal eating routine, eating three times a day.

To emphasize once again, if we have undertaken three days of fasting-prayer, we must be cautious about eating for three days after the fast; if five days of fasting-prayer, five days of caution; if ten days, ten days of caution; if thirty days, thirty days of caution—in accordance with the method and order of the intake as spelled out in these instructions.

25

The Grieving Rite: A Protestant Response to Confucian Ancestral Rituals

James Huntley Grayson

Before examining the grieving rite, a Protestant practice unique in Korea, two points need to be made. First of all, "Protestantism in Korea" in this chapter shall refer principally to those churches that stem from the Methodist and Presbyterian traditions, including groups such as the Salvation Army and the Holiness Church (Sŏnggyŏl kyohoe), as well as other groups in the traditions of the Baptist movement and the Assemblies of God. The definition of "Protestantism" used here excludes the Anglican Church because the Church of England mission in Korea was of the "High Church" tradition and identified itself as being "catholic" and not "protestant." Secondly, Protestant missions in Korea derived largely from denominations in the United States, with some input from Canadian and Australian missions. Consequently, the Protestant churches in Korea have come to reflect these American roots in the context of Korean culture. This statement is true ecclesiastically and liturgically as well as theologically.

Protestant Religious Practices

Following the conclusion of the Civil War in the United States in 1865, religious revivals there led to the development of a movement for world missions. Regardless of denomination, the evangelical and missionary movements were characterized by three features: pietism in worship and religious life, a focus on scripture, and an emphasis on social concerns. Each of these features has left its imprint on contemporary Protestant practice in Korea. An important feature of Protestant missions in Korea was the substantial extent of mutual interdenominational cooperation between all mission groups, which culminated in the proposal of 1905 made by all Protestant missionaries to create a single united church of Christ in Korea. Although this proposal was turned down by the mission boards in the United States, the high degree of cooperation in the early stages of mission has

left its mark on Protestant practice today. In spite of certain differences from denomination to denomination, the structure of Sunday services is remarkably similar across the denominations, a sense of similarity heightened by the use of a
common hymnbook rather than a denominational one, and the use since 1910 of
a single authorized translation of the Bible. The most recent revision, called the
P'yojun sae p ŏnyŏk (Standard New Translation, or New Korean Standard Version),
was published in 1993.

Although many Korean Protestants have a strong personal identification with a
particular denominational group, the actual ecclesiology of the Korean Protestant
denominations is remarkably similar. Two key aspects of American Methodism
are episcopacy ("bishops") and itinerancy. Episcopacy means that the bishop is
appointed for "life" (until retirement), and, while being responsible for chairing
annual meetings called "conferences," he or she has "the power of appointment":
the authority to appoint the clergy wherever and whenever he or she desires. Itinerancy means that the clergy expect to move from one clerical charge to another
within a matter of years. Lay officials in a church are elected regularly and never
serve for "life." The Presbyterian system is very different. Annual regional meetings, or "synods," are chaired by annually elected chairmen or "moderators," who
serve to represent the church but have no authority to appoint clergy. Clergy are
appointed to a church by the local membership, and once in office can be moved
or removed only with difficulty. Ecclesiastical authority lies at a more local level
with the "presbyters," or lay elders, who are selected for "life." Consequently,
Methodism can be said to have a more centralized structure of authority, reflecting its Anglican roots, while Presbyterianism has a more localized structure.

In Korea, the Methodist Church's ecclesiology has been significantly "presbyte-
rianized" in that the bishops are elected to hold office for a very short period of
time and act mainly as a symbolic chairman for a particular conference like a
Presbyterian moderator. They have no power of appointment. Selection of the
minister of a Methodist church in Korea is done in effect at the local level. The
Methodist churches, like the Presbyterian churches of Korea, which are called
Changnohoe, have elders (*changno*) elected for "life." Both denominations also
have a lower tier of local church leaders called *kwŏnsa* (deacons) who are subordinate to the *changno*. However, there is a significant difference between the
Methodist and Presbyterian groups in that in Methodism men and women can be
either a *kwŏnsa* or a *changno*, whereas in Presbyterianism generally only men are
changno, and only women are *kwŏnsa*.

There is a third and lower level of church leadership called a *chipsa* (class
leader). These leaders have responsibility for local study groups (home groups)
which meet on a weekly basis to study the Bible and to pray together. These
groups are not a feature of Presbyterianism but of Methodism. Methodism began
in the mid–eighteenth century as a pietistic revival movement within the Church
of England. Its chief feature was the "class meeting" for the study of the scriptures, prayer, and mutual spiritual encouragement. Although these cell groups
are not characteristic of traditional Presbyterian or any other denominational

practice other than Methodism, they have been adopted by all Protestant groups in Korea. Known in the Korean Methodist Church as *sokhoe* (class meeting) and in the Presbyterian churches as *kuyŏkhoe* (local meeting), these groups are the backbone of congregational life in Korea.

Ch'udo Yebae

With the establishment of the Chosŏn kingdom (1392–1910) at the end of the fourteenth century, a process of the thorough "Confucianization" of society was gradually undertaken. In practice this meant the government placed a strong emphasis on the Confucian value of "filial piety," or *hyo* in Korean: respect for your parents and reverence toward one's ancestors as being the key moral value personally and socially. In Confucianism, the expression ritually of values such as *hyo* was seen to be the outer sign of the inner moral condition of the person. Consequently, elite families were encouraged to maintain family ancestral shrines and to perform regularly ancestral rituals, called *chesa* in Korean, as a means to give ritual expression to their sense of filial piety, as well as to provide a means for the moral disciplining of their self. Over the course of centuries, the elite of this very long-lived dynasty pursued a policy of thoroughly "Confucianizing" all aspects of society. Over many years, local communities were encouraged to adopt village covenants or *hyangyak*, which bound the members of village society to adhere to Confucian moral concepts and patterns of behavior. As ritual became increasingly important in this project as a means to express Confucian values, the use of books of ritual practice was also encouraged in order to create a uniformity of practice. The standard handbook in use throughout Korea was the *Chuja karye* (The Book of Family Ritual by Zhu Xi), which contains precise descriptions of how to perform the four types of rites that were thought to maintain proper social etiquette. These rites were the capping (coming of age), marriage, mourning, and ancestral ceremonies. This text contains a precise outline of every stage in each ceremony, providing the words to be used, and indicating the precise actions to be taken (kneeling, movement to a new place, and so forth). In this sense, the *Karye* is the Confucian equivalent of the Anglican Book of Common Prayer. Among the ancestral rituals the *k'ilche*, or death-date memorial rite, was a key family ceremony as it was *the* means for ritually expressing filial piety.

Thus by the late eighteenth century, when Roman Catholic Christianity began to spread into Korea, filial piety had come to be seen as the core moral value upholding society, which was ritually expressed through *chesa*. However, at the same time, and contrary to the urgings of earlier Jesuit missionaries to China, the Vatican had defined Confucian ancestral rituals as idolatrous because they were thought not to be memorial rites but to be the worship of spirits other than Almighty God. In Christian theology, the uniqueness of God and the consequent worship of him alone is a key moral and theological value. Consequently, Christianity in its earliest stages in Korea had to deal with a clash of two core values:

the Confucian values of Korean society and the values of the newly imported religion. The result of this clash was more than three-quarters of a century of severe persecution of Catholicism, in which successive Korean governments attempted to eradicate what was seen to be a pernicious doctrine, resulting in the deaths of thousands of early Catholic believers.

Following the signing of Western-style diplomatic treaties by the Korean government in the mid-1880s, various Protestant missionary bodies, largely from North America, began to establish missionary work there. Protestant missionaries of all denominations took the same view toward the performance of the *chesa* rites as had the Catholic Church, with the result that converts to either Methodism or Presbyterianism were forbidden to participate in them. Although the Korean government of the late nineteenth century did not pursue a policy of persecution for noncompliance in the practice of ancestral rituals, centuries of Confucian moral discipline had created in the minds of the early converts a strong desire to find a way to ritually express their feelings for their deceased parents, especially on their death date.

By the end of the 1890s, it had become common among early converts to Methodism to perform death-date rituals called *ki'il yebae* (death-date rite) or *ch'udo yebae* (grieving rite). The earliest record of a ritual of this type appears in a newspaper article of 1897, which states that on the death date of his mother a member of Chŏngdong Methodist Church in Seoul invited members of the church to his home to attend a ceremony on behalf of his deceased mother. A candle was lit, prayers were offered to God on behalf of his mother, a hymn was sung, his mother's faith in God and her moral virtues were publicly recalled, there was lamentation for her death, and concluding prayers. The article said that as the people who had attended this informal ritual felt it was a beautiful form of *chesa*, the rite had subsequently become common practice within their congregation. Within ten years or so of the arrival of foreign missionaries, the first generation of Korean Protestants had themselves found a way to resolve the major conflict of values between the moral values of their society and the theological values of their newly accepted religion, and to do so in a ritual way that was acceptable to both sides in the conflict.

Since the late eighteenth century, Methodism in the United States has followed a liturgical practice contained in a book of liturgy that derives from the Anglican Book of Common Prayer, the various services of worship of which were modified equivalents of the Anglican services. This American Methodist book of liturgy, The Book of Worship, was translated into the Korean language from a very early date, forming the liturgical section (*yemun*) of a book called *Kyori wa changjŏng* (Doctrines and Discipline). Among the specialized services were liturgies for baptism, confirmation, communion, and funerals. In 1935, the first *Kyori wa changjŏng* published by a newly independent Korean Methodist Church contained—in addition to those rituals—a new ritual called *Pumonim k'il kinyŏmsik sunsyŏ* (Order of Service for a Memorial Rite on the Death Date of a Parent). This is first time that any denomination had created a formal *ch'udo yebae* liturgy, which specified the precise order of service, the words to be used in each element of the service, the form of the prayers to be said, and the portion of scripture to be read. Early formalization of ch'udo yebae practice by the Methodists reflects the stronger liturgical sense of American Methodism compared with Presbyterianism. It also reflects the Korean Confucian practice of formalized ritual observance as represented by the Karye.

Styling the new ritual as a "Memorial Rite on the Death Date of a Parent" reflected the Korean Confucian tradition of holding a chesa ceremony on the precise death date of a relative or ancestor. The specification of the ritual as being as a commemoration of the parent reflected both the emphasis on filial piety in Confucianism and the Christian emphasis on honoring one's parents, the fifth of the Ten Commandments. The choice of the term kinyŏmsik, or memorial ritual, reflects the Christian concern not to contravene the first and second of the Ten Commandments to worship no other gods but God. The new ritual was to be a memorial rite on behalf of the deceased parent, but not to be the worship of their spirit, which was said to be the case by some people regarding chesa. Thus, Pumonim ki'il kinyŏmsik was a carefully crafted ritual that represented one of the earliest examples of a formal resolution of the conflict of values between the indigenous Confucian culture of Korea and Christian theology and is thus a prime example of what some theologians refer to as "indigenization."

The order of the service in Pumonim ki'il kinyŏmsik followed the pattern of hymn, prayer, three readings from scripture, a reflection on the life of the deceased, a hymn, and a memorial prayer followed by the benediction, following the pattern of usage since the 1890s. In 1955, the Salvation Army and the Holiness Church, denominations in the Methodist/Wesleyan tradition, added a death-date memorial ritual to their books of liturgy, which were styled for the first time as a ch'udosik or ch'udohoe (grieving ritual). Until 1978, none of the branches of Presbyterianism in Korea had a denominational book of liturgy. Instead, patterns for services of worship were suggested in handbooks for ministers such as the Moksaŭi p'irhyu (The Minister's Requisites), but these handbooks did not provide the tight liturgical format of the Methodist Kyori wa changjŏng. In 1978, the Kijang (Christ Presbyterian) Church published its Yesik sŏ (Book of Ritual), which included a formalized ch'udosik rite. Subsequently, all denominations in the Yejang (Jesus Presbyterian) bloc and all other Protestant groups including the Baptists and Assemblies of God have come to use books of liturgy, and these books all include liturgies to be used on the death date of a relative.

Popularly, these rituals became known as a ch'udosik or ch'udo yebae. By 1973, the Methodist book of liturgy compromised by using the term ch'udosik in place of ki'ilsik by referring to the ritual as a Pumonim ch'udosik. By using the term pumonim for parents, the ritual still maintained its association as a rite solely for one's parents. In the denomination's 2002 book of liturgy, however, the reference to parents is dropped and the term ch'umo sik (memorial rite) is substituted for ch'udosik, turning the rite into a general commemoration ritual—although commemoration does not go as far back as in the usage of the Confucian chesa rite.

In Presbyterian and conservative circles, there has been noticeable dissatis-faction with the term *ch'udosik*, which is felt to carry a strong sense of grieving, leading to the general adoption of the term *ch'umosik* (memorial rite), which is thought to convey a stronger sense of commemoration and to be freer from po-tential pagan influences. Generally, non-Methodist liturgical books preface the words of the liturgy with strong theological statements that the rite is addressed to God giving thanks for the life of the deceased, and emphasizes that it is in no way the worship of their spirit. This indicates that in conservative circles, al-though death-date rituals are performed, there is a higher degree of concern for the potential pagan character of the memorial rites than there is in Methodist circles.

The last quarter of a century has seen the development of additional rituals fo-cused on the commemoration of the dead, many of which have not yet found their way into denominational books of liturgy. Among these new rituals are *Ch'ŏt sŏngmyo* (First Visit to the Grave Mound), *Sŏngmyo* ([Annual] Visit to the Grave Mound), and *T'alsang yebae* (Mourning-Period Final Worship). The creation of these new rites illustrates the concern of a Confucian society for the appropriate and visible expression of filial and familial attitudes. The creation in the 1890s of an informal ritual specifically to commemorate one's parents led eventually to the emergence of a wider definition of ritual usage to incorporate other family mem-bers, leading in turn to the creation of a range of rituals dealing with the various aspects of traditional ritual expressions of filial piety, in particular regular visits to grave sites. Thus the initial informal *ch'udosik* rituals of the end of the nineteenth century, which had been a Christian response to the cultural values of a Confucian society, have led to the development of a complex of Confucianized Christian ritu-als. This "Confucianization" of Protestant Christian ritual practice is an excellent marker of the extent to which Korean Protestantism has successfully accommo-dated itself to Korean culture, in spite of numerous, superficial appearances to the contrary.

Ch'umosik and *Ch'ŏt sŏngmyo* are translated from *Yemun* (*Book of Liturgy*) (Seoul: Korean Methodist Church, Board of Communication and Publication, 2002), pp. 125–34. Passages of scripture are taken from Holy Bible: New International Version.

Further Reading

James H. Grayson, *Korea: A Religious History*, rev. ed. (Richmond, Va.: Routledge-Curzon, 2002); Don Baker, "Christianity 'Koreanized,'" in *Nationalism and the Construction of Korean Identity*, Korea Research Monograph 26, edited by Hyung Il Pai and Timothy R. Tangherlini (Berkeley: Institute of East Asian Studies, 1998); Donald N. Clark, *Christianity in Modern Korea* (Lanham, Md.: University Press of America, 1986); Kwang-ok Kim, "Ritual Forms and Religious Experiences:

Protestant Christians in Contemporary Korean Political Context," in *Religion and Society in Contemporary Korea*, Korea Research Monograph 24, edited by Lewis R. Lancaster and Richard K. Payne (Berkeley: Institute of East Asian Studies, 1997).

LITURGICAL TEXTS

CH'UMOSIK (MEMORIAL RITE)

The Leader of the Ritual: The Person in Charge

(If there is a photograph, this may be placed on the altar; candles and flowers may be used as decorations. Members of the family and members of the church should sit around the altar; the leader will stand or sit in front. In the case of an elderly person who has no specific title, it is appropriate to address them as orŭn [elder], sŏnsaengnim [teacher; mister], haraböji [grandfather], halmŏni [grandmother], and so forth.)

Opening Words: The Leader

As today is the memorial date (*ch'umo il*) of (*changno* [elder], *kwŏnsa* [deacon], *chipsa* [class leader], church member, etc.), we now commence the ritual of rememberance [*ch'umosik*] for him/her.

Silent Prayer: Together

"Do not let your hearts be troubled. Trust in God; trust also in me. In my Father's house are many rooms; if it were not so, I would have told you. I am going there to prepare a place for you. And if I go and prepare a place for you, I will come back and take you to be with me that you also may be where I am. You know the way to the place where I am going." Thomas said to him, "Lord, we don't know where you are going, so how can we know the way?" Jesus answered, "I am the way and the truth and the life. No-one comes to the Father except through me" (John 14:1–6).

Hymn (No. 543): Together

I'm Pressing on the Upward Way

Prayer: The Leader (Choose one of the following prayers).

Prayer 1:

O ever-living God who has control of the life, death, and happiness of humanity! Today we have gathered together in this place on the date on which you called the late (*changno* [elder], *kwŏnsa* [deacon], *chipsa* [class leader], church member, etc.). We beseech you to have compassion on us by giving us your blessing and the peace of heaven.

God of Compassion!

We feeble ones beseech you to forgive the sins which we have committed against you and our fellow men.

O Lord who blesses when we believe in the unseen hope rather than the seen hope which is not hope!
You govern your kingdom; grant that we may work only for your kingdom on earth and its righteousness.

We recall and bewail the many sins which we have committed not only against you but also against our earthly parents. Please forgive these our sins. Give to us an even stronger faith. Continually strengthen the faith of this family.

(If the deceased was a member of the church, the following words may be used)

Gracious God!
We give you thanks for strengthening the faith of the late (*changno* [elder], *kwŏnsa* [deacon], *chipsa* [class leader], church membe, etc.) while he/she was alive on earth. We too, following him/her, in faith wish to live a sincere life.

We pray that you will truly guide and direct every element [of this service] so that to You will be the glory. Give us anew grace and blessing.

We pray in the name of our Lord, Jesus Christ.
Amen.

Prayer 2:
O ever-living God who has control of the life, death, and happiness of humanity!

On the day on which you called the late (*changno* [elder], *kwŏnsa* [deacon], *chipsa* [class leader], church member, etc.) to your kingdom, we have gathered together in this place in order to commemorate that day. We beseech you to have compassion on us by giving us your blessing and the peace of heaven.

God of Compassion!
We feeble ones beseech you to forgive the sins which we have committed against you and our fellow men.

We recall and bewail the many sins which we have committed not only against you but also against our earthly parents. Please forgive these our sins. Give to us an even stronger faith. Continually strengthen the faith of this family.

(If the deceased was a believer, the following words may be used).

We give you thanks for strengthening the faith of the late (*changno* [elder], *kwŏnsa* [deacon], *chipsa* [class leader], church member, etc.) while he/she was alive on earth. Grant that we too, following him/her, may in faith live a sincere life.

We pray that you will truly guide and direct every element [of this service] so that to You will be the glory. Give us anew grace and blessing.

We pray in the name of Jesus Christ Who is the guardian of our life and death.
Amen.

Reading from Scripture: The Leader

"My son, do not forget my teaching, but keep my commands in your heart, for they will prolong your life many years and bring you prosperity.

Let Love and faithfulness never leave you; bind them around your neck, write them on the tablet of your heart. Then you will win favor and a good name in the sight of God and man.

Trust in the Lord with all your heart and lean not on your own understanding; in all your ways acknowledge him, and he will make your paths straight.

Do not be wise in your own eyes; fear the Lord and shun evil. This will bring health to your body and nourishment to your bones.

Honor the Lord with your wealth, with the firstfruits of all your crops; then your barns will be filled to overflowing, and your vats will brim over with new wine."
Proverbs 3:1–10.

(Supplementary Readings: Psalms 90:1–6; 1 Corinthians 15:20–22, 422–44; Gospel According to St. Luke 16:19–31, 23:39–43; Revelation 21:1–8.)

Words of Recollection: The Leader

(*Members of the family and close friends may speak about the life, work, last words, character, and deep impressions of the deceased.*)

Proclamation of the Word: The Leader

Hymn (541): Together
Face to Face with Christ My Saviour.

Prayer: The Leader

(*If the leader is a minister, he/she may finish with the Benediction.*)

God of Glory!
We are sinful people who do not know that which hinders us. However, through the Word of God we know of your eternal kingdom. Grant that we may have a faith which overcomes all trials while living in this world, always joyful in hope, and that we may see that eternal kingdom. Each day send down blessings on this family; grant that the work of the eternal God may spread to the descendants [of the deceased].

We pray in the name of Jesus Christ who gives us eternal life.
Amen.

(After worship, there may be a time for greetings, fellowship, and the exchange of good wishes.)

CH'ŎT SŎNGMYO (FIRST VISIT TO THE GRAVE MOUND)

The Leader of the Ritual: The Person in Charge

(Usually the first visit to the burial mound is on the fourth day after the burial. Excepting on the Lord's Day, the surviving family members should gather on a convenient day. When they arrive at the burial site, they should first place a flower basket or bunch of flowers in an appropriate place, and then pray silently. When everyone is gathered in front of the burial mound and worship is to begin, either a minister or an adult of the family may lead [the worship].)

Opening Words: The Leader

With silent prayer, let us begin the first graveside worship as we recall the late (*changno* [elder], *kwŏnsa* [deacon], *chipsa* [class leader], church member, etc.) who has left this world to go the Lord's kingdom.

Silent Prayer: Together

"I am the resurrection and the life. He who believes in me will live, even though he dies; and whoever lives and believes in me will never die. Do you believe this?"

"Yes, Lord! I believe that you are the Christ, the Son of God, who was to come into the world."
Amen

Hymn (543): Together

(Or a hymn which the deceased enjoyed and sang.)

I'm Pressing on the Upward Way.

Prayer: The Leader

God of Grace!

We, who at the time of the death of the late (*changno* [elder], *kwŏnsa* [deacon], *chipsa* [class leader], church member, etc.), were fearful and did not know what to do, were able through the grace and comfort of the Lord to hold the funeral of the deceased. Today, we come to the graveside to hold the first graveside memorial service. We truly thank You that until now You have guarded and guided this grieving family. Comfort the members of the family who have gathered here. Lord, grant that you will guide them by the cloud and fiery pillar; encourage them so that as they pass through this stormy world, by living only by depending on you, they will be victorious.

Lord!
Give to those gathered here a new resolve, living from now only in the Holy
Spirit. According to the wish of the deceased, grant that they may have a life
filled with the fruits of a firm faith. Grant them a harmonious life in the
Lord, a life of mutual love without any regrets.

We pray in the name of Jesus Christ who loved us to the end.
Amen.

Reading from Scripture: The Leader

(Select and read one of the Scriptures below.)

1. I lift up my eyes to the hills—where does my help come from?
   My help comes from the Lord, the Maker of heaven and earth.
   He will not let your foot slip—he who watches over you will not slumber;
   Indeed, he who watches over Israel will neither slumber nor sleep.
   The Lord watches over you—the Lord is your shade at your right hand;
   The sun will not harm you by day, nor the moon by night.
   The Lord will keep you from all harm—he will watch over your life;
   The Lord will watch over your coming and going both now and for
       evermore.
   (Psalm 121)

2. Now we know that if the earthly tent we live in is destroyed, we have a
   building from God, an eternal house in heaven, not built by human
   hands. Meanwhile we groan, longing to be clothed with our heavenly
   dwelling, because when we are clothed, we will not be found naked. For
   while we are in this tent, we groan and are burdened, because we do not
   wish to be unclothed but to be clothed with our heavenly dwelling, so
   that what is mortal may be swallowed up by life. Now it is God who has
   made us for this very purpose and has given us the Spirit as a deposit,
   guaranteeing what is to come.
   (2 Corinthians 5:1–5).

Confession of Faith (The Apostles' Creed): Together
I believe in God, the Father Almighty, creator of heaven and earth;

And in Jesus Christ, His only son, our Lord, who was conceived by the Holy
Spirit, born of the Virgin Mary, suffered under Pontius Pilate, was crucified,
died and was buried; he descended to the dead. On the third day he rose
again, ascended into heaven, he is seated at the right hand of the Father, and
he will come again to judge the living and the dead.

I believe in the Holy Spirit, the holy catholic church, the communion of
saints, the forgiveness of sins, the resurrection of the body, and the life everlasting.
Amen.

Hymn (424): Together
  Saviour More Than Life to Me.

The Lord's Prayer: Together

> Our Father in heaven, hallowed be your name.
> Your Kingdom come, your will be done, on earth as in heaven.
> Give us today our daily bread.
> Forgive us our sins, as we forgive those who sin against us.
> Lead us not into temptation, but deliver us from evil.
> For the kingdom, the power and the glory are yours, now and forever.
> Amen.

(after worship)

1. *Go around the site of the grave mound and tidy up [the grave site].*
2. *Examine the condition and location of the earthen grave mound and the stone stele and other graveside items.*
3. *If any food and drink has been prepared, they may be shared together.*

New Religions

26

The Great Transformation:

Religious Practice in Ch'ŏndogyo

Don Baker

Ch'ŏndogyo (Religion of the Heavenly Way) is Korea's oldest indigenous organized religion, dating back to 1860. Korea, of course, had its own indigenous religious beliefs and practices long before the formation of Ch'ŏndogyo (which was originally called Tonghak, or "Eastern Learning"). However, the folk religion of Korea, like most folk religions the world over, lacked canonical texts like those that standardize doctrine and practice in organized religions. It also lacked three other characteristics of organized religions: standardized procedures for certifying ritual specialists, a clearly defined hierarchy of those ritual specialists, and permanent buildings of wood, stone, or brick built for the performance of rituals by those specialists. Buddhism, Confucianism, and Catholicism (a relatively new arrival, having reached Korea at the end of the eighteenth century) are all organized religions and were active on the Korean peninsula before Tonghak, but they were imported religions. Ch'ŏndogyo, on the other hand, originated in 1860 from the revelations of Ch'oe Cheu (1824–64) near the Yongdam waterfall in the vicinity of Kyŏngju. By the beginning of the twentieth century, Ch'ŏndogyo had grown into a fully organized religion. On Sunday morning, Ch'ŏndogyo believers went to churches where specialists led standardized rituals and preached sermons on the doctrines and practices of the religion, as explained in the *Ch'ŏndogyo kyŏngjŏn*, a collection of canonical writings by Ch'oe Cheu and the subsequent leaders of Ch'ŏndogyo.

As an indigenous Korean religion, Ch'ŏndogyo is a product of Korea's pluralistic religious culture. It uses terminology, promotes practices, and extols virtues that are similar to the terminology, practices, and virtues found in shamanic, Buddhist, Confucian, and even Catholic circles. However, Ch'ŏndogyo is a religion in its own right. Its ritual specialists are not shamans. Its rituals are not Buddhist rituals. Its virtues are similar to, but nevertheless different from, Confucian virtues. And though it sometimes borrows the Catholic name for its God, its God is clearly not the God of Catholicism. That is clear in both the way Ch'ŏndogyo believers talk about God and the way God is discussed in the Ch'ŏndogyo scriptures.

The God of Ch'ŏndogyo goes by three names. The most common name in the twentieth century is Hanullim. However, in the nineteenth century, when Ch'ŏndogyo leaders wrote essays in Chinese, they tended to call God Ch'ŏnju (the Lord of Heaven), a term adopted from Catholicism, or Sangje (the Lord Above), an ancient Chinese term. In poems written in vernacular Korean, however, these leaders often referred to God with the Korean word for heaven with an honorific suffix attached. Early in the twentieth century, that indigenous Korean term, Hanullim, became the standard Ch'ŏndogyo name for God. No other religions in Korea use that particular name for God, though Protestant Christians use a similar term (Hanŭnim).

The proper name it uses for God is not the only unique feature of Ch'ŏndogyo. The Ch'ŏndogyo concept of God is also distinctive. The God of Ch'ŏndogyo is neither a supernatural personality like the God of Christianity nor an impersonal metaphysical concept like the absolute of Neo-Confucianism. Rather, Hanullim is something in between. Ch'oe Cheu's accounts of his revelations, such as the account translated here as "On Propagating Virtue," often sound as though he was interacting with a being who could talk with him. However, the canonical writings of the second and third patriarchs, Ch'oe Sihyŏng (1827–98) and Son Pyŏnghŭi (1861–1921), make clear that they never had any conversations with God. In their essays, God appears as the animating force in the universe that we can experience personally when we ask Ultimate Energy to fill our hearts with spiritual energy; we should also recognize that God as present not only in ourselves but also in all other human beings and, indeed, in all other animate objects in the universe.

Neo-Confucians never had any personal encounters with their abstract absolute. So the Ch'ŏndogyo God is not the same as the Neo-Confucian absolute. However, neither is Hanullim the sort of supernatural personality seen in popular Buddhism or Korea's folk religion. Instead, Hanullim is an impersonal force with whom we can have an intimate, personal encounter. We do so by chanting over and over again the incantation revealed by Sangje to Ch'oe Cheu: "Ultimate Energy being all around me, I pray that I feel that Energy within me here and now. Recognizing that God is within me, I will be transformed. Constantly aware of that divine presence within, I will become attuned to all that is going on around me."

A careful examination of this incantation, and of explications of it by Ch'oe Cheu and his two immediate successors, reveals that God is Ultimate Energy. In other words, God is what the Koreans term *ki*. *Ki* is a very difficult term to translate precisely into English, since it has such a wide range of meanings. Even in the Ch'ŏndogyo scriptures, it has two quite different meanings. Ch'ŏndogyo borrows those two meanings from Neo-Confucianism but adds to them in the process.

In its broadest sense, *ki* is the matter and energy out of which the universe is constructed. This is the Neo-Confucian understanding of *ki*. Ch'ŏndogyo adds to this basically passive notion of *ki* both creative and controlling powers. In Ch'ŏndogyo, *ki* is Ultimate Energy, the animating force of the cosmos that not only provides the material of which every object in the universe is made but also creates those objects and directs their operation. Heaven was often given that commanding role in Neo-Confucianism, but in Neo-Confucianism heaven was not *ki*, which caused a dilemma for Neo-Confucians who wanted to explain how an otherwise passive heaven exercised its power. By combining the energy of *ki* with the creative and controlling power of heaven, Ch'ŏndogyo provided a way to envision the moral guiding force in the universe having the power to implement its directives. Moreover, it also provided a way for individual human beings to experience that moral power within themselves.

Ki is not only the primordial energy of the cosmos but also the air that we breathe and the food we eat. In other words, *ki* is not only all around us; it is also inside us. Even our minds are *ki*, which allows us to understand the world around us, since everything around us is made from the same *ki* we are made of. (Ch'ŏndogyo, like Neo-Confucianism, does not draw the sharp lines between the material and the mental realms so often seen in Western religions and philosophies.) The fact that we, too, are *ki* not only allows us to understand the material and human worlds in which we find ourselves but also allows us to share in the creative activity of the cosmos. In doing so, however, we must keep in mind that *ki* also provides the foundation for our existence as moral beings. Whenever we interact with people and things around us, we should remember that, because of our common participation in cosmic *ki*, we are not isolated individuals but are instead integral components of both human society and nature. We should, therefore, always act for the common good rather than seek our own individual selfish interest.

This is all rather abstract. However, Ch'ŏndogyo supplements its philosophical reasoning with concrete advice on how we can confirm the truth of these assertions through direct experience. Ch'ŏndogyo teaches that, by chanting the incantation taught by Ch'oe Cheu, we can increase our awareness of the *ki* within our own bodies. It will not happen every time we chant that incantation over and over again, but there will be occasions when we will feel as though our bodies have suddenly been flooded with powerful energy. As we see in the translation here of the section on incantations in the Ch'ŏndogyo ritual handbook, when that happens, we will not just know with our mind but will also feel with our whole body that we are part of something much greater than ourselves. This awareness will jolt us out of a tendency to think and act selfishly, as though we were isolated individuals, and stimulate us to treat other human beings, and other natural objects as well, with the respect they deserve.

The inner cosmic *ki* we encounter in this way is Hanullim. Hanullim is not a God existing above and beyond us. Instead, Hanullim is the power we experience within ourselves to join with the rest of the universe to continue the process of creation and build a better, more harmonious world. This is what Ch'ŏndogyo means by one of the key tenets of this religion, that every human being has a spark of the divine within them (*in nae ch'ŏn*).

Once we understand that Hanullim is the cosmic *ki* within, we can then understand another key tenet of Ch'ŏndogyo, *Si Ch'ŏnju*. Ch'ŏnju is the Lord of Heaven, the term Korean Catholics use for God. However, the Ch'ŏnju of Ch'ŏndogyo is not a God living in heaven above but a power within our own heart. Ch'oe Cheu explained that the character *si* in this phrase does not carry the usual meaning of "to serve someone higher than yourself. " Instead *si* means "to bear within the power to penetrate with your mind and therefore understand (*sinnyŏng*) everything around you, and to bear without the power to transform the material world (*kihwa*)" ("Nonhak" [On Learning], in the Ch'ŏndogyo scriptures, p. 34). In other words, *si Ch'ŏnju* may literally mean serving or bearing God, but God here is more a power than a divine person. To bear God is to become one with the cosmos and therefore share in both the penetrating intelligence of *ki* and its creative transforming power.

Such experiential theology was a new concept in Korea. Neo-Confucians had not sought to experience cosmic *ki* within. Nor had they sought a personal encounter with heaven. They sought only to understand heaven and its Way so that they could act in accordance with it. To do so, however, they understood that they needed to discipline their bodies and quiet selfish emotions. Ch'ŏndogyo agrees on the need for self-discipline, and it expresses that agreement with a phrase in which *ki* appears with the second meaning we find in both Neo-Confucian and Ch'ŏndogyo writings. When Ch'ŏndogyo stresses the need to *susim chŏnggi* (the syllable *gi* here is the same word spelled elsewhere as *ki*), *ki* does not mean Hanullim, the cosmic *ki* that unifies, but individual *ki* that separates. This four-syllable phrase can thus be translated as "preserving our original pure mind and rectifying our psycho-physical endowment." *Ki* in this phrase means our body, including the emotions and desires our body generates. *Ki* is not only the matter and energy that constitutes the universe in its entirety; it is also the individual coagulations of that matter and energy. When *ki* coagulates and forms individual entities, it creates distinctions between and among those various entities and, by so doing, can create barriers to the moral good of cosmic harmony.

In other words, the fact that my body is a particular coagulation of *ki* that is different from the coagulations of *ki* that form those around me can lead me to think of myself as separate and distinct. This can therefore encourage me to seek what is best for myself, even if it comes at the expense of the good of my community. It is precisely the pursuit of narrow self-interest that creates disharmony both within human society and in the cosmos as a whole. In both the Neo-Confucian and the Ch'ŏndogyo worldview, such disharmony is the very definition of evil.

The Ch'ŏndogyo prescription for fighting such evil is to "preserve our original pure mind and rectify our psycho-physical endowment." Ch'ŏndogyo agreed with Neo-Confucians that human beings are essentially good—that all human beings have an originally pure mind that gives them the ability to perceive and respond to their environment without any distortions introduced by selfish considerations of personal interest. (Ch'ŏndogyo differs from Neo-Confucianism, however, in that sometimes it calls this pure mind "Hanullim.") As we have seen, they also agree with Neo-Confucians on the need to discipline our bodies so that selfless thoughts and emotions replace selfish thoughts and emotions. They argue that this can be done by "rectifying our *ki*." How can we do this?

The unique answer Ch'ŏndogyo provides to this question can be seen in the portions of two essays by Ch'oe Sihyŏng translated here from the Ch'ŏndogyo scriptures. The passage titled "Preserving Our Original Pure Mind and Rectifying Our Psycho-physical Endowment" tells us that we can rectify our *ki* by following the standard Confucian prescription to respect our parents, love our siblings, treat our friends with respect and affection, and be deferential to elders. But how can we make sure we are in the right frame of mind to consistently follow such prescriptions? The passage "How to Cultivate a Moral Character" tells us how. We need to both understand and chant the inscription that Ch'oe Cheu taught us so that we will be attuned to the divine presence within us all. A third passage, "Ch'ŏndogyo Cultivation Practices," from a Korean government–compiled description of the rituals and ceremonies of various Korean religions, provides more information on how to chant in order to achieve such a result.

Chanting to awaken ourselves to the divine presence within is the core of Ch'ŏndogyo practice, as we see in the statement translated here by a convert to Ch'ŏndogyo, "Why I Joined Ch'ŏndogyo." However, there is more to Ch'ŏndogyo than just chanting. It also has distinctive rituals, which were standardized by Son Pyŏnghŭi, the third patriarch, in 1906 and 1907. One feature of a Ch'ŏndogyo ritual is the presence of a bowl of clean water on an altar, meant to symbolize the purity of the heart of a Ch'ŏndogyo practitioner who is inspired by Hanullim within. Another distinctive feature of Ch'ŏndogyo is the daily collection of spoonfuls of rice to present as offerings at church later. This "sincerity rice" is a material expression of the selfless concern for the common good that all Ch'ŏndogyo believers are supposed to display. Both practices are described here in translation from the Ch'ŏndogyo ritual handbook.

The goals of Ch'ŏndogyo also distinguish it from many other religious traditions. Ch'ŏndogyo does not promise its faithful followers rebirth in paradise after death. Nor does it promise that it will help them develop detachment from this world and the suffering that living in this world entails. Instead, it asks them to contribute to the creation of a paradise on this earth for the living who follow them. Ch'ŏndogyo uses language reminiscent of Daoism in describing both that paradise and those who help create it. Perhaps that is because Ch'ŏndogyo shares the Daoist fascination with *ki*

Daoists sought through breathing practices and physical exercises to increase their life-enhancing *ki*, and therefore gain a longer life span. However, they did not stress the moral connotations of that *ki*. Ch'ŏndogyo, on the other hand, took the Daoist term for someone who had enhanced their *ki* to the point that they were free of the normal decay to which the body was subject and extended that term (*sinsŏn*) to refer to people who had enhanced their awareness of the presence of cosmic life-giving *ki* within themselves to the point that they thought and acted as part of the universal social and natural community rather than as isolated individuals. In other words, in Ch'ŏndogyo, to be a *sinsŏn* means to be a person who thinks and acts morally.

Moreover, when enough people have followed the prescriptions of Ch'ŏndogyo and become *sinsŏn*, then the world will become a *sŏn'gyong*, a realm of immortals. Ch'ŏndogyo promises that human beings will not need to fear disease once a *sŏn'gyŏng* has been established on this earth. That is not the most important characteristic of life in a *sŏn'gyong*, however. More important than freedom from disease is that, in such a paradise, everyone will live in harmony with every other human being and with nature. In such an ideal world, there will be no discrimination based on race, social class, age, or gender. Everyone will recognize that everyone, including him- or herself, is a bearer of Hanullim, the creative and unifying animating force in the cosmos,

Such a paradise will be achieved after the earth has gone through a Great Transformation (Kaebyŏk). Hanullim choose Ch'oe Cheu as his prophet because the time for such a Kaebyŏk was near and Ch'oe Cheu appeared to be the best man to prepare humanity for such a dramatic change. In contemporary Ch'ŏndogyo writings, Kaebyŏk is interpreted as primarily a transformation of consciousness, in which human beings come to realize through the chanting of the incantation that they all bear Hanullim. However, in the nineteenth century, many Koreans thought Kaebyŏk referred to a political and social transformation of revolutionary import. The Tonghak rebellion of 1894, a rebellion against corrupt government officials and the intrusions of foreign imperialism, was partially inspired by the belief that the time was ripe for radical political and social change. It was partially to distance itself from such an overly political interpretation of Ch'oe Cheu's message that the Tonghak religion was renamed Ch'ŏndogyo in late 1905.

"On Propagating Virtue" (*P'odŏk mun*) is translated from *Ch'ŏndogyo kyŏngjŏn* (The Scriptures of Ch'ŏndogyo) (Seoul: Ch'ŏndogyo Headquarters, 1993), pp. 15–22. "Preserving Our Original Pure Mind and Rectifying Our Psycho-physical Endowment" (*Susim chŏnggi*) is translated from *Ch'ŏndogyo kyŏngjŏn*, pp. 295–301. "How to Cultivate a Moral Character" (*Sudobŏp*) appears in *Ch'ŏndogyo kyŏngjŏn*, pp. 335–36. "Ch'ŏndogyo Cultivation Practices" are translated from *Han'guk Chonggyo ŭi ŭisik kwa yejŏl* (The Rituals and Ceremonies of Korean Religions), edited by the Ministry of Culture and Sports (Seoul: Hwasan Munhwa Publishing, 1996), p. 338. "Ch'ŏndogyo Rituals" appears in the *Ch'ŏndogyo ŭijŏl* (The Ch'ŏndogyo Ritual Handbook) (Seoul: Ch'ŏndogyo Headquarters, 2000), pp. 26–32. "Why I Joined Ch'ŏndogyo" is related in Ok Soong Cha (Ch'a Oksung), *Han'gugin ŭi chonggyo kyŏnghŏm: Ch'ŏndogyo. Taejonggyo* (The Religious Experience of Koreans: Ch'ŏndogyo and Taejonggyo) (Seoul: Sŏgwangsa, 2000), pp. 81–83.

Further Reading

A team of translators is currently working on an English translation of the scriptures of Ch'ŏndogyo, the *Ch'ŏndogyo kyŏngjŏn*. It will not be available for several more years, however. In the meantime, the following English-language materials are available: Yong Choon Kim, *The Ch'ondogyo Concept of Man: An Essence of Korean Thought* (Seoul: Pan Korean Book Corporation, 1989); Benjamin B. Weems, *Reform, Rebellion, and the Heavenly Way* (Tucson: University of Arizona Press, 1964); Susan Shin, "The Tonghak Movement: From Enlightenment to Revolution," *Korean Studies Forum*, no. 5 (Winter–Spring 1978–79): 1–80; Carl Young, "Tonghak and Son Pyŏnghui's Early Leadership, 1899–1904," *Review of Korean Studies* 5, no. 1 (June 2002): 63–83; Paul Beirne, "The Eclectic Mysticism of Ch'oe Cheu," *Review of Korean Studies* 2 (September 1999): 159–81; Kirsten Bell, "Cheondogyo and the Donghak Revolution: The (Un)Making of a Religion," *Korea Journal* 44 (Summer 2004): 123–48; Kirsten Bell, "The Gendering of Religious Experience: Ecstatic Trance in Cheondogyo," *Asian Journal of Women's Studies* 9, no. 2 (2003): 7–37

On Propagating Virtue (*P'odŏk Mun*)

From the distant past up to the present day, every year without fail spring has eventually turned into autumn, and all four seasons have come and gone in the proper sequence. This is a display for the entire world to see of how the Lord of Heaven [Ch'ŏnju] regulates the changes and transformations in the universe. Yet ignorant folk know only that rain and dew are natural phenomena and do not know how it is that they are able to benefit from them.

Ever since the reigns of the first five emperors of China, we have been fortunate to have a number of sages who have recorded in writing the patterns governing the movements of the sun, the moon, and all the stars in heaven. They attributed when something moved and when it was still, and when something waxed and when it waned, to the decrees of heaven. That is why they revered heaven and tried to act in accordance with the principles of heaven. Because they revered heaven and tried to act in accordance with the principles of heaven, they became the superior men we respect today. The focus of their scholarly endeavors became the Way and how it manifests itself in appropriate actions. The Way they studied was the Heavenly Way. The actions they studied were Heavenly virtues. When they had a clear vision of what the Way of heaven was and disciplined themselves to act in accordance with it, they then became superior human beings and even sages. How can we not admire them for that?

Recently, however, people have tended to do whatever they feel like doing instead of acting in accordance with heavenly principles. They no longer pay any attention to the decrees of heaven. I had been worried about this night and day, but did not know what to do about it.

It got worse in 1860. That is when I learned that Westerners, claiming that they were only doing what the Lord of Heaven wanted them to do and were not trying to be rich or to lord it over others, began using military force to seize territory all over the world. Everywhere they went they set up churches and promoted their way of doing things. I asked myself if this really could be happening, and if so, how could such things happen?

Then a totally unexpected event occurred one day in the fourth month of that year. All of a sudden a chill came over my heart and my whole body shivered. It was as if I had abruptly fallen ill, but I couldn't tell what sort of illness had attacked me. Then my ears seemed to pick up a strange voice. It is difficult to describe. The closest I can come to describing it is to say that it sounded like the voice of one of those immortals who lives deep in the mountains. I was frightened and asked, "Who are you?" An answer came back, "You don't have to be afraid. I am the one whom human beings call the Lord Above (Sangje). Don't you know who the Lord Above is?" Startled, I asked why he was talking to me. He replied, "So far I haven't been able to accomplish all that I have wanted to accomplish. Therefore I have sent you into this world so that you can teach human beings the right way to do things. So cast all fear and doubt aside and listen to me."

I then asked, "Do you want me to teach people the Western way of doing things?" He replied, "No, not at all. I have a talisman that is called the "medicine of the mountain immortals." It resembles the Great Ultimate [the name Neo-Confucians give to the wellspring of all existence]. It is written with the Sino-Korean characters Kunggung. Take this talisman and use it to heal people of the various diseases that afflict them. Also, I am giving you an incantation of mine that I want you to use to teach human beings on my behalf. If you do this, you will live a long life and will propagate virtue all over the world."

Persuaded by what he had to say, I accepted that talisman from him. I copied it onto a piece of paper that I immersed in water and then swallowed. Right away I felt completely healthy again. Truly this was a "medicine of the mountain immortals," an elixir of long life. I then began offering it to others who were ill. Some were cured but others were not. At first, I couldn't figure out why. Then I realized that all those who were sincere and showed proper respect for the Lord of Heaven were cured, but no one benefited from that talisman who did not follow the Way and was therefore not a person of virtue. Doesn't this indicate that the effectiveness of this talisman is determined by the sincerity and respectful attitude of the person who consumes it?

This all happened at a time when terrible diseases were sweeping across our country. Everyone was worried day and night that they or someone dear to them might be the next victim. It was our bad luck that this was happening at the same time that Westerners were on a rampage. It looked like nobody could stop them and they would roam and conquer at will. If they succeeded in taking over the rest of the world, wouldn't we suffer that same terrible fate? I wondered if there wasn't some way to help our country and put the minds of the people at ease.

Unfortunately, people these days don't understand what a precarious situation we are in. If they happen to hear what I have to say, it goes in one ear and out the other. Even worse, some of them criticize me publicly. They are ignorant of the Way and don't follow it. This is really a pitiful situation. Even the wise among them, after listening to me, have doubts about my message. I am getting really frustrated but there doesn't seem to be anything I can do about it. Nevertheless I am going to prepare a written summary of the message I have been asked to deliver in the hope that there will be some who will read it with proper respect and take that message to heart.

Preserving Our Original Pure Mind and Rectifying Our Psycho-physical Endowment (*Susim Chŏnggi*)

If we human beings are able to keep our heart-and-mind basically clean of contamination and are also able to remove all impurities in the energy that runs through and animates our psycho-physical endowment, then there will be no pollution from the mundane world on our heart-and-mind and we will not have to worry about selfish desires welling up from within. Our body will then be able to contain the mind of heaven and earth.

If our heart-and-mind is not clean, we will be ensnared in ignorance. However, if our heart-and-mind is free of the dust of the mundane world, then we will be as wise as a sage. Our heart-and-mind is like a lamp that can shine brightly only after it has been given some oil. It's like a mirror that can only reflect clearly when it has been polished with mercury. It's like a brass vessel that can be as solid as it is supposed to be only after it has been forged in a flame. We human beings can reach the clarity and purity of thought and intention of which we are capable only after the spiritual light within our heart-and-mind is activated and tells us what to do and what to think.

Our physical body is the home of those wondrous powers of our heart-and-mind that make it possible for us to perceive, think, evaluate, and choose properly. The heart-and-mind, with those wondrous powers, can control our body. When those wondrous powers of the mind-and-heart are active, then our body is calm and stable. However, when selfish desires are active instead, then our body is in a tumultuous state. . . .

That four-character phrase *susim chŏnggi* tells us that a decline in psycho-physical endowment can be reversed. Our sacred writings tell us that Our Great Teacher Ch'oe Cheu said, "Benevolence, righteousness, propriety, and wisdom were what the sages of the past taught. I have added to that the phrase 'Preserve your original pure mind and rectify your psycho-physical endowment' " [Ch'oe Cheu, "On Cultivating Virtue" (*Sudŏk mun*), *Ch'ŏndogyo kyŏngjŏn*, p. 51.] If you don't preserve your original pure mind and rectify your psycho-physical endowment, then it will be very difficult to act benevolently and righteously or to act with wisdom and in accordance with the demands of propriety. . . .

If we truly understand how to preserve our original pure mind and rectify our psycho-physical endowment, then we will have no difficulty becoming a sage. However, preserving our original pure mind and rectifying our psycho-physical endowment is the most difficult of all the tasks we face. If you are able to know when someone enters or leaves your room even when you are in a deep sleep, or if you are able to hear other people talking and laughing even when you are in a deep sleep, then you can be said to have preserved your original pure mind and rectified your psycho-physical endowment.

How can you preserve your original mind and rectify your psycho-physical endowment?

You can do both those things by showing love and respect for your parents, by showing affection and concern for your siblings, by being kind and generous to your friends, and by being respectful and deferential to your elders. If you protect such a pure heart-and-mind as you would protect a newborn child, then your heart-and-mind will be so calm that it will never erupt into anger, and your heart-and-mind will see things so clearly that it will never be confused about anything.

How to Cultivate a Moral Character (*Sudobŏp*)

If you only recite the incantations and do not delve into the principles behind them, then your chanting is a waste of time. Similarly, if you only delve into the principles behind the incantations and don't chant those incantations, then you have wasted your time. You need to both chant the incantations and understand thoroughly what they mean. You cannot slack off on either task for a minute.

[The basic principle behind the incantations is that] I am Heaven, and Heaven is I. In other words, Heaven and I are essentially the same. However, if my psycho-physical endowment is not rectified and therefore my heart-and-mind wavers from the straight and narrow, then I will not do the things I should do, and instead will do things I shouldn't do. On the other hand, if my psycho-physical endowment is free of the distortions introduced by selfishness and therefore my mind-and-heart is steady and unwavering, then I will follow the Way of virtue. Whether the Way prevails, or not, depends entirely on whether our psycho-physical endowments as well as our minds-and-hearts are rectified, or not.

Ch'ŏndogyo Cultivation Practices

Ch'ŏndogyo believers experience the presence of God within, both in their bodies and in their minds, by regularly intoning the incantations and undergoing spiritual training. They seek to awaken their true inner nature by experiencing the unity of heaven and humanity. There are three types of spiritual training: ordinary training, special training, and intensive training.

Ordinary training refers to spiritual exercises you engage in during the course of everyday life. During ordinary religious training, you do not have to engage in those spiritual exercises at a specific time or for a specified period of time, nor do you have to worry about what you eat or drink. Special training refers to engaging in religious exercises for a specified period of time, such as 7, 21, 49, or 105 days, while abstaining from alcohol, tobacco, and meat. During special training, specific times during the day are set aside for those spiritual exercises. Special training takes place at a specific location, such as your home, a church, or a retreat center. Special training is done in order to achieve some special objective. Intensive training is similar to special training except that you put aside all secular activities, including family affairs, for the duration of that training so that you can concentrate solely on those spiritual exercises.

When you are undergoing such training, sit up straight with your legs tucked beneath you. Don't let your legs sprawl out across the floor. Keep your eyes closed lightly. Focus your attention on how much you owe both heaven and our great teacher [Ch'oe Cheu] for all they have provided you. At the same time, chant an incantation over and over again either to yourself or aloud. Count your incantations with counting beads you hold in your hands. Some of those undergoing such training set a goal of reciting an incantation 10,000 times or even 30,000 or 50,000 times a day, in order to cultivate a moral character and awaken their true inner nature.

Ch'öndogyo Rituals

INCANTATIONS

The incantations are ways of using language to show the utmost respect for Hanullim. They are religious formulas that both earn a long life for the person who recites them and extend the influence of Hanullim over the whole world. By reciting them, you recover your original virtuous inner nature, are enlightened to truth, make sure you do not forget the debt of gratitude you owe Hanullim, and become attuned to all that is going on around you. They constitute prayers which make it possible for you to transform your physical existence into a spiritual life and link the moral power of God with human power so that you can actualize the Way and make virtue a reality instead of an unrealized dream. There are four incantations recited by Ch'öndogyo believers these days: the 21-syllable incantation; the 8-syllable incantation, which is the first part of the 21-syllable incantation; the 13-syllable incantation, which is the second part of the 13-syllable incantation; and the incantation of the Great Spiritual Guide Ch'oe Cheu.

The 21-syllable incantation is "*Chigigŭmji wŏnwidaegang sich'ŏnju chohwajŏng yŏngseipulmang mansaji*" (Ultimate Energy being all around me, I pray that I feel that Energy within me here and now. Recognizing that God is within me, I will be transformed. Constantly aware of that divine presence within, I will become attuned to all that is going on around me). This incantation is chanted either to oneself or aloud when praying and when undergoing spiritual training.

The 8-syllable incantation, also known as "the incantation for inviting the descent of the Divine Presence," is "*Chigigŭmji wŏnwidaegang*" (Ultimate Energy being all around me, I pray that I feel that Energy within me here and now).

The 13-syllable incantation, also known as the "Sacred incantation," is "*Sich'ŏnju chohwajŏng yŏngseipulmang mansaji*" (Recognizing that God is within me, I will be transformed. Constantly aware of that divine presence within, I will become attuned to all that is going on around me). It is chanted three times by a congregation chanting in unison during various rituals, such as initiation rituals, Sunday services, celebratory occasions, holy day services, funeral services, and on other such special occasions.

The incantation of the Revered Founder Ch'oe Cheu is as follows: "*Sinsayŏnggi asimjŏng mugungchohwa kŭmilchi*" (The founder's spiritual power settles my heart and mind. Today I am one with infinite creation). This incantation is recited 105 times either to oneself or aloud during the 9 P.M. Sunday evening prayers.

CLEAN WATER

Our founder, Ch'oe Cheu, made an offering of a bowl of clean water every time he prayed. Of particular note is that on March 10, 1864, right before he was beheaded in Taegu, he offered a bowl of clean water while praying. He then accepted martyrdom for our faith.

That is why every time Ch'ŏndogyo believers pray or enact a ritual, whether individually or in a group, we offer a bowl of clean water to remind us of his great sacrifice. A bowl of clean water is presented as an offering at daily 9 P.M. prayers as well as at Sunday services, holy day services, celebratory services, weddings, funerals, and ancestor memorial services.

The families of Ch'ŏndogyo believers gather in their respective homes every evening at 9 P.M. to offer a bowl of pure water and to pray. This is called "daily prayer." Here is how it is done. First of all, shortly before nine, all the family members clean up the site set aside for those prayers. They then gather in a circle around an altar on which sits a bowl of clean water. They are then ready to pray together as follows. First, the head of the family declares that it is time for daily prayer. Next he lifts the lid off that bowl of clean water and says, "We present this bowl of clean water as a sacred offering." This is followed by a period of time during which each family member prays silently. The head of the family then signals the next stage of daily prayers, in which the family members quietly chant the 21-syllable incantation 105 times. (On special occasions, they may chant it together aloud 21 times.) This daily ritual ends when the lid is put back on that bowl of clean water and everyone again prays silently for a while.

If someone is not able to be with the rest of their family for those 9 P.M. prayers, they should still make an offering of a bowl of clean water wherever they happen to be at that time. If that is not possible, they should at least pray silently at 9 P.M. and then offer a bowl of clean water when they finally get home.

SINCERITY RICE

As a material manifestation of the sincerity of their dedication to the Ch'ŏndo-gyo goals of enlightening all human beings to the True Way, liberating people all over the world from pain and suffering, protecting the Korean nation and comforting the Korean people, and constructing a paradise on this earth, Ch'ŏndogyo families set aside a receptacle into which every day the mother of the family places one spoonful of uncooked rice per family member whenever she prepares rice for breakfast or dinner. She offers up a silent prayer with every spoonful of rice she puts in the "sincerity rice" receptacle. At the end of every month, with their hearts filled with gratitude toward heaven and toward our revered founder, each family presents that "sincerity rice" to the Ch'ŏndo-gyo church they attend.

When rice is not part of the meal or there is no uncooked rice to put into that receptacle, money should be set aside, instead.

By sincerely offering this "sincerity rice," Ch'ŏndogyo believers enlist the aid of Hanullim and of our Revered Founder in the creation of a strong and healthy family and a strong and healthy church.

In addition every month Ch'ŏndogyo believers should donate a portion of their income to the church they attend as a way of displaying gratitude to Han-ullim and the Revered Founder for all Hanullim and the Revered Founder have done for them.

Why I Joined Ch'ŏndogyo

FROM AN INTERVIEW IN 1998 WITH A THIRTY-NINE-YEAR-OLD
GOVERNMENT WORKER

My hometown is P'aju, in Kyŏnggi province nor far from Seoul. My father ran a factory. I am the third of his four sons, but I was the most full of mischief. In fact, I was known in my neighborhood for getting into fights. Because I was short and skinny, I was actually afraid of others, but I didn't want to show it. When other kids pushed us around, I was always the one who led the counter-attack.

When I was in middle school, my father had an affair, which threw our fam-ily into turmoil. However, when I was in high school, Dad returned to Mom. I was able to go to university, and the atmosphere in my home was tranquil again. My father didn't have any religious affiliation but my mother frequented Buddhist temples. Several times, when I was a child, my mother took me with her to those temples. However, when I was in middle school, I started attending a Christian church. Later on, after I finished my military service, for two or three years I was active in a Chŭngsan'gyo group.

In 1988 I quit my job. Three years later, in 1991, I began studying for the bar exam. Two years after that, I gave up studying for the bar and went back to being a government clerk.

In 1988 I married a women who was a devout Christian. Before I joined Ch'ŏndogyo, she was after me all the time to go to church with her. I gave in a few times and accompanied her to the neighborhood church she attended. She also took our daughter to that church.

My wife worked in the public health center in the P'aju city hall. She kept trying to introduce me to a doctor who worked there. She said he was about my age, and was a religious man of good moral character. At that time, I was quite proud of my knowledge of religions. I thought I understood the core principles of any religion that anyone had heard of and had concluded that no one religion was particularly better than any other. I didn't think that anyone could talk me into adopting one religion to the exclusion of all the others.

One day, when I was home on vacation from my job as a civil servant, our five-year-old daughter kept pestering me to take her to her mother's office so that we could walk home with her when she got off work. That health center was close to our home, so we arrived there a little early, about five minutes before my wife was due to leave for the day. My daughter then insisted that we go inside to let her mother know we were there. That was when I was met the various people who worked with my wife. Among them was that doctor she had told me about. He introduced himself to me, mentioning that he had heard a little about me from my wife. He told me that he was a believer in Ch'ŏndogyo and that he was able to heal heart problems. I responded that I knew that many religions claimed they could heal diseases, but didn't know that Ch'ŏndogyo made a similar claim.

We went on talking about this and related matters for a while and then I mentioned that I did not believe that God was all-good. He agreed, saying that it was inappropriate to use terms like "good" or "bad" when talking about God. That was when I really got interested in what he had to say. Over the next week I met with him almost every day to discuss this and other religious questions. Through him, I came to realize that religious orientation is not a theoretical or academic matter but must be grounded in personal spiritual experience. He told me that 95 of out every 100 Ch'ŏndogyo believers who spend a week at a Ch'ŏndogyo retreat center undergoing religious training are able to personally experience a divine presence within their heart, and therefore experience being one with the Ultimate Energy that fills the entire universe.

He then introduced me to a local Ch'ŏndogyo church, which I began attending. When I saw how the elderly members of that church bowed respectfully to everyone they met, regardless of age, I decided to formally join the Ch'ŏn dogyo community. My wife joined at the same time. She hoped that joining Ch'ŏndogyo would turn me into a better person who would be respected by others. Moreover, she didn't see herself as converting from Christianity to Ch'ŏndogyo. Instead, she believed that she had simply moved up to a higher level of religiosity.

When my wife first went to a retreat center for religious training, after only three days she experienced Ultimate Energy descending from on high and filling her with awareness of a divine presence within. She also felt her hands being moved by that divine spirit within to draw a talisman of spiritual power. As for me, after I formally enrolled in the Ch'ŏndogyo community, I decided to pray at home for an hour every morning for a period of twenty straight days. From the third day on, whenever I prayed I felt a tingling in my spine. Though this continued until the end of that twenty-day period, I wasn't quite sure what was going on or if what I was experiencing was of any spiritual significance. Then I went to a retreat center and, when I prayed, I first felt my hands shake and then my whole body begin to vibrate. However, I fought against such spontaneous movement and forced my body to be still. Since I wasn't quite sure what was happening to me, I was not able to move up to a deeper level of religiosity.

I told Rev. Wŏlsan [Kim Sŭngbok, the director of spiritual training for Ch'ŏndogyo] that I was still a little uncomfortable and wasn't sure if I really believed in Ch'ŏndogyo, or not. He advised me to continue fighting those spontaneous bodily movements and see what happened. I followed his advice but finally I couldn't resist any longer and my whole body began to vibrate even though I told it not to. That is when I discovered that how people experience the descent of Ultimate Energy and the awakening to the divine presence within differs from person to person.

While I was undergoing religious training, I kept asking myself "Who am I? What is the real me?" At first I couldn't keep from feeling that I was an independent entity in a universe filled with a multitude of independent entities. Nevertheless, I struggled to understand that actually the universe is not many things but one thing, and I am just one of a multitude of interconnected beings who constitute that all-encompassing and integrated universe. As I began to internalize this new view of the universe and my place in it, I became a different person. For one thing, I became much calmer and collected. In the old days, I was frequently distracted by sexual fantasies but now I exercise self-control over what I think and do. I constantly discipline myself so that I can be focused and calm. I want to achieve that peace of mind which is sometimes referred to as the state of "no-mind" or "no-ego."

—— 27 ——

The Korean God Is Not the Christian God:

Taejonggyo's Challenge to

Foreign Religions

Don Baker

Taejonggyo (Religion of the Great Progenitor) is the most overtly nationalistic of Korea's major new religions. Taejonggyo defines itself as the original religion of the Korean people, which was forgotten for centuries and then was revived in the first decade of the twentieth century. The man responsible for that revival was Na Ch'ŏl (1863–1916), an anti-Japanese activist who founded Taejonggyo in 1909. He believed that Korea had once been a powerful nation but had lost its strength when it replaced its own religion with the foreign religions of Buddhism and Confucianism. He argued that, in order for Korea to regain its rightful position in the world, Koreans had to return to the worship of the same God their ancestors worshiped, the three persons in one God that Taejonggyo calls Hanŏllim.

According to Taejonggyo teachings, Hwanin, Hwanung, and Tan'gun, who appear in the foundation myth of Korea, are the three persons in that one God. According to that myth, Hwanin (sometimes spelled Hanin) is the Lord of Heaven, Hwanung (sometimes spelled Hanung) is his Son whom he dispatched to earth, and Tan'gun is the product of the union on earth between Hwanung and a bear-turned-beautiful-human-female. Tan'gun is widely believed in Korea, by both Taejonggyo believers and nonbelievers, to be the first ruler of the first Korean kingdom, more than forty-three hundred years ago. In Taejonggyo theology, Hwanin represents God as Creator, Hwanung represents God as Educator, and Tan'gun represents God as Ruler. Taejonggyo also teaches that the ruling philosophy of Tan'gun was to broadly benefit humanity (*hongik in'gan*) and create a paradise on earth (*ihwa segye*), and that should be the governing philosophy of Korea today as well.

Over the course of the twentieth century, Taejonggyo accumulated a number of texts that it considers sacred. The most important are three works it believes date back to the time of Tan'gun, or even earlier. The *Ch'ŏnbugyŏng* (The Classic of the Seal of Heaven) is the best known of those works and has come to be accepted even by many people outside of Taejonggyo as an authentic ancient text. Only eighty-one characters long, it is difficult to decipher, but Taejonggyo teaches that this work is its equivalent of Genesis, providing an explanation of how the world came to be. Less well known is the *Samil sin'go* (The Teachings of the Trinitarian God), which provides much of the basis for Taejonggyo theology. The third text is even less well known. The *Ch'amjŏngyŏng* (The Classic of the Wise One) details the behavioral implications of Taejonggyo doctrines. Taejonggyo believes that, in these and other sacred texts, God broadly benefits humanity by providing specific advice on how to be both spiritually and physically healthy. Some of that advice appears in a section of the Taejonggyo scriptures called the "Three Rules for Self-Cultivation" (*Sambŏp hoet'ong*), which is translated here. Written in 1944 by Yun Sebok, who was then the leader of Taejonggyo and was in prison on charges of leading an anti-Japanese organization, this treatise is an explication and expansion of a chapter of the *Samil sin'go*.

The "Three Rules for Self-Cultivation" (*Sambŏp hoet'ong*) appears in *Taejonggyo yogam* (n.p.), pp. 306–13. Since this section of the Taejonggyo scriptures is rather brief and sometimes cryptic, I have supplemented it with explanatory notes from the section on Taejonggyo in *Han'guk Chonggyo ŭi ŭisik kwa yejŏl* (The Rituals and Ceremonies of Korean Religions), edited by the Ministry of Culture and Sports (Seoul: Hwasan Munhwa Publishing, 1996), pp. 375–76. These explanatory notes are in brackets. "Why I Believe in Taejonggyo," is translated from Ok Soong Cha (Ch'a Oksung), *Han'gugin ŭi chonggyo kyŏnghŏm: Ch'ŏndogyo, Taejonggyo* (The Religious Experience of Koreans: Ch'ŏndogyo and Taejonggyo) (Seoul: Sŏgwangsa, 2000) pp. 233–34. "Christians Have No Right to Call Their God 'Hananim'" is translated from An Ch'angbŏm, "Kidokkyochŭk ŭi Hananim myŏngho ch'amch'ing bulganon" (Christians Have No Right to Use the Name "Hananim" for Their God), in *Hananim sasang kwa Pulgyo ŭi kiwŏn* (Hananim Philosophy and the Origins of Buddhism) (Seoul: Samyang Publishing, 1994), pp. 47–55.

Further Reading

There is not much available in English on Taejonggyo. Ho-sang An, "Dae-Jonggyo: Religion of God-Human Being," *Korea Journal* 3, no. 5 (May 1963): 9–13, provides a brief introduction to Taejonggyo doctrines by a German-trained philosopher (and former minister of education in the Republic of Korea) who later became the leader of that religious organization. Information on the founder of Taejonggyo, and why he founded this nationalistic religion, can be found in Hwan Park, "Na, Chŏl and the Characteristics of His National Movement," *International Journal of Korean History* 3 (December 2003): 225–54.

The Three Rules for Self-Cultivation (*Sambŏp hoet'ong*)

1. CONTROL YOUR EMOTIONS

There are six emotions you should watch out for so that you can keep them under control. They are happiness, fear, sadness, greed, anger, and hate.

2. CONTROL YOUR BREATHING

You should keep your breathing calm and regular. In doing so, you must make sure your breath is neither too fresh nor too stale, neither too cold nor too warm, and neither too dry nor too wet.

3. CONTROL SENSORY DISTRACTIONS

In order to protect your mind against disturbances from the outside world, you should watch out for loud noises and bright colors, you should ignore all enticing smells and tastes, and you should abstain from all pleasures of the flesh.

The Three Techniques for Self-Cultivation

1. CONTROLLING YOUR EMOTIONS

These three rules should be engraved on your mind. They must be given equal weight and practiced continually. You have to keep your body healthy, your breath fresh, and your mind calm. You also must keep all your thoughts sincere, free of any taint of self-interest. [A weak mind makes it impossible for you to control your emotions. When your mind is not strong, you become a slave to your emotions. The technique for controlling your emotions outlined below will give you the mental strength you need to make sure your mind, rather than your emotions, is in charge.]

Set aside a specific time during the day when you can sit up straight in a quiet place and for quite a while do nothing more than focus your attention on the "palace of mystery," a spot between your eyebrows. This will nurture clear vision and inner strength, and will transform that "palace of mystery" into the abode of God. This will produce in you a feeling of deep joy.

Once you have brought the six emotions under control and have forgotten about the pleasures of the flesh, then evil spirits will no longer have any power over you. You will rise above distinctions of mundane good and evil and will find inner peace. The end result will be the recovery of the essential core of goodness that lies within you.

2. CONTROL YOUR BREATH

[Controlling your breath means to take long quiet breaths. When you control your breathing, you both clear your mind and make your body healthier.]

When the first dim light of dawn comes streaming in through your windows, while all is still quiet in your study, breathe deeply and slowly, making sure you inhale and exhale at the same steady rate. As your chest opens up, you will feel energy gathering in that place right below your navel known as the "sea of energy" and you will feel cool and refreshed. That energy will then move down lower in your abdomen, to the bottom of your digestive tract, where it will grow more palpable. Next you will feel energy moving through your tailbone and up your spinal cord and into the bones at the base of your skull. As it moves, it will open up energy portals that had been closed. Finally, that energy will reach the "heavenly palace" in your skull, which is the equivalent in your head of the "sea of energy" in your abdomen, and you will find yourself breathing in more life-enhancing energy with every breath.

Breathing in this way sends that life-enhancing energy downward from your nose and mouth into your abdomen and then back up to your head again, while at the same time expelling depleted energy. Don't overdo it. Just breathe naturally at an even rate.

[Specific steps to take in controlling your breath:

1. Sit up straight with your legs crossed.
2. If you keep your back and your upper buttocks perpendicular to the floor, it will keep pressure off your waist and will allow you to breathe comfortably with your lower abdomen.
3. Place one hand on top of the other, palm to palm, and rest them on your ankles.
4. Keep your eyes open, and bending your neck downward slightly, focus on a spot between your knees.
5. Keep your lips closed gently and put the tip of your tongue lightly between the roof of your mouth and the back of your upper front teeth.
6. Taking longer breaths than you would normally, breath slowly in and out through your nose only.
7. Be sure that, with every breath, you breathe out the same amount you breathe in.
8. Do this every morning and every evening for thirty minutes or an hour. You will find that your breathing will naturally become softer, lighter, and more regular.
9. Breathing in slowly and deeply, direct the air you inhale down toward the cinnabar field, which lies just below your navel. Once you have become accustomed to this sort of breathing, the energy you take in every time you inhale will naturally gravitate toward that cinnabar field without any specific effort on your part.]

3. CONTROL SENSORY DISTRACTIONS

Begin each day by bowing [four times] to Han Paegŏm (Tan'gun, the Celestial Ancestor). Then recite the "words of enlightenment" (a sixteen-syllable phrase said while focusing attention on the trinitarian God in heaven above). That phrase can be loosely translated as "There are three persons in One God in heaven above who see and hear everything we do. It is that God who brought us into this world and that God who keeps us alive. May He continue to bestow His grace on humanity for tens and thousands of years." Next quietly pray [as follows: "We pray that those who have neglected You will repent of their sin and return to Your love. We pray that You will forgive their sin and enlighten them so that they can once again be Your humble servants."]. While offering up that prayer, light some sandalwood incense. Then read the "Teachings of the Trinitarian God."

Protect your vital energy. Bathe in cold water. Make sure your clothes and your hat are on straight. Guard your ears and eyes against sensory distractions. Avoid alcohol as well as foods with a strong smell. Abstain from indulging your carnal desires.

If you keep your mind free of evil thoughts, you will not be distracted by things from the material realm. You will be able to enter the Jade Hall and feel the providence of God. Your heart will be filled with joy and your body will be strong and healthy.

Why I Believe in Taejonggyo

Many followers of Taejonggyo are drawn to that religion by a combination of nationalism and a desire to improve both their physical and their mental health. One such person was interviewed by Ok Soong Cha of Hanil University in 1998. This report is taken from Cha's interview with a forty-two year-old man working as the director of a center in downtown Seoul teaching Kich'ŏnmun, a combination of martial arts and longevity-enhancing exercises and breathing practices.

I was born in Seoul as the oldest son of what became a family of three sons and one daughter. We had a comfortable existence when I was a child. My father was a businessman and my mother was a housewife. I was a shy and quiet kid who from an early age was fascinated by metaphysical issues. When I was in middle school, I started to read a lot of fantasy tales about great heroes. When I read those novels, I believed I was learning a lot from them and acquiring deep philosophical insights. They made me feel more mature than I actually was. Those books talked a lot about the cosmos, so, even though I didn't know much about outer space yet, I began to get very interested in it.

After I entered high school, I began to read a lot of Buddhism. After high school I entered Yonsei University and majored in business administration. I really liked reading new books and learning from them, so I joined a political study group and started reading radical literature. We called our group the "Cotton Club." Our aim was to learn from each other, develop a Korean philosophy, and push for improvements in the situation in which the Korean nation and the Korean people found themselves at that time. That is when I first became interested in the indigenous philosophy of the Korean people. When I was exposed to the basic concepts and doctrines of Western religion during chapel, rather than rejecting them outright, I compared them with what I knew about the religions of East Asia and decided to learn more about my own heritage.

After I graduated and began working for a company, I continued studying Korea's traditional philosophy in my spare time. Then I read the best-selling novel *Tan* (The Elixir) and learned about Kwŏn T'aehun, the real-life hero of that novel. That inspired me to learn more about Taejonggyo, the religion that preserved the spirit of the Korean people and had been the center of the struggle against Japanese colonial rule. [Kwŏn was the head of that religion from 1982 to 1992.] This is how I came to be involved with Taejonggyo.

I have worked in the youth organization of Taejonggyo and for a while was the head of the Young Taejonggyo Believers Association. These days I am an ordinary staff member in our education department, supporting the work of that department in teaching and spreading Taejonggyo teachings. In November a couple of years ago, I was placed in charge of the section responsible for teaching our creed. I have become particularly interested in the ancient history of Korea, especially the history of the ancient states of Parhae, Koryŏ, Puyŏ and the Old Chosŏn of Tan'gun.

According to the trinitarian philosophy that lies at the core of Taejonggyo beliefs, although we associate God the Creator with business, God the Educator with religion, and God the Ruler with politics, these three divine persons are actually one God. However, in the world today, business, politics, and religion are treated as three separate and distinct spheres. I think they should instead be treated as simply different aspects of the same thing.

Taejonggyo once assumed a leading role in politics, when it led the movement for independence from Japanese rule. It should assume a leading role in politics once again, this time by promoting the reunification of Korea. I helped build the altar to Tan'gun and would like to unify the Korean peninsula around that altar. This is not a task only for Taejongogyo. Since 1986 we have worked with young people across Korea who want reunification.

True enlightenment is not self-centered enlightenment but an awakening to our own true nature, which includes the power to promote the common good. By actualizing our own true nature, we are able to benefit broadly those around us and even humanity as a whole. What I want from Taejonggyo is precisely that ability to contribute to my community and to humanity as a whole. Moreover, I believe that helping others helps us become more like our revered Grandfather Tan'gun. Taejonggyo is composed of people who share that belief and that desire.

I have learned how to open the Celestial Gate, the Ch'ŏnmun, through which life-enhancing energy (*ki*) can enter our bodies. In order to do this, I use the physical exercises and breathing practices bequeathed us by Grandfather Tan'gun. At first I relied on mental exercises such as meditation, but I found physical exercises to be more effective than mental exercises. You can only have a sound mind if you first have a sound body. That is how I came to be interested in the *ki*-enhancing practices of *Kich'ŏnmun*.

Christians Have No Right to Call Their God "Hananim"

Taejonggyo is not a very large religion. The most recent South Korean government census found only a few thousand people who said they were believers in Taejonggyo. However, it has influence far beyond those limited numbers. In a bow to the nationalist cachet attached to Taejonggyo teachings, the South Korean government has designated October Third National Foundation Day and made it a national holiday. According to Taejonggyo, that is the date Tan'gun assumed the throne in 2333 B.C.E. Moreover, many Koreans who have never attended Sunday services in a Taejonggyo worship hall share the Taejonggyo belief that Koreans believed in a trinitarian God long before Christian missionaries began preaching their particular brand of trinitarian theology on Korean soil. These believers in the indigenous origins of trinitarian monotheism do not always use the Taejonggyo term for God, Hanŏllim. Some of them believe instead that Hananim, the name Korean Christians use for their God, is more appropriately applied to Tan'gun.

The God of the Korean people, whom we call "Hananim" (the Supreme One), is fundamentally different from the god of the Jewish people, whom they call Jehovah. Jehovah is a jealous god who violently punishes those who offend him. That means he is an immoral god, one we cannot accept. That alone is enough of a reason for us to protest when Christians apply the sacred name "Hananim" to Jehovah.

Christians have appropriated the term "Hananim" for their god to make him appear no different from the God our ancestors worshiped. We cannot tolerate this attempt to deny the unique Korean characteristics of Hananim and make him a generic god for all humanity. There are a number of ways in which the god of Christianity is different from Hananim and make the Christian use of that name for God inappropriate.

First of all, the term "Hananim" is the name for the revered progenitors of our race (Hanin, Hanung, and Han'gŏm [Tan'gun]) when we talk about them as essentially one and the same God. However, Christians denounce worship of those divine ancestors as idolatry. Therefore they have no right to use the term "Hananim" for their god.

Second, Hananim is the spirit that animates Korean indigenous religious culture. That name represents the core belief of our race that distinguishes us from other peoples and, as such, represents the flowering of our unique religious traditions. Christians violate the very core of our religious beliefs when they appropriate the name "Hananim" for Jehovah, who was the tutelary god of the Jewish people. This is totally unacceptable.

Let me explain in greater detail. The term "Hananim" means both the Dao of heaven as well as the three revered progenitors of our nation (Hanin, Hanung, and Han'gŏm) when we talk about them as essentially one and the same God. Because these founders of our nation were such great men, everything they did aligned perfectly with the Dao of heaven. As a result our race came to worship heaven and the nation's progenitors as one and the same, and we came to be known as the descendants of heaven. Not only does the name "Hananim" appear in our national anthem, we call out the name "Hananim" when we are happy and when we are in distress. This shows that Hananim is the core of those religious beliefs that define us as a people, and that our concept of Hananim represents the flowering of our unique religious traditions.

However, Christians have stolen this name "Hananim" from us. And that is not all. Instead of teaching us about our people, our history, and our traditions, they teach us about the history, philosophy, and religion of another race, the people of Judea. This is exactly the same as what the Japanese did when they had us in their colonial grip and made us study Japanese history, philosophy, and religion. Consequently, the ten million Christians who live on this peninsula may have Korean bodies and eat, sleep, and enjoy themselves in the land called Korea, but in their hearts they long for Israel, so they are not really Koreans. Moreover, because of these Christians our children, as well as adult nonbelievers, are confused about what the name "Hananim" refers to. They do not know whether Hananim (Hanŭnim) is the Jehovah the Christians worship or is the God of our forefathers. How can anyone deny, therefore, that Christians have undermined the very foundations of our nation? That is why I say that we cannot tolerate Christians appropriating the name of our God for their god.

Third, since the religious beliefs of our nation are based on belief in Hananim, Hananim forms the core of our national consciousness. When Christians apply the name for our God to their god, they weaken our pride in our own distinctive racial identity and threaten the very existence of Koreans as a separate people. That is another reason I say we cannot tolerate Christians misappropriating the name of our God for their god.

In our Korean society, we say that somebody who does not know who they are, who thinks they are someone different than their bodies say they are, is mentally unbalanced. Such people cause trouble for their parents rather than paying them the respect a child owes a parent. They sell off their family's financial assets, set their family home on fire, or steal from their family.

The relationship between an individual and his race is the same as the relationship between an individual and his family. A person can act as a proper member of their race only if they keep in mind that they are a member of that race. If people abandon the defining beliefs of their race and adopt the beliefs of another race, they lose their sense of who they are and lose their ability to feel pride in their own race or country. When that happens, they will not be able to carry out properly their duties as a citizen of their mother country. If such a person ends up in an important position in which their actions affect the fate of their nation, that will almost guarantee that their nation is doomed.

For example, look at how the huge nation of Koguryŏ was wiped out of existence by the little nation of Silla. There are a number of explanations for why that happened, but religion was clearly one important factor. Koguryŏ was originally a Buddhist country. However, Yŏn Kaesomun did not think there were any significant differences among Buddhism, Daoism, or Confucianism, so he switched the official religion to the Five Pecks of Rice branch of Daoism and established a Daoist temple at the Koguryŏ court, pushing Buddhism aside. As a result, the masses began frequenting that Daoist temple instead of the Buddhist temples they had flocked to before. The number of practicing Daoists in Koguryŏ swelled while the number of practicing Buddhists shrank. Just then Silla joined forces with Tang China and invaded Koguryŏ. Instead of defending their country as they should have, those Daoists adopted the path of nonresistance. Even the few remaining Buddhists did not resist those invading forces, since Buddhists felt they no longer had any stake in the survival of the Koguryŏ government. Usually when their government is in moral danger from foreign invaders, the masses spontaneously organize into righteous armies to defend it. However, that did not happen when Koguryŏ was invaded. That is why the combined Silla-Tang armies were able to topple Koguryŏ without meeting any serious resistance.

This is an example of a foreign religion undermining a people's consciousness of being a separate and distinct people. When someone abandons the defining beliefs of their race, they are uprooting the plant on which the flowers of patriotism and ethnic pride appear. Such a person won't risk his life for his country even when it is on the verge of extinction. Not all Christians are that bad but if they want to be true to who they really are, they need to know who they really are. I'm not saying that there were no Christians among those who fought for Korea's independence when we were under Japanese colonial rule. However, the number of Christian independence fighters pales in comparison with the number of independence fighters who were followers of Korea's indigenous religions. Moreover, there were certain religious organizations that argued that, whether or not Japan's annexation of Korea was legal, the anti-Japanese independence movement was a political movement, and religious organizations should remain aloof from political activities. That gave Christians a pretext for not joining with the rest of us in our patriotic struggle. As a matter of fact, there were quite a few Christians who supported the Japanese war effort during the final years of colonial rule. The newspaper *Religious News* pointed out after liberation that most of the collaborationist landlord class was just that sort of Christian. Now that the winds of reform are blowing across our land, even the president of our country has pointed out (according to *Reli-*

ginus News) that "As embarrassing as it is to admit it, we can't deny that there are some Christians among those found to be tarred by corruption."

What kind of religion is this Christianity we see in our country these days? Shouldn't Koreans living in churches in Korea teach their fellow Koreans Korean history, Korean philosophy, and Korean religion? Can it really be that the opposite is true, that it is all right for them to teach the history, religion, and philosophy of Israel, a Western nation, and sing words of praise to Jehovah, the god of the Israeli people?

Let's think a minute how it would look if that situation were reversed. Wouldn't it seem a little strange if Israelis taught Korean history, religion, and philosophy to other Israelis in houses of worship in Israel? Wouldn't it seem a little strange if Israelis gathered together in houses of worship in Israel to worship Tan'gun? Yet ten million Korean Christians enter churches once or twice a week to listen to lectures about Israeli history, philosophy, and religion. In doing so, they deny the value of the history, religion, and philosophy of their own race. What effect do you think such disdain for their own heritage has on national identity and ethnic pride? Not only do these Christians forget their own racial identity, they also weaken the soul and spirit of the nation and threaten the very notion of Koreans as a separate people. This is completely contrary to what the term "Hananim" represents. That is why I say it is unacceptable for Christians to use the name "Hananim" for their god.

A fourth reason I reject the Christian misappropriation of the name "Hananim" is that all filial piety originates in Hananim. That is why it is unacceptable for Christians, who deny the cardinal importance of filial piety, to use the name "Hananim" for their god.

Let me explain in detail. Filial piety means strong love for our parents and other ancestors. If our love for our parents is as strong as it should be, then that love will extend not only to our parents but will reach all the way down the family tree to the first ancestor of our family, the progenitor of our lineage. Such love for the progenitor of our own lineage will naturally also extend to love for the progenitors of the entire Korean race, the three divine beings (Hanin, Hanung, and Han'gŏm) who together are the Supreme One, Hananim. To the same extent that we cannot forget how much we owe our mother and father, as well as our grandfathers and grandmothers, who gave us life and educated us, we also cannot forget how much we owe Hanin, Hanung, and Han'gŏm. That is why the *Classics* talk of the "filial piety that has its origin in heaven," which means that filial piety begins with Hananim. That is also why belief in Hananim is the foundation of an education in filial piety. And that is why we both worship Hananim and show respect and love for our ancestors with proper ritual.

Whether or not the spirits of dead ancestors actually partake of the food we provide for them in those rituals is beside the point. What is important is that bowing before something which has their names on it reminds us that they were once alive. It doesn't make any difference whether we bow before a piece of paper on which we have written the names of our revered ancestors or we bow before an actual wooden ancestral tablet. Similarly, placing offerings on the altar, putting on the appropriate ritual costume, and reading the prayers prescribed for such a ritual is a way of showing how much we respect our ancestors and how grateful we are for what they did for us. Such rituals showing love and respect for our parents and grandparents are just like rituals showing respect for Hananin. They are ways of reminding us where we came from and serve as wellsprings of filial piety.

However, not only do Christians deny that Hanin, Hanung, and Han'gŏm (in other words, Hananim) are the progenitors of our race, they also condemn rituals honoring ancestors, saying such displays of ritual respect constitute idolatry. That is a rejection of the wellsprings of filial piety and therefore of filial piety itself. That is why I say Christians are not qualified to speak the name "Hananim."

Fifth, a philosophy centered on Hananim is a philosophy of cosmic unity and peace. Christianity, however, rejects both cosmic unity and peace in favor of a philosophy that posits differentiation, contradictions, and struggle. That is why I say that we cannot tolerate Christians using the name of our God for their god.

Let me explain in detail. Hana (one) in Hananim (the Supreme One) means that all things in the universe are essentially the same thing, in that everything in the universe is interrelated and intermingled and forms one and only one universe. This means that Hananim, human beings, and all the animals in the animal kingdom have the same foundation—the universe itself. That is why a philosophy with belief in Hananim at its core must be a philosophy that emphasizes peace and life. Let's see what the ethical implications of such a philosophy would be.

We should treat the simplest forms of life with the same respect we show Hananim and should hold them just as dear. If that's the case, how much more should we human beings respect each other, love each other, and treat each other as valuable in our own right? If we all do that, then there will be peace on earth.

However, Christians don't think the way real Koreans do. Christians believe in creation and a Creator. According to this creation theory, Jehovah, who is the Creator, is far above human beings, animals, and the other things he created. Moreover, Jehovah's creations are placed on a vertical ladder of being, with some creatures ranking above others. That is the reason Christians deny that animals have souls; it is also the reason Christians believe that all creation is governed by a law of the jungle in which the strong dominate the weak. Such a concept of creation makes peace on earth impossible. For that reason, wherever we find Christians we also find war. Christians not only make peace on earth impossible: since they reject the essential unity of all existence they also are guilty of discrimination. That is contrary to the Hananim philosophy of us Koreans. That is why I say we cannot tolerate Christians misappropriating the name of our God for their god.

Sixth, the Hananim philosophy assumes the essential equality of all human beings. Christianity, on the other hand, makes the opposite assumption. Christians treat some people as better than other people. That is why I say we cannot allow Christians to use the name of our God for their god.

As noted above, the term "Hananim" means that heaven, earth, and humanity, since they are all essential elements of the one universe, constitute a cosmic unity. This means that white people, black people, and yellow people are one and the same. In other words, Hananim philosophy sees all human beings as equally valuable and equally worthy of respect. Christianity, however, is descended from Judaism and as such is a religion that elevates the Jewish people as a chosen people above other peoples. Therefore it can't escape being guilty of racial and religious prejudice. It is incapable of viewing all human beings and their religions as equally deserving of respect. That is why I say that it is unacceptable for Christians to use the name of our God for their god.

— 28 —

The Wŏn Buddhist Practice of
the Buddha-Nature

Jin Y. Park

Wŏn Buddhism, founded by Pak Chungbin (1891–1943; now known by his so-briquet Sot'aesan) after his enlightenment in 1916, is a representative Korean new religion with Buddhist affinities. The initial organization for the school was established in 1918 under the name Society for the Study of the Buddhadharma (Pulbŏp yŏn'guhoe). The school was known by that name until 1947, when the second Dharma Master Chŏngsan (1900–1962) renamed the order Wŏn Buddhism (Wŏnbulgyo).

The "Treatise on the Renovation of Korean Buddhism" (*Chosŏn Pulgyo hyŏksil-lon*, 1935), the second half of which is translated in this chapter, provides a blueprint for Pak's approach to reforming Korean Buddhism. At the beginning of this treatise, Pak Chungbin identifies the main issues of his reform agenda as changing Korean Buddhism in all aspects, "from the Buddhism from abroad to Buddhism for Koreans; from the Buddhism of the past to the Buddhism of the present and future; from the Buddhism of a few monks residing in the mountains to the Buddhism of the general public." Pak claims that Korean Buddhism during the early twentieth century needs serious renovation. According to him, the situation of Korean Buddhism at the time was double-edged. On the one hand, the suppression of Buddhism under the Neo-Confucian ideologues of the Chosŏn dynasty (1392–1910) had lasting effects. It left the Korean Buddhism of his time alienated from the general public, rejected by many as superstitious and ill suited to people living outside a monastic setting. On the other hand, the changes in Korean society prompted by foreign cultural influences entering the peninsula from both East and West demanded the integration of religious prac-tice into daily life. By combining these two issues, Pak fashions his proposal for renewing Korean Buddhism by revitalizing both its institutions and its social status.

First Pak proposes radical changes for Buddhist practice. These include mov-ing Buddhist temples, most of which were isolated deep in the mountains, into ordinary society. Situating temples closer to communities would help unify the curriculum of educating the laity and the priesthood, in turn making Buddhist teachings more relevant and Buddhist practice available in the context of everyday life. In summary, in its social aspect, Pak's reform agenda focuses on expanding Buddhism beyond the monastic community by popularizing and simplifying its teaching and practice. In philosophical terms, Pak's reform is solidly anchored in the Mahāyāna Buddhist idea of the existence of the Buddha-nature in all beings. Combining the Buddhist theory of the Buddha-nature and Buddhism's social commitment, Pak proposes replacing buddha images with what he calls the One Circle Symbol of the Buddha-nature (*Pulsŏng Irwŏnsang*). This symbol marks one of the most visible distinctions between Wŏn Buddhism and traditional Buddhism.

In explaining the relationship between the Buddha-nature and the One Circle Symbol, Pak grounds his theory on the Buddha's teaching that all the dharma world, including heaven, earth, the myriad living things in between, and empty space, represents the nature of the Buddha. If all the existence in the world is a manifestation of the Buddha-nature, then spatial confinement such as the separation between the monastic setting and secular world, or institutional devices such as the division between the priesthood and laity, or methods of practice such as how and to whom to make offerings have only provisional, not ultimate, meaning. Therefore the separation between the monastery and the outside world, priesthood and laity, and eventually that between the Buddha and sentient beings need be overcome in order to truly realize and embody the Buddha's teaching of the omnipresence of the Buddha-nature in the world.

This can be explained in terms of the Buddhist doctrine of dependent co-arising. Things do not have any unchanging and intrinsic essence but instead exist through the cooperative functioning of numerous things in the world that constantly interact with one another. In an attempt to provide a practical understanding of this potentially abstract idea, Pak explains dependent co-arising through the idea of the fourfold beneficence (*saŭn* in Korean), which becomes one of the major doctrines in Wŏn Buddhism.

The fourfold beneficence explains dependent co-arising through four concrete categories in our life. They are the Beneficence of Heaven and Earth, the Beneficence of Parents, the Beneficence of Brethren, and the Beneficence of Law, which explicate the Buddhist nonsubstantialist view of being in terms of environmental, biological, and social ties or in the context of one's relation to nature, family, nation, and society. By understanding one's existence as being situated within the net of the fourfold beneficence, the practitioner realizes that an individual is the dependent co-arising and not an independent entity. Since being is a part of this net of the fourfold beneficence, properly exercising one's role in that network means fully activating one's original nature, which Mahāyāna Buddhism identifies as the Buddha-nature. According to the Wŏn Buddhist canon, to recompense the "beneficence of heaven and earth" is to embody the Dao of the heaven and earth; to recompense the "beneficence of parents" is to take care of the helpless as one's parents do and to protect them; to recompense the "beneficence of brethren" is to realize the virtue of "doing good for others as well as for oneself"; and finally to recompense the "beneficence of law" is to realize humanity and righteousness in the same manner that law protects an individual.

Changing the focus of Buddhist doctrine from dependent co-arising to the fourfold beneficence demonstrates the distinctiveness of both the nature and scope of Pak Chungbin's reformation and shows as well how he sought to differentiate Wŏn Buddhism from traditional Buddhism. First of all, his reformation reinterprets major Buddhist doctrines in the context of the daily lives of practitioners. Second, by doing so, it makes an appeal to lay practitioners and the general public, again changing the focus of Buddhist training from the teaching of monastic communities to teaching laities. Third, the fourfold beneficence transforms the seemingly ontological and abstract language of dependent co-arising into a moral and ethical reformation; this move, in turn, activates Pak's intention to transform Buddhism from the solitary endeavor of achieving enlightenment for oneself to a communal practice of living out enlightenment together.

Another example of Wŏn Buddhism's practical approach to Buddhist doctrine is reformulating the traditional concept of the three trainings in morality (śīla), concentration (samādhi), and wisdom (prajñā) and into the threefold practice (Kor. samhak). In this treatise, Pak identifies the core of the Wŏn Buddhist curriculum as the three major subjects, which later evolve into the threefold practice. The three major subjects of study include training in the investigation of things, training in the cultivation of mind, and training in mindful choice. The Mahāyāna tradition holds that the attainment of wisdom for oneself and its transformation into compassion for others takes place naturally and simultaneously. The bodhisattva path, through which one delays eventual enlightenment until all sentient beings are delivered from saṃsāra, is a symbolic as well as practical statement of the Mahāyāna Buddhist view of compassion's important role in the realization of wisdom. In reality, however, the relationship between one's practice to obtain enlightenment and its social implications has been far from clear. Does gaining wisdom (awakening) naturally produce compassion toward others? Traditional Buddhism remained unclear on the process by which wisdom was transformed into compassion. Because of this, Buddhism was subject to criticism for its lack of social commitment toward fellow human beings. The threefold practice (or the three major subjects) proposed by Pak Chungbin in this "Treatise" provides a blueprint to overcome the gap between an individual's practice and its communal implications. The threefold practice together with the fourfold beneficence effectively demonstrates Wŏn Buddhism's efforts to bring Buddhist doctrines into the context of practitioners' daily life.

The One Circle Symbol of the Buddha-nature is the symbol of the transformation and renovation Pak Chungbin was eager to introduce into Korean Buddhism. Unlike the traditional Buddha statue, whose form is an image of the Buddha and may promote idolatry, the One Circle Symbol is free from such danger because of its abstract nature. Unlike the traditional Buddha statue, it is easy to create and can be enshrined anytime and anywhere.

The treatise is an important document for understanding modern Korean Buddhism as well as Wŏn Buddhist practice. The agenda Pak Chungbin proposes in this "Treatise" reveals the state of Korean Buddhism during the first half of the twentieth century. Pak was not alone in voicing a need for radical changes in Korean Buddhism at the time and, in that sense, Buddhist reform movements were one major trend pursued by Buddhist intellectuals and religious leaders in Korea. One document frequently compared with Pak Chungbin's treatise is "Treatise on the Revitalization of Korean Buddhism" (Han'guk Pulgyo yusillon) by Manhae Han Yongun (1879–1944). In addition to Manhae's "Treatise," movements to create vernacular versions of Buddhist texts, to bring Buddhism back into the milieu of daily life by creating connections between Buddhist doctrine and various social activities, to undertake mass proselytization, to educate both the laity and the monkhood—all are part of the spirit of the modern reformation of Korean Buddhism. These efforts were not merely theoretical but reveal an awareness that religious practice in the twentieth century should be different from that in previous times. As part of a centuries-old tradition in Korea, Buddhism was keen to this changing nature of society and of people's lifestyles, and if one wanted to make Buddhist practice viable in the modern world, renovation was inevitable.

The text translated here provides the very foundation of Wŏn Buddhist doctrine and practice. The "Treatise," together with several other writings by Pak, served as major teachings of Wŏn Buddhism as they were included in the school's first scripture, the Chŏngjŏn (The Principal Book, or Canon; 1943). Most of the contents of the "Treatise" are now reflected in modified format in Taejonggyŏng (The Scripture of the Founding Master), which, together with the revised version of The Principal Book, makes up the current Wŏn Buddhist scripture, The Teachings of Wŏn Buddhism, published in 1962.

The translation is based on the "Treatise on the Renovation of Korean Buddhism" (Chosŏn Pulgyo hyŏksillon) by Sot'aesan Pak Chungbin, in Wŏn pulgyo kyogoch'onggan (Collected Publication of Wŏn Buddhist Teachings), vol. 4 (Chŏnbuk, Korea: Wŏn Pulgyo Chŏnghwasa, 1970), pp. 100–104.

Further Reading

Bongkil Chung has published a complete, annotated translation of the first two major texts of Wŏn Buddhism in The Scriptures of Wŏn Buddhism: A Translation of the Wŏnbulbyo kyojŏn with Introduction, Classics in East Asian Buddhism (Honolulu: University of Hawai'i Press, A Kuroda Institute Book, 2003). Recently, the Department of Edification of Won-Buddhism has published an entirely new English translation of the Chŏngjon by an international team of scholars: The Principal Book of Won-Buddhism: Korean-English (Wonbulgyo Chongjon) (Iksan: Won Kwang Publishing, 2000); a new rendering of the Taejonggyŏng is forthcoming from the same source. See also Bongkil Chung, "Wŏn Buddhism: The Historical Context of Sot'aesan's Reformation of Buddhism for the Modern World," in *Buddhism in the Modern World: Adaptations of an Ancient Tradition*, edited by Steven Heine and Charles S. Prebish (Oxford: Oxford University Press, 2003), pp. 143–67; Ray Key Chong, *Wŏn Buddhism: A History and Theology of Korea's New Religion*, Studies in Asian Thought and Religion, vol. 22 (Lewiston, N.Y.: Edwin Mellen Press, 1997); James Huntley Grayson, *Korea: A Religious History* (Oxford: Clarendon Press, 1989), pp. 250–54; Bokin Kim, *Concerns and Issues in Wŏn Buddhism* (Philadelphia: Won Publications, 2000); Jin Young Park, "Religious Conflict or Religious Anxiety: New Buddhist Movements in Korea and Japan," *Religious Studies and Theology* 17, no. 2 (December 1998): 34–46; Kwangsoo Park, *The Wŏn Buddhism (Wŏnbulgyo) of Sot'aesan: A Twentieth-Century Religious Movement in Korea* (San Francisco: International Scholars Publications, 1997).

Treatise on the Renovation of Korean Buddhism

SECTION 5. FROM THE BUDDHISM OF THE FEW TO THE BUDDHISM OF THE PEOPLE

Korean Buddhism in the past was rejected by society, and thus practiced by only a small number of people. Its doctrine and systems had been tailored for the lifestyle of monks who left the secular world to lead a monastic life, and not all of its aspects could fit into the life of people living outside the monasteries. Sometimes, facets of Buddhism were in direct contradiction to life in the secular world. Lay Buddhist practitioners were not able to play a principal role in this system and instead remained on the periphery. If someone had special business or had cultivated himself exceptionally, his situation might be different; but it was difficult for lay practitioners in general to be recognized as legitimate disciples of the Buddha or be recognized as patriarchs in the Buddhist school as were monks in a monastic setting. How can such doctrines and systems appeal to the laity? Let me provide some examples of how the doctrines and systems focused on monastic life are at odds with lay practitioners.

Religious teaching exists in order to edify people. However, since [Buddhist] temples have been built in places where people do not live, how can those people who are busy with their livelihood in the secular world find time to escape society and learn from this teaching? In terms of making a living, monks did not labor as scholars, farmers, craftsmen, or merchants; instead they depended on providing services for making offerings to the Buddha for the laity as well as on donations or almsgivings by them. How can such methods of livelihood be practiced by the general public? With regard to marriage, celibacy was a requirement for those leading a monastic life. Not only does such a lifestyle limit one's vision, but as a religious teaching it is completely unfit for those who live outside monastic settings. How can we call such teachings universal? How, then, do we resolve these problems?

There shall be no distinction with regard to primary or auxiliary status between monks and laity. The difference will be marked only through the degrees of their practice and public service. As for the dharma-lineage as well, there should be no distinction between priesthood and laities. The places for practice should be built wherever practitioners live. Practitioners should also be able to choose their own occupations and have the freedom to make decisions as to whether they want to maintain celibacy or not. I would not specify special vows for lay and ordained practitioners. However, in terms of training, during childhood one should learn letters; during adulthood one should cultivate oneself and devote time to the deliverance of others; and after the age of sixty, one should join a monastery on the mountainside with beautiful scenery where one should sever all the attachments to love and greed in the mundane life and deal with the grave matter of birth and death. At this stage, during the six months of spring and fall when the weather is neither cold nor hot, one should travel among temples in the society and lead practitioners to be born in the upper three levels of the wheel of life. During the six months of summer and winter, one should refrain from visiting the mundane world but maintain life on the mountain, surrounded by the joy of nature amid the sound of water and the singing of birds. Heartened by the unsurpassed teachings of the Buddhadharma and taking refuge in Amitābha Buddha, one will spend the rest of one's life in this manner and there will then be nothing that is lacking in daily life. Also everyone, whether lay or ordained, should try to popularize the teaching. In that context, with regard to doctrines, instead of focusing exclusively on "seeing the nature of things" (Kor. *kyŏnsŏng*) and "cultivating one's mind" (Kor. *yangsŏng*), we should also include "the application of the understanding of the nature of things to daily life" (Kor. *solsŏng*). These three principles should be at the core of our doctrine. In other words, we should create the essential path for ordained practitioners to practice the life of the monkhood, we should also create the essential path for lay practitioners to practice life in the secular world, and finally we should create a curriculum to train both the laity and the monks in how to practice appropriately. The institutions should also be structured so that there will be no obstacles in actualizing the above teachings in the context of the current historical situation as well as people's orientations. All practitioners should try their best to realize this goal.

SECTION 6. FROM AN INCONSISTENT TO A UNIFIED CURRICULUM

The curriculum of traditional Buddhism has been a combination of studying Buddhist texts, meditating with the *hwadu* [keyword or critical phrase], chanting, and incantations. Each teaching has its own function. Through the study of sūtras one learns Buddhist doctrine, its systems and history. By practicing meditation with the *hwadu*, one attains the realization of the profound truth that is difficult to express in Buddhist texts or in language in general. Having developed various attachments and greed while living in the complex world, people have difficulty getting onto the right path and, as a result, when first encountering Buddhist teachings, they find it difficult to concentrate their minds. The techniques of chanting and repeating incantations are used to teach people how to concentrate. The ritual of making offerings to the Buddha is taught in order to help monks maintain their vocation.

Believers are required to master all of the above teachings. However, those who lack a profound understanding of the Buddhadharma study only one or two of the above teachings and claim that "I" am right and "you" are wrong. By creating divisions in this manner and forming different sects, such people hamper the spirituality of those who first encounter the teachings of the Buddha. They impede the practitioners' unity and further damage the dignity of Buddhist practitioners in general while also hindering the development of Buddhism. In order to prevent such a situation, the curriculum will be unified: various different *hwadus* in the Sŏn (Meditation) school and all the sūtras in the Kyo (Doctrinal) school will be condensed. Complicated *hwadus* and complicated sūtras will be left out and only those *hwadus* and sūtras that contain the primary principles and essential teachings will be incorporated in the curriculum so that by studying them people will obtain results in their understanding of facts as well as in the investigation of things. Also chanting, meditation, and incantation will be combined in the teaching of practicing concentration of mind. All the precepts, the contents of karmic retribution, and the four principles of beneficence will be condensed to create a curriculum that will be suitable for proper practice in mundane life. All practitioners will practice equally the three major subjects in our curriculum. Through the training in investigation, practitioners will earn, like the Buddha himself, the power of nonobstruction with the principle itself and with phenomena; through the training in cultivation, practitioners will earn, like the Buddha himself, an energy which will not be carried away by things; through the training in mindful choice, the practitioners will earn, like the Buddha himself, the power to distinguish injustice from justice and then to realize that justice. If one uses these three great powers of investigation, cultivation, and mindful choice as a foundation for making offerings to the Buddha so that one can fulfill all the vows, then the teachings will naturally be unified and the practitioners will feel a sense of unity.

SECTION 7. FROM THE VENERATION OF THE BUDDHA STATUE TO THE VENERATION OF THE ONE CIRCLE SYMBOL OF THE BUDDHA-NATURE

Paying homage to the Buddha statue has its specific function in the development of Buddhist teaching. However, if we consider the current state of our society and the future world, not only is its function dubious, but it can be an obstacle to the development of Buddhism. Let me give you an example. In the fall, when the crops in the field are ripening, the farmers who took pains to grow the crops set up a scarecrow in a place where birds flock in order to protect their crops. The dummy will scare birds away for days. Birds will try various methods—or have they attained some awakening?—but they will eventually come for the crops again, eating them, and even using the dummy scarecrow as a resting place, covering it with their droppings. If we think about this, we know that even birds, which are uneducated, come to learn the difference between a dummy and a real person. Why wouldn't human beings who have the highest intelligence and who have been venerating the immobile dummy Buddha statue for over two thousand years come to a certain kind of disillusionment? If they become disillusioned without realizing the unsurpassed great path of the Buddhadharma, they will take the ineffectiveness of what is only a means instead to be the ineffectiveness of the Buddha's teaching. If there are many such individuals who introduce Buddhism in a negative way to those who have no knowledge of the religion, how will it not be an obstacle to the development of Buddhism?

In addition, in various places in this country people use the sacred Buddha statue as a sign for their business and make a living out of it. If practitioners of the religion make offerings to the same Buddha statue as those who use it for business, ignorant onlookers will make no distinction between practitioners and those who use the Buddha statue for business. As the food offerings increase, the dignity of the temples will be damaged, discouraging practitioners from joining the monastery. Study of the Buddhadharma will in turn dissipate, as Buddhist temples turn into places of business. Even nowadays, our society has the false belief that all Buddhists do is to chant and make offerings to the Buddha. If people are identified as Buddhist who know nothing about the true dharma of the Buddha, the meaning of the deliverance of all sentient beings, or the differences between good and bad realms, those who manage Buddhist doctrines and systems will be treated in the same manner as these people. How, then, wouldn't this create obstacles to the development of the religion?

Also if believers are to venerate a Buddha statue, then that statue should be available for all the believers to own and venerate it. However, since it is not easy to produce a Buddha statue, those who do own a statue might feel they are closer to the Buddha, as if they were immediate disciples of the Buddha. Thus, the Buddha statue to them will be a thing to rely upon, something that brings comfort. Those who cannot afford to own a statue, however, will feel the opposite. They will feel as if they are not close to the Buddha, nor can they get comfort from or rely on it. This is a pity. For this reason, we have decided to venerate and worship the One Circle Symbol of the Buddha-nature (Kor. *pulsŏng irwŏnsang*).

What does the One Circle Symbol of the Buddha-nature stand for? The Buddha mentioned that all the things in the dharma world, including heaven, earth, the myriad things in between, and empty space, are representations of the nature of the Buddha. If we say this in one word, it is called the Buddha-nature; if we draw a picture of the Buddha-nature, it will be the symbol of one circle. If we talk about the contents of this symbol of one circle, it includes the entire dharma world of heaven, earth, the myriad things in between, and empty space. That being the case, it becomes obvious that the One Circle Symbol will benefit sentient beings in ten thousand ways. To put it another way, since all the things in the dharma world reflect the Buddha, one should make offerings to appropriate objects based on what one seeks and what one does in order to expiate misdeeds and earn merit. To expiate misdeeds and earn merits that are related to heaven and earth, one should make offerings to heaven and earth; to expiate misdeeds and earn merits that are related to one's parents, one should make offerings to one's parents; as for the misdeeds and merits that are related to one's brethren, one should make offerings to one's brethren; and as for the misdeeds and merits related to the law, one should make offerings to the law. If we concentrate on our practice and venerate and worship the One Circle Symbol of the Buddha-nature, even the spectators who do not have a deep understanding of the Buddhadharma will begin to see the difference. Our society used to identify Buddhists with those who do not have an understanding as to what the right teachings of the Buddha are, what the meaning of delivering sentient beings is, or the differences between evil and good realms, lumping practitioners together with those who go to see a blind person to inquire about their fortune or who call in a shaman for a shamanic ritual. Such a tendency will gradually disappear. Also, if we replace the Buddha statue with the One Circle Symbol of the Buddha-nature, there will be no difficulty in each and every believer obtaining one.

This is the time when humankind is entering into the stage of adulthood. People will become wiser, and accordingly good and bad events in life will make people understand the difference between misdeeds and the merit made from those events. This will in turn make people seek the source of misdeeds or merit-making. Such a search will reveal one's will, and that will should enhance one's faith. If one finds and practices a religion that explains their reality, one will find peace of mind as well as friends in religion.

In the old customs of Buddhism, one relied upon others to make offerings to the Buddha, and now one will make offerings to the Buddha oneself. It follows that all believers need to learn how to make offerings to the Buddha. And how do we make offerings to the Buddha? That should be based on the doctrines and systems that renovated the Buddhism of old. Once one has learned how to make offerings to the Buddha, one should also learn that making offerings produces different effects in different situations. For example, some works need a thousand rebirths to be completed; other works need only a hundred rebirths; still others dozens of rebirths, and others only several rebirths. Furthermore, there are works that can be done in several decades, several years, several months, or several days. Depending on the nature of the work, the length required for its completion varies. Consequently, whether one has a good relationship with others, creates good or bad karma, or whether one is born into a wealthy upper class or a poor lower class in this life depends on

Figure 28.1. The *Irwŏnsang* (One Circle Symbol) of Wŏn Buddhism.

how well one made offerings to the Buddha during the lives one lived through rebirths.

Those who have accumulated merit and wisdom will obtain awakening to the teaching of the One Circle Symbol of Buddha-nature and venerate heaven and earth, the myriad things in between, and empty space, as the Buddha did. Since such people have a clear understanding about the time needed for different works to be completed, they will know the ground of misdeeds and merit-making and make offerings accordingly, so their vows will always be realized.

Those who do not understand the source of misdeeds and merit-making will not only make their vow exclusively to the Buddha statue but will lack the understanding of how different amounts of time are required to complete different types of works. For example, such people will make offerings to heaven and earth when they actually need to make offerings to their parents; they will make offerings to heaven and earth when they actually need to make offerings to their brethren; they will make offerings to heaven and earth when they actually need to make offerings to the law. They will stop trying after a couple of months for work that actually requires a year of effort to be successful. They will stop trying after a couple of days for work that actually requires a month of effort to be successful. Such individuals will eventually consider making offerings to the Buddha a vain effort and thus will not be able to achieve success. For this reason, instead of exclusively venerating the Buddha statue, we venerate the One Circle Symbol of the Buddha-nature so that we will venerate as the Buddha the dharma world of heaven and earth, the myriad things in between, and empty space.

How to Create the One Circle Symbol of the Buddha-Nature

The physical shape of the Buddha-nature can be represented by the One Circle Symbol, and the details of this One Circle Symbol are represented by the fourfold beneficence. In venerating this One Circle Symbol of the Buddha-nature, each individual will create it, based on his situation, in the shape as shown [above (figure 28.1)]. It can be a golden symbol on wood; one can also sew it on silk cloth; or one can draw it in ink with a brush on a paper or on hemp cloth. Enshrine it on the wall by hanging it neatly. Make vows and pray to it.

─── 29 ───

Renewing Heaven and Earth:
Spiritual Discipline in Chŭngsan'gyo

Don Baker

Of all of Korea's major new religions, Chŭngsan'gyo is the least influenced by Christianity. The primary worship halls of Wŏn Buddhism, Taejonggyo, Ch'ŏndogyo, and, of course, the Unification Church resemble Christian churches. Moreover, Sunday is a regular day of worship for members of those religious communities. In addition, the Sunday services they attend normally include sermons and the singing of hymns, just as Christian services do. Even the names of the gods of Taejonggyo and Ch'ŏndogyo resemble the names Christians use for God. (Wŏn Buddhism is an exception.) Hanullim (Ch'ŏndogyo) and Hanŏllim (Taejonggyo) are variations on Hanŭnim, one of the Christian names for God (along with Hananim).

Chŭngsan'gyo is different. Its worship halls do not look like churches. From the outside, they look more like temples than churches. Moreover, you will hear no hymns being sung at a Chŭngsan'gyo service. In addition, Chŭngsan'gyo has its own name for its Supreme God, Sangjenim. Sangje (to which the honorific *nim* is added) is the Korean pronunciation of an ancient Chinese term (Shangdi) meaning "the Lord on High" or "Lord Above" and has no relationship to Christian theological nomenclature.

Chŭngsan'gyo does resemble Christianity in two key features. First of all, like Christianity, it is divided into many denominations, all worshiping the same God and revering roughly the same holy book, but each insisting that they are the true followers of Sangjenim and all others are misguided. Second, its scriptures are the record of the words of their God when he walked on earth as a human being. In other words, Chŭngsan'gyo, just like Christianity, believes in incarnation of the deity.

However, in the case of Chŭngsan'gyo, when God walked on this earth, he walked on Korean soil, where his name was Kang Chŭngsan. Born in 1871, he returned to heaven in 1909 and, his followers believe, resumed his post as the Lord of the Ninth Heaven and the Supreme Ruler of Heaven and Earth. All the various Chŭngsan'gyo denominations teach that he descended to earth so that he could teach human beings how to prepare for the Great Transformation. Using the same term used by Ch'ŏndogyo, Chŭngsan'gyo shares the belief that the current cosmic era is coming to an end soon. Through a Great Transformation, a new and better era will appear, in which all the causes of human suffering will disappear and the earth will become a paradise of immortals. However, in order to prepare for that transition, and hasten its arrival, it is necessary to rectify the current disorder in heaven, on earth, and in the human community. This can best be done with the Great Work of Renewing Heaven and Earth (ch'ŏnji kongsa), rituals created and taught by Sangjenim before he returned to heaven.

Chŭngsan'gyo teaches that the proper performance of the rituals taught by Sangjenim, as well as adherence to the ethical guidelines he preached, will lead to a number of positive consequences. First of all, the imbalance between yin and yang that has led to male domination of females will end. In the new era, such unjust inequality will be abolished, as yin and yang are brought to parity, and women are treated the same as men. Second, gods and spirits will no longer have the power to intervene unfairly in human affairs. Instead, human beings and spiritual beings will coexist in perfect harmony. Third, the dog-eat-dog atmosphere of the contemporary world will be replaced by a culture of cooperation. Rather than trying to take advantage of our fellow human beings, we will instead try to help them, just as they will try to help us. Fourth, all those who feel resentment for their unfair treatment, including the dead who still feel the pain of being poorly treated when they were alive, will have their grievances resolved. Rather than looking back at past mistreatment, everyone will instead look ahead to a new era of justice and equality. Finally, a paradise will be created on this earth, as the Dao (the Way things should be) will prevail. The name for this paradise is "a realm of immortals," reminding us that it is more like the utopian Peach Blossom realm of Daoist immortals who do not have to worry about disease, old age, or death than it is like the heavenly paradise after death that Christians long for.

These are the basic beliefs of all the various denominations of Chŭngsan'gyo. The divisions between them arose primarily over disputes over the correct line of transmission of Kang Chŭngsan's teachings. The largest Chŭngsan denomination, Daesun Jinrihoe (Taesŏn chillihoe; the Truth of the Great Peregrinations of Sangjenim), traces its lineage to Cho Ch'ŏlche (1895–1958), who never met Kang Chŭngsan while he was on this earth but encountered him in a vision in 1917. In 1919, Cho founded a religious organization that came to be known as T'aegŭkto (the Way of the Grand Ultimate) to promote worship of Sangjenim and action in accordance with Sangjenim's instructions. Before Cho died, according to Daesun Jinrihoe, he passed on leadership of his organization to Pak Hangyŏng (1917–96). An internal dispute led to Pak leaving Mugŭkto and founding Daesun Jinrihoe in 1969. Daesun Jinrihoe now runs its own university (Daejin University, north of Seoul), as well as several secondary schools and one general hospital. It claims a membership of more than six million. The other major Chŭngsan'gyo denominination is Jeungsando (Chŭngsando). It traces its lineage through Kang Chŭngsan's widow but took its current form in 1974 under the leadership of An

Unsan (b. 1922) and his son An Kyŏngjŏn (b. 1954), Jeungsando is known for its best-selling book *Igŏsi Kaebyŏk ida* (This Is the Great Transformation) and for its attempts, unusual among Chŭngsan'gyo denominations, to spread its message overseas. It now has temples in ten countries, including seven in the United States. It also is the most visible Chŭngsan'gyo denomination on university campuses in South Korea. Like Daesun Jinrihoe, it claims a membership of more than six million.

Further Reading

One of the first scholarly studies of Chŭngsan'gyo, now somewhat outdated, is by Lee Kang-o, "Chungsan-gyo: Its History, Doctrines, and Ritual Practices," translated by Richard Rutt, *Transactions of the Royal Asiatic Society* 43 (1967): 28–66. Somewhat more up-to-date is Gernot Prunner, "The Birthday of God: Sacrificial Service of Chŭngsan'gyo," *Korea Journal* 16, no. 3 (March 1976): 12–26, which is recent enough to deal with Daesun Jinrihoe. A concise overview of Chungsan'gyo is Kang-Nam Oh, "The Chŭngsan Tradition in the History of Korean Religions," *Korean Studies in Canada* 3 (1995): 145–58. A critical look at the rapid rise to prominence of Taesun Jinrihoe is John Jorgensen, "Taesun Chillihoe: Factors in the Rapid Rise of a Korean New Religion" (paper presented at the 2001 conference of the Korean Studies Association of Australasia and available at http://www.arts.monash.edu.au/korean/ksaa/conference/programme.html).

For a study of the Chŭngsan'gyo view of Korean history, focusing on Jeungsando, see Boudewijin Walraven, "The Parliament of Histories: New Religions, Collective Historiography, and the Nation," *Korean Studies* 25, no. 2 (2001): 157–78. English-language Web sites are available for both Daesun Jinrihoe (http://www.daesun.or.kr/English/htm/main.htm) and Jeungsando (http://www.jeungsando.org/welcome/).

Jeungsando Rituals

Jeungsando, because of its books which are best-sellers in Korea and because of the non-Korean believers it has attracted, is one of the most visible of the many new religions in Korea centered on worship of Kang Chŭngsan. (They prefer to spell his name Jeungsan.) Jeungsando, which means the Dao of Kang Chŭngsan, differs from most of the other Chŭngsan'gyo religions in that it places Kang Chŭngsan's wife alongside him both in the sanctuaries of its temples and in heaven. The title it uses for its God, Sangjenim, is the same name all the Chŭngsan religions use for God. However, of the major Chŭngsan religions, only Jeungsando also prays to T'aemonim, "Great Mother," the title they give his wife. Jeungsando teaches that, after Sangjenim returned to heaven, his wife assumed leadership of the religious community he had established and preserved the rituals he had devised and taught to save humanity. The description of Jeungsando rituals here is taken from Han'guk Chonggyoŭiŭisik kwa yejŏl (The rituals and ceremonies of Korean religions), edited by the Ministry of Culture and Sports (Seoul: Hwasan Munhwa Publishing, 1996), pp. 470–75.

There are two basic types of rituals in Jeungsando. There are communal rituals that are performed in temples. There are also rituals performed by individual believers either at home or as they go about their daily life.

A. RITUALS PERFORMED AT SET INTERVALS

1. Rituals Performed in the Temple Sanctuary

Every Wednesday and Sunday, services are held in the sanctuary in a temple. Those services follow a prescribed format as follows: the beginning of the service is announced, incense and candles are lit, the participants bow four times while praying silently in their heart, they read a prayer aloud with reverence, they read aloud from the scriptures with reverence, they chant the mantra, they bow to the chief celebrant, and then they leave the sanctuary.

2. Rituals Performed at the Home Altar

The services performed before the home altars are essentially the same rituals as the ones performed in the temple sanctuary. First of all, there are the household rituals performed as part of a daily routine. That would include the spiritual discipline of offering a bowl of clean water in the morning and again in the afternoon. There are also rituals that are performed over a set period of time in order to seek a resolution to a specific problem through worship and spiritual discipline. Finally, there are the special rituals that are held on such specials occasions as a marriage, an opening of a new business, moving to a new home, the birth of a new family member, or a death in the family.

Before you perform a ritual at home, you should wash your face, brush your teeth, comb your hair, and make sure your clothes are on straight. Only then can you offer the bowl of clean water that signals the start of that service. If you plan to pray any special prayers during that ritual, or burn a sacrificial paper as an offering to the spirits, you should prepare the prayer book or the sacrificial paper beforehand.

You need to keep a picture of Sangjenim on the home altar, along with such ritual utensils as the bowl that you use to make an offering of clean water. The home altar is different from the altar in the temple, since when you go to the temple, that altar is already set up for the service. At home, you have to prepare the altar yourself. If you can, you should have a separate room just for your altar. However, if that is not possible, you can set aside a corner in your living room or in another room in your house for the altar. Since the altar represents the flow of air and water that sustains life, it should be placed at the northern end of that room. [In geomancy and traditional Korean science, the north is associated with water.] However, if the layout of the room makes it difficult to do that, you can place the altar so that it faces the same direction your head is in when you lie down to sleep. The most important thing is to make sure that the altar does not face the same direction your feet point to when you lie down.

On your altar you need to have a picture of Sangjenim, a picture of T'aemonim, bowls for clean water, candles, an incense burner, a box of incense sticks, candlesticks, sacrificial paper, and a pot for the burning paper. If possible, in addition to the pictures of Sangjenim and T'aemonim, you could also have on your altar pictures of the three founding gods of our nation (Hwanin, Hwanung, and Tan'gun) as well as pictures of your ancestral spirits. The rituals you perform in your home (whether they are the rituals of offering clean water, the rituals asking for help with a problem, or the rituals for special occasions) should follow the basic format of the services performed in a temple.

B. RITUALS OF PRAYER AND MAKING REQUESTS

Prayer is a way for believers in Jeungsando to have a spiritual encounter with Sangjenim. When you pray to Sangjenim or T'aemonim, the supreme objects of faith in Jeungsando, and talk to them from the depths of your heart, you will be able to hear them speaking to you as well. This is how you can engage in a conversation with Sangjenim or T'aemonim through prayer.

C. THE INITIATION RITUAL

The initiation ritual of Jeungsando is a sacred ceremony in which you take a solemn oath before Sangjenim and the many other spirits of heaven and earth that you will become a laborer for Sangjenim. To become a laborer for Sangjenim means much more than just becoming a simple worker. It means that you assume responsibility for achieving in the here and now the great task which Sangjenim, T'aemonin, the founder of Jeungsando, and his son-and-successor have assigned you.

D. THE SACRED CALENDAR OF JEUNGSANDO

There are five days set aside each calendar year for special ritual celebrations. On those days we worship the Father and Mother of heaven and earth, whom we call Sanjenim and T'aemonim, as well as the myriad spirits of heaven and earth. On those days we also show our humility and sincerity by bowing to heaven and to earth.

1. The Chŏngsam Service. This is celebrated on the third of January every year, according to the lunar calendar. This is the day we proclaim to Sangjenim, to T'aemonim, and to the myriad spirits of heaven and earth that we are beginning another year of working to realize the Dao.

2. The Service Celebrating the Birthday of T'aemonim. This is celebrated on March 26, according to the lunar calendar. It is a celebration in commemoration of the birthday of T'aemonim, who is the mother of all that lives under heaven.

3. The Service Celebrating Sangjenim's Return to Heaven. This is celebrated on June 24, by the lunar calendar. That is the date Jeungsan Sangjenim returned to his throne in heaven after completing the Great Work of Renewing Heaven and Earth through which he set the three realms of heaven, earth, and humanity back on the right path.

4. The Service Celebrating the Birthday of Sangjenim. This is celebrated on September 19, by the lunar calendar. On this day, we celebrate the historic date on which Jeungsan Sangjenim, who is the ruler of heaven and earth, descended to earth to live as a human being among human beings on the Korean peninsula. This is a holy day for thanking Sangjenim for all he has done for us.

5. The Winter Solstice Service. This service is held on December 22, by the lunar calendar. This service prepares us to say good-bye to the old year, which is coming to an end, and to get ready for the new year, which is fast approaching.

There are also various rituals that can be performed either at home or in a temple but are not performed at the same time every year since they are rituals for particular purposes. For example, services are held to strengthen resolve at the beginning and at the end of a retreat. "Relieving Resentment at Injustice" services are held to relieve the pain of injustice suffered by our ancestors and by aborted fetuses. Prayer services are held to offer prayer for help in resolving someone's personal problems. And thanksgiving services are held to offer thanks for having an earlier prayer answered. Furthermore, rituals celebrating a marriage, the opening of a new business, or the birth of a new family member, or rituals mourning a death of a family member, are usually held at home, but if you want to share your joy with many friends and neighbors or have your grief eased by the support of many friends and neighbors, you may hold such rituals in a temple. This is in accordance with the saying "If you share your grief with others, your pain will be halved. And if you share your joy with others, your joy will be doubled." This is also a good way to strengthen friendship and solidarity among believers.

E. SPIRITUAL DISCIPLINE AND TRAINING

The primary method Jeungsando uses for spiritual training is chanting incantations. By incantation, we mean mantras that contain within them the concentrated essence of heaven and earth. When you chant them over and over again, the energy they contain will enter your body. There are a number of different mantras, each with their own specific effect. The most powerful of them is the T'aeŭl mantra. Chanting that mantra properly and frequently will help you overcome all sorts of mental anguish as well as misfortune, accidents, and disease. When you chant this mantra properly and frequently, you will find that your problems will disappear. Therefore this mantra is the key to solving not only family problems but all the problems we face during the course of our life on this planet.

Chŭngsan'gyo Believers in Their Own Words

Although there are many denominations within the Chŭngsan family of religions, they all share several elements in common. First of all, they believe that Kang Chŭngsan was the incarnation of Sangjenim, the Supreme Lord in Heaven. Chŭngsan'gyo believers are not monotheists. They believe that there are many gods and spirits. However, they believe there is a hierarchy of gods and spirits, with Sangjenim at the top. Second, they believe that Sangjenim descended to earth to prepare humanity for the coming Great Transformation. They believe that the current cosmic era, one characterized by gender, class, racial, religious, and national inequality and conflict, will soon come to an end. With the guidance of Sangjenim and the Great Work of Renewing Heaven and Earth that he taught while he was on this earth, the transition to the new era will be smoother and faster than it would be otherwise. This new era, the era of the Later Heaven, will usher in paradise on earth. In this paradise, there will be no disease or poverty, and conflict will be replaced by universal cooperation.

Chŭngsan'gyo believers are also convinced that the troubles we see around us in the world today, troubles heralding the end of this particular cosmic era and the coming of the new era, are the result of thousands of years of accumulated resentment by those who have been treated unfairly and have been unable to do anything about that unfair treatment. The spirits of deceased women, aborted fetuses, and subjects of colonial rule are particularly resentful, since they have suffered particularly unfair treatment. If the transition from the current cosmic era of Prior Heaven to the coming era of Later Heaven is to proceed smoothly, it is necessary to relieve the resentment at unjust treatment that has accumulated over the course of the current cosmic era. That can be done, Chŭngsan'gyo teaches, by following the injunctions of Sangjenim to treat everyone fairly and performing the rituals Kang Chŭngsan taught.

The following first-person accounts of what Chŭngsan'gyo means to two representative believers are taken from Ch'a Oksung, Han'gugin ŭi chonggyo kyŏnghŏm: Chŭngsan'gyo, Wŏnbulgyo (The Religious Experience of Koreans: Chŭngsan'gyo and Wŏnbulgyo) (Seoul: Sŏgwangsa, 2003), pp. 58–59, 64–65.

AN INTERVIEW ON MAY 24, 1996, WITH A SIXTY-SIX-YEAR-OLD FEMALE BELIEVER IN SEOUL

My hometown is Chinju, in South Kyŏngsang province. I was the youngest of four children. My father was a Confucian scholar who read books every day. He was a very calm and gentle person. My mother was a typical demure housewife. My brother assumed responsibility for supporting our family financially. We were not poor, and we all got along quite well. I got married when I was twenty-four and had our first child, a daughter, when I was twenty-five. My husband was a section chief at an agriculture field research station. However, he died and left me alone when I was only twenty-seven. I found being a widow very difficult at first.

I now live in Puch'ŏn, near Seoul. After my husband died, my two daughters and I felt very lonely. Then my brother-in-law said to me, "Why don't you try to cultivate the Dao? I think you will find that a great help." So, in June of my 31st year, I was initiated into the Samdŏkkyo branch of Chŭngsan'gyo, of which my brother-in-law was a member. I thought joining such a religion would help me overcome my loneliness.

A year after my initiation, I started going to Mount Chiri twice each season to pray and take part in religious services, spending either a week, two weeks, or even twenty-five days each trip. After hearing a couple of sermons by the preacher there, I began to pray that I could act in accordance with Sangje's will and become a laborer working for heaven and earth. I also prayed that I could help spread salvation widely. I have never prayed for some private benefit for myself only. I never prayed for my children to turn out well, nor did I ever pray to be blessed with good luck. All I asked in my prayers was that I be given the strength to follow the will of Sangjenim and work hard to save the entire world. However, I must confess that, whenever we held a ritual to honor my departed husband, I told him about all the things that weighed heavily on my mind and about the difficulties his children were facing, and I asked him to help us as best he could.

The very first time I went on a retreat, I felt a divine spirit take over my body. My whole body shook and began moving spontaneously. When that spirit possessed me, my mind became totally clear and I felt really happy. It appeared that for a moment a bright light was shining down from heaven into my body. That's when my body began to shake and move of its own accord. This went on for twenty to thirty minutes. The first time this happened I knew I had found the true Dao. Since then I have not wavered from my belief in this practice. I have had many more experiences like that while undergoing spiritual training. Now I see the world and all that happens in it clearly, and I pray that, with the help of Sangjenim's Great Work of Renewing Heaven and Earth, everything will go according to his plan. I like what my religion says about relieving resentment that has built up because of past injustice, cultivating a feeling of gratitude for everything that has been done for us, and creating a world in which mutual aid and cooperation replace conflict. Over the course of my long life, I have learned a lot from many different teachers, but I have yet to fully comprehend these profound truths.

AN INTERVIEW IN PUCH'ŎN CITY ON MAY 24, 1996, WITH A FORTY-TWO-YEAR-OLD FEMALE JUNIOR HIGH SCHOOL TEACHER

I already knew about Chŭngsan'gyo from the time I was a child, since my mother was a believer. Chŭngsan'gyo is different from other religions. It doesn't demand belief with no doubts or questions. Nor is it like Buddhism, which tells you to become enlightened to your own inner Buddha-nature. Instead, Chŭngsan'gyo is based on scientific explanations of the cosmic order. It teaches us to prepare for the coming change from the old order of the Prior Heaven, which is now coming to an end, to the new order of the Later Heaven and the paradise it will bring.

According to Chŭngsan'gyo, we are now entering the time of Autumn Harvest in the cosmic seasonal cycle. That is why we see the flourishing of material civilization, and that is why we need to start harvesting the fruits of that civilization in preparation for the Great Transformation that lies ahead. In the new cosmic era, men and women will be equal.

In my opinion, the Chŭngsan'gyo precept of *Haewŏn sangsaeng* [relieve the grievances caused by past injustice and create a society of mutual aid and co-operation] is not much different from the love Christians talk about or the compassion Buddhists preach. For me, *haewŏn sangsaeng* defines Chŭngsan'-gyo. Chŭngsan'gyo teaches us to avoid mistreating others so that they won't see us as their enemy. It teaches us to make sure that we don't give others any reason to harbor resentment at unfair treatment.

Chŭngsan'gyo warned us that, during the transition from the Prior Heaven to the Later Heaven, there will be growing disorder both on heaven and on earth. If you look around you, you can see that his prophecy is coming true.

Over the course of the era of Prior Heaven, many sages handed down rules governing our daily lives. In the Later Heaven, those rules will be different. We must prepare for that change by helping each other and cooperating with each other.

Among the more important pieces of advice Chŭngsan gave was that we need to clear our minds of greed and personal ambition and instead concentrate on cultivating a pure heart. Since I believe in Chŭngsan Sangjenim, I don't worry too much or let things upset me. Three different times my husband's business failed and we had to sell our home. However, whenever I began to get worried about that, I would make sure that I invoked the name of Sangjenim and chanted the T'aeŭl incantation before I headed off to school to teach my classes. That put my mind at ease. Since I trusted that Sangjenim would help us, I was relatively calm and did not let our financial troubles wear me down. Since I believed my husband suffered such business failures because either our ancestors, or myself in a previous life, had treated others unfairly, and that the harm we had done to others had rebounded to us, I resolved to try my best to make sure that I did not mistreat others in the future. This is precisely what Chŭngsan'gyo is talking about when it tells us to avoid mistreating others, causing them to see us as their enemy, and to make sure we don't give others any reason to harbor resentment at unfair treatment at our hands.

I believe that, although the broad parameters of the path our life will follow are predetermined, within that limitation we can change our lives for the better through hard work and determination. That is why I don't simply passively accept the teachings of Chŭngsan'gyo. However, I do believe that if we sincerely ask our ancestors and those gods who are close to us to help us, they will do so. I believe that Chŭngsan Sangjenim is far superior to all other gods, but I don't call him Hanŭnim, since that is the term for the Lord of Heaven who is the one and only God.

30

Rites of Passage in

the Unification Church

Don Baker

Of all of Korean's new religions, the Unification Church of the Reverend Sun Myung Moon (Mun Sŏnmyŏng) is the best known outside of Korea. Though the Holy Spirit Association for the Unification of World Christianity (the original full name of the Unification Church) was founded in Korea in 1954, Moon moved to the United States in 1971, and for most of the time since he has led that religion from his headquarters outside of New York City. There are no reliable figures on the total worldwide membership of the Unification Church, or even accurate comparative national membership figures. However, the Unification Church claims it has followers in well over one hundred different countries. Besides Korea, sizable Unification Church communities can be found in Japan, the United States, the United Kingdom, and Brazil.

Despite its high visibility outside of Korea, the Unification Church remains essentially a Korean religion in both its theology and its rituals. Though it is one of the few Korean new religions that has its roots in Christianity rather than in Confucianism, Buddhism, or folk religion, there are nevertheless many characteristically Korean elements in Unificationist thought and practice.

For example, the teachings of the Unification Church reflect the influence national and ethnic pride have had on Korean religions in modern times. The Unification Church proclaims that Korea, Japan, and the United States have been chosen by God to lead humanity into a new era by serving as the cornerstones on which a United Nation of Cosmic Peace will be established to usher in the kingdom of God on this earth. However, Korea, not Japan or the United States, will play the leading role, since the man chosen by God to prepare for this unification of humanity under God's authority is a Korean—none other than Sun Myung Moon himself—who was crowned in 2003 as the King of All Blessed Families.

Since God has anointed a Korean to carry out this sacred task, the Unification Church teaches that the language of the kingdom of God is Korean and that therefore all those planning on living in the kingdom of God should begin learning

Korean now, if they do not already speak it. As Moon himself explained in a speech delivered November 21, 1982, "When you go to the Kingdom of Heaven, you will discover that its language is Korean. English is spoken only in the colonies of the Kingdom of Heaven!" In another manifestation of the link between Unificationist thought and Korean national pride, an advertisement placed in the Unification Church–owned *Washington Times* on December 30, 2000, stated that, because of the esteem with which Moon is viewed both in heaven and on earth, Korea has become "the motherland of faith of all peoples of the world. . . . That means that Korean culture will shine to all the world, and Korea will become the holy land, and Korean shall become the world's language."

One more sign of the Korean origins of the Unification Church is that Unificationist doctrines and rituals emphasize the family more than they do the individual. Though both today and in centuries past many Koreans have pursued individual enlightenment, immortality, or salvation, religious rituals were usually performed for the sake of a family or community. Whether it was a housewife asking her household gods to protect the health of all the members of her family, a village ritual asking the village tutelary deity to protect the villagers from disease and give them bumper crops, or a memorial service at the Royal Ancestor Shrine asking those ancestors to protect their descendants for generations to come, traditional Korean religion was generally more concerned with the health and wealth of a particular group or community rather than with whether or not a specific individual went to heaven after he or she died. That changed somewhat in the twentieth century, with the rise of Christianity to prominence on the peninsula, but the legacy of a family-centered religiosity survives. The influence of that legacy is particularly obvious in Unificationist thought and practice.

In 1994 the Unification Church changed its full name from the Holy Spirit Association for the Unification of World Christianity to the Family Federation for World Peace and Unification. It did so for a couple of reasons. First of all, it wanted to make clear that its goal was the unification of all humanity and all of the religions of humanity, not just Christians and their various Christian denominations. However, the more important reason for that name change is the Unificationist belief that only families can enter the kingdom of heaven. Single individuals will be kept outside the gates. In fact, a defining teaching of Unificationism is that Jesus himself was not able to enter the kingdom of heaven until Moon opened those gates for him.

The Unification Church teaches that Jesus failed to complete the mission God assigned him. That mission required that he marry and raise a family. Only by marrying a woman as pure as he was and therefore bringing into this world children free of the lineage of Satan (which human beings had belonged to ever since Eve sinned with Satan) would Jesus have been able to establish the pure lineage necessary for the establishment of the kingdom of heaven. Unfortunately, he was crucified before he could settle down with the right woman. Therefore, both he and all other human beings (in Unificationist thought, Jesus is not God but a human being) had to wait another two thousand years, until God anointed another messiah. That messiah is Sun Myung Moon. However, Moon, like Jesus, could not save humanity all by himself. He had to find a pure bride. The Unification Church teaches that he found such a bride in Hak Ja Han (Han Hakcha). They married in 1960 and soon began producing children free of the original sin that had kept humanity in Satan's dominion for six thousand years. Rev. and Mrs. Moon thus became the True Parents who have ushered in a new age for humanity, the age of the completed testament in which the state God intended for humanity before Satan intervened and seduced Eve will be restored. The messiah is therefore a family, not an individual.

Mainstream Christians were shocked in 1992 when Moon declared that he was the Messiah the world had been waiting for. However, part of that shock came from a misunderstanding of what Moon meant when he said he was a messiah. He was not declaring that he was God (that is why it is incorrect to call Unificationists "Moonies," as if they worship Moon in the way mainstream Christians worship Christ). Nor was he declaring that he was the one and only messiah, or even that he and his wife were the one and only messiah the world would ever see. In fact, Unificationists believe that Jesus, too, was a messiah, in that he brought spiritual salvation to humanity. Moon simply completed the mission Jesus began by bringing physical salvation to humanity with the restoration of a pure lineage. Moreover, Moon promised that he has made it possible for others to become messiahs as well.

The Unification Church teaches that the appearance of the True Parents on this earth has made possible a ritual that allows others to become messiahs as well, so that they too will be able to beget a pure lineage qualified to enter the kingdom of heaven. That ritual is called the Blessing but is best known to outsiders as the mass marriages the Moons are known for presiding over. Once a pure lineage had been restored, that purity can be passed on to the children of other couples if those couples are properly blessed by the True Parents. According to Unificationist thought, whether or not a couple follows the Unification Church, if their marriage is blessed, they will be able to enter the kingdom of heaven. If their marriage is not blessed, or, even worse, if someone never marries, they may be able to go to paradise but will not be able to move up to the next level, the kingdom of heaven. Even Jesus had to be married by Rev. Moon in a spirit wedding before he could take his rightful place in the kingdom of heaven. The same is true of the Moons' second son, Heung Jin, who died in a car accident at the age of seventeen, before he was able to marry. Two months after his death, he was married to the daughter of one of Moon's top aides so that there would be no questions about his ascension to the kingdom of heaven.

Because of the belief that salvation is for families, not for individuals, the most important rituals in the Unification Church are family rituals, some of which are translated in this chapter. These rituals, with the exception of the Blessing, are for couples who have already been blessed. That is why there is no ritual of baptism. The children of Blessed couples are born without original sin, so they do not need the cleansing power of baptism. However, to protect their purity, when they are born they need to be shielded from the power of Satan by sacred "birth candles" as well as by the prayers of Unificationists who know their parents. In addition, eight days after they are born, their parents should dedicate them to God as an affirmation that they are all now a True Family.

In addition to birth and marriage, another important turning point in the life of a family is the departure of a member of that family through death. The Unification Church therefore has a funeral ritual, just as it has a birth ritual. However, Unificationists see death as more a joyful than a sad experience, since the dead have ascended to a higher plane. That joyful attitude is expressed in the clothing worn by the mourners. Women are told to wear white or light-colored clothing to the "ascension ceremony" and to wear a red corsage as well. Men should wear a dark blue suit, but with it they should wear a white shirt and a white tie. They should also pin a white carnation or rose to their jacket.

The most important ritual for Unificationists is the Blessing, since it is the Blessing that forms the family that makes salvation possible. Moreover, it is the Blessing, in the form of mass weddings, that is the Unificationist ritual best known to outsiders, and is also the most misunderstood. Therefore, in addition to translating a statement on the meaning of the Blessing, I also include a more detailed account of the various steps of the Blessing ritual reprinted from a Unificationist Web site: http://www.tparents.org/Library/Unification/Topics/U-Stuff/ET-Bless.htm (accessed June 14, 2004).

In the description of the various rituals here, the reader will notice several references to candles and salt. The Unification Church teaches that burning sacred candles, such as "birth candles," weakens the power of Satan at the same time that it renders the spiritual atmosphere in the place they are burning more holy and pure. Holy Salt reinforces the sanctifying power of sacred candles. Both are utilized to protect a vulnerable newborn from Satan's grasp, for example. Holy Salt is also used to sanctify the casket at a Unification Church ritual for the dead, and to sanctify the place where newlyweds consummate their marriage. Sacred candles similar to birth candles are also used at farewell services for the dead and can be used during the ceremonies signaling the beginning of a conjugal relationship.

This account of Unification Church rites of passage is translated from *Han'guk Chonggyo ŭi ŭisik kwa yejŏl* (The Rituals and Ceremonies of Korean Religions), edited by the Ministry of Culture and Sports (Seoul: Hwasan Munhwa Publishing, 1996), pp. 646–52.

Further Reading

George D. Chryssides, *The Advent of Sun Myung Moon: The Origins, Beliefs, and Practices of the Unification Church* (New York: St. Martin's Press, 1991), provides an outsider's nonjudgmental account of the Unification Church. Nansook Hong, *In the Shadow of the Moons: My Life in the Reverend Sun Myung Moon's Family* (Boston: Little, Brown, 1998), is a more critical account by Moon's former daughter-in-law, who has left the church.

The Unification Church is a modern religion that uses the Internet to its full advantage. One Web site, http://www. unification.net, includes a book-length guide in English to Unification Church rituals, *The Tradition: Book One,* by Hwan Kwak Chung, available in its entirety for downloading. Other useful sites are http://www.unification.org and http://www.ffwpui.org.

Rites of Passage in the Unification Church

BIRTH

One of the most important things on this earth is the bond of love formed by husband and wife. Moreover, one of the main reasons God created human beings is that he wants them to find true love as a family. In this unrighteous world, there is a lot of false "love" and sexual misbehavior, but if a husband and wife build a truly harmonious household centered on God, then God will be by their side to help them maintain a healthy and happy family life. This is a big difference between the love between a husband and a wife, on the one hand, and sexual ties between male and female animals on the other, since the only purpose of sexual intercourse between animals is procreation. The love a husband and wife feel for each other is an emotion to be treasured which will grow even stronger and deeper as they build their lives together. The closer a husband and wife grow to one another, the more God wants to be part of their lives. When we understand this, we can also understand that no new life comes into this world without the direct involvement of God.

In the Unification Church, the family that is awaiting the imminent arrival of their first child receives from either their pastor or from older Blessed couples from their congregation a "birth candle" and a box or book of "birth matches," both items needed for the ritual accompanying birth. It is essential that a "seed birth candle" is passed on to the parents-to-be before their first baby arrives. In addition, if possible, a space for group prayer during birth should be sanctified with holy salt. The seed birth candle should be placed in the center of a candelabra which rests on an altar. Another six candles should then be placed on that candelabra around that "seed birth candle." Usually those candles are lit five minutes before the baby enters the world and stay lit for five minutes afterward.

Close family friends of the expectant couple should gather together to pray for a good delivery while the mother is giving birth. Traditionally, church members gather together once they hear that a midwife has entered the delivery room and pray for the midwife to do a good job. There is no particular form those prayers should take or particular format that prayer meeting should follow.

DEDICATING A NEWBORN CHILD TO GOD (THE EIGHTH-DAY CEREMONY)

The dedication ceremony is a way for parents to thank God for giving them children. It is a ritual in which parents accept responsibility for the children God has given them and pledge to raise them properly. It is important for the parents to keep in mind during this ceremony that, though they have brought those children into this world, those children are actually the children of God, whom God has entrusted to their care. This ritual will help them cultivate a feeling of gratitude to God for giving them the responsibility for looking after his children. Since God has chosen the family as his medium for promoting ideal love, after their children are born parents should dedicate themselves to raising those children as proper sons and daughters of God. The inner spirit with which they perform this ritual is more important than external adherence to the proper procedures. The primary focus of this ritual is gratitude toward God.

Unificationist parents should hold this ceremony at seven in the morning eight days after the child is born. The actual day the child is born should be counted as the first of those eight days, no matter whether the child was born in the morning or in the evening. The parents cannot ask anyone else to conduct this ceremony for them. They have to conduct this ceremony totally by themselves. (If there is some unavoidable reason why one of the parents cannot be there, the other parent must assume sole responsibility for conducting the ritual.) Before the ritual can begin, they have to bathe themselves and their baby, and then don the proper ritual clothing (white Holy Robes).

To begin the ceremony, either the father or the mother should light a candle that has been placed on the altar in preparation for this moment. Then the mother and father should pick up their child together, with both of them using both their arms. Still holding their child, they should both pray silently, meditating on the fact that their child belongs to God. Next, they should both kneel while lifting their child slightly as a sign that they are dedicating that child to God. After that, they should lay the baby on the floor in front of the altar, with the baby's head pointed north. This ceremony then ends with both the mother and the father showing their respect for God by bowing, followed by the father offering a prayer of dedication as the representative of both parents.

THE BLESSING

As one of the most important rites of passage for the Unification Church family, the Blessing encompasses the engagement benediction, the Holy Wine Ceremony, and the actual wedding ceremony itself. The Blessing is the ritual through which human beings, who have fallen under the sway of Satan, are restored to their proper place as sons and daughters of God. In other words, it is the ritual that restores the family of God. The Blessing plays the same role in the Unification Church that baptism and marriage play together in Protestant

Christianity. Through this ritual, God uses individuals and families to bring his creation to completion.

The Unification Church's Blessing ritual is much more than just a ceremony to join a man and a woman in holy matrimony. It also is a manifestation through religious ritual of creation and salvation. The Unification Church is well known for marrying large numbers of couples at the same time. That's because the Blessing is not some private ritual off-limits to the outside world but is a public display for the whole world to see of the love God has for each and every human being.

The term "Blessing" originally referred to Adam and Eve, the ancestors of all humanity, escaping the clutches of Satan and forming an ideal family through God's love. The eternal love of God would in that case have been manifest through the marriage of Adam and Eve but that did not happen since they sinned and fell from grace. According to the Bible, Jesus, who is the savior of humanity, is also known as the second Adam, since he was given the mission of serving as the progenitor of a reborn humanity. That is why Christianity today is known as a religion that preaches being born again through Jesus and the Holy Spirit.

The Unification Church interprets the Christian rite of Holy Communion as a symbolic way for Christian believers to establish a lineage relationship, a bloodline relationship, with Jesus, since it provides the conditions through which Christians can make the flesh and blood of Jesus their own. This means that the ritual of Holy Communion is a ritual for Christians to gain rebirth and salvation. The equivalent ritual in the Unification Church is the Holy Wine Ceremony. The Holy Wine Ceremony is nothing other than a ritual for gaining rebirth and salvation through religious symbols.

The Blessing is also a ritual similar to a ritual the people of Israel performed as a chosen people. In their fallen state, human beings have both a link to God, in their hearts and in their basic human nature, and a link to Satan, since they are of Satan's lineage. As fallen creatures, human beings thus fall between God and Satan and they can use their in-between state to break with Satan completely. The Blessing is a way to make that break, just as circumcision was used by the people of Israel in the Old Testament age to show that they were a chosen people who had separated themselves from the realm of Satan. In the New Testament age, that tradition survived in the ritual of baptism practiced by Christians, the spiritual Israel. The Unification Church invests Christian baptism with great significance. That is why the Unification Church has transformed the formal and obligatory way baptism has been carried out and says that everyone should have a baptism of the Holy Spirit, in other words, a baptism of fire (The Gospel according to John, 1:33).

The Unification Church Blessing ritual takes us out of the clutches of Satan. It starts us down the road to becoming a holy family that looks only to God, and to being part of the people of God centered on such a family. The Blessing is thus like a stone laid as a foundation for the project of forming a people of God. We believe that the true meaning of rebirth through Jesus and the Holy Spirit is concretely realized in the Blessing of the Unification Church. The actual significance of the Blessing is that it makes us the sons and daughters of God, as well as members of the family of God, through the link we have with God in our hearts. Moreover, Blessed families lead to the kingdom of God on this earth.

[This description tells us the rationale behind the Blessing, but it doesn't tell us what the Blessing itself is. Here are the actual steps in becoming a Blessed Family:]

Explanation of the Blessing

The Blessing has five steps, each with its own purpose and significance. It is important to understand and appreciate the value of each.

Repentance and Forgiveness: The Chastening Ceremony

The Chastening Ceremony creates the foundation to cleanse the historical sin between men and women. In man-woman relations, to one degree or another, we have all erred. So have our ancestors. In this ceremony, the husband and wife chasten each other three times from a position representing God. This simple act opens the door to God's forgiveness and grace. At the same time it is an occasion for the couple's mutual chastening and forgiveness. This allows us to begin a new life of pure love.

[The Chastening Ceremony involves a ceremonial wielding of a stick by the bride to hit the groom on his hips, and by the groom to hit the bride on her hips. Each hits the other three times. However, the "beatings" should cause no injury or even pain. Instead, this ceremony is a way for the couple to force Satan from their partner's body through religious ritual.]

Grace for the Blessing: The Holy Wine Ceremony

God created man and woman to become true husbands and wives and to create ideal families through unselfish love. As we know from the biblical record, however, something went wrong in the beginning. The first parents created a dysfunctional, fallen family, in which disunity between parents and children, and intense sibling rivalry, led to murder. Such a family was clearly separated from God's love, life, and lineage. We all are descended from the false parents of that family.

In the Holy Wine Ceremony, we make the spiritual transition from the lineage of false parents to that of the True Parents. Through this ceremony, we each are restored conditionally to the position of "original man" and "original woman," like Adam and Eve before the Fall.

In the ceremony, the officiator gives the Holy Wine to the woman. She bows to him and drinks half of it. She then gives the Holy Wine to her husband, who bows to her and drinks the remainder. He bows and gives the empty cup to his wife, who bows and returns it to the officiator.

[The Unification Church teaches, first of all, that drinking the Holy Wine in this ritual replaces the blood of Satan that flows through our spiritual body with the blood of God. It thus ends our membership in the lineage of Satan and restores us to the lineage of God. The woman drinks the wine first in this ceremony since Eve was the first to sin and therefore the woman should be the first to be restored.]

The Spiritual Blessing of Marriage: The Holy Blessing Ceremony

The Holy Blessing is a simple and beautiful event. For betrothed couples, it is their wedding ceremony. For previously married couples it is a ceremony of rededication of their marriage and family to God.

The ceremony includes several traditional elements. One is a sprinkling of Holy Water. This represents the rebirth or renewal of the husband and wife together as a Blessed couple. Then there is a recitation of vows. Here the couples pledge to consummate the ideal of the creation of God as an eternal husband and wife, to rear their children to live up to the will of God, and to love the people of the world as God does. Finally, the bride and groom exchange rings and the officiator offers a prayer and proclaims the participants husband and wife standing within the realm of God's original and eternal Blessing.

Thanksgiving: The Separation Period

The forty days following the Blessing is a historical time period for each couple. Just as Jesus began his mission on the foundation of forty days of fasting, couples who have received the Blessing are enjoined to offer a period of sexual abstinence for a period of forty days after the Blessing.

Many couples have discovered from experience that the Separation Period can be a significant step in the process of transformation and renewal. Sexual abstinence is an honored religious tradition. On the spiritual level, problems are often worked out during the Separation Period. Moreover, the act of love itself takes on a new dimension of sacredness after offering the period of separation.

Consummation of the Blessing: The Three-Day Ceremony

After the separation period, the couple come together to carry out the Three-Day Ceremony. This is the completion of sanctification, in which the couple is restored to the position of true husband and wife. Over a three-day period, the wife gives rebirth to her husband from the position of mother and then receives him in the position of wife. Then in the position of father, the husband gives rebirth to his wife and receives her in the position of husband. Through this process, God breathes into the couple a new conjugal life.

[This is the first time the newly married couple are allowed the physical intimacy that characterizes a loving relationship between a husband and a wife. However, it is treated more like a religious ritual than a carnal experience. First, it should take place in a sacred site, such as a Unification Church building or some other place with a good spiritual atmosphere. Second, the husband and wife should use Sacred Salt to sanctify the

room in which this ceremony takes place, as well as the bedding in that room. Third,
they should wash themselves with a Holy Handkerchief and then put on Holy Gowns.
Finally, there are strict rules governing how they express their love for each other over
the course of these three days. It must take place over three consecutive nights, and no
close physical contact can take place outside of this ritual context during those three
days. Finally, the first two nights the wife must take the initiative and lie on top of the
husband. By doing so, she reenacts the behavior of Eve which led to the fall of humanity.
However, the third night, the man must take the initiative and lie on top of his wife. By
doing so, he signals that the relationship between husband and wife has been restored to
the way God intended it to be.]

THE ASCENSION CEREMONY

The ascension ceremony is a ritual announcing that a spiritual being has departed for a new life. Death is usually seen as the end of something but in the
Unification Church death means being reborn in another world. That is why we
call death "ascension" and call the service for someone recently departed from
this life an "ascension ceremony." Accordingly, we do not find the prospect of
death discouraging. Instead, we face death with a joyful heart, grateful that, with
this victory of the spirit, we will be born again.

There are three stages to the ascension ceremony: the ceremony celebrating
a return to joy (*kwihwansik*), the ceremony celebrating the ascension of the
spirit to harmony (*sŭnghwasik*), and the ceremony to celebrate the return to
the palace that is home (*wŏnjŏnsik*). These three stages are a reflection of traditional Korean mourning ritual in that they follow each other in the same order
as do the stages of a traditional funeral (preparing the body for burial, escort-
ing the body to the burial ground, and lowering the body into the ground).
That is because the Unification Church believes that Korea traditional ritual
has provided a model of how we should show respect for our ancestors and for
Heaven.

The *kwihwansik* is a visitation that is held after the body has been laid in the
coffin but before the body has been moved to the burial ground. It is held in
the room which holds the coffin in which the body had been laid. The *kwihwansik* provides an occasion for direct descendants, close friends in the
church, and relatives in general to stay good-bye and can be held either in the
room set aside for such a purpose at a hospital or in the home in which the
death occurred. Usually the coffin is open during this part of the ascension
ceremony. The ceremony has silent prayer, the burning of incense, communal
prayer, and the offering of flowers, in that order.

The *sŭnghwasik*, like ordinary burial services, is held three, five, or seven
days after death. It provides one last opportunity for the living to say good-bye
to the soul that is ascending to heaven. The leader of the church the deceased
attended should make the arrangements for this stage of the ascension ritual,
and a Blessed elder should lead the service. This stage consists of the singing

of hymns, followed by communal prayer, testimonies to the life the ascending individual led, the lighting of incense, a sermon, and then a final hymn, in that order.

The *wŏnjŏnsik* corresponds to the ordinary ritual of lowering the coffin into the grave. *Wŏnjŏn* means "whence you came." Pallbearers carry the coffin to the burial ground and lower it to the ground in front of the grave. The portrait of the ascending individual should be placed in front of the coffin. (It is all right at this time to bring some simple food offerings to the grave site and make a simple memorial offering.) This stage of the ritual begins with the singing of hymns, a representative prayer, a sermon, a closing prayer, the lowering of the coffin into the ground, and the tossing of dirt onto the coffin. Three days after the burial, direct descendants of the ascended individual, or close friends and other family members, should visit the grave site to offer a final memorial service in the form of a resurrection service.

—31—

Internal Alchemy in the Dahn World School

Don Baker

There has been an explosion of interest in internal alchemy recently in contemporary Korean religion. Much of this interest has been catalyzed by the growth in practice of Taejonggyo breathing techniques. The breathing techniques discussed in Taejonggyo scriptures focus on the "sea of energy," which is also often referred to as the cinnabar field or the elixir field, known in Korean as the *tanjŏn*. Internal alchemy is an English term used to refer to similar breathing techniques and the accompanying physical exercises intended to enhance the *ki* (life-giving energy) in the *tanjŏn* and circulate it smoothly through the rest of the body. As shown in the guidelines for Taejonggyo self-cultivation translated in a previous chapter, meditation to calm the mind is an essential component of such *ki*-enhancing practices.

We have already seen in the chapter on Taejonggyo that one school of internal alchemy, Kich'ŏnmun, is directly associated with Taejonggyo. Moreover, the modern Korean revival of interest in the ancient practice of internal alchemy began in the 1970s, when the head of Taejonggyo was Kwŏn T'aehun, who was so well known for his internal alchemy practices that the best-selling novel *Tan* was written about him and the unusual abilities his enhanced *ki* gave him. Other important Korean internal alchemy schools, though they deny a direct connection to Taejonggyo, echo the Kich'ŏnmun claim that their particular style of meditation, breathing practices, and physical exercises are revivals of techniques originally taught by Tan'gun more than four thousand years ago. The best known of those internal alchemy schools now calls itself Dahn World, though it began in the mid-1980s as Tanhak sŏnwŏn (Institute for the Pursuit of Immortality through Cinnabar-Field Breathing).

Dahn World (Dahn is their spelling of the *tan* in *tanjŏn*) originally appeared to many outsider observers to be an offshoot of Taejonggyo. Not only did Dahn World claim that its techniques were the same practices that Tan'gun taught when he ruled over the first Korean kingdom; it also heralded the three Tan'gun-era sacred texts of Taejonggyo as authentic scripture. In the 1990s, practitioners at

Institutes for the Pursuit of Immortality through Cinnabar-field Breathing were even taught to memorize the *Classic of the Seal of Heaven* (Ch'ŏnbugyŏng) and to perform a *Classic of the Seal of Heaven* dance, in which each one of the eighty-one syllables of that text was associated with a particular dance step.

Moreover, Dahn World proclaims that it is guided by the *hongik in'gan ihwasegye* philosophy associated with Tan'gun. In recent years, however, as it has reached beyond Korea and established centers overseas (its international headquarters is now located in Sedona, Arizona), it has downplayed its connections with Taejong-gyo (though it has erected a large outdoor statue of Tan'gun near that Sedona headquarters). It also explicitly denies that it is a religion, though it proclaims that its leader, Ilchi Seung Heun Lee, is one of the early twenty-first century's foremost spiritual leaders. The spiritual character of Dahn World is obvious in the Declaration of Humanity it began promoting in the first years of the twenty-first century. Dahn World, through its affiliated World Earth Human Alliance for Peace, is asking people all over the world, whether or not they are practitioners of Dahnhak (its new spelling for the standard transliteration *tanhak*), to sign this declaration.

Further Reading

There are as yet no academic studies of Dahn World or Tanhak in English. However, since Dahn World is active outside of Korea and has practice centers all over the world, it publishes much material in English. Lee Seung-heun, *Dahn Meditation* (Seoul: Dahn Publishing, 1997), provides a general introduction to Dahn World teachings and practices. Ilchi Lee, *Brain Respiration: Making Your Brain Creative, Peaceful, and Productive* (Las Vegas, Nev.: Healing Society, 2002), explains the latest Dahn World approach to internal alchemy. Seung Heun Lee, *Healing Society: A Prescription for Global Enlightenment* (Charlottesville, Va.: Hampton Roads Publishing, 2000), provides a glimpse of Dahn World's soteriological vision. Ilchi Lee, *Mago's Dream: Communing with the Earth's Soul* (Las Vegas, Nev.: Healing Society, 2002), suggests the direction Dahn World is now moving.

TEXTS OF THE DAHN WORLD SCHOOL OF INTERNAL ALCHEMY

DAHN WORLD'S DECLARATION OF HUMANITY

1. I declare that I am a Spiritual Being, an essential and eternal part of the Soul of Humanity, one and indivisible.
2. I declare that I am a Human Being whose rights and security ultimately depend on assuring the human rights of all people of Earth.
3. I declare that I am a Child of the Earth, with the will and awareness to work for goals that benefit the entire community of life on Earth.

4. I declare that I am a Healer, with the power and purpose to heal the many forms of divisions and conflicts that exist on Earth.

5. I declare that I am a Protector, with the knowledge and the responsibility to help the Earth recover her natural harmony and beauty.

6. I declare that I am an Activist, with the commitment and the ability to make a positive difference in my society.

This text of Dahn World's Declaration of Humanity is taken from one of Dahn World's many Web sites: http://www.healingsociety.org/activities/declaration.html.
This declaration was first disseminated to the public in June 2001 at a Humanity Conference in Seoul organized by Ilchi Lee's New Millennium Peace Foundation and attended by, among others, the former U.S. vice president Al Gore and the New Age writer Neale Donald Walsch, the author of Conversations with God.
    At that conference, Ilchi Lee declared:

Only humans can revive the environment and establish peace on Earth. Therefore we must set a new identity for ourselves as "Earth Humans" and share this with all humans in the world. "Earth Human" is another word for Hong-Ik-Ingan [*hongik in'gan*], a traditional Korean term for someone who lives for the betterment of all. "Earth Humans" are those who live out the philosophy of love for humanity and love for the Earth. "Earth Humans" are our hope for the future. The key to overcoming the limit of materialistic civilization is the philosophy of harmony that integrates heaven, earth, and human into one. This is the essence of the Hong-Ik-Ingan philosophy. The Declaration of Humanity is the flower of the Humanity Conference. (http://www.healingsociety.org/activities/summaraise.html#ilchi).

Though Lee does not mention Tan'gun here, he clearly proclaims the need for the modern world to adopt a philosophy associated with Tan'gun, and with Taejonggyo. He also makes references to the unity of heaven, earth, and man, a unity proclaimed by many of the religions in Korea, both old and new.
    In his many publications, Lee insists that Dahn World is a spiritual-cultural movement rather than a religion. However, his constant references to the need for "enlightenment"— and his claim that, if enough people practice the internal alchemy techniques his Dahn World centers teach, there will be an Enlightenment Revolution that will create a paradise on earth—are reminiscent of language heard in churches and temples that do not shy away from the "religion" label. The following passage is from Lee's best-known English-language publication, Healing Society (Charlottesville, Va.: Hampton Roads, Publishing, 2000).

To make enlightenment an everyday and worldwide reality, we need three separate yet related phases: the enlightenment of the individual, the enlightenment of the group, and the enlightenment of all of humanity

The first will be accomplished with Brain Respiration, through which the individual will learn how to get in touch with the Creator Within and access the highest Truth, riding on a stream of his or her own energy into a higher awareness. The second will be accomplished through a culture of New Human Society, in which enlightened individuals join together in harmony to help others reach the Creator Within and share their enlightenment with as many as possible. "New Human" is just another world for "Hong-ik Ingan," the traditional Korean term for someone who lives for the betterment of all. The third will be accomplished via a worldwide spiritual-cultural movement that sweeps the earth in a blaze of harmony and cooperation, led by those New Humans who have made enlightenment a natural and obvious part of our society (*Healing Society*, p. xxi).

BRAIN RESPIRATION

As he has grown farther away from his Taejonggyo roots, Ilchi Lee has changed some of the traditional terminology for the internal alchemy techniques his Dahn World centers teach. Instead of "cinnabar-field breathing," the term that was used in his earlier Institutes for the Pursuit of Immortality through Cinnabar-Field Breathing, he now talks of "brain respiration," which he defines as "a method that seeks to elevate a person's spiritual awareness by teaching him or her how to control the type of information that remains in the brain" (Healing Society, p. 48). *He adds the following explanation.*

Brain Respiration is a revolutionary relaxation and guided meditation technique that will allow you to feel the *ki* energy flowing throughout your body, and eventually tap into the most powerful reservoir of energy in your physical body, your brain. You will use your brain to raise your awareness to the point at which you can consciously communicate with the Cosmic Mind. You will use your brain for the fulfillment of your spiritual needs (*Healing Society*, p. 27).

MAGO, THE MOTHER GODDESS

Though in his Healing Society book, Ilchi Lee does not use such terms as "sea of energy" or "heavenly palace," the roots of his Dahnhak school in Taejonggyo internal alchemy and religious orientation are obvious. Less traditional is the shift he has made in recent years away from Tan'gun, going even farther back in ancient Korean history to an age of Mago, the Mother Goddess of the Korean people.

Until recently, the name Mago was found only in various folktales about female mountain goddesses in Korea. (See Kang Chinok, "Mago halmi sŏrhwa-e nat'anan yŏsŏngsin kwannyŏm" [The concept of the goddess as seen in the folk tales about Grandmother Mago], Han'guk minsokhak, no. 25 (1992), pp. 3–47.) However, near the end of the twentieth century, a text was "recovered" that was declared to be the ancient history of an era thousands of years before Tan'gun ruled. That text, the Pudoji (The Chronicle of the Capital of the Seal of Heaven), tells the story of a goddess named Mago who ruled over a paradise in which the first human beings lived. Ilchi Lee's publishing house published that text. He has also begun promoting the Mago story in his recent publications, such as Healing Society *(pp. 71–73) and, more recently,* Mago's Dream: Communing with the Earth's Soul *(Las Vegas, Nev.: Healing Society, 2002). In addition, he has named the garden at the Sedona Ilchi Meditation Center the Mago Garden.*

This excerpt from the opening chapters of the Pudoji *is translated from Kim Ŭnsu,* Pudoji *(The Chronicle of the Heavenly Seal Capital), Korean translation by Pak Chesang (Seoul: Han Munhwa Wŏn, 2002), pp. 17–37. The* Pudoji *is claimed to have been composed during the fifth century and then preserved as a family secret by the Pak family for generations. The original, it is said, was lost during the chaos that swept across the Korean peninsula during the twentieth century, but the text itself was recovered when a member of the Pak family wrote it down from memory in 1952.*

Mago's castle-town was situated in the highest spot of any walled town on the face of the earth. Based on respect for the Seal of Heaven, it carried on the traditions of the era of Prior Heaven. Within that walled town, there lived four kinds of celestial beings who played heavenly music on pipes. They were, in order of seniority, the Yellow Sky people, the White Nest people, the Blue Sky people, and the Black Nest people. The mother of the first Yellow Sky couple and the first Blue Sky couple is called the Sky Maiden. The mother of the first White Nest couple and the first Black Nest couple is called the Nest Maiden. Both the Sky Maiden and the Nest Maiden are the daughters of Mago. Mago was born in our time, after the era of the Prior Heaven. She had a pure character that was undisturbed by such emotions as joy or anger. The era of Prior Heaven was an era of male domination but in the era of the Latter Heaven, women will come into their own. Mago gave birth to the Sky Maiden and the Nest Maiden without the help of any male partner. Those two maidens inherited the same pure disposition their mother had and each gave birth to two celestial male beings and two celestial female beings, bringing a total of four celestial men and four celestial women into this world. . . .

Mago ordered those four celestial males and four celestial females to remove a rib so that they could give birth. Those four celestial males then married those four celestial females and each couple gave birth to three sons and three daughters, who were the first human beings and the ancestors of the entire human race. Over several generations of intermarriage, the number of human beings living in Mago's castle rose to 3,000. . . .

One day a member of the White Nest lineage joined a group going to the spring within the castle, from which gushed nourishing milk from the earth, on which they all depended. However, so many people had gathered there that he could not get some of that milk. This happened five times in a row. Finally, he went back home and climbed into the nest that was the family home. There he became so hungry that he grew faint and could hardly stand up. He even heard ringing in his ears. He then reached out and grabbed for something, anything, that he could thrust into his mouth. What he found was a delicious grape growing on a vine on the outer wall of his nest. He couldn't resist that delicious taste and began grabbing grapes right and left and stuffing them into his mouth. He then rushed out of the nest and cried out with joy, "I'm saved! This grape has given me more energy than I ever got from that nourishing milk from the earth." Crowds gathered around him to ask him what he was shouting about. He told them about the grapes and urged them to try them as well. They did so and found out that those grapes were as delicious as he said they were. They all began eating lots of grapes.

Members of the White Nest family grew alarmed and began putting restrictions on how many grapes any one individual could consume. This was the first time human beings needed such rules. It was also the first time human beings began relying on fruits and vegetables to sustain themselves. When Mago, who had previously provided humanity with everything it needed, heard about this, she threw them out of the castle and locked the gates behind them.

Once human beings began eating fruits and vegetables, they developed teeth. These teeth were as dangerous as the venom of a snake. They used them to begin consuming other living beings. . . . As a result, human beings lost the heaven-bestowed nature they had in Mago's castle and instead found that their bodies decayed over time and that they grew weaker as they aged.

North Korea

32

The Sociopolitical Organism:
The Religious Dimensions
of Juche Philosophy

Eun Hee Shin

North Korean Juche (*chuch'e*) philosophy is typically interpreted to be a North Korean version of Marxist atheist thought, but this is just one of its aspects. Although Juche thought has its origins in Marxist-Leninist philosophy, it has evolved into the elaborate indigenous national religion of North Korea. Although the average North Korean would of course not think of Juche thought as a religion, it does include a godlike figure, Kim Ilsŏng (Kim Il Sung), who is worshiped by approximately twenty-three million adherents in North Korea. They believe in him as "Father," in the sense of being the national provider, healer, and even savior. Juche is thus no longer a merely political ideology but has become the national religion of North Korea.

What Is Juche? From Political Ideology to National Religion

What is Juche? Etymologically, *Ju* (*chu*) means "the main principle" and *che* (*ch'e*) "body" or "self"; the compound is interpreted as "sovereign autonomy," "self-determination," or "self-reliance." Juche thought has been assumed to be a "Marxist-Leninist political ideology," but this understanding falls far short of the mark today. Although Juche thought captures some essential elements of Marxist-Leninist concepts of the Communist Workers' Party and the masses, Juche deviates from Marxist-Leninist philosophy in its alternative interpretation of history, in which people's sovereignty is seen as being of greater significance than class struggle. Kim Ilsŏng (1912–94), the former leader of North Korea, created the Juche idea of self-reliance in order to emphasize the importance of developing the nation's potential using its own resources and reserves of human creativity. For him, the people's primary requirement was to establish the Juche idea in order to achieve sovereignty (*chajusŏng*), and he made Juche ideology the guiding principle for all the actions of the Workers' Party. Juche emerged during the early 1950s as a strong, self-reliant nationalism and an indigenous system of Korean humanistic thought. Kim Ilsŏng explains Juche as follows:

> *Juche* is a Korean word. It means "subjectivity" in English. The revolution in each country should be carried out responsibly by its own people, the masters, in an independent manner, and in a creative way suitable to its specific conditions. It raised the fundamental question of philosophy by regarding human as the main factor, and elucidated the philosophical principle that the human being is the master of everything and decides everything. (*Korean Central News Agency*, December 1997)

Although the interpretation and application of Juche thought have varied depending on the historical context, the core idea of Juche is based on a "human-centered view on the world." Here, the notion of human-centrism should be understood not in terms of a negative anthropocentrism without ecological sensitivity but in light of humanist thought. The historical development of Juche thought can be divided into three major periods.

Juche Thought as Anti-imperialism Ideology, 1950–1960s

The term Juche first appears in a speech Kim Ilsŏng delivered on December 28, 1955, to the propaganda and agitation workers of the Korean Workers' Party. He declared the idea of Juche to be an indigenous expression of Korean sovereignty and autonomy. Kim's speech sets forth the core idea of national self-reliance and pride, emphasizing that a person without Juche is worthless and a state without Juche is a colony. Juche in this period is primarily directed against the political influence of the Soviet Union and China, as expressed in Kim's attempts to purge his political rivals, especially those in the Soviet and Chinese factions of his party. The early ultranationalist quality of Juche served Kim's regime well during the Soviet-Chinese rivalry. He strongly criticizes the imitation of foreign ways, which eventually leads the people into slavishness. He claims that "we are not engaged in any other country's revolution, but solely in the Korean revolution." By saying so, Kim attempts to unify Korean nationalism and internationalism. The opposite of Juche is "servility" or "reliance on others" (*sadaejuŭi*). Juche thus explicitly denounces all types of dependence, including reliance on foreign powers for economic aid and military support. Early Juche ideology can thus be characterized as a combination of national self-reliance and Korean resistance to foreign influences.

Juche Thought as Korean Humanism, 1970–1980s

Juche thought evolves into a philosophy of Korean humanism during this period. Although the initial connotation of Juche as a political ideology remains strong, Juche becomes more philosophical, to distinguish it from Marxist-Leninist social ideology. Juche no longer retains the Marxist concept of "dialectic," which views cultural change and social evolution as being driven by ongoing contradictions in terms of class struggles and materialism. Proponents of Juche thought point out that Juche should not be interpreted in terms of the materialistic understanding of Marxism. As Yi Hwarang, a Juche philosopher, states:

> Juche is different from the dialectical stance of the preceding [Marxist] philosophy, which considers that the world consistently changes and develops, so everything should be viewed as undergoing a process of change and development. The might of Juche idea as an instrument of practice can be increased only when the people have a correct understanding of its independent and creative strands and adhere to them in the revolution and construction. (*Korean Weekly Web*, September 1997)

The focus of Juche is not on materialism but on life-centrism, from which the theory of the sociopolitical life emerges. Juche thought in this period is closer to a nondualistic philosophy, in which spirit and matter are not in conflict but in harmony. Life cannot be interpreted as exclusively spiritual or material but should instead be viewed as involving both spirit and matter. Furthermore, human consciousness and free will, as the driving forces in sociohistorical development, occupy a central position in Juche thought. Kim Ilsŏng says that the motive force of the revolution and the work of construction are the masses, who are responsible for their own destiny and also have the capacity to forge their own destiny. Juche in this period emphasizes a humanistic spirit, free will, consciousness, and the organic nature of life, from which a Korean form of communitarianism can develop.

Juche Thought as North Korea's State Religion, 1990–2000s

During this period, Juche becomes North Korea's national religion. Although Juche has been consistently defined as a "revolutionary new atheistic philosophy," it in fact has profound religious implications. Juche involves three features common to many religions: doctrine, ritual, and priesthood. With the introduction of the theory of the sociopolitical life and the immortality of that life, which are now considered to be its major doctrines, Juche comes closer to being an institutionalized religion. Juche also has unique ritual observances, such as Sun Day, which is observed on President Kim Ilsŏng's birthday (April 15). For North Koreans, 1912, the year of Kim's birth, is considered to be the first year of the Juche Era (Juche 1). Sun Day is the biggest national holiday in North Korea. As the *Korean Central News Agency* announced in April 1997: "The Juche era is a symbol of the eternal harmony of the Korean people with the President. With its institution, our nation and humankind can always live in Kim Ilsŏng's era, in the history of the sun. It is an immortal milestone symbolic of the immortality of the era of Juche created by the President." The doctrine of leader (*suryŏng*) justifies not merely political leadership but also a clergy, whose role includes proclamation of words, leadership, visiting, and pastor care. Kim Ilsŏng worship continues to be an integral part of the Juche religious faith of North Korea. New applications of Juche such the "army-first policy," the "ideology of the red flag," and the theory of the "great strong nation" emerge in the "arduous march" under the leadership of Kim Chŏngil (Kim Jong Il; 1942–), the hereditary leader. Kim Chŏngil made Juche an article of faith rather than a guide to practice. Through his efforts, Juche has been transformed from a political ruling ideology into an indigenous national religion.

The Sociopolitical Life of Juche Thought

According to Juche thought, a human being has both a physical life and a sociopolitical life. An individual's physical life span is mortal, whereas one's sociopolitical life span is immortal. A person's eternal sociopolitical life shares the same fate as the associated "sociopolitical organism." Juche philosophers advocate that the physical life is given by one's biological parents, but the sociopolitical life is given by society. The social group represented by the working masses will live forever together with the party, the leader (suryŏng), and the history of the fatherland and the people. A human being is thus neither a purely spiritual being nor a simple biological being: he or she is a social being who lives and acts in social relationships.

Kim Chŏngil explains the idea of a sociopolitical life in *Socialism Is a Science* (November 1994):

> The Juche idea also newly clarified the essence and the value of a human being's life. When a human being is regarded as an organic body, his life means a physical life. However, he is not a being who only leads a physical life. The Juche idea indicated, for the first time in history, that a man/woman has a socio-political life, as well as a physical life. Physical life is a man/woman's life as an organic body, whereas socio-political life is a man/woman's life as a social being. Socio-political life is the life which is unique to a human being as a social being.

This relational view of Juche places the people at the center of everything, in that they are the masters of the world and play the decisive role in transforming the world and in shaping their own destiny. Establishing Juche in their lives is the primary requirement of the masses' struggle for sovereignty and political autonomy.

Juche philosophers argue that one's biological life might be independent but not one's sociopolitical life, which represents the locus of several relationships. The sociopolitical life can only be discovered within the context of a fluctuating network of relations. Juche thinkers deconstruct the notion of an individual self, which is viewed merely as the transitory intersection of a plethora of relationships, thus undermining the integrity of its autonomous nature. As postmodern thinkers advocate, Juche philosophers stress that the "other" is extremely important to any notion of the self and its development; indeed, one cannot be fully understood without the other. Therefore, the self is always defined in terms of, and functions only within the context of, its communal value. Juche thought places both self and other inextricably within the web of sociopolitical life, in which both are completely co-relative and codependent.

This particular interpretation of Juche thought is radically different from Marxist-Leninist philosophy. Kim Ilsŏng and Juche philosophers wrestled with the problem of reconciling the claim that Juche was people-centered with the Marxist-Leninist idea of community. References to Marxism-Leninism were eventually dropped from the 1980 charter of the Korean Workers' Party and from the 1992 version of the North Korean constitution, which states as follows: "The Democratic People's Republic of Korea makes Juche ideology—a revolutionary ideology with a people-centered view of the world that aims toward the realization of the independence of the masses—the guiding principle of its actions." They engage in a philosophical argument, by claiming that the major distinction between the two systems of thought is their differing interpretations of the human being. For instance, Juche regards a human being as an individual social life, whereas Marxist-Leninists view a human being as a means of production. Juche thinkers perceive a human being as a social being with relational independence, creativity, and consciousness. As members of society, each individual forms the social collective and lives in it in a socially cooperative relationship with other members of society. According to Juche theory, a society governed by Juche is "the most ideal society," for it is developed on the basis of a collective view of life. The sociopolitical integrity of the masses as a whole is emphasized, while the comparative value of any individual is instead fused within the community.

The Sociopolitical Life and Communitarian Relationality

A philosophical interpretation of the sociopolitical life is based on the theory of relationality, the concrete unity of the life-generating process of an individual life. All finite appearances of one's physical life are merged together in an all-embracing sociopolitical life, in which each of its many parts breathe and share the same organic life. The unifying principle of Juche creates an interrelational social fellowship; the parts are distinguished by their individual roles and yet are all one in their relation. The doctrine of the leader (suryŏng), which derives from this theory of relationality, has been particularly criticized by many in the Western media for validating North Korea's totalitarian government and enabling Kim Ilsŏng's regime to justify the eventual father-to-son succession of Kim Chŏngil in the 1990s. The present political reality of North Korea may seem to provide some justification for this view, but, at least in theory, the leader is considered to be a co-relational partner, not a power that controls or dominates the people or the party. The unity of the people, the party, and the leader is profoundly social, as each of the three is interpenetrated by the other two. This is the core principle of Juche thought, which maintains the relational and social character of the people, the party, and the leader.

The leader is not merely a specific person or figure but a virtuous and benevolent entity who functions like the "nerve center" or "top brain" of the nation. The leader's existence is meaningless, if he or she does not serve the people. According to Juche thought, the "people are God [lit. heaven]," and the leader must listen to the voice of the people in order to know their needs and wishes. This is known as the "mass line," which suggests the inseparability of the leader and the people: the leader is always present among the people, and the people are always subsumed within the existence of the leader. Kim Chŏngil, in explaining the idea of the mass line, notes that the leader and the working-class party must always go out among the masses and listen to their desires. The people should be treated like God, and the leader and the party are nothing more than their servants. "Serving the people" has been the stated concern of the North Korean leadership and one of Kim Chŏngil's mantras.

The mass line has been regularly exercised in the "movement of the thousand-mile march," a strategy designed not only to enhance economic production but also to reorient or reeducate people with a communitarian spirit through cooperative works in the field. People are grouped in small units that create a new sociopolitical life, until they achieve their final task together. There is no room for individual identity or activity; rather, the working unit gives them a totally new and collective identity as one body of life. The "movement of the thousand-mile march" is considered to be one of the representative examples of the mass line still practiced in North Korea. In this context, the leader cannot be viewed as a totalitarian dictator but instead constitutes the totality of the sociopolitical life; he is a powerful agent of relationality, in which a multitude of individual lives are integrated into a structured, coexistent whole. This vision of interconnectedness fostered by Juche thought has deeply permeated North Korean culture and functions as a peculiarly North Korean variety of religion or spirituality.

The unity of the leader and the people through the connection of the party derives from the cyclical movement of two theoretical driving forces in the mass line: centripetal force from above and centrifugal force from below. The constant and continuous movement of this unity ensures social rhythm and order, which in turn gives rise to the transformation of the people through the inner process of renewal and re-creation. The political and spiritual unity of the leader and the people subsequently occurs in a cyclical and sequential way, creating a novel social synthesis: the new Juche communitarian society.

Despite the predictions of internal collapse made by many North Korean "experts," we have to ask why it is that North Korea has been able to maintain its own political system at such a level of intensity for such a long period of time. It is true that North Korea's Juche mentality, as a defensive focus of unity against the threat of imperialist subversion, has helped to maintain Kim Ilsŏng's cultic system for nearly half a century. The influence of Juche thought can be seen most strongly in North Korean attitudes toward sovereignty. However, there has been a more fundamental reason why the Kim Ilsŏng cult has been kept so strong and powerful. This is the religio-cultural dimension of Juche, which is intimately conjoined with traditional Korean Confucian culture. The religious dimension of the relationship between father and son should not be neglected in understanding the cultural aspects of Juche thought, which enhance the durability of the Kim-to-Kim succession.

The vestiges of Confucian thought are primarily influential in shaping the vertical structure of the North Korean socialist bureaucracy. The hierarchical structure and the ritualistic aspects of Confucianism, although influenced by socialist interpretations, are important determinants for understanding and interpreting North Korean behavior at both the personal and the national level. Confucian culture is deeply based on filial piety. In Western writings, the idea of filial piety is often misunderstood as an authoritarian impulse to dominate children or the powerless. However, the original teaching of filial piety is profoundly reciprocal and relational: if the duty of children to parents is clearly defined, so too is the duty of parents to children. For example, if parents fail to maintain ideal standards of conduct, their children's obligation to obey them is diminished. If parents make a wrong decision, children should protest. In order to be a filial son and daughter, the children too need to know the difference between right and wrong. Therefore, filial piety does not imply the one-sided authority of parents over children or the powerful over the powerless. Filial piety always includes the idea of "remonstrance," which refers to the duty of a child to dissuade the parent from an immoral course of action. The ethic of filial piety continues to influence North Korean society today. The Russian scholar Alexandre Mansourov calls the North Korean system a "politics of filial piety." Kim Chŏngil's legitimacy hinges on his filial piety, and his piety toward his father reinforces the power of Kim Ilsŏng's legacy from beyond the grave. For instance, Kim Chŏngil places his father in the pantheon of Korean rulers, thus equating him with Tan'gun, the mythical founder of the Korean nation, whose tomb was reconstructed in the mid-1990s. Also, Kim Chŏngil demonstrates his filial piety by observing the longest mourning period in modern Korean history.

In North Korea, society is viewed as one big family, led by a benevolent father to whom unconditional respect and gratitude are owed. The leader is revered like a parent by the whole society. Kim Chŏngil describes the "theory of a family nation" as follows:

> Children love and respect their parents not because their parents are always superior to those of others or because the children receive benefits from them, but because the parents are the benefactors of their lives who gave birth to them and have brought them up. . . . All the communist revolutionaries of Korea have been accorded immortal political integrity by the fatherly leader. . . . Therefore, the loyalty of our party members and working people to the great leader is unconditional.
> (*Nodong sinmun* [Labor Newspaper], November 1994)

Confucian cultural roots have been deeply associated with Juche thought in thus establishing the nation as family. In this Confucian-oriented Juche culture, some unique ethical systems and criteria have developed. North Koreans reject the absolutism of value systems imposed mainly from without by powerful nations. They claim that they have their own internal value system based on the ethics of Juche thought. Of course, the values of a particular community should be compatible with the values of the global community, but this compatibility is not a principal concern of the North Koreans at present. Instead, their primary concern is maintaining their own political autonomy and sovereignty. The virtues of morality and human rights need to be viewed within the framework of national sovereignty, without which the moral order would be fundamentally shattered. The idea of a right to self-expression, or the notion that people have individual rights of their own, develops only in conditions of what the North Koreans term Juche corporatism. In the constant cyclical movement of the mass line through the dynamic combination of centripetal and centrifugal forces, all moral decisions are made based on certain communal values, rather than individual interests. Some of the consequences of this particular ethical premise of Juche communitarianism may tend toward moral relativism, but the North Koreans contend that morality cannot be conceived in universal terms. In a communitarian society, ethical values are conceived of as a substantive conception of the morality that defines the community's "unique way of life." These common moral criteria constitute a common culture, which is the precondition of moral autonomy. Therefore, the community's way of life forms the basis of the "normative conceptions" of good and bad, and the significance of an individual's preferences depends on the degree to which each member conforms or contributes to that communal value.

North Koreans think of themselves as sovereign, both politically and morally. They alone have the capacity to judge what is valuable for them and what constitutes their common good. This does not mean that they totally reject any type of social confirmation from other communities. What they have consistently claimed, however, is that there is neither a single version of what constitutes a good society nor any single criterion of justice. Worthwhile freedom requires cultural pluralism in interpreting the virtues of morality. We might say, then, that it is essential for Christians to become better Christians, Muslims to become better Muslims, humanists to become better humanists, and Juche persons to become better Juche persons.

Toward a Life-Centered Juche Organism

The emphases in Juche may have changed over the years—or, more accurately, new concepts may have been incorporated into Juche—but the basic concepts that sustain the North Korean people remain: the commitment to socialism, an insistence on achieving economic self-sufficiency, the cult of personality surrounding the leader, and political and moral sovereignty. All these ideas are woven together in the cultural framework of the sociopolitical life of the Juche organism.

The organic and communitarian perspective of Juche thought is a corrective to the modern liberal notion of self that is based on individualism, according to which individuals are self-sufficient and hence need no cultural or social contexts in which to exercise their moral power. In a communitarian society like that of North Korea, an individual is instead viewed as profoundly relational. The relationality of the sociopolitical life is stated in Article 63 of the North Korean

Constitution: "One is for many and many are for one." In this symmetrical and symbiotic relation between one and many, life is structured both conceptually and metaphorically as a monistic multiplicity, in which the ideas of individuality and the unity of life can both be made fully manifest. The idea of oneness in Juche thought does not imply the superordinateness of the leader, to which the many reduce. In other words, this is not a reduction of the multiplicity of life but the production of multiplicity from out of unity. The notion of a sociopolitical life represents both the individuality and multiplicity implicit in the one-and-many relationship. The one-and-many principle represents the totality of reality as a powerful agent of change, in which a great multitude of things are integrated into the structured whole of coexistence through Juche thought. The sociopolitical life unifies "many" through its own creativity and is the foundation of the ontological unity of the people, the party, and the leader.

As explained earlier, the organic and communitarian community is more than a mere association; it is a unity in which the individuals are essential members of this larger web of life. Their membership is not artificial or instrumental, but spiritual, and has its own intrinsic value. Therefore, it is essential to recognize that the cultural and political morality of North Korea cannot be understood except in terms of the shared values of their own interpretative community. When viewed from this standpoint, the ideological power of Juche thought offers the potential for the holistic liberation of the people and the transformation of every dimension of life in North Korea.

"The Philosophical Principle of the Juche Idea" was written by Kim Chŏngil and published in *Kim Jong Il: On the Juche Philosophy* (P'yŏngyang: Foreign Language Publishing House, 1982), pp. 9–11. *The Workers' Party of Korea Is the Party of the Great Leader Comrade Kim Il Sung* was written by Kim Chŏngil (P'yŏngyang: Foreign Language Publishing House, 1995), pp. 15–17. *Socialism Is a Science* was written by Kim Chŏngil (P'yŏngyang: Foreign Language Publishing House, 2001), pp. 12–22.

Further Reading

Additional descriptions of Juche thought appear in Kim Ilsŏng, *Reminiscences with the Century*, vol. 1 (New York: JAMS, 1999); Kim Ilsŏng, *For an Independent World* (Honolulu: University Press of the Pacific, 2001); Kim Chŏngil, *Kim Jong Il: On Carrying Forward the Juche Idea* (P'yŏngyang: Foreign Language Publishing House, 1995). For background on North Korean state ideology, see Suh Dae-sook, *Kim Il Sung: The North Korean Leader* (New York: Columbia University Press, 1988); Bruce Cumings, *North Korea: Another Country* (New York: New Press, 2004). Helpful discussions of North Korean politics and religion appear in Ch'oe Sŏng, *Pukhan chŏngch'isa* (The History of North Korean Politics) (Seoul: P'ulbit, 1997); Pak Chaegyu, ed., *Saeroun Pukhan ilgirŭl wihayŏ* (Toward a New Reading of North

Korea) (Seoul: Pŏmmunsa, 2004); Kim Heung-Soo and Ryu Dae-Young, eds., *Pukhan chŏnggyo ŭi saeroun ihae* (Religion in North Korea: A New Understanding) (Seoul: Tasan Kŭlbang, 2002); Pak Hyŏngjung, *Pukhan ŭi chŏngch'i wa kwŏllyŏk* (Power and North Korean Politics) (Seoul: Paeksanch'aryowŏn, 2002); Eun Hee Shin, "Pukchosŏn ŭi kongdongch'e munhwa wa t'ongil tawŏnjuŭi" (North Korea's Communitarian Culture and the Pluralism of the Unification) in *Tongbuga chŏnŏl* (Northeast Asia Institute of Sŏnmun University) (February 2004): 79–99.

"The Philosophical Principle of the Juche Idea," by Kim Chŏngil

The Juche idea is a new philosophical thought that centers on the human being. As our leader [*suryŏng*] said, the Juche idea is based on the philosophical principle that the human being is the master of everything and decides everything. The Juche idea raised the fundamental question of philosophy by regarding the human being as the main factor, and elucidated the philosophical principle that the human being is the master of everything and decides everything.

That "the human being is the master of everything" means that he is the master of the world and of his own destiny; that "the human being decides everything" means that he plays the decisive role in transforming the world and in shaping his destiny. The philosophical principle of the Juche idea is the principle of human-centered philosophy, which explains his position and role in the world. The leader made it clear that the human being is a social being with independence, creativity, and consciousness.

The human being, though existing materially, is not a simple material being. He is the most developed material being, a special product of the evolution of the material world. The human being was already outstanding as he emerged from the world of nature. He exists and develops by cognizing and changing the world to make it serve him, whereas all other material lives maintain their existence through their subordination and adaptation to the objective world.

The human being holds a special position and plays a special role as master of the world because he is a social being with independence, creativity, and consciousness. The leader gave a new philosophical conception to humanity by defining independence, creativity, and consciousness as the essential features of the human being, a social being. Independence, creativity, and consciousness are the human being's social qualities, which take shape and develop socially and historically. The human being alone lives and conducts activity, his aim only socially. Independence, creativity, and consciousness are peculiar to the human being, a social being.

Man/woman is a social being with independence, that is, an independent social being. Independence is an attribute of a social being who is desirous of living and developing in an independent way as master of the world and his own destiny. On the strength of this quality, man/woman throws off the fetters of nature, opposes social subjugation of all forms, and puts everything at his own service. Independence is the life and soul of man/woman, the social being. When independence is referred to as his life and soul, it means social and political life. Man/woman has a physical life and also a social and political life. The physical life is what keeps man/woman alive as a biological organism; the social and political life is what keeps him alive as a social being.

Man/woman is a being with creativity, that is, a creative social being. Creativity is an attribute of a social being who transforms the world and shapes his destiny purposefully and consciously. By virtue of his creativity, man/woman transforms nature and society to be more useful and beneficial to him, by changing the old and creating the new. Creativity, like independence, constitutes an essential quality of man/woman, the social being. Independence finds expression mainly in his position as master of the world; creativity is expressed mainly in his role as transformer of the world.

Man/woman is a being with consciousness, that is, a conscious social being. Consciousness is an attribute of the social being, which determines all his endeavors to understand and reshape the world and himself. Because he has consciousness, man/woman understands the world and the laws of its motion, and development reshapes and advances nature and society as he desires. Consciousness guarantees the independence and creativity of the human being, the social being, and ensures his purposeful cognition and practice.

Independence, creativity, and consciousness, after all, are what enable man/woman to be superior to any other being and to be the most powerful being in the world, to approach the world not fatalistically but revolutionarily, not passively but actively, and to reshape the world not blindly but purposefully and consciously. Man/woman, the social being, who has independence, creativity, and consciousness, is precisely the only dominator and re-maker of the world.

"The Workers' Party of Korea is the Party of the Great Leader Comrade Kim Il Sung," by Kim Chŏngil

Fifty years has elapsed since our Party was founded.

Greeting the 50th anniversary of the foundation of the Workers' Party of Korea, and looking back with deep emotions upon the glorious road of struggle our Party has traversed, scoring a historic victory and effecting the greatest change by acclaiming respected Comrade Kim Il Sung as its head and under his leadership, our Party members and our people express the warmest gratitude and pay the highest respect to the great leader Comrade Kim Il Sung, who founded and led the Party.

Under Comrade Kim Il Sung's wise leadership, the Workers' Party of Korea was established as a working-class party of a new type and has developed in the flames of struggle for half a century into a trained and seasoned veteran revolutionary party, an unconquerable party enjoying the unqualified support and trust of the people. Under his leadership, our Party created a brilliant new history in the people's cause of independence, the cause of socialism, and made great, imperishable achievements in this cause.

The history of the Workers' Party of Korea is precisely the history of respected Comrade Kim Il Sung's great revolutionary activities. Both the thorny path of our Party's struggle and its road of glorious victory bear his sacred footprints. Both our Party's great achievements and its unbreakable strength and high prestige are associated with his respectful name.

The Workers' Party of Korea belongs to the great leader Comrade Kim Il Sung. It is his great time and exploits that have made our Party's fifty years brilliant. His name and exploits will be immortal together with our Party's history. The Workers' Party of Korea is a glorious party, which under the leadership of the great leader Comrade Kim Il Sung has paved a new road of building a revolutionary party in the ages of independence, setting a shining example in this work.

Respected Comrade Kim Il Sung was the great leader of the people and their father. His ideology, leadership, and virtue were based on love for, and trust in, the people. All his life he was among the people, shared joy and sorrow with them, and devoted his all to them. He placed deep trust in the strength, wisdom, and excellent qualities of our people and solved all problems by relying on them and by giving rein to their revolutionary zeal and creative force.

Our Party has fully applied in all its activities the noble idea of Comrade Kim Il Sung, "The people are my God," and his revolutionary method of leadership. It has always formulated its lines and policies by reflecting truthfully and incorporating the opinions and requirements of the popular masses, and implemented them by enlisting their efforts and resourcefulness. It has given definite priority to ideological work, namely, the political work of awakening the popular masses ideologically, rallying them organizationally, over all other undertakings; it has also worked tirelessly to oppose abuse of authority and bureaucratism and establish a revolutionary method and popular style of work among officials. The iron rule in the activities of our Party and in the work of our officials is to go among the people, breathe the same air with them, work devotedly for them, and execute revolutionary tasks by relying on them under the Party's slogan, "We serve the people." Our Party is a motherly party, which takes care of the destiny of the popular masses under its charge, and its politics is a benevolent one in that it is politics of love for the people and trust in them.

Because of genuine comradeship and their inseparable relationship, in which the Party and leader trust and love the people, place unqualified trust in them, and support them with loyalty, the single-hearted unity of the leader, Party, and masses has been strengthened and developed, and the revolutionary enthusiasm and creative force of the popular masses have been fully displayed on a high plane. Relying on the popular masses and welding itself to them in the struggle—this is the secret of how our Party has been able to promote the revolution and construction with vigor in such complicated circumstances and trying ordeals, and has won victory after victory by turning misfortune into a blessing and unfavorable conditions into favorable ones.

From the first days of his revolutionary activity, the great leader Comrade Kim Il Sung blazed the trail of independent development of the Korean revolution, holding aloft the banner of independence. He made it a fundamental principle to establish Juche and maintain independence in the revolution and construction, then led the effort to implement it. The line of Juche in ideology, independence in politics, self-sufficiency in the economy, and self-reliance in defense, as advanced by Comrade Kim Il Sung, is a revolutionary line of independence run through with the principle of Juche and the spirit of independence. Our Party has staunchly safeguarded this line and implemented it to the letter.

Respected Comrade Kim Il Sung was a great communist revolutionary and a genius in revolution and construction. With unshakable revolutionary faith and steel-like revolutionary will, he led our arduous and tortuous revolution along the straight road to victory, with unfailing loyalty to the cause of the popular masses for independence, the socialist cause of Juche. Comrade Kim Il Sung led our Party and people by setting a brilliant example of the art of leadership. He defended the revolutionary principle under all circumstances and conditions, and skillfully combined principle and adroitness in revolution and construction.

We must defend his great ideas, theories, and revolutionary methods of leadership, and thoroughly apply them in Party building and activities. We must do all the work of revolution and construction just as Comrade Kim Il Sung planned and intended and showed in his personal example, and we must conduct everything in the same way as Comrade Kim Il Sung. This is the way to develop our Party as the Party of Comrade Kim Il Sung, the way to brilliantly inherit and complete the revolutionary cause of Juche. We must resolutely safeguard the revolutionary idea of the great leader Comrade Kim Il Sung and thoroughly put it into effect.

"Socialism Is a Science: Sociopolitical Life," by Kim Chŏngil

Our socialism is based on the Juche-oriented view of, and attitude toward, the human being. The view of and attitude toward the human being are the basic questions concerning what view and attitude one has in one's understanding of the development of society and the revolution. They constitute the standard for the scientific character and validity of ideas and theories, and of lines and policies. The scientific character and truth of our socialism lies in the fact that it is based on the absolutely correct, Juche-oriented view of and attitude toward human being.

The Juche idea has given a scientific definition of human being's essential qualities, for the first time in history. Understanding man/woman's essential qualities is not merely a matter of science but a sociopolitical issue, which reflects class interests. Throughout history, serious philosophical arguments have taken place on this issue between progressive and reactionary classes.

The reactionary ruling classes and their mouthpieces distorted man and woman's essential qualities in the interests of the exploiting class in order to justify their exploitative society. Philosophical arguments on man/woman's essential qualities formerly boiled down to two dominant views; one regarded the human being as a spiritual being, and the other considered him a material being. According to the religious, idealist view, which regards human being as a purely spiritual being, man/woman is a product of a certain supernatural, mysterious being and his destiny is also decided by the latter. By means of their religious, idealist view of man/woman, the reactionary ruling class and its spokespersons preached that the miserable life of working masses who suffered exploitation and oppression was their unavoidable fate and, therefore, they had to submit to their predestined life. The view that regards man/woman as simply a natural, biological being makes it impossible to understand the qualitative difference between man/woman who acts purposefully and consciously under the regulation and control of consciousness, and a biological being which is governed by instinct. The reactionary ruling class and its spokesperson used this view to justify capitalist society, which is ruled by the law of the jungle. Having recourse to the reactionary viewpoint and attitude toward man/woman, the renegades of socialism are restoring capitalism through the introduction of bourgeois liberalism and the capitalist market economy.

The human being is neither a purely spiritual nor a simple biological being. The human being is a social being who lives and acts in social relationships. The fact that man/woman is a social being is the major quality that distinguishes him from other biological beings.

Marxism defined man/woman's essential quality as the ensemble of social relations. This definition rendered a historic service by shattering the unscientific, reactionary view that regarded man/woman as a purely spiritual being or a simple biological being. However, the definition of man/woman's essential quality as the sum total of social relations does not provide a comprehensive elucidation of man/woman's own essential qualities. Consequently, it cannot correctly explain the relations between the human being and the world, or the position and role of the human being in the world. The Juche idea has, for the first time, found a scientific solution to the question of man/woman's own essential qualities. On this basis, it has thrown a new light on his position and role in the world.

In the past, too, many attempts were made to elucidate man/woman's essential qualities by dealing mainly with his own features, for example, attempts to define man/woman as a speaking, working, or thinking being. These attempts, however, all dealt with some aspects of man's actions, which are the expression of his essential qualities. The human being is a social being with independence, creativity, and consciousness. Herein lie his essential qualities.

Independence is an attribute of a social being, who wants to live and develop independently as the master of the world and his destiny, free from any fetters or restrictions. Creativity is an attribute of a social being, who transforms the world and shapes his destiny purposefully and consciously in order to meet his needs. Consciousness is a social being's attribute. It regulates all his activities for understanding and transforming the world and himself. Independence and creativity are ensured by consciousness. The human being is distinguished qualitatively from animals, which act instinctively, in that he conducts independent and creative activities with consciousness. The course of a human being's activities is a process whereby he expresses his independence, creativity, and consciousness. Independent, creative, and conscious activities constitute man/woman's mode of existence.

Man/Woman as a social being with independence, creativity, consciousness is inconceivable outside his developed organism, especially his highly developed brain. His developed organism is the biological basis of his independence, creativity, and consciousness. However, the organism itself does not give birth to independence, creativity, consciousness. Man/Woman's independence, creativity, and consciousness are social attributes which are formed and developed through a sociohistorical process, where he acts in social relationships.

The Juche idea also newly clarified the essence and the value of the human being's life. When the human being is regarded as an organic body, his life means a physical life. However, he is not a being who only leads a physical life. The Juche idea indicated, for the first time in history, that a man/woman has a sociopolitical life, as well as a physical life. Physical life is a man/woman's life as an organic body, whereas sociopolitical life is a man/woman's life as a social being. Sociopolitical life is the life which is unique to the human being as a social being.

For a man/woman, physical life is valuable. Only when he has a physical life can he acquire sociopolitical life. In this sense, we can say that the material life that implements the demand for physical life is the life that implements his primary needs. As man/woman is a social being who is different from a simple biological being, his demand for material life constantly increases as his independence, creativity, and consciousness develop and as society develops. His material life affects his sociopolitical life. A stable and sound material life fully guarantees his demand for physical life, and at the same time, it constitutes a material guarantee for the maintenance and development of his sociopolitical life.

For a man/woman, physical life is precious, but his sociopolitical life is more precious. It is the intrinsic need of man/woman as a social being to value his sociopolitical life more than his physical life. If a man/woman only seeks to satisfy his demand for physical life, and not his demand for a sociopolitical life, his life can never be an honorable one, no matter how affluent he is. Such a material life will be reduced to a deformed and abnormal life, no better than an animal life, and will run counter to man/woman's intrinsic nature.

Independence is the life and soul of man/woman. Man/woman, an independent social being, desires to live independently, free from any subordination or shackles. The fact that man/woman lives independently means that he lives as the master of the world and of his own destiny, maintaining his position and exercising his rights as such. Only when a human being lives as a social being, exercising his right to independence and implementing his demand for independence, can he be said to enjoy a dignified life, maintaining sociopolitical life. If he loses his independence and is subordinated to others, he is as good as dead socially and politically, even though he is alive. Man/woman's desire to live independently is realized, first of all, through an independent political life. When man/woman is subordinated socially and politically, he cannot lead any kind of independent life.

As sociopolitical life is man/woman's precious life, a noble life for him is to maintain and exalt sociopolitical life. Man/woman receives sociopolitical life from the social collective. The social collective is the parental body of man/woman's sociopolitical life. Therefore, the worth of man/woman's life depends on how he is connected with the social collective. Man/woman's life becomes noble when he is loved and trusted by the social collective; it is worthless when he is forsaken by it. Man/woman enjoys the love and trust of the social collective when he considers the interests of the social collective to be dearer than those of individuals and when he faithfully serves the social collective. In the final analysis, the greatest value and worth of man/woman's life is to lead an independent and creative life, enjoying the love and trust of the social collective, while at the same time combining his own destiny with that of the social collective and serving it heart and soul. This is the way for man/woman to enhance his sociopolitical life and lead a worthy human life as a social being.

Today, the bourgeois reactionaries and renegades of socialism regard the exploitation and domination of man/woman by man/woman as something normal and consider man/woman as a base being who only pursues his own material desires. This clearly demonstrates the reactionary nature of the bourgeois viewpoint and attitude toward the essence and worth of man/woman's life.

True human life, which enables everyone to enhance their most precious sociopolitical life and fully meet the demands of their physical life, can only be realized admirably in a socialist society based on collectivism. In this society, people are free from all manner of exploitation and oppression, domination, and subordination and can lead an independent and creative life in social, political, and all other areas. In socialist society, we must organize people's organizational and ideological life properly, as well as their cultural life, in order to enable them to lead an independent and creative life with a high consciousness and an ability that befits the masters of society. People can make great contributions to society and the collective and lead a worthy life as proud members of society and the collective, only when they are fully equipped with an independent consciousness and have comprehensively developed creative ability, through a moral and rich cultural life.

Our socialism is genuinely human-centered socialism. It regards the human being as most precious and fully meets his intrinsic requirements. It thus enables everyone to keep and greatly enhance their sociopolitical life. It also fully meets the demands of their physical life. Human-centered socialism enables all members of society to live in harmony, enjoying the love and trust of the society and the collective, and to lead a completely noble and worthy life, while working devotedly for society and the collective with a high degree of consciousness and creative ability.

INDEX

Amitābha (Amitāyus), 19, 67–69
ancestor worship/memorialization: Buddhism
and, 91; Catholicism and, 25, 167, 356–57,
364, 377–78, 382, 436; Confucianism/
Neo-Confucianism and, 6–7, 23, 164, 166–69,
436; Protestantism and, 167, 434–45; [texts]
172–74, 383–91. *See also* filial piety
An Chunggŭn, 362
Anglican Church, 434
animism, 16
An Kyŏngjŏn, 489
ansu kido (laying-on-of-hands prayer), 422
Anthology of Korean Literature. See
Tongmun sŏn
An Unsan, 489
archaeological evidence, 43–46, 66, 235
Array of Critiques of Buddhism. See *Pulssi
chappyŏn*
Articulation of Orthodoxy. See *Hyŏnjong non*
Assemblies of God, 438
Assembly of the Eight Commandments. See
P'algwanhoe
Avalokiteśvara, 19–20, 67–70, 116–17

Balmer, Randall, 393
baptism, 26, 499
Baptists, 438
behavioral rules, 11–12; in Buddhism, 52, 87;
in Confucianism/Neo-Confucianism, 21–23,
52, 164, 168–69, 174–76, 453
Bhaiṣajyaguru, 19, 113
birth, 6, 245, 307; [texts] 309–10, 501–2
birth dreams, 146
bodhisattvas, 19, 70–71
Book of Family Ritual (*Chuja karye*), 436
Book on Choosing Settlements (*Taengniji*), 206,
[text] 217–19
books, "how-to," 146–48
bowing, 10, 381
Buddha lands (*pulgukt'o*), 47, 54, 77
Buddha-nature, 13, 21, 149, 476–80, [texts]
152–53, 480–86

Buddhism, 18–21; adherents of, 2–3; ancestor
worship/memorialization and, 91; behavioral
rules and, 11–12, 52, 87; cause and effect in,
145, 181, 183, 200; Confucian critique of,
21–22, 177–204; devotional practices in,
8–10, 26, 28, 65–75, 130–31, 178; exorcisms
in, 112–29; geomancy and, 76–85; gods/
buddhas/bodhisattvas in, 13–14, 19–20,
238–39; monastic rules of, 54–55, 77; monks
and *śramaṇa,* as practitioners of, 21–22,
69–71, 101; poetry and, 100–101; prenatal
education and, 144–60; rituals of, 20, 26,
86–99, 112–29; salvation/suffering in, 4–5,
18–19, 21; self-cultivation in, 5–6, 131–32;
state authority and, 36–37, 43, 46–47,
51–54, 77, 90, 180, 236; urbanization of, 20,
28, 476–77; women/gender and, 53–54;
worlds beyond in, 101–11, 239. *See also* Sŏn
Buddhism; Wŏn Buddhism

Cao Cao, 234
Catholic Bible Life Movement, 363–64
Catholicism, 24–25; adherents of, 2–3,
24–25, 360, 363, 377; ancestor worship/
memorialization and, 25, 167, 356–57, 364,
377–78, 382, 383–91, 436; devotional practices in, 8–10, 359–60, 363, 381–82; inculturation and, 376–78; mass practices in,
379–81; missionaries and, 361; monotheism
of, 25–26, 29, 357; in North Korea, 363, 365;
openness to other religions and, 364–65;
open practice of, 362–66; persecutions and,
25, 356, 359–62, 377; rituals of, 376–92;
self-cultivation in, 5; Shintōism and, 362–63;
social activism and, 362, 365–66, 378; state
authority and, 25; underground practice of,
355–62; urbanization of, 377; women/gender
and, 358–61; worlds beyond and, 358, 377
cause and effect, 145, 181, 183, [texts] 200
Cespedes, Gregorio de, 355
Ch'ae Chŏngnye, 326
Chajang, 51–56; biography of [text], 60–64